ENCYCLOPEDIA OF THE SOCIAL AND SOLIDARITY ECONOMY

Encyclopedia of the Social and Solidarity Economy

A Collective Work of the United Nations Inter-Agency Task Force on SSE (UNTFSSE)

Edited by

Ilcheong Yi

United Nations Research Institute for Social Development (UNRISD), Switzerland

With

Peter Utting

Jean-Louis Laville

Barbara Sak

Caroline Shenaz Hossein

Sifa Chiyoge

Cecilia Navarra

Denison Jayasooria

Fernanda Wanderley

Jacques Defourny

Rocio Nogales-Muriel

Cheltenham, UK • Northampton, MA, USA

© United Nations Research Institute for Social Development 2023

This is an open access work distributed under the Creative Commons Attribution-NonCommercial-NoDerivatives 4.0 Unported (https://creativecommons.org/licenses/by-nc-nd/4.0/). Users can redistribute the work for non-commercial purposes, as long as it is passed along unchanged and in whole, as detailed in the License. Edward Elgar Publishing Ltd must be clearly credited as the rights holder for publication of the original work. Any translation or adaptation of the original content requires the written authorization of Edward Elgar Publishing Ltd.

Published by
Edward Elgar Publishing Limited
The Lypiatts
15 Lansdown Road
Cheltenham
Glos GL50 2JA
UK

Edward Elgar Publishing, Inc.
William Pratt House
9 Dewey Court
Northampton
Massachusetts 01060
USA

A catalogue record for this book
is available from the British Library

Library of Congress Control Number: 2022950550

This book is available electronically in the Elgaronline
Sociology, Social Policy and Education subject collection
http://dx.doi.org/10.4337/9781803920924

Printed on elemental chlorine free (ECF)
recycled paper containing 30% Post-Consumer Waste

ISBN 978 1 80392 091 7 (cased)
ISBN 978 1 80392 092 4 (eBook)

Printed and bound in the USA

Contents

List of figures ix
List of tables x
About the editors xi
List of contributors xii
Foreword xv
Foreword xvi
Preface xviii
List of abbreviations xxi

PART I   HISTORIES, CONCEPTS AND THEORIES

1   Activism and social movements   2
     Hamish Jenkins and Yvon Poirier

2   Community economies   12
     Stephen Healy, Ana Inés Heras and Peter North

3   Contemporary understandings   19
     Peter Utting

4   Ecological economics   27
     Dražen Šimleša

5   Feminist economics   37
     Suzanne Bergeron

6   Globalization and alter-globalization   44
     Carmen Marcuello, Anjel Errasti and Ignacio Bretos

7   Heterodox economics   53
     Jean-Louis Laville

8   Indigenous economies   61
     Luciane Lucas dos Santos

9   Moral economy and human economy   68
     Jean-Louis Laville

10   Origins and histories   73
     Jean-Louis Laville

11   Postcolonial theories   83
     Luciane Lucas dos Santos

vi *Encyclopedia of the social and solidarity economy*

| 12 | The Black social economy
Sharon D. Wright Austin | 92 |
| 13 | The commons
Anabel Rieiro | 97 |

PART II ACTORS AND ORGANIZATIONS

14	African American solidarity economics and distributive justice *Jessica Gordon-Nembhard and Ajowa Nzinga Ifateyo*	105
15	Associations and associationalism *Bruno Frère and Laurent Gardin*	113
16	Community-based organizations *Kiran Kamal Prasad*	121
17	Cooperatives and mutuals *Chiyoge B. Sifa and Caroline Shenaz Hossein*	131
18	LGBT* inclusion *Vincenza Priola and Saoirse C. O'Shea*	138
19	Migrants and refugees *Giulia Galera and Leila Giannetto*	147
20	Non-governmental organisations and foundations *Edith Archambault*	155
21	Social enterprises *Jacques Defourny and Marthe Nyssens*	163
22	Women's self-help groups *Christabell P.J.*	172
23	Youth *Davorka Vidović*	180

PART III LINKAGES TO DEVELOPMENT

24	Care and home support services *Christian Jetté, Yves Vaillancourt and Catherine Lenzi*	187
25	Culture, sports and leisure sectors *Nadine Richez-Battesti and Francesca Petrella*	194
26	Education sector *Christina A. Clamp and Colleen E. Tapley*	200
27	Energy, water and waste management sectors *Waltteri Katajamäki*	209

28	Finance sector *Riccardo Bodini and Gianluca Salvatori*	216
29	Food and agriculture sector *Judith Hitchman*	224
30	Gender equality and empowerment *Bipasha Baruah*	231
31	Health and care sector *Jean-Pierre Girard*	240
32	Housing sector *Alice Pittini*	248
33	Information and communication technology (ICT) *Raymond Saner, Lichia Saner-Yiu and Samuel Bruelisauer*	255
34	Local community development *Luis Razeto Migliaro*	264
35	Peace and non-violence *Smita Ramnarain*	272
36	Reduction of hunger and poverty *Judith Hitchman*	281
37	Reduction of multidimensional inequalities *Andrea Salustri*	287
38	Social services *Susanne Elsen*	295
39	Sustainable investment, production and consumption *Cynthia Giagnocavo*	303
40	The Sustainable Development Goals *Denison Jayasooria and Ilcheong Yi*	310
41	Tourism sector *Gilles Caire*	321
42	Work integration *Kate Cooney, Marthe Nyssens and Mary O'Shaughnessy*	329

PART IV ENABLING ENVIRONMENT AND GOVERNANCE

| 43 | Access to markets
Darryl Reed | 338 |

44	Co-optation, isomorphism and instrumentalisation *Nadine Richez-Battesti and Francesca Petrella*	348
45	Financing *Gianluca Salvatori and Riccardo Bodini*	356
46	Legal frameworks and laws *David Hiez*	365
47	Local and territorial development plans *Hamish Jenkins*	372
48	Management *Sang-Youn Lee*	382
49	Participation, governance, collective action and democracy *Jeová Torres Silva Junior*	388
50	Partnership and co-construction *Marguerite Mendell*	394
51	Public policy *Peter Utting*	400
52	Resilience in the context of multiple crises *Beverley Mullings and Tinyan Otuomagie*	409
53	Social policy *Ilcheong Yi*	416
54	Statistical measurement *Marie J. Bouchard*	425
55	Supporting organizations and intermediaries *Hamish Jenkins*	434
56	The institutional ecosystem *Jean-Marc Fontan and Benoît Lévesque*	443
57	Working conditions and wages *Kunle Akingbola and Carol Brunt*	452
Index		462

Figures

2.1	Diverse Economies Iceberg by Community Economies Collective	14
3.1	The solidarity economy within the broader economy	20
3.2	Positioning both the social and the solidarity economy	22
4.1	Nested model of sustainability	30
4.2	Planetary boundaries	31
21.1	Institutional logics and resulting SE models	166
36.1	The vicious circle of food access	282
36.2	The virtuous circle of resilience	282
40.1	Five dimensions of the SSE	313
40.2	How Seoul's SSEOEs contribute to the SDGs: tracing the pathways	314
54.1	Filters to identify SSE entities in national statistics accounts	427
54.2	The SSE field and its coverage by international SSE statistics frameworks	429

Tables

6.1	Examples of organizations utilizing control-based international scaling strategies	49
6.2	Examples of organizations utilizing altruism-based international scaling strategies	50
6.3	Examples of organizations utilizing hybrid international scaling strategies	50
6.4	Examples of international public–private partnerships	51
12.1	Different names of ROSCA in different regions or countries	94
26.1	Universities with degrees in co-operative business studies	201
40.1	Five SDG dimensions of development	311
40.2	SDGs and SSE local community potential	313
45.1	Social base	358
45.2	Surpluses and assets (management)	358
45.3	Grants	359
45.4	Debt	360
45.5	Equity	361
55.1	Types of relationship between supporting organizations and government	435
57.1	Working conditions and wages in the SSE	457

About the editors

Ilcheong Yi, Senior Research Coordinator, United Nations Research Institute for Social Development (UNRISD), Switzerland.

With

Peter Utting, Senior Research Associate, United Nations Research Institute for Social Development (UNRISD), Switzerland.

Jean-Louis Laville, Professor, Conservatoire national des arts et métiers (Cnam, France).

Barbara Sak, Senior Economic Researcher and Director, International Centre of Research and Information on the Public, Social and Cooperative Economy (CIRIEC), Belgium.

Caroline Shenaz Hossein, Associate Professor, Global Development and Political Science, the University of Toronto, Scarborough, Canada

Sifa Chiyoge, Regional Director and CEO of International Cooperative Alliance – Africa.

Cecilia Navarra, Policy Analyst, the European Parliamentary Research Service, Belgium.

Denison Jayasooria, Practice Professor for Public Advocacy, the Institute of Ethnic Studies (KITA), National University of Malaysia (UKM), Malaysia.

Fernanda Wanderley, Director of the Institute for Social and Economic Research, the Catholic University (IISEC-UCB), La Paz, Bolivia.

Jacques Defourny, Professor of Non-Profit and Cooperative Economics, and Comparative Economic Systems, HEC – Management School of the University of Liège, Belgium.

Rocio Nogales-Muriel, Managing Director of the EMES International Research Network.

Contributors

Kunle Akingbola, Lakehead University, Canada.

Edith Archambault, University of Paris I: Panthéon-Sorbonne, France.

Sharon D. Wright Austin, University of Florida, USA.

Bipasha Baruah, Western University, Canada.

Suzanne Bergeron, University of Michigan Dearborn, USA.

Riccardo Bodini, EURICSE.

Marie J. Bouchard, Université du Québec à Montréal, Canada, and CIRIEC International.

Ignacio Bretos, University of Zaragoza, Spain.

Samuel Bruelisauer, University of Bern, Switzerland.

Carol Brunt, University of Wisconsin-Whitewater, USA.

Christabell P.J., University of Kerala, India.

Gilles Caire, CRIEF, Université de Poitiers, France.

Christina A. Clamp, Southern New Hampshire University, USA.

Kate Cooney, Yale University, USA.

Jacques Defourny, University of Liège, EMES, Belgium.

Susanne Elsen, Free University of Bolzano, Italy.

Anjel Errasti, University of the Basque Country, Spain.

Jean-Marc Fontan, University of Quebec, Montreal, Canada.

Bruno Frère, Fonds National de la Recherche Scientifique, Liege University, Belgium.

Giulia Galera, EURISE.

Laurent Gardin, Institut du Développement et de la Prospective (IDP), France.

Cynthia Giagnocavo, University of Almería, Spain.

Leila Giannetto, European University Institute.

Jean-Pierre Girard, École des sciences de la gestion/Université du Québec à Montréal, HEC Montréal, Canada.

Jessica Gordon-Nembhard, City University of New York, USA and Grassroots Economic Organizing.

Stephen Healy, Western Sydney University, Australia and the Community Economies Institute.

Ana Inés Heras, Universidad de San Martín, Argentina; CONICET; and the Community Economies Institute.

David Hiez, University of Luxembourg.

Judith Hitchman, RIPESS Intercontinental and Urgenci International Community Supported Agriculture Network.

Caroline Shenaz Hossein, University of Toronto Scarborough, Canada.

Ajowa Nzinga Ifateyo, Grassroots Economic Organizing.

Denison Jayasooria, Asian Solidarity Economy Council (ASEC).

Hamish Jenkins, United Nations Research Institute for Social Development.

Christian Jetté, Université de Montréal, Canada.

Waltteri Katajamäki, International Labour Office (ILO).

Jean-Louis Laville, Conservatoire National des Arts et Métiers à Paris (Cnam), France.

Sang-Youn Lee, Sungkonghoe University, South Korea.

Catherine Lenzi, HES-SO/Haute École de Travail Social, Switzerland.

Benoît Lévesque, University of Quebec, Montreal, Canada.

Luciane Lucas dos Santos, Centre for Social Studies of the University of Coimbra, Portugal.

Carmen Marcuello, University of Zaragoza, Spain.

Marguerite Mendell, Karl Polanyi Institute of Political Economy, Concordia University, Canada.

Luis Razeto Migliaro, Universitas Nueva Civilización, Chile.

Beverley Mullings, Queen's University, Canada.

Peter North, University of Liverpool, UK and the Community Economies Institute.

Marthe Nyssens, Université catholique de Louvain, Belgium, EMES.

Mary O'Shaughnessy, University College Cork, Ireland, EMES.

Saoirse C. O'Shea, Open University, UK.

Tinyan Otuomagie, Queen's University, Canada.

Francesca Petrella, Aix Marseille Université et LEST-Cnrs, France.

Alice Pittini, Housing Europe.

Yvon Poirier, Intercontinental Network for the Promotion of Social Solidarity Economy.

Kiran Kamal Prasad, JEEVIKA, India.

Vincenza Priola, Open University, UK.

Smita Ramnarain, University of Rhode Island, USA.

Darryl Reed, University of British Columbia, Canada.

Nadine Richez-Battesti, Aix Marseille Université et LEST-Cnrs, France.

Anabel Rieiro, University of the Republic, Uruguay.

Andrea Salustri, Sapienza University of Rome, Italy.

Gianluca Salvatori, EURICSE.

Raymond Saner, Centre for Socio-Eco-Nomic Development (CSEND), Switzerland.

Lichia Saner-Yiu, Centre for Socio-Eco-Nomic Development (CSEND), Switzerland.

Chiyoge B. Sifa, International Cooperative Alliance-Africa.

Jeová Torres Silva Junior, Federal University of Cariri (UFCA), Brazil.

Dražen Šimleša, Institute of Social Science Ivo Pilar, Croatia.

Colleen E. Tapley, Southern New Hampshire University, USA.

Peter Utting, United Nations Research Institute for Social Development.

Yves Vaillancourt, Université du Québec à Montréal, Canada.

Davorka Vidović, University of Zagreb, Croatia.

Ilcheong Yi, United Nations Research Institute for Social Development (UNRISD).

Foreword

In order to ensure resilience in a context of crisis, we must absolutely accelerate the change towards the economy of tomorrow: just and sustainable to meet current and future social and societal challenges. The social and solidarity economy (SSE) can play a substantive role in achieving the Sustainable Development Goals leaving no one behind.

The online platform SSE Knowledge Hub for the SDGs already aimed at enhancing awareness of and contributing to the body of knowledge on the social and solidarity economy as a means of implementation of the Sustainable Development Goals by featuring more than 100 draft and working papers.

In my view, supporting the United Nations Inter-Agency Task Force on Social and Solidarity Economy (UNTFSSE) *Encyclopedia of the Social and Solidarity Economy*, and thus providing policymakers and academics with a reference tool that contains information and knowledge on a wide range of topics associated with the SSE, is key for fostering the development of the ecosystem.

By providing legitimate and credible information and knowledge on key issues of the SSE, the *Encyclopedia* will introduce the SSE to those not familiar with it, offer them with an overview of a wide range of topics associated with the SSE, and allow stakeholders to check facts or gain additional knowledge.

In the upcoming years, I will remain strongly committed to raising awareness of the SSE and offer SSE organizations the necessary support to grow.

Georges Engel

Minister of Labour, Employment and the Social and Solidarity Economy, Luxembourg

Foreword

A series of rolling global crises – environmental, social, economic and political – have exposed the shortcomings of our current development system. The social deficit and level of hardship and human suffering have increased over the last decades, in particular during the COVID-19 pandemic. This is partly due to the manner in which we have incentivised and governed economic behaviour in the last 40 years, as well as our overreliance on the power of the market, left to its own devices.

Although the implementation of the Sustainable Development Goals (SDGs) is steadily progressing, a number of challenges are yet to be addressed to make a transformative aspiration a reality. One of these challenges is how to embed the SDGs into our economic activities, relations and systems, and align them through an integrated approach in which we explore linkages between goals and targets.

One vehicle that has the potential to make a big positive impact in addressing these challenges is the social and solidarity economy (SSE). The SSE is defined as economic activities and market relations prioritising social (and often environmental) objectives over profit motives, and which are guided by principles and practices of cooperation, solidarity and democratic self-control. A United Nations Research Institute for Social Development (UNRISD) study on the SSE in South Korea shows its importance in almost all economic sectors, contributing to all 17 SDGs.

It comes as no surprise that policymakers and practitioners are increasingly paying attention to the SSE as a viable alternative approach to development, rebalancing economic, social, environmental and democratic objectives. Responding to this increasing interest in the SSE, several United Nations (UN) agencies, including the International Labour Organization (ILO), UNRISD and United Nations Non-Governmental Liaison Service (UN-NGLS), organised an international meeting to discuss Potential and Limits of Social and Solidarity Economy in May 2013, the first of its kind within the UN system. This in turn led to the establishment of the UN Inter-Agency Task Force on Social and Solidarity Economy (UNTFSSE), comprising UN agencies and international and regional organisations working in the SSE.

Since its establishment, the UNTFSSE has played a significant role in raising awareness of the SSE and has called on the international development community to recognize it as an alternative paradigm of development and a means of implementing the SDGs. One of the first initiatives of the UNTFSSE was to establish an SSE Knowledge Hub with the aim of enhancing awareness of and contributing to the body of knowledge on the SSE. This *Encyclopedia* is one of the research outputs of this SSE knowledge platform.

Although the SSE can play a significant role in achieving the SDGs, it has not yet reached its full potential, mainly due to a lack of it being mainstreamed in national policies and thinking, which is mostly due to a lack of information and discussion on the SSE in the policymaking process and everyday lives. This *Encyclopedia* provides lessons and findings on the positive contribution of the SSE that prioritises people and the planet over profit, and democratises the economy and society. It is available as a tool for education and communication on the SSE for all audiences, and will assist policymakers, raise awareness and create opportunities to promote the SSE at international, national and local levels.

We would like to thank members and observers of the UNTFSSE for supporting this project, and the authors who contributed excellent entries to the *Encyclopedia*. Our special thanks go to the members of the Editorial Committee who have coordinated and managed the whole process of this project to add value and academic credibility to this *Encyclopedia*, the research assistants who edited the manuscripts of the entries, and the staff of Edward Elgar Publishing who provided timely advice and consistent support and encouragement.

This *Encyclopedia* is the outcome of a research project of the UNTFSSE Knowledge Hub. We gratefully acknowledge the financial support for this project from the Luxembourg government.

Vic Van Vuuren
Chair of the UNTFSSE and Director, ILO Enterprise Department

Paul Ladd
Director, United Nations Research Institute for Social Development (UNRISD), the Implementing Agency of the UNTFSSE Knowledge Hub

Preface

Over several decades, neoliberalism has shaped economic activities and relations in much of the world. Although there are many variants of neoliberalism, they all share in common two fundamental assumptions: that we human beings can maximize self-interest based on an economic calculation of costs and benefits; and that the market is inherently efficient and self-regulated. The policy conclusion drawn from these assumptions is that a stronger free market enhances human wellbeing.

These assumptions, and the policy conclusion, are patently false. Calculated self-interest may be one element that determines our behaviour, but so too are non-economic interests and values associated with social norms, rights, obligations, reciprocity and morals. An inherently efficient and self-regulating market is just a utopian idea whose original imposition and catastrophic collapse was the subject of Karl Polanyi's (1944) *The Great Transformation*.

The social and solidarity economy (SSE), which has gained currency across the world over the past two decades, provides an alternative approach to promoting human wellbeing, social justice and economic and sustainable development. Although the meaning of the SSE and its key features are contested, its constituent organizations such as cooperatives, associations, mutuals, women's self-help groups and social enterprises play a significant role in creating and protecting economic activities and social relations from commercialization and bureaucratization, and transforming them into participatory and democratic ones. In a nutshell, the SSE is all about social control and democratization of the economy understood as a vast set of social relations.

Despite the growing recognition of the transformative potential of the SSE and the amount of academic and policy-oriented research related to the SSE, it remains a relatively new concept to many. There is therefore a need for high-quality knowledge on this topic, and information to guide policymakers, practitioners and researchers. Yet, there are very few sources that comprehensively examine the attributes, dynamics, opportunities and challenges associated with the SSE in various contexts. This is what has motivated the United Nations Inter-Agency Task Force on Social Solidarity Economy (UNTFSSE) to convene leading experts to produce the *Encyclopedia of the Social and Solidarity Economy* (the SSE *Encyclopedia*), which is intended as an essential tool for raising awareness of SSE and promoting SSE organizations and enterprises at local, national and international levels.

The SSE *Encyclopedia* is divided into four parts. Part I, 'Histories, Concepts and Theories', includes entry 10, 'Origins and Histories', which reveals the collective amnesia about the origins of social and economic organizations based on democratic solidarity initiated by various groups (indigenous self-organization in South America, women and African Americans in North America, and pioneering workers in Europe). It also includes entries dealing with the contested contemporary meanings of the SSE, and how the SSE relates to alternative and heterodox economic approaches and social movements. Part II, 'Actors and Organizations', has entries explaining and introducing the key actors and organizations constituting the SSE, ranging from cooperatives and mutuals, to associations, non-governmental organizations and foundations, and social enterprises, to women's self-help groups and community-based organizations. Entries on actors who play an increasingly important role but receive less research attention, such as LGBTIQ+, youth, and migrants and refugees, are also featured in Part II. The contribution of SSE to inclusive and sustainable development is the overarching theme of Part III, 'Linkages to Development'. The entries highlight the SSE's linkages with aspects of the United Nations Sustainable Development Goals (SDGs) related to hunger and poverty, health care, education, gender, energy and water, inequality, housing, tourism, sustainable production, social services, peace, culture, sports and leisure sectors, finance and investment. In Part IV, 'Enabling Environment and Governance', the entries address the question of how to promote the SSE in global, national and local contexts; what institutions and policies are necessary; and how SSE organizations and enterprises are or should be governed and managed. Key elements examined include the institutional ecosystem of the SSE; challenges and obstacles related to the management and governance of SSE organizations and enterprises; and the SSE as a source of resilience in the context of multiple crises.

Through these entries, this *Encyclopaedia* aims to address several challenges of research on the SSE. Firstly, it adopts a global perspective, departing from the national perspectives, Eurocentrism and transatlanticism in dealing with the key themes and issues. The examples of SSE organizations and enterprises introduced in the entries are from the countries of all continents, which highlights the universal applicability of the SSE to diverse contexts. Secondly, given the diverse backgrounds and experience of the authors and editors, the *Encyclopedia* aims to communicate with a broad international readership.

The entries in this *Encyclopedia* bring out the complex relationship between economic, social and political dimensions, and how SSE actors and organizations are positioned differently in relation to the aspiration of transforming the economy, polity and society. We hope that this *Encyclopedia* will provide policymakers, academics and practitioners with a guide on how to further the utilitarian purpose and realize the transformative potential of the SSE in terms of democratization, systemic change and, ultimately, emancipation. By providing legitimate and credible information and knowledge on key issues, we also expect to introduce the SSE to those not familiar with it, offer them an overview of a wide range of topics associated with it, and allow SSE stakeholders to check facts or gain additional knowledge on the topic.

The *Encyclopedia* (subtitled "systematic dictionary of the science, arts and crafts"), edited by Denis Diderot and Jean Le Rond d'Alembert (1776), was an exemplary work of those who led the 18th-century Enlightenment in France. It contributed to the progress and a positive transformation of human society. We hope that our SSE *Encyclopedia* will play a similar role and will inform both current and future generations.

The SSE *Encyclopedia* Editorial Committee would like to express our gratitude to all the authors who contributed entries, as well as to the UNTFSSE members and observers who provided valuable advice. We also thank Daniel Mather and Catherine Elgar of Edward Elgar Publishing who have supported this project from beginning to end by providing advice and encouragement. Our special thanks go to Natalie Taylor, Emily Kostanecki, Billy Southern and Carl Hughes who copyedited all the entries in such a short time frame.

The SSE Encyclopedia Editorial Committee

REFERENCES

Diderot, Denis, and Jean Le Rond d'Alembert. 1776. *Encyclopédie ou Dictionnaire raisonné des sciences, des arts et des métiers*, vol. 5. Pergamon Press.
Polanyi, Karl. 1944. *The Great Transformation: Economic and Political Origins of Our Time*. New York: Farrar & Rinehart.

Abbreviations

ABONG	Brazilian Association of Non-Governmental Organizations
AERé	Action Emploi Réfugiés
AI	artificial intelligence
AIAB	Italian Association for Organic Agriculture
Alliance PEC	Alliance Paysans–Écologistes–Consommateurs
ALMPs	Active Labour Market Policies
AMAP	Associations pour le Maintien d'une Agriculture Paysanne/ Association for the Preservation of Small-Scale Farming
AMC	Ahmedabad Municipal Corporation
ASA	Amigos Siempre Amigos
ASD	autistic spectrum disorder
ASEC	Asian Solidarity Economy Council
ASSEFA	Association for Sarva Seva Farms
ATTAC	Association for the Taxation of Financial Transactions and Aid to Citizens
AYB	Alashanek ya balady/Association for Sustainable Development
B2B	business to business
B2C	business to consumer
BMGF	Bill & Melinda Gates Foundation
BRI	Bank Rakyat Indonesia
BSCP	Brotherhood of Sleeping Car Porters
CAKHS	Coopérative Agricole Kavokiva du Haut Sassandra
CBD	community-based development
CBHI	community-based health insurance
CBO	community-based organization
CD	community development
CE	community economies
CEiS	Community Enterprise in Scotland
CEO	chief executive officer
CEPES	Confederación Empresarial Española de la Economía Social
CERN	Community Economies Research Network
CES	critical entrepreneurship studies
CFI	Cooperazione Finanza Impresa

CHCA	Cooperative Home Care Associates
CIRIEC	International Centre of Research and Information on the Public, Social and Cooperative Economy
CLGSSE	Council of Local Governments on the Social Solidarity Economy
CLT	community land trust
CLU	Cooperativa Lavoratori Uniti
CNCRESS	Conseil National des CRESS
CNS	Co-op Network Studies
CO	community organization
CO_2	carbon dioxide
COP	Conference of the Parties
CORD	Chinmaya Organisation for Rural Development
CPRs	common-pool resources
CREA	Creating Resources for Empowerment in Action
CRESS	Chambres Régionales de l'Économie Sociale et Solidaire
CSA	community supported agriculture
CSF	credit surety fund
CSMO-ESAC	Comité Sectoriel de Main-d'œuvre – Économie Sociale Action Communautaire
CSO	civil society organization
CSP	Community Services Programme
CSR	corporate social responsibility
CUT	Central Única dos Trabalhadores
DAY-NRLM	Deendayal Antyodaya Yojana – National Rural Livelihoods Mission
DE	diverse economy
DG ECHO	Directorate-General for European Civil Protection and Humanitarian Aid Operations
ENP	entrepreneurial non-profit
ERDF	European Regional Development Fund
ESF	European Social Fund
ESG	environmental, social and governance
ESIFs	European Structural and Investment Funds
ESSFI	SSE International Forum
EU	European Union
EURICSE	European Research Institute on Cooperative and Social Enterprises
FAO	Food and Agriculture Organization
FARC-EP	The Revolutionary Armed Forces of Colombia – People's Army

FASE	Framework Act on the Social Economy
FBES	Fórum Brasileiro de Economia Solidária/Brazilian Solidarity Economy Forum
FDT	Fonds de développement des territoires/Territorial Development Fund
FE	feminist economics
FEW	Forum for the Empowerment of Women
FFC	Freedom Farm Cooperative
FPI	Foundation for Public Interest
FPO	for-profit organization
FRA	European Union Agency for Fundamental Rights/Fundamental Rights Agency
FSF	Free Software Foundation
GATT	General Agreement on Tariffs and Trade
GB	Grameen Bank
GCMMF	Gujarat Co-operative Milk Marketing Federation Ltd
GDP	gross domestic product
GEM	Global Education Movement
GHG	greenhouse gas
GILRHO	Global Index on Legal Recognition of Homosexual Orientation
GMF	guarantee mutual fund
GNGO	governmental non-governmental organization
GPI	genuine progress indicator
GRIN	Global Respect in Education
GSEF	Global Social Economy Forum
HDI	Human Development Index
HI	Hostelling International
HLPF	High-Level Political Forum
HRD	human resource development
ICA	International Cooperative Alliance
ICMIF	International Cooperative and Mutual Insurance Federation
ICSEM	International Comparative Social Enterprise Models
ICT	information and communication technology
IGLYO	International LGBTQI Youth and Student Organisation
IHCO	International Health Cooperative Organisation
ILC	International Labour Conference
ILGA	International Lesbian, Gay, Bisexual, Trans and Intersex Association
ILGLaw	International Lesbian, Gay, Bi, Trans, and Intersex Law Association

ILO	International Labour Organization/International Labour Office
ILO COOP	ILO Cooperatives Unit
ILO GED	ILO Gender, Equality and Diversity Branch
IMF	International Monetary Fund
INCOOP	Incubadora Regional de Cooperativas Populares
INGO	international non-governmental organization
IOT	internet of things
IPC	International Planning Committee for Food Sovereignty
ISEE	International Society for Ecological Economics
ISEW	Index of Sustainable Economic Welfare
ISTO	International Social Tourism Organisation
IT	information technology
ITCP	Incubadora Tecnológica de Cooperativas Populares/Technological Incubators for Popular Cooperatives
ITMAV	Initiatives de travail de milieu auprès des aînés en situation de vulnérabilité
IUCN	International Union for Conservation of Nature
IYHF	International Youth Hostel Federation
JEEVIKA	Jeeta Vimukti Karnataka/Bonded Labour Liberation Karnataka
JLG	joint liability group
JOAA	Japan Organic Agriculture Association
KMBL	Khushhali Microfinance Bank Limited
KoSEA	Korea Social Enterprise Promotion Agency
LCD	local community development
LED	light-emitting diode
LETS	local exchange trading system
LGBT*	lesbian, gay, bisexual, transgender and minority sexuality and gender people
LGBTQ	lesbian, gay, bisexual, transgender and queer
LGBTQI	lesbian, gay, bisexual, transgender, queer and intersex
LSPA	local solidarity-based partnership for agroecology
MARDEF	Malawi Rural Development Fund
MDGs	Millennium Development Goals
MFI	microfinance institution
MGNREGA	Mahatma Gandhi National Rural Employment Guarantee Act
MGNREGS	Mahatma Gandhi National Rural Employment Guarantee Scheme
MHT	Mahila Housing SEWA Trust

MPA	Small Farmers Movement
MST	Movimento dos Trabalhadores Sem Terra/Landless Rural Workers' Movement
MTA	Mondragon Team Academy
MU	Mondragon University
MYRADA	Mysore Resettlement and Development Agency
NABARD	National Bank for Agriculture and Rural Development
NAFTA	North American Free Trade Agreement
NEET	not in employment, education or training
NFCF	National Federation of Colored Farmers
NGO	non-governmental organization
NHG	neighbourhood group
NPA	non-performing asset
NPISH	non-profit institutions serving households
NPO	non-profit organization
OECD	Organisation for Economic Co-operation and Development
OSI	Open Source Initiative
PAC	Alternative Community Project
PIESS	Pla d'Impuls de l'Economia Social i Solidària
PPPPSES	Public–Private Policymaking Partnership for the Social Economy in Seoul
PRI	programme-related investment
PSE	popular and solidarity economy
PSE	public sector social enterprise
PSSEPs	public-social and solidarity economy partnerships
PT	Partido dos Trabalhadores
PTCE	Pôles territoriaux de coopération économique/Territorial Business Clusters for Economic Cooperation
RIPESS	Intercontinental Network for the Promotion of Social Solidarity Economy
ROSCA	rotating savings and credit association
SACCOs	savings and credit cooperatives
SAFRA ADAP	San Francisco Association of Differently Abled Persons
SB	social business
SBI	social business initiative
SC	social cooperative

SCIC	Société Coopérative d'Intérêt Collectif/Collective Interest Cooperative Company
SDGs	Sustainable Development Goals
SE	social enterprise
SEI	Social Enterprise Initiative
SEL	French local exchange system
SELP	Social Economy Leadership Program
SENAES	National Secretariat for Solidarity Economy
SEWA	Self Employed Women's Association
SHG	self-help group
SHG-BLP	Self-Help Group–Bank Linkage Programme
SIGI	Sisterhood Is Global Institute
SMEs	small and medium-sized enterprises
SNA	System of National Accounts
SOLAWI	Solidarischelandwirtshaft/Solidarity Agriculture
SPA	social provisioning approach
SPC	sustainable production and consumption
SPG	solidarity purchasing group
SR	social reproduction
SSE	social and solidarity economy
SSEC	Seoul Social Economy Centre
SSEN	Seoul Social Economy Network
SSEOEs	social and solidarity economy organizations and enterprises
SSET	social and solidarity economy tourism
SSF	social and solidarity financing
STEAM	science, technology, engineering, the arts and mathematics
STEM	science, technology, engineering, and mathematics
SWAPO Party	South West Africa People's Organisation
TEEB	The Economics of Ecosystems and Biodiversity
TEKB	Association of All Pharmacists Cooperatives
TIDE	Technology Informatics Design Endeavour
TRP	The Rainbow Project
TYM	Tao Yeu May Fund
UCIRI	Union of Indigenous Communities of the Isthmus Region
UK	United Kingdom
UNDP	United Nations Development Programme
UNEP	United Nations Environment Programme

UNESCO	United Nations Educational, Scientific and Cultural Organization
UNICEF	United Nations Children's Fund
UN-NGLS	United Nations Non-Governmental Liaison Service
UNRISD	United Nations Research Institute for Social Development
UNTFSSE	United Nations Inter-Agency Task Force on Social and Solidarity Economy
UPOV	Union for the Protection of New Plant Varieties
UPR	Universal Periodical Review
US	United States
USAID	United States Agency for International Development
VHSNC	Village Health, Sanitation and Nutrition Committee
VNR	Voluntary National Review
WCED	World Commission on Environment and Development
WHO	World Health Organization
WIEGO	Women in Informal Employment: Globalizing and Organizing
WISE	work integration social enterprise
WLUML	Women Living Under Muslim Laws
WSF	World Social Forum
WTO	World Trade Organization
WWF	World Wide Fund for Nature

PART I

HISTORIES, CONCEPTS AND THEORIES

1. Activism and social movements
Hamish Jenkins and Yvon Poirier

INTRODUCTION

Given the diversity of social and solidarity economy (SSE) experiences within and between countries and continents, it is not surprising that scholarly studies on the SSE and social movements are fraught with divergent views and understandings, especially since they tend to be associated with distinct fields of academic research that so far rarely intersect. Should we think in terms of a relationship, or lack thereof, between the SSE and social movements, or is the SSE in itself a social movement that is part of broader movements (from local to global levels) aiming to challenge the dominant neoliberal economic model (Laville et al. 2017)? This entry proposes that it is both: SSE entities and ecosystems are often the result of various forms of social movements' activism in different parts of the world, whether or not they stay connected to social movements thereafter. And significant parts of the overall SSE constellation can be described as a converging social movement (or 'movement of movements') with a plurality of views that are in articulation with other social movements; not only to resist the harmful socio-environmental effects of the current economic model but also to demonstrate, through practice, concrete alternatives. These experiments, at the level of the organization/enterprise and the local territory, given the right political conditions and motivation of the actors concerned, can be scaled up or 'mainstreamed' through enabling public policy changes. Advocacy, contestation, policy influence, and the co-construction of policy via SSE intermediary organizations and their allies play an important role in this process (see also entry 55, 'Supporting Organizations and Intermediaries' and entry 47, 'Local and Territorial Development Plans').

At this juncture, the question is whether the end result of such developments is the incremental growth of economic activity undertaken through SSE principles at the micro and meso levels, in a context where unsustainable production and consumption patterns remain relatively unchanged. Alternatively, these advances can be seen as stepping-stones to consolidate social movements aiming at more fundamental macro-changes to democratize the overall economy and politics itself (Laville et al. 2017).

1.1 DEFINING SOCIAL MOVEMENTS IN THE CONTEXT OF THE SSE

Since the 1970s, social movements have become a subject of multidisciplinary academic studies, presenting slightly varying elements to define what constitutes a social movement. For the purposes of this entry, we will use the definition provided by James and van Seters (2014) in the context of their study of social movements' mobilization against neoliberal globalization, or the 'alter-globalization' movement:

Defining a social movement entails a few minimal conditions of 'coming together': (1.) the formation of some kind of collective identity; (2.) the development of a shared normative orientation; (3.) the sharing of concern for change of the status quo and (4.) the occurrence of moments of practical action that are at least subjectively connected together across time addressing this concern for change. Thus, we define a social movement as a form of political association between persons who have at least a minimal sense of themselves as connected to others in common purpose and who come together across an extended period of time to effect social change in the name of that purpose. (James and van Seters 2014, xi)

In addition to these generic elements, a distinctive feature of social movements related to the SSE (especially compared to primarily protest-based movements) is the combination of political activism with solidarity-based forms of economic activities that can change material conditions in people's daily lives and demonstrate in concrete terms that alternative economic models (especially at local and territorial levels) are possible (Laville et al. 2017; Zimmer and Eum 2017). In section 1.4, we suggest that large parts of the myriad entities throughout the world that recognize themselves as part of the SSE are converging, from local to global levels, into a *de facto* social movement (or 'movement of movements') that meets these minimal conditions; albeit with their own tensions and contradictions, as well as their own strengths and weaknesses vis-à-vis other social movements with which they seek to cooperate. First, however, this entry examines social movements as catalysts of SSE.

1.2   SOCIAL MOVEMENTS AS CATALYSTS OF THE SSE

SSE initiatives are typically the result of the activism of social movements and alliances that have common affinities, whether thematic (for example, environmental protection, agroecology, food sovereignty, health, social and economic justice, anti-extractivism, the commons) or identity based (for example, small and landless farmers, consumers, workers unions, informal workers' associations, feminist movements, indigenous peoples, religious groups). The forms of action are in part determined by the political context in which they operate. They may include relatively soft forms of mobilization, such as bypassing agro-industrial production and distribution through short local organic food supply networks, or the creation of SSE initiatives to combat unemployment and (re)generate sources of livelihoods. Another option may involve more radical operations such as the illegal or semi-legal occupation of land/ territories, wherein SSE 'microcosms' can develop with some degree of autonomy vis-à-vis capitalistic relations, such as the Zapatista movement in Chiapas, Mexico, the Landless Rural Workers' Movement (Movimento dos Trabalhadores Sem Terra, MST) in Brazil, or the more recent Zones à Défendre (*zadiste*) movements in France (Laville et al. 2017). SSE social movements, like other social movements, are best understood through a 'multi-organizational field' approach: namely, the need to understand them in relation to the confluence of different currents of thought and pre-existing movements (Curtis and Zurcher 1973; Laville et al. 2017). Using this approach, this entry illustrates the role of social movements in catalyzing and accompanying SSE agroecological consumer–producer networks in South Korea and France (Box 1.1), and in generating jobs and livelihoods in Colombia and Brazil (Box 1.2).

BOX 1.1   SSE AGROECOLOGICAL CONSUMER–PRODUCER MOVEMENTS

The Republic of Korea

The Republic of Korea (or South Korea) today is one of the countries with the most vibrant SSE ecosystem in the world, backed by many local authorities, as described in entry 47, 'Local and Territorial Development Plans'. The beginnings of the SSE can be traced to the creation of credit unions by the ecclesiastical movement in the 1970s, inspired by the Antigonish movement in Canada (blending adult education, cooperatives, microfinance and rural community development). From the mid-1980s onward, building on earlier rural agricultural cooperative experiments, a new form of consumer cooperatives called Hansalim brought together consumers and producers with the aim of developing solidarity-based relations between urban consumers and rural organic food producers. A coalition of environmental, feminist and neighbourhood movements and citizen mobilization helped to organize the daily provisioning of healthy organic products. It has been observed that these movements are a continuum of earlier pro-democracy movements from the 1970s against military dictatorship (notably students, intellectuals, church groups) that are still active today, notably through the mass demonstrations in 2016–17 calling for the impeachment of President Park Geun-hye over a corruption scandal. The 'social movement' dimension of consumer cooperatives also remains alive through their participation in the organization of public demonstrations in favour of environmental protection and food sovereignty (Zimmer and Eum 2017).

France

Similarly in France, the Associations pour le Maintien d'une Agriculture Paysanne, AMAP (Associations for the Preservation of Small-Scale Farming), which also promotes solidarity partnerships between smallholder farmers and consumers, began operation in 2001 through the combined efforts of an alliance of small farmer, environmental and consumer movements, Alliance Paysans–Écologistes–Consommateurs (Alliance PEC) created in 1991. Among them is the Confédération Paysanne, the national union of smallholder farmers and agricultural workers which defends a 'realistic alternative' to industrial agriculture, based on social, solidarity and ecological principles, and is one of the founders of the global small farmers movement, Via Campesina, campaigning for the principles of food sovereignty and solidarity worldwide (http://confederationpaysanne.fr). According to the latest surveys in France, there are well over 2000 AMAP and over 250 000 people involved in the movement, in both producer–consumer networks and awareness-raising campaigns (Zimmer and Eum 2017; http://miramap.org). The national network (Mouvement inter-régional des Amap) is part of URGENCI, which is an international network of grassroots organizations that is present in 32 countries. It follows similar principles and types of action through different names, such as community supported agriculture (CSA), and is generally referred to as local solidarity-based partnerships for agroecology (LSPAs). The AMAP are part of the wider ecologist movement in France, which formed a political party (Les Verts, now called Les Écologistes) that played an important role in supporting the elaboration and adoption of the 2014 framework law on SSE proposed by the Socialist Party then in power (Laville et al. 2017; Zimmer and Eum 2017).

BOX 1.2 MOVEMENTS FOR EMPLOYMENT AND LIVELIHOODS

Colombia

In Colombia, SSE initiatives emerged in the 1960s, although solidarity-based economic principles date back to pre-Hispanic times through indigenous practices of mutual help and reciprocity (named *minga, manos vueltas, convite*). Since the 1960s, the movements developing concrete SSE projects in the field had already been promoting the idea of incorporating solidarity economy principles into law. These movements were significantly driven by Catholic activists adhering to the Theology of Liberation through the diocesan social pastoral secretariat (Sepas). They also drew on the experiences of cooperativism in Europe and Canada. Caught between a repressive oligarchic regime and armed rebel guerrillas, activists found in SSE a non-threatening manner to implicitly express their ideological position against capitalistic development, while providing alternative livelihood opportunities to those proposed by the armed revolutionaries. In the southern region of the Department of Santander, activities included support for the creation and development of cooperatives principally in rural development, but also finance, transport, education and health. A third of the population (450 000 persons) work in 200 created cooperatives. In addition, an intermediary organization, El Commun, was established to enable dialogue with the state and to promote SSE territorial development, as well as networks bringing together academics, non-governmental organizations (NGOs) and community organizations to plan and implement local SSE development initiatives.

Elements of the concept of the solidarity economy were first introduced in the Constitution of 1991. The legal framework for SSE entities, regrouped in two categories (solidarity enterprises and economic organizations for solidarity-based development), was later spelt out in law 545 of 1998 on 'the solidarity economy and entities of a cooperative nature'. It is noteworthy that solidarity economy was also recognized in the peace agreement between the Colombian Government and Revolutionary Armed Forces – Peoples' Army (FARC–EP) in 2016 (Hataya 2017).

Brazil

In neighbouring Brazil, the ecclesiastical movement also played a leading role in generating SSE initiatives throughout the country together with other social movements, especially the workers' movement and its extension into a major political party. The draconian neoliberal policies of austerity, privatization and trade liberalization undertaken in the 1980s and 1990s generated mass long-term unemployment, poverty and social exclusion throughout the country. From the 1990s onward, SSE initiatives developed initially as a survival strategy for a growing number of unemployed workers through Alternative Community Projects (PACs). These were established by the Catholic NGO Caritas and SSE incubators called Incubadora Tecnológica de Cooperativas Populares (ITCP) and hosted by public universities and NGOs, and resulted from the mobilization of university professors, students, workers and grassroots activists. SSE initiatives began spreading with the involvement of a wider number of movements and groups, including landless rural workers, waste collectors, artisans, indigenous peoples and Afro Brazilian groups, women's movements, and neighbourhood assemblies.

> One of the two major national trade union confederations, the Central Única dos Trabalhadores (CUT) embraced the solidarity economy as a creative response to severe economic crises and the devastating impact on the labour market. In 1999, it set up an Agency for Solidarity Development with other NGOs and SSE organizations, in order to support the creation and consolidation of solidarity cooperatives and enterprises as means to generate employment and income. In parallel, solidarity economy was increasingly being supported at municipal and state levels by elected officials from the political party emanating from the workers' movement, the Partido dos Trabalhadores (PT). After it gained power at the federal level in 2002, between 2003 and 2016 the PT government developed a wide range of public policies and programmes to support the SSE through the newly created National Secretariat for Solidarity Economy (SENAES), as described in entry 47, 'Local and Territorial Development Plans'. Upon creation of the Secretariat, a plenary meeting with representatives of the entire SSE movement in the country was held to create two major national entities: the Fórum Brasileiro de Economia Solidária (FBES) regrouping all solidarity economy-based initiatives and civil society organizations supporting the SSE; and a network of officials from municipal and state governments promoting the SSE in their territories. According to some estimates, over 30 000 organizations and enterprises (SSEOEs) and supporting organizations were created nationwide, involving around 3 million individuals. (Singer and Schiochet 2017; Addor and Rolim Laricchia 2018; CUT 1999).
>
> Some of the main actors propelling the SSE movement in Brazil were also instrumental in the process leading to the World Social Forum discussed in section 1.3.

Many initiatives are the result of a cross-fertilization of ideas and practices from across countries and continents. The success of initiatives has in many cases brought political momentum toward the adoption of public policies in favour of the SSE, notably through political parties with affinities to the leading social movements. In some cases, the actors of SSE initiatives, once well established, distance themselves from activism, prioritizing the daily economic operations of their enterprise or organization ('routinization'), marking a partial or complete break from the social movement that created them. In other cases, the ties with the social movement remain active or evolve into new movements (Zimmer and Eum 2017).

1.3 THE SSE: AN EMERGING GLOBAL MOVEMENT WITHIN THE ALTER-GLOBALIZATION MOVEMENT

The spread of the SSE through social movements is not the fruit of a fully fledged theory or blueprint imposed through a top-down approach. Rather, it reflects a bottom-up process representing very diverse experiences, where actors respond to challenges within their own context; some *de facto*, undertaking activities involving SSE principles without recognizing themselves as part of a collective identity called 'social and solidarity economy'. As noted in Boxes 1.1 and 1.2, some movements have studied the experience of cooperativism from other countries and applied its principles to their own realities. However, cooperatives are only a part of the broader set of SSEOEs described in other entries of this *Encyclopedia*. This section examines: (1) the conditions of coming together of significant parts of the overall SSE community as a global social movement as defined by James and van Seters (2014) cited above; and (2) the relationship and articulation between the SSE movement and other social movements mobilizing against the neoliberal agenda, increasingly referred to as the alter-globalization movement.

The SSE: An Emerging Global Social Movement

The gradual construction of collective identity and shared normative orientation among SSE actors around the world has been a slow process of dialogue and mutual learning. To simplify what is in fact a much larger nomenclature, it has been the convergence of two major currents: the 'social economy' tradition, originating notably from Europe and Canada; and the 'solidarity economy', predominant notably in the Latin American experience, but also increasingly used in other continents. The exchange of experiences and visions from actors across different continents has greatly contributed to this convergence. The main differences and elements in common among scholars and activists are presented in a stylized fashion in entry 3, 'Contemporary Understandings', whereby social economy places the emphasis on SSEOEs as part of a 'third sector' complementing the capitalist economy and the public sector, while solidarity economy aims at more systemic change, social transformation and political engagement at multiple levels of governance.

The Intercontinental Network for the Promotion of Social Solidarity Economy (RIPESS) is one international SSE coalition that has been instrumental in forging a common identity among strands of social versus solidarity economy. The first in a series of international meetings on the Globalization of Solidarity was held in Lima in 1997, where activists from a wide range of social movements, NGOs, researchers and practitioners from around the world gathered to begin developing the elements of a more concrete global SSE movement. This set the stage for the formal establishment in 2002 of RIPESS, as 'a global network of continental networks committed to the promotion of Social Solidarity Economy' in Latin America and the Caribbean, North America, Europe, Africa, Asia and Oceania. Each continental network is composed of national and sectorial networks which provide strong territorial and substantive anchoring to promote intercontinental cooperation and advocacy at different levels.

In the words of former RIPESS board member Emily Kawano, the 'Social Solidarity Economy is actually a marriage of the solidarity economy and the more radical end of the social economy'. Namely, this refers to social economy actors who see its value in addressing problems such as poverty, unemployment and social exclusion caused by neoliberal capitalism in the short term, but also understand it as a stepping stone toward a more fundamental transformation of the economic system. 'It is this end of the social economy spectrum that converges with the concept of the solidarity economy' (Kawano 2013). This reflects the view of many solidarity economy scholars and activists who argue that the SSE agenda must extend beyond the promotion of SSE principles within an organization or enterprise (limited profit, collective ownership and democratic governance). It should not satisfy itself with solely obtaining legal frameworks that guarantee SSEOEs distinct statutory identity without also engaging in the systemic transformation of the prevailing economic system, starting with the promotion of broader solidarity economy ties in the local community and beyond (Laville et al. 2017).

The intercontinental nature of SSE social movements coordinated by established international organizations, such as RIPESS, is an acceptance of nuances in the meaning of terminologies that forges a common identity within a diversity of historical practices and cultural heritage. In Europe, the social economy is quite strongly rooted and pre-dates the framework of the solidarity economy, which has been gaining more support. The RIPESS Europe network, therefore, works with both social economy and solidarity economy organizations and includes sectoral as well as territorial organizations/networks. Quebec builds on the concept of the social economy and seeks to create a movement for transformation that is very practical and grounded at the local and territorial levels. In the rest of Canada, the emphasis is on the territorial framework of local economic development. RIPESS Latin America and the Caribbean uses the solidarity economy framework. Despite some differences in definition, there is broad agreement about its systemic and transformative agenda and is built around a core of ethical principles. The United States Solidarity Economy Network deliberately chose, from the outset, to work within the solidarity economy framework as an unambiguously transformative movement. The Asia Solidarity Economy Council (ASEC) takes the social enterprise as a starting point, along with the need to build solidarity economy supply chains. RIPESS networks in Africa work with both the social economy and solidarity economy frameworks (RIPESS 2013). One of the achievements of RIPESS was to bring under the SSE umbrella organizations and enterprises that had been practising social and solidarity economy for decades without knowing it.

The SSE Movement and Other Social Movements

From the mid to late 1990s, SSE movements began to converge as a global movement, around the same time that other social movements were coalescing against neoliberal globalization. The mass protests at the 3rd Ministerial Conference of the World Trade Organization in Seattle in 1999 (the so-called 'Battle of Seattle') made this global 'anti-globalization' movement visible to the mass media and the general public. In previous years, however, a variety of historical events had already revealed distinctive critiques of neoliberal globalization with global interconnections. The Zapatista uprising in Mexico in 1994 was connected to the resistance to the North American Free Trade Agreement (NAFTA), the worldwide protests against the corporate-driven Multilateral Agreement on Investment that had been initiated by the Organisation for Economic Co-operation and Development (OECD) in 1995, the mobilization against the International Monetary Fund (IMF) in the wake of the 1997–98 East Asian financial crises, and the massive demonstration of the Jubilee 2000 debt cancellation campaign at the G8 meeting in Birmingham in 1998. All were indicative of a deepening popular discontent against globalization (James and van Seters 2014).

From an initial position primarily focused on being 'against' ('anti-globalization'), prominent actors within the movement took steps to enable this unprecedented global mobilization to move to a new stage of resistance: over and beyond the demonstrations and mass protests, it seemed possible to offer specific proposals 'for' ('alter-globalization') to seek concrete responses to the challenges of building 'another world', one where the economy would serve people and not the other way around. The World Social Forum (WSF) became the vehicle for this effort, spearheaded by a group of Brazilian organizations affiliated to the SSE movement, including CUT (mentioned in Box 1.2), the Landless Peasants' Movement (MST) of Brazil, the Brazilian Association of Non-Governmental Organizations (ABONG) and the French Association for the Taxation of Financial Transactions and Aid to Citizens (ATTAC). The organizers received the logistical support of the Governor of the Brazilian state of Rio Grande do Sul and the Mayor of Porto Alegre (elected on the pro-SSE workers' party – PT – platform) where the Forum would be held. A form of global validation of this initiative took place in June 2000, during an 'alternative' summit of social movements opposed to globalization organized in coordination with the United Nations Non-Governmental Liaison Service (UN-NGLS) in parallel with the Copenhagen+5 World Summit on Social Development. On that occasion, an International Committee was set up in support of the organization of the first WSF, which was held in late January 2001 and timed to coincide with the World Economic Forum of corporate leaders held annually in Davos (Whitaker 2005).

From the outset, the SSE movement was active in World Social Forum processes to contribute to the contents of alternatives to the neoliberal agenda at local, national and global levels. This was within the framework of the Forum's slogan 'Another World is Possible' and the motto 'Resist and Build', which then framed the content of the 2nd Globalization of Solidarity meeting in Quebec City in October 2001. There were difficulties in making the SSE visible among the multitude of issues and agendas brought by thousands of organizations and movements which gathered in the series of WSF editions that took place since. Some also saw as a handicap the fact that article 1 of the WSF Charter prohibited WSF spokespersons or resolutions from representing the Forum as a whole. The dilution of coherent substantive messaging contributed, among other shortcomings, to a gradual loss of media interest and the lack of any clear normative demands that governments and international institutions could concretely respond to (Savio 2019).

However, a major breakthrough was an agreement to hold a Thematic World Social Forum in Porto Alegre in preparation for the Peoples' Summit, which was held in parallel with the 2012 United Nations Summit on Sustainable Development (Rio+20). This occasion brought together diverse social movements from around the world, but this time organized around clearly defined cross-cutting thematic clusters, including the SSE, in which RIPESS played a major role, most notably through the Fórum Brasileiro de Economia Solidária (FBES). Among the normative demands emanating from the dialogue between the People's Summit spokespersons and United Nations (UN) officials was the need for the United Nations to take up the SSE as an alternative to neoliberal globalization capable of addressing the major sustainable development challenges discussed at the official Summit. These demands were heeded, starting with the International Conference on Potential and Limits of Social and Solidarity Economy, organized by the United Nations Research Institute for Social Development (UNRISD) in collaboration with the International Labour Organization (ILO) and UN-NGLS in May 2013 in Geneva. At that meeting, it was decided to create the United Nations Inter-Agency Task Force on Social and Solidarity Economy (UNTFSSE) which was established in September 2013. Its mission, in collaboration with international SSE networks acting as observers, is to raise the visibility of the SSE within the UN system and beyond, notably by showcasing the SSE as a strategic means of implementation of globally agreed Sustainable Development Goals that originated from the follow-up to the Rio+20 Summit (www.unsse.org).

1.4 LOOKING FORWARD

This entry has demonstrated the considerable achievements of the SSE movement, especially over the last two decades. Looking forward, compared to some other social movements that are able to garner global media attention through mass mobilization (such as the climate justice movement and Black Lives Matter), the SSE movement is less visible, in part because the SSE is a more complex concept to convey and it does not lend itself easily to mass mobilization around a catchy slogan. On the other hand, its strength lies in its rootedness at the local level and the fact that it offers concrete benefits to people that are more tangible and immediate than, say, the possible benefits of a hypothetical global Tobin tax, or systemic reforms of the international financial architecture – however much needed these may also remain.

The future of the SSE movement should also be seen in the light of the advent of new social media. While this communication revolution has provided formidable means for rapid mobilization of social movements, it has led to what James and van Seters (2014) have described as a shift from group-based solidaristic movements and place-making to 'mediated networked politics', which has engendered limitations to the depth of individual engagement in a transformative politics. When accompanied by a subjectivity that emphasizes autonomy and freedom over other values such as mutuality and reciprocity, networked politics tends to be reduced to symbolic action. Most contemporary activism, rather than producing a transitional practice that might set up alternative ways of living, tends to be reduced to acts of protest and 'mediated communication'. Mass mobilizations in the age of new social media, such as the Arab Spring of December 2010 and the Occupy Wall Street movement that followed in September 2011, tend to remain limited to 'communicative protest politics' with all its strengths and weaknesses. In response, James and van Seters (2014) propose what they call a 'grounded globalization approach', suggesting that:

> [A]nother world only becomes possible when globalizing social movements are grounded in the local and address the human condition in its fullness: production, exchange, enquiry and organization as well as communication. Prefiguring the claim that 'another world is possible', the slogan of the Porto Alegre World Social Forum, requires that exemplary practices are initiated across the full range of human life. (James and van Seters 2014, xxvi)

Therein lies the inherent strength of the global SSE movement in the years to come.

REFERENCES

Addor, Felipe, and Camilla Rolim Laricchia. 2018. 'Incubadoras Tecnológicas de Economia Solidária.' Rio de Janeiro: Universidade Federal do Rio de Janeiro (UFRG). https://base.socioeco.org/docs/incubadoras-tecnologicas_v1_1ed2018_web.pdf.

Curtis, Russell L., and Louis A. Zurcher. 1973. 'Stable Resources of Protest Movements: The Multi-Organizational Field.' *Social Forces* 52 (1): 53. https://doi.org/10.2307/2576423.

CUT (Central Única dos Trabalhadores). 1999. 'Sindicalismo e Economia Solidária – Reflexões Sobre o Projeto da CUT.' http://docvirt.com/docreader.net/DocReader.aspx?bib=bibliotms&pagfis=10810.

Hataya, Noriko. 2017. 'Des Mouvements Promoteurs D'Économie Solidaire en Colombie et au Japon.' In *Mouvements Sociaux et Économie Solidaire*, edited by Jean Louis Laville, Elisabetta Bucolo, Geoffrey Pleyers and Jose Luis Coraggio, 163–80. Paris: Desclée De Brouwer.

James, Paul, and Paul van Seters. 2014. 'Global Social Movements and Global Civil Society.' In *Globalization and Politics. 2: Global Social Movements and Global Civil Society*, edited by Paul James, Nevzat Soguk, Paul van Seters and James H. Mittelman, vii–xxx. Los Angeles, CA: SAGE.

Kawano, Emily. 2013. 'Social Solidarity Economy: Toward Convergence across Continental Divides.' UNRISD. https://www.unrisd.org/thinkpiece-kawano.

Laville, Jean-Louis, Elisabetta Bucolo, Geoffrey Pleyers and Jose Luis Coraggio, eds. 2017. *Mouvements Sociaux et Économie Solidaire*. Paris: Desclée De Brouwer.

RIPESS (Inter-continental Network for the Promotion of Social Solidarity Economy). 2013. 'RIPESS Working Paper: Differences and Convergences in Social Solidarity Economy Concepts, Definitions and Frameworks.' RIPESS. https://ccednet-rcdec.ca/sites/ccednet-rcdec.ca/files/ccednet/pdfs/doc2_global_vision_base_document_en.pdf.

Savio, Roberto. 2019. 'Farewell to the World Social Forum?' Great Transition Initiative, 7 October. https://greattransition.org/gti-forum/wsf-savio.

Singer, Paul, and Valmor Schiochet. 2017. 'Économie Solidaire et Parti des Travailleurs Au Brésil.' In *Mouvements Sociaux et Économie Solidaire*, edited by Jean Louis Laville, Elisabetta Bucolo, Geoffrey Pleyers and Jose Luis Coraggio, 355–63. Paris: Desclée De Brouwer.

Whitaker, Francisco. 2005. 'World Social Forum: Origins and Aims.' Transnational Institute, 6 June. https://www.tni.org/en/article/world-social-forum-origins-and-aims.

Zimmer, Magali, and Hyungsik Eum. 2017. 'L'Émergence D'Initiatives Solidaires en France et en Corée du Sud.' In *Mouvements Sociaux et Économie Solidaire*, edited by Jean-Louis Laville, Elisabetta Bucolo, Jose Luis Coraggio and Geoffrey Pleyers, 181–97. Paris: Desclée de Brouwer.

2. Community economies

Stephen Healy, Ana Inés Heras and Peter North

INTRODUCTION

Community economies (CE) is a key term in the interdisciplinary subfield of diverse economies, growing from the pioneering feminist political economy scholarship of J.K. Gibson-Graham (Gibson-Graham and Dombroski 2020). Scholarship in this subfield has been influential in many academic fields including geography, anthropology, sociology, business and organization studies, as well as the humanities and arts. It has also informed movement activism in countries throughout the world. In keeping with this tradition this entry uses the term 'community economies' to emphasize the plurality of economic forms of life but recognize the meaning of the suffix 'ic' as of or pertaining to something. Both 'community' and 'economy' have distinct pluralist and open meanings that contrast with their common-place understanding. Accordingly, community economies are spaces where humans negotiate the terms of their coexistence (Gibson-Graham 2006). From the CE perspective, 'economies' are always plural, containing diverse forms of economic organization, exchange, remuneration, finance, care, and ownership. Consequently, economies are not understood as a systematic totality. Correspondingly, 'community' is understood as always open. Coexistence is the basis for belonging, rather than being from a particular place, community of interest, class, or any conception of 'imagined community'. From this perspective, 'solidarity' both names an aligned stance and disposition towards one another as well as designating (economic) spaces where these negotiations unfold. What community economies offer is a way of understanding what these stances entail, as well as a further opening up of the 'with whom', or 'what' we humans are in solidarity with.

These theoretical starting points of 'economies always plural' and 'communities always open' play a decisive role in shaping how CE relates to the social and solidarity economies (SSEs). In what follows, this entry makes three conceptual contributions: (1) it aligns the SSEs' commitment to pluralist politics with the theory of community economies as already defined above; (2) it uses the theory of community economy as a way of theorizing the different ethical dilemmas that attend being together in solidarity in place; and (3) in conclusion, drawing on the theory of community economy it makes the case for the necessity of a commitment to solidarity that includes the 'more than human' world as crucial for our shared survival.

2.1 PLURALISM AND COMMUNITY ECONOMY: WHAT'S IN A NAME?

The SSEs' theoretical and political commitment to pluralism is one of their distinctive features. Rather than imagining one path to social change, pluralism commits the movement to paths, where there may be many roads to social transformation. The role of the state, market exchange, formal or informal institutions and practices in constituting the SSEs are all up for debate. One consequence for the movement is that solidarity becomes a process of discerning how the elements of this plurality can connect with and support one another. This pluralism is one point of contiguity with the theory of community economies. What CE adds to this debate is an insistence that both the ethical and political vitality of social movements, like the SSEs, hinges upon the opening of how community and economy are understood.

Gibson-Graham's (1996) early intellectual interventions drew on array of scholarly and theoretical perspectives, including Marxian, feminist, economic anthropology and queer theory, to understand the economy in anti-essentialist terms. Writing just a few years after the collapse of the Soviet Union, their aim was to challenge the conflation of the economy, singular, with a capitalist totality. 'Capitalocentrism' is a diagnostic term they developed to describe an ideological consensus, that capitalism was now the 'only game in town'. They challenged capitalocentric thinking in two ways. First, they brought capitalism down to size, making capitalism one form of enterprise organization among many. Drawing on a nuanced reading of Marx, they defined the capitalist class process as an enterprise that employs wage labour to produce goods and services and to generate a surplus in the process that is appropriated and distributed by the capitalist. With this 'thin' definition, capitalism is no longer a totality, and the capitalist class process sits alongside various forms of non-capitalist organizations.

The second move has been to populate this non-capitalist exterior with an increasing diversity of organizational forms, processes of exchange and remuneration, finance and ownership, work and non-work; a diversity that can no longer be contained or subordinated to a systemic logic. Accompanying this second move was a call to other scholars, artists and activists to develop new understanding and appreciation for the hidden, alternative and non-capitalist economies that had been pushed to the discursive and material margins. Many have answered this call, leading to the formation of the Community Economies Research Network (CERN), circa 2008. The Diverse Economies Iceberg (Figure 2.1) is a visualization, initially developed in the context of action research projects, to emphasize that capitalism is only the tip of the iceberg: far more is going on below the waterline, and this matters. There is a need to learn to see the economy differently.

Over the years, this diagram has been elaborated upon, redrafted and translated into other diagrams and visualizations as part of an evolving programme of action research (CEC 2021), making visible the diverse economy (DE) and, furthermore, the theoretical consequences of taking this stance. When the 'economy' is no longer a space driven by a totalizing logic, it becomes a space open to other possibilities, and allows for an understanding of what kinds of economies might be enacted, and to specify the terms of coexistence. A principal inspiration is the late philosopher Jean-Luc Nancy's inessential conception of community as 'being in common' (Nancy and Connor 1991). For Gibson-Graham what this redefinition of community did was to separate community from scale, especially the local, and fixed notions of identity (for example, a local community, the 'working class') and as such the work of enacting community economy is opened as well.

What does the reconfiguration of 'economy as always plural' and this sense of 'community as always open' do for us? It allows us to identify the dilemmas and difficulties of 'being in common', and to identify potentialities of living in common on a planet that has been overexploited over the centuries. In this line, Gibson-Graham et al. (2013) explored the possibility for 'taking back the economy' by identifying efforts throughout the world, seen as efforts at enacting economies of solidarity (whether they use the term or not), and by enacting provisional answers to the questions of how humans and non-humans (other species, machines,

14 *Encyclopedia of the social and solidarity economy*

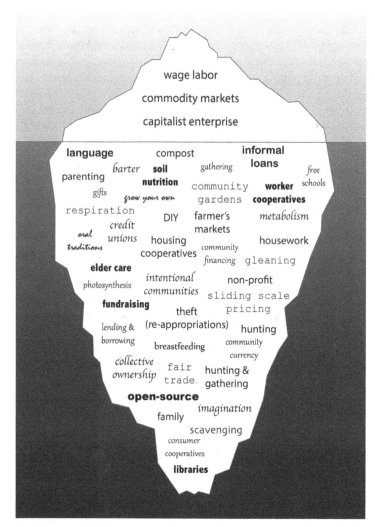

Source: Community Economies (2022).

Figure 2.1   Diverse Economies Iceberg by Community Economies Collective

the material world) are to live together. Key concerns are expressed as questions that reprise familiar Marxian and feminist concerns: What is necessary for shared survival? What is to be done with surplus? What are the terms of fair exchange? How do communities care for a common world or invest in a common future? In DE scholarship, art and activism over the last decade the answers to these questions have increasingly been inflected by planetary concerns, and a growing recognition that human livelihood depends upon renegotiating the terms of coexistence with a life-giving planet, and this means including non-humans (other species, things) as well as future generations.

These questions foreground both community and economy as dilemmatic spaces of problem posing and decision making in interdependence. Their relevance to the solidarity economy movement becomes apparent when one considers the persistent questions that preoccupy the movement: are the SSEs a movement that aims at social transformation, or does it aim to address the shortcomings of so-called free market societies? Is the movement experiencing 'mission creep' as it becomes more professional? What role does/should the state play in supporting the solidarity economy movement? What is the relationship between more formal solidarity economy institutions (for example, cooperatives) and everyday practices of mutuality? How does the solidarity economy connect to the concerns of other social movements? Each of these questions expresses genuine ethical dilemmas; the struggle to answer these questions is ongoing. In a sense, they re-pose the central questions raised by the theory of community economy – 'What is an economy?' and 'With whom are we in community (solidarity)?' – for which there can be no final answer.

The sections that follow sketch out some of the ethical dilemmas that shape and in part define solidarity economies in different regions of the world.

United Kingdom: What is a Solidarity Economy?

Home to the Rochdale Pioneers (see entry 17, 'Cooperatives and Mutuals') and Owen, the United Kingdom (UK) was foundational in the development of the SSEs but is also now perhaps a place where processes of professionalization and neoliberalization have gone the furthest. For this reason, it becomes important to understand how the movement arrived at this point, and to also describe what count as SSEs.

The end of World War II saw the development of a 'nationalized' social economy in the United Kingdom. The aspiration was to replace locally inadequate and piecemeal local provision with comprehensive welfare services. Critics felt that there would never be enough money to meet everyone's needs, and often these hoped-for comprehensive services were poor quality and not targeted on local needs. The economic volatility of the 1970s brought this approach into crisis.

At a local level, vibrant community-based, solidarity economies grew in response to criticism of inadequacy and bureaucratization as young people squatted in derelict housing, and workers occupied factories that were closed. Cooperatives thrived and local authorities often supported them. The rise of Thatcherism in the 1980s closed off these experiences and many social economy initiatives were 'translated' into social enterprises engaged in service delivery (see entry 53, 'Social Policy'). For some, this translation was class war, pure and simple, while others saw opportunities to deliver services tailored to local needs. By the 1990s, New Labour's 'enterprise state' sought to enlist social enterprises into its agenda of social inclusion, a 'solidarity economy' in which 'everyone was included' (in a market economy).

After the financial crisis of 2008, state support was cut off. Some survived in the new harsh environment by, they said, running their affairs in conventionally business-like ways, while others failed in this new competitive 'market'. While this story of social entrepreneurship, professionalization and privatization is an important part of the UK experience, it is not the whole story. The Transition Initiatives movement, emerging from south-west England, has seen an effervescence of local action to avoid the dangers of extreme exploitation (of human and non-human). These processes count as solidarity economies in action. For example, in Preston, the local council is engaged in community wealth building to grow social enterprises and co-ops, meeting local needs. The Welsh Government is supporting the foundational economy, consisting of things needed for everyday life – haircuts, green groceries, bread –

rather than encouraging multinational businesses to invest in the area, hopefully bringing jobs. Liverpool's social economy is starting to speak the language of solidarity in the face of an unsympathetic national government. As elsewhere, COVID-19 saw a mushrooming of mutual aid, both online and from placed-based community businesses. In this sense, it would appear the last chapter on social solidarity economy in the UK has not yet been written. Perhaps what the UK needs is a little more of the anger at injustice that has inspired solidarity economy activities elsewhere, as outlined in the section below (North et al. 2020), where the aim is not to include everyone in what we have now, but build something better.

United States: Who is Involved?

In the United States (US) context the solidarity economy is a new name for practices of cooperation, mutual aid and solidarity interconnection, particularly in communities that face daily challenges to sustain life. The term became associated with an organized and intentional movement US Social Forum in Atlanta with the unfolding of the 2008 global financial crisis (Allard et al. 2008). Given the context of economic crisis and instability it is perhaps unsurprising that jobs were a focus of the movement, as well as other aspects that support immediate survival.

Over the past decade, particularly in the wake of Occupy, the Ferguson protests of 2015 and the rise of Black Lives Matter, the movement became more attuned and connected to the struggle for racial justice, against anti-black white supremacist violence and state violence (Akuno et al. 2017). For other theorists, such as diverse economies scholar Lauren Hudson (2020), part of what needs to be defended are the structures of everyday solidarity in communities that organize effectively to respond to ecological disasters such as Superstorm Sandy and health emergencies such as the global coronavirus pandemic.

This type of work necessarily involves a reflexive confrontation within the movement of forms of supremacist thinking, including forms of internalized racism. As in the UK, in the US solidarity is vitally connected to the question of shared survival, but the context is different. In the UK the history is one of the state first absorbing, rationalizing and then partly abandoning a shared commitment to solidarity. In the US context, as one anonymous Detroit activist wryly observed, 'for the state to abandon you, it needs to have been there in the first place'. To be certain, there are many places in the US (for example, New York, Philadelphia, Boston, Cleveland) where the city government and other institutions have started to foster solidarity economies. But in this context, who is a part of the SSEs cannot be divorced from the history of colonization, slavery and state violence, which also means that the questions of reparations, prison abolition and other animating concerns of social justice are movements that link solidarity to shared survival (see entry 12, 'The Black Social Economy').

Latin America: How to Decide?

In the territories usually referred to as América Latina, a myriad of coalitions, enacting solidarity in difference, have existed, struggling to secure life, challenge oppression, domination and exploitation, and construct solidarity practices, over centuries. Recently, Vieta and Heras (2022) have analysed several of these enactments as 'organizing solidarity in practice', and they have started to map out several of these experiences in present times.

This work has started to identify the commonalities amongst these processes:

- Practices of collective decision making, creating different ways of doing this (for example, *asambleas, comisiones, células, mesas*).
- Communal ownership (often naming common property as both *comunal y comunitario*, which means that it is not only owned jointly but also cared for in common).
- Support parity and mutual caring for each other (even if there may be different perspectives at play about how this is enacted, which is explicitly discussed).

These practices are important because they stage an encounter between oppressed and exploited individuals, groups and organizations with others who have already transformed their conditions, and now operate *autónomos, autogobernados y autodeterminados*. Encounters like these take place throughout Latin America; their defining features are their mixed composition, that is, enacting solidarity in difference; and the fact that they do not necessarily seek as a goal to remain stable over time, but seek to transform the living conditions as they are, towards justice, openness and living well together.

2.2 CONCLUDING THOUGHTS

The preceding sections foregrounded a working definition of community and diverse economies, and sketch an outline of how the theory helps to understand how SSEs are enacted in and by different communities around the world. The entry poses some foundational questions to be addressed when thinking about the mutual relationships across community/diverse economies and SSEs over space and time, such as: What counts as SSEs, as defined contextually? Who is involved and who is in solidarity with whom, and to do what? How and when are decisions made, and by whom? Introducing as well the notion of 'solidarity in difference', that is, an always-to-be-defined notion of solidarity, when it is enacted, and not as a reified concept or practice.

The theory of community economy puts forward a challenge for the terms enacting interdependent existence: what is necessary for shared survival in the Anthropocene, and how to respond to the baleful effects of the great acceleration, the period between 1950 and the present, when the planetary impact of human communities became more pronounced. The need to attend to planetary wellbeing has consequences for the distribution of surplus, the terms of exchange and how a shared understanding of economy, interdependent with life-giving ecologies, is crucial to care for what is held in common and how communities invest in a common future. For many community economy theorists and practitioners, the last decade has been defined by an increasing recognition that shared survival depends upon extending these negotiations to the 'more-than-human' world. This is a first point of contiguity between the fields of solidarity economy and community/diverse economies. For us, the solidarity economy can be a place where these discussions happen in concrete ways as people think about how they want to live and how they can actualize this.

In some parts of the world such as the US, the solidarity economy movements espouse a commitment to sustainability or environmental justice. In other places, solidarity economy movement practitioners have been shaped by agroecological praxis. What the theory of community economies might meaningfully contribute is a different way of thinking about the terms of human and more-than-human coexistence. This renegotiation of terms must take place locally: one cannot and will not try to define how or where this should happen in advance.

REFERENCES

Akuno, Kali, Ajamu Nangwaya and the Cooperation Jackson Project. 2017. *Jackson Rising: The Struggle for Economic Democracy and Black Self-Determination in Jackson, Mississippi*. Montreal, Québec: Daraja Press.

Allard, Jenna, Carl Davidson and Julie Matthaei. 2008. *Solidarity Economy: Building Alternatives for People and Planet; Papers and Reports from the U.S. Social Forum 2007*. Chicago, IL: Changemaker Publications.

Community Economies. 2022. 'Community Economies. 24 May. http://www.communityeconomies.org.

Gibson, K., Cameron, J., Dombroski, K., Healy, S., Miller, E., and Community Economies Collective. 2021. Cultivating community economies: tools for building a livable world. In J. G. Speth & K. Courrier (Eds.), *The New Systems Reader: Alternatives to a Failed Economy*. 410–32. https://doi.org/10.4324/9780367313401

Gibson-Graham, J.K. 2006. *A Postcapitalist Politics*. Minneapolis, MN: University of Minnesota Press.

Gibson-Graham, J.K., Jenny Cameron and Stephen Healy. 2013. *Take Back the Economy: An Ethical Guide for Transforming Our Communities*. Minneapolis, MN, USA and London, UK: University of Minnesota Press.

Gibson-Graham, J.K. and Kelly Dombroski. 2020. 'Introduction to the Handbook of Diverse Economies: Inventory as Ethical Intervention.' In J.K. Gibson-Graham and Kelly Dombroski (Eds.), *The Handbook of Diverse Economies*, 1–26. Cheltenham, UK and Northampton, MA, USA: Edward Elgar Publishing.

Hudson, Lauren. 2020. 'Building Where We Are: The Solidarity-Economy Response to Crisis.' In Vincent Lyon-Callo, Yahya M. Madra, Ceren Özselçuk, Jared Randall, Maliha Safri, Chizu Sato, & Boone W. Shear (Eds.), *Pandemic and the Crisis of Capitalism: A Rethinking Marxism Dossier*, 172–80. Cambridge, MA: ReMarx Books. http://rethinkingmarxism.org/Dossier2020/.

Nancy, Jean-Luc, and Peter Connor. 1991. *The Inoperative Community*. Minneapolis, MN: University of Minnesota Press.

North, Peter, Vicky Nowak, Alan Southern and Matt Thompson. 2020. 'Generative Anger: From Social Enterprise to Antagonistic Economies.' *Rethinking Marxism* 32 (3): 330–47. https://doi.org/10.1080/08935696.2020.1780669.

Vieta, Marcelo and Ana Inés Heras. 2022. 'Organizational Solidarity in Practice in Bolivia and Argentina: Building Coalitions of Resistance and Creativity.' *Organization* 29 (2), 271-294. https://journals.sagepub.com/doi/full/10.1177/13505084211066813

3. Contemporary understandings
Peter Utting

INTRODUCTION

The uptake of new terms is often accompanied by contestation over their meaning. This is very much the case with the concept of the social and solidarity economy (SSE), which has gained currency during the past two decades. In practice, different countries, actors and organizations may adopt one or several terms, also including 'social economy', 'solidarity economy', 'plural economy', 'community economies' and 'social enterprise'. While each emphasizes particular aspects, they share common features that are captured by the broader term, 'the SSE'.

Referring to the actors, institutions, principles and practices involved, this entry identifies the key features of the SSE. It contrasts different perspectives regarding the nature and potential of the SSE, highlighting both their commonalities and substantive differences. In doing so, the entry examines how the SSE is positioned both in the broader economy, vis-à-vis the state or public sector, the private for-profit sector and the popular or informal economy, as well as in relation to the possibilities for systemic change. It also questions whether the meaning of 'the SSE' is being diluted as the term is mainstreamed. To guard against this possibility, the entry suggests the need for an encompassing definition that acknowledges both its attributes associated with social and environmental purpose, and its democratic and transformative potential.

3.1 SOCIAL VERSUS SOLIDARITY ECONOMY

The task of defining the SSE was complicated from the outset given that the term was an amalgam of two others: the 'social economy' and the 'solidarity economy'. While the 'social economy' is interpreted differently in different parts of the world, the term has increasingly come to be associated with a particular set of organizations. In much of Europe and Asia, the 'social economy' focuses on certain statutory organizations that emerged in 19th century Europe and contemporary variants of social enterprise. The 'solidarity economy' broadened the purview further by focusing on the 'popular economy' and informal community practices. While also having adherents in the Global North, the 'solidarity economy' was articulated most prominently in Latin America, beginning in the late 20th century (Razeto 1999; also see entry 10, 'Origins and Histories'). While each of these terms continues to be used differently by different actors, certain stylized facts suggest that the coupling of social and solidarity economy brought together not only different sets of actors but also different perspectives regarding development strategy and social-economic and political change.

Concerning actors, the 'social economy' often focuses on third-sector organizations, notably cooperatives, mutual societies, foundations and associations or non-governmental organizations (NGOs). Such organizations operate in an economic space that can be distinguished from both the public sector and conventional for-profit private enterprise. More recently, the focus has broadened to include various forms of social enterprise and social entrepreneurship that blend economic or commercial and social objectives (Defourny et al. 2019; see also entry 21, 'Social Enterprises'). This development extends the purview of the SSE to the private sector, via not only philanthropy but also so-called blended value organizations and various forms of private–SSE partnerships. The relationship with the state centres primarily on its role as an external actor that regulates and potentially supports the SSE via public policy (see also entry 51, 'Public Policy').

The 'solidarity economy' also enlarged the third-sector frame. In this case, however, a key focus was on myriad indigenous and community-based organizations and local-level solidarity and collective self-help practices. Furthermore, it emphasized contemporary organizational forms such as bought-out enterprises (*empresas recuperadas*) and fair trade, food sovereignty, ecology, artisanal networks and their constituent organizations, as well as solidarity finance. The last of these included not only micro-credit and concessionary lending but also old and new modalities, such as barter and complementary currencies, respectively. Furthermore, this approach emphasized the role of social movements as both SSE constituents and allies. And it saw certain state or public sector organizations and institutions as a key component of the SSE, not least universities, municipal governments and other state entities tasked with supporting the SSE.

Drawing on research in Latin America on solidarity economy, Figure 3.1 illustrates the interconnections between the SSE and other sectors of the economy.

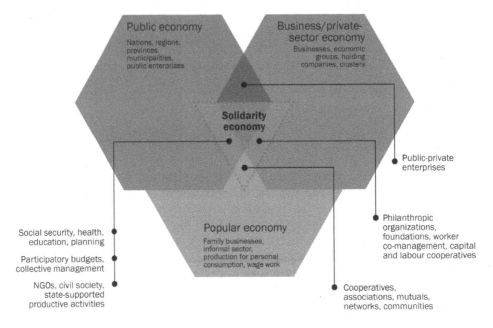

Source: Based on Coraggio (2015), published in UNRISD (2016, 121).

Figure 3.1   The solidarity economy within the broader economy

Concerning strategy, proponents of social economy often emphasize two key roles. First, its capacity to foster well-being via the production and distribution of basic needs and decent work, the term popularized by the International Labour Organization (ILO) to refer to employment promotion, labour rights, social protection and social dialogue. And second, its potential as a sector that can grow in a way that complements the roles of the public and private sectors, as well as cultivate a more people- and planet-sensitive market economy.

The strategic orientation of the 'solidarity economy' is somewhat different. The remit of SSE actors extends beyond income-generating activities, basic needs provisioning and micro-level interactions. At a philosophical level, solidarity economy resonates with what is referred to in the Andean region as *Buen Vivir*, a notion of living well in harmony with people and the planet, thereby respecting both human rights and the rights of nature (Gudynas 2011).

The solidarity economy perspective is also concerned with systemic change, social transformation and political engagement at multiple levels of governance (Hillenkamp and Wanderley 2015). People's well-being and planetary health depend on subordinating economic principles and processes that characterize contemporary capitalism. These include the commodification of nature and the commons; the concentration of wealth; financialization; and capital accumulation and profit maximization centred on exploitative labour relations, dispossession and the externalization of social and environmental costs.

The solidarity economy, therefore, emphasizes the need for an economic system where the dominant institutional logic is fundamentally different. In addition to market-based activities that are regulated to control for contradictory social and environmental impacts, the solidarity economy emphasizes the importance of decommodifying economic circuits (Laville 2022; Loritz and Muñoz 2019; Novkovic 2021).

The transformative project also extends to reconfiguring power relations via democratization, active citizenship and new coalitions. To enable the SSE and to level the playing field for SSE organizations and enterprises (SSEOEs), it is necessary to alter power structures involving complementary and synergistic relations between economic and political elites. Such relations reinforce corporate power and market relations through, for example, subsidies, deregulation and privatization. As an emancipatory project, the solidarity economy approach focuses on not only relieving the symptoms of oppression and disadvantage via basic needs provisioning and decent work, but also transforming the structures that historically have reproduced deprivation, inequality and other forms of injustice. Beyond the skewed distribution of income and wealth, such structures involve patriarchy, racism, colonialism and dependency related to trade, corporate-led global value chains and geopolitical relations (Coraggio 2015). Transformation requires, then, institutional and technological innovation, as well as deep changes in power relations at multiple scales.

Figure 3.2 illustrates the contrast between the SSE as a sector or sub-sector of the wider economy, and the SSE as a sphere that not only interfaces with other sectors, but also seeks to transform them.

This broad-brush interpretation of differences in approach should not mask important variations in how each term is interpreted. The social economy label, for example, can refer to a relatively narrow focus on income and employment generation and social service provision via social enterprises. Or it can refer to a broader process of change via active citizenship and an institutional ecosystem that scales SSEOEs to an extent that has systemic implications as, for example, in Emilia Romagna in Italy and Quebec, Canada (Mendell and Alain 2015).

22 *Encyclopedia of the social and solidarity economy*

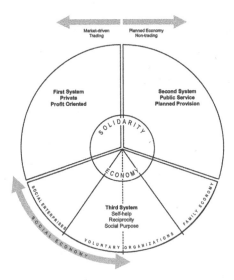

Source: Lewis and Swinney (2007).

Figure 3.2   Positioning both the social and the solidarity economy

Similarly, while some strands of solidarity economy thought explicitly support a policy agenda that is antithetical to neoliberalism (Santos 2007), others see scope for progressive change by taking advantage of spaces linked to neoliberal policy. Place-based activism and non-capitalist practices and relations can emerge not only in response to neoliberal failures but also by taking advantage of institutional and policy changes linked to neoliberal reform, such as decentralization and targeted poverty reduction programmes (Gibson-Graham 2006).

3.2   COMMON GROUND

Despite the differences captured by these stylized versions of the social economy and the solidarity economy, the commonalities were sufficient to allow different actors, notably regional and international research and advocacy entities and networks (see entry 27, 'Energy, Water and Waste Management Sectors' and entry 43, 'Access to Markets') to adopt and promote an overarching term. Commonalities concerned the key role of principles or mechanisms of reciprocity and redistribution in resource allocation, and the primacy of social objectives within circuits of production and exchange of goods and services. Other aspects related to democratic governance within SSE organizations, participation or 'co-construction' within the policy process, local community and territorial development, and environmental protection. In contrast to the profit-maximizing firm, SSE organizations either adopted a non-profit orientation or practised some form of constraint on profit distribution and the sale of assets. More generally, the SSE concept promoted the idea that the economic system should be biased in favour of inclusion, equality and planetary health (Vail 2010). This bias is achieved by reordering priorities and objectives: for example, social and environmental purpose instead of profit maximization and shareholder primacy; democratic governance rather than hierarchy; cooperation and partnership over competition; and solidarity as opposed to self-centred individualism.

Both perspectives also see SSEOEs as an important avenue for transitioning from contexts of precarious employment and poverty that characterize much of the popular or informal economy. While the emphasis may vary, key mechanisms include:

- Organizational and enterprise forms involving self-help, collective action and social entrepreneurship that facilitate economic and political empowerment, as well as social and cultural emancipation of individual workers or families; the case, for example, of landless or small farmers forming agricultural cooperatives.
- Associations representing and advocating for informal economy workers representing, for example, home-based workers, waste pickers and street vendors.
- State policy, such as social and labour rights policies, that proactively support informal economy workers in relation to social security and decent work.

3.3 TOWARDS A UNIVERSAL DEFINITION?

How a somewhat cumbersome term such as 'the SSE' gained currency within international development discourse relates to both the fairly broad coalition of actors and approaches which came together in the early 21st century, and the fertile terrain for thinking and policy related to alternatives to capitalism and neoliberalism, not least in the wake of various financial crises. It also coincided with the retreat of socialism as an idea and a strategy within some mainstream academic, policy and advocacy circles. While core principles of the SSE related to social justice, democracy and the subordination of the economy to social power (Wright 2010) overlap with basic tenets of the socialist tradition, the SSE was concerned with alternatives to centralized state control. It also made explicit the possibilities for intersectoral complementarities and coexistence with market principles in a mixed and plural economy.

Ongoing differences related to ideology and strategy within the coalition of actors that support the SSE, as well as the acknowledged need to respect and recognize variations in terminology in different regional, cultural and political contexts, complicate the task of crafting a universal definition. The task has been further complicated as governments and parliaments attempt to design laws regulating and supporting the SSE. The legislative process can have the effect of narrowing or diluting the meaning of the term. Certain aspects are likely to be sidelined for purposes of both legal precision and political expediency.

As a result, attention often focuses on less controversial aspects of the SSE, namely the organizations and enterprises involved, social and environmental objectives, non-profit or 'less-for-profit' orientation, and participatory governance arrangements.

In Uruguay a more conceptually rigorous definition of the SSE, along the lines of the solidarity economy perspective outlined above, was dropped in the process of designing the 2019 law (Guerra and Reyes Lavega 2020). Nevertheless, it retained key elements, including:

- the absolute primacy of people over capital;
- relations based on solidarity, cooperation, reciprocity, democratic control, with the collective interest prevailing over that of the individual;
- autonomous, democratic and participatory management;

- a commitment to community and local and territorial organization and development, while caring for the environment;
- where legally permitted, the distribution of profit will reflect primarily the work performed and the services or activity of members and producers;
- the promotion of gender equity and social inclusion via work integration.

In France, the 2014 law promoted a vision of the SSE more in line with the interpretation of the 'social economy' perspective noted above. It sought to strengthen and legitimize the SSE, which was seen as comprising both traditional statutory actors, such as cooperatives and mutuals, and certain commercial enterprises with a social utility purpose, a profit distribution constraint and an asset lock. It recognized the SSE as a specific entrepreneurial approach, and supported social innovations such as bought-out enterprises and modernizing cooperatives, for example, by allowing them to join together for increased efficiency. It also promoted the role of the SSE in local development through territorial economic cooperation hubs, involving multiple (SSE, private and public sector) actors and institutions, as well as networking to gain policy influence (OECD and European Union 2017).

While definitions adopted by international networks supporting the SSE often broaden its scope in terms of organizations and practices, there remains a tendency to focus on the sectoral or micro level. The United Nations Inter-Agency Task Force on Social and Solidarity Economy, for example, states:

> SSE encompasses organizations and enterprises that have explicit economic and social (and often environmental) objectives; involve varying degrees and forms of cooperative, associative and solidarity relations between workers, producers and consumers; and practice workplace democracy and self-management. SSE includes traditional forms of cooperatives and mutual associations, as well as women's self-help groups, community forestry groups, social provisioning organizations or 'proximity services', fair trade organizations, associations of informal sector workers, social enterprises, and community currency and alternative finance schemes. (UNTFSSE 2014)

Focusing on particular types of organizations and the micro level, as well as social utility, can detract from the transformative potential of the SSE. Some academic and advocacy networks insist on highlighting the transformative dimension associated with the solidarity economy approach (Poirier 2014). According to the Intercontinental Network for the Promotion of Social Solidarity Economy, for example:

> The Social Solidarity Economy is an alternative to capitalism and other authoritarian, state-dominated economic systems. In SSE ordinary people play an active role in shaping all of the dimensions of human life: economic, social, cultural, political, and environmental. SSE exists in all sectors of the economy: production, finance, distribution, exchange, consumption and governance. It also aims to transform the social and economic system that includes public, private and third sectors. SSE is not only about the poor, but strives to overcome inequalities, which includes all classes of society. SSE has the ability to take the best practices that exist in our present system (such as efficiency, use of technology and knowledge) and transform them to serve the welfare of the community based on different values and goals. (RIPESS 2015)

Such a definition emphasizes not only the transformation of multiple sectors but also the need to look beyond the micro or sectoral level, to the macro scale where structural change has to occur. A way of viewing the transformative nature of the SSE is in terms of a dual process, whereby diverse relations of solidarity and cooperation are cultivated, reproduced and reinforced in the broader plural or mixed economy in order to meet people's needs, demands and aspirations (both material and non-material), and where democratic practices by workers, producers and citizens play out at multiple scales of decision-making and governance. From this perspective, the focus widens from particular types of organizations that prioritize social purpose to the transformation of social and power relations. The objectives of SSE organizations expand: from the social, environmental or cultural, to the political, via agency, contestation, democratic participation and emancipatory struggles. The SSE, then, is concerned with democratizing both the economy and the polity (Dacheux and Goujon 2011; Laville 2022; Razeto 1999).

As the SSE gains visibility and the term is mainstreamed, there is a danger that its meaning is being diluted and that core elements are ignored. To guard against this risk, it is important that the essence of both the social economy and the solidarity economy variants outlined above is retained when defining the SSE: one should not eclipse the other. This points to the need for an encompassing definition that highlights both utilitarian purpose and transformative potential in terms of emancipation, democratization and systemic change.

From this perspective, the SSE comprises autonomous forms of organization that produce and exchange goods and services, giving primacy to: (1) social, cultural and environmental objectives and the equitable distribution of surplus over profit maximization and financial returns to investors; (2) democratic governance over hierarchy and bureaucratic control; and (3) principles and practices of solidarity, mutual help and cooperation over self-centred individualism and competition. Additionally, it refers to the institutionalization of collective action for emancipatory purposes within economic circuits and the wider political economy. Such purposes include freedom from want and social exclusion via livelihood security and a sense of belonging or community; and freedom from oppressive forms of domination and elite control via contestation, meaningful participation and active citizenship.

REFERENCES

Coraggio, José Luis. 2015. 'Institutionalizing the Social and Solidarity Economy in Latin America'. In *Social and Solidarity Economy: Beyond the Fringe*, edited by Peter Utting, 130–49. London: Zed Books/Geneva: UNRISD.

Dacheux, Eric and Daniel Goujon. 2011. 'The Solidarity Economy: An Alternative Development Strategy?' *International Social Science Journal* 62 (203–4): 205–15. https://doi.org/10.1111/j.1468-2451.2011.01804.x.

Defourny, Jacques, Marthe Nyssens and Olivier Brolis. 2019. 'Mapping and Testing Social Enterprise Models Across the World: Evidence from the International Comparative Social Enterprise Models (ICSEM) Project', ICSEM Working Papers No. 50. Liege: International Comparative Social Enterprise Models (ICSEM) Project. https://orbi.uliege.be/bitstream/2268/233219/1/SE%20Models%20-%20Defourny%20et%20al..pdf.

Gibson-Graham, J.K. 2006. *A Postcapitalist Politics*. Minneapolis, MN: University of Minnesota Press.

Gudynas, Eduardo. 2011. 'Buen Vivir: Today's Tomorrow'. *Development* 54 (4): 441–7. https://doi.org/10.1057/dev.2011.86.

Guerra, P. and S. Reyes Lavega. 2020. 'Ley de Economía Social y Solidaria en Uruguay: Texto y Contexto'. *Revista Jurídica de Economía Social y Cooperativa* 37: 53–80. https://doi.org/10.7203/ciriec-jur.37.16918.

Hillenkamp, Isabelle and Fernanda Wanderley. 2015. 'Social Enterprise in Bolivia: Solidarity Economy in Context of High Informality and Labour Precariousness', ICSEM Working Papers No. 21. Liege: International Comparative Social Enterprise Models (ICSEM) Project. https://horizon.documentation.ird.fr/exl-doc/pleins_textes/divers17-08/010070758.pdf.

Laville, Jean-Louis. 2022. *The Social and Solidarity Economy*. Minneapolis, MN: Minnesota University Press.

Lewis, Mike and Dan Swinney. 2007. 'Social Economy? Solidarity Economy? Exploring the Implications of Conceptual Nuance for Acting in a Volatile World'. BALTA/Canadian Centre for Community Renewal.

Loritz, Erika and Ruth Muñoz (eds). 2019. *Más allá de la supervivencia: experiencias de economía social y solidaria en América Latina*. Buenos Aires: Universidad Nacional de General Sarmiento.

Mendell, Marguerite and Béatrice Alain. 2015. 'Enabling the Social and Solidarity Economy through the Co-construction of Public Policy'. In *Social and Solidarity Economy: Beyond the Fringe*, edited by Peter Utting, 236–49. London: Zed Books/Geneva: UNRISD.

Novkovic, Sonja. 2021. 'Cooperative Identity as a Yardstick for Transformative Change'. *Annals of Public and Cooperative Economics* 93 (2): 313–36. https://doi.org/10.1111/apce.12362.

OECD and European Union. 2017. 'The Law on the Social and Solidarity Economy (SSE), France'. In *Boosting Social Enterprise Development Good Practice Compendium*. Paris: OECD Publishing. https://www.oecd.org/publications/boosting-social-enterprise-development-9789264268500-en.htm.

Poirier, Yvon. 2014. 'Social Solidarity Economy and Related Concepts. Origins and Definitions: An International Perspective'. Socioeco.org http://www.socioeco.org/bdf_fiche-document-3293_en.html.

Razeto, Luis. 1999. 'Economía de Solidaridad: Concepto, Realidad y Proyecto'. *Persona y Sociedad*, 13 (2). https://emes.net/content/uploads/publications/Razeto_La_economia_de_solidaridad_061.pdf.

RIPESS (Intercontinental Network for the Promotion of Social Solidarity Economy). 2015. 'Global Vision for a Social Solidarity Economy: Convergences and Differences in Concepts, Definitions and Frameworks'. http://www.ripess.org/wp-content/uploads/2017/08/RIPESS_Vision-Global_EN.pdf.

Santos, Boaventura de Sousa (ed.). 2007. *Another Production is possible: Beyond the Capitalist Canon*. London: Verso.

UNRISD. 2016. 'Promoting Social and Solidarity Economy through Public Policy'. In *Policy Innovation for Transformative Change*, 115–39. Geneva: UNRISD.

UNTFSSE (United Nations Inter-Agency Task Force on Social and Solidarity Economy). 2014. 'What is the Social and Solidarity Economy?' https://unsse.org/sse-and-the-sdgs/.

Vail, John. 2010. 'Decommodification and egalitarian political economy'. *Politics and Society* 38 (3): 310–46. https://doi.org/10.1177/0032329210373069.

Wright, Eric Olin. 2010. *Envisioning Real Utopias*. London: Verso.

4. Ecological economics
Dražen Šimleša

4.1 EARLY DAYS AND CONCEPTUALIZATION

The origins of ecological economics can be dated back to the debate on the political philosophy of the 19th century, or even before. However, it only began to be accepted as a field of study, or an academic subdiscipline in economics influencing academic debate, during and after the interwar period. As a countermovement to mainstream economics, such as neoclassical economics or Keynesian economics, which neglected natural resources and environmental concerns, ecological concerns emerged which contributed to the formation of ecological economics. Seminal works such as Frederick Soddy's (1926) *Wealth, Virtual Wealth and Debt*, Karl Polanyi's (1944) *Great Transformation* and John Kenneth Galbraith's (1958) *The Affluent Society* contributed to forming the concepts and theories of ecological economics (for bibliographical information on these works, see Spash 2018). All these works warned about a malfunction in the design of time economy, advocating for changes that would secure more fairness and well-being in societies. However, such works all focused on the analysis of the economy and did not make a clear connection between the economy and the ecosystems, which became the basis of ecological economics. One that led in that direction was Kenneth E. Boulding with his famous presentation of planet Earth as a spaceship with limited area and resources. Highlighting the connection between the economy and the environmental ecosystem in the essay 'The Economics of the Coming Spaceship Earth' (Boulding 1966), he interpreted economy within an ecological system by describing the transition from the 'frontier economics' of the past, where growth in human welfare meant growth in material consumption, to the 'spaceship economics' of the future (for bibliographical information, see Spash 2018). This form of economics was fundamentally different from those of the past, with growth in welfare no longer fuelled by growth in material consumption. The author who had an incomparable effect on the later framework and development of ecological economics was Nicolas Georgescu-Roegen. In his seminal book *The Entropy Law and the Economic Process* (Georgescu-Roegen 1971), he positioned himself as a prominent critic of the growth paradigm, and a strong proponent of emphasizing Earth's carrying capacity as the crucial variable in any economic theory and practice. Georgescu-Roegen's theories had a huge influence on numerous ecological economics thinkers and researchers (for bibliographical information, see Spash 2018). Among these, Herman Daly has made a significant contribution to the development of ecological economics since the 1970s by (re)integrating nature into economics and elaborating the concept of a steady-state economy (for bibliographical information on Herman Daly, see Spash 2018). According to him, the human economy is an open subsystem embedded in a finite natural environment of scarce resources and fragile ecosystems. Therefore the human economy, which is a finite non-growing system, should at some point become non-growing and start to maintain itself in a steady state. This steady-state economy is composed of a constant stock of physical wealth (capital), a constant stock of people (population) and a flow of natural resources that maintain these two stocks. In this steady-state economy, the durabilities of two stocks should be maximized, since a more durable stock of physical wealth demands a smaller flow of natural resources, and a more durable population means a higher life expectancy, maintained by a low birth rate and an equally low death rate.

Many economists, such as Georgescu-Roegen and Daly, who took alternative approaches to dominant neoclassical and Keynesian economics, contributed to establishing ecological economics as a unique subdiscipline within economics. They brought into economics a new view about the issues intersecting economy and ecology, such as limits to growth, weak versus deep sustainability, Earth's ecosystem services, balance, and so on. After several meetings of early ecological economics pioneers, the International Society for Ecological Economics (ISEE) was founded in 1989, publishing the *Journal of Ecological Economics*.

4.2 ECOLOGICAL ECONOMICS AS A TRANSDISCIPLINE

It is often emphasized that ecological economics is not a subdiscipline of economics, ecology or any other academic discipline. It is not a purely academic field either. It therefore takes a transdisciplinary approach to understand the world, which exists as a complex, interdependent and continually evolving system in which the economy is embedded within society, which is embedded within nature. Scholars and practitioners who consider ecological economics as a transdisciplinary approach generally characterize its goals, worldviews and methodology (Costanza et al. 2020). For them, the overarching goal of ecological economics is the sustainable well-being of humankind and all other forms of nature, with three broad subgoals, of sustainable scale, fair distribution, and efficient allocation of resources. These overarching goals of ecological economics resonate with the objectives of the social and solidarity economy (SSE), in particular the objectives associated with equal distribution of surpluses and sustainable local resource management. The worldview of ecological economics includes an interdependent, coevolving, complex system perspective of economies embedded in societies, which are embedded within nature. The perspective of economies embedded in societies is also central to the ideas underpinning the SSE. The methodology emphasizes intelligent pluralism and integration across disciplines. This methodological feature is partly based on the importance of understanding and solving complex and evolving world demands, moving beyond disciplinary boundaries and the so-called 'argument culture', in which problems or discussions are cast as polar opposites (such as zero-sum, win–lose, either–or dichotomy). The methodology manifests that understanding or managing the complex, highly interdependent system that human beings now inhabit requires the transcendence of both disciplinary and academic boundaries.

To solve the problems of well-being; material standards of living; social, cultural and community interactions and institutions; and ecological life-support systems, ecological economics integrates three basic elements: tools for analysis and synthesis, promoting system thinking (for example, systems analysis and modelling) in particular; a vision of how human beings would like to exist; and implementation, which includes concrete and specific institutions, policies and strategies that can realize the vision (Costanza et al. 2020). System thinking is highly important for ecological economics because it is grounded in the science-based 'system view of life', meaning thinking in terms of relationships, patterns and context (Capra and Luisi 2014).

Ecological economics is also defined as the 'union of economics and ecology, with the economy conceived as a subsystem of the Earth ecosystem that is sustained by a metabolic flow or "throughput" from and back to the larger system'. This elucidates the meaning of embedded economy in ecological economics (Daly and Farley 2004, 431). Another definition explains ecological economics as 'the study of the relationships between human housekeeping and nature's housekeeping. Put another way, it is about the interactions between economic systems and ecological systems' (Common and Stagl 2005, 1). Linked to the Greek root *oikos* (literally meaning 'house', but often meant as 'the world') shared by both ecology and economics, it highlights the interests of ecological economics in the management of the world in an integrated way.

The following summary shows crucial aspects of ecological economics discussed above (Costanza et al. 2020):

- It is a transdisciplinary concept and discipline receiving inputs from many fields, where all involved appreciate the existence of economy as a subsystem of the environment (and society, of course), and the requirement for us as a species to be aware, respectful, and work within the limits of Earth's carrying capacity. However, divergences exist regarding how progression is made from this initial appreciation.
- The interrelations and interconnectedness between the human system and the natural system are complex. Ecological economics is here to help us understand these ties and their impact on us.
- The ultimate goal of ecological economics is mutually enhancing the well-being of all life on our planet.

4.3 ECOLOGICAL ECONOMICS AND SUSTAINABILITY

Since the 1970s, ecological economics has grown increasingly more prominent in the academic and policy discourse, as the world has become more and more aware of the dangerous effects and long-term devastation to the environment that the modern economy gives rise to. For example, concerns have been increasing regarding environmental degradation and pollution, greenhouse effects and changes in climate, biodiversity losses, resource depletion, population growth, energy conflicts and wars, welfare state crisis, and social polarization.

In this context, it is interesting to note that ecological economics has evolved in parallel with important discourses on the environment and society, which have led to the emergence of the concept of sustainable development. The major contributions to these discourses include *The Limits to Growth* report (Meadows et al. 1972) and the subsequent quest for 'global equilibrium', and the World Commission on Environment and Development (WCED) and the *Our Common Future* report (World Commission on Environment and Development 1987), often been labelled as the Brundtland Report, which defined the concept of sustainable development. In this document the concept of sustainable development was explained as 'development that meets the needs of the present without compromising the ability of future generations to meet their own needs' (World Commission on Environment and Development 1987, 40). The concept of sustainable development resonated with the values of those advocating for ecological economics. Ecological economics seemed to provide the best theoretical and operative tool to achieve sustainable development. Although the importance of sustainable development was widely accepted at the global level, policies and strategies for development were still shaped by the goal of economic growth.

The 'Caring for the Earth – A Strategy for Sustainable Living' report co-produced by the United Nations Environment Programme (UNEP), the International Union for Conservation of Nature (IUCN) and the World Wide Fund for Nature (WWF) in 1991 used the definition of sustainable development that was much more aligned with the theories and concepts of ecological economics: 'Sustainable development improving the quality of human life while living within the carrying capacity of supporting ecosystems' (The World Conservation Union, United Nations Environment Programme and World Wide Fund for Nature 1991, 10).

As the discourse on sustainable development became more prominent in international discourses, ecological economics also elaborated its views, concepts and theories on sustainable development. Notable are the discussions on the concept of the nested sustainability system or the so-called 'Levett's model' of sustainability (see Figure 4.1). This new concept puts aside the outdated, and even misleading, visualization of sustainable development as three equal-sized circles representing the three pillars (environment, economy and society), in which the overlapped space indicates sustainable development, being expanded on all three circles. In reality, however, these three pillars are not equally represented and do not hold equal power in today's political and economic system. Rather more accurately, year by year the economic circles have started to expand and spread over the environmental and societal circles. A nested sustainability system follows one of the main principles of ecological economics: observing the human economy as a subsystem of ecology, and not as something that should subordinate other systems to itself. This view still has economic, societal and environmental components, but these pillars are positioned within nested circles, with the economy being central and shaped by the needs for well-being and good quality of living within society. These needs are encircled by the limits of the world's ecosystem, what are today called the nine planetary boundaries (see Figure 4.2).

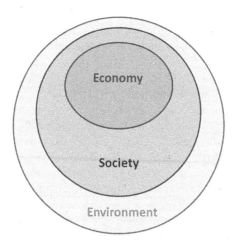

Note: This file is licensed under the Creative Commons Attribution-Share Alike 3.0 Unported licence.
Source: commons.wikimedia (2022).

Figure 4.1   *Nested model of sustainability*

Ecological economics 31

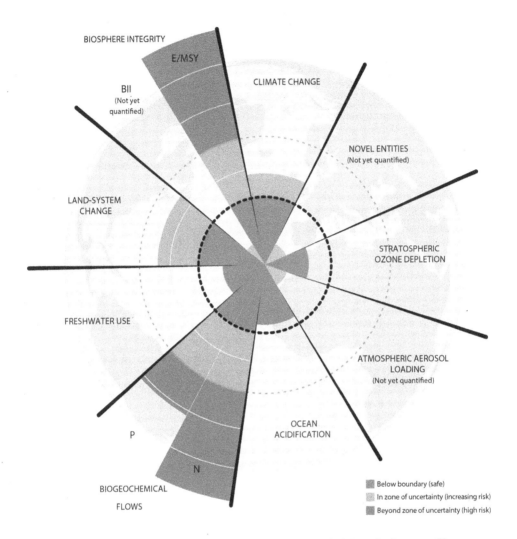

Note: BII – Biodiversity Intactness Index. N – nitrogen. P – phosphorus. E/MSY – extinctions per million species-years.
Source: Stockholm Resilience Centre (2012) (CC BY 4.0) (Credit: J. Lokrantz/Azote based on Steffen et al. 2015).

Figure 4.2   *Planetary boundaries*

Observing this nested model of sustainability, ecological economics aims to address all three pillars of sustainable development at once. In this framework, the environment regards system-carrying capacity and resilience; society regards the distribution of wealth and rights, social capital and coevolving preferences; and the economy regards the efficient allocation of resources, especially natural capital and ecosystem services (Costanza et al. 2020).

With its focus on both environmental limits and the unique value of nature and ecosystems, ecological economics paved the way for the profiling of a deep or strong sustainability approach versus a weak sustainability approach. A weak sustainability approach postulates the substitutability of natural ecosystems or resources. It argues that with technological improvements and profit gained from the economy, natural ecosystems or resources can be compensated. Based on the theories and concepts of ecological economics, strong sustainability considers natural ecosystems as a set of complex systems that are inseparable from the 'web of life' (Capra 1997) on our planet. This idea of strong sustainability is well practised in various SSE organizations and enterprises (SSEOEs), in particular those which have emerged from grassroots, indigenous and community-based movements to develop a sustainable model to manage the commons (see entry 13, 'The Commons' and entry 29, 'Food and Agriculture Sector'). The point of departure and principles these SSEOEs are based upon are a commitment to the ethical organization of society and all of its activities, meeting the needs of all people in the community and enabling provision for the well-being of future generations (Barkin 2018). Additionally, the importance and impact of the natural ecosystem were researched and verified by the Millennium Ecosystem Assessment (2005). The report was the result of scientific research that presented conditions and trends in the global ecosystems, and it concluded that 15 out of 24 planet ecosystem services had already been significantly degraded or were close to the tipping point. It also highlighted four ecosystem services crucial to the quality of life: supporting, provisioning, regulating and cultural. According to the Millennium Ecosystem Assessment (2005), these four ecosystem services, with different strengths, correspond to the main components of well-being, including the accessibility of basic materials for a good life, health, security and good social relations. The authors of this research conclude that the condition of Earth's ecosystem and the ability to run a standard set of services is crucial for the human opportunity for freedom of choice and action. Without a good and balanced environment, there is no good and balanced society; and, in turn, there is no good and balanced economy. This mirrors the interconnected levels of the nested concept of sustainability. From awareness of ecosystem services, some went further and started to research the economic value of nature and its services. According to this research, the amount was estimated to be in the range US$16–54 trillion per year, much more than the global gross national product at that time (Costanza et al. 1997). The intention of calculating the value of nature was to highlight the importance and preciousness of ecosystems and discover to what extent the value of nature exceeds what the economy produces, even in terms of economic standards. This research trend continued within studies such as *The Economics of Ecosystems and Biodiversity* (TEEB) from 2010, which also highlighted the scale of economic losses as a result of biodiversity degradation (Spash 2018).

However, some criticized this approach in ecological economics as the path that 'has served to blur the meaning of ecological economics' (Brown and Timmerman 2015, 5) or as an 'infiltration of inappropriate mainstream economic approaches' (Kish and Farley 2021, 4). The point is that it is not possible to measure the real or actual value of nature or ecosystems, since some of its characteristics are not measurable and cannot be presented in monetary terms, being much deeper and broader. In this vein, some authors also pointed out that 'ecosystem services should not be defined as nature's benefits to people, but rather as fund-services that benefit all members of the biotic community, not simply humans' (Washington 2020, 37). This debate has some similarities to the debate on the monetization of social values created by the SSE, which indicates the cross-fertilization of ecological economics and SSE studies (see entry 54, 'Statistical Measurement').

Others viewed this as methodological and content-oriented pluralism within the whole ecological economics. For instance, Clive Spash identifies three schools of thought in ecological economics: mainstream new resource economists who mostly focus on the inclusion of ecological costs into economic decisions; new environmental pragmatists who embrace any new theory or concept; and radical social-ecological economists who focus on alternatives to capitalism and recommend transformative social measures (Kish and Farley 2021). According to Spash, only the last school is based on the key concepts and theories of ecological economics.

4.4 CRITIQUE OF THE GROWTH FETISH

Ecological economics is strongly critical of the growth imperative or even growth addiction of the modern economy. The modern economy pursues linear, ever-rising growth, without any limits or boundaries. This is in direct conflict with ecosystem principles and services, and with the design and operation of a 'web of life' on our planet (Daly and Farley 2004, 226). Notable researchers criticizing growth include Peter Victor and Tim Jackson (Victor and Jackson 2012), both being ahead of their time.

The idea underpinning such a degrowth movement is Georgescu-Roegen's 'declining state' (opposite to Daly's steady state) of the late 1970s. The movement originated in France (Muraca and Schmelzer 2017) with the name translating into *décroissance* (decay) in French. Degrowth is defined as 'a socially sustainable and equitable reduction (and stabilization) in society's throughput, where throughput denotes the materials and energy a society extracts, processes, transports and distributes, to consume and return back to the environment as waste' (Charonis 2012, 2).

These concepts of degrowth or declining (decay in French) share in common a very critical position toward growth, and even green growth, which has been promoted within the sustainable development framework because growth in whatever form will not bring the absolute decoupling required for ecological economics. Although diverse schools employ these degrowth concepts, sometimes with different meanings and in different contexts, they are all on the same unique quest for the radical transformation of social institutions and structural (economic and institutional) and socio-cultural (modes of subjectivation, social imaginary and colonization of the lifeworld) critique of economic growth.

4.5 IMPORTANCE OF WELL-BEING

From the very beginning of the formation period of ecological economics, many authors and researchers emphasized why, instead of the rise in material outputs and resources flow, society should focus on equality, human potential and life satisfaction. Daly advocated for decreasing pressure on the planet's ecosystems, in place of an increase in human well-being. He also developed new tools for measurement of well-being or quality of life, instead of growth-dependent gross domestic product (GDP). Together with John and Clifford Cobb, Daly initiated a new approach in testing the level and scope of development success in some countries with their Index of Sustainable Economic Welfare (ISEW) tool, later known as the Genuine Progress Indicator (GPI). They showed how GDP was constantly rising, but GPI in some countries had stagnated, and in many cases, decreased. Along this line, many similar concepts and approaches were developed which aimed to count not the amount of money going through the economy, but the effect of that amount on the quality of living and the environment. Since 1990, the United Nations Development Programme (UNDP) has announced its Human Development Index (HDI), which today still has regular modifications and improvements. Questioning GDP as an indicator of society's success became particularly prevalent after the global financial crisis in 2008–09. It is not by accident that in 2011 an ecological footprint report was announced, with the title 'What Happens When an Infinite-Growth Economy Runs Into a Finite Planet?'. From there we can follow the development of the European Union-based Quality of Life Index, the new United Nations-initiated World Happiness Report, or even the Organisation for Economic Co-operation and Development's (OECD's) Beyond GDP programme, which has resulted in its Better Life Index. Although they have a long way to go in matching the values and points of view of ecological economics, these new measurement tools all share the same goal of disconnecting societal progress from linear economic growth. Instead, they are balancing economic achievements with areas such as education, health, security and safety, gender rights, community bonds and trust, human rights, democracy, and transparency. Although it is not certain how much influence these new concepts, approaches and measurements exert on policy discourses, it is certain that these have become prominent in various contexts. For instance, well-being economics provides a basis for a political agenda, and since 2018, countries such as Scotland, Iceland and New Zealand (later joined by Finland and Wales, and considered by Canada) expressed their commitment to the collective well-being and quality of living for their citizens, instead of focusing on the constant rise of economic growth through the lens of GDP. Many cities also started to use measurement tools based on Kate Raworth's idea of the 'Doughnut Economy' (Raworth 2017). She combined the nine planetary boundaries researched by the Stockholm Resilience Centre with the 12 areas of social foundations that are linked to the quality of living and level of satisfaction/happiness in life. Following Daly's analyses, Raworth developed a tool for sustainable and resilient adaptation of cities where the use of the outer section of the doughnut (which houses the planetary boundaries) must be limited or shrunk, while the inside part of the doughnut (which houses social foundations) must be spread and made affordable to as many citizens as possible.

4.6 LINK TO THE SSE

The development of the SSE, in particular its goals, world perspectives and operational norms and practices, are very much in line with ecological economics, although they do not have explicit linkages to each other. Ecological economics came from the care for Earth's ecosystems and natural resources. The SSE came from the care for a more just, fair and solidarity society. However, both concepts are seeking the same goal: a democratic transformation of the economy (see entry 10 'Origins and Histories' and entry 3 'Contemporary Understandings').

In terms of world perspectives, as was explained earlier, ecological economics understands the world through the nested system of sustainability, in which the economy is embedded in society, and society is embedded in nature. Similarly, the fundamental premise or idea underpinning the SSE is that the economy needs to be re-embedded in society, that is, 'in ethical and social norms and democratizing the economy through active citizenship' (Utting et al. 2014, 1).

Both ecological economics and the SSE also share in common the pursuit of a wide and deep transformation of the social/economic system. Ecological economics pursues transformation, since without transformation the large ecological footprint and pressure on Earth's carrying capacity and ecosystem would perpetuate. The SSE also explicates the need for transformation of the economic system from current market-based capitalist model that is dependent on endless growth and profit above all to the one that puts people and the planet at its core. This pursuit of transformation by the SSE is not only underpinned by social concern, but is also an ecological concern. For instance, the Intercontinental Network for the Promotion of Social Solidarity Economy (RIPESS), in its 'Global Vision for a Social Solidarity Economy: Convergences and Differences in Concepts, Definitions and Frameworks' report, announced that it advocates for a world in which of rational use of resources and respect for the balance of ecosystems is promoted, with a clear rejection of the 'neoliberal model of economic growth that threatens life on the planet' (RIPESS 2015, 5).

Some of the best-known proponents of ecological economics advocate for measures to address social problems. For instance, they argue for quotas and taxes on basic resources and fossil fuel use, considering affordability for the poor and impoverished; limits to the inequality of society with maximum and minimum income; working weekdays adaptation; reform of international trade agreements and the financial sector in order for people to work for the benefit of the common good and well-being; and free use of cultural/knowledge commons (Daly and Farley 2004). Many, if not all, of these actions and policies are also mentioned within the agenda and campaign manifestos of the SSE.

CONCLUSION

There is no doubt that our world is in a systemic crisis. Ecological economics is conceptualized as a core solution to this crisis, especially in an environmental capacity. Endless linear economic growth which encapsulates the modern system is neither practical (in the long term, on the planet with limited resources) nor ethical (causing other crises, including increased inequality due to resource wars and debt-dependent societies). Ecological economics provides a solution for the future and can 'help society move from an endless growth economy to one in balance with the world that sustains human society' (Washington 2020, 341). The SSE also aims to achieve this by assuming responsibility for transitioning to more appropriate production and consumption patterns to meet 'the needs of all people in the community (Utting et al. 2014, 9), 'while also making provision for the well-being of future generations' (Barkin 2018, 374).

The elective affinity between the SSE and ecological economies, and the possibility of cross-fertilization, is also found in Karl Polanyi's remark that provides the basis of both ecological economics and the SSE: 'the economy needs to be embedded in social relations, but capitalist society is diametrically opposite' (Kish and Farley 2021).

REFERENCES

Barkin, David. 2018. 'Popular Sustainable Development, or Ecological Economics From Below.' In *The Essential Guide to Critical Development Studies*, edited by Henry Veltmeyer and Paul Bowles. New York: Routledge.
Brown, Peter and Peter Timmerman, eds. 2015. *Ecological Economics for the Anthropocene: An Emerging Paradigm*. New York: Columbia University Press.
Capra, Fritjof. 1997. *The Web of Life: A New Synthesis of Mind and Matter*. London: Flamingo.

Common, Mick and Sigrid Stagl. 2005. *Ecological Economics – An Introduction*. Cambridge: Cambridge University Press.
commons.wikimedia. 2022. 'File:Nested Sustainability-V2.Svg – Wikipedia.' Commons.wikimedia.org. Wikipedia. 25 May. https://en.m.wikipedia.org/wiki/File:Nested_sustainability-v2.svg.
Costanza, Robert, Jon D. Erickson, Joshua Farley and Ida Kubiszewski, eds. 2020. *Sustainable Wellbeing Futures – A Research and Action Agenda for Ecological Economics*. Cheltenham, UK and Northampton, MA, USA: Edward Elgar Publishing.
Daly, Herman E. and Joshua Farley. 2004. *Ecological Economics: Principles and Applications*. Washington, DC: Island Press.
Kish, Kaitlin and Joshua Farley. 2021. 'A Research Agenda for the Future of Ecological Economics by Emerging Scholars.' *Sustainability* 13: 1557. https://doi.org/10.3390/su13031557.
Meadows, Donella H., Dennis L. Meadows, Jorgen Randers and William W. Behrens. 1972. *The Limits to Growth: A Report for the Club of Rome's Project on the Predicament of Mankind*. New York: Universe Books.
Millennium Ecosystem Assessment. 2005. *Ecosystems and Human Well-Being*. Washington, D.C: Island Press.
Raworth, Kate. 2017. *Doughnut Economics: Seven Ways to Think like a 21st-Century Economist*. London: Random House Business Books.
RIPESS (Intercontinental Network for the Promotion of Social Solidarity Economy). 2015. 'Global Vision for a Social Solidarity Economy: Convergences and Differences in Concepts, Definitions and Frameworks.' http://www.ripess.org/wp-content/uploads/2017/08/RIPESS_Vision-Global_EN.pdf.
Spash, Clive L. 2018. *Routledge Handbook of Ecological Economics: Nature and Society*. London: Routledge.
Stockholm Resilience Centre. 2012. 'Planetary Boundaries – Stockholm Resilience Centre.' 19 September. https://www.stockholmresilience.org/research/planetary-boundaries.html.
TEEB. 2010. *The Economics of Ecosystems and Biodiversity Ecological and Economic Foundations*, edited by Pushpam Kumar. London, UK and Washington, DC, USA: Earthscan.
Utting, Peter, Nadine van Dijk and Marie-Adélaïde Matheï. 2014. 'Social and Solidarity Economy – Is There a New Economy in the Making?' UNRISD. http://www.unrisd.org/80256B3C005BCCF9/search/AD29696D41CE69C3C1257D460033C267?OpenDocument.
Washington, Haydn, ed. 2020. 'Ecological Economics: Solutions for the Future.' https://www.isecoeco.org/wp-content/uploads/2020/07/EESolutionsFutureRoyalEbook.pdf.
World Commission on Environment and Development. 1987. *Our Common Future*. Suffolk: Oxford University Press. https://sustainabledevelopment.un.org/content/documents/5987our-common-future.pdf.
The World Conservation Union, United Nations Environment Programme and World Wide Fund for Nature. 1991. *Caring for the Earth: A Strategy for Sustainable Living*. Gland, Switzerland: International Union For Conservation Of Nature And Natural Resources.

5. Feminist economics
Suzanne Bergeron

INTRODUCTION

The struggle for a more equitable, democratic, and sustainable economic system has resulted in a plurality of efforts to reimagine and transform the socio-economy that is encapsulated within the term the "social and solidarity economy" (SSE). While once relegated to the fringe, there is growing interest in the SSE as a viable alternative within development policy circles (Utting 2015). Yet this interest in the SSE has been largely gender-blind, as outcomes of gender equality in the SSE are assumed rather than analyzed (Verschuur et al. 2021). There is also the issue of the SSE's ongoing productivist bias, which sidelines crucial aspects of the economy, such as women's unpaid work in social reproduction (Laville 2021), including women's self-organization through collective SSE entities to secure decent livelihoods (notably in Africa, Asia, and Latin America). Adding to this disconnect is the fact that gender and development policy has not yet engaged significantly with the SSE. Dominant neoliberal gender policy frameworks have focused on integrating women into the existing capitalist system, rather than fostering alternatives along SSE lines. Feminists critical of these policy frameworks often view all possible paths to the SSE as foreclosed, either already coopted by neoliberalism or too fragile to succeed (Bergeron and Healy 2015). This entry aims to bring the SSE and feminism into a more robust conversation with each other by introducing some key analytical insights from feminist economics (FE) and tracing out connections to the SSE. It begins by briefly introducing the field, then turns to the FE revision of economics, paying particular attention to the social provisioning approach of FE and the centrality of social reproduction within it.

5.1 WHAT IS FEMINIST ECONOMICS? A BRIEF INTRODUCTION

Feminist economics is an interdisciplinary field of scholarship that exists to challenge the biased and incomplete accounts of economic life found in dominant economic theories, particularly those of the neoclassical, free-market school of thought. Feminist challenges to economics date back to at least the mid-19th century, but the foundation for FE as it exists today can be traced to the 1970s and 1980s, when the growing feminist movement in the United States and Europe gave rise to critiques of the received ideas about women and gender in economics. FE research at that time focused on women's labor force participation, the gender wage gap, and the failure to account for household production and women's unpaid domestic labor. By the 1990s, this work coalesced into a distinct subfield of the discipline, with its own journal, organized under the banner of "feminist economics." It also expanded its critique of the male bias of mainstream economics on a number of fronts. In addition to tackling the failures of neoclassical economics to address discrimination in the market or adequately account for and value activities outside of the market, such as unpaid domestic labor, FE has shown that troubling gender assumptions operate at virtually all levels of economic thought and practice. Take, for instance, the representative agent of neoclassical economics, an abstract *Homo economicus* defined as a self-sufficient and self-interested rational economic agent. FE analysis has shown that this supposedly universal figure reflects a White, Western, masculine ideal of detachment, individualism, and rationality. It also pushes to the margins human motivations associated with devalued feminine characteristics and resting on obligation, altruism, connection, solidarity, and care. In contrast, FE views people as relational subjects with multiple motivations, and for whom gender, race, class, sexuality, power, social norms, and other factors are at play in the economic processes in which they are involved (Ferber and Nelson 1993). In addition, FE scholarship has critiqued the mainstream's false standard of objectivity and scientific detachment, which is propped up by its use of abstract, mathematical models. Over the past decades, FE has continued to critique and reformulate economics, tackling issues at the core of the mainstream's foundational assumptions as well as addressing questions in particular subfields such as development, household economics, macroeconomics, political economy, labor market discrimination, and more.

5.2 FE AND THE SOCIAL PROVISIONING APPROACH

Currently, the field of FE is wide-ranging, and the entry points and perspectives of FE are diverse. Still, beyond the obvious shared project of making gender a central category of analysis, there is a methodological convergence of a wide range of FE's various strands around the social provisioning approach (SPA) (Power 2004). The SPA redefines economics as the study of provisioning for human life, rather than the study of choices in markets. It recognizes that provisioning includes activities that lie both within and outside of markets, including paid work, unpaid labor, community networks, cooperation (and SSE), the natural world, and the public sector. It views women's unpaid domestic labor and care work as an essential, if heretofore neglected, part of the economic system. It further analyzes how economic processes and outcomes are shaped by gender and other identities. The SPA acknowledges motivations such as care and cooperation in addition to those of self-interest. It rejects the idea that our current mode of provisioning reflects the "natural" workings of the market, for which there is no alternative, and instead views economic organization as the outcome of power dynamics and struggle. Finally, the SPA embraces ethics as a part of economic analysis, as economics should be in the service of not just analyzing, but also improving human well-being. The same commitments to ethics, justice, caring, and cooperative motivations, and social provisioning for well-being, are where the SSE, in its diverse perspectives and pluralistic strategies, tends to engage (see entry 3, "Contemporary Understandings"). Consequently, what follows will focus on key themes that emerge from the SPA framework.

5.3 FE AND THE EVALUATION OF ECONOMIC SUCCESS

How FE evaluates economic success around social provisioning for well-being distinguishes it from the dominant economic approach. Mainstream neoclassical economics evaluates the economy in terms of market efficiency, profitability, and growth of gross domestic product

(GDP) per capita, measured in terms of market-produced goods. FE finds these goals to be narrow, insufficient, and misleading, since other types of output and outcome can be, and are, achieved or obtained. The emphasis on GDP growth to measure economic success rests on the assumption that all economic activity is "priced" and takes place in markets, leaving out the enormous amount of production and resource use that takes place in households, communities, and the natural world outside of markets. The emphasis placed on market efficiency is also troubling. Some strands of FE have made an "efficiency case" for pursuing gender equality through the removal of obstacles to women's participation in labor and financial markets, and these ideas have been taken up enthusiastically in institutions such as the World Bank and the International Monetary Fund. But those employing the SPA are more skeptical of this "business case" for pursuing gender equality. Subordinating the goals of gender equality to efficiency enhancement does little to challenge the structural inequalities of the economy that have contributed to the immiseration of so many in the first place. Further, this approach fails to challenge the mainstream idea that an underlying logic, in which we cannot interfere, guides the economy even when current economic approaches are not working for most of us. This "logic we must obey" approach of the dominant neoclassical school, and the neoliberal policies that it informs, fails to present the economy as it is: something that humans create through struggle, in which ethical commitments are always present (Bergeron and Healy 2015).

In this respect, FE joins other non-mainstream economists and many working in the SSE to reject strict market criteria and focus on outcomes related to achieving broad-based human well-being. Such efforts focus on reframing economic success outside of per capita GDP, through alternative measures and indicators. One such alternative indicator, adopted by some in FE, is the Genuine Progress Indicator. This was developed by ecological economists, and combines economic, social, and environmental aspects to provide a more robust measure of sustainable well-being. Amartya Sen's capabilities approach, which defines the success of the socio-economy in terms of enhancing human agency to allow people to better lead lives that they value, has been particularly influential in FE. Using this approach, the goals of improving women's access to economic opportunities and knowledge, increasing voice and ability to make decisions, living secure lives, having control over income, and other freedoms are viewed as ends to strive for in and of themselves, not solely for their effects on the income of women, or the efficiency and growth of the economy at large (Sen 1999). A rich literature on FE has drawn upon and extended these insights. Naila Kabeer (2021), for instance, has variously drawn upon the capabilities approach in her work, shifting the focus to empowerment—defined in terms of challenging the constraints that oppress people—to make the role of power in structuring human agency more explicit. These insights have been incorporated into gender-aware measures of well-being such as the Gender Equality Index, which accounts for a range of gender inequalities related to labor rights, participation and earnings, reproductive and maternal health, gender-based violence, political participation and leadership, literacy, and other factors that impact the development of women's capabilities. All those elements are to be found as underlying concepts and intrinsic values of the SSE.

5.4 CONCEPTUALIZING AND ADDRESSING GENDER INEQUALITIES

FE has provided a corrective to dominant neoclassical economics as well as to a variety of heterodox economic theories of inequality. These theories focus only on market-related factors such as labor market earnings and financial assets which, while important, do not tell the whole story. A rich literature on FE has documented the inequalities that occur in the sphere of the household and family life that are left out of the mainstream theories, including the myriad ways that rights, voice, work, resources, and leisure are unequally distributed in households, as well as the lack of autonomy that many women experience in patriarchal contexts (Folbre 2020). It has also examined the ways that gender relations can shift as access to resources inside and outside of the household changes, with implications for how inequalities play out in both market and household (Agarwal 1997). Further, there is attention to structural and institutional factors for which FE offers an intersectional framework that can explain the complexities and interactions of gender, race, class, caste, sexuality, and coloniality (Brewer et al. 2002; Ruwanpura 2008).

Liberal feminism has long connected the fight for equality with women's integration into the labor market as workers or entrepreneurs. Some strands of FE have adopted a similar position, viewing the household as the primary site of women's oppression, and extolling the liberatory effects of participation in labor or credit markets to provide women with their own income. But more critical perspectives have shown that the results of integration into the market have had mixed effects. While women gaining access to their own income has, in many cases, increased their bargaining power at home in ways that challenge patriarchy (including supporting their ability to live autonomous lives outside of patriarchal household structures), it also heightens exploitation and gender inequality in some contexts (Benería et al. 2015). While feminist efforts to foster equal opportunity have led to successes for some groups of women, labor markets remain segregated by race, caste, sexuality, class, and gender in ways that make low-paid and precarious work the only option for many poor women. Further, fostering women's success "inside" the existing system contributes to multiple crises, including those related to climate, energy, water, underemployment, and more, that threaten the well-being of all individuals (Matthaei 2009). With regard to the argument that microcredit is a "magic bullet" to resolving poverty and liberating women from patriarchal confines, many strands of FE have been highly critical. They point to the increased commercialization of microfinance and the huge profits gained by drawing women into global debt relations. They also point to the precarities associated with the informal sector activities that these loans support. In many cases, recipients' overall workload of paid and unpaid labor increased to nearly breaking point. It is also not clear that inequalities in households are reduced as women's income increases. While in some cases additional income can improve women's status and decrease their workload at home, in other cases women earners may end up doing more domestic labor as their incomes rise, and they may face increased incidence of domestic violence (Barker et al. 2021).

Women's integration into paid work and financial circuits that are more in line with SSE principles of democratic participation and cooperation can, however, foster alternatives to the mechanisms of gendered exploitation that drive more neoliberal contexts. Hossein (2018) discusses the important role of women-led cooperative financial institutions in both empowering women and provisioning for well-being within African diaspora communities. The work of SSE organizations such as the Self Employed Women's Association in India, which operates through women-run cooperatives and unions, has helped to secure the livelihoods of many hundreds of thousands of women through training that leads to increased wages and fighting for enhanced social protections from the state (see entry 30, "Gender Equality and Empowerment"). Domestic workers' cooperatives and unions have provided poor, racialized, and immigrant women with the ability to improve their working conditions and pay in this line of work (Eşim 2021). These initiatives—especially at the local and community level—are but a handful of examples of how the SSE can offer an alternative to capitalist "business as usual" to reduce gender inequality and foster women's empowerment. But, as Verschuur et al. (2021) argue, additional attention to a key concept in FE—the gendered organization of social reproduction—by the SSE could further strengthen the development of more equitable alternatives. It is thus a discussion of social reproduction that this entry now turns to.

5.5　CARE AND SOCIAL REPRODUCTION

One of the major contributions of FE has been to highlight the essential contribution that unpaid domestic labor and care work makes to social provisioning. This labor has been ignored and devalued in mainstream economics because of gender divisions and hierarchies that privilege the historically masculine sphere of production and the market over activities in the feminine sphere of reproduction and maintenance of life. While men do engage in these activities, the disproportionate share of household care, domestic labor, and unpaid farming work is done by women (and young girls). FE has also brought attention to the essential but often undeclared and low-paid care work done largely by poor, racialized, and immigrant women. As an aside, one can critically note that the SSE is barely starting to make inroads into this sector with more equitable alternatives such as mutuals or collective self-managed initiatives. The neglect of these activities has many negative effects. At the level of ontology, J.K. Gibson-Graham highlights that it obscures the diverse economic processes and motivations that make up the socio-economy in ways that constrain our ability to imagine and build on existing alternative values and practices (Gibson-Graham 1996). At the level of macroeconomic policy, the absence of unpaid and undocumented domestic and care work in official statistics such as GDP presents a false picture of the economy. There are also deeply flawed macroeconomic policy initiatives that, by failing to take this important work into account, have resulted in a significant increase in women's labor burdens and depletion of care. At the level of the labor market, workplaces organized around the masculine ideal of an unencumbered worker result in a double burden of unpaid household work and wage labor for those with care responsibilities (Barker et al. 2021). The ongoing failure to recognize and support this work at all levels has created a depletion of and crisis of care.

In addition to highlighting the value of previously ignored household labor, more critical strands of FE scholarship have also challenged the mainstream economics presentation of market and household as completely separate spheres. A rich literature on social reproduction (SR) has been debating and tracing out the crucial interrelationships between capitalism and care work since the 1970s. "Social reproduction" is a term that refers to the crucial role that activities and processes of sustaining and reproducing life play in the development of capitalism. The understanding of SR has evolved since the term was first coined by feminist scholars examining the relationship between gender oppression, housework, and the reproduction of the labor force. It has expanded to include an analysis of all activities—market and non-market, encompassing a diversity of economic sites and practices—that are engaged in the reproduction of life. For instance, as thinking around these issues developed, attention to the ways that complexities of race, class, and global circuits were implicated in SR extended the analysis to include the paid labor of social reproduction (such as paid domestic work). Other theoretical developments have emphasized the ways that increasingly informalized and fragmented systems of labor have turned many households into sites where paid work and SR occur simultaneously, and the distinctions between them are blurred. Still others have pointed to the ways that the disappearance of natural commons around the world has intensified SR labor for those who once relied upon these commons for much of their sustenance and well-being. Central to the FE analysis of SR is the contradictory relationship between capitalist accumulation and provisioning for well-being. The unlimited search for profits has increased exploitation in ways that have made it more difficult for the majority of people to meet their SR needs, destabilizing the very processes of maintenance and reproduction of life on which capitalism relies.

These debates about and insights from SR are summarized and extended to SSE in an important volume by Verschuur et al. (2021). They argue that reframing our understanding of work to include SR can greatly enhance the transformative potential of the SSE. As people around the world address the crises of SR that they face—along with the gender, race, class, colonial, and other power relations that structure these crises—the current organization of the economy is being rejected, and people are searching for SSE alternatives. For instance, social movements have created community-based programs for providing SR outside of capitalist logics. In fact, there is a long history of racialized and otherwise marginalized communities mobilizing to provide collective care and mutual aid. This represents not only a survival strategy, but one of political resistance and social transformation. Verschuur et al. (2021) examine a range of emerging women-led SSE SR alternatives that offer a more equitable form of social provisioning characterized by solidarity relations. These include: collective efforts for providing childcare, education, food, and other goods; sharing knowledge and resources; a variety of articulations with the state to support SSE SR activities and processes; organizing paid SR workers to reduce exploitative practices; and mobilizing community workers engaged in SR to demand recognition and rights. Examples offered in the book include the development of community centers in Argentina, people's canteens in West Africa, the Self Employed Women's Association in India, and more. Throughout, the authors highlight the importance of recognizing and valuing women's SR activities in SSE practices, as well as the potential of the SSE for addressing the crisis of SR that so many poor people are experiencing around the world.

CONCLUSION

This entry has offered a brief introduction to some key contributions of FE to an alternative understanding of the economy outside of the mainstream. While acknowledging that the field of FE is wide-ranging and, at times, hard to pin down, the entry identified a few central elements of FE scholarship that could expand thinking about the scope and nature of SSE activities. While for many years the SSE has been somewhat gender-blind in its approach, it is heartening to see an emerging literature bringing an explicit FE analysis to understanding SSE activities and processes. Continued engagement between FE and SSE is crucial to understanding the conditions under which inclusive, gender-equitable SSE processes can foster democratic participation, cooperative governance, and social provisioning for the well-being of all people and the planet.

REFERENCES

Agarwal, Bina. 1997. "Bargaining and Gender Relations: Within and Beyond the Household." *Feminist Economics* 3 (1): 1–51. https://doi.org/10.1080/135457097338799.

Barker, Drucilla K., Suzanne Bergeron, and Susan F. Feiner. 2021. *Liberating Economics: Feminist Perspectives on Families, Work, and Globalization*, 2nd edn. Ann Arbor, MI: University of Michigan Press.

Benería, Lourdes, Günseli Berik, and Maria Floro. 2015. *Gender, Development, and Globalization Economics as If All People Mattered*. New York: Routledge.

Bergeron, Suzanne, and Stephen Healy. 2015. "Beyond the Business Case: A Community Economics Approach to Gender, Development and Social Economy." In *Social and Solidarity Economy: Beyond the Fringe?* edited by Peter Utting. London: Zed Books.

Brewer, Rose M., Cecelia Conrad, and Mary King. 2002. "Gender, Color, Caste, and Class." *Feminist Economics* 8 (1): 3–17.

Eşim, Simel. 2021. "Cooperatives." In *The Routledge Handbook of Feminist Economics*, edited by Günseli Berik and Ebru Kongar. Abingdon, UK and New York, USA: Routledge.

Ferber, Marianne A., and Julie A. Nelson. 1993. *Beyond Economic Man: Feminist Theory and Economics*. Chicago, IL: University of Chicago Press.

Folbre, Nancy. 2020. *Rise and Decline of Patriarchal Systems*. London: Verso Books.

Gibson-Graham, J.K. 1996. *The End of Capitalism (as We Knew It): A Feminist Critique of Political Economy*. Cambridge, MA, USA and Oxford, UK: Blackwell Publishers.

Hossein, Caroline Shenaz. 2018. *Politicized Microfinance Money, Power, and Violence in the Black Americas*. Toronto: University of Toronto Press.

Kabeer, Naila. 2021. "Capabilities, Empowerment, and Citizenship." In *The Routledge Handbook of Feminist Economics*, edited by Günseli Berik and Ebru Kongar. Abingdon, UK and New York, USA: Routledge.

Laville, Jean-Louis. 2021. "Afterword: The Cross-Fertilization between Feminism and the Solidarity Economy." In *Social Reproduction, Solidarity Economy, Feminisms and Democracy: Latin America and India*, edited by Christine Verschuur, Isabelle Guérin, and Isabelle Hillenkamp. Cham: Palgrave Macmillan.

Matthaei, Julie. 2009. "Beyond Economic Man: Economic Crisis, Feminist Economics, and the Solidarity Economy." Paper presented at the International Association for Feminist Economics Conference. Boston, MA: International Association for Feminist Economics.

Power, Marilyn. 2004. "Social Provisioning as a Starting Point for Feminist Economics." *Feminist Economics* 10 (3): 3–19. https://doi.org/10.1080/1354570042000267608.

Ruwanpura, Kanchana N. 2008. "Multiple Identities, Multiple-Discrimination: A Critical Review." *Feminist Economics* 14 (3): 77–105. https://doi.org/10.1080/13545700802035659.

Sen, Amartya. 1999. *Development as Freedom*. Oxford: Oxford University Press.

Utting, Peter. 2015. "Introduction: The Challenge of Scaling Up Social and Solidarity Economy." In *Social and Solidarity Economy: Beyond the Fringe?* edited by Peter Utting. London: Zed Books.

Verschuur, Christine, Isabelle Guérin, and Isabelle Hillenkamp. 2021. *Social Reproduction, Solidarity Economy, Feminisms and Democracy: Latin America and India*. Cham: Palgrave Macmillan.

6. Globalization and alter-globalization
Carmen Marcuello, Anjel Errasti and Ignacio Bretos

6.1 GLOBALIZATION

Globalization is an extremely complex phenomenon, from both a theoretical-conceptual and a practical point of view, and has received the attention of a multitude of research from various disciplines (sociology, political science, anthropology, geography, economics, and so on) due to its multidimensional nature. Moreover, the development of globalization is associated with serious negative and positive consequences. The alter-globalization movements emerged strongly to counteract these negative effects and to propose other ways of understanding the relationships between the global economy, environment and people. Among them, the social and solidarity economy (SSE) is one of the most comprehensive proposals which address the problems caused by globalization. The SSE confronts future challenges by prioritizing social and environmental needs in economic decisions.

Globalization can be understood as a dynamic process of capitalism that has structured the different forms of capital accumulation throughout history: from the 15th century with the logic of the accumulation of mercantile capital, which allowed the dominance of the Atlantic centres over the peripheries of the Americas and other continents, to the current paradigm of technology as the basis for capital accumulation. Although the term 'globalization' began to be used in the late 1960s and early 1970s, it became popular from the 1980s onwards with Levitt's (1983) famous work, 'The Globalization of Markets'. It is no coincidence that this fact occurs at this particular historical moment: since the late 1970s and early 1980s, capitalist globalization experienced an unprecedented dynamism in our time, driven by neoliberalism, which encompasses political, geographical, cultural, social and economic spheres (Harvey 2005).

Since then, this phenomenon has attracted considerable attention. The lack of consensus across academic spheres suggests that there remains great complexity in the analysis of globalization, and demonstrates why it is still the focus of a multitude of debates from different disciplines. In this sense, there is a strong controversy due to the wide diversity of approaches to different aspects of globalization, such as its definition and meaning, its historical origin, its dimensions, its ideological bases or its implications.

We can understand globalization as an ongoing process of intensifying cross-border social and economic interactions which is enabled by the decreasing costs of connecting distant places through communication. The process of globalization facilitates the transfer of capital, goods and people across space, and leads to an increasing transnational interdependence of economic and social actors, an increase in both opportunities and risks, and an intensification of competition. Globalization is accelerated by factors such as political decisions (reduction of barriers to trade, foreign direct investment, capital and services, privatization and deregulation policies), technological developments (communication, media, transport) and socio-political developments (migration, diffusion of knowledge, creation of new identities).

6.2 CONSEQUENCES OF GLOBALIZATION

Economic globalization, understood as an open practice through the mobility of capital, goods and services, is associated with multiple processes of regional economic integration that exposes the national productive fabric to increasing foreign competition (Dicken 2011). Globalization experienced an extraordinary escalation in the first years of the 21st century, driven by a paradigm known as neoliberalism (Harvey 2005). These processes are boosted by transnational corporations, which play a key role in the economic, social and political changes of globalization (Dicken 2011). The effects of neoliberal globalization on local economies can be studied from four perspectives: economic, socio-labour, democratic and environmental.

The Economic Instability

There is a certain consensus that economic liberalization has brought development to many countries. However, the neoliberal model of globalization that has been implemented has led to serious inequalities between and within countries. There is a strong concentration of trade flows in the geographic areas with the greatest wealth, creating dependence on other regions such as Latin America, Eastern Europe and Africa (Dicken 2011). In this way, extremely unequal geography is produced through processes of social/territorial exclusion and inclusion that affect countries, regions, cities or neighbourhoods. Through this, large segments of populations are excluded, while linking trans-territorially everything that can be of value in the global networks that accumulate wealth, information and power. In addition, another (and perhaps most potent) source of destabilization of the productive economy has been the process of financialization of the economy. Financial capital has become more important in relation to labour income, creating processes outside the productive economy in a way that has increased the risk of cyclical economic crises and their global transmission.

The Socio-Labour Instability

The processes of internationalization of corporations together with the delocalization of production and the increase of imports in national markets have increased net unemployment rates, the precariousness of workers' working conditions and social exclusion. Globalization has facilitated the international mobility of goods, production and capital in the quest for lower labour costs in other countries (Bretos and Marcuello 2017). This situation has provoked significant socio-labour tensions in the affected territories. Overall, this context has fostered increasingly individualized patterns of social relations in public and community life, thus undermining levels of social capital in local communities.

The Weakening of Democratic Sovereignty

The third aspect is concerned with how the growing processes of globalization, and the emerging sets of rules governing the international economy and its power structures, can affect the capacity for democratic self-management of local communities. In this area, we observe that in a globalized world, nation-states are losing their capacity to control the impact of the dynamics of globalization, with the consequent weakening of their political-territorial power. At the same time, the process of individualization generated by neoliberal globalization – reflected in more individualistic behaviour in the social, labour and civil spheres of community life – has undermined the creation of democratic organizations and the individual's participation in collective decision-making. Globalization thus leads to a reduction in democratic spaces and decision-making processes shaped by people in local territories and, in turn, to a gap between the extent of their participation and its direct impact on the economic and social configuration of these territories, thus reducing their capacity to influence the democratic construction of their communities.

The Environmental Consequences

Domestic economies are largely exposed to the economic and financial fluctuations of other countries. The impact of economic and environmental policies at the territorial level may be reduced by such interrelation and openness to the outside world. Furthermore, there is global environmental degradation which is generated by international trade relations and by the behaviour of many companies, especially transnationals, which benefit from lax environmental regulations in many emerging countries (Bretos and Marcuello 2017). These free-trade dynamics have the potential to undermine democratically established rules and norms at the local level, especially those relating to environmental legislation. In this area, the enormous power and pressure exerted by multinational companies, some larger than many national economies, plays a fundamental role in shaping the environmental configuration of countries. This is achieved by establishing legislation, policies and measures that are far removed from democratic decision-making procedures and that often go against the general interests of societies and environmental sustainability (Rodrik 1999).

6.3 ALTER-GLOBALIZATION AND THE SSE

Neoliberal globalization has generated different responses worldwide to try to counteract its effects and propose alternative models of globalization. Among them are the movement represented by the global social justice movement, alter-globalization, or the alter-global movement, which is not against globalization but for another globalization, where the economy could be regulated and where human beings and the environment are more important than transnational profits. The alter-globalization movement has its origins in the World Social Forum in 2001 in Porto Alegre, and arises as a counterpoint to the annual event of the World Economic Forum. The alter-globalization movement consists of networks of international organizations and movements present on all continents. These networks have various themes of mobilization and work, including the improvement of working conditions, the revitalization of democracy, the protection of the environment, human rights, and the situations of exclusion and vulnerability of populations.

The SSE, one strand of this alter-globalization movement, is a global movement that is characterized by strategic organizations which foster social cohesion and promote sustainable and inclusive economic development in the context of economic globalization (Monzón and Chaves 2012). The SSE has a relevant role to play in developing a model of globalization based on people and the environment. In this sense, the principles and values that define the SSE are essential in the promotion of local sustainable development of territories through its contribution to the economic, socio-labour, democratic and environmental stability of local territories.

The SSE and Economic Stability

The special characteristics and the resilience of SSE organizations and enterprises (SSEOEs) make it possible to address situations of economic instability and the financialization of the economy (see entry 52, 'Resilience in the Context of Multiple Crises'). SSEOEs are founded on democratic decision-making models and are based on the members of the organization and not on the ownership of capital. In this way, we can affirm that decisions will be aligned with the needs of the territory and the community where the members live. Other relevant characteristics are the benefit distribution model which is based on effort and reinvestment in a member's local area, the capacity to mobilise resources and investments, and the generation of local accumulation processes (Bretos and Marcuello 2017). Moreover, in rural areas, the SSE is supporting traditional activities and fostering new economic directions. Finally, SSE financial institutions are key to avoiding financial exclusion processes through services for low-income individuals and community-oriented projects.

The SSE and Socio-Labour Stability

The operating model of the SSE is based on principles and values in which the needs of the people, the members of the organizations and the communities where the organizations operate are at the core of their activities. As a result, the employment generated by SSEOEs has better working conditions and also offers greater stability, especially in times of crisis (see entry 52, 'Resilience in the Context of Multiple Crises'). SSE salaries are often higher than in other companies in the surrounding area, and wage inequality is lower (Roelants et al. 2014). On the other hand, these principles and values guide SSE entities to generate inter-cooperative processes and inclusive governance models that favour social cohesion. In other words, SSEOEs foster the social capital of communities through people-oriented management models with open and plural governance structures, and the formation of social networks within the community together with inter-cooperation processes between people and producers.

The SSE and Democratic Strengthening

The democratic participation of the members of the SSE entities in the management model is one of the hallmarks of the SSE. This democratic model has effects both within the organization and in the territory in which they operate in such a way that it generates processes of empowerment and democratization of local communities. Moreover, within the organization, members of SSEOEs participate in the governance structure of the entity, assemblies and the boards of directors, which involves learning civic and relational skills, as well as solidarity and democratic values. Members also have a shared responsibility in the social capital of the entity, as well as in the financial profits and losses. Further, these processes of empowerment of the entity's members have external effects on the communities, as it is observed that an individual is more likely to involve themself in other community structures by actively participating in public life. Furthermore, SSEOEs themselves foster the creation of networks based on reciprocity and cooperation with other local actors, both economic and political. This is a fundamental contribution to the democratic construction of communities and territories.

The SSE and the Environmental Contribution

The contribution of the SSE to the environmental problems generated by globalization is based on the organization's strong roots in the territory and communities in which they operate. In this sense, the processes of self-management and local development based on the needs of the people and future generations are a model for the construction of processes generated from the bottom up, and which make it possible to counteract the pressure of the large multinational power groups. Furthermore, in response to the negative effects of the liberalization of international markets, the SSE is forming new networks that seek to promote economic development in local territories. Examples of SSEOEs involving the promotion of environmental protection include agricultural cooperatives engaged in organic agriculture and farming, fishery and forestry cooperatives achieving more sustainable management of natural resources, and renewable energy cooperatives providing ecologically friendly alternatives in the field of energy production and consumption, among others (see entry 27, 'Energy, Water and Waste Management Sectors' and entry 36, 'Reduction of Hunger and Poverty').

6.4   GLOBAL SCALING OF SSEOES

SSEOEs are often considered small-sized enterprises that tend to carry out their economic activity exclusively within the local context. However, throughout recent decades a key trend in the SSE sector at a global level lies in the growing adoption of internationalization strategies by SSEOEs (Bretos and Marcuello 2017). The main reasons for this international expansion are the growing pressures faced by many SSEOEs to internationalize if they are to maintain their competitive position in increasingly globalized and dynamic markets. There is a growing demand to scale the social impact and wider innovations across borders in a context of growing economic, social and environmental problems that are not being effectively addressed by the market and the state. The vast majority of the largest 300 cooperatives and mutuals in the world operate across borders, through different strategies ranging from contractual operations such as direct exports, franchising and licensing, to equity operations such as greenfield investments, joint ventures and full acquisitions (Bretos et al. 2018). Smaller SSEOEs and social ventures are equally producing and offering their goods and/or services on a global scale. Information and communication technologies (ICTs) are critical for these organizations to achieve a global dimension and to scale the social impact across borders. ICTs allow SSEOEs to identify and exploit global social entrepreneurship opportunities, access a wider range of funding sources (for example, crowdfunding) and create social networks and entrepreneurial alliances to drive international growth (see entry 33, 'Information and Communication Technology (ICT)'). Not surprisingly, many of the new international SSEOEs and social ventures are born globally from their inception (Marshall 2010).

Three major scaling strategies could be identified: control-based, altruistic and hybrid. These strategies can be placed along a continuum in terms of increasing the degree of central control and resource requirements (Bretos et al. 2021).

Table 6.1   Examples of organizations utilizing control-based international scaling strategies

Mondragón Corporation	Mondragon industrial cooperatives have pursued extensive acquisitive growth in international markets since the mid-1990s in order to maintain their competitiveness and safeguard the jobs of the worker-members at the parent Basque plants. There are 132 subsidiaries all over the world with more than 14 000 foreign employees.
The Up Group	Combines economic development, social innovation and respect for the environment. Its mission is twofold: to contribute to social progress, and to provide solutions for a better daily life. With 3600 workers, it has operations and sales in 30 countries.

Control-based international scaling strategies rely on a considerable degree of centralized control and coordination and generally require the greatest investment of resources by the parent organization. These strategies, which basically include cross-border mergers, acquisitions and greenfield investments, involve the parent organization creating branch structures beyond national borders in the form of company-owned stores, offices or plants with all units legally belonging to the parent organization. Control-based strategies are often pursued by SSEOEs seeking to increase the scale of operations, to acquire new capabilities and to access resources while entering new geographic markets, with this approach acting as a way to preserve or stimulate their competitive position in highly globalized and dynamic markets. Table 6.1 gives examples of organizations utilizing control-based international scaling strategies.

Similar internationalization strategies have been equally adopted by SSEOEs in the manufacturing industry (for example, SACMI – Società Anonima Cooperativa Meccanici Imola), the banking industry (for example, Crédit Agricole, Raiffeisen Banking Group, Crédit Mutuel and Rabobank) and agri-food industry (for example, Danish Crown, Fonterra, Arla Foods and FrieslandCampina). These multinational cooperatives tend to centralize major strategic, technical, financial and commercial decisions in the parent company, based on a dual cooperative–noncooperative model.

Altruism-based international scaling strategies involve a disseminating organization that makes its social innovation internationally available by actively sharing information and/or providing technical assistance to one or more recipient organizations that seek to replicate the approach or model. Also referred to as dissemination, scaling across, diffusion or spread, altruist strategies rely on few resources, and there is little or no centralized control by the source organization over the replication of the social innovation by the adopter, which tends to use the shared information and knowledge as it deems appropriate. Hence, the source organization is not interested in owning and appropriating the value created using its approach, but rather in altruistically spreading its model, ideas or tools to generate broader social impact. The focus of these strategies is on replication, diffusion by other actors and adoption, rather than organizational control. Common mechanisms for the diffusion of knowledge and information in altruist strategies include open sourcing, training, consultancy and loose networks. Food Assembly, REScoop.eu and Cycling Without Age can be considered examples of expansion through the use of loose networks (Table 6.2 gives examples).

Hybrid international scaling strategies offer the broadest range of possibilities for SSEOEs to expand across borders and scale their social impact. They rely on long-term contractual organizational arrangements in which both the parent organization and the partners maintain their autonomy, although they usually require a commitment from both parties to share information and pool some level of resources. In hybrid strategies, the relationship between the

50   *Encyclopedia of the social and solidarity economy*

Table 6.2   *Examples of organizations utilizing altruism-based international scaling strategies*

Food Assembly	This organization operates an online platform enabling direct trade between communities and local farmers and producers. Anyone can set up their own local branch. Food Assembly operates as a central body that provides the technological platform and support, as well as guidance and assistance to implementers, but without a formal contract or agreement. Indeed, the central association is small and reports no shared results. Originated in France, today the Food Assembly model is spread across Europe in different countries such as Spain, Italy, Belgium and Germany.
REScoop.eu	This European network of renewable energy cooperatives (REScoops) was informally established in 2011 in Belgium, when the founders of six of them met to explore ways of promoting the REScoop model across Europe. Today, the network comprises 1500 REScoops which are owned by roughly 1 million citizens from a wide variety of European countries. REScoop.eu basically coordinates the collaboration between members in different thematic working groups, aiming to provide their members with direct access to experts, and to build a forum for exchange.

Table 6.3   *Examples of organizations utilizing hybrid international scaling strategies*

Cafédirect	This well-known British farmer-owned and fair trade social enterprise was founded as a joint venture between four United Kingdom (UK) organizations involved in poverty alleviation: Oxfam, Traidcraft, Equal Exchange and Twin Trading. Much of the subsequent national and foreign expansion pursued by Cafédirect has been achieved through partnerships with other organizations.
Divine Chocolate	Divine Chocolate Ltd is a British purveyor of fair trade chocolate. The company operates in the UK and the United States. It is owned by Kuapa Kokoo, a Ghanaian cocoa farmers' cooperative, and Twin Trading, a UK-based non-governmental organization (NGO) working on market access. The farmers own the biggest stake in the company and share its profit.
Specialisterne	This is a Danish social innovator company using the characteristics of people with autistic spectrum disorder (ASD), including autism and Asperger's syndrome. The company transforms these features into competitive advantages in the business market (highly developed logical and analytical skills, the capacity to concentrate for long periods of time, zero tolerance of errors or attention to detail). It provides services such as software testing, quality control and data conversion for business companies in Denmark and other countries. In addition, Specialisterne assesses and trains people with ASD to meet the requirements of the business sector. In 2011, Specialisterne opened a subsidiary in Scotland with the social enterprise company Community Enterprise in Scotland (CEiS), which was funded by the Scottish Government and Glasgow City Council. Specialsterne has partnered with the large German multinational SAP SE to train and recruit people with autism across its global operations.

parent organization and the partners can range from loose cooperation to strongly linked structures. Hybrid strategies represent an intermediate solution in terms of resource commitment and control. In comparison to altruist strategies, hybrid modes allow the source organization to gain greater control over its adopters and the process of transfer of knowledge and information. However, hybrid strategies also require more resources and support from the source organization. In addition, hybrid strategies are capable of achieving more varied incremental impacts, as they can scale social impact both directly, by reaching a larger number of users, and indirectly, in a process through which the partners of the alliance or network can induce one another to carry out new activities and processes aimed at increasing social value creation. Common hybrid forms of scaling include social franchising, social licensing, joint ventures and other strategic partnerships. Table 6.3 gives examples.

Table 6.4   Examples of international public–private partnerships

AdapCC	The German federally owned international cooperation enterprise GTZ and the British social enterprise Cafédirect formed a public–private partnership that operated between 2007 and 2010 in Kenya, Mexico, Nicaragua and Peru. The aim was to support small coffee and tea producers in their developing strategies and to cope with the risks and impacts of climate change.
Honey Care	The Kenyan social enterprise that strives to raise incomes for rural farmers through apiculture was established in 2000 as a private sector social enterprise to promote sustainable community-based beekeeping in eastern Africa. In partnership with a number of local NGOs and international development and financial institutions, as well as the governments of Kenya and Tanzania, Honey Care undertakes village-level demonstrations and provides microfinance, training and community-based extension services. It also provides a guaranteed market for the honey produced by smallholder farmers at fair trade prices through the Honey Care Africa and Beekeeper's Delight brands.

International public–private partnerships (Table 6.4) between organizations from the public and the not-for-profit sectors are also commonly used to address social concerns and unresolved needs more effectively, and to increase the efficiency and quality in the provision of public services.

Nevertheless, international growth and scaling involve great challenges for international SSEOEs to maintain a sustainable balance between social and financial performance. This involves not only preserving their community embeddedness and socially oriented practices and values, but also extending these across their international networks which are made up of branches, partners and/or implementers. When operating on an international scale, SSEOEs have to pursue the societal needs of a broader range of local communities and mutual benefits of the diverse stakeholders affected by their activities. At the same time, some SSEOEs must meet the increased efficiency and financial performance requirements associated with competing in highly globalized markets, while others seek to fulfil the challenge of implementing their social innovations in culturally and institutionally distant contexts.

It is also worth noting that several international organizations and associations have played an important role in the creation and global dissemination of the SSE. The International Cooperative Alliance (ICA) is the voice of cooperatives worldwide. It was established in 1895 to promote the cooperative model and unite the world cooperatives along with different sectors, such as agriculture, fisheries, industry, craft and services, banking, insurance, retail, housing and health care services. For instance, CICOPA is the international organization of industrial and service cooperatives of the ICA. It gathers 49 members from 32 countries, who affiliate with 65,000 enterprises employing 4 million persons across the world. There are many other international organizations, including: the Intercontinental Network for the Promotion of Social Solidarity Economy (RIPESS), research networks such as EMES, Ciriec and Rulescoop, international forums such as the Global Social Economy Forum (GSEF) and SSE International Forum (ESSFI; formerly known as the Mont-Blanc Meetings). All of them contribute to strengthening the ties among SSE actors and developing global models of cooperation and democracy.

REFERENCES

Bretos, Ignacio, Millán Díaz-Foncea and Carmen Marcuello. 2018. 'Cooperativas e internacionalización: un análisis de las 300 mayores cooperativas del mundo'. *CIRIEC-Espana Revista de Economia Publica, Social y Cooperativa*, 92: 5–37.

Bretos, Ignacio, Anjel Errasti and Aurélie Soetens. 2021. 'International Social Economy Organizations'. In *The New Social and Impact Economy*, ed. Benjamin Gidron and Anna Domaradzka, 245–68. Cham: Springer Nature Switzerland.

Bretos, Ignacio and Carmen Marcuello. 2017. 'Revisiting Globalization Challenges and Opportunities in the Development of Cooperatives'. *Annals of Public and Cooperative Economics*, 88 (1): 47–73. https://doi.org/10.1111/apce.12145.

Dicken, Peter. 2011. *Global Shift: Mapping the Changing Contours of the World Economy*, 6th edn. New York: Guilford Press.

Harvey, David. 2005. *A Brief History of Neoliberalism*. Oxford: Oxford University Press.

Levitt, Theodore. 1983. 'The Globalization of Markets'. *International Executive*, 25 (3): 17–19. https://doi.org/10.1002/tie.5060250311.

Marshall, R. Scott. 2010. 'Conceptualizing the International For-Profit Social Entrepreneur'. *Journal of Business Ethics*, 98 (2): 183–98. https://doi.org/10.1007/s10551-010-0545-7.

Monzón, José Luis and Rafael Chaves. 2012. *The Social Economy in the European Union*. Brussels: European Economic and Social Committee.

Rodrik, Dani. 1999. *The New Global Economy and Developing Countries: Making Openness Work*. Washington, DC: Overseas Development Council.

Roelants, Bruno, Eum Hyungsik and Elisa Terrasi. 2014. 'Co-operatives and Employment: A Global Report.' CICOPA. https://www.cicopa.coop/wp-content/uploads/2018/03/cooperatives_and_employment_a_global_report_en__web_21-10_1pag.pdf.

7. Heterodox economics
Jean-Louis Laville

INTRODUCTION

Recurrent crises have challenged the standard form of economic thought which largely influences methods of government. Therefore, heterodox approaches make methodological choices that set them apart from mainstream economics in the sense that they combine economic analysis with other social sciences to study the relations between economy and society. After the fall of the Berlin Wall, while orthodox economics defended the idea of the end of history, other approaches resurrected heterodox approaches either by embedding themselves in the Marxian framework, as with the theory of regulation, or by distancing themselves from it, as with the new economic sociology and the theory of conventions.

The regulation school (Hollingsworth and Boyer 1997) moves beyond the overly simplistic distinction between infrastructure and superstructure. It seeks to revitalize the approach inspired by Marx by showing how the market can assume different forms depending on sets of rules and stabilized arrangements, codifying social relations within capitalism. The regulation of different varieties of capitalism thus rests on hierarchical sets of rules and stabilized arrangements, which link the economic domain to other fields of society. These sets of rules and arrangements constitute institutional forms, of which there are five: social relations, forms of competition, monetary regimes, state–economy relations, and international integration. Despite acknowledging the diversity of forms of capitalism, the regulation school still comes close to the critical philosophy of the Frankfurt School and the critical sociology of Bourdieu, for whom capitalism is an immense cosmos that pre-exists individuals, and cannot be changed by them. Its main concern is to draw our attention to market forces in Weber's sense. It is the dynamic of capitalism that occupies centre stage in an approach focused on the factors that explain the system's durability.

For its part, new economic sociology focuses on the social construction of economic action (Granovetter 1973). It has been an important trend in recent decades, at least in the English-speaking world. It proposes a form of social network analysis that, based on empirical observations, questions the atomism of orthodox economics: economic actors are not considered as monads, but as maintaining relationships that influence their behaviour. Although markets are not the only phenomenon to which this form of analysis has been applied, it is around markets that the new economic sociology's proponents have entered into dialogue, shaping an approach that is as distinct from functionalist sociology as it is from orthodox economics. Other heterodox currents on the frontier between sociology and economics also refute the postulates of neoclassical theory. Joining economic sociology – particularly in its questioning of the rational choice model through the study of values – the school of the economy of conventions emphasizes the plurality of forms of rationality and modes of coordination. Optimizing rationality and market coordination are considered to be an overly narrow set of conceptual tools. In order to broaden our understanding of economic phenomena, the school of the economy of conventions draws attention to the role that conventions play in the economy, as well as to its diversity of modes of coordination, notably through models of 'justice' that are essential to different forms of agreement (Boltanski and Thévenot 2006).

Working outwards from ordinary activities, the school of the economy of conventions, and new economic sociology, demonstrate the diversity of market situations that affect the course of economic events.

In sum, while macro-syntheses such as regulation theory may overestimate market forces by depicting capitalism as implacable, both the new economic sociology and the economy of conventions may underestimate these forces by focusing on micro-arrangements. Thus, on the one hand, the focus of macro-syntheses on market forces can lead them to notice only institutional forms of capitalism. On the other hand, insufficient consideration of market forces by new economic sociology (according to Granovetter) and the school of the economy of conventions concentrate on markets' extreme variability. All these approaches – which are, in fact, very diverse – ultimately endorse the centrality of the market to the economy. The originality of Karl Polanyi's heterodoxy lies in its questioning of the economics fallacy of reducing the economy to the market, which is considered a major problem of our time. To counter this fallacy – which corresponds to the formal definition of the economy, according to which scarcity determines the relationship between means and ends – Polanyi gives us a substantive definition of the economy. This definition recognizes our dependence on nature and on our fellow human beings, and holds that the satisfaction of human needs requires institutional interaction. This substantive understanding of the economy is illustrative of an approach relevant to the social and solidarity economy (SSE), both because of its own characteristics and because of its epistemological proximity to other important approaches, such as feminist economics (see entry 5, 'Feminist Economics').

7.1   THE FEATURES OF SUBSTANTIVE ECONOMICS

Substantive economics presents a theoretical framework that allows us to re-interpret history.

A Theoretical Analysis

Substantive economics replaces the focus on the market with an openness to the plurality of principles of economic integration. These are principles of behaviour that ensure order in the production and circulation of goods and services. There are four such principles:

- The market principle allows the equilibrium of the supply and demand of goods and services; exchange happens on the basis of price-setting. The relation between supply and demand is established through contracts informed by the calculation of interest. The market principle does not presuppose immersion in social relations and it is not necessarily produced by the social system, unlike the other economic principles described below.
- Redistribution is the principle according to which central authority is responsible for allocating what is produced, which presupposes procedures defining the rules of levy and their use. A relation has become established over time between the central authority that imposes an obligation and the agents who submit to it.
- Reciprocity corresponds to relations established between groups or persons through actions that only make sense insofar as they express a will to demonstrate a social link

among the stakeholders. The cycle of reciprocity contrasts with the market exchange in that the former is inseparable from the human relations involving the desire for recognition and power; reciprocity also differs from redistribution insofar as it is not imposed by a central authority.
- Householding does not involve relations between groups, but concerns the basic group in the society under consideration (the *oikos*, the nuclear family, and so on). It refers to the production and sharing that takes place within this group in order to satisfy its members' needs.

This pluralist approach emphasizes the process of disembedding, through which public authorities promote the formal economy while hiding this support through the naturalization of the self-regulating market. By destroying social bonds and exercising violence towards nature, this disembedding threatens the substance of society. For this reason, disembedding generates a need for re-embedding, but this can take two directions: one authoritarian, the other emancipatory. Crises are dangerous periods, at once fraught with the risk of totalitarian regression but they are also charged with democratic potential. This is exemplified by Polanyi in *The Great Transformation*, which explains the emergence of fascism in the 1930s (Polanyi 1945). But crises can also represent an opportunity for deepening democracy, by inventing new institutional compromises. Through its critique of positions that reduce the economy to the formal economy, substantive economics joins up with bioeconomics and ecological economics, which blame these formalist positions for introducing a complete rupture between the economy and the living. In formal economics, both labour and land are equated to commodities, which is untenable from the point of view of both human and non-human beings. This extractivist way of thinking – for which these beings are only human or natural resources – denies the interdependencies of life.

On an epistemological level, substantive economics also converges with feminist analyses questioning the reductionism of formal economics, which values production and neglects reproduction. Taking up the discussion of care, economists such as Silvia Frederici, Nancy Folbre, Julie-Katherine Gibson-Graham have criticized this view as neglecting the activities of provisioning, in which the purpose is not profit but rather the preservation of life and the concern for wellbeing. They argue that to reintegrate the dimensions of race and gender into the economy, it is crucial to take into account all forms of production and reproduction: those that make room for monetary flows as well as those that occur through non-monetary flows. Thus, they advocate a change in perspective that involves developing economic activities, such as the people's canteens in South America and West Africa, the local food networks in Senegal, the collective kitchens in Peru, the Self Employed Women's Association in India, and so on (Verschuur et al. 2021).

Polanyi's argument also joins up with that of the epistemologies of the Global South, which prescribe a 'sociology of absences and emergencies'. It is important, according to the sociology of absences, to show that 'what does not exist is in fact actively produced as non-existent' and, according to the sociology of emergences, to replace 'linear time ... with plural, concrete possibilities, which are both utopian and realistic' (Santos 2014). Finally, this approach is both critical of capitalism, and possibilist in its attention to initiatives coming from societies that exhibit other logics.

Because the process of disembedding generates a need for re-embedding, substantive economics, feminist economics and epistemologies of the Global South speak of a double movement that helps to elucidate how societies have changed over the last two centuries.

A Historical Analysis

It is worth noting that the forms of re-embedding adopted in the 19th century were insufficient, and that this was due to a deficit in how civil society was understood (see entry 10, 'Origins and Histories'). At least, this is what becomes clear considering the genesis of the compromises between the economy and politics.

Polanyi rejects Smith's assumption of a propensity to exchange good for good, service for service, which reduces civil society to the market. He shares with Marcel Mauss (1997) the belief in institutional creativity within local civil society. Both authors recognize civil society's contribution to democracy, while acknowledging that it may also have an economic dimension that is not simply that of the market alone. In doing so, Mauss and Polanyi move beyond a contractual framework to see democratic solidarity not as an involuntary consequence of market exchanges, but as a form of egalitarian reciprocity linked to the birth of modern democracies. Multiple forms of reciprocity are largely linked to kinship, to the division between genders, and to religion. However, egalitarian reciprocity – in other words, the social link defined by its hallmark, equality – involves an openness towards emancipation: associationalism arose not out of inherited ties, but rather from collective action in which freedom of commitment and equality in law are respected. In a way, self-organization extends the achievements of political democracy into economic and social life. The first version of democratic solidarity thus results from social practices that exhibit an egalitarian form of reciprocity inextricably linked to protests in the public sphere.

In the second half of the 19th century, as productivism and capitalism progressed, this solidarity-based associationalism, weakened by repression, ran out of steam (see entry 15, 'Associations and Associationalism'). Solidarity gradually took on a different meaning: that of a social debt which social groups owed to each other and to past generations, and which the state had to settle by channelling redistribution. At the same time, pioneering associationalism gained ground, giving rise to various institutions such as trade unions, mutual societies, cooperatives and non-profit associations. Association thus gave way to social economy organizations, and trade unions and political movements retreated. Some of these movements made the revolutionary promise of a new world and a new human being. This vision centred on seizing power, a necessary step towards collectivizing ownership of the means of production. But far from providing the expected solution, upon collapse, 'communist' countries reinforced the belief in the inevitability of capitalism.

This is not the end of the story: the debate on the democratization of society is more topical today than ever. Nevertheless, it must learn the lessons of the last century, in particular the failure to take into account political interactions, and interactions between politics and the economy symptomatic of Bolshevism. The failure of this project invites us to re-examine other strategies for change. In contrast to totalitarianism, Keynesianism, but also – albeit to a lesser degree – the social economy, has progressed through the welfare state. Though we should not deny these achievements, an in-depth assessment of these strategies must also include an examination of their limits (see entry 53, 'Social Policy'). Behind their apparent success during the post-World War II economic expansion lie long-neglected problems.

The one is that redistributive solidarity remains dependent on market growth. This dependency was imperceptible until the 1960s, but became increasingly significant with the decline in the rate of growth, which deprived social democracy of some of its key resources. This trend destabilized Keynesian methods and social transfers. In the traditional social democracy, while the state has a monopoly on legitimate violence, the market remains the natural mechanism through which needs are satisfied since it is based on individual interests and ensures their compatibility. The state limits itself to providing an institutional framework suitable for the operation of market mechanisms and for the limitation of the inequalities it generates.

The second problem is the tendency to consider users of public services as subjugated and concentrate decision-making in the spheres of representative democracy (government, employers' and unions' representatives), the voice of ordinary citizens being largely ignored. While Fordism reigned in companies, resulting in the exclusion of workers from decision-making in return for an increase in their income, according to P.R. Bélanger and B. Lévesque (1990), providentialism developed in the welfare state. Here, the recipients of social services remained distant from their design, with compensation for this exclusion taking the form of almost free access to such services.

The state ensures that each person's individual freedom does not encroach on that of others; it maintains the conditions for negative freedom. But this focus on negative freedom hides another side of freedom, namely positive freedom based on the ability to act together, and participate in public discussions and decisions. Consequently the deliberative dimension of democracy, the importance of consulting citizens, and the fact that individual preferences are modified through the establishment of a common public language, can be forgotten.

That is the case with social democracy, it has focused primarily on macroeconomic policies and state redistribution. It has been more concerned with solidarity than with economic initiative, acting as if democratic decisions could only pertain to the distribution of wealth already produced. Leaving the market economy to capitalist enterprises appears to be one of its constitutive weaknesses, long hidden behind the scale of economic expansion.

This elucidates the importance of the social economy tradition, which has stressed the various different forms that enterprises can take. It emphasizes legal statuses that break the link between economic activity and shareholder power, while sharing a key feature: they impose a limit on the individual distribution of profits. With its entrepreneurial culture, the social economy has focused on the collective enterprise without considering the extent to which this type of enterprise is dependent on the institutional framework in which it is embedded. It has done little to question the regulation of markets, continuing to see non-capitalist enterprises as the main lever for change. Yet, as one cooperative leader put it: 'Cooperatives wanted to change the market, but it is the market that has changed cooperatives.' Over time, social economy enterprises have increasingly lost their distinctiveness, and the representative democracy established in their statutes by the principle of formal equality (one person equals one vote) has not been enough to maintain effective member participation over time.

Unaware of their potential to complement one another, social democracy and the social economy have run out of steam. This may explain their absence in the fight against economic reductionism: their restriction of the market's effects through redistribution and collective enterprises has made them forget the potential of reciprocity. Meanwhile, the solidarity economy, which is motivated by reciprocity, reaffirms a socio-political dimension by allowing those concerned by an issue to self-organize and express their views in the public sphere.

A new configuration thus emerges: one that combines the experience of the social economy and the emergence of the solidarity economy.

7.2 THE CHALLENGES OF THE SSE

The resulting union of the SSE contests the capitalist paradigm but faces the challenge of joining up entities that have economic significance but are afflicted by a certain normalization, on the one hand, and entities more inclined to protest but which are undeniably economically fragile, on the other. The future of the SSE hangs on its capacity to build solidarity between the entities within this composite group. It also depends on its ability to increase its collective strength by respecting its internal differences and establishing itself as an interlocutor of the public authorities. Finally, it turns on its ability to find a conceptual framework that is less Western-centric and more open to the experiences of the rest of the world.

In any case, in its effort to legitimise itself and make its various components cohere, the SSE can draw on the analytical grid provided by substantive economics and reinforced by bio-economics and ecological economics, feminism, and the epistemologies of the Global South. Two features bring together these heterodox perspectives, which are all points of reference for the SSE.

An Institutionalist Analysis

Capitalism can only be regulated if the market economy is both respected and complemented by other economic principles. These principles can be seen through an analysis that combines history and theoretical reflection, such as that which Polanyi conducted from 1947 to 1964, leading to a conception of the economy as an institutionalized process (Polanyi 1945, 2008, 2011). These activities remind us of the current relevance of Mauss, who stresses the importance of constructing institutions that can preserve effective solidarity. Associationalism creates institutions based on democratic solidarity that have an economic dimension, countering the dominant tendency to equate the economy and the market, as well as the belief in capitalism's omnipotence.

Two major lessons emerge from the 19th and 20th centuries. Firstly, the promotion of a market society underpinned by a concern for individual freedom has increased inequality. Secondly, the subjugation of the economy to political will under the pretext of equality has led to the suppression of freedoms. These two solutions have thus come to challenge democracy. Not only is this what totalitarian systems wanted, but it is also, alternatively, what the subordination of political power to that of money leads to.

The crises therefore raise the question of which institutions are able to ensure the pluralization of the economy in order to embed it in a democratic framework; a framework in which the logic of material gain has to be limited. The answer lies in institutional inventions rooted in social practices; it is these inventions that can show us how to re-embed the economy in democratic norms. The significance of the SSE lies in the fact that it is a 'real economic movement' and not a project of social reform that has been plastered over reality. The conception of social changes found in the SSE is one of the changes that 'in no way demand...brutal choices between two contradictory forms of society', but which 'are made and will be made by constructing new groups and institutions alongside and above the old ones' (Mauss 1997, 265).

It is due to their ability to initiate such changes that the convergences between the heterodox approaches mentioned above should be highlighted. More broadly, they support the citizen's search for a 'good life', to use Aristotle's expression, or '*buen vivir*', to use the phrase adopted in the Andean countries, by outlining the theoretical foundations of a plural democracy and a plural economy, with the SSE examining the practical conditions for their recognition.

An Aim for Democratic Social Change

'The alternative is as follows: the extension of the democratic principle of politics to the economy or the outright abolition of the democratic "political sphere"' (Polanyi 2008, 393). This statement, made in 1935, is even more relevant today, as we see the emergence of a service economy with a strong immaterial and relational component. Indeed, within this economy, informational interactions are much more numerous and constitute a form of work that participates in the public sphere in a new way.

In any case, democratization of society cannot occur without democratization of the economy, which itself depends on new alliances between civil society and public authorities. There are signs of mutual rejection, as governments become more technicized, and citizens are becoming increasingly distrustful of institutional politics. Yet such alliances are emerging in areas such as the defence of common goods, whether local or global, from water to free licences (see entry 13, 'The Commons'). As Elinor Ostrom (1990) has shown, it is not possible to recognize these common goods if we start from a dichotomy between market and state. This can be achieved, however, through a combination of an engaged citizenry and new policies. To counter the excesses of capital and to maintain ecodiversity – which is equally as necessary to a living democratic society as to biodiversity – it is important to diversify forms of resistance, drawing on aspects of the real economy that are made invisible by its formal definition. This is why the SSE, understood from a Polanyian perspective, can no longer be scorned or dismissed in thinking about emancipation, as the proliferation of research in this direction shows.

Furthermore, the SSE requires an approach in which ideas and practices are interwoven. The separation between 'material' and 'ideal' motivations has, in Polanyi's view, produced 'disastrous' consequences for the vision that 'Western man' has of 'himself and his society', with hunger and profit the only real motives for the individual's participation in economic life, and other incentives seen as 'distant and hazy' (Polanyi 2011, 45–6).

However, if democratic possibilities are to be opened up, then what is material and what is ideal must not be separated. Economic motivations cannot be mistaken for material motives; ideas cannot be the prerogative of experts who are supposedly alone in having access to the truth about reality. 'It is the interdependence of thought and experience that gives us the method to follow. For terms and definitions established without reference to data would be hollow, while a simple collection of facts without readjustment of our perspective would be sterile' (Polanyi 2011, 31). To avoid this vicious circle, conceptual and empirical research must go hand in hand. The need to debate the interpretations made of SSE initiatives is taken up with vigour by major authors such as Jose Luis Coraggio (2015). According to him, these initiatives give agency back to citizens, countering the economic determinism that has dominated approaches to social change for far too long.

REFERENCES

Bélanger, Paul R. and Lévesque, Benoît. 1990. *La Théorie de la régulation. Du rapport salarial au rapport de consommation*. Montréal: UQAM.
Boltanski, Luc and Laurent Thévenot. 2006. *On Justification: Economies of Worth*. Princeton, NJ: Princeton University Press.
Coraggio, José-Luis. 2015. 'L'économie Sociale et Solidaire et Son Institutionnalisation En Amérique Latine: Cinq Pays, Cinq Processus.' *Revue Française de Socio-Économie* 15 (1): 233. https://doi.org/10.3917/rfse.015.0233.
Granovetter, Mark S. 1973. 'The Strength of Weak Ties.' *American Journal of Sociology* 78 (6): 1360–80. https://doi.org/10.1086/225469.
Hollingsworth, J. Rogers and Robert Boyer. 1997. *Contemporary Capitalism. The Embeddeness of Institutions*. Cambridge: Cambridge University Press.
Laville, Jean-Louis. 2023. *The Solidarity Economy*. University of Minnesota Press.
Mauss, Marcel. 1997. *Ecrits politiques*. Paris: Fayard.
Ostrom, Elinor. 1990. *Governing the Commons. The Evolution of Institutions for Collective Action*. Cambridge: Cambridge University Press.
Polanyi, Karl. 1945. *Origins of Our Time: The Great Transformation*. London: Victor Gollancz.
Polanyi, Karl. 2008. *Essais*. Paris: Seuil.
Polanyi, Karl. 2011. *La Subsistance de 'Homme – la Place de l'Économie dans l'Histoire et la Société*. Paris: Flammarion.
Santos, Boaventura de Sousa. 2014. *Epistemologies of the South: Justice against Epistemicide*. London: Routledge.
Verschuur, Christine, Isabelle Guérin and Isabelle Hillenkamp, eds. 2021. *Social Reproduction, Solidarity Economy, Feminisms and Democracy: Latin America and India*. Cham: Palgrave Macmillan.

8. Indigenous economies
Luciane Lucas dos Santos

INTRODUCTION

This entry addresses some common points and particularities between the social and solidarity economy (SSE) and indigenous economies, aiming to highlight how the SSE framework can contribute to a deeper comprehension of communities' resilience and agency within a community economy framework. This entry, distancing from neoliberal policies grounded on the reduction of state involvement in welfare matters, refers to resilience as being the capacity of the communities to deal with adversity, and simultaneously reinforce social ties through grassroots knowledge and creative solutions based on self-organisation and popular technologies.

Based on the premise that popular resilience and other rationales regarding material life are key aspects of SSE initiatives and indigenous economies, this entry presents a threefold contribution: (1) a discussion on the principles of economic integration and the everyday economy embeddedness; (2) a reflection upon community-based aesthetics and its connection with these economies; (3) the political dimension that the domestic domain might assume in both economies.

8.1 SOME KEY ASPECTS IN THE INDIGENOUS ECONOMIES

Important differences with regard to rationales might be found between indigenous peoples living in forests and rural indigenous communities (*campesino-originarios*). However, some characteristics of these two constitute a common set of concerns within the heterogeneous indigenous economies. Some of them are listed as follows: the way territoriality is experienced; the entanglements between the spiritual dimension and the material life production; and the connection with the surrounding nature, which is understood as shared with more-than-human beings. These three aspects are intertwined with each other.

Different from market societies and their exchange strategies, indigenous economies are shaped in line with a sense of sacredness. It means that the material culture both forges and expresses the interplay with non-human worlds (Santos-Granero 2009; Viveiros de Castro 2014; Van Velthem 2014). Materiality will thus be attached to cosmovisions in such a way that the production of food and artefacts relies on an ongoing covenant with the supernatural dimension (Zannoni 1999). Broadly speaking, there are underlying meanings with regard to what is produced or circulated that cannot be accounted for by an economic explanation. Communities' ways of living, producing, sense-making and constituting their territoriality are grounded on a social and spiritual dimension, being thus embedded from the very beginning.

The embeddedness of the economy has been reinforced by a prevalence of reciprocity over trade, despite the fact that both are expected to play a role regarding the needs of provisioning. However, it is noteworthy that indigenous groups take their dynamics from an ongoing feeding process of rites and covenants. Departing from Marcel Mauss, and attempting to move a step further, Temple (2003) argues that indigenous societies are essentially economies of reciprocity, in the sense that a relational structure prevails over the trade itself. Analysing the Andean indigenous economies, he argues that reciprocity is at the heart of the matter. According to Temple, 'if it is necessary to give for being, it is likewise necessary to produce to make gift-giving possible' (Temple 2003, 81–93, translated by author).

Although there are some epistemological differences between the ways of understanding reciprocity, gift-giving and trade/exchange as driving forces in the indigenous economies – which could be seen in anthropological readings by Lévi-Strauss, Marcel Mauss, Éric Sabourin and Dominique Temple – it can be said that reciprocity gains a prominence associated with the need of both strengthening the social fabric and maintaining strategic political alliances (see also entry 9, 'Moral Economy and Human Economy'). In this sense, even when money is present, the indigenous communities' trade is more related to a sociability structuring factor rather than the Western sense of self-interested, individual-based perspective disseminated by market societies.

Reciprocity has also left a footprint on the way the space is organised. The Andean territoriality is a good example as it relies on the very concept of complementarity. The spatial complementarity that characterises the territorial occupation mode – named by Murra (1984) as a 'vertical archipelago' – has revealed the economic relevance of a collective dimension within the communities (*ayllus*) and the value of popular knowledge that allows local people to cope with inhospitable environments. Additionally, this knowledge constitutes popular technologies of production – and should be properly recognised as such – not only because they shape innovative crop production methods at extremely high altitudes, but also because of the local wise elders' capacity of unveiling some biological markers, such as the fox howl change as a sign of the proximity of the sowing time. As is also the case of the SSE regarding its creative potential to forge popular technologies and solutions to deal with material constraints, indigenous and other popular knowledges have not been properly recognised as an innovation in themselves, regardless of their contribution to providing different looks and frameworks towards old challenges (Banerjee et al. 2021).

One example is the system of ecological floors – that is, the vertical archipelago – that implies a set of crop-growing grounds dedicated to different cultures according to specific heights (Murra 1984). The families and the community as a whole are committed to this collective dimension both by cultivating in different ecological floors and by adopting a community crop rotation (*aynuqa*) where the system, involving practical decisions and rites, is closely scrutinised by the community to guarantee good harvests. Complementarity might be thus witnessed in different aspects of the *comuneros*' (communards' or community members') economy, such as the interdependence between the ecological floors with regard to provisioning, the commitment of the community to cultivate land parcels in different ecological floors, and the collective monitoring of the *aynuqa* system, to name but a few (see also entry 4, 'Ecological Economics').

However, this complementarity does not simply exist in aspects concerning the use of the land and the organisation of the production. Reciprocity practices, trade and consumption of goods from different ecological floors at local fairs (*qhatu*) and annual festivals, as well as the caravans along with these ecological floors, have reinforced this sense of complementarity, with mobility being the lever that shapes and strengthens complementarity as the major driver of indigenous economies in the highlands (Lucas dos Santos 2017).

Whether it be in rural areas or in the forest, a balance between the humans' presence and the surrounding environment is assumed as a tacit rule. However, as remarked by Viveiros de Castro (2014), this conviviality is not to be idealised or stifled in time, but understood as the result of social processes, where the agency is not recognised as being a monopoly of the human being. There has been a vivid circulation of symbolic meanings between humans and other beings (Viveiros de Castro 2014), in such a way that indigenous communities might be said to depart from a much more complex idea of surroundedness. They do not follow suit with the dual codes of Western modernity, where the split between nature and culture makes the former the hostage of the decisions with regard to the latter.

8.2 RECIPROCITY AND REDISTRIBUTION

Common features and political alliances between diverse indigenous economies and the SSE as a movement towards social emancipation may be located in different countries and contexts. The borders between the two might be blurred, not only because some principles animating solidarity initiatives may coincide with ancestral forms of organising material life, but also because this dialogue can reinforce the political dimension of non-capitalist economies, highlighting some issues of public interest such as food and water sovereignty, the right to seeds, and the commons agenda, to name but a few.

With respect to matters of public interest, the proximity between the agendas of the indigenous economies and of the SSE has increased, and despite eventual mismatching the fact is that the SSE and indigenous economies have been put together in different agreements documents, particularly in Latin America. In this sense, the Popular and Solidarity Economy (PSE) Law in Ecuador, created in 2011, refers to the need for the PSE to be aligned with the indigenous concept of *Buen Vivir*. Similarly, indigenous communities are constantly assumed as part of the solidarity economy movement in the 1st Brazilian National Plan on Solidarity Economy (2015–19). Specific educational programmes were also outlined, targeting indigenous peoples and other traditional communities (such as *quilombos*, fishing, resource extraction communities, and so on).

Although there are some common features, such as self-organisation, community property, shared management of resources, and community-based production, it is noteworthy that some indigenous communities might prefer not to be labelled as part of the solidarity economy or the SSE. Likewise, the solidarity economy may appreciate the non-capitalist dimension within indigenous economies without necessarily waiving the usual classifications or formats that characterise its own arrangements. Regardless of this possible mismatching, there is indeed a set of features related to production, consumption, trade and popular savings that consist of spaces for dialogue and political alliance. Five of them are listed below in order to reveal these feasible bridges for political alliance or channels for dialogue.

The first one has to do with the Polanyian principles of economic integration – exchange, reciprocity, redistribution and householding – the last of these being less disseminated both in the literature on the SSE and in Polanyi's work (Hillenkamp 2013). Despite the literature on solidarity economy being inspired by these principles, and the different ways in which they might be combined in popular economic initiatives (Hillenkamp 2013), many projects on local development have still been focused on trade and the initiatives' capacity of fitting into the market. A representative number of SSE initiatives, however, have promoted groundbreaking experiences in terms of social and economic justice, challenging the way scholars have theorised thus far about issues such as everyday economy, poverty, resilience and inclusion policies, or innovation.

By putting into action community redistribution strategies, minority women in peripheral and indigenous communities, for example, have demonstrated that practical knowledge is as valuable as scientific theories with regard to social change (see entry 29, 'Food and Agriculture Sector'). Inspiring new theoretical frameworks without being lenient with respect to the welfare state's progressive erosion, they have disrupted the assumption that redistribution is always a state issue. Similarly, the SSE and indigenous economies have proven that popular and community-led solutions can play a pivotal role in the re-embeddedness of the economy, by reconnecting the economic and the social dimensions.

Reciprocity has also been a common element of the SSE and indigenous economies, contributing to social ties and giving support to people dealing with material constraints. Going against the grain, reciprocity practices and community redistribution have not been properly valued as assets within local development guidelines and innovation projects. This is a challenge that the SSE as a field needs to overcome, debating to what extent community knowledge and activities have been repeatedly neglected on behalf of outside-modelled technical solutions.

Reciprocity and redistribution do not replace trade or exchange in market societies, but they can support people by enhancing their capacity for provisioning. In SSE arrangements, individual scarcity may be rebalanced by a collective supply that results from gathering sparse but diversified community resources. This engine can be found in different SSE initiatives, such as exchange fairs (using complementary currencies or otherwise), community repair shops and popular rotating savings, to name but a few. Despite the difference between an indigenous economy of reciprocity (where equivalence does exist but may be replaced at any time by generalised reciprocity) and an SSE exchange economy (where gift-giving and generalised reciprocity are common, but balanced reciprocity is expected), generalised and balanced forms of reciprocity are part of an invisible economy that makes everyday material life more feasible.

8.3 SUBALTERN AND INSURGENT COMMUNITY-BASED AESTHETICS

Consumption in capitalist societies cannot be uncoupled from social distinction (Bourdieu 1984). What is more, the social distinction has laid the cornerstone upon which the circulation of material and symbolic goods relies. By promoting other logics of sense-making, the SSE and indigenous economies have contributed to causing a disruptive effect on the way these social asymmetries are reified in market societies. Although each of them does so in its own way, new theoretical and epistemological issues have resulted, thus generating empirical and political implications for how subaltern aesthetics will be addressed thereafter.

A multifaceted indigenous aesthetic rationale has unveiled non-Western systems of perception (Santos-Granero 2009). What is at stake is the epistemological potential for indigenous aesthetics to challenge some certainties claimed by modern, Western aesthetic rationality. Indigenous aesthetics, for example, argues for the plasticity of the beautiful, elucidating different patterns of sensibility, plural semantics of the taste, and non-Western criteria with regard to aesthetic judgement. Questioning what could be taken as beautiful and what is worthy in aesthetic terms rattles the value criteria that underlie and strengthen markets.

Within their economies, indigenous communities might foster forms and codes of expression that cannot be explained by Western-based theories. Given indigenous practices such as ritual basketry, body painting, weaving techniques and native pottery designs, it might be said that their crafts constitute a means to communicate a system of values and representations in which material culture and supernatural dimensions appear intertwined. Some remarks below reveal how untranslatable this sense-making might be for Western societies:

> the Yanesha theory of materiality is multi-centric, based on the notion that there are multiple ways of being a thing ... The Yanesha claim that objects possess different degrees of animacy and agentivity is tantamount to saying that they have different degrees of power. This power depends on, and can only be ascertained by, their particular ontological trajectories, social histories, and/or personal biographies ... The Yanesha believe that things that are in permanent close contact with a person become gradually infused with that person's vitality (yecamquem) ... The most important among these objects are tunics ... which in Yanesha thought are equivalent to a person's body. Because of the process of ensoulment, the relationship between bodies and tunics is not metaphorical but rather literal: bodies are tunics, as tunics are bodies ... The Yanesha and other Amerindian peoples conceive of bodies as including the objects more closely linked to a person through frequent use.
> (Santos-Granero 2009, 106–22)

> The formal aspect of the tipiti [an artefact made of braided straw to have cassava roots drained] reproduces a supernatural serpent, Kutupxi, although it does not faithfully correspond to its appearance, as it lacks the extremities, the head and the tail, as mentioned. What properly associates the artefact with the supernatural is the reproduction of its constricting movements and the presentation of its 'body painting', or rather, its epithelial structure, which is possible through extensible braiding techniques.
> (Van Velthem 2014, 8, translated by author)

With regard to a community economy theory, indigenous peoples' artefacts are of great importance because they stress a threefold contribution: (1) they unveil other modes of producing the material culture as well as different forms of sense-making, whose meanings extrapolate the modern Western thought; (2) they forge other perspectives on social belonging attached to the material culture that contradict the Western-based connection between consumption and distinction; and (3) they stress other possible aesthetic criteria that give rise to other patterns of sensibility and politics of taste (see entry 2, 'Community Economics').

It is noteworthy that crafts have not only played a pivotal role within indigenous economies but also constitute one of the major income sources in the SSE. Notwithstanding the differences they might present regarding value criteria or the association with consumption issues, crafts consist of the majority of commercialised goods by both indigenous women and the women in the SSE initiatives. In this sense, demands regarding spaces for commercialisation are shared by women in indigenous communities and SSE arrangements.

As is the case in indigenous economies, different patterns of valuing have also been fostered by the SSE. However, belonging and identity-building processes are aspects that remain in need of further analysis. If it is appropriate for the literature on the SSE to address issues such as overconsumption, climate-neutral and circular economy, and fair trade systems, it is worrying that some underlying aspects of the everyday consumption engine remain practically unspoilt. Amongst the subjects in need of further discussion, one must consider: (1) the way different social asymmetries (of gender, race/ethnicity, class, sexuality) might be reinforced by a distinction-based discourse, regardless of effective attitudes towards consumerism reduction; (2) the need for a collective approach regarding solidarity consumption, by building up different logics of sense-making and alternative sociabilities; (3) the need to propose less-often-controlled impacts associated with productive consumption, given the prevailing individual accountability in the responsible consumption discourse; and (4) new imaginaries on consumption beyond the capitalist market, by exploring reciprocity and redistribution mechanisms.

Although there is still so much lacking in terms of theoretical advances on solidarity consumption, it might be said that the practices themselves have provided clues on what to do. Solidarity exchange circuits in many countries, for example, have stimulated different logics of belonging to the group, with goods in circulation being less valued for a class-based idea of the beautiful than for the perspective of being in connection with the Otherness. More than the goods themselves, artisans' and peasants' life stories behind the goods seem to be the key to animating local purchases and exchanges (Mascarello and Machado, 2014).

It is also worth recalling that, by evoking community-based ideas on the beautiful and the useful, SSE initiatives have contributed to promoting other forms of valuing laid down and fed by community-based bargaining processes (see also entry 7, 'Heterodox Economics'). This happens, for example, when a collectivity decides to apply the same price to all available services (in a number of local currency units) to make them affordable to some people within an exchange group. It also happens when products are chosen due to other value criteria than compliance with class-based market standards.

8.4 THE DOMESTIC DOMAIN AS A POLITICAL ARENA

A third feature to be stressed regarding commonalities between the SSE and indigenous economies has to do with the domestic domain and its political dimension. Being socially gendered, the domestic domain has been repeatedly neglected as a potential seedbed for a political arena. Notwithstanding this misinterpretation, the domestic domain has accounted for the provisioning, which is one of the key concepts in a community-based economy framework (see also entry 24, 'Care and Home Support Services').

Even underestimated when compared to other principles of economic integration, householding was not absent in Polanyi's work (Hillenkamp 2013). His concern with the re-embeddedness of the economy in market societies has made room for feminists in the fields of economic sociology and the solidarity economy to stress the role played by women in preventing the everyday economy from being uncoupled from the social dimension (Hillenkamp 2013; Hillenkamp and Lucas dos Santos 2019).

Both indigenous and peripheral women have contributed to this ongoing re-embeddedness process, having departed from their private provisioning concerns to raise alliances with other women towards issues of public interest, such as food and water sovereignty, the right to the land and to the seeds, and the struggle against transgenic food and pesticides (see also entry 12, 'The Black Social Economy' and entry 14, 'African American and Distributive Justice'). What is taken as an issue of the private sphere is brought to the public one, intertwining economic, social and political domains through provisioning concerns.

Going against the grain, since the householding is usually associated with gender imbalance, women from indigenous communities and the SSE movement – but not restricted to them – have reframed the positioning of householding within the set of economic integration principles. Being at the forefront of many struggles for land, food and territory, heterogeneous women all over the world have not only forged alliances to guarantee their ways of living and producing, but also creatively reshaped and upscaled reciprocity and redistribution in their communities. What is at stake is the prominence that women from indigenous communities and the SSE movement have assumed with regard to the re-embeddedness of the economy (see also entry 1, 'Activism and Social Movements').

It is also worth recalling that this reframing of the domestic domain, thereafter considered as a potential political zone, has allowed feminist economies to question the split between the economic and the domestic domains as a possibly universal issue (Lucas dos Santos, 2016; see also entry 5, 'Feminist Economics'). However, since this split does not make sense when applied to indigenous communities – the domestic and the economic being coupled from the very beginning – it might be said that this epistemological surveillance has provided a more accurate picture of minority women's agency over time.

REFERENCES

Banerjee, Swati, Luciane Lucas dos Santos and Lars Hulgård. 2021. 'Intersectional Knowledge as Rural Social Innovation.' *Journal of Rural Studies*. https://doi.org/10.1016/j.jrurstud.2021.04.007.

Bourdieu, Pierre. 1984. *Distinction: A Social Critique of the Judgement of Taste*. London, UK and New York, USA: Routledge.

Hillenkamp, Isabelle. 2013. 'Le Principe de Householding Aujourd'hui. Discussion Théorique et Approche Empirique par L'Économie Populaire.' In *Socioéconomie et Démocratie. L'Actualité de Karl Polanyi*, edited by Isabelle Hillenkamp and Jean-Louis Laville, 215–40. Toulouse: Érès.

Hillenkamp, Isabelle, and Luciane Lucas dos Santos. 2019. 'The Domestic Domain Within a Post-Colonial, Feminist Reading of Social Enterprise: Towards a Substantive, Gender-Based Concept of Solidarity Enterprise.' In *Theory of Social Enterprise and Pluralism: Solidarity Economy, Social Movements, and Global South*, edited by Jean-Louis Laville, Philippe Eynaud, Luciane Lucas dos Santos, Swati Banerjee and Lars Hulgård, 90–115. London, UK and New York, USA: Routledge.

Lucas dos Santos, Luciane. 2017. 'Economias Indígenas, Cosmovisão e Territorialidade: Os *Qhatu* No Altiplano Andino.' In *Solidariedade e Ação Coletiva: Trajetórias e Experiências*, edited by Luiz Inácio Gaiger and Aline Mendonça dos Santos, 13–42. São Leopoldo: Editora Unisinos.

Lucas dos Santos, Luciane. 2016. 'Polanyi through the lens of epistemologies of the South and Postcolonial Feminist Economics: different glances at the concept of disembeddedness.' Selected Papers. 2nd EMES-Polanyi International Seminar. http://hdl.handle.net/10316/41607

Mascarello, Magda, and Maria Izabel Machado. 2014. 'The Solidarity Economy and its things: among production, trade, consumption and discard.' *The Brazilian Journal of Labour Studies* 13 (2): 236–47.

Murra, John. 1984. 'Andean Societies.' *Annual Review of Anthropology* 13 (1): 119–41. https://doi.org/10.1146/annurev.an.13.100184.001003.

Santos-Granero, Fernando. 2009. *The Occult Life of Things. Native Amazonian Theories of Materiality and Personhood*. Tucson, AZ: University of Arizona Press.

Temple, Dominique. 2003. *Teoria de la Reciprocidad. La Reciprocidad y el Nacimiento de Los Valores Humanos* 1. La Paz: Garza Azul editores.

Van Velthem, Lúcia. 2014. 'Serpentes de Arumã. Fabricação e Estética Entre Os Wayana (Wajana) Na Amazônia Oriental.' *PROA: Revista de Antropologia e Arte* 5: 1–12.

Viveiros de Castro, Eduardo. 2014. *Cannibal Metaphysics for a Post-Structural Anthropology*. Minneapolis, MN: Univocal Publishing.

Zannoni, Claudio. 1999. *Conflito e Coesão: o Dinamismo Tenetehara*. Brasília: Cimi.

9. Moral economy and human economy
Jean-Louis Laville

INTRODUCTION

From the 17th century, the theorists of political economy developed a so-called 'classical' economic science. This recognized self-interest as the precondition for exchange: 'it is not from the benevolence of the butcher, the brewer, or the baker that we expect our dinner, but from their regard for their own self-interest', Adam Smith (1998) wrote. The multiplication of acts of buying and selling then produces an unintentional social order; each individual is 'led by an invisible hand' and 'by pursuing his own interest he frequently promotes that of the society more effectually than when he really intends to promote it'. In the 19th century, the 'neoclassical' school proposed to go further, founding a 'pure political economy' which they understood as a 'science quite similar to the physical and mathematical sciences' (Walras 1988, 52 §30). Leon Walras did still accept the existence of both applied economics, 'a theory of the economic production of social wealth' (ibid., 61 §34) and social economics, which dealt with 'the distribution of social wealth' (ibid., 65 §38), but they only had a secondary role.

9.1 THE CONCEPT OF THE MORAL ECONOMY

It is this way of seeing the economy that E. Thompson contests. He sets out not to claim 'that Smith and his colleagues were immoral or were unconcerned for the public good' (Thompson 1993, 201–2), but to challenge the 'abbreviated view of economic man' when it becomes 'a crass economic reductionism, obliterating the complexities of motive, behaviour, and function' (ibid., 187). One example of this oversimplicity is the spasmodic view of popular history, according to which social unrest is merely a consequence of rising food prices. Through an examination of the actions of the English 'mob' in the 18th century, Thompson puts forward the concept of the moral economy to refute this excessively superficial explanation. He shows that 'riots' were forms of direct action, 'disciplined and with clear objectives', involving 'definite, and passionately held, notions of the common weal'. They had a 'popular consensus' legitimized by 'a consistent traditional view of social norms and obligations, of the proper economic functions of several parties within the community' (ibid., 188).

James C. Scott employs this idea to consider 'peasant conceptions of social justice, of rights and obligations, of reciprocity' (Scott 1985, 341). Like Thompson, he does not see these shared rules as inciting passivity, but rather as leading to revolts that occur when collective principles are flouted and the protections provided by inherited redistributive institutions are swept away. So protests do not arise suddenly as a result of events but are rooted in the values and affects that characterize everyday resistance. They are the weapons of the weak (Scott 1976).

The term 'moral economy' is also used by Lorraine Daston to refer to values and affects, but this time among scientific researchers, according to an approach that Didier Fassin endorses when he defines the 'moral economy as the production, distribution, circulation and use of emotions and values, norms and obligations in the social space' (Fassin 2012, 37). This development is valuable in the sense that it does not confine the concept of the moral economy to a defence of ways of life that predate the market society. On the other hand, however, it loses the critical edge it has when deployed by Thompson and Scott. This is why, starting again from these authors, this entry will move beyond chronological divisions, making it possible to preserve the concept's epistemological contribution. It will neither restrict its use to a particular historical period nor equate it to a set of rules in any particular social sphere. A moral economy can emerge at any time; what matters is its ability to effectively challenge the monopoly on understanding the economy that orthodox economics has granted itself.

Thus, solidarity-based associationalism – the forgotten source of the social and solidarity economy (SSE); see also entry 10, 'Origins and Histories' and entry 15, 'Associations and Associationalism' – can be understood as a form of moral economy that, in the 19th century, was inspired by customs established in different settings (villages, trades, families, and so on), and transformed them by introducing principles of freedom and equality emanating from the democratic revolutions (see entry 15, 'Associations and Associationalism'). So both transmission and invention played a role here. Social bonds anchored in the *longue durée* were preserved and modified to bring about forms of self-organized reciprocity that contrasted with previous hierarchies.

9.2 THE MORAL ECONOMY: FROM OBLIVION TO RENAISSANCE

The political economy was not enough to guarantee civil peace (Thompson 1963). Faced with the risks generated by social inequality, the ruling classes supplemented this with a form of philanthropic solidarity advocated by Frederic Bastiat, Thomas Malthus and David Ricardo. As Thompson said, it was necessary to eradicate the moral economy so that it could be replaced by this moralization of the poor (Thompson 1963). With philanthropy, morality was no longer something produced by the groups concerned, but became a condition of access to relief – which was reserved for the deserving poor – imposed by the authorities. Philanthropy was in turn marginalized by the welfare state, which seemed sufficient for restricting and regulating the operation of the market. The moral economy thus experienced a long eclipse.

At the end of the 20th century, new social movements – whose appearance demonstrated that social conflict could not be reduced to class struggle alone – attacked the impasses of a mode of development premised on the complementarity of market and state. The environmental movement challenged a conception of the economy based on endless expansion without regard for the planet's limits, while the feminist movement revealed the residual paternalism and gender inequalities embedded in the traditional welfare state's modes of intervention. These movements were controversial, but they pointed to transformations in modes of engagement. Compared with previous movements, they were both more concerned with concrete actions on the ground and more prefigurative, that is, the means they mobilized had to anticipate the objectives pursued. This re-emphasis on alternative experiences, which is expressed in alter-globalization (one of whose slogans is: 'resist and build: another world is possible ... and it is already here') has given rise to the rebirth of a moral economy perspective (see entry 6, 'Globalization and Alter-globalization'). This perspective is advanced through the idea of a human economy, inspired by Thompson's economics 'from the bottom up'. Its main assumption is that economics which focuses on mathematical calculations rooted in the rational individual's utility maximization has an implicit normative stance that makes it inappropriate for safeguarding human and non-human beings in the 21st century. As a consequence, it is necessary to return to a more realistic conception of the economy embedded in most people's everyday experiences. So a human economy is a form of moral economy characterized by four features:

- It is made and remade by people; economics should be of practical use to us all in our daily lives.
- It should address a great variety of particular situations in all their institutional complexity.
- It must be based on a more holistic conception of everyone's needs and interests.
- It has to address humanity as a whole and the world society we are making. (Hart et al. 2010, 5)

This human economy does not have to be created, it 'is already everywhere' (ibid.); the problem is that it is made invisible by mainstream economics. And, as the epistemologies of the South point out, this absence explains why it remains so difficult for the SSE to flourish.

9.3 THE SSE AS A FORM OF HUMAN ECONOMY

It is now possible to summarize the relationship between the moral economy, the human economy and the SSE. It is clear that many forms of moral economy prioritize social protection, and are liable to forget about emancipation. Among the different types of moral economy are nationalist protectionism and conservative values, and elites also have moral norms that legitimize inequalities (Hann 2010, 187–98). Within this wide range of moral economies, the social and solidarity economy will gain strength if it is defined as a form of human economy that emphasizes the values and rules of democratic solidarity-based practices: one that takes account of long-term links between human and non-human beings and aims at more than just short-term utility maximization. The SSE fulfils this definition as it combines protection and emancipation, helping to bring about a transformative solidarity and environmental transition. But this project of the SSE uses the language of social struggles for emancipation, and for this reason it is being contested by a new wave of philanthropic solidarity.

First-generation neoliberalism, formulated by Friedrich Hayek (1983), centred on reaffirming the primacy of competition and limiting democracy. It did so by weakening the mechanisms for collective expression and putting the state at the service of a re-marketization, by shrinking the domain of public services, through financialization or through deregulation according to the principles condensed in 1989 in the Washington Consensus. Today, the ode to competition typical of Hayek's writings is coupled with a concern to establish a form of social-purpose capitalism. In fact, social business, is based on the promise of eradicating poverty and is presented as a miracle recipe. Social business initiatives have only rarely been subject to independent evaluations, and these are hardly conclusive (Humberg 2011). The discourse of social business is nevertheless welcomed by public authorities absorbed in their own budgetary problems, and is supported by private interests anxious for new investment opportunities. Some of these are already being offered by 'bottom of the pyramid' marketing methods targeted at the poorest populations, and by social impact bonds. The mechanism through which these social impact investments operate is revealing: one of its key features is that it shifts the financial risk within social services from the public authority to a private intermediary. Financed by institutional investors, this intermediary takes on the entrepreneurial risk and allocates funds to operators. It receives payment from the public authority – and investors make a return on their investment – only if its results are judged to be successful. Such projects rest on a new philosophy of financializing the social sector, since it is private actors who determine where interventions take place. They have spread to many different countries, expanding into the culture, international solidarity and development. A whole set of tools is now available for the private redeployment of solidarity. Social business limits discussion to questions about initiatives' effectiveness and efficiency in fulfilling social objectives, without worrying about the distribution of power.

This tendency to adopt social business and social impact bonds is partly explained by the inadequacy of social democracy that placed its faith in redistribution alone to protect society. But rather than solidarity coming from private business it is important to reassert the strength of the principle of solidarity. It is also necessary to rediscover the complementarity of the two forms of public and democratic solidarity: one based on rights and public redistribution, the other on civil ties and egalitarian reciprocity (Laville, 2023). This will involve both the SSE and public authorities acknowledging their interdependence while recognizing that, in the present as in the past, these two entities are neither separable nor substitutable.

Current levels of social and environmental damage are such that it is no longer enough to simply check economic activity through taxation and redistribution for social purposes. The welfare state's achievements must be supported by a concern for public participation. Representative democracy can now be reinforced by forms of deliberative democracy that are not only granted, but also won through collective action. What is now needed is a new model that is both opposed to neoconservatism, but also distinct from welfare-statism or the 'third way'. This new model must include a project to renew public debate and deliberation; a project that corresponds to what can be called plural democracy. Its future depends on public authorities' capacity to consolidate representative democracy by feeding it with voices from a more open public sphere, extending the social dialogue between social partners to include other components of civil society. This is a paradigm shift in public action.

If modes of production and consumption are to change, then capitalism cannot be seen as the only mode of economic activity; other ways of valuing goods and services must be recognized (see entry 2, 'Community Economies'). We are at the end of a period of growth based on scientific arrogance and the belief in human omnipotence. In the future, economic means must be chosen according to environmental, social and cultural ends.

Transforming our societies in a way that addresses environmental and social crises will largely depend on the rejection of the orthodox definition of the economy, which is based on the principle of self-interest alone. It is crucial both to limit commodification and to pluralize economic logic. In short, the neoclassical approach developed at the end of the 19th century is becoming inappropriate for the challenges of the 21st century. Hence the revival of a moral economy perspective. This approach should not be reserved for analysing the societies of the past. Its current relevance is empirically supported by the existence of the SSE, which can be understood as a form of human economy, one that offers both protection and emancipation opportunities.

REFERENCES

Fassin, Didier. 2012. 'Vers une théorie des économies morales'. In *Economie Morale Contemporaine*, 19–47. Paris: La Découverte.
Hann, Chris. 2010. 'Moral Economy'. In *The Human Economy: A Citizen's Guide*, 187–98. London: Polity.
Hart, Keith, Jean-Louis Laville and David Antonio Cattani. 2010. 'Building the Human Economy Together'. In *The Human Economy. A Citizen's Guide*, 1–20. London: Polity.
Hayek, Friedrich A. 1983. *Law, Legislation and Liberty, Volume 3: Political Order of a Free People*. London and Henley: Routledge & Kegan Paul.
Humberg, Kerstin Maria. 2011. *Poverty Reduction Through Social Business? Lessons Learned from Grameen Joint Ventures in Bangladesh*. Munchen: Oekom.
Scott, James C. 1976. *The Moral Economy of the Peasant: Rebellion and Subsistence in Southern Asia*. New Haven, CT: Yale University Press.
Scott, James C. 1985. *Weapons of the Weak. Everyday Forms of Peasant Resistance*. New Haven, CT, USA and London, UK: Yale University Press.
Laville, Jean-Louis. 2023. *Solidarity Economy*. University of Minnesota Press.
Smith, Adam. 1998. *The Wealth of Nations*. Oxford: Oxford University Press.
Thompson, Edward Palmer. 1963. *The Making of the English Working Class*. London: Victor Gollancz.
Thompson, Edward Palmer. 1993. *Customs in Common*. London: Penguin.
Walras, Léon. 1988. *Elements of Pure Economics*. Paris: Economica.

10. Origins and histories
Jean-Louis Laville

INTRODUCTION

The tensions between capitalism and democracy have become obvious in the past few decades, and the social and solidarity economy's (SSE) significance has to be seen in this context. But there is also a longer story that this entry aims to reconstruct by identifying three periods in the past two centuries.

Generally speaking, the official narrative claims that a few utopian experiments initiated by pioneer worker and peasant movements failed in the early 19th century. To counter this superficial view, this first period will be described through a closer examination of the content of these 'real utopias' (Wright 2010), which constituted a form of associationalism based on democratic solidarity (see also entry 15, 'Associations and Associationalism').

The second period saw the recognition of different legal statuses: those of the cooperative, the mutual society and the nonprofit organization (see also entry 46, 'Legal Frameworks and Laws'). Since the end of the 19th century, they have been the components of a social economy, defined as a set of non-capitalist organizations operating within an institutional framework based on the separation between the market economy and the welfare state, particularly during the post-Second World War economic expansion (1945–75).

The third period links the different crises of the late 20th century with the emergence of the solidarity economy during the same period, which can also be considered as a resurgence of the associationalist movement. The origins and histories allow us to consider the significance of the SSE in the 21st century, and to address the conditions to concretize its transformative potential.

10.1 A MULTIDIMENSIONAL, SOLIDARITY-BASED ASSOCIATIONALISM: THE HIDDEN SOURCES OF THE SSE

The shockwaves of revolutions in the 18th and 19th centuries created new social demands all over the world. In South America, as well as in North America and Europe, they generated movements calling for emancipation through a new relationship between the political and economic spheres.

The Diverse Profiles of Solidarity-Based Associations

During colonization, South America was pillaged. Millions of Africans were enslaved, torn from their countries to be used as forced labour. They gathered together in mutual assistance organizations, mainly for religious celebrations and tributes to the dead. Elsewhere, poor colonists, peasants and artisans settled in lands unwanted by the oligarchy. All of them constituted a popular economy.

In the first half of the 19th century, anti-colonialist social movements escalated in South America. While the popular economy in its diverse forms survived, its internal structure was modified. For example, in Colombia, the Democratic Republican Society of Progressive Artisans and Laborers was created. In Brazil, former slaves resorted to economic survival strategies, collectively taking possession of the land. These *kilombos* (or *quilombo*, the term derived from Angola Jaga *kilombo*) (Nascimento 1977) were extensions of the semi-formal organizations through which they tried to deal with day-to-day problems. In Chile, a form of popular entrepreneurship was developed by the *labradores* over almost 150 years – from 1700 to 1850 – in agriculture, animal husbandry, pre-industrial mining and forestry operations, the small businesses run by women and also in artisanal production. In Santiago in the mid-19th century, more than half of the population was involved, in one way or another, in the popular industry established by artisans. Using local resources, they relied on community labour known as *la minga*.

The associative impulse allowing to change the popular economy in South America was also used in North America to demand civil rights. From the beginning of the 19th century, African Americans succeeded in building their own institutions: small mutual aid groups promoting self-organization and civic virtue (see also entry 12, 'The Black Social Economy' and entry 14, 'African American and Distributive Justice') (Hossein 2019; Gordon-Nembhard 2014). For example, in the mid-1820s, the African Methodist Episcopal Church, founded by Bishop Richard Allen in 1816, had more than 1000 members. Almost a century later, this stance led famous African American activist and scholar William E.B. Du Bois (quoted in George 1973) to conclude that this church was one of the greatest Black organizations in the world, where religious and economic activities always had a political dimension. The church supported members in need by providing start-up capital to help small entrepreneurs. It also became a seat of protest. As they published petitions and newspapers and set up national antiracist conventions, African American churches were transformed into spaces of struggle against continuing discrimination.

Women, meanwhile, were kept away from the public sphere through an established separation between the domestic and political domains, reinforced by customary law. To avoid endlessly coming up against a wall of incomprehension, some women made their way toward a political existence through economic organizations: mainly refuges and daily support for poor women and their children. They benefited from donations from rural public authorities in North Carolina, as well as urban areas such as Philadelphia, Baltimore, New Orleans and New York. Women were less reluctant than men to seek government funding, even soliciting help from local councils for this purpose. Progressively, they gained a reputation and influenced policies through a variety of means: public meetings, petitions, lobbying, and so on.

In Europe, workers' associative practices – which centred on the protection of professional skills – were experienced as an extension of their political emancipation. In the UK, with the development of forms of solidarity among artisans and manual workers determined to collectively defend their interests, the mutually supportive alliance between political emancipation and economic independence assumed an unexpected scale when these artisans and workers forcefully demanded that their collective forms of the organization be recognized.

In France, during the 1830s, the meaning of purposeful political action was re-examined in direct relation to social inequality. In 1848, a number of decisions were quickly made regarding the right to work, the abolition of the death penalty and slavery, and the freedom of the press, of assembly and of association. *Compagnonnages*, or French guilds, which were mutual help organizations, secularized and became associations where workers were no longer subject to a hierarchy but determined their own governance. Meanwhile, mutual aid societies, which evolved from guilds, developed in a similar way to those in the UK and they provided unemployed or striking workers with help. These tools of struggle, which wove together corporatism, mutualism and republicanism, laid the groundwork for trade unions.

Although the UK and France are emblematic examples, others can be cited in the countries of the Iberian Peninsula, such as Spain, where the 1836 legislation against guilds failed to prevent the development of a labour movement. Thus mutual aid societies came into being in 1841; in 1887 there were 664 of them, and in 1904 they numbered 1271, with 238 351 members. They were combined with other forms of advocacy in multifunctional associative initiatives. Little by little, a patchwork of collective entities was established that borrowed from the popular economy but also demonstrated a desire for independence and collective pride.

The Common Features of Solidarity Associationalism

Despite their diversity, all the initiatives mentioned above share certain characteristics. They create social relationships based on freedom of membership and equality between participants. These are relationships of solidarity that aim to bring lived realities into line with the principles adopted following the democratic revolutions. Social groups that have been discriminated against can decide to self-organize to fight the inequalities of which they are victims, sharing the idea that they alone can contribute to their own emancipation.

Thus the democratic solidarity invented amid the proliferation of associations differed from the traditional solidarities that endorsed age and gender differences, but it nonetheless originated in previous forms of belonging. Social change would not be achieved by breaking away from pre-existing communities, but by building on them and transforming them. Thus, mutual societies in South America changed their internal rules to give everyone the same formal power to make decisions; mutual aid societies in Europe adopted a more horizontal way of operating, soliciting the participation of all.

These changes also reflected a desire to escape the control exercised by the elites. Workers and peasants affirmed their pride in being able to act without the permission of those who had previously oppressed them. Collective dignity was asserted through street demonstrations, public events that expressed the pride of being rid of the tutelage of the elites.

This societal movement linked together economic, social and political issues. Women and African Americans in North America organized forms of mutual aid, but these social activities were inseparable from protests against exclusion from the political sphere (see also entry 12, 'The Black Social Economy' and entry 14, 'African American and Distributive Justice'). When providing these social services, their aim was to make an argument, to engage with local administrations and prove to them that their activities were useful, and demonstrate that they should therefore be included in democratic debate. Their economic activities thus had a social dimension as well as a political impact. The project of change implicitly defended by associationalism is also fundamentally governed by the rejection of violence. It places its faith in mutual learning and shared experience, which it believes will foster the recognition of more inclusive forms of citizenship.

Recovering the forgotten memory of solidarity-based associationalism allows us to show that it was not simply the application of utopian doctrines (by Fourier, Owen, Saint-Simon, and so on). This phenomenon of self-organization was much broader. The importance of its message for today's SSE lies in the fact that it sought to embrace diversity in order to broaden and deepen democracy, which is considered to be a form of life (Dewey 1939, 240–45) that encompassed the economic sphere.

10.2 FROM ASSOCIATIONALISM TO SOCIAL ECONOMY

When the 'second' 19th century, the era of capital and empires, succeeded the 'first' 19th century, the era of revolutions – to use Erik Hobsbawm's evocative terms – associationalism and its demand for democratization gave way to the economic priority of industrial development. This was supposed to bring wealth to nations and their populations, ultimately resolving the social question.

In this productivist vision, solidarity was redefined in a more restrictive way. As mentioned above, the first form of solidarity was democratic. Based on mutual aid as well as on the expression of demands, it drew on both self-organization and social movement forms, which presupposed equal rights among the people committed to it. In opposition to this approach to solidarity, another approach was increasingly put forward, replacing notions of equality with those of benevolence and solicitude. This second form of solidarity was philanthropic solidarity, which referred to the vision of an ethical society where citizens motivated by altruism voluntarily fulfil their duties toward one another.

From Philanthropic Solidarity to the Welfare State

The emergence of this second form of solidarity was accompanied by discrimination against democratic solidarity. The existence of a popular economy in the countries of the South was considered proof that they were lagging behind others. From this progressivist perspective, history was seen as a succession of 'stages' of development, and the popular economy became a sign of economic backwardness. It was defined by what it lacked (legality, rationality, structure, social and legal protection, and a barrier to entry), and by its weaknesses (in terms of capital invested, skill levels, technological development and size).

Women and African Americans were persecuted, while charitable organizations saw their political aspirations stifled by male elites' benevolence. This process of normalization was achieved either through men taking direct control, or through paternalism that offered protection to middle-class white women as long as they complied with the behaviours that men considered appropriate to their gender (Ryan 1990). Although the organizations run by these women were weakened by male pressure, the situation of African American women was much worse (see also entry 12, 'The Black Social Economy' and entry 14, 'African American and Distributive Justice'). As victims of overt hostility, they had to fight with their limited resources for education and assistance, as well as for the assertion of their identity.

In parallel to this, the first-ever Farmers' Alliance was established, with its 400 000 members aiming to organize cooperatives to sell their produce. Large farmers' and workers' movements emerged between 1880 and 1890. Unionist troops were mobilized, and recent immigrants, who were prisoners of their own material distress, were used to break the strikes. The year of the 'big labour revolt' was 1886, with 1400 strikes mobilizing 500 000 workers. The scale of these confrontations led to their being referred to as a 'civil war' by Howard Zinn (2015).

Similar cleavages opened up in the UK. Aiming for a productive system based on mutualism as an alternative to capitalism, the working class defended themselves. But they were unable to bridge the differences between skilled workers undergoing a loss of status and unskilled workers, nor to form an alliance with the bourgeoisie, whose inegalitarian ideology was reinforced by the fear of revolution. The separation between the 'two nations' was inscribed in the 1832 electoral franchise, and the force of the counter-revolution isolated a movement toward equality, which remained a workers' movement. As in Great Britain and Germany during the same period, more stringent legislation was passed relating to the poor, who were considered responsible for their own plight. Murders and atrocities, coupled with the infiltration of movements and the violation of freedoms, sometimes led to their radicalization.

Through the repression and control of independent associations, and with the discouragement of workers' associations and the concomitant promotion of charitable organizations and patronage structures, this period redefined the contours of the associative map in favour of the social elites. But despite all the advantages conferred on philanthropic solidarity, social problems persisted. Their threat to social stability made the philanthropic solution – which attributed unequal conditions solely to individual responsibility – untenable.

This is why, from the end of the 19th century onwards, a democratic version of solidarity once again came to the fore, but this time it took on a new shape. Now democratic solidarity became the responsibility of the state, which enforced the rule of law. The social domain was framed as different from the economy and complementary because it was supposed to re-embed market capitalism in collective norms determined by representative democracy.

The institutional architecture that characterized the 20th century separated the economy, defined as the market, and the social, understood as the domain in which the state intervenes. The state's corrective role was emphasized after the Second World War when an international consensus emerged that, as stated in the 1944 Philadelphia Declaration, economic development was not an end in itself, but a means to achieve social development. Even though it took the form of various regimes, during this period the welfare state expanded on all continents, as social security systems were extended and the resources allocated to social policies increased.

The Recognition of the Social Economy: Benefits and Limitations

Both before and after the emergence of the welfare state, popular struggles and philanthropic concerns led to the recognition of social economy organizations in which a category of stakeholders other than investors was given beneficiary status.

That said, these legal statutes introduced distinctions contrary to the initial associationalist ethos. Cooperatives were distinguished from mutuals and nonprofit organizations. They became part of the market economy and were engaged in sectors of activity with low capital intensity. The general logic of concentration of the means of production forced them to specialize in one core activity related to their members' identity.

The emergence of the welfare state in turn modified the role played by mutuals. As noted previously, many initiatives were organized in the 19th century to deal with the problems of work incapacity, sickness and old age on a solidarity basis by bringing together the members of a profession, sector or locality. They were tolerated and monitored by the authorities. Later, the levels of contributions and benefits, and the way they were collected and distributed, were standardized at the national level. After the end of the Second World War, the types of economic activity that these mutuals were engaged in led to their interdependence with social security systems, and mutual health insurance societies became social protection organizations that complemented compulsory schemes. Increasing competition in the insurance sector put them under severe strain, similar to that experienced by mutual insurance companies covering property-related risks.

In the United States, as in many southern countries, the weak development of the state largely left social services in the hands of families, resulting in gender inequalities that nonprofit organizations rarely questioned. In Europe, however, where the state's functions were more expansive, nonprofits participated in the development and delivery of social services and were incorporated into welfare state regimes.

The social economy consequently gained economic significance, but it was also neglected in the political and economic debates focused on the respective roles of the market and state. The cost of this expansion was that its constituent entities became subject to institutional isomorphism: cooperatives in competition with capitalist enterprises underwent market isomorphism, while mutuals and associations were reframed by welfare state regimes and submitted to state isomorphism.

10.3 THE EMERGENCE OF SOLIDARITY INITIATIVES

When the synergy between market and state entered into crisis in the last decades of the 20th century, new types of solidarity became visible (detailed for Europe, South America, Laville, 2023).

Some Local and International Initiatives

In South America, there has been a rediscovery of the popular economy. Based on mutual help and shared ownership of the means of production, new popular initiatives have sprung up, including worker takeovers; organizations of the unemployed who sought work collectively; community food groups, such as collective kitchens and vegetable gardens; organizations dedicated to problems of housing, electricity and drinking water; pre-cooperative self-building organizations; and associations for providing healthcare and cultural services to the community. These initiatives can be seen in Argentina, Brazil, Chile, Colombia, Ecuador, Mexico, Peru or Uruguay. They are supported by Black and indigenous movements (Alvarez et al. 1998, 333), as in the countries of the Andes, where the principles of the indigenous organizations have been reactivated to generate original development models, such as the United Nations prize-winning Nasa project in Colombia.

Another example is the Landless Rural Workers' Movement (MST) in Brazil, which came into being in 1984. By 2000, 250 000 families had reappropriated unoccupied and unproductive land. At that point, the movement included around 50 farming cooperatives involving 2300 families, and around 30 service cooperatives benefiting 12 000 families.

In these cases, the public dimension of popular economic activity is obvious. In these cases, the fight for better living conditions is intrinsically linked to the fight for the rights of citizenship. This struggle oscillates between protests and the self-resolution of problems, without separating material questions from questions related to living conditions and coexistence. The same point is made by women's groups that are opposed to the dichotomy between public and private, production and reproduction (Verschuur et al. 2021). Women are in the majority in popular initiatives because they believe these collective initiatives might help to identify and contextualize their needs so that they can express them and bring them into the public sphere. Given the failure of standardized universal measures, these initiatives are a means of consolidating rights and translating them into capacities for action, thanks to the collective, which is a resource for developing self-confidence, relieving the weight of responsibilities assumed in the family sphere, and reconciling them with a commitment to social justice. These collective actions aim first and foremost to be pragmatic responses to the problems of daily life. However, they also formulate societal and environmental claims, establishing a link with ecological feminism in opposition to an economist's conception of wealth.

These popular economic activities in the South have prompted a shift in attitudes to activities that involve caring for others, including a more equal distribution of these tasks and heightened awareness as to the wealth that they generate. In this respect, they are very similar to initiatives established in the North in the 1980s under the name of 'proximity' or 'community' services. These initiatives proposed new organizational forms and solutions to local social problems.

In the Scandinavian countries, the 'cooperatization' of social services is primarily a way of increasing the role of users – as demonstrated in parent-run crèches – and was accepted under the pressure of financial constraints affecting the public sector. In France, one of the main examples of these innovations has been the movement for childcare involving parents' participation. In the United Kingdom in the 1990s, associations representing cultural minorities and disabled people developed radical approaches that also encouraged user participation. In the sphere of local development, grassroots community approaches appeared, including community enterprises (which are numerous in Scotland), community foundations and community development trusts.

Among the attempts to regenerate local economies, there is also a movement to revive the concept of popular credit present in Proudhon's exchange bank project in France, Raiffeisen's mutual agricultural credit bank and Schulze-Delitzsch's popular bank in Germany, and the credit unions in the United Kingdom. This revival is being led by the old mutualist and cooperative banks, who are returning in a certain sense to their original aims, as well as by new players. The idea that money should be at the service of social ties is being extended in the exchange of goods, services and knowledge, organized through social currencies. The goal is no longer to democratize access to the official currency, but to create a unit of calculation that is shared among the members of the same association. Unlike national currencies, social and alternative currencies, which are issued by a group of citizens that gives them a name, are currencies that escape state monopolies. They are designed to develop interpersonal relations, constituting spaces of trust where rules of trade are negotiated, which enables local capabilities other than those mobilized by mercantile production to be valued. Among them are Local Exchange Trading Systems (LETS), which appeared in 1983 and involve – as far as can be gleaned from the scant information available – over 1.5 million members spread over more than 2500 associations in around 30 countries, particularly in the West, South America and Japan. A few examples are the Italian time banks, French Local Exchange Systems (SEL) and the German Tauschringe.

Another novelty was the emergence of cooperation between the North and South. Resulting from the encounter between representatives of the South, who demanded that development aid be converted into fair trading practices, and environmentalist and human rights associations in the North, fair trade established two aims from the outset. The first was to improve the lives of small producers in the South, marginalized due to their lack of financial resources and experience, by creating channels for their agricultural produce and handicrafts to be sold to consumers in the North who wished to contribute to greater solidarity between North and South. The second was to build a network of consumers by raising public awareness about the injustices of the rules of international trade, and through activism that targeted political and economic decision-makers. The issues addressed by fair trade are also tackled by initiatives such as responsible solidarity consumption and solidarity tourism networks.

10.4 A NEW PROBLEM

None of these initiatives, which have gained legal recognition in various countries, can be fully understood through the third sector approach, which establishes a watertight separation between associations and cooperatives. This separation is increasingly challenged by reality when initiatives use either associative or cooperative status to carry out economic activities that they see as means at the service of ends related to democratic solidarity. Thus, in the case of organic farming, renewable energy and economic integration, such initiatives internalize environmental and social costs that are externalized by other companies. In fair trade, solidarity finance and proximity services, there is also respect for criteria of social justice and the accessibility of services. By raising the question of the aim of economic activities, the solidarity economy has brought notions of social utility and collective interest to the public's attention.

The dual focus – both political and economic – of the solidarity economy approach underlines the need for associative, cooperative and mutualist initiatives to influence institutional arrangements. The social economy has not been able to counter the institutional isomorphism created by the division and complementarity between the market and welfare state. The social enterprise approach is also insufficient because it is too centred on the economic success of organizations, and it has put the political to one side. Indeed, as a reaction to the perverse effects of this focus on economic success, initiatives that aim to be both citizen-oriented and entrepreneurial have reinforced the political aspects of their activities. But this will have a limited effect if these initiatives are unable to promote democracy in both their internal functioning and their external expression. Beyond looking inwards at their own organization, they must also reflect on the reasons why they find it so hard to scale up. Through its dual focus, the solidarity economy questions the categories of economics at both conceptual and empirical levels, refusing to limit economic phenomena to those that are defined as such by economic orthodoxy. It also questions orthodox economic science's power to delimit reality, fostering more general reflection on how the economy is defined and instituted (see also entry 7, 'Heterodox Economics').

CONCLUSION

The social and solidarity economy might be nothing more than a tactical compromise, but it might also generate new momentum by combining the social economy tradition with the emergent solidarity economy. One of the reasons why this entry focuses on the origins and histories of the SSE is to create this new momentum.

To ensure that this new momentum is generated, three key questions are required:

- Better cooperation between the components of the SSE, so that established initiatives are linked to less-established ones, is necessary for the improvement of collective strength in particular countries.
- Alliances with all the social movements, such as trade unions, and collective actions working to bring about a solidary and ecological transition, are necessary to avoid isomorphic tendencies.
- Participation of the SSE in co-constructing public policies, in order both to move beyond the margins and to prevent a loss of distinctiveness through absorption into the mainstream.

The economy cannot be conflated with the market alone, and social solidarity cannot be conflated with the state alone. The SSE approach by no means has all the virtues – it can often drift towards the commercial and the bureaucratic – but it gives form to social practices that cannot find a home elsewhere. For this reason, it can give politics a place that economism refuses to give it, without thereby focusing on the state. It transforms economic activities and their institutionalization into phenomena that are simultaneously economic and democratic.

This penetration of democratic principles into activities of production, trade, commerce, savings and consumption is necessary to strengthen democracy and avert a slide into technocracy or authoritarianism. Without rebalancing economic conditions, political equality cannot be preserved. The SSE is the new label for initiatives that have long argued for a democratization of the economy. Its further development is crucial for the future of democracy (Gibson-Graham 2006; Laville 2015, 2023; Hart et al. 2010).

REFERENCES

Alvarez, Sonia E., Dagnino Evelina and Escobar Arturo, eds. 1998. *Culture of Politics, Politics of Culture*. New York: West View Press.

Dewey, John. 1939. 'Creative Democracy – The Task Before Us.' In *John Dewey: The Later Works, 1925–1953, vol. 14*, edited by Jo Ann Boyden, 224–30. Carbondale, IL: Southern Illinois University Press.

George, Carol V.R. 1973. *Segregated Sabbaths: Richard Allen and the Emergence of Independent Black Churches, 1760–1840*. New York: Oxford University Press.

Gibson-Graham, J.K. 2006. *A Postcapitalist Politics*. Minneapolis, MN: University of Minnesotta Press.

Gordon-Nembhard, Jessica. 2014. *Collective Courage: A History of African American Cooperative Economic Thought and Practice*. Philadelphia, PA: Penn State University Press.

Hart, Keith, Jean-Louis Laville and David Antonio Cattani. 2010. 'Building the Human Economy Together.' In *The Human Economy: A Citizen's Guide*, edited by Keith Hart, Jean-Louis Lavelle and David Antonio Cattani, 1–17. London: Polity.

Hossein, Caroline Shenaz. 2019. 'A Black Epistemology for the Social and Solidarity Economy: The Black Social Economy.' *Review of Black Political Economy* 46 (3): 209–29. https://doi.org/10.1177/0034644619865266.

Laville, Jean-Louis. 2015. 'Social and Solidarity Economy in Historical Perspective.' In *Social and Solidarity Economy: Beyond the Fringe*, edited by Peter Utting, 41–56. London: Zed Books.

Laville, Jean-Louis. 2023. *Solidarity Economy*. University of Minnesota Press.

Nascimento, Maria Beatriz. 1977. 'Historiografia do Quilombo.' *Quilombola e Intelectual: Posibilidades nos Dias da Destruição*, 125–49. Africa: Editora filhos de Africa.

Ryan, Mary P. 1990. *Women in Public: Between Banners and Ballots, 1825–1880*. Baltimore, MD: Johns Hopkins University Press.

Verschuur, Christine, Isabelle Guérin and Isabelle Hillenkamp. 2021. *Social Reproduction, Solidarity Economy, Feminisms and Democracy: Latin America and India*. London: Palgrave Macmillan.
Wright, Erik Ollin. 2010. *Envisioning Real Utopias*. London: Verso.
Zinn, Howard. 2015. *A People's History of the United States*. New York: Harper.

11. Postcolonial theories
Luciane Lucas dos Santos

INTRODUCTION

Postcolonial theories have been increasingly applied to different fields of knowledge. Having started in literary studies, they have contributed to challenging a set of universal assumptions in various areas of research, such as sociology, anthropology, architecture, economics, semiotics and feminist thought.

By criticising the Eurocentric bias that many theories might contain and reproduce, postcolonial theories have focused on the asymmetries between nations or social groups due to colonial pasts and one-sided colonial wounds. Despite their overarching approach, the focus in postcolonial theories remains on the representations of Otherness and the hegemony developed from this (Said 2003). Building non-Western nations and peoples as underdeveloped and unskilled, Eurocentric strategies and policies have brought about symbolic and material consequences for minorities, whether in the Global South or in the 'South' of the Global North (Santos 2014).

This entry aims to: provide an overview of the main ideas regarding the postcolonial approach; reflect upon the narrative of development; and analyse how biases in interpretation might forfeit initiatives, programmes and policies bridging the social and solidarity economy (SSE) and goals such as inclusion, resilience, participation, gender and racial equity, to name but a few.

11.1 POSTCOLONIAL THEORIES

Postcolonial theories have focused on the issues of (mis)representation, being critical of modern Western-based universalised concepts and perspectives. Usually associated with the Anglo-Saxon world and located in the cultural studies field, the postcolonial theory might not be so easily distinguishable, at first glance, from other approaches focused on the colonial wounds. Three strands are worth mentioning here: the anti-colonial readings (Aimé Cesaire, Frantz Fanon, Albert Memmi and Edward Said having provided the early founding texts to further support postcolonial thought); the subaltern studies (where scholars such as Ranajit Guha, Dipesh Chakrabarty and Gayatri Spivak also laid the foundation, being further considered as postcolonial authors); and the decolonial movement (in which Anibal Quijano, Walter Mignolo and María Lugones stand out for their groundbreaking work). Despite some important differences among these theoretical frameworks, the fact is that the frontiers are not always obvious.

Likewise, other theoretical approaches with ongoing ties to the postcolonial theories – such as the anti-orientalism (where Said is also placed), the third world approach and the epistemologies of the South – have consistently contributed either to pave the way to the postcolonial entrenchment or to amplify some issues raised by them. The epistemologies of the South

(Santos 2014), for example, have not only highlighted the narrow-mindedness of reducing the epistemological diversity of the world to Western thinking, but also called for attention to the plasticity behind the sociological categories of the Global South and the Global North. Santos (2014) originally argues that this 'South' might be found in the Global North, being represented by minorities who are commonly treated as 'unworthy citizens' due to the remaining colonial roots where they live – for example, Roma and indigenous peoples, Muslim communities, intra-European Union migrants and refugees, and minority women (see also entry 12, 'The Black Social Economy'). This 'South' plasticity offers a broad understanding of how different Europes might coexist, albeit the prevalent European cohesion discourse.

Postcolonial theories might be said to gain prominence during the 1990s, even though their roots date back some decades, with the works of Edward Said, Homi Bhabha and Gayatri Spivak (Said 2003; Bhabha 1994; Spivak 1988). Drawing upon the colonialism associated with the French and British empires, postcolonial theories analyse the colonial roots laid down in these regions during the 19th and 20th centuries (Bhambra 2014). Heading in a different direction, decolonial thought has focused on Spanish and Portuguese colonisation processes, going back to 1492 and the conquest of what was later called the American continent. This defining moment, according to Dussel (1990), not only gave rise to a history of invasions but was also the foundation stone for modernity. The latter has been inspired by the post-Marxist world-systems theory, proposed by Immanuel Wallerstein, being also in dialogue with both the dependency and the underdevelopment theories (Bhambra 2014). The decolonial approach has been more focused on the relations between the West and Latin America, whereas the postcolonial perspective draws upon the ties between the West and different contexts, namely Africa, South Asia and the Middle East.

Generally speaking, postcolonial criticism remains focused on representations and discourses. Some ideas might be said to set up the core of this approach: (1) making a criticism of the modern binaries, questioning universalised concepts that have, all in all, reaffirmed the Western hegemony with regard to knowledge production; (2) unveiling the Othering processes that were moulded and fed by shallow representations of the difference; (3) highlighting that the narrative of modernity is, in fact, one of its possible versions – the Western one – that is in contradiction with other readings of what Modernity meant; and (4) calling for the attention to a 'politics of location' (Brah 1996), according to which the situatedness of embodied subjects cannot be neglected when it comes to analysing identities, contexts and relations.

11.2 POSTCOLONIAL THEORIES APPLIED TO ECONOMICS AND THE NARRATIVE OF DEVELOPMENT

Contrary to other disciplines in social sciences, economics has resisted being heckled by postcolonial theory. However, as a discipline, the more economics steps aside from recognising its underlying ties with cultural issues, the more its discourse is allowed to legitimise biases, having an impact on nations, institutional decisions and ordinary people's lives. If it is true that there are perspectives considering the role played by culture in shaping the everyday economy, it is also a fact – a worrying fact, indeed – that a dualistic-based approach (developed/underdeveloped, universal/particular, and so on) still prevails, now focused on identifying and measuring the cultural determinants of economic development (Zein-Elabdin 2016, 11). By establishing causality links between cultural variables and economic growth, this approach has also led to Western-based assumptions on what development should be.

The mainstream approaches continue to rely on neoclassical, mathematical models. On behalf of a supposedly neutral approach, economics has veiled culturally based assumptions feeding methods and models. This is the reason for Zein-Elabdin (2004, 22) to argue that a postcolonial analysis of economics 'must begin with a scrutiny of the cultural construction of the subject matter of economics itself, namely, *its non-economic core*' (emphasis in the original). Culture is to be understood here, first and foremost, as the context which supports the shaping and the prevalence of certain theoretical and epistemological perspectives instead of others. It is thus connected with the mindset and context in which the theories have been forged.

Proposing an original research agenda where different economic strands are analysed, Zein-Elabdin and Charusheela (2004), along with a small group of scholars (Robert Dimand, Jennifer Olmsted, Karen Graubart, Antonio Callari, among others) have elaborated on three main issues: (1) the prevalent discourses on poverty and richness and the way they have been handled in public policies, funding programmes and other institutional uses over time, particularly in formerly colonised countries; (2) the narrative of development and the way it has been used to support 'the ontological precedence of modern European societies' (Zein-Elabdin and Charusheela 2004, 2); and (3) the orientalist mindset that can persist and feed some international organisations when thinking of economic recovery plans.

If postcolonial theories in economics constitute a brand new approach, a dialogue between the SSE and postcolonial economics is even more recent and unusual. This entry is an attempt to signal what this dialogue could be, particularly in European countries. Allowing us to recognise biased policies and routines on civic betterment and community facility support, on the one hand, and cultural assets of a responsiveness-positive community on the other, postcolonial lenses can provide governments and institutions with fine-tuned guidelines for stimulating and assessing social transformation. Postcolonial theories on the SSE can also demonstrate to what extent commonly undervalued issues such as self-organisation, minorities' power of choice and non-hierarchical forms of solidarity are primary concerns in decolonising local development goals.

Some scholars (Özkazanç-Pan 2017; Essers and Tedmanson 2014; Sambajee 2015; Verduyn et al. 2017) have already been discussing neighbouring concepts in the light of postcolonial theories. Highlighting the importance of feminist and ethnicity-based lenses, they have interpreted some trendy concepts in a very different way, dissecting market-based discourses and perspectives. This approach, mainly grounded on critical entrepreneurship studies (CES), has otherwise privileged concepts other than social and solidarity economies. They show how close to solidarity economy initiatives some popular formats of social entrepreneurship might be, given the presence of a minority perspective or an enriched blend of economic principles. However, a distinction between social economy, solidarity economy and social entrepreneurship is still needed.

These differences are associated with three main aspects: the promoting agent, the relationship with the state, and the relationship with the market (Hespanha and Lucas dos Santos 2016). Aiming at covering the social gaps in the territories and existing in a close relationship with the state and its social welfare agenda, social economy organisations are not allowed to adopt shared management with the aid recipients who they cover. In a different direction, and supporting individuals and groups in situations of precariousness or inequality, social entrepreneurship is commonly committed to innovative and efficiency-based models, products and services being adapted to market requirements. Social entrepreneurship distinguishes itself from social economy and solidarity economy by waiving the state's intervention and grasping some market-based concepts such as efficiency, replicability and upscaling. With major differences from the previous concepts, solidarity economy privileges the communities' autonomy and horizontal participation rather than the adaptation to market requirements or state guidelines. As remarked by Laville (2023, 196), 'the solidarity economy approach has brought notions of social utility and collective interest into the public debate' in such a way that the benefits for the community take on the leading role, by overriding the economic goals (see also entry 10, 'Origins and Histories', entry 3, 'Contemporary Understandings' and entry 49, 'Participation, Governance, Collective Action and Democracy').

Embodied in formal or informal economic arrangements and not being focused on individuals, solidarity economy is grounded on self-organising, shared management and non-hierarchical forms of solidarity, thus having a political and a collective dimension. This political dimension is said to follow a threefold perspective: (1) the fight against different social asymmetries (of gender, class, race and so on) through popular and horizontal alliances among marginalised people and groups; (2) the validation of non-Western knowledge, aesthetic codes and logics of sense-making that are usually undervalued by the market and the state; and (3) the valuing of economic integration principles beyond the market (reciprocity, community redistribution and householding within the communities).

Considering this political dimension, it is surprising that research on the relationship between solidarity economy and postcolonial theories is still underdeveloped, and the same could be said about social economy. Research on postcolonial approaches in the SSE framework is scarce. They have mainly focused on solidarity economy initiatives in the Global South (Lucas dos Santos and Banerjee 2019; Hillenkamp and Lucas dos Santos 2019; Calvo Martínez et al. 2019), but have also started to provide an analytical framework for the social economy and voluntary sector in Western contexts (Lucas dos Santos forthcoming). It is worth recalling the huge potential for postcolonial theories to critically analyse how minorities have been supported by social welfare policies and included in projects by social economy organisations in Europe. Similarly, postcolonial lenses could deepen the analysis on the level of minorities' participation (or absence) in European solidarity economy arrangements. Given that there is a 'South' in the North – represented by a number of marginalised citizens, such as Roma and indigenous peoples, refugees and internally displaced people, immigrants, black and ethnic communities, Muslim and other minority women, transgender people, and individuals who are homeless – there remains a large set of issues to be analysed through postcolonial lenses in a very heterogeneous Europe (see also entry 18, 'LGBT* Inclusion' and entry 19, 'Migrants and Refugees').

Generally speaking, a postcolonial approach to SSE should be grounded on a set of premises including the following:

- It is not possible to perceive the inherent power dynamics related to the production of knowledge in the absence of a subaltern understanding of modernity. By assuming Western modernity as an encompassing perspective that fits all, the West is taken as the ruler according to which other economies and societies are compared and expected to follow suit.

- Theories – and scholars who gave rise to them – should not be decoupled from the context in which they were forged.
- Discourses and visual approaches that contribute to the overrepresentation of minorities as unchanged aid recipients by Western-based organisations revive colonial imagery.
- The identification of biases in the discourse of institutions, governments, organisations and even collectivities is a cornerstone of decolonising approaches in SSE.

Aiming at proposing a road map toward postcolonial theories in the SSE, the next section presents a set of issues that could characterise a further dialogue between the two perspectives.

11.3 A POSTCOLONIAL AGENDA OF SSE

More recently, mobilisations towards civic engagement, community resilience and co-governance through participative methods have become trends in the European context. Although these efforts to realise them are undoubtedly a breath of fresh air, the underlying conditions to make them achievable goals are as important as the drive towards them. Some challenges are thus presented under a postcolonial framing to highlight some aspects that might be overlooked. These challenges are related to poverty reduction, sustainable development, inclusion policies and assessment guidelines.

Poverty Cannot be Decoupled from Other Forms of Othering

Poverty reduction has been assumed to be one of the main targets in SSE policies and projects. Being measurable through a set of indicators that allow the calculation of resource deficit, poverty might also be a trapped concept if misinterpreted as a problem to be technically solved. To put it simply, poverty cannot be decoupled from other forms of Othering.

Poverty has been the material consequence, rather than the cause, of intersected asymmetries. Without combating what has made groups of people vulnerable on a daily basis, the efforts towards the reduction of resource deficit will just attenuate the circumstances. Likewise, without the participation of subaltern groups in the forging of tailor-made solutions, their resistance to vested interests and power imbalances will be permanently undermined.

Besides, material constraints experienced by some minority groups in terms of labour opportunities and/or job mobility, social welfare services, credit access, fair housing policies and unhindered access to public equipment should be seen as the outward face of tacit forms of discrimination due to gender, race, ethnic background, religion or sexual identity, to name but a few.

For instance, the situation of black people in Europe shows how material constraints might be associated with or aggravated by discrimination. According to the 2018 Fundamental Rights Agency (FRA) report *Being Black in the EU* (FRA 2018, 12), 'skin colour affects access to adequate housing'. The disproportionate ratio of the access to decent housing by black people compared to other citizens demonstrates how material constraints might be related to non-economic issues. In a group of 6000 black people interviewed in the 12 European countries with a high proportion of black residents, 'nearly half of the respondents live in overcrowded housing (45%), compared to 17% of the general population in the EU' (ibid.). Peripheral black women, likewise, are overrepresented in low-paid jobs and are likely to be misinterpreted as being poor because of their unskilled jobs. Notwithstanding their low wages, it is worth stressing that these women are stuck in a permanent situation of in-work poverty exactly because they are repeatedly selected for these unskilled job vacancies. Another finding of the FRA report (FRA 2018, 45) demonstrates that education is not the reason behind the overrepresentation of black people in low-paid jobs: 'almost twice as many respondents with tertiary education (9%) are employed in elementary occupations – usually manual work involving physical effort – than the general population (5%)'.

Grounded on findings such as these, postcolonial thinking calls for attention to the following issues: (1) inequality cannot be properly understood without a deeper comprehension of power relations and prevalent social imageries that might reinforce stereotypes; (2) the tacit mechanisms of Othering need to be detected and dismantled, be they in social dynamics, public policies or local projects; (3) discourses and pictures disseminating the Other as a permanent aid recipient, stuck in a position of someone who is always in need of learning and direction, need to be removed from institutional communication, be they in the SSE or third sector frameworks, in public policies or even in international organisations; (4) recognising minorities' agency and power of choice is the stepping stone to reinforce their resilience and to contribute to social cohesion.

Achieving Sustainable Development Requires the Capacity of Overcoming the 'One-Size-Fits-All' Approach

As discussed by Zein-Elabdin and Charusheela (2004), there has been a strong drive in disseminating Western-based patterns as the parameters to follow. It encompasses values, aesthetic codes, priority definitions, ways of living and sense-making. The narrative of development has not only naturalised a kind of ontological precedence of Western societies (Zein-Elabdin and Charusheela 2004; Zein-Elabdin 2016), but also has made other coexisting rationalities fade in time, seen as inconsistent or illogical (Santos 2014). Indigenous rationales and forms of knowledge could be said to be among them.

Even when development is addressed according to the United Nations' Sustainable Development Goals, one might question to what extent Western societies have accepted that other contexts have knowledge worth learning about in a more balanced North–South dialogue. Popular and non-Western forms of knowledge has been constantly neglected, despite its solutions to old and brand-new challenges. While Western-based solutions are assumed as a deliverable for everyone everywhere, innovative knowledge from other contexts might be refused under the excuse that it was tailored to specific settings. As examples of that, it is worth recalling the indigenous knowledge of large and antiseismic structures (Moassab 2020), and their capacity for developing crop production methods to deal with extremely high altitudes (see also entry 8, 'Indigenous Economies' and entry 29, 'Food and Agriculture Sector').

The very concept of sustainable societies should also give more attention to its capacity of overcoming the 'one size fits all' approach to environment-related issues. Solidarity economy, through popular alliances toward food and water sovereignty, plays an important role by directing attention to environmental justice and the way that different groups are disproportionately impacted upon by growth strategies. For example, those gated in devalued areas with higher levels of toxic waste and industrial pollution, such as the case of Roma people – a situation that was recently reported by the European Environmental Bureau (Heidegger and Wiese 2020).

Postcolonial lenses can thus contribute to a more critical and sensitive look towards the way minorities have been placed in an overarching sustainable society project. They can also increase attention to a remaining unequal production of space (for minority women, persons in situations of homelessness, Roma people, and so on) even in the light of sustainable cities.

Inclusion Should Not be Misinterpreted with the Depletion of Otherness

Inclusion might also be a trapped concept if the differences associated with minorities are expected to fade out over time. A postcolonial approach, on the contrary, requires organisations, public bodies, technical staff – and even solidarity economy collectivities, usually animated by a political dimension – to stimulate active participation of minorities in designing the solutions to combat their inequality situation.

It means that the idea of inclusion should not imply total compliance with prevailing Western-based perspectives, nor should it be reduced to a labour inclusion issue. The Otherness must be respected as such – a condition which is only possible if Europe recognises its own heterogeneity. Likewise, minorities should not be seen as homogeneous or frozen in time; which is, unfortunately, a very common perspective in public policies and inclusion strategies. It is worth bearing in mind that minorities' cultural values and/or traditions have also undergone changes, although this happens on their own terms.

Through a postcolonial perspective, the following issues are to be taken into account: (1) inclusion should not be reduced to the acquisition of competencies to fit into the host societies' labour market; (2) inclusion policies should not undermine the power of choice and the agency of minorities; (3) participation must not be misunderstood as a mere opinion poll, and the possibility of dissent by disadvantaged people in consultation processes should be safeguarded; (4) participatory methods imply tailor-made consultation processes aimed at enlarging minorities' conditions for expressing dissent and negotiating.

A Different Approach Starts by Changing Metrics and Assessment Guidelines

One of the major problems regarding the SSE framework is the growing isomorphism, a result of the pressure for efficiency from funding sources. Although upscaling, at first sight, may seem the most effective way of driving forward a previously tested solution to a wider context, the excessive concern with scale has led initiatives and support organisations to deviate from long-lasting solutions on behalf of more quantifiable and time-bound objectives (see entry 44, 'Co-optation, Isomorphism and Instrumentalisation').

Scale-based solutions focused on efficiency-based answers usually overlook how cultural changes require prior recognition of usual biases and factors of lock-in within the communities. This means that the connivance with stereotypes, or flimsy approaches to combat exclusion and discrimination – in the community or in the public bodies – contributes to both deviating from what is at the core of the problem and masking the one-sided focus on the market. The fact is that community resilience – outside a neoliberal understanding of that – demands new sociabilities and collective practices capable of reinforcing the social ties in the community. Being concerned with reciprocity and community redistribution, the solidarity economy might contribute to long-lasting community-based solutions.

With regard to this topic, contributions brought by a postcolonial theory on the SSE can thus be summarised as follows: (1) community-based popular technologies should be seen as assets in the assessment guidelines' scope, since they foster both community resilience and social cohesion; (2) other economic integration principles should be evaluated as being as relevant as the capacity of having products and services circulating in the market; (3) the capacity of solidarity economy arrangements to simultaneously reframe the redistribution of community surplus and reduce the burden of individual scarcity – through short supply chains, exchange circuits, community vegetable gardens, community repair shops and popular rotating savings – evinces the empirical but also the theoretical contribution to rethinking small-scale solutions to foster social and environmental justice.

REFERENCES

Bhabha, Homi K. 1994. *The Location of Culture*. Brantford, Ont.: W. Ross Macdonald School Resource Services Library.
Bhambra, Gurminder. 2014. 'Postcolonial and decolonial dialogues.' *Postcolonial Studies*, 17(2): 115–21.
Brah, Avtar. 1996. *Cartographies of Diaspora: Contesting Identities*. London: Routledge.
Calvo Martínez, Sara, Andrés Pachón Morales, José María Martín Martín and Valentín Molina Moreno. 2019. 'Solidarity economy, social enterprise, and innovation discourses: understanding hybrid forms in postcolonial Colombia.' *Social Sciences*, 8(7): 205.
Dussel, Enrique. 1990. '1492: diversas posiciones ideológicas.' In: *1492–1992: La interminable conquista. Emancipación e Identidad de América Latina*, edited by Joaquin Mortiz, 77–97. Mexico: Grupo Editorial Planeta.
Essers, Caroline and Deirdre Tedmanson. 2014. 'Upsetting "others" in the Netherlands: narratives of Muslim Turkish migrant businesswomen at the crossroads of ethnicity, gender and religion.' *Gender, Work and Organization*, 21(4): 353–67.
FRA (European Union Agency for Fundamental Rights). 2018. *Being Black in the EU*. Second European Union Minorities and Discrimination Survey. Luxembourg: Publications Office of the European Union. https://fra.europa.eu/sites/default/files/fra_uploads/fra-2018-being-black-in-the-eu_en.pdf.
Heidegger, Patricia and Katy Wiese. 2020. *Pushed to The Wastelands: Environmental Racism Against Roma Communities in Central and Eastern Europe*. Brussels: European Environmental Bureau.
Hespanha, Pedro and Lucas dos Santos, Luciane. 2016. 'O nome e a coisa. Sobre a invisibilidade e a ausência de reconhecimento institucional da Economia Solidária em Portugal.' *Revista da Aceesa – Associação Centro de Estudos de Economia Solidária do Atlântico*, 9: 22–66.
Hillenkamp, Isabelle and Luciane Lucas dos Santos. 2019. 'The domestic domain within a postcolonial, feminist reading of social enterprise: towards a substantive, gender-based concept of solidarity enterprise.' In *Theory of Social Enterprise and Pluralism: Solidarity Economy, Social Movements, and Global South*, edited by Jean-Louis Laville, Philippe Eynaud, Luciane Lucas dos Santos, Swati Banerjee and Lars Hulgard, 90–115. Abingdon: Routledge.
Laville, Jean-Louis. 2023. *The Social and Solidarity Economy*. Minneapolis, MN: Minnesota University Press.
Lucas dos Santos, Luciane. Forthcoming. 'Economic democracy through the lenses of the epistemologies of the South.' In *The Handbook of Critical Perspectives on Nonprofit Organizing and Voluntary Action: Concepts, Applications and Future Directions*, edited by Roseanne Mirabella, Tracey Coule and Angela Eikenberry. Cheltenham, UK and Northampton, MA, USA: Edward Elgar Publishing.
Lucas dos Santos, Luciane and Swati Banerjee. 2019. 'Social enterprise: is it possible to decolonise this concept?' In *Theory of Social Enterprise and Pluralism: Solidarity Economy, Social Movements, and Global South*, edited by Jean-Louis Laville, Philippe Eynaud, Luciane Lucas dos Santos, Swati Banerjee and Lars Hulgard, 3–17. Abingdon: Routledge.
Moassab, Andreia. 2020. 'De que lado a arquitetura está? Reflexões sobre ensino, tecnologia, classe e relações raciais.' *Revista Projetar – Projeto e Percepção do Ambiente*, 5(1): 8–19.

Özkazanç-Pan, Banu. 2017. 'On entrepreneurship and empowerment: postcolonial feminist interventions.' In *Critical Perspectives of Entrepreneurship*, edited by Caroline Essers, Pascal Dey, Deirdre Tedmanson and Karen Verduyn, 192–205. Abingdon: Routledge.
Said, Edward. 2003. *Orientalism*. London: Penguin Books.
Sambajee, Pratima. 2015. 'Rethinking non-traditional resistance at work: the case of the Indian Diaspora in Mauritius.' *Culture and Organization*, 21(5), 386–408.
Santos, Boaventura de Sousa. 2014. *Epistemologies of the South: Justice Against Epistemicide*. Abington: Routledge.
Spivak, Gayatri. 1988. *Can the Subaltern Speak?* Basingstoke: Macmillan.
Verduyn, Karen, Pascal Dey and Deirdre Tedmanson. 2017. 'A critical understanding of entrepreneurship.' *Revue de l'Entrepreneuriat*, 16(1), 37–45.
Zein-Elabdin, Eiman. 2004. 'Articulating the postcolonial (with economics in mind).' In *Postcolonialism Meets Economics*, edited by Eiman Zein-Elabdin and S. Charusheela, 21–39. Abingdon: Routledge.
Zein-Elabdin, Eiman. 2016. *Economics, Culture and Development*. New York: Routledge.
Zein-Elabdin, Eiman and S. Charusheela. 2004. 'Economics and postcolonial thought.' In *Postcolonialism Meets Economics*, edited by Eiman Zein-Elabdin and S. Charusheela, 1–18. Abingdon: Routledge.

12. The Black social economy
Sharon D. Wright Austin

INTRODUCTION

This entry provides a definition and analysis of the Black social economy in the African diaspora. People of African descent around the world have engaged in this political economy as a way to gain political and economic power. The term 'the Black social economy' was first coined by Hossein in 2013 because there was a need to expose the assumption that the social economy interacts with state and private sector actors. Hossein (2013) examined the politicized economic cooperation between historically excluded people of African descent when they use informal banks, known as rotating savings and credit associations (ROSCAs). This has been, and remains, difficult because of the institutional racism and discrimination they have encountered. As a way to overcome these obstacles, many people have participated in solidarity economic undertakings. These strategies require them to collaborate and pool their resources with individuals from their same background for material gain shared by all.

This entry is significant because it describes how marginalized people can prosper despite the discrimination they endure and, even more importantly, are able to enhance their financial gain. The Black social economy pushes against this understanding that the third sector can interact with the public and private sectors. In 2018, cases were compiled for the first time to define and to show through case study analysis the various organizations that make up the Black social economy (Hossein 2018).

This form of the Black social economy is termed solidarity economics, the solidarity economy or the social economy: people working in solidarity with one another and profiting financially in communities deprived of substantial political and economic resources. Men and women around the world engage in these political economy strategies as a way to counter the barriers posed by racial capitalism, defined as the economic profit whites receive from exploiting the labour of Black individuals (Robinson 1983) and to make more equitable economies for all.

12.1 DEFINING THE BLACK POLITICAL ECONOMY

Put simply, the Black political economy can be defined as the concerted attempts of Black people to advance their political and economic status. Black intellectuals such as Carter G. Woodson, W.E.B. DuBois, E. Franklin Frazier and Harold Cruse believed that African Americans would be better served by focusing on the enhancement of their economic, rather than political, power (Tauheed 2008, 693). However, African American scholars have often lamented their lack of political rights, out of the belief that these rights would result in an improved quality of life. The Black political economy emphasizes both political and economic gains simultaneously. In fact, the pursuit of economic power is a political act. By engaging in the solidarity economy, such as mutual aid, individuals have benefited themselves and their communities financially, but have also indicated their power to challenge political and economic barriers.

This point leads to the question: How can people of African descent pursue these political and economic goals when they constantly must combat political and economic discrimination? Voter suppression is a growing problem for Black voters in elections worldwide. Discrimination is also still prevalent today in banking, financial, real estate, and other industries. As a result, some people have difficulty in gaining access to credit, loans, mortgages, and other fiscal resources. Philosopher Charles W. Mills once discussed the presence of a 'political, moral, and epistemological' racial contract that has often relegated African Americans to an inferior status (Mills 1997, 9). Throughout history, individuals, corporations, and other entities reaped political and economic benefits while at the same time denying an equal status to people of African descent. The denial of equal status is rather common in all racially structured societies. For instance, in countries such as Australia and India, respectively, Aborigine and Dalit citizens are members of their nation's 'untouchable' classes, at the bottom of their respective racial caste systems. Because they endure vehement discrimination on a constant basis, they must find innovative ways to improve their political and economic plight. For instance, Curtis Haynes and Jessica Gordon Nembhard (1999) examined the presence and effectiveness of cooperative economic efforts in impoverished American inner-city communities. As a way to enhance their financial wealth, these individuals and others throughout the diaspora engage in the collaborative efforts outlined in the next section. However, the discriminated peoples engaging in cooperative endeavours also involves risks, as Jessica Gordon Nembhard (2014), author of *Collective Courage: A History of African American Cooperative Economic Thought and Practice*, discusses the great risks that African Americans took when engaging in cooperative endeavours during and after their enslavement.

12.2 THE PRACTICE OF THE SOCIAL AND SOLIDARITY ECONOMY

The social and solidarity economy (SSE) encompasses organizations and enterprises that seek to accomplish both economic and social goals, encourage cooperative relationships that build solidarity among participants, and allow participants to have an equal say in how the cooperative enterprise operates. Examples of SSE endeavours include, but are not limited to, cooperative financial structures, mutual women's aid groups, and self-help groups (see entry 3, 'Contemporary Understandings'). The United Nations Inter-Agency Task Force on Social and Solidarity Economy (UNTFSSE) educates the public about social and solidarity economic endeavours that result in economic, social, environmental, and political development.

One example of the Black social economy is ROSCAs. Throughout the world, women and men participate in ROSCAs, also known as money pools, giving circles and *sou-sous*. Through ROSCAs, individuals are able to save money, pool resources, allocate money to each other, purchase necessities, and increase wealth. These organizations allow groups of people to work in solidarity with each other as a method to reap increased returns. These practices constitute the very essence of mutual aid because men and women work together to aid themselves and others who they trust in their networks. ROSCAs have been particularly useful in countries with either few banks and financial institutions, or hostile banking institutions.

Table 12.1   Different names of ROSCA in different regions or countries

Name	Region or country	Name	Region or country
equp or *idir*	Ethiopia	*sandooq*	Sudan
higgler	Jamaica	*gama'yia*	Egypt
susu	Ghana	*cheetu*	Sri Lanka
sol or *main*	Haiti	*chits*	India
hagbad or *ayuto*	Somalia	*community*	Pakistan
restourne	Congo	*hui*	Vietnam
jangui	Cameroon	*arisan*	Indonesia
esusu or *ajo*	Nigeria	*jou*	Japan
itega	Kenya	*kye*	Korea
tontines	francophone West Africa	*esusu*	West Africa

Source: Hossein (forthcoming).

So, how do these ROSCAs work? Every month, each person contributes the same amount of money. One group member receives the untaxed funds which are referred to as the 'hand' (Hossein 2018, 2013). Thus, they allow members to avoid banking fees, loan interest, and bureaucracy. After each group member has received funds, the group then decides whether any changes need to occur in terms of the composition of the group, the amount of funds contributed, and so on. The monthly, bi-weekly, or weekly investments may be small or large, but must be made for an allotted period of time. The group selects a treasurer who collects the funds, selects the dates that funds will be distributed (unless members have requested that they receive their hand on a certain date), and determines who will contribute what amount. Members also have the option of doubling their contribution and receiving two hands in one cycle. A 'fund manager' then distributes the hand to a different contributor every month until the pool is empty (Hossein forthcoming).

ROSCAs are used in different forms in countries around the world. The term and practice originated in West Africa, where the Yoruban term for this type of programme is *esusu* and refers to the savings accumulated from the pooled money of several people. In many countries, ROSCAs are the only method for individuals to profit from their monetary investments. Some of the different names are highlighted in Table 12.1.

In the Americas, these groups are referred to as the Mexican *tanda*, Peruvian *pander*, Bahamian *asousous*, Bajan *lodge*, Haitian *main* or *sol*, Trinidadian *susu*, Dominican Republic *sociedad*, Guyana *box hand*, or the South African *stokvel*.

12.3   POLITICIZED MICROFINANCE AND FEMINISM

'Politicized microfinance' is a term that was developed to characterize the political significance of solidarity economic strategies. Microfinance is a banking system used mostly by poor and lower-income individuals who lack access to established banking systems. Politicized microfinance occurs when people make their own independent banking systems that are not encumbered by state regulations. It comes in two forms. The first is primarily used in Caribbean countries such as Trinidad and Guyana when people pool their resources and provide a hand to each member. In these countries, ROSCAs provide enough funds for individuals to open their own businesses in some cases. In the other form, politicized microfinance enlightens people about the discrimination endured by people of African descent in countries such as Haiti, Jamaica and Grenada (Hossein 2016, 12). For example, in Jamaica, the Rastafari community developed a cooperative form of the economy after being ostracized by other Jamaicans who rejected their way of life.

This concept has also been discussed as an example of contemporary feminism. ROSCAs and other solidarity economic methods empower women of colour financially, but serve an even greater purpose: they allow these women to enhance their economic capital (at times in communities where they lack political influence). In *Politicized Microfinance: Money, Power, and Violence in the Black Americas*, Professor Caroline Shenaz Hossein (2016) discusses the challenges that marginalized women encounter when seeking assistance from financial institutions. Many of these women reside in communities that are not only racist but patriarchal as well. Because of the obstacles they encounter when seeking to utilize their countries' financial establishments, money pools and ROSCAs provide a beneficial alternative offering shared resources. Female participants receive a sense of autonomy in addition to tools for financial wealth in countries that deprive women of equal rights. These problems are exacerbated for women of colour because many rely heavily on their male family members for their own and their children's subsistence. In some situations, women of colour are forced to flee abusive relationships. When seeking independence and safety for themselves and their children, they benefit from solidarity economic initiatives that allow them to amass the funds necessary to take care of themselves and their families. By pooling their money with allies, they are able to bypass banks that historically have refused to lend money to women from their racial, immigrant, and/or class backgrounds.

Although they are engaging in feminist work by working collectively to empower themselves and other women, many of these women do not refer to themselves as feminists. The poor women who utilize these methods believe that they are simply doing what is necessary for their survival and self-sufficiency. In the United States, Mississippi civil rights activist Fannie Lou Hamer provides an example of a Black feminist who influenced the residents of her community to pool their resources to enhance their political and economic capital. Hamer lived in poverty all of her life but developed the Freedom Farm Cooperative (FFC) in 1969. She purchased 40 acres of land with the assistance of a charitable donation in Ruleville, Mississippi, and used it to empower her community.

This collective allowed poor Black farmworkers in Mississippi to work on and own land in a state that once had laws prohibiting Black Mississippians from doing so. Because land ownership had always been equated with wealth and influence, the 1865 Black Codes (and an environment of terror) placed strict restrictions on Black land ownership. Eventually, the members of the FFC purchased a total of 640 acres and 'provided a crucial means for local farmers to have some sense of financial and even political autonomy' (Blain 2021, 121–2). Thus, Hamer provided a means for her neighbours (most of whom lived in poverty) to gain financial resources, she empowered her community, and engaged in feminist political work without referring to it as such.

This entry has provided an analysis of the Black social economy in which people of the African diaspora have utilized mutual aid as a form of politicized economic cooperation in response to their business and social exclusion. People of African descent have benefited immensely from the SSE. Women of African descent in both urban and rural communities have especially benefited from cooperatives, in particular informal ones known as ROSCAs, that have allowed them to escape oppressive family situations, support their families, and achieve financial gain. Despite their circumstances in oppressive societies, cooperatives reveal that poor people can always find innovative ways to empower themselves.

REFERENCES

Blain, Keisha N. 2021. *Until I Am Free: Fannie Lou Hamer's Enduring Message to America*. Boston, MA: Beacon Press.
Gordon Nembhard, Jessica. 2014. *Collective Courage: A History of African American Cooperative Economic Thought and Practice*. University Park, PA: Penn State University Press.
Haynes, Curtis, and Jessica Gordon Nembhard. 1999. 'Cooperative Economics: A Community Revitalization Strategy'. *Review of Black Political Economy* 27 (1): 47–71. https://doi.org/10.1007/s12114-999-1004-5.
Hossein, Caroline Shenaz. 2013. 'The Black Social Economy: Perseverance of Banker Ladies in the Slums'. *Annals of Public and Cooperative Economics* 84 (4): 423–42. https://doi.org/10.1111/apce.12022.
Hossein, Caroline Shenaz. 2016. *Politicized Microfinance: Money, Power, and Violence in the Black Americas*. Toronto: University of Toronto Press.
Hossein, Caroline Shenaz. 2018. *The Black Social Economy in the Americas: Exploring Diverse Community-Based Alternative Markets*. New York: Palgrave Macmillan.
Hossein, Caroline Shenaz. Forthcoming. *The Banker Ladies*. Toronto: University of Toronto Press.
Mills, Charles W. 1997. *The Racial Contract*. Ithaca, NY: Cornell University Press.
Robinson, Cedric W. 1983. *Black Marxism: The Making of the Black Radical Tradition*. Chapel Hill, NC: University of North Carolina Press.
Tauheed, Linwood F. 2008. 'Black Political Economy in the 21st Century: Exploring the Interface of Economics and Black Studies: Addressing the Challenge of Harold Cruse'. *Journal of Black Studies* 38 (5): 692–730. https://doi.org/10.1177/0021934707310292.

13. The commons
Anabel Rieiro

INTRODUCTION

The concept of the commons or common goods has been incorporated into economic theory – along with those of public goods and private goods – largely due to the contributions of Elinor Ostrom in 1990 who, based on the empirical study of different forms of self-government that manage resources for common use, made its importance and specificity visible.

The debate has not ceased, and different re-elaborations have been carried out, proposing to take up the commons as a type of social relations through which people can propose shared goals and the mechanisms to achieve them, thus generating modes of existence with certain autonomy from the market and the state, rather than as a good or resource.

The heterogeneous experiences of self-management and self-organization centred on the production of the commons are beginning to arouse the interest of several authors as new ways to re-think antagonisms and social transformation. From this point of view, approaching the debate on the commons from the perspective of the social and solidarity economy (SSE) could help to re-politicize and re-think the role that the commons could play in social change.

13.1 THE COMMONS AS OPPORTUNITY OR TRAGEDY

The origin of the discussion on the commons can be traced back to the age-old discussion on individual behaviour and its collective/social effects. The concept, however, evolved over the last half-century, starting with Garret Hardin's provocative article 'The Tragedy of the Commons' published in *Science* in 1968. The article discusses how the sum of rational behaviour at the individual level can result in irrational results at the societal level. Using an example of herders using a common pasture, it shows how everyone is driven to 'increase their livestock without limit, in a world that is limited' (Hardin 1968, 1244). Overgrazing, which results in the destruction of the rangeland, is the metaphor through which the tragedy of the commons is analysed. Hardin's central argument about the commons can be found in a wide range of authors who analyse the particular relationship between individual choices/strategies and emergent collective outcomes.

The prisoner's dilemma – which comes from game theory – is perhaps the most widely used example to illustrate the difficulty of cooperation between rational and selfish human beings. It shows that, even if the players have all the information they need to be able to decide their strategy, because of the lack of communication between them, the decisions made produce the least desired outcome for both players. Olson (1965) even analyses this dilemma in mutually supportive groups, that is, groups with self-recognized collective interests that still fail to deploy group-wide action to achieve the common benefit. What causes rational individuals to act against their group's interests? This could happen, according to the author, because some individuals – 'free riders' – feel little incentive to voluntarily cooperate with the effort or cost involved in collective action since once the group goal is achieved, they will benefit from it anyway, whether they have participated or not. The paradox of collective action, then – similar to the tragedy of the commons proposed by Hardin – would be that if all individuals act in the same way, no one ends up benefiting.

Elinor Ostrom, winner of the 2009 Nobel Prize in Economics, warned in 1990 how, faced with the dilemmas posed by theories of rational action, political analysts, instead of re-thinking the incentives necessary for cooperative behaviour, end up proposing solutions that are external to the commons. According to her, some political analysts recommend that the state should control most natural resources to avoid their destruction, while others suggest that their privatization will solve the problem. What is observed around the world, however, is that neither the state nor the market has been successful in getting individuals to sustain long-term, productive use of natural resource systems (Ostrom 1990, 25–6).

Ostrom takes up the dilemmas posed by Hardin, Olson and others to develop a theory of collective action, aiming to explain how individuals, using a common pool resource, can circumvent several of the problems outlined above by building capacities, agreements, binding contracts and cooperative strategies that enable them to effectively direct and manage those resources.

With her theory of collective action, Ostrom systematized and empirically analysed diverse institutions of self-organization and self-management of common-pool resources (CPRs). Reviewing the theoretical models that methodologically start from individual rationality, she demonstrated that under certain circumstances individuals could generate their own mechanisms of regulation in a collective and socially rational manner. The approach to concrete cases allowed her to identify, from the contradictions of the processes studied, how in some contexts it was possible to appropriate common goods through different agreements. For Ostrom, institutional provision, credible commitments and mutual supervision would explain to a large extent the creation of particular institutionalized ways of collective action with the capacity to manage CPRs sustainably. Through the different experiences analysed, she identified some central principles to generate institutionally strong collective designs for CPR users. These would be: clearly defined boundaries of the CPR; congruence between the resource environment and its governance structure or rule; effective agreements between resource appropriators; effective supervision and monitoring; gradual sanctions in case of non-compliance with agreements; low-cost and easy-to-access mechanisms for conflict resolution; and recognition of the right of the resource appropriators to self-govern; and in the case of larger CPRs, rules organized and enforced through multiple layers of nested enterprises.

Based on these dynamics of commons management, Ostrom proposed to re-think public policy. 'If the theories used in political science do not include the possibility of self-organized collective action, then the importance of a court system used by self-organized groups to monitor and enforce contracts will not be recognized' (Ostrom 2001, 37). Furthermore, Ostrom warns that public policies based on the notion that all appropriators of CPRs are incompetent, and therefore rules should be imposed on them, may end up destroying the institutional capital that has been accumulated over years of experience in particular locations. CPRs include both natural and man-made systems, emphasizing the resources or assets that are manageable by self-organized groups. Ostrom's research findings and analysis on the governance of the commons have been taken up by renowned economists such as the French economist Jean Tirole (2017), who has written his latest book on 'the economics of the commons', but

Ostrom's work has also become an indispensable reference in other disciplinary fields, thus feeding new re-working and problematizations.

Finally, Ostrom in her studies on the existence of different self-organization ways to manage resources for common use did not deny the validity of theories formulated by the tragedy of the commons, which is based on individual rational actions. But she questioned their capacity for generalization and their universal character. In this sense, Ostrom suggested that common goods are not antagonistic to capital, but can coexist with public goods and privately owned goods.

13.2 THE COMMONS FROM AN ANTAGONISTIC POINT OF VIEW

With the neoliberal advance from the 1990s onwards, different European and North American authors highlighted different forms of resistance, re-appropriation and recreation of the social relationship for the sustainability of collective life and nature. They reworked the debate on the commons from a critical and antagonistic perspective to capitalism. Within the SSE sector – especially in the cooperative sector – the sustainability crisis has been taken up. Many SSE organizations support the Sustainable Development Goals of the 2030 Agenda. However, those considering the commons as antagonistic to capitalism started to question the approach of these SSE organizations.

The antagonistic approach to the commons proposed a shift of the approach to the commons from one centred around contradictions between capital and labour (based on the social relations structured on the relation with the means of production) to one centred around the contradictions between capital and life (based on the social relations resulting from the relation with the means of production, but also from the modes of existence). It highlighted capitalist accumulation as a historical process that puts the very sustainability of life at risk. Through analysis of the material and symbolic reproduction of life – that is, the life of humans and the whole environment – it explained capitalist accumulation as the development of strong individualistic rationality that destroys community networks and generates a tendency toward inequality. And it argued that capitalist accumulation and expansion are sustained by processes of commodification of nature, enclosure, dispossession and privatization of essential goods.

For instance, Silvia Federici explains that the commons existed a long time ago, and the contemporary world retains many elements based on them. These 'communalizing practices that are created in emergency situations do not disappear without trace … they are part of our collective memory and our cultural symbols' (Federici 2020, 27–8). Federici argues that capitalism requires the destruction of communal goods and relations in order to develop its process of large-scale accumulation. One of the key examples is the enclosures that allowed the expropriation of English farmers from their land and commons, establishing the conditions for capitalist development in 16th century Europe. It was a starting point of the historical process of accumulation that continues to act today, advancing on the means of production and also modes of existence. Federici pointed to both the separation of the producer from the means of production (to generate the wage society) and the re-functionalization of the means of existence (reproductive work to the sphere of 'the private'), as the beginning of two accumulation processes of the market society.

In the same vein, Dardot and Laval (2015) argue that what we are experiencing today is a tragedy of the uncommon, highlighting the contradiction created by the advance of capital over life. From a political economy perspective, they point out that the notion of common goods, although it makes visible the inadequacy of the public–private dichotomy, is a concept based on the neoclassical tradition since it separates the economic from the political. In this sense, Dardot and Laval propose to use the term 'commons' (instead of 'common goods') to emphasize the political use and meaning. To them, the commons is the political principle that defends the right of public/private non-appropriability through social practices and ways of life based on self-governance. The co-obligation of men and women engaged in public activity creates alternative practices to those practices based on the principle of competition and the dynamics of privatization of all spheres of life. In this way, the commons has a counter-hegemonic political movement to neoliberal rationality and its logics of accumulation, privatization and enclosure.

Hardt and Negri (2009), like Dardot and Laval, take up the commons from a political perspective. They argue that different experiences can lead to an overall process in which the multitude (that is, all those who labour and produce under capitalism, which is not restricted to those associated with the traditional industrial working class but includes those with reproductive roles, the poor, and the unemployed and underemployed) learns the art of self-government and invents durable forms of democratic organization. Hardt and Negri (2009, 10) understand 'the commons' as both the common wealth of the material world and the results of social production necessary for interaction and further production such as knowledge, languages, codes, information, affects, and so on. Their idea of the commons does not place humanity as something separate from nature. They focus on practices of interaction, care and cohabitation. Hardt and Negri criticize that neoliberal government policies have established power over life and naturalized the argument that the only possibility of decision-making lies in the public–private dichotomy. They proposed a counter-argument that there is also the commons where there is a production of the subjectivity of individuals who resist power while not losing sight of their own individuality.

While for Hardt and Negri the commons is understood mainly from the spontaneity of the multiple forms of connection, Dardot and Laval agree with Ostrom on the importance of creating a system of rules and norms that could institute new practices and forms of government. Further, they argue for the importance of implementing ways of radical democracy and direct participation beyond the representational logic on which delegative democracies are based. For her part, Federici (2020) suggests a bias in Hardt and Negri's approach which conceptualizes the commons only from their views on the transformations of labour from Fordist (material labour) to post-Fordist (immaterial labour), without managing to fully incorporate the spheres of reproduction and care.

Federici has also a critical view of the lack of practical advice on how the multitude wins the struggle. According to her, Hardt and Negri just urged patience, hoping for the event that will secure the multitude 'becoming prince', not offering any concrete practical advice to those in the movements or struggles for the commons. For Federici, winning the struggle for the commons demands the time-consuming, yet indispensable, work that is needed for organizing and reproducing what are otherwise short-lived, sensational moments of struggle.

From the perspective of seeing the commons as antagonistic to capital, the commons, as a free association of self-governed people with the aim of sustaining life, can either become a means to fight for a more cooperative society, or become self-enclosed or re-functionalized by capitalism. The fact that the commons are not fully capitalist does not mean that they are anti-capitalist; far from being pure entities, they are produced, reproduced, updated. And the commons build up different perspectives of struggle on a daily basis.

In Latin American practices and discourses that understand coloniality and modernity as two sides of the same coin, the production of the commons is mainly based on the practices of indigenous and peasant communalities. In this concept of the commons, autonomy is highlighted to defend heterogeneity.

In this sense, with the study of the Ch'ixi world of Bolivia, Rivera-Cusicanqui (2018) explains how heterogeneity of conceptions about space and time coexist in the present, different from the neoliberal linear proposal. The spatiotemporal multiplicity found in the Ch'ixi world enables different cosmovisions and forms of self-government. Rivera-Cusicanqui also highlights the importance of understanding 'the indigenous' from the current heterogeneity that characterizes its communitarian component, neither from a folkloric-homogeneous vision nor as a pre-capitalist economy. According to Rivera-Cusicanqui, it is from the daily plots and their collective memory – strongly orally transmitted – that the moments of Andean insurgency can be understood.

On the other hand, Gladys Tzul Tzul points out the power of Guatemalan indigenous governance where decisions are produced through deliberation and consent by the assembly. 'These are concrete and situated historical-social relations, which through a set of strategies and practices of the communal organization seek to conserve, share, defend and recover the territory from which to deploy the material means for the reproduction of life' (Tzul Tzul 2018, 15). Everyday life finds in these communities formal spaces for decision-making by the assembly, but also non-assembly spaces for meeting, celebration and work from where the commons is inhabited and produced. From the study of these indigenous communities, Tzul Tzul shows the difference between politics centred on the citizen/individual and the politics that emanates from community networks and the production of the commons.

While the wefts of relationships and social ties sustained over time are clearly visible in indigenous, and peasant communities in their way of (self-)regulating coexistence, as Gutiérrez (2015, 22) tells us, they are also present outside of them. 'They function below and partially outside of the state and capital accumulation, they have preserved and recreated colourful associative networks for the preservation and reproduction of life. Such wefts are the product of diverse conversations and coordination intertwined in an autonomous manner, establishing their own ends, scopes and activities' (Gutiérrez 2015, 110). According to Gutiérrez, community networks would be constellations of social relations – not harmonious or idyllic, but full of tensions and contradictions – that manage to operate in a coordinated and/or cooperative manner in a more or less stable way over time, with multiple concrete objectives to satisfy the needs that make for the material and symbolic reproduction of human and non-human life.

In summary, the expansive creativity of living labour and the production of the commons emerges both from social relations generated within capitalism and from experiences that inhabit the territory from multiple anticolonial, decolonial or transcolonial cosmovisions. From Latin America – as a colonial context – the politics of the commons is taken up again in terms of the 'reproduction of life', recognizing a multiplicity of interdependent relations that human beings produce between humans and with nature in order to reproduce our ways of life. In this sense, rather than proposing the commons as a destiny, they are taken up as a seedbed of intermittent alternative 'modes': autonomous meanings that can strengthen their actions in moments of deepening social antagonism to capitalism.

13.3 THE COMMONS AND THE SOCIAL AND SOLIDARITY ECONOMY

The great transformation that explains how today's society has become a 'market society' (Polanyi 1989) by basing its economy solely on a liberal conception can be complemented by the vision of the commons as the new forms of capitalist exploitation affect bodies and territories. In this way, a heteronomous dynamic is configured, characterized by the enclosure and progressive privatization of all areas of life, with new cycles of appropriation of both the means of production and modes of existence. Making visible and taking up the different ways of producing the commons allows us to tune in to the creative and autonomous capacity that in turn enables processes of politicization and with them new possible modes of subjectification. This autonomous project historically accompanies the experiences of the social and solidarity economy and can therefore generate new synergies and re-elaborations.

The commons, as forms and modes of self-organization, can coexist with, resist or contest neoliberal logic. The production of the commons is shaped in diverse contexts through the defence, recovery or re-appropriation of goods, material and/or symbolic. There is a great heterogeneity of the commons today, both in cities and in rural areas, which can be created from tangible human needs (housing, food, work, and so on) and/or environmental needs (defence of goods such as water, soil, seeds and territories as a whole), as well as from intangible needs (creation of free software, cooperative digital platforms, knowledge, cultural creations, among others).

Re-thinking the SSE, in the face of the multiple processes of dispossession that are affecting territories, makes visible new community and solidarity meanings on which alliances can be built. These meanings are not limited to institutionalized forms of cooperation such as cooperatives, organizations and formalized networks, but also include strongly territorialized communities, such as indigenous communities, and even virtual communities, as in the case of free software and different digital platforms.

The SSE has been developed and institutionalized as an alternative socioeconomic form to both the market economy and the public economy. In this sense, as proposed by Ostrom, it has historically demonstrated that there are collective capacities that, through self-organization, can manage different projects in common without leading to overexploitation or misuse of resources. The entities traditionally recognized within the SSE sector, that have managed to produce, distribute and consume in an associative way, generally became institutionalized as alternatives in contexts where the economy is based on the market. Thus, mutual aid practices, in many cases, are consolidating and adopting classic formats within the SSE, such as cooperatives, which are recognized – by Ostrom and several others – as empirical institutions of self-organization.

In the face of theories that explain the economy solely through rational, competitive and utilitarian individuals acting within the framework of self-regulated markets, both the experiences of the commons and the SSE share some common aspects:

1. They focus on a relational economy, strongly supported by the concept of care and human interdependence and interdependence with nature.
2. They highlight the inadequacy of the public–private dichotomy.

In this sense, the dialogue between entities that make up the SSE and experiences of the commons can revitalize practices and theories on social transformation, as follows:

1. It highlights the importance of the relational and community component, within the economy in particular, and the reproduction of life in general.
2. It provides singular experiences of combining economic and social objectives explicitly in the same project. The SSE – such as the development of almost two centuries of the cooperative movement – provides concrete examples of producing the commons that are based on associativism and self-government.
3. It points out new connections and openings to multidimensional relational compositions and multiscale alliances between the SSE and the commons based on the capital–life tension.
4. It breaks down some productivist biases that make invisible some essential work for reproduction, broadening the conceptions of wage work to the integral work that allows sustaining life (paid and unpaid).
5. It highlights new dimensions such as care among humans and care about the environment.
6. It elaborates on the principle of democracy and self-management.

It can be concluded that the discourse on the antagonistic nature of the commons can become a renewed impetus for politicization within the different forms of the SSE. It helps to revitalize visions of cooperation and strengthen the SSE's potential in the context of neoliberalism.

REFERENCES

Dardot, Pierre and Christian Laval. 2015. *Commun: Essai Sur la Révolution au XXIe Siècle*. Paris: La Découverte.
Federici, Silvia. 2020. *Reencantar el Mundo. El Feminismo y la Política de los Comunes*. Buenos Aires: Tinta limón.
Gutiérrez, Raquel. 2015. *Horizonte Comunitario-Popular. Antagonismo y Producción de lo Común en América Latina*. Puebla: Instituto de Ciencias Sociales y Humanidades-BUAP.
Hardin, Garret. 1968. 'The Tragedy of the Commons.' *Science* 162: 1243–8.
Hardt, Michael and Antonio Negri. 2009. *Commonwealth*. Cambridge, MA: Belknap Press of Harvard University Press.
Olson, Mancur. 1965. *The Logic of Collective Action: Public Goods and the Theory of Groups*. Cambridge, MA: Harvard University Press.
Ostrom, Elinor. 1990. 'Reflections on the Commons.' *Governing the Commons: The Evolution of Institutions for Collective Action*. Cambridge: Cambridge University Press.
Ostrom, Elinor. 2001. 'Reformulating the Commons.' In *Protecting the Commons: A Framework for Resource Management in the Americas*, edited by Joanna Burger, Elinor Ostrom, Richard Norgaard, David Policansky and Bernard D. Goldstein, 17–41. Washington, DC: Island Press.
Polanyi, Karl. 1989. *La Gran Transformación. Crítica del Liberalismo Económico*. Madrid: La Piqueta.
Rivera-Cusicanqui, Silvia. 2018. *Un Mundo Ch'ixi es Posible. Ensayos Desde un Presente en Crisis*. Buenos Aires: Tinta Limón.
Tirole, Jean. 2017. 'Economics for the Common Good.' *Economics for the Common Good*. Princeton University Press.
Tzul Tzul, Gladys. 2018. *Sistemas de Gobierno Comunal Indígena. Mujeres Tramas de Parentesco en Chineq'ena'*. México: Instituto Amaq'.

PART II

ACTORS AND ORGANIZATIONS

14. African American solidarity economics and distributive justice

Jessica Gordon-Nembhard and Ajowa Nzinga Ifateyo

INTRODUCTION

Racial capitalism and neoliberal economics create huge gulfs between the 'haves' (mostly white males) and the 'have nots' (people of African descent, indigenous peoples, immigrants, and other people of colour) with increasing wealth inequality that threatens human survival, undermines human dignity and is destroying Mother Earth. The World Social Forums and solidarity economy movements started in the late 20th century have developed out of this need to create and rediscover values-based humane economic models that recognize existing solidarity practices and deliver distributive justice to all (see also entry 10, 'Origins and Histories').

Solidarity economics and practices include cooperatives, collective and/or nonprofit businesses, community dollars or local currencies, bartering, gifting, and/or a process where work is exchanged, fair trade, as well as regional federations or cooperative regional associations that may include multi-stakeholder cooperatives and enterprises (US Solidarity Economy Network 2022). There are many ways that social and solidarity economy (SSE) practices enable distributive justice, equalizing both the benefits and the burdens of human existence and social reproduction. Human beings in every era of history, and in every part of the world, practise some form of solidarity economics, mutual aid and economic cooperation. These are strategies and practices older than capitalism and mercantilism, yet they have been consumed by and overwhelmed by capitalist practices, especially over the last few hundred years. This entry summarizes ways that cooperative economics, especially worker co-ops, contributes to distributive justice. As an example, the entry explores ways that African American mutual aid and economic cooperation (even during enslavement and American apartheid segregation) provide some measure of social and economic development as well as distributive justice to some of the most marginalized communities in the United States of America (USA).

14.1 COOPERATIVES: BENEFITS AND IMPACTS

Cooperative businesses are community-owned private enterprises that combine consumers with owners, and buyers with sellers, in a democratic structure (Gordon Nembhard 2014). Cooperatives are member-based and member-controlled, values-based enterprises (see entry 17, 'Cooperatives and Mutuals'). In worker cooperatives, the workers are known as worker-owners, owners or employee-owners. In consumer and housing cooperatives, they are known as member-owners, or simply members. However they are referred to, members of cooperatives put energy and equity into a cooperative enterprise. If the cooperatives are successful, they provide a return: sometimes annual dividends or patronage refunds (often distributed upon exit from membership); and sometimes the return takes the form of job security and living wages and benefits, or reduced costs of products and services.

Individual cooperatives decide democratically how much of the surplus should be allocated to members and how much is unallocated or retained in the business. Because of the democratic nature of cooperatives, distribution occurs in an equitable fashion, which places the wealth generated from the business into the hands of the owner-members (and sometimes other stakeholders). This means that cooperatives as a business are also a democratic mechanism for wealth creation (Gordon Nembhard 2008, 2014, 2015). Cooperatives are a form of communal, joint and democratic ownership of a business whose equity is an asset that can contribute to an individual member's wealth portfolio in addition to group wealth. Cooperatives have enabled people who are exploited, asset-stripped and left out of the mainstream economy to provide affordable, quality goods and services, generate jobs, create income, stabilize their communities, accumulate some assets, and at the same time be family- and community-friendly (Gordon Nembhard 2015, 2014). In addition, cooperatives tend to survive longer than other small businesses (Borzaga and Galera 2012; Logue and Yates 2005; Williams 2007), providing greater longevity than many traditional businesses.

Cooperatives address market failure and the negligence of profit-maximizing investor-owned businesses and corporations, as well as the lack of will in the public sector, to meet the needs of people neglected by investor-owned, profit-maximizing companies (Borzaga and Galera 2012; Gordon Nembhard 2015). Cooperative and collective ownership enable the provision, for example, of affordable healthy and organic foods, or even any kind of groceries in urban food deserts; of rural electricity or other utilities in sparsely populated areas; or enable access to credit and banking services, affordable housing and markets for culturally sensitive goods and arts. Meeting member needs rather than maximizing profits on investment is the major purpose of a cooperative business.

Collectively and cooperatively owned enterprises often not only provide economic stability, but also develop many types of human and social capital: skills, institutional knowledge and organized groups of people (Shipp 2000; Gordon Nembhard 2014; Borzaga and Galera 2012). Cooperative members acquire a variety of general business and industry-specific skills. They also develop leadership and team-building skills. The workers or members learn first-hand what democracy is, because they vote on issues of major importance to the business, or a representative they elected votes on policies that speak to their needs.

Worker cooperatives are often established to meet needs in a community such as lack of childcare or eldercare; or to save a company that is being sold off, abandoned or closed down; or to start a company that exemplifies workplace democracy and collective management. Worker-owned businesses offer economic security, income and wealth generation, and democratic economic participation to employees, as well as provide meaningful and decent jobs and environmental sustainability to communities. Workers form cooperatives to jointly own and manage a business themselves, to create employment because of race- and/or gender- or sexuality-based discrimination, or immigration status, to stabilize employment, make policy and share the profits. Many worker-owned cooperatives, in particular, increase productivity and increase industry standards in wages and benefits, as well as provide self-management or teamwork between management and 'labour', job ladder opportunities, skill development and capacity building, job security, and general control over income and work rules (Gordon Nembhard 2004, 2014, 2015; Artz and Younjun 2011; Logue and Yates 2005). Women-owned catering and house cleaning cooperatives, for example, provide women with control over the hours of work, work rules, health and safety, benefits and income generation that allow them to balance home, family and work lives and own their own business. Worker cooperatives pay better wages, and give workers more pride in, ownership of and commitment to the business.

Because worker-owned businesses are community-based business anchors that distribute, recycle and multiply local expertise and capital within a community, cooperative businesses stabilize communities, unlike investor-owned private enterprises (Novkovic and Gordon Nembhard 2017). Often the cooperative that is formed to meet the needs in the community also helps to develop the community by hiring local residents, providing livable wages and utilizing local resources and businesses to partner with or support. This stabilizes the economy and makes other opportunities likely, and the community more attractive to people who live there and for new residents and businesses. Cooperatives generally have a social commitment to supporting other community and nonprofit projects in the community in which they are located. Borzaga and Galera (2012, 7) note that cooperatives tend to address the needs of communities, and 'should be regarded as collective problem solvers'. These problem-solvers use their expertise to participate in distributive justice, in their neighbourhoods and elsewhere.

In addition, the process of making decisions about the internal workings of a business and its external relations creates more engaged citizens and leaders with experience in advocating for themselves; experience that can be utilized and mobilized when advocating for policies that might involve distributive justice opportunities. Participation in cooperatives has also been found to encourage involvement in state and local government affairs (Gordon Nembhard 2014). This participation can be a means for the needs of the community to find a voice in the political arena (see also entry 49, 'Participation, Governance, Collective Action and Democracy').

14.2 AFRICAN AMERICAN COOPERATIVE ECONOMIC THOUGHT AND PRACTICE

One hundred and sixty-five years after the legal end of the African-enslaved economic system, African Americans have been denied distributive justice in a country which billed itself as a democracy, but which has not only failed to compensate African Americans for hundreds of years of unpaid labour, but has also shut them out of the economic opportunities to change their situation of being disproportionately poor (see also entry 10, 'Origins and Histories'). Racial capitalism – a system that benefits from exploitation of labour and pitting different racial and ethnic groups and genders against each other – and neoliberal economics exploit Black bodies, labour, skills, creativity and humanity, and undermine Black communities.[1] For those African Americans not institutionalized, unemployment and underemployment, and low wages among those employed, significantly curtail the ability of a substantial number to earn a decent living, to afford basic healthcare or education to ensure upward mobility, even as a handful of African Americans become wealthy or obtain the stature of President of the United States. The gap between African American well-being and wealth, and that of white Americans, is growing. According to McIntosh et al. (2020), for example:

> during the most recent economic downturn, median net worth declined by more for Black families (44.3 per cent decline from 2007 to 2013) than for White families (26.1 per cent decline). In fact, the ratio of White family wealth to Black family wealth is higher today than at the start of the century.

Black-owned businesses are particularly vulnerable (Washington 2021), and people of colour, especially African Americans, are suffering more long-term health, employment and other economic insecurities than the rest of the population during the COVID-19 pandemic (Andrew 2021; McIntosh et al. 2020).

In addition, African Americans remain disproportionately represented in the US prison system, the largest, and among the most ruthlessly exploitative and dehumanizing, in the world. A Black person can still too often be murdered on the streets, with the prosecution of their killers, be they police officers or armed white citizens, still doubtful (but more likely not to take place, or a guilty verdict not obtained if they are tried). A new study by the GBD 2019 Police Violence US Subnational Collaborators (2021), for example, finds that incidents of fatal police violence reported by the National Vital Statistics System are underreported by 59 per cent. Their analysis indicates that Black men are killed by police at a rate of three and a half times that of whites, instead of the rate of two and a half previously reported. In every year in which statistics were compiled, the rate of fatal police violence was higher for Black Americans than for white Americans.

Despite these challenges, in every era of history, and especially starting in the 20th century, African Americans have used economic cooperation and cooperative ownership to survive and thrive. Cooperative business ownership, cooperative financial institutions and co-op housing have been solutions to past economic challenges, such as debt peonage under Jim Crow, and lack of food, affordable housing and financial services during the Great Depression; and can be solutions to current and continuing economic challenges, as well as a vehicle for distributive justice. No specific data exists on how many African Americans participate in cooperatives, but their numbers are significant across a variety of cooperatives around the country, such as housing cooperatives, food and retail co-op stores, agricultural cooperatives, marketing co-ops, utility cooperatives, and so on; and there is a continuous history in the USA of African Americans creating many different kinds of mutual aid networks and cooperatives.

In the 20th century, Black leaders increasingly promoted the benefits of cooperatives. W.E.B. Du Bois had already been writing about Black economic cooperation in the late 1890s, and held a conference and published a book on Black cooperatives in 1907 (Du Bois 1907). For over 40 years he argued that a successful cooperative economy would better serve the common good (Gordon Nembhard 2014). George Schuyler, *Pittsburgh Courier* columnist, contended early in his career that co-ops were a better ownership strategy for Black advancement. He and cooperative and civil rights organizer Ella Jo Baker founded the Young Negroes' Co-operative League in 1930 to promote that strategy and train a new generation of Black cooperators. A. Philip Randolph, founder of the Brotherhood of Sleeping Car Porters (BSCP), along with Halena Wilson, president of the Ladies Auxiliary to the BSCP, connected the consumers' cooperative movement to the labour movement (Gordon Nembhard 2014). Throughout the Black reparations movement in the USA, leaders and organizations have argued that reparations money should include financing for Black cooperative development (Gordon Nembhard 2018; National African American Reparations Commission 2022; Movement for Black Lives 2022). African American economist Jeremiah Cotton in some way sums up this thought by rationalizing that Blacks should exercise 'community cooperation' since Blacks suffer common 'materialities' (Cotton 1992, 24).

In *Collective Courage*, Gordon Nembhard (2014) finds that African Americans have used cooperatives to survive depressions, economic exclusion, discrimination, marginalization and economic inequality. African Americans used mutual aid and economic cooperation because they did not have any wealth, or even own their own bodies during enslavement, and were often excluded from the best jobs and wealth accumulation even after emancipation; also because of Jim Crow segregation, apartheid and institutional racism. Gordon Nembhard documents over 162 legally incorporated cooperative enterprises owned by African Americans from the mid-1800s to the present. These housing cooperatives, credit unions, retail grocery and other stores, marketing cooperatives, farmers' markets, shared services cooperatives, health centres, craft co-ops, worker co-op factories, mills, construction companies, catering, house cleaning/ janitorial services, transportation services, and so on, were found in rural and urban areas throughout the United States (Gordon Nembhard 2014). Many were very successful and well sustained, and lasted for years. Others were successful at addressing the original problems they were created to address, and then no longer used. And many were thwarted and attacked by white competitors and white supremacist terrorists (Gordon Nembhard 2018, 2014).

Below we provide four examples from US history of the economic, social and distributive benefits, and other achievements, of Black co-ops: the National Federation of Colored Farmers in the 1920s; Cooperative Industries of Washington, DC in the 1930s; the North Carolina Council for Credit Unions and Associates in the 1930s–40s; and Cooperative Home Care Associates from the late 1980s to the present.

The National Federation of Colored Farmers (NFCF), founded in 1922, had a mission to stabilize African American farm ownership and improve farm living, using 'cooperative buying, production and marketing' (Hope 1940, 48). The cooperatives saved members 25 to 40 cents on the dollar for every truckload of goods they bought together. Members also shared machinery and trucks, and established livestock processing plants. The NFCF provided access to more favourable credit for its members, which significantly reduced their interest payments so that land and equipment purchases were possible. Over the ten years of the cooperative's existence most of the members, who started out as tenants and sharecroppers, became farm owners and were now less dependent on the government for relief or loans (Gordon Nembhard 2018).

During the Great Depression, Black women activists started the Northeast Self-Help Cooperative to put unemployed women to work in good manufacturing jobs in Washington, DC. After receiving grant funding, they opened as a hybrid co-op, Cooperative Industries of Washington DC, which combined a variety of industries such as sewing, canning, laundry services, shoe repair, broom, chair and handicrafts production, and beauty culture training, along with a farm. They established a co-op grocery store that sold fresh produce and chickens from the co-op farm, as well as other groceries, to members and their neighbours in the city. This co-op society consistently provided good jobs, especially for women (paying more than domestic service), as well as access to healthy food for the neighbourhood (Gordon Nembhard 2014).

Two Black education institutions in North Carolina, Bricks Rural Life School and Tyrrell County Training School, established cooperative networks in the 1930s and 1940s, providing co-op education to their students' families, and helping the families to establish farmers' cooperatives, equipment co-ops, credit unions, buyers' clubs and health insurance (Gordon Nembhard 2014). At first, they operated in relative isolation, but soon joined forces, and in 1939 organized the regional Eastern Carolina Council, a federation of Black North Carolinian cooperatives that worked closely with the credit union division of the state Department of Agriculture. In 1945 the Tyrrell County Training School held a co-op workshop co-sponsored by all the major co-op development groups in the state, the Eastern Carolina Council, and two Black colleges. The coalition established a state-wide organization called the North Carolina Council for Credit Unions & Associates to design a cooperative economic education curriculum and other materials to support Black co-op development throughout the state. The result was that Black credit unions increased from three to 98 between 1936 and 1948, and an additional 48 Black co-op enterprises were started in the state: nine consumer stores, 32 machinery co-ops, four 'curb markets', two health associations and a housing project (Gordon Nembhard 2014).

The final example is a pathbreaking worker cooperative in the South Bronx (NYC), the largest worker cooperative in the USA. Founded in 1985, Cooperative Home Care Associates (CHCA) was established to provide quality home care to clients by providing quality jobs for direct-care workers (CHCA 2022; Shipp 2000; Glasser et al. 2002; Schneider 2009). CHCA employs about 2000 mostly Latina and African American women as home care paraprofessionals, the majority of whom are worker-owners. CHCA provides benefits that are unprecedented for the traditionally low-wage and unstable home care industry: full-time consistent work, paid vacations and health insurance, training, job ladder mobility, retirement plans and union membership. This is another example of a cooperative that sets standards for wages, benefits, training and workplace democracy in a low-wage industry that traditionally does not provide any benefits, let alone full-time work (Gordon Nembhard 2014).

In sum, Gordon Nembhard (2014) finds that African Americans established cooperative enterprises often in response to market failure and exclusion, and created alternative economic solutions that not only enabled survival but also provided non-exploitative, democratic collective economic ownership and production, which led to meaningful profit-sharing and some level of individual and community self-determination. Many of the examples through history also show how essential access to high-quality cooperative economics and co-op business education was to the success of African American cooperatives and their communities.

African American cooperative ownership provides marginalized people with a chance to design and manage needed goods and services in culturally sensitive ways to benefit their families and communities. The African American cooperative movement combines retentions from early African mutual aid and self-help ideologies, and spiritual notions of communalism, with the need to survive but also to liberate themselves from their colonized and exploited experiences, and to create economic justice through economic democracy. Because racial capitalism has structural and long-term impacts on racial economic inequality, more economic democracy and economic justice are needed to address racial discrimination and exploitation. For these reasons, cooperatives are prime vehicles for addressing community needs, developing viable strategies, and implementing solutions that include democracy and equity. Deliberate development of cooperative ownership and other solidarity economic practices, with participation by those traditionally overlooked, can achieve distributive justice and create concrete and meaningful change in people's lives and their communities.

NOTE

1. By 'racial capitalism' we mean to emphasize the ways that capitalism and economic exploitation build on and utilize false notions of racial inferiority in order for capitalists to maintain their power over labour and others. The term 'racial capitalism' also serves to remind us that capitalism developed and flourished not just because of industrialization and gender discrimination, but also

because of anti-Blackness, colonialism and enslavement of Africans. For more details about the consequences of racial economic inequality in the USA, see Darity and Mullen (2020).

REFERENCES

Andrew, Scottie. 2021. 'Reparations for Slavery Could Have Reduced Covid-19 Transmission and Deaths in the US, Harvard Study Says.' CNN. https://www.cnn.com/2021/02/16/us/reparations-covid-black-americans-disparity-trnd/index.html.

Artz, Georgeanne and Younjun Kim. 2011. 'Business Ownership by Workers: Are Worker Cooperatives a Viable Option?' Iowa State University, Department of Economics. https://www.researchgate.net/publication/254425279_Business_Ownership_by_Workers_Are_Worker_Cooperatives_a_Viable_Option.

Borzaga, Carlo and Giulia Galera. 2012. 'Promoting the Understanding of Cooperatives For a Better World.' Euricse. https://www.euricse.eu/wp-content/uploads/2015/03/promoting-the-understanding-of-cooperatives-for-a-better-world-full.pdf.

CHCA (Cooperative Home Care Associates). 2022. 'About.' Cooperative Home Care Associates. 27 January. https://www.chcany.org/about.

Cotton, J. 1992. 'Towards a Theory and Strategy for Black Economic Development.' In *Race, Politics, and Economic Development: Community Perspectives*, edited by James Jennings, 11–32. London: Verso.

Darity, William A. and A. Kirsten Mullen. 2020. *From Here to Equality: Reparations for Black Americans in the Twenty-First Century*. Chapel Hill, NC: University of North Carolina Press.

Du Bois, William Edward Burghardt. 1907. *Economic Co-operation Among Negro Americans: Report of a Social Study Made by Atlanta University Under the Patronage of the Carnegie Institution of Washington, DC Together with the Proceedings of the 12th Conference for the Study of the Negro Problems, Held at Atlanta University, on Tuesday, May the 28th, 1907. No. 12*. Atlanta: Atlanta University Press.

GBD 2019 Police Violence US Subnational Collaborators. 2021. 'Fatal Police Violence by Race and State in the USA, 1980–2019: A Network Meta-Regression.' *The Lancet* 398 (10307): 1239–55. https://doi.org/10.1016/S0140-6736(21)01609-3.

Glasser, Ruth, Jeremy Brecher, Cooperative Home and System Center. 2002. *We Are the Roots: The Organizational Culture of a Home Care Cooperative*. Davis, CA: Center for Cooperatives, University of California.

Gordon Nembhard, Jessica. 2004. 'Non-Traditional Analyses of Cooperative Economic Impacts: Preliminary Indicators and a Case Study.' *Review of International Co-operation* 97 (1): 6–21.

Gordon Nembhard, Jessica. 2008. 'Asset Building Through Cooperative Business Ownership: Defining and Measuring Cooperative Economic Wealth.' University of Wisconsin Center for Cooperatives. 1 December. http://reic.uwcc.wisc.edu/discussion/papers/nembhard.pdf.

Gordon Nembhard, Jessica. 2014. *Collective Courage: A History of African American Cooperative Economic Thought and Practice*. University Park, PA: Pennsylvania State University Press.

Gordon Nembhard, Jessica. 2015. 'Understanding and Measuring the Benefits and Impacts of Co-operatives.' In *Co-operatives For Sustainable Communities: Tools to Measure Co-operative Impact and Performance*, edited by Leslie Brown, Chiara Corini, Jessica Gordon-Nembhard, Lou Hammond-Ketilson, Elizabeth Hicks, John McNamara, Sonja Novkovic, Daphne Rixon and Richard Simmons, 152–79. Ottawa and Saskatoon: Co-operatives and Mutuals Canada and Centre for the Study of Co-operatives (University of Saskatchewan).

Gordon Nembhard, Jessica. 2018. 'African American Cooperatives and Sabotage: The Case for Reparations.' *Journal of African American History* 103 (1–2): 65–90. https://doi.org/10.1086/696361.

Hope II, John. 1940. 'Rochdale Cooperation among Negroes.' *Phylon (1940–1956)* 1 (1): 39–52. https://doi.org/10.2307/271171.

Logue, J. and J. Yates. 2005. *Productivity in Cooperatives and Worker-Owned Enterprises: Ownership and Participation Make a Difference!* Geneva: International Labour Office.

McIntosh, Kriston, Emily Moss, Ryan Nunn and Jay Shambaugh. 2020. 'Examining the Black–White Wealth Gap.' Brookings. 27 February. https://www.brookings.edu/blog/up-front/2020/02/27/examining-the-black-white-wealth-gap/.
Movement for Black Lives. 2022. 'Policy Platforms: Vision for Black Lives.' Movement for Black Lives. https://m4bl.org/policy-platforms/.
National African American Reparations Commission (NAARC). 2022. 'What Is NAARC's 10-Point Reparations Plan?' NAARC. https://reparationscomm.org/reparations-plan/.
Novkovic, Sonja and Jessica Gordon Nembhard. 2017. 'Beyond the Economy: The Social Impact of Cooperatives.' *Cooperative Business Journal* Fall 2017: 12–22.
Schneider, Stu. 2009. 'Cooperative Home Care Associates.' Paper presented at Fair Work Conference.
Shipp, Sigmund C. 2000. 'Worker-Owned Firms in Inner-City Neighborhoods: An Empirical Study.' *Review of International Co-operation* 93 (1): 42–6.
US Solidarity Economy Network. 2022. 'U.S. Solidarity Economy Network.' https://ussen.org/.
Washington, Kemberley. 2021. 'Covid-19 Has Had a Disproportionate Financial Impact on Black Small Businesses.' Forbes Advisor. 3 June. https://www.forbes.com/advisor/personal-finance/covid19-financial-impact-on-black-businesses/.
Williams, Richard C. 2007. *The Cooperative Movement: Globalization from Below*. London: Ashgate Publishing Group.

15. Associations and associationalism
Bruno Frère and Laurent Gardin

INTRODUCTION

Many people still think of citizens' associations either as unrealistic utopias or as offering social or cultural services that neither the state nor the market wants to provide. This entry will define associationalism, showing that its project for society has never been a mere pipe dream, nor has it been confined to addressing poverty or to the socio-cultural sector. In the 19th century, an association between workers was thought of as an economic model. It was a relatively successful attempt to restore the economy to civil society via a serious political movement. Sometimes described as associationalist socialism, and sometimes as libertarian socialism (Frère 2009), this movement's goal was not so much the disappearance of all forms of political and economic coordination at a supra-local level, as the end of capitalism. Basically, it was less about replacing public action and more about replacing capitalism, which at the time was in rapid industrial expansion.

This entry first presents the emergence of associationalism in the 19th century by introducing Proudhon, its main theorist. This emergence rested on a few major ideas that are still quite easy to discern today in a range of civil society organisations: self-management, collective ownership of the means of production, political participation, and so on. In a second step, the entry tries to show how serious reflection on associationalist socialism cannot be separated from a question that was already crucial when it first emerged: What place should be given to the state, or to any form of collective political and economic organisation related to it? The entry shows how, by redefining state power in a federative and radically democratised way, associationalism can still provide an answer today.

The entry particularly focuses on why associationalism cannot be reduced to the idea of the third sector, social entrepreneurship or the charitable economy. And then it further describes the relationship that a radically democratised and federalised state might have with the associations that constitute it (see entry 49, 'Participation, Governance, Collective Action and Democracy'). Finally, by way of conclusion, this entry will try to show that if the associationalist project is to have a future at a time when some claim the end of ideologies, then it must avoid conceiving of social relations as devoid of conflict. Associationalism was born in the context of workers' struggles. If it is to endure today, then it must do so within the framework of a more global struggle: a struggle that opposes capitalism, the injustices it entails and all the neoliberal policies that support it by destroying more and more public and environmental goods.

15.1 ASSOCIATIONALISM AS MUTUALISM

The works of Pierre-Joseph Proudhon (e.g. 1846, 1851, 1857, 1860, 1863) are generally considered associationalism's founding texts, alongside those of certain other socialists such as

Pierre Leroux (Frère 2018). In the mid-19th century, this perceptive observer of working-class practices developed an economic project that he initially described as 'mutualism'. For the workers in various workshops at the time, mutualism involved training themselves in economic autonomy through mutual aid with a view to emancipating themselves, not only from the grip of the market but also from the state. Although Proudhon developed the idea of mutualism at length, notably in a few key texts such as *De la Capacité Politique des Classes Ouvrières* (*On the Political Capacity of the Working Classes*) (Proudhon 1865), he was also one of those self-taught intellectuals who ventured to put their economic ideas into practice. In France, he initiated the People's Bank, which he based on an alternative local currency. Along with Owen's National Equitable Labour Exchange in England, the People's Bank can be considered one of the first modern experiments in social currencies (Proudhon 1865). It allowed various professionals to offer their services in exchange for a quantity of an alternative currency indexed to the number of hours worked. Proudhon also formalised interest-free mutual credit (or 'free credit'), the forerunner of credit unions, by studying some of the rural practices of the time that sought to enable small farmers to buy back the land they farmed. His 'mutual credit fund' was intended to finance agricultural associations so that they could compete with the first large industrial consortia (Proudhon 1846, 1851). This kind of initiative contributed to the birth of the 'cooperative' status in France, notably with the so-called Waldeck–Rousseau law in 1884 (some 20 years after Proudhon's death).

Proudhon also often mentions the Canut workshops. These forerunners of the workers' cooperatives put up resistance to the big factories, as well as to the silk merchants who tried to subject their goods to (very low) international prices. The Canuts made a point of recruiting journeymen with few, or even no, qualifications to train them in the silk trades and, in the best cases, to integrate them into the management and ownership of the workshop (Frère 2018).

Proudhon thought that all of these initiatives should come together on a regional and then a national scale, forming federal economic governments whose members, elected at the grassroots level, would only have short-term mandates that could be revoked to ensure the permanent rotation of representatives. This economic federation should be responsible for coordinating trade and all macroeconomic regulations on the basis of a principle of reciprocity distinct from strict market exchange. Preventing the accumulation of surplus value beyond what was necessary to meet vital needs, workers would exchange service for service, credit for credit, and labour for labour (Proudhon 1865, 210).

The idea of reciprocity is at the heart of mutualism. It is intended to govern workers' organisations internally (Proudhon 1846) through a few major principles, which can be used to characterise the typical format of an associative enterprise even today (Frère 2018): serving the members of local communities by involving their representatives; democratic self-management; social ownership of capital and the means of production; the primacy of people over the capital in the redistribution of profits; rotation of management tasks; wage equity (maximum ratio of lowest to highest wage); anti-capitalist struggle.

15.2 DEMOCRATISING AND FEDERALISING AS A RESPONSE TO SOCIAL ENTREPRENEURSHIP AND THE WITHDRAWAL OF THE SOCIAL STATE

As with economic power, Proudhon wished to alter political power to become radically more democratic, so that it would incorporate self-management. He would continually refine his stance on this, notably in *Du Principe Fédératif* (*The Federative Principle*) (Proudhon 1863). In this text, he sought to limit the state's prerogatives without denying them all. So the government is subalternized by:

> the representatives or institutions of liberty, namely: the central state by the deputies of the departments or provinces; the provincial authority by the delegates of the communes and the municipal authority by the inhabitants; so that liberty thus aspires to make itself predominant, authority to become the servant of liberty, and the contractual principle to be substituted everywhere, in public affairs, for the authoritarian principle (ibid., 81)

Using the concept of contract, Proudhon emphasises that the parties to the federation do not submit to the federation itself; thus he rejects 'any measure or initiative that tends to strengthen the power of the federal state or federation and consequently to compromise the (political) sovereignty of the contracting parties on which his federalist theory is based' (Cagiao y Conde 2011, 292). It is here that Proudhon develops the idea of subsidiarity: a decision can only be taken by a higher level of federal organisation if it cannot be taken by a lower level – the region, the commune or the association (Millon-Delsol 1993, 22–4).

This political federalism enters into a dialogue with the economic federalism based on mutualism mentioned above. The state then becomes one actor among others:

> The state has retained its power, its strength ... but it has lost its *authority* ... it is itself, so to speak, a kind of citizen, it is a civil person just like families, trading companies, corporations, communes. Just as it is not sovereign, it is not a servant either ... it is the first among its peers. (Proudhon 1860, 68)

Proudhon's thinking embraces diversity. '[He] invokes the noisy dialectic of a pluralist society, in which each individual, each group, participates in determining the general interest' (Chambost 2004, 247). More broadly, the pluralist management of public affairs described by Proudhon is a form of regulation (Vaillancourt and Laville 1998, 131) which goes beyond that of tutelage, whereby the public authorities alone decide on the general interest, with associations applying its directives. In France, such tutelary management can be found in the financing of organisations promoting social and economic inclusion, which take the 'labour market' to be a sacred space into which the 'defective parts of the social body' must reintegrate at all costs. The fact that unemployment is a structural invariant of capitalism is thus passed over in silence by the elected representatives in charge of this sector 'under tutelage'. If Proudhon's associationalism cannot tolerate such public supervision, it also rejects all forms of quasi-market regulation aimed at making associations compete with each other to fulfil missions in the public interest, financed through 'project-based' funding; missions that are once again defined by the state alone in the name of the new public management.

It is because they focus only on 'tutelised' associations that some people see in associationalism the disengagement of the state or subversion of 'the foundations of the status of the civil service' (Hély and Moulévrier 2009, 41). But from a Proudhonian perspective, it is the private capitalist economy rather than the civil service that must be supplanted, even if the latter is to be radically federalised. For Proudhon, mutualism or associationalism does not constitute a third sector that compensates for the failings of the state. In his vision, the state (or the federation) continues to provide funding streams for social security, unemployment, health care, pensions, culture, schools, public spaces, and so on. Better still, it can – and indeed should – strengthen them. It is just that the tax collected to fund all of these redistributive activities is levied on an economy that is entirely associative, cooperative and mutualist rather than capitalist. A form of secondary solidarity – both large-scale and universal – thus replaces the primary forms of solidarity embedded locally in associations and cooperatives.

Today, it is actors involved in social entrepreneurship who reduce associationalism to quasi-market regulation. They advocate the introduction of laws in the health and social sectors that 'replace the historical *bottom-up* process based on civil society initiatives with a *top-down* process that enshrines ... the planning of supply and the placing of actors in competition with one another' (Itier 2016, 43). To this end, the sector has a policy of issuing calls for projects, which can be seized on by capitalist companies, for example in the field of temporary work and professional training (see entry 53, 'Social Policy'). This new post-welfare state social model is clearly neoliberal. As well as restoring power to the state that Proudhon's subsidiarist and pluralist logic wanted to take away once and for all, it abandons associations to the throes of competition that Proudhonian economic federalism aimed to eradicate. For Proudhon, federations of non-capitalist economic organisations should be allowed to share the production of goods and services democratically, rather than opposing each other.

15.3 NEITHER CHARITY NOR UTOPIAN COMMUNISM

From an associationalist perspective, democratising the economy and the state in no way implies that the latter should relinquish its social prerogatives (see entry 10, 'Origins and Histories' and entry 49, 'Participation, Governance, Collective Action and Democracy'). In contrast to associationalism, neoliberal political currents are keen to transfer the social responsibilities of what, in Western Europe, has long been called the 'welfare state' to a charitable civil society populated by voluntary associations and/or to the neoliberal market. This was true, for example, of the United Kingdom Conservative Party, which sought to promote 'the radical devolution of power and greater financial autonomy to councils, local residents and community groups' (Conservatives 2010). But they do not think for a moment that these local residents – principally those living in the poorest communities – could play a direct role in controlling all the country's economic resources and political responsibilities on a larger scale (see entry 2, 'Community Economics'). For if such localism were really to take on its associationalist logic, it would have to recognise that empowering local residents must also logically lead to the redistribution of economic power and resources that have been concentrated in the hands of private shareholders.

On the other hand, associationalism does not refer to the inaccessible possibility of a post-revolutionary society (as many variants of Marxism-Leninism did). It is practised here and now, as Proudhon said. Of course, it is marginal. But it is not utopian. In France, the Associations pour le Maintien d'une Agriculture Paysanne (AMAP, or Associations for the Preservation of Small-Scale Farming), wind power cooperatives, solidarity finance, local exchange trading systems, local food networks and Sociétés Coopératives d'Intérêt Collectif

(SCICs, or Collective Interest Cooperative Companies) are multiplying faster than ever. These initiatives are based on the mutualist principles from which Proudhonian theory was constructed, as well as the practices of the first workers' cooperatives and associations (those of the Canuts, for example). Contemporary associationalism owes its success to the fact that it is not subservient to a 'tutelary state' and that it refuses to be subjected to the rules of the market. There is no capitalist principle that can enable us to understand its mode of operation: not the invisible hand, nor free competition, nor the pursuit of financial interests, nor private property, nor even the idea of growth, be it social or cultural. Instead, the idea of reciprocity and the principles outlined above in the discussion of Proudhon remain relevant.

But beyond the enthusiasm this development may generate, a pressing question has arisen over the last two decades. As many other entries in this *Encyclopedia* show, associations are growing all over the world. At the end of the 19th century, libertarian socialism lost its struggle against statist socialism and trade unionism within the Workers' International in Europe. State socialism – which was authoritarian and involved economic planning – emerged in the East. In the West, trade unionism was confined to defending workers against capitalist exploitation, as the project of a market society had, it was thought, triumphed once and for all. So can a collaboration between trade unions and contemporary civil society organisations now succeed where this collaboration failed as part of associationalist socialism 150 years ago? Can this associationalist socialism recompose a project for society today? At present, nothing could be less certain. At a time of platform capitalism, the complete virtualisation of financial transactions, and the overexploitation of human and natural resources, the power of neoliberalism seems to be unparalleled (Frère 2019) (see entry 33, 'Information and Communication Technology (ICT)'). If associationalism – as a project that is as economic as it is political – is to have a future, it will undoubtedly have to reconceptualise itself as a joint struggle to be waged with the unions towards a radically federalised and democratised redistributive social state.

15.4 RETHINKING THE STATE FORM BASED ON THE SOCIAL STATE, IN OPPOSITION TO THE NATION-STATE

If contemporary associationalism must rethink the form of the state from top to bottom in order to revitalise a socialist-libertarian societal project, it must also do so in order to eliminate everything in this project that is deleterious: patriarchy, inhuman migration policies, and low taxes on wealth or capital, for example. But all these things can be fought against while trying to safeguard the progressive institutions that the state has been forced to develop following a century of worker and popular struggles in Western Europe, for example in health, education and social protection. For these are institutions that we care about today (Hache 2013). The anthropologist James Scott, much of whose work consists of a radical critique of the nation-state, declares his inclination towards anarchism while also conceding that human rights have become unsurpassable and that it is no longer possible for many states to discard them. He writes:

> I do not believe that the state is everywhere and always the enemy of freedom. Americans need only recall the scene of the federalised National Guard leading black children to school through a menacing crowd of angry whites in Little Rock, Arkansas, in 1957 to realise that the state can, in some circumstances, play an emancipatory role. (Scott 2012, xiv)

Everything depends on the form it is given in a democracy. When we understand it simply as one public policy tool among others, it can be horizontalized.

Meanwhile, the linguist Noam Chomsky, still in a socialist-libertarian vein, develops this idea further: what is called the 'state' today, in Western societies, is no longer only a superstructure in the service of the bourgeoisie's interests. In contrast to its pre-democratic forms, its function today is also to protect a set of rights and the political culture of a population accustomed to freedom. We can no longer one-sidedly reject everything that comes together in the form of the state if we understand this as the collective public organisation that goes beyond the scale of the locality. Evidently, Chomsky confesses, the socialist-libertarian vision he espouses ultimately consists in dismantling the power of the state and all its discriminatory tools: armies, prisons, bureaucracy, patriarchy, and so on. But in the world we live in at the beginning of the 21st century, destroying the state in one fell swoop would be dangerous. In the face of advancing neoliberal policies, it may be appropriate 'to defend and even strengthen certain elements of state authority that are now under severe attack', he adds, when asked about the social services and welfare state programmes that are being laid into by the political right worldwide (Chomsky 2013, 39). It is a safe bet that in the hands of the far-right, which at the time of writing in 2020 is making steady progress in North America (Trump), South America (Bolsonaro in Brazil) and Europe (Italy, Poland, Hungary and Austria have already been severely affected), the state apparatus will continue its backward march. It will put an end to social security (which is already inadequate) once and for all, abolish taxation on capital (which is already too low), threaten paid leave, challenge free health care and freedom of the press, abandon the financing of public services and public education. It will put a stop to all the collaborations that have developed in recent years between local authorities and associations on a number of emancipatory social, environmental and cultural projects. And the list of dangers could be continued ad infinitum. As Chomsky again points out:

> given the accelerating effort that's being made these days to roll back the victories for justice and human rights which have been won through long and often extremely bitter struggles in the West, in my opinion, the immediate goal of even committed anarchists should be to defend some state institutions, while helping to pry them open to more meaningful public participation, and ultimately to dismantle them in a much more free society. (Chomsky 2013, 40)

CONCLUSION: REINSTITUTE

To sum up, as the 21st century seems to be moving increasingly down an associative path, it is vital to remember that this is not a third sector (it aims to replace the market capitalism sector, not to constitute a third one), nor social entrepreneurship (which aims to make 'moral capitalism' and social purpose compatible), nor a charitable economy (which aims to relieve the excluded in order to keep social violence and potential revolution on the horizon), nor a substitute economy that aims to discharge the state of its social responsibilities. In this respect, associationalism can help to redefine the functions of the social state.

Proudhon, the first theorist of associationalism, already thought that associations could potentially establish fruitful relations with local state organisations if the latter agreed to allow them complete freedom of action. Recent research on his 'people's bank' has shown that it was not his work alone, but that it was developed together with the elected representatives of the Luxembourg Commission created by Louis Blanc (Chaïbi 2010, 17–18). These elected officials not only gave the necessary authorisation for the Bank; they also played a key role in its management and development, while Proudhon was busy with his political and journalistic activities. In short, they helped to establish the Bank through their political support.

Thus, from an associationalist perspective, it is not only a question of asking which institutions we want to eliminate, since many institutions exist independently of those of the nation-state, which the associationalist tradition has always rightly criticised. We must also correctly distinguish between those institutions we want to create and those we want to keep. The danger would be to believe that, in a society that is as ideal as it can be, 'we cannot institute at all' (Latour 2018, 99). We can certainly do without the state in its nation-state form, the form that institutions have taken in modernity. We probably cannot do without institutions, namely the 'state' form understood in its broader sense as the organisation of the collective, together with the intersubjective norms and rules of coordination that this collective gives itself. What we can do, however, is to make these institutions participatory, horizontal, democratic; in short, associationalist:

> There are institutions in all (or almost all) societies; there will be institutions in an emancipated society. But we can conceive of institutions differently: not as authorities claiming a kind of absolutism, but as fragile constructions that accept that they will be constantly confronted with critique ... We must not throw out the institutions that, in certain respects, are indispensable to social life, with the bathwater of the nation-state, a quite recent historical form that has nothing universal about it. Our task is thus to construct a framework that allows us to critique institutions – as does, for example, the notion of symbolic violence forged by Bourdieu – and, at the same time, to defend them against the temptation of autonomous anarchism, which does not account for all of libertarian thought. (Boltanski and Jeanpierre 2011, 480)

Once it has freed itself from capitalism, the associative society will nonetheless still need large-scale economic institutions. It is a fiction to believe that in the future of a society without economic exploitation we will all agree on the rules for collective life and the directions to be taken. Conflicts and differences of opinion will persist, which makes democracy unavoidable, even in the society we aspire to. Whatever form society takes, it will not be pacified unless we assume that humans can become clones of each other, able to agree on everything, which would be reminiscent of the worst totalitarian fantasies. If there is one task that associationalist thought can give itself, it is to assume the inevitable agonistic contingency of human political relations (Mouffe 2016). It is crucial that we think about how to organise disagreement over the common good, even in its economic dimension, as democratically as possible.

REFERENCES

Boltanski, Luc and Laurent Jeanpierre. 2011. 'Critique Sociale et Émancipation.' In *Penser à Gauche. Figures de la Pensée Critique Aujourd'Hui*, edited by Laurent Jeanpierre, 466–85. Paris: Éditions Amsterdam.
Cagiao y Conde, Jorge. 2011. 'Fédéralisme.' In *Dictionnaire Proudhon*, edited by Chantal Gaillard and Georges Navet, 278–92. Brusseles: Editions Aden.
Chaïbi, Olivier. 2010. *Proudhon et la Banque du Peuple*. Paris: Editions Connaissances et Savoirs.
Chambost, Sophie. 2004. *Proudhon et la Norme, Pensée Juridique d'un Anarchisme*. Rennes: Presses Universitaires de Rennes.
Chomsky, Noam. 2013. *On Anarchism*. New York: New Press.

Conservatives. 2010. 'Where We Stand'. Conservative Party. http://www.conservatives.com/Policy/Where_we_stand/Local_Government.aspx.
Frère, Bruno. 2009. *Le Nouvel Esprit Solidaire*. Paris: Desclée de Brouwer.
Frère, Bruno. 2018. 'Back to materialism. Reflections on Marx's Conception of Labour, Praxis, Cooperative and Libertarian Socialism in the 19th Century.' *International Journal of Politics, Culture and Society*, 31 (1): 69–94.
Frère, Bruno. 2019. '"Politics Without Politics": Affordances and Limitations of the Solidarity Economy's Libertarian Socialist Grammar.' In *The Everyday Resistance*, edited by Bruno Frère and Marc Jacquemain, 229–62. London: Palgrave.
Hache, Emilie. 2013. *Ce à Quoi Nous Tenons. Propositions Pour une Écologie Pragmatique*. Paris: La Découverte.
Hély, Matthieu and Pascal Moulévrier. 2009. 'Économie Sociale et Solidaire: Quand les Sciences Sociales Enchantent le Travail.' *Idées Économiques et Sociales*, 2009/4 (158): 30–41. https://doi.org/10.3917/idee.158.0030.
Itier, Christophe. 2016. 'Réinventer le Modèle Social Post-État Providence!' Direction[s].fr. 2016. https://www.directions.fr/Piloter/organisation-reglementation-secteur/2016/5/-Reinventons-le-modele-social-post-Etat-providence---2047691W/.
Latour, Bruno. 2018. 'Où la ZAD Donne à l'État une Bonne Leçon.' In *Eloge des Mauvaises Herbes*, edited by Jade Lindgaard, 93–102. Paris: Les Liens Qui Libèrent.
Millon-Delsol, Chantal. 1993. *Le Principe de Subsidiarité*. Paris: PUF.
Mouffe, Chantal. 2016. *L'Illusion du Consensus*. Paris: Albin Michel.
Proudhon, Pierre-Joseph. 1846. *Système des Contradictions Économiques ou Philosophie de la Misère*. Paris: Groupe Fresnes-Antony de la Fédération anarchiste.
Proudhon, Pierre-Joseph. 1851. *Idée Générale de la Révolution Au Xixe Siècle*. Paris: Marcel Rivière.
Proudhon, Pierre-Joseph. 1857. *Manuel du Spéculateur à la Bourse*. Paris: Librairie de Garnier Frères.
Proudhon, Pierre-Joseph. 1860. *Théorie de L'Impôt, Texte Commenté et Présenté par Thierry Lambert*. Paris: Editions L'Harmattan, Logiques Juridiques.
Proudhon, Pierre-Joseph. 1863. *Du Principe Fédératif et de la Nécessité de Reconstituer le Parti de la Révolution*. Paris: E. Dentu.
Proudhon, Pierre-Joseph. 1865. *De la Capacité Politique des Classes Ouvrières*. Paris: Editions du Monde Libertaire.
Scott, James C. 2012. *Two Cheers for Anarchism*. Princeton, NJ, USA and Oxford, UK: Princeton University Press.
Vaillancourt, Yves and Jean-Louis Laville. 1998. 'Les Rapports Entre Associations et État: un Enjeu Politique.' *Revue du MAUSS* 11, 2ᵉ semestre: 119–35.

16. Community-based organizations
Kiran Kamal Prasad

INTRODUCTION

Community-based organizations (CBOs) are mechanisms that encourage individuals and communities to take control of different issues impacting their life, be they economic, social, cultural, environmental or even political. In the context of the increasingly centralizing tendencies of state agencies to deprive individuals and groups of an opinion regarding such issues, there is a need to ensure that not just the marginalized but also the 'ordinary' citizens take centre stage in their own life's concerns. Also, in the context of extreme wealth concentration in a few and the pauperization of many (characterized by increasing jobless growth led by technological inventions in information and communications technology, artificial intelligence and biotechnology) within the neoliberal economy, there is an acute need to find solutions not just to reduce, but to eradicate poverty, or find alternatives to the dominant mode of production, thus enriching human life through empowerment. CBOs encapsulate various attempts in this direction. They occur in geographically, socially, psychologically, culturally and digitally bounded communities to meet community needs. They are meant to supplement and not replace the state, local, territorial laws, rules and regulations. They also create alternative systems and societal structures outside the established power structures. They are guided by some ideology rooted in humanity and are ultimately based on the values of justice, equality, freedom and fraternity. CBOs are developed from the earlier practices of community organization (CO) and community development (CD). The concepts 'community' and 'development' are very much implied in the concept of CBO (see Box 16.1).

BOX 16.1 RELATED CONCEPTS: COMMUNITY DEVELOPMENT (CD) AND COMMUNITY ORGANIZATION (CO)

'Community' is a widely used term with various definitions. It is essentially 'formed by people connected to each other in distinct and varied ways' (Walsh et al. 2012, 14). The four main components for defining the concept of the community are: people, place, social interactions, and the idea of common attachment or psychological identification with a community (Christenson and Robinson 1989, 6). 'Development' has many connotations. It mainly implies improvement, growth and change (Christenson and Robinson 1989, 9). There are questions regarding development over whether it is to be measured in terms of overall economic growth or social justice, gender justice, ecological sustainability, human rights and even happiness.

CO has mainly a connotation of a method or 'a way of working on an orderly conscious basis to affect defined and desired objectives and goals' (Government of India 1987, 112). It occurs when 'a group of citizens, recognizing a need, band together to see that the need is met' (Government of India 1987, 113). Thus, people have to get together over a problem or a need, form social relationships, develop cooperative attitudes and structures, and work out solutions. There is a distinction between CO and community organizing, where the former is considered more as a structure with a community perspective, and the latter more as a process aimed at creating change. 'New Community Organizing' is a contemporary CO, having glocalized perspectives and organizing methods.

The different phases of CO are: problem (identification), study, diagnosis, treatment, and evaluation. In addition to all these, CO includes the following elements, according to the practitioners and theoreticians of CO in India, Sri Lanka and Bangladesh in the 1980s:

> (1) importance ... of philosophy, vision or ideology of the kind of a just society worth struggling for, together with a deliberate option and commitment to the poorest of the poor, often leading to living and working with them. (2) Their ability to use the tools of structural analysis on micro and macro levels in analyzing the basic causes of poverty in the situation, identifying, innovating, designing and using indigenous and culture-based communication methods and materials. (Tellis-Nayak 1987, 118)

From practice, the concept of CO was developed and became a part of teaching subjects in schools of social work. The term:

> was used in the United States before World War I. It has been taught as a professional practice in American schools of social work since 1940 and Indian schools of social work since the 1950s. However, the Council on Social Work Education (USA) recognized it as a field of specialization only since 1962 (Tellis-Nayak 1987, 112)

James A. Christenson and Jerry W. Robinson have formulated CD from the various definitions of different authors, including that of the United Nations up to the 1980s. CD is defined as 'a group of people in a locality initiating a social action process (i.e., planned intervention) to change their economic, social, cultural, and/or environmental situation' (Christenson and Robinson 1989, 14). It is viewed in four ways: as a process, a method (process and objectives), a programme (method and content), and a movement (programme and emotional content) (Christenson and Robinson 1989, 13).

Thus the two terms, CO and CD, are interrelated and complement each other.

The term 'CBO' is used very loosely by various authors to indicate various groups or organizations. CBOs could simply be called COs or sometimes named community-led/driven organizations. Self-help groups and cooperatives are some specific forms. Usually, civil society organizations (CSOs), voluntary organizations and non-governmental organizations are differentiated from CBOs. Social and solidarity economy organizations and enterprises (SSEOEs) has recently become the overarching term connoting all the above terms (including CBOs).

16.1 THE ORIGINS OF AND DEVELOPMENTS IN CO/CBOS

The needs of a community and its individuals were addressed during different phases of the development of Western society before the industrial era. In the Global South, various indigenous systems organized – and in some regions continue to organize – the life of the communities. For example, the Indian subcontinent had a village system characterized by a graded caste hierarchy, which governed all life aspects. This system provided many different privileges to the few at the top of the hierarchy, while encouraging the exclusion of many by promoting severe indignities to those on the lowest rung. Some basic features of the village system continue to exist even today in rural areas. The essentials of the caste system are still to be found in rural areas and urban localities, and the Indian diaspora worldwide. From the industrial society had sprung up new forms of inequality, resulting in acute poverty for the many propertyless people, who exist only on labour, and wealth for a few propertied class people. Gender inequalities were also part of the system. In the neoliberal global era, the social and environmental consequences have become enormous. Different CO efforts have taken place from the beginning of the industrial revolution to address these issues.

The first CO efforts that emerged were for charity and relief to overcome the problem of acute poverty leading to beggary, and provide settlement houses for the rural poor who flocked into the cities. These efforts appeared first in the United Kingdom (UK) during the 19th century and then subsequently in the United States (US). Community councils sprang up in the US in the early 20th century 'to increase efficiency, encourage specialization, set standards for service and provide leadership to member agencies for joint planning. Later, World War I gave rise to war chests in many communities to promote fundraising, coordination of services, and spending control' (Tellis-Nayak 1987, 113). Thus from the 1920s to the 1950s, CO came to be considered as working with member agencies for the above services, and not directly with communities.

Gradually, government public welfare departments took up welfare activities, and the focus was shifted from the voluntary effort to institutionalized welfare departments of government. CO was also restricted when casework became prominent in social work. Since the 1950s, developing countries have carried out CD programmes under the auspices of the United Nations, alongside consultants from national governments and academic experts from the Western world. Previously, CD was used for colonial domination in Nigeria, with T. R. Batten, the author of Training for Community Development, attempting to give rise to a different type of CD there as a result of his trainings between 1927 and 1949 (Ledwith 2005, 9).

During the late 1960s, urban renewal projects and the war on poverty refocused on direct services to people and communities (Tellis-Nayak 1987, 113). There was a surge in organizing people for radical change in Latin America and the Philippines. Paulo Freiere's *Pedagogy of the Oppressed*, first published in Portuguese in Brazil in 1967 and then in English in the UK in 1970, set the tone for radical CO worldwide. Freire 'has made more impact than any other thinker on community development worldwide since the 1970s' (Ledwith 2005, 53). The main focus was on the increasing agency of individuals and communities to produce a radical change in various domains, including the political sphere. There was a surge of CBOs and people's movements worldwide, attempting to radically restructure society through peaceful means. This occurred particularly in the Global South.

The 1990s saw the emergence of neoliberalism, with emphasis on worldwide structural transformation and globalization, catering to the needs mainly of capital. Even the communist regimes were affected by these trends. The wealth produced is increasingly concentrated in a few, and the vast majority are marginalized, with enormous social and environmental consequences. Issues of gender justice and child rights came to the forefront. Such trends have initiated the development of many types of CBOs in rural and urban areas, not only in the Global South but also in most Western countries. The projects funded by Western governments, the World Bank and other international financial institutions also started supporting various projects through partnerships with government and non-governmental organizations (NGOs), with a deliberate emphasis on collaboration with CBOs. Where CBOs were initially concentrated in rural areas, urban-based CBOs became more common. Governments, United Nations agencies and NGOs have realized the importance of promoting CBOs throughout all project phases. In Western countries, especially in the US, local governments and professional institutions carry out their services in collaboration with CBOs. This is mainly in healthcare, especially of the elderly and the disabled, and during epidemics such as COVID-19.

In this context, the International Labour Organization (ILO) Declaration on Social Justice for a Fair Globalization in 2008, which called 'for the promotion of Social Economy Organizations within a pluralist economy' (Fonteneau et al. 2011, vii), indicates a renewed interest of the ILO in the social economy and its impact on CBOs. From its beginning in 1920, through setting up a Cooperative Branch, the ILO 'has built a long tradition and developed thorough expertise on SSE enterprises and organizations' (Fonteneau et al. 2011, vi). The first reference to the SSE (social and solidarity economy) in an ILO document was in 1922 in the 11th Session of the Governing Body proceedings. The concept of 'social finance', covering various microfinance institutions and services, was developed in the 1980s. The ILO began promoting community-based protection schemes and mutual benefit societies in the area of social protection in the 1990s. More recently, the ILO has become involved in the promotion of 'social enterprises' and 'social entrepreneurship' through its Recommendations on Job Creation in Small and Medium-sized Enterprises and on Promotion of Cooperatives (Fonteneau et al. 2011, vi). The concepts of SSE and SSEOEs are now an integral part of ILO initiatives and programmes, such as: the Social Protection Floor Initiative; labour-intensive programmes; ecotourism and fair trade; support to indigenous minorities; local economic development projects; the fight against HIV/AIDS; the promotion of green jobs; and, more broadly, sustainable enterprises (Fonteneau et al. 2011, vii).

16.2 VARIOUS AREAS OF ACTIVITIES OF CBOS

CBOs can be grouped into broad categories, including income generation, service provision, human rights, Sustainable Development Goals (SDGs), environment or a combination of two or more of these categories. Income generation could be carried out by micro-enterprises through collectives such as self-help groups (SHGs) or cooperatives, enhancing agricultural production, animal husbandry, and so on. The services relate to education, skill enhancement, recreation, events and gatherings, youth sports, home visiting, health, food, water, sanitation, children, vulnerable children, orphans, women, domestic violence, the elderly, the disabled, the homeless, immigrants, refugees, victims of natural and human-made disasters, vulnerable individuals at higher risk of severe illness, HIV/AIDS, pandemics such as COVID-19, and so on. The various human rights and entitlements addressed by CBOs include gender issues, child rights, indigenous people, racial and caste-affected groups, communities carrying out descent and caste-related occupations, forced labour and trafficking, accessing entitlements from the state agencies, implementing various government welfare programmes, peace issues regarding communal harmony and arms conflict, and so on. Environmental issues dealt with by CBOs include conservation of forests, planting trees, conservation of wildlife, protection of common property resources, watershed management, conservation of water and water bodies, replacing plastics, and so on. Some CBOs participate in the local governance structures to encourage participation in self-governance.

The CBOs in the Global South, including most of the countries in Asia, Latin America and Africa, mainly concentrate on the various income generation activities, agricultural production, animal husbandry, human rights, peace, harmony and environmental issues, as well as education and health. These activities are mainly promoted by NGOs. United Nations agencies also promote CBOs through collaboration with government agencies. In the US and European countries, they are mainly concentrated on service provision in health and education. Professional institutions, both independent or extensions of universities and local governments, deliver their services mainly in collaboration with CBOs.

Of late, marginalized communities or individuals with specific needs have taken their own initiative to form CBOs to secure their rights or entitlements. They could be specifically termed community-led/driven organizations. Spontaneous movements sometimes get formalized into CBOs. Citizens or community leaders concerned for issues affecting their communities or with a radical ideology may inspire their community members to come together, forming organized groups with a clear plan of action to address various social, environmental or human rights concerns, and more significant societal issues. They may also initiate the development of local SSEOEs.

16.3 ORGANIZATIONAL STRUCTURE OF CBOS

Most of the CBOs are promoted by NGOs or CSOs. Some enlightened and motivated leaders from communities may themselves promote CBOs within their communities. CBOs are formed within a village or a larger geographical region; at a particular community level; between segments of the community such as women, men, youth, girls and children; or to address particular issues. A CBO could be a single unit or a federation of many units. Each CBO has a few selected leaders. The NGO-promoted CBOs are likely to be more structured and very well formalized compared to those that emerge from the innate leadership within communities. The NGOs which promote the CBOs provide constant training on leadership and management, carrying out group meetings, keeping records, identifying issues to be addressed, addressing such issues, and reviewing or evaluating CBOs periodically. To ensure ownership and sustainability, the members pay regular fees. All CBO leaders may be more motivating when compared to managers of organizations that work to set targets; however, the leaders of CBOs from within communities are more inspirational than those from NGO-promoted CBOs. These community-led/driven CBOs are likely to be more informal, setting up structures as the need arises, and learning from their own experience addressing their issues.

Below is an example of an NGO, Chinmaya Organisation for Rural Development (CORD), promoting various CBOs as its mechanism to deliver various services in villages in different states in India.

BOX 16.2 CHINMAYA ORGANISATION FOR RURAL DEVELOPMENT (CORD)

CORD, originating in Himachal Pradesh in India and now spread to other states such as

Odisha and Tamil Nadu, has CBOs of women, men, youth and children. These CBOs, particularly the women's groups, are the heart of CORD's constituent programmes, and around these CBOs other programme components evolve.

Each CBO elects its president, secretary and, if required, a treasurer. They learn to conduct monthly meetings, maintain records of finances, delegate responsibilities, establish priorities and resolve multiple issues. Besides their active role in decision-making and taking up responsibilities, their ownership in the CBO is established further by a small donation (denoted Chanda) of Rs. 2 to Rs. 10 per month per member. They are empowered to access funds directly from the government.

Once these CBOs are nurtured in each village ward for various issues, they are encouraged to participate in local self-governance, first in the Up-gram Sabha at each of the wards in a Gram Panchayat, and then at the Gram Sabha of the Gram Panchayat.

The CBOs nurtured since 1985 include Mahila Mandals (Women's Groups), Self Help Groups, Men and Farmers' Clubs, Adolescent Girls' Groups (Yuvathi Samuh), Children's Groups (Bal Vihar), Advocacy Groups, Chinmaya Umang for persons with disability, single women groups, women in agriculture and local self-governance, old-age people, promotion of education through school management committees, and so on. CBOs also focus on promoting health, nutrition, hygiene and sanitation through government-promoted groups such as the Village Health, Sanitation and Nutrition Committee (VHSNC). CORD also offers youth leadership programmes (Kevalananda 2021).

Government agencies, on their own or through the support of international agencies such as the World Bank, United Nations Development Programme (UNDP), and so on, carry out various projects in partnership with local NGOs which, in turn, directly build up CBOs to carry out the project or link with other NGOs to deliver various services through CBOs. Box 16.3 gives an example of a partnership in the late 1990s between the Gujarat Government, Ahmedabad Municipal Corporation (AMC), six NGOs and the CBOs they promoted to run a water and sanitation programme in the slums of Ahmedabad in Gujarat. The World Bank supported it.

BOX 16.3   PARTNERSHIP OF CBOS

The Approach Paper to the 9th Five Year Plan of the Government of India, the Country's Economic Memorandum of the World Bank and the Government of Gujarat envisaged the involvement of CBOs in most urban programmes. The AMC planned to build partnerships with six NGOs which, in turn, promoted many CBOs in a range of projects, including Parivartan. Some NGOs were working directly with CBOs, while some were working through other NGOs to support those CBOs. The six NGOs included the Self Employed Women's Association (SEWA), Mahila Housing SEWA Trust (MHT), VIKAS, Foundation for Public Interest (FPI), CHETNA and SAATH. Each is described below.

SEWA is a membership-based CO working for the economic development of poor women for over 40 years. Work is focused on local income and employment generation needs. SEWA identifies local women leaders and connects poor women by promoting people's organizations. This focus on women leaders and connection among women facilitates poor women's access to urban resources, policies and programmes. SEWA also builds the capacity of CBOs through training, organizing support services, savings, credit, and policy development.

MHT, a subsidiary organization of SEWA, was formed to meet the need for housing-related services. MHT developed a unique tool called 'Housing Clinics' for the community, which facilitates easier access to housing finance and social security schemes, raises awareness about housing-related schemes and initiates participatory capacity-building within the community (see entry 32, 'Housing Sector'). MHT worked in 12 of the 18 slums and was upgraded within the Parivartan programme. Besides motivating the members of each slum community to participate in the programme through their one-third cash contribution, MHT also facilitated linkages between all the partners and coordinated the overall upgrading process. Additionally, MHT helps to form Community Associations within each slum and enables the community to organize the Associations into electing a Working Committee, which carries out day-to-day functions, including the operation and maintenance of the services by the Parivartan programme.

With its many years of experience working with CBOs in Ahmedabad, VIKAS responds to the needs of CBOs and promotes decision-making through democratic structures. It motivates CBOs to work for basic urban needs through the LINK project. It has a directory of 304 CBOs in Ahmedabad slums and was also involved in establishing the Urban Resource Center.

FPI has dual experience in small towns such as Idar and large cities such as Ahmedabad. Linking up CBOs with the state and city governments is FPI's main focus, along with the joint CBO–NGO government policy formulation. FPI also trains CBOs and develops planning and monitoring tools.

CHETNA provides training and develops training materials for CBOs for health and education activities. It focuses on coordination between CBOs and the government, and sensitizes CBOs to local urban issues, particularly health, education and women. CHETNA also advocates simplifying policies that affect women and their economic status. Sanchetana, a subsidiary organization of CHETNA, promotes local groups and CBOs of women and minorities. It provides training to CBOs on health, savings and credit, and aims to raise awareness amongst CBOs of social issues such as alcoholism, corruption and social injustice. Dissemination of official information to local CBOs is an expanding activity.

SAATH has formed CBOs in several Ahmedabad slums. It concentrates on youth development and focuses on the creation of social awareness. SAATH supports activities for savings and credit and disseminates information to communities.

The AMC has been successfully working with the CBOs involved in Parivartan and was planning to involve more CBOs in future urban management programmes (Ahmedabad Municipal Corporation 1998).

16.4 GENERAL TRENDS IN CBOS

Some general trends and suggestions for improvements in a CBO partnership were articulated at a workshop organized by the AMC in 1998. They are still relevant today for any CBO partnership. They are the following (Ahmedabad Municipal Corporation 1998):

- Rural and urban CBOs function differently. In rural areas, issues of caste, religion or occupation are more common, while in urban areas, CBOs are mainly formed based on minority, ethnicity and locality of migrants.
- At times of crisis such as riots, floods, and so on, defunct CBOs revive themselves.
- It is challenging to organize women as active members of CBOs.
- Male leadership is common in CBOs, while women make most of the operational decisions.
- Except in savings and credit groups, mismanagement of funds is common when amounts handled become larger.
- CBOs are good at marketing and building marketing links for income-generating activities.
- There is a lack of information about the government's plans and policies and the availability of essential services among CBOs, feedback from the community to government policies is very limited and mechanisms for the dissemination of information to CBOs are lacking.
- Political events such as elections cause seasonal orientation changes.
- There is a mismatch of CBO, NGO and government activities.
- There is a lack of coherence in policies, programmes and resources at state and city levels.
- There is no coordinated information for CBOs in city and state governments.

16.5 SUGGESTIONS FOR IMPROVEMENTS IN CBOS

Since working with CBOs can be complex, it requires a high degree of flexibility on the part of the partners involved:

- Local settlement needs should be reflected in the programme.
- CBOs need to link with other CBOs.
- There is a great need for capacity building in leaders and among members of CBOs.
- Investment of time by partners to gain the trust of the CBO members is essential, especially when dealing with finances.
- Partners must recognize the seasonality of the flow of finance at the community level.
- The complicated policies, rules and regulations of governments hampering CBOs should be simplified and made accessible to CBOs.

Apart from the NGO/CSO and government or international agency-sponsored CBOs, many CBOs emerge from within the communities or the affected groups of people. They might be formalized or continue to function as informal groups purely based on the leadership from the community or the affected groups of people or funded by the community or the group. These are more like movements, since they mainly work on rights, justice and environmental issues and undertake various types of struggles, agitations and advocacy associated with the community or the affected groups of people. They may also address the economic security of the community or the group members. Some movements may take on the features of CBOs (see entry 1, 'Activism and Social Movements'). Apart from providing leadership, management and administrative skills training, strengthening the community's social capital, meaning networks of civic engagements engendering societal norms of reciprocity and trust, is of primary importance (Saxton 2007, 1). An example is given in Box 16.4 of JEEVIKA, a movement on bonded labour in India.

> ## BOX 16.4 JEEVIKA (JEETA VIMUKTI KARNATAKA / BONDED LABOUR LIBERATION KARNATAKA), INDIA
>
> JEEVIKA is a movement on bonded labour that started in Karnataka, India and is now spread to the neighbouring state of Andhra Pradesh. It follows a human rights approach and addresses fundamental rights associated with bonded labourers and Dalits and Moolanivasis from which most bonded labourers come. It promotes the agency of the bonded labourers through awareness-raising and organization building. Using scientific data, and through advocacy and lobbying, it aims to bring policy changes at the highest levels of governance and tries to bring about systemic change. While doing all these, it also secures the economic interests of bonded labourers through promoting CBOs such as self-help groups (SHGs) and cooperatives.
>
> The movement began with the initiative of one individual who identified himself with the Dalits and the Moolanivasis in villages, and through the cooperation of youth from those communities. Though clear on strategies and broad approaches to be followed, a detailed plan of action was not formulated beforehand. The issues and the concrete programmes and activities emerged as the movement spread. Not just bonded labourers, but also Dalits and Moolanivasis have emerged and are emerging to take leadership in the movement. More and more freed bonded labourers lead independent and dignified lives through their CBOs (Prasad 2022).

CONCLUSION

The CBO concept evokes noble sentiments regarding people's affirmation and agency. It refocuses people as the central factor in the development and societal structure. Without their participation, without their full involvement, without their taking ownership, without them taking decisions, no programme of government, NGOs or any society can be successful. From charity and relief work to welfare and poverty eradication programmes, from service deliveries to rights-based actions, to gender justice, to environment protection and ecological sustainability, CO and CBOs have taken many forms and continue to manifest in newer forms. There are many varieties of CBO. Because of the high valorization of CBOs, there is a trend of calling any NGO or CSO a CBO. Since it is realized that no programme for whatever purpose can be effectively implemented without people at its centre, many NGOs, CSOs, governmental agencies, various international bodies, and so on, incorporate the formation of CBOs as a primary strategy of carrying out their projects. Both as a process and as an entity, the full potential of CBOs is yet to be realized.

REFERENCES

Ahmedabad Municipal Corporation. 1998. 'Field Note: Community Based Organizations.' UNDP World Bank. https://documents1.worldbank.org/curated/pt/679721468257943651/585559324_20050010001826/additional/multi0page.pdf.

Batten, T. R. 1962. *Training for Community Development, A Critical Study of Method*. London: Oxford University Press.

Christenson, James A. and Jerry W. Robinson, Jr. 1989. *Community Development in Perspective*. Ames, IA: Iowa State University Press.

Fonteneau, Bénédicte, Nancy Neamtan, Fredrick Wanyama, Leandro Pereira Morais, Mathieu De Poorter, Carlo Borzaga, Giulia Galera, Tom Fox and Nathaneal Ojong. 2011. 'The Reader 2011: Social and Solidarity Economy: Our Common Road towards Decent Work, Social and Solidarity Economy Academy.' ILO. Montreal, Canada: The Reader. https://www.ilo.org/wcmsp5/groups/public/---ed_emp/---emp_ent/---coop/documents/instructionalmaterial/wcms_166301.pdf.

Freire, Paulo. 1970. *Pedagogy of the Oppressed*. London: Penguin Books.

Government of India. 1987. *Encyclopedia of Social Work in India: Vol 1*. New Delhi: Ministry of Social Welfare.

Kevalananda, Swami. 2021. 'CORD – Chinmaya Mission.' Chinmaya Misson. https://www.chinmayamission.com/what-we-do/cord-chinmaya-organisation-for-rural-development/#.YYtyozV8TB4.gmail.

Ledwith, Margaret. 2005. *Community Development, A Critical Development*. Jaipur: Rawat Publications.

Prasad, Kiran Kamal. 2022. 'Bonded Labourers Leading Their Liberation.' Webinar. Presented at the International Conference on Cooperatives, Mutual Aid and Solidarity Economies. https://www.youtube.com/watch?v=hy6IrQ7r2Dk&list=PLxtVCaJrq1t1D59a1MJGTN_FKfdSALHQS&index=3.

Saxton, Gregory D. 2007. 'Social Capital and the Vitality of Community-Based Organizations.' Paper accepted for presentation at the Annual Meeting of the Western Academy of Management in Christabell P.J. 2022. Social and Solidarity Economy, Experiments and Experiences. New Dehli: SSDN Publishers and Distributors.

Tellis-Nayak, Jessie B. 1987. 'Community Organisation.' In Government of India (eds.), *Encyclopedia of Social Work in India: Vol 1*, 112–22. New Delhi: Ministry of Social Welfare.

Walsh, Aisling, Chishimba Mulambia, Ruairi Brugha and Johanna Hanefeld. 2012. 'The Problem Is Ours, It Is Not CRAIDS', Evaluating Sustainability of Community Based Organizations for HIV/AIDS in a Rural District in Zambia.' *Globalization and Health* 8 (40), 1–16. http://www.globalizationandhealth.com/content/8/1/40.

17. Cooperatives and mutuals
Chiyoge B. Sifa and Caroline Shenaz Hossein

INTRODUCTION

More than 1 billion humans belong to formal member-owned co-op institutions. Millions more engage in informal cooperatives, self-help groups, and the commons. Cooperatives are voluntary organizations usually born out of a crisis (see also entry 52, "Resilience in the Context of Multiple Crises"). They often exist to fill a need in business and society. These organizations are democratic and rules are determined by the members who created them. The more we study social and solidarity economies, the clearer it becomes that people around the world have and are engaged in formal and informal cooperatives. The International Cooperative Alliance (ICA) defines a cooperative as an autonomous association of persons united voluntarily to meet their common economic, social, and cultural needs and aspirations through a jointly owned and democratically controlled enterprise, and they are guided by a set of seven principles that make them distinct from commercial firms.

To locate the origin of cooperatives and mutuals is no easy task because of the global reach of the co-op system (see also entry 10, "Origins and Histories"). Canadian scholar Lou Hammond Ketilson (2006) made the point more than a decade ago that there is a need to rethink how we understand the development of cooperatives, especially for people who do not identify with Europe's industrial revolution. In *The Cooperative Movement: Globalization from Below*, Richard Williams (2007) has argued that the cooperative movement owes its start (and growth) to the Global South (see also entry 8, "Indigenous Economies"). Today, India is the country with the largest number of cooperatives in the world, both formal and informal (ICA 2018; Williams 2007).

The story of cooperative and mutual sector beginnings is usually located in 19th century Europe. It is the story of the Rochdale Equitable Pioneers Society founded in 1844, also known as the Rochdale Pioneers, regarded as the "founders" of the cooperative movement. However, once we adjust for timelines and geographies, a global understanding of the cooperative sector emerges (Williams 2007).

17.1 WHAT ARE COOPERATIVES AND MUTUALS?

The cooperative model has a governance structure that gives members a say—and usually a vote—in how the institution is organized, with dividends distributed to its members. An example of a global cooperative firm is the Mondragon Cooperative Corporation in the Basque region of Spain, which was born of exclusion and crisis, and today is one of the leading cooperative firms in household appliances, as well as an actor in banking and education. Unlike commercial investor-owned firms, cooperatives and mutuals are member-owned businesses formed to prioritize the needs of their members, rather than corporate shareholders who may be focused solely on profit. Examples of mutuals include credit unions, building societies, and mutual insurers.

Mutuals are distinct from cooperatives in that a large proportion of the business should be owned by either employees and/or the local community, with the organizations being owned by and run for the benefit of their current and future members (Mutuo 2009).

Mutuals consist of people making a commitment to each other which guarantees sustainability through their commitment in bringing their trade to the organization and responding to any further changes. They are able to do this because, as members, they own and control the organization. In a report by the World Cooperative Monitor (2020, 7), it explained why cooperatives and mutuals are in the top 300 rankings:

> The Top 300 by turnover ranking this year (data reference year 2018) presents an overall total of US$2146 billion with the agricultural (104 enterprises) and insurance sectors (101 enterprises) dominating the list. The wholesale and retail trade sector mainly composed of retailers' cooperatives (33 enterprises) and consumer cooperatives (21 enterprises) represents the third biggest economic sector followed by the financial service sector (21 enterprises). In terms of cooperative type, almost half of the Top 300 are producer cooperatives (133 enterprises) mainly representing agricultural cooperatives and retailers' cooperatives, whereas mutuals (83 enterprises) and consumer/user cooperatives (65 enterprises) mainly composed of consumer cooperatives and financial service cooperatives represent the other half. Only a small number of worker cooperatives (3 enterprises) and multi-stakeholder cooperatives (2 enterprises) are included in the Top 300 rankings by turnover.

Cooperatives and mutuals are owned by and run for the benefit of the membership and the community values of the society. The worker voice and membership in a co-op challenge the notion that there is only one way to do business. The strive for lateral and democratic governance—as seen in *empresas recuperadas* in Argentina, the MST (Movimento dos Trabalhadores Sem Terra / Landless Workers' Movement) in Brazil, and the Gung-Ho (Gōngyè Hézuòshè) in China—enables greater autonomy in the capitalist process, and allows workers to run the organizations themselves (see also entry 49, "Participation, Governance, Collective Action and Democracy"). The origin of cooperatives is about the plurality of experiences, because so many people have found refuge in these collective businesses that are rooted in struggle and transforming the economic conditions from the bottom up (see Boxes 17.1 and 17.2).

BOX 17.1 GUNG-HO (GŌNGYÈ HÉZUÒSHÈ)

Gung-Ho is one the oldest cooperatives, founded during the invasion of China by Japan in 1938, with a set of values including mutual aid and rooted in national identity. Gung-Ho, or the International Committee for the Promotion of Chinese Industrial Co-operatives, was founded in 1938 in Hong Kong to organize unemployed individuals and refugees to take part in productive activities during wars with Japan (Bernardi 2016).

BOX 17.2 THE FIRST MUTUAL IN SOUTH AFRICA

The Old Mutual Group was established in Cape Town, as South Africa's first mutual life insurance company, offering financial security during uncertain times in 1845. The company was founded by John Fairbairn as a mutual insurance company under its first name of the Mutual Life Assurance Society of the Cape of Good Hope (see https://www.oldmutual.com/about). This mutual operates in 14 countries and has a membership made up of individuals, small and medium-sized businesses, corporates, and institutions.

17.2 LOCATING THE ORIGINS OF THE COOPERATIVE MOVEMENT

Much of the co-op origin stories we know about are Western, but those stories come much later. American scholar John Curl (2012) provides early examples of economic cooperation such as First Nations, the Shoshone Nation, the Lakota, Southwest Pueblos, Northwest Coast tribes, and the Iroquois Confederacy as the original cooperators, because of their communal systems and potlatches embedded into the local economy. Metis (Indigenous peoples in the three Prairie Provinces of Manitoba, Saskatchewan, and Alberta, as well as parts of Ontario, British Columbia, the Northwest Territories, and the Northern United States) business scholar Wanda Wuttunee (2010) has explained that Indigenous Canadians have potlatches (a gift-giving feast practiced by Indigenous peoples of the Pacific Northwest Coast of Canada and the United States), and wisdom circles (gatherings which help elders to create and maintain social connections with other like-minded persons) as ways to rethink cooperativism. According to University of Jordan Professor Adnan Obeidat (1975), cooperative guilds were formed by craftsmen in ancient Egypt in 3000 BC. There are many cooperative institutions that have had a long history in Indigenous communities and in non-Western societies.

One of the early co-op institutions documented was that of the Dutch Eendragt Maakt (meaning "unity creates strength"), an investment trust in 1774. As early as 1843, Japan had a cooperative known as Hotokusha, which was a mutual savings and credit society (Fisher 1938). The term *kyoritsu* or *doeki* means "cooperation," yet these expressions are not known as part of the origin story (Saito 2010). In the mid-19th century, the Japanese had a growth of consumer cooperatives, such as the Kyoritsu-Shosha and Doeki-Sha in Tokyo, Osaka Kyoritsu Shoten, and the Kyoritsu Shoten in Kobe around 1879 (ibid.). Ela Bhatt (2007), the founder of the Self Employed Women's Association (SEWA), has shown the world that India has a long-standing tradition of self-help groups and informal cooperatives.

During the European violent conquest and plantation economies in the Americas, African people were enslaved as a way to finance the Industrial Revolution, and they resorted to collective and hidden cooperatives to cope with this brutality. It was the knowledge of collectivity and cooperative systems that helped people to form the Quilombola system in Brazil and the Maroons colonies across the Caribbean to live free (Farfán-Santos 2015; St Pierre 1999). Historian Maurice St Pierre (1999) described how African enslaved people in Guyana organized buying clubs to buy their freedom and land when they were freed. By 1932, the Kilimanjaro Native Cooperative Union Ltd was the first coffee cooperative established despite considerable opposition from colonizers (*East African Agricultural Journal* 1946). Renowned

African American scholar W.E.B. Dubois hailed the Underground Railroad as a series of cooperatives, born out of a struggle for freedom since the 19th century (Haynes 2019). In the archives, Benjamin Drew (1856) recorded True Bands systems, which were cooperatives of formerly enslaved Africans who fled to Canada. Locating the cooperative origins is vast and varied in terms of the kinds of cooperative institutions that many people have had a stake in inventing.

17.3　MAKING THE DISTINCTION BETWEEN COOPERATIVES AND MUTUALS

Seven principles form the cooperative identity: voluntary and open membership; democratic member control; member economic participation; autonomy and independence; education, training, and information; cooperation among cooperatives; and concern for the community. Cooperatives and mutuals choose "one member, one vote" governance directly or indirectly, and they both share this commitment to democracy building and yielding to the membership. During the early 1900s in Lévis, Quebec, the Desjardins created the *caisses populaires* in response to the financial exclusion of a French-speaking Catholic minority (Lévesque et al. 1997). Today, Desjardins is one of the largest financial institutions in Canada and has an extensive global reach. Much of the organization is committed to the concern for community co-op value and it educates and supports cooperative development in Canada and worldwide.

The differences between co-ops and mutual institutions are subtle. Cooperatives require members to contribute to the capital of the business through direct investment and savings, whereas mutuals can derive profits through their customer relationship and direct it to the will of the membership. Cooperatives by design adhere to the "one member, one vote" rule (Bernard and Spielman 2009), and in mutuals the voting principle can also be operationalized through the use of delegates or interest groups. Though mutuals do not have to abide by the cooperative principles, many of them share values of open membership and members' voices. The goal is that cooperative and mutual institutions share the power in the organization, and this is fundamental to the classic definition of a "mutual entity."

17.4　THE IMPACT OF COOPERATIVES AND MUTUALS

Cooperatives and mutuals have wide appeal around the world because of their impact on community development. The United Nations General Assembly declared 2012 as the Year of Cooperatives, based on the major impact that cooperatives and mutuals have had in social and economic development, with cooperativism acting as a formal human intervention across the planet. In Uganda, precarious youth created a shoe-shining cooperative (see Box 17.3). The autonomous nature of cooperatives guarantees that they are not manipulated into fulfilling the needs and aspirations of external agents at the expense of members' needs and aspirations, which makes these institutions valuable to people around the world. It is why cooperatives are a critical component of the social and solidarity economy (Hossein 2018). Through the establishment of the United Nations Inter-Agency Task Force on Social and Solidarity Economy in 2013, cooperative institutions are viewed as an integral part of the United Nations agenda.

These global efforts signify that no single region in the world can claim to be the only authority on cooperatives or mutuals.

> ### BOX 17.3 UGANDA SHOE-SHINERS
>
> In 1975, Uganda shoe-shiners, homeless street boys and girls, organized themselves into a cooperative. Having attained legal status, they requested that the city authority grant a permit to carry out their business on city streets. Success followed, and in a couple of years they started manufacturing shoe brushes using environment-friendly materials. In 2007, the cooperative had more than 600 members and had created branches in other cities of Uganda. Their affiliation to the Uganda Cooperative Alliance assisted them in capacity building and training, and the Cooperative Savings and Credit Union of Uganda provided loans to their members (Mshiu 2003).

The cooperative principles are not only about business results: these co-op values are also about making positive impacts in the community. A mutual venture, for instance, is one where people come together to achieve something that none of them can on their own. By pooling a shared need through a willingness to do something collaboratively, they provide a mechanism to meet the needs of all. Author Nici Nelson (1996) has documented the Kiambu women's banking co-ops actively since the 1970s to show that informal co-ops existed in Kenya long before the colonial period. In East Africa, savings and credit cooperatives (SACCOs) have an ancient history of mobilizing goods, and they are well recognized as cooperative institutions.

The principle of "cooperation among cooperatives" enables cooperatives and mutuals to utilize the benefits of economies of scale and enhances the sustainability of the organisations, and this is why they have a tremendous impact on human development. The case of the Amul Dairy cooperative in India speaks to the value chain which supports a number of cooperative producers and marketing organizations (see Box 17.4).

> ### BOX 17.4 AMUL
>
> Amul in India was formed in 1946 at the very end of colonial rule. Amul emerged as a co-operative movement, as a way to end the monopoly of Polson Dairy, and to foster the economic liberation of farmers in Anand, Gujarat (http://www.amuldairy.com/index.php/about-us/history). Amul is managed by a cooperative body, the Gujarat Co-operative Milk Marketing Federation Ltd (GCMMF). Amul is jointly owned by 3.6 million milk producers, and the apex body of 13 District Milk Unions, spread across 13 000 villages of Gujarat. Unlike corporate companies, Amul is owned by villagers who contribute tirelessly to the development of their cooperative (Heredia 1997).

Another important aspect for cooperatives and mutuals is the price point for members. When the profit motive is not the only focus for shareholders, then these member-owned institutions can ensure transparent prices to members. In co-ops, the goods and services can be sold at a lower cost to members (and consumers) because of various decisions the institution will make, and the cost savings go to the membership to decide how to use these surpluses. In terms of equity-sharing, a cooperative institution rewards its membership in relation to its engagement with the cooperative or mutual, rather than in proportion to investor shareholding. Mutuals can also offer competitive interest rates and fee tariffs on savings, deposit accounts, mortgages, and loans.

Cooperatives contribute to better socio-economic development because of communities' concern with poverty reduction, employment generation, and social integration. In 2002, the International Labour Organization (ILO) approved a specific instrument for cooperatives, called the Promotion of Cooperatives Recommendation no. 193 (ILO 2002), which recognized the importance of cooperatives in job creation, mobilizing resources, generating investment, their contribution to the economy, and how they promote the fullest participation in the economic and social development of all people.

CONCLUSION

Humans around the world have created cooperatives and mutuals to shape their local context because these systems allow people to partake in an alternative economic model. Given economic and environmental crises and a global pandemic, cooperatives and mutuals stand as a reminder that non-capitalist origins, markets that put people first, and making a strong human economy are very much embedded in the world economy.

Situating the plural origins of cooperatives and mutuals is to give credence to the emergence and growth of cooperatives and mutuals as a global bottom-up movement. Co-ops put people before profit, and no one place or person can take credit for these origins. Crises are not unique to any one country, and people have sought camaraderie as a way to navigate complex arenas. The plurality of the historical origins only makes the movement a strong one. Once we understand that the cooperative movement is global, then we can fully appreciate how to build a movement that is a viable alternative to the dominant firm.

The timeline solely based on the experiences in the West would limit our understanding of the development of co-ops and mutuals. Informal and formal cooperative institutions have evolved with a purpose that seeks to achieve equity-sharing outcomes for members first and foremost. Cooperatives need not be subservient to the commercial firm and beholden to the goal of profit-making only. These member-owned institutions present a new way of doing business, one that is accountable to community well-being and human development.

REFERENCES

Bernard, Tanguy and David Spielman. 2009. "Reaching the Rural Poor through Rural Producer Organizations? A Study of Agricultural Marketing Cooperatives in Ethiopia." *Food Policy* 34 (1): 60–69. https://doi.org/10.1016/j.foodpol.2008.08.001.

Bernardi, Andrea. 2016. "Gung-Ho, The Chinese Co-operative Movement." In *The Co-operative Firm: Keywords*, edited by Andrea Bernardi and Salvatore Monni, 51–60. Rome: RomaTre-Press.

Bhatt, Ela Ramesh. 2007. *We Are Poor But So Many: The Story of Self-Employed Women in India*. Oxford: Oxford University Press.

Curl, John. 2012. *For All the People: Uncovering the Hidden History of Cooperation, Cooperative Movements, and Communalism in America*. Oakland, CA: PM Press.

Drew, Benjamin. 1856. *A North-Side View of Slavery: The Refugee: Or, The Narratives of Fugitive Slaves in Canada. Related by Themselves, with an Account of the History and Condition of the Colored Population of Upper Canada*. Boston, MA: JP Jewett.

East African Agricultural Journal. 1946. "A Short Account of the Kilimanjaro Native Co-operative Union, Ltd." *East African Agricultural Journal* 12 (1): 45–8. https://doi.org/10.1080/03670074.1946.11664524.

Farfán-Santos, Elizabeth. 2015. "'Fraudulent' Identities: The Politics of Defining Quilombo Descendants in Brazil." *Journal of Latin American and Caribbean Anthropology* 20 (1): 110–32. https://doi.org/10.1111/jlca.12108.

Fisher, Galen M. 1938. "The Cooperative Movement in Japan." *Pacific Affairs* 11 (4): 478–91. https://doi.org/10.2307/2751318.

Hammond Ketilson, Lou. 2006. "Revisiting the Role of Co-operative Values and Principles: Do They Act to Include Or Exclude?" Centre for the Study of Co-operatives, University of Saskatchewan. https://usaskstudies.coop/documents/books,-booklets,-proceedings/revisiting-the-role.pdf.

Haynes, Curtis. 2019. "From Philanthropic Black Capitalism to Socialism: Cooperativism in Du Bois's Economic Thought." *Socialism and Democracy* 32 (3): 125–45. https://doi.org/10.1080/08854300.2018.1562824.

Heredia, Ruth. 1997. *The Amul India Story*. New Delhi: Tata McGraw-Hill Publishing Company.

Hossein, Caroline Shenaz. 2018. *The Black Social Economy in the Americas: Exploring Diverse Community-Based Markets. Perspectives from Social Economics*. New York: Palgrave Macmillan.

ICA. 2018. *World Cooperative Monitor*. Brussel: ICA.

ILO (International Labour Organization). 2002. "Promotion of Cooperatives Recommendation, R193 No. 193." https://www.ilo.org/dyn/normlex/en/f?p=NORMLEXPUB:12100:0::NO::P12100_ILO_code:R193.

Lévesque, Benoît, Marie-Claire Malo, and Ralph Rouzier. 1997. "The 'Caisse de dépôt et placement du Québec' and the 'Mouvement des Caisses populaires et d'Économie Desjardins': Two Financial Institutions, the Same Convergence towards the General Interest?" *Annals of Public and Cooperative Economics* 68 (3): 485–501. https://doi.org/10.1111/1467-8292.00060.

Mshiu, Sam. 2003. "The Cooperative Enterprise as a Practical Option for the Formalization of the Informal Economy." https://www.ilo.org/wcmsp5/groups/public/ed_emp/emp_ent/coop/documents/publication/wcms_754087.pdf.

Mutuo. 2009. What is a mutual? http://www.mutuo.co.uk/latest-from-mutuo/what-is-a-mutual/.

Nelson, Nici. 1996. "The Kiambu Group: A Successful Women's ROSCA in Mathare Valley, Nairobi (1971 to 1990)." In *Money-Go-Rounds: The Importance of Rotating Savings and Credit Associations for Women*, edited by Shirley Ardener and Sandra Burman, 49–71. Oxford: Berg.

Obeidat, A. 1975. "The Concept of Cooperation in Islam and in Arab Society." *International Journal of Rural Cooptation* 3 (1): 3–12.

Saito, Yoshiaki. 2010. *A Brief Chronicle of the Modern Japanese Consumer Cooperative Movement*, translated and edited by Takeshi Suzuki. Tokyo: Japanese Consumers' Co-operative Union.

St Pierre, Maurice. 1999. *Anatomy of Resistance: Anticolonialism in Guyana 1823–1966*. London: Macmillan Education.

Williams, Richard C. 2007. *The Cooperative Movement: Globalization from Below*. Farnham: Ashgate Publishers.

World Cooperative Monitor. 2020. "Exploring the Cooperative Economy Report."

Wuttunee, Wanda A. 2010. *Living Rhythms: Lessons in Aboriginal Economic Resilience and Vision*. Kingston, ON: McGill-Queens University Press.

18. LGBT* inclusion

Vincenza Priola and Saoirse C. O'Shea

INTRODUCTION

This entry explores meanings and possibilities for the work and social inclusion of lesbian, gay, bisexual, transgender and minority sexuality and gender people (LGBT*), and considers the role that the social and solidarity economy (SSE) may have in promoting their social, political and economic inclusion (see also entry 42, 'Work Integration'). In this entry, the SSE is viewed with reference to a wide range of non-capitalist practises and organising principles across the economic, social, political and communitarian spheres, which aim to build an economy and society that support people and the environment (see also entry 3, 'Contemporary Understandings').

Research shows that discrimination against LGBT* people is persistent and pervasive, affecting work organisations (Colgan and Rumens 2018), housing (Romero et al. 2020), quality of life, and basic human rights (Katz-Wise and Hyde 2012). LGBT* people continue to endure limitations in human, social and economic rights across the world. Homosexuality remains illegal in more than 70 countries across the world, with LGBT* people experiencing open hostility and violence. On the other hand, legal rights and social recognition have been achieved by gay, lesbian and transgender people in many nations in the Global North, where legislation exists which protects their equal rights in work and society. Despite the legal protection offered by this legislation, discrimination remains common, whilst it is more subtle and sometimes more difficult to prove. Furthermore, although the acronym used in this entry embraces many sexualities, it is important to emphasise that transgender and gender-fluid people continue to be subjected to considerably more violence and exclusion than gay or lesbian individuals, with no recent evidence of improvements to their social and economic opportunities. This discrimination often results in mental and physical health issues and social isolation, alongside estrangement from family (Potoczniak et al. 2009), as social stigma often negatively impacts upon family support and the benefits which can be derived from it (Hazel and Kleyman 2019).

This entry defines inclusion as distinct from equality and diversity. The concept of 'equality' is generally embedded in legislation designed to address harassment and discrimination, focusing on the provision of equal opportunities to all (that is, everyone is treated the same), regardless of sexuality, sexual orientation, gender, race, colour, ethnicity, disability, religion, age, and so on. On the other hand, while equality addresses equal treatment, 'diversity' acknowledges and recognises differences among people. Human rights and individual freedom are at the core of the diversity approach, with the differences that exist among people inherently respected and valued. Meanwhile, the concept of 'inclusion' focuses on outcomes, and refers to the individual's experience of the extent to which they feel valued, welcomed and able to fully participate in decision-making. It also encapsulates the availability and accessibility of development opportunities for individuals within organisations and society. The following section considers LGBT* inclusion in more detail and explains how the SSE can contribute to LGBT* inclusion in work and society.

18.1 WHAT IS LGBT* INCLUSION?

Efforts of organisations to consider the needs of LGBT* individuals have focused on diversity and diversity management approaches, often influenced by national legislation and/or social movements. For example, in the European Union (EU), the Employment Equality Framework Directive of 2000 has established a legal agenda to be incorporated into the legislation of EU countries, making it illegal to discriminate in the workplace on the basis of sexual orientation, among other categories. The diversity management approach taken by commercial organisations has often focused on the business case, which argues that employing a diverse workforce that represents the customer/consumer base brings a competitive advantage to the firm (Otaye-Ebede et al. 2020). However, it can be argued that the business case is not sufficient to sustain the commitment to diversity, as organisations should also uphold a moral argument to support minority groups. Commercial and social enterprises, in particular, ought to take into account the moral case for social justice, which highlights an obligation to compensate for the oppression that minority groups, especially LGBT*, have endured (and continue to endure) in society. Furthermore, the diversity approach adopted by organisations generally focuses on numerical differences and similarities of employees, heavily relying on statistics and often neglecting the different needs of diverse individuals. Some scholars (e.g. Kumra and Manfredi 2012) argue that organisations should instead focus on inclusion as a means to involve, support and value employees as unique individuals so that they can be fully recognised in their identities, feeling a sense of belonging and recognition when participating and contributing to the organisation. Inclusion therefore means the involvement of individuals in the decision-making process in order to ensure that their input is integrated into the organisational actions. It is an outcome measured by the scale to which LGBT* people (and all individuals who belong to minority groups) feel that they are welcomed and supported.

18.2 THE SSE AND THE WORK AND SOCIAL INCLUSION OF LGBT* PEOPLE

Whilst there have been few empirical studies that have considered economic development in relation to LGBT* people (Badgett et al. 2019), research shows that positive changes in LGBT* rights and inclusion lead to improved economic development (Badgett et al. 2014). The inclusion and acceptance of LGBT* people 'is an indicator of an underlying culture that's open and conducive to creativity' (Florida and Tinagli 2004, 25) and can contribute to a country's economic development. Badgett et al. (2019) estimated the relationship between per capita gross domestic product (GDP) and LGBT* legal rights (as measured by the Global Index on Legal Recognition of Homosexual Orientation – GILRHO) across a large range of countries between 1966 and 2011. They reported that the inclusion of LGBT* people is linked to a stronger economy, with one additional legal right in the GILRHO index (out of eight legal rights in total) associated with US$2065 more in per capita GDP.

LGBT* people are widely discriminated against in many countries, experiencing: violence; workplace, health and educational discrimination, resulting in loss of productivity; economic deprivation; social and familial marginalisation and exclusion; and lowered life expectancy (Badgett et al. 2019; Badgett 2014). A United Nations (UN) source (UN Human Rights 2015) cites that the costs of homophobia and transphobia to the economy is US$32 billion a year, an amount equal in size to India's economy. In the case of transgender people, discrimination and marginalisation result in increased rates of under- and unemployment, poverty, homelessness, substance misuse, suicidal ideation and suicide, and criminalisation (Grant et al. 2011). LGBT* people commonly present as forced migrants and refugees, as a consequence of fleeing repressive regimes, persecution and torture (Forced Migration Review 2013; Jordan 2011), or further, fleeing exploitation and victimisation by, for example, sex traffickers. There is therefore an economic, social and ethical necessity to consider how LGBT* people may be best included in work organisations that recognise and value their contribution. Due to their commitment to supporting people and society, SSE organisations and enterprises (SSEOEs) represent a key channel for the work and social inclusion of LGBT* people.

Priola et al. (2014, 2018) conducted a study with social cooperatives based in Italy which were founded to support the employment of people who are disadvantaged in the labour market, such as disabled individuals, drug addicts and ex-convicts, among others. The authors of the study analysed the inclusion practises of these cooperatives to assess whether, and how, such organisations extended their core aim of inclusion to other groups, such as LGBT*, who are not formally considered disadvantaged, but are often ostracised and discriminated against at work and in society. In view of the fact that such organisations are part of the SSE and work 'against normativity' in supporting people who do not fit within the normative standards of the 'typical worker', they were expected to show a culture of inclusion extending to a diverse workforce in general. However, the authors found that the efforts of these social cooperatives to 'include' their employees remained grounded on heteronormativity, which is defined as 'the expectations, demands and constraints produced when heterosexuality is taken as normative within a society and thus when biological gender roles fit with sexuality' (Priola et al. 2014, 489). In these social cooperatives, interventions to support the inclusion of socially disadvantaged groups were clearly based on individual psychological support and group-based actions aimed at developing individual resilience. However, alongside their supportive ethos, the authors found that these cooperatives were characterised by a heterosexist culture, revealed in discriminatory practices such as silence, gossip and derogatory comments that were generally accepted and justified as banter. The importance of considering sexual orientation in the workplace was neglected by these social cooperatives on the basis of the fact that sexuality and sexual orientation belonged to the private sphere of life rather than to the work environment. LGBT* individuals were 'included' as long as they did not flaunt their diversity. Most lesbian and gay workers remained in the closet. As an example, transgender employees felt excluded because they visibly did not conform to normative conventions associated with the fit between gender and sex. They reported that they had been asked to move from a customer-facing position to a 'hidden' role, and that colleagues often avoided conversations beyond mundane daily exchanges, preventing them from establishing friendships. Priola et al. (2018) suggest that the organisational practises observed reproduce cultural discourses present at the national level, characterising the Italian society and reinforcing the view that LGBT* sexualities should remain confined to the private aspect of life, and excluded from work organisations. The authors of the study reconnect these aspects to the importance that Italian society places on the institution of the family in its traditional form, which is embedded in the historical legacies of fascism and the influence of the Catholic church.

While this study shows how these specific social cooperatives have missed the opportunity to be fully inclusive, we argue that SSE organisations of all types have a great potential to be inclusive of LGBT* individuals. We now turn our attention to consider specific SSE LGBT* organisations.

18.3 SSE ORGANISATIONS SUPPORTING LGBT* PEOPLES

LGBT* organisations vary in size, who they represent and how, and the issues that they cover. They include large national organisations such as Stonewall in the United Kingdom (UK), Gay and Lesbian Alliance Against Defamation (GLAAD) in the United States of America (USA) and Arcigay in Italy, which campaign on all issues that are of importance to their national LGBT* communities. As well as these LGBT* national organisations there are single-issue organisations and/or those that focus on a specific group within the LGBT* community, such as transgender people. Examples of these organisations include Mermaids in the UK (a charity focused on supporting transgender children) and the Sylvia Rivera Law Project in the USA (focused on the legal rights and protections of transgender people in the USA), and other regional and local, self-organised groups. Some organisations support the economic development of the LGBT* community, for example, by listing LGBT* businesses in specific areas. Among these, Pink Spots, the LGBT directory in San Francisco (USA), lists LGBTQ owned and friendly businesses in the area (divided across many categories), as well as events and LGBTQ news.

LGBT* people are diverse and have multiple needs, which may reflect the local realities of indigenous people. Such individuals have been marginalised both by their country and by the concerns of a Global North which focuses on economic development (Budhiraja et al. 2010). In this sense, sexual and gender identities may have a cultural context rather than a simple, uniform one (Altman 2004; Katyal 2005). For example, many countries and cultures have, for centuries, included diverse gender identities, such as *muxe* people in Mexico, *kinnar* people in the Indian subcontinent, *kathoeys* people in Thailand and third-gender indigenous American people in the United States. The term 'transgender', as a 20th century Anglo-American term, reflects neither these histories nor the difference between these peoples. On this account, local SSEOEs may have a better understanding and ability than a multinational non-governmental organisation (NGO) to appeal to, represent and aid fragmented and disparate communities. Doan (2010) argues that there is a need to: (1) undermine social control mechanisms, through personal and local acts that question normative assumptions of 'correct' sex and gender behaviour and presentation; (2) mitigate social control through international conditions by building international coalitions that question repression, such as the Sisterhood Is Global Institute (SIGI) and Women Living Under Muslim Laws (WLUML) in the Middle East, both of which resist Islamic fundamentalism through regional and international coalition building; and (3) strengthen local coalitions: whilst international NGOs can help, local groups must lead local action.

In addition to specific LGBT* organisations, other SSEOEs can support the inclusion of LGBT* individuals in the economy and society due to their mission of prioritising the welfare of people over profit and business imperatives. In a 2021 document, the International Labour

Organization (ILO) advocates the cooperative advantage for the transgender community, suggesting that it:

- helps to create employment and improve income;
- supports the transition from the informal to the formal community;
- provides access to services such as finance, housing and care;
- generates resources and bargaining power;
- promotes education and training, and supports economic democracy; and
- lobbies for workers' rights and inclusion.

It provides a few examples of LGBT* cooperatives, such as:

- Estilo Diversa: the textile cooperative in Argentina, formed in 2010 by a LGBT* collective that specialises in producing theatre costumes and fashion wear for the LGBT* community. After the first cooperative was formed in Buenos Aires, other LGBT* cooperatives were formed in Bahía Blanca, Comodoro Rivadavia and Còrdoba.
- Trans Welfare Cooperative Society: formed in 2018 in Kerala, India, by the Left Democratic Front government to provide financial assistance facilitating hospitality business ventures, the creation of temporary shelters for homeless transgender people, and the creation of pension schemes for transgender people over 60.
- LGBT Place of Refuge Multipurpose Cooperative in the Philippines, formed in 2010 by a LGBT* collective to provide a wide range of opportunities including business credit, capacity development, health and accident insurance, and other benefits.

18.4 EXAMPLES OF INTERNATIONAL ORGANISATIONS SUPPORTING LGBT* PEOPLE ACROSS THE WORLD

Many international organisations supporting LGBT* individuals share SSE principles or have SSE organisations as their members. Among the international associations and organisations supporting LGBT* people are:

- The International Lesbian, Gay, Bisexual, Trans and Intersex Association (ILGA) World. It brings together more than 1600 organisations from over 150 countries and campaigns for lesbian, gay, bisexual, trans and intersex human rights.
- The International Lesbian, Gay, Bi, Trans, and Intersex Law Association (ILGLaw). It specifically provides legal information and policy support.
- The International Lesbian, Gay, Bisexual, Transgender, Queer and Intersex (LGBTQI) Youth and Student Organisation (IGLYO). It is the largest LGBT* youth and student network in the world, operating in more than 40 countries.
- Global Action for Trans Equality (GATE), an international advocacy organisation supporting justice and equality for transgender, gender-diverse and intersex communities. It works with global partners to provide knowledge, resources and access to UN mechanisms and bodies.
- Global Respect in Education (GRIN), a transatlantic non-profit organisation and advocacy group which campaigns primarily for lesbian, gay, bisexual, transgender and queer/questioning (LGBTQ) people's social and political equality in education. It seeks to end

discrimination, harassment and bullying based on sexual orientation, gender identity and gender expression in all educational institutes. It is run by students.
- Kaleidoscope Trust. It works to uphold the human rights of lesbian, gay, bisexual and transgender (LGBT+) people in countries around the world where they are discriminated against or marginalised due to their sexual orientation, gender identity and/or gender expression.

18.5 EXAMPLES OF NATIONAL AND LOCAL ORGANISATIONS SUPPORTING LGBT* PEOPLE

While listing national SSE organisations that support LGBT* people is a challenging task, in this section we want to give a few examples from countries in the Global South. We have chosen to focus on the Global South in this section because there is often a tendency to consider the Global North as more egalitarian than the Global South. Puar (2007) discusses homonationalism as a process by which the claims of the LGBT* social movement are used by some groups, such as far-right parties, to justify racism and xenophobic positions, particularly against Muslim people and migrants from countries considered homophobic. Far-right parties in the Global North often use LGBT* rights and sexual diversity to sustain their political stance against migration. Alexander (2005) argues that scholars in the Global North generally view the degree of development of LGBT* movements and rights by Global North standards and neoliberal ideologies, and presuppose that the Global North has the answers to the Global South's problems. However, as Puar (2007) argues, the use of LGBT* social movements by certain groups generally focuses on the rhetoric of equality, and neglects to acknowledge the homophobia and discrimination that LGBT* people still experience in Western societies. The exceptionality of the simplistic homonationalistic accounts used by some groups in the Global North is questioned by LGBT* communities in many countries in the Global South. Rights such as same-sex marriage reflect heteronormativity, but do not always correspond to full equality or equal treatment. The remainder of this section lists a few organisations supporting LGBT* people.

In Bolivia, Mujeres Creando is a feminist collective that participates in actions tackling homophobia, anti-poverty and racism via participatory methods such as street theatre, workshops and also via publishing and TV programmes. Familia Galan, another Bolivian organisation, formed in 2001 by a group of transgender artists and activists, challenges the machismo that dominates Bolivia's public and political lives. It produces a TV show, and a magazine, using street theatre and performance to question repression and oppression. This local organising through the arts is important as it can involve people across classes, ages, races, and so on. It also brings the LGBT* community and its issues into the spotlight.

In India, Creating Resources for Empowerment in Action (CREA) works with structurally excluded women; individuals of diverse sexualities, genders and sex characteristics; disabled individuals; and sex workers to advocate their broader inclusion and solidarity. It organises a range of programmes and events, develops resources to advance human rights, builds feminist leadership, and expands sexual and reproductive freedoms.

In Turkey, Lambda Istanbul is an LGBT* organisation that reports human rights violations and runs campaigns to amend the Constitution of Turkey to include sexual orientation and sexual identity among the categories protected by the discrimination legislation. Lambda

Istanbul organises panel discussions, LGBT* film screenings, symposia and a variety of LGBT* solidarity activities.

Helem was established in Beirut, Lebanon, in 2001 to support the civil, political, economic, social and cultural rights of LGBT* people and any non-conforming sexualities or gender identities in Lebanon, and the South West Asia and North Africa regions. It works with young LGBT* leaders to empower local actions through education and community building, and creates initiatives and spaces to build community power and mobilise changes in legislation, policies and practices to improve the quality of life of the LGBT* communities.

In the Dominican Republic, Amigos Siempre Amigos (ASA) is a social advocacy organisation that promotes HIV/AIDS prevention and fights for the rights of LGBT* people in the Dominican Republic, which currently has no legislation protecting LGBT* people from discrimination.

In South Africa, the Forum for the Empowerment of Women (FEW) is an organisation raising issues of violence affecting black lesbians and the wider LGBT* community. It works to build alliances with the state and creates networks across the regions.

In Namibia, The Rainbow Project (TRP) and Sister Namibia are two SSE organisations that oppose the South West Africa People's Organisation's (SWAPO Party) 'homosexuality is un-African' message and its subsequent hostility against the LGBT* community, including threats and penalties for sodomy. As highlighted by Currier (2011), state leaders in some African nations position LGBT* as a colonial import, arguing that LGBT* sexualities did not exist within pre-colonial African societies (hence the SWAPO argument that homosexuality is 'un-African').

CONCLUSIONS

Limited research has explored LGBT* inclusion and the SSE. This entry has discussed some of the issues that LGBT* people face in society and in the workplace, and argued that SSEOEs have the potential to support the economic and social inclusion of LGBT* people. SSEOEs are diverse, operating through a variety of models, and according to different aims, by providing services and goods to meet the needs of specific groups. In relation to LGBT* inclusion, they can have an important role that extends beyond their immediate aims and can generate awareness of the oppression that LGBT* people experience, as well as a willingness to change on a much wider scale. The entry has provided examples of organisations that operate internationally and nationally in the Global South, to support the needs of LGBT* people.

REFERENCES

Alexander, M. Jacqui (2005) *Pedagogies of Crossing: Meditations on Feminism, Sexual Politics, Memory and the Sacred.* Durham, NC: Duke University Press.

Altman, Dennis. 2004. 'Sexuality and Globalization.' *Sexuality Research and Social Policy* 1 (1): 63–8. https://doi.org/10.1525/srsp.2004.1.1.63.

Badgett, M.V.L. 2014. *The Economic Cost of Stigma and the Exclusion of LGBT People: A Case Study of India.* World Bank. https://documents1.worldbank.org/curated/en/527261468035379692/pdf/940400WP0Box380usion0of0LGBT0People.pdf.

Badgett, M.V.L., S. Nezhad, C. Waaldijk and Y. van der Meulen Rodgers. 2014. *The Relationship between LGBT Inclusion and Economic Development: An Analysis of Emerging Economies.* Los Angeles, CA: US Agency For International Development (USAID) and Williams Institute (UCLA).

Badgett, M.V.L., Kees Waaldijk and Yana van der Meulen Rodgers. 2019. 'The Relationship between LGBT Inclusion and Economic Development: Macro-Level Evidence.' *World Development* 120: 1–14. https://doi.org/10.1016/j.worlddev.2019.03.011.

Budhiraja, S., S.T. Fried and A. Teixeira. 2010. 'From Alphabet Soup to Sexual Rights and Gender Justice.' In *Development, Sexual Rights and Global Governance*, edited by Amy Lind. London, UK and New York, USA: Routledge 131–44.

Colgan, Fiona and Nick Rumens, eds. 2018. *Sexual Orientation at Work: Contemporary Issues and Perspectives.* New York, USA and London, UK: Routledge Taylor & Francis Group.

Currier, A. 2011. 'Decolonising the Law: LGBT Organising in Namibia and South Africa.' In *Social Movements/Legal Possibilities: Special Issue*, edited by Austin Sarat. Bingley: Emerald 17–44.

Doan, P. 2010. 'Disrupting Gender Normativity in the Middle East: Supporting Gender Transgression as a Development Strategy.' In *Development, Sexual Rights and Global Governance*, edited by Amy Lind. London, UK and New York, USA: Routledge 145–54.

Florida, Richard and Irene Tinagli. 2004. *Europe in the Creative Age.* Pittsburgh, PA: Carnegie Mellon Software Industry Center.

Forced Migration Review. 2013. 'Special Issue – Sexual Orientation and Gender Identity and the Protection of Forced Migrants.' *Forced Migration Review* 42: 1–64.

Grant, J.M., L.A. Mottet and J. Tanis. 2011. *Injustice at Every Turn: A Report of the National Transgender Discrimination Survey.* Washington, DC: National Center For Transgender Equality and National Gay and Lesbian Task Force.

Hazel, Kelly L. and Kerry S. Kleyman. 2019. 'Gender and Sex Inequalities: Implications and Resistance.' *Journal of Prevention and Intervention in the Community* 48 (4): 281–92. https://doi.org/10.1080/10852352.2019.1627079.

ILO. 2021. 'Why Cooperatives for Transgender Community? An ILO Perspective.' https://www.ilo.org/global/topics/cooperatives/news/WCMS_776103/lang--en/index.htm.

Jordan, Sharalyn R. 2011. 'Un/Convention(Al) Refugees: Contextualizing the Accounts of Refugees Facing Homophobic or Transphobic Persecution.' *Refuge: Canada's Journal on Refugees* 26 (2): 165–82. https://doi.org/10.25071/1920-7336.32086.

Katyal, S.K. 2005. 'Sexuality and Sovereignty: The Global Limits and Possibilities of Lawrence.' *William and Mary Bill of Rights Journal* 14: 1429–92.

Katz-Wise, Sabra L. and Janet S. Hyde. 2012. 'Victimization Experiences of Lesbian, Gay, and Bisexual Individuals: A Meta-Analysis.' *Journal of Sex Research* 49 (2–3): 142–67. https://doi.org/10.1080/00224499.2011.637247.

Kumra, Savita and Simonetta Manfredi. 2012. *Managing Equality and Diversity: Theory and Practice.* Oxford: Oxford University Press.

Otaye-Ebede, Lilian, Samah Shaffakat and Scott Foster. 2020. 'A Multilevel Model Examining the Relationships between Workplace Spirituality, Ethical Climate and Outcomes: A Social Cognitive Theory Perspective.' *Journal of Business Ethics* 166 (3): 611–26.

Potoczniak, Daniel, Margaret Crosbie-Burnett and Nikki Saltzburg. 2009. 'Experiences Regarding Coming out to Parents among African American, Hispanic, and White Gay, Lesbian, Bisexual, Transgender, and Questioning Adolescents.' *Journal of Gay and Lesbian Social Services* 21 (2–3): 189–205. https://doi.org/10.1080/10538720902772063.

Priola, Vincenza, Diego Lasio, Francesco Serri and Silvia De Simone. 2018. 'The Organisation of Sexuality and the Sexuality of Organisation: A Genealogical Analysis of Sexual "Inclusive Exclusion" at Work.' *Organization* 25 (6): 732–54. https://doi.org/10.1177/1350508418790140.

Priola, Vincenza, Diego Lasio, Silvia De Simone and Francesco Serri. 2014. 'The Sound of Silence. Lesbian, Gay, Bisexual and Transgender Discrimination in "Inclusive Organizations".' *British Journal of Management* 25 (3): 488–502. https://doi.org/10.1111/1467-8551.12043.

Puar, Jasbir K. 2007. *Terrorist Assemblages: Homonationalism in Queer Times.* Durham, NC: Duke University Press.

Romero, A.P, S.K. Goldberg and L.A. Vasquez. 2020. *LGBT People and Housing Affordability, Discrimination, and Homelessness*. Los Angeles, CA: Williams Institute (UCLA).

UN Human Rights. 2015. 'UN Free & Equal – the Price of Exclusion.' YouTube. https://www.youtube.com/embed/DvSxLHpyFOk.

19. Migrants and refugees
Giulia Galera and Leila Giannetto

19.1 WHY IS THE LINK BETWEEN MIGRANTS, REFUGEES AND THE SSE RELEVANT?

The arrival, reception and inclusion of refugees, asylum seekers and migrants in receiving localities have yet to be carefully investigated through the lens of the social and solidarity economy (SSE). Here, the SSE is defined as a wide set of organizations, including cooperatives, mutual associations, foundations, voluntary and community organizations, registered charities and non-governmental organizations, as well as informal entities, all sharing a number of peculiar features. These features of SSE organizations include the following: they prioritize meeting the needs of people over making a profit; they are guided by values such as equity, solidarity, sustainability, participation and inclusion; they are concerned about the communities wherein they operate; and they are democratic and transformative in nature (see also entry 3, 'Contemporary Understandings').

So far, little attention has been paid to the impact of welcome initiatives aiming to host asylum seekers and refugees which are promoted by the SSE in receiving communities. Neither have the peculiar organizational characteristics that allow SSE organizations to ensure the provision of high-quality welcome services, and to facilitate the effective integration of recipients in receiving communities, been adequately investigated. Additionally, the initiatives of migrants who have made recourse to the SSE through self-organization, instead of setting up traditional enterprises, have been overlooked by research.

Investigating the role of the SSE in addressing the multiple problems faced by migrants and refugees is nevertheless particularly relevant for at least two main reasons. By providing the institutional architecture to manage complex phenomena from a bottom-up approach, while taking the peculiarities of local territories into account, the SSE provides targeted solutions to the global challenge of international migrations. International migrations are structural in nature and are expected to grow in relevance, given, among other factors, the increase in the number of environmental migrants who will flee their countries as a result of climate change over the coming decades. The topics of migration and asylum have turned into a battlefield for electoral purposes worldwide. However, the SSE, which has proved itself to be effective in creatively managing conflicts, encapsulates efforts to design and implement innovative solutions in hosting territories (Patuzzi et al. 2019). Indeed, when faced with the migration crisis, local communities, in many instances, have proven to be unprepared and significantly divided internally. This has resulted in complex situations in which traces of extraordinary spontaneous solidarity exist together with manifestations of deep hostility (European Committee of the Regions 2020). Against this backdrop, the local responses of the SSE appear as extremely valuable not only in light of xenophobia and populist politics, but also due to welfare state retrenchment, which has resulted in the inability of public agencies to detect and address new emerging needs arising in society, amongst which those connected to migration are among the most challenging.

148   *Encyclopedia of the social and solidarity economy*

Previous research shows that SSE initiatives are the most resourceful measures to respond to the asylum and migration challenge because they have proven to be able to both develop concrete solutions and heal profound divisions in local communities (Perlink et al. 2019). This has proven possible thanks to the unique position of SSE organizations and enterprises (SSEOEs) that have operated often in response to emergency situations, especially during the last decade. The SSEOEs had leeway to experiment with the design and provision of new services, tailored to meet the needs not only of asylum seekers and refugees, but also of the local communities, using bottom-up approaches (Galera et al. 2018). This entry presents the main patterns of evolution and the main challenges faced by SSEOEs active in the field of migrants' and refugees' integration. It explains the added value of SSEOEs when dealing with the issues associated with migrants and asylum seekers. In particular, the entry underlines the attention SSEOEs pay to relational aspects, and their knowledge of, and anchorage to, local communities, together with their 'holistic' approach to integration, encompassing concerns not only for labour market inclusion but also for socio-cultural and housing dimensions.

19.2   THE SSE: PATTERNS OF EVOLUTION

Observing the evolution of the SSE, especially in the Global North, shows that many organizations have expanded their activities with a view to welcoming asylum seekers and refugees (see also entry 10, 'Origins and Histories'). Drawing on the active engagement of stakeholders sharing common concerns, who have self-organized so as to provide, for instance, first aid to newcomers, new models of services have been designed by the SSE using bottom-up approaches. While experimenting with new methodologies to assess and take stock of unexploited skills of recipients, they have provided dispersed accommodation, organized innovative language courses, and delivered job orientation and integration services. These initiatives, led by the most innovative SSEOEs, have emerged by taking stock of the collective engagement of volunteers, social workers and the community at large (Galera et al. 2018).

Numerous associations and social enterprises have activated innovative social inclusion paths (Patuzzi et al. 2019), often in cooperation with local communities, which in some instances have facilitated the matching of labour market needs with the supply of labour at the local level. In other cases, inclusion paths have resulted in new economic activities based on taking stock of the formal, survival and practice-oriented skills of recipients in a variety of economic fields of activity, which range from recycling to community tourism and social farming, all of which generate a beneficial impact in terms of welfare, employment and economic development at the local level. Commonly, new SSEOEs have been set up by groups of volunteers who have self-organized spontaneously to provide support to asylum seekers, and then formalized the creation of new organizations specifically designed to deliver innovative welcome and integration services, sometimes in cooperation with public administrations and mainstream enterprises.

Thousands of individuals engage daily in both voluntary and professional activities aimed at improving the welfare of people who have been forced to flee their countries for different reasons. Interestingly, the form of volunteering that emerged out of this new wave of civic commitment, notably within the last decade, is very different from that of the past. It is cross-cutting across social classes and age groups, and rather than reflecting the willingness to donate time and energy for the benefit of other people in a community, it is strongly linked to the commitment to help migrants specifically, and change society for the better (Galera et al. 2018).

Given its peculiar features, the SSE is able to channel these new forms of civic activism so as to meet the needs of newcomers and host communities alike, through organized and sustainable solutions which are able to support a progressive transformation of the social and economic system, including a change in mindset of those who tend to be hostile due to an irrational fear of strangers. In this way, the SSE contributes to the designing of innovative solutions to problems that public authorities would have been unable to cope with (see also entry 51, 'Public Policy' and entry 53, 'Social Policy'). In the context of the recent increase in the number of asylum seekers, which peaked in 2015 in Europe, without SSEOEs, shelter and food, housing, legal assistance and language training would not have been ensured, and innovative social and integration paths would not have been experimented with (Simsa 2017; Galera et al. 2018).

At the same time, many migrants have chosen the SSE to institutionalize their collective efforts in diverse fields of economic activity, in order to meet the specific needs of their members, rather than to respond to the rationale of profit maximization (see Box 19.1). This is the case of many migrants' worker cooperatives, which have enabled the creation and preservation of decent jobs in domains where migrants are often exploited (such as agriculture, cleaning, and so on; see also entry 42, 'Work Integration').

BOX 19.1 UP & GO (USA): MIGRANTS' SELF-ORGANIZATION IN THE GIG ECONOMY

Up & Go (www.upandgo.coop) is a platform cooperative that offers an online booking service for domestic and commercial professional cleaning. It was launched in New York in 2017 and was spearheaded by three immigrant-led, local and eco-friendly cleaning cooperatives. Up & Go is owned by, and employs, women with migrant backgrounds, who have started to collaborate thanks to the support of, and the networking opportunities created by, the non-profit community job centre La Colmena, the Center for Family Life, the tech support of the CoLab Cooperative, and partial funding by the Robin Hood Foundation. The sustainability of this platform is ensured thanks to investment in customer service and towards advancing the technology of the app. While 95 per cent of the profits made by Up & Go are allocated to support the cooperatively owned business, 5 per cent are reinvested in the further development of the platform itself.

While the app supports workers with migrant backgrounds by overcoming the language barrier during the search for job opportunities, the main strength of Up & Go is the innovative use of the platform economy to benefit its workers and their community. The ownership of the app by the self-organized migrant workers ensures that they receive a fair income, have reasonable and flexible working hours which are more compatible with their personal lives and family time, and have a better understanding of their rights and potential not only as workers but also as entrepreneurs. Tapping into the potential of technology and making use of data, Up & Go can provide a different model of the gig economy, fighting precarious labour (Hayes 2019) but also stereotypes and prejudices, by empowering women with migrant backgrounds to provide high-quality services to clients residing in New York.

> Finally, this cooperative model unearths the talents and skills of the workers/entrepreneurs and motivates them to train further.
>
> *Source:* Up & Go (2022).

19.3 WHAT MAKES THE SSE SO SPECIAL IN SUPPORTING MIGRANTS' INTEGRATION?

One of the reasons for the success of the SSE in tackling the migration and asylum challenges is that SSEOEs are not motivated to maximize the rate of profit for investors, but rather to address the needs of recipients and communities (Utting 2015; Borzaga et al. 2017). As such, they can be regarded as collective problem-solvers.

The capacity to design innovative and effective solutions results from the close connection of SSEOEs with the communities wherein they operate. SSEOEs have distinctive ownership structures and governance models, enabling them to actively engage diverse stakeholders with different relations to the organizations, namely: workers, volunteers, recipients, donors and local authorities. The involvement of diverse stakeholders allows the identification of key needs arising in local communities, which in many instances would remain unheard, and to attract unexploited resources which would otherwise not be allocated for welfare or development goals such as community assets, building, spaces and land.

A peculiar trait of many SSEOEs assisting asylum seekers, refugees and migrants is the attention they pay to relational aspects, which has proven to be crucial in both ensuring their social inclusion and autonomy, as well as in the building of bridges between the hosting community and recipients.

The 'holistic approach' promoted by many SSEOEs does not limit itself to linking integration exclusively to supporting labour market inclusion. It also pays attention to a number of crucial structural, social and cultural dimensions influencing the path toward social inclusion (see Box 19.2). Especially relevant is the capacity to empower recipients by encouraging their active participation in SSEOEs to help them gain control over their own projects, and by taking stock of their skills and previous work experiences. Many SSE organizations have specialized in designing individualized integration pathways that often draw on the unexploited skills of fragile workers. Skills assessment practices, experimented by SSE organizations by taking stock of their holistic and inclusive approaches, have proven to be particularly effective; the more sensitive they are to recipients' implicit, practice-oriented skills – appreciated via extended and tailored interaction with them (see Box 19.3 in section 19.4) – the more effective they are. Cases in point are SSE organizations which build on recipients' manual, informal skills, and on their 'survival' skills, as a basis for fostering their entrepreneurial skills (Galera et al. 2018; Galera 2010).

BOX 19.2 JOBEL (ITALY): TRANSFORMING REFUGEES' NEEDS AND TALENTS INTO LOCAL DEVELOPMENT OPPORTUNITIES

Jobel (www.jobel.it) is a locally rooted social cooperative, founded in 2005, which aims to provide social and educational services at the local level. With the arrival of asylum seekers and refugees in small towns and rural areas in Italy, as elsewhere in Europe (European Committee of the Regions 2020), social cooperatives such as Jobel started providing reception and integration services for asylum seekers and refugees. Jobel's experience is particularly interesting because the cooperative's activities of reception and integration are all located in small towns and rural areas with declining populations, even though these localities still retain some tourist vocation. The intuition of the cooperative's members was to develop several entrepreneurial projects, not only to support the training and labour market inclusion of people hosted in their reception centres, but also to foster the local development of these remote areas. The businesses developed include a restaurant, a tailoring workshop and a woodworking shop, among others.

The main strength of Jobel is to have a holistic approach to the inclusion of not only the hosted asylum seekers and refugees, but also other vulnerable persons, such as victims of sex trafficking and people with mental health issues, living in the areas of activity of the cooperative. Moreover, Jobel's knowledge of the local context and of the local key actors is a crucial asset to tailor entrepreneurial projects that can benefit not only the workers and trainees, but also the hosting territory, and boost local development in economically depressed areas (Martini and Bartolini 2020). The main challenge faced by SSEOEs such as Jobel, which hosts asylum seekers and refugees, is the closure of reception projects or the end of the reception period for refugees in small towns and rural areas. These could push refugees to leave the welcoming but remote and depopulated territories to move to larger urban areas, thus leading to the closure of the businesses themselves.

19.4 CHALLENGES AHEAD

SSEOEs active in this field often strive for scale in order to activate new services and/or serve additional recipients (Moore et al. 2015). Scaling, however, poses numerous challenges as well as opportunities. New opportunities include the possibility to serve a larger number of asylum seekers or other target groups (see Box 19.2) and to design new models of services that may address new needs. Threats are connected to the consequences of growth, which often pushes SSEOEs to behave like mainstream enterprises (for example, by adopting strategies and tools consistent with a for-profit nature), which in turn may put at risk the local anchorage that distinguishes SSEOEs (Borzaga et al. 2016) (see entry 44, 'Co-optation, Isomorphism and Instrumentalisation').

Therefore, effective scaling strategies that are able to safeguard the local embeddedness of SSEOEs are needed. The observation of successful SSE initiatives suggests that effective scaling should be understood not only as organizational growth, but also as 'scaling deep' (Moore et al. 2015). This implies, for instance, tackling a larger set of needs of a given target group – such as helping recipients to find a suitable job and supporting their social inclusion in addition to offering housing and food – rather than increasing the overall number of persons served.

Developing strategic partnerships with other organizations presents an opportunity to increase the number of recipients served. Strategic partnerships could, for instance, allow for the replication of given models of service that have proven to be effective, such as micro forms of accommodation, or strategies to boost constant interaction with civil society. Moreover, networking could support the diffusion of skills assessment tools, which have proven to be more successful in matching the needs of local populations and labour markets with the skills, competencies and qualifications of asylum seekers, refugees and migrants.

Crucial in the case of SSEOEs supporting the work integration of migrants are partnerships with conventional enterprises that are facing labour shortages but are not equipped to select workers with migration backgrounds who, for example, lack language skills, or to facilitate their work integration (see Box 19.3).

BOX 19.3 ACTION EMPLOI RÉFUGIÉS (FRANCE): REFUGEES' LABOUR MARKET INTEGRATION

Action Emploi Réfugiés (AERé) (www.actionemploirefugies.com) is a social enterprise that emerged in 2016 in Paris as a digital platform created to unearth and match refugees' skills with French businesses' demand for workers. AERé's main objective is to 'level the playing field' for refugees in accessing the labour market of the country of destination. On the one hand, it offers refugees the social capital that they lack when settling in a new country, which is crucial to finding a job (Bakker et al. 2017), and the necessary information about the country of destination (in this case, France) regarding how the labour market works and how to access it. On the other hand, AERé recognizes the need for traditional enterprises, as well as other SSEOEs, to learn how to deal with diversity and the specific challenges that refugees face when accessing the new labour market (for example, trauma, language barrier, difficulties in the recognition of their qualifications, among others) (Federico and Baglioni 2021).

AERé's main strength is its founders' and members' ability to create a solid network with traditional enterprises and with other social enterprises (for example, through the Tent Partnership for Refugees), as well as with public services working for labour market inclusion. A strong network and partnership with traditional enterprises is key to learning about the issues of traditional enterprises in relation to the inclusion of refugees and migrants, and thus to addressing business concerns through tailored support. This, in turn, provides AREé with the opportunity to scale up its activities in terms of the number of available job postings for refugees, to replicate AERé's model in other territories (such as the Bordeaux area, where AERé is also present), and possibly to collaborate with other traditional enterprises in a wide variety of sectors.

Additional challenges result from the contracting out of reception services (accommodation, food, legal support, and so on) to private providers by public authorities, which in most countries include both for-profit enterprises and SSEOEs. Challenges arise particularly from competitive tenders evaluating offers on value-for-money grounds, which tend to crowd out grass-roots SSEOEs and favour for-profit enterprises with the economy of scale generated by the large number of recipients hosted, and low-cost (and low-quality) welcome services delivered (Del Biaggio 2020). The possibility to provide housing to asylum seekers and refugees has indeed attracted a growing number of self-interested actors, including mainstream enterprises and even non-profit organizations, that enter this business to make a profit.

Effective enabling environments or institutions for SSEOEs include procurement procedures through competitive bids that value the contribution of SSEOEs to meeting specific conditions (locally based, engagement of the community, empowerment of recipients), as well as collaborative interactions between SSEOEs and public authorities inspired by cooperation rather than competition.

SSEOEs tackling asylum and migration issues also face key management challenges as they pursue economic performance while seeking to remain faithful to their values and founding principles. These challenges are particularly prevalent when SSEOEs develop out of voluntary initiatives. They are normally pushed to adopt management and governance methods as similar as possible to those of conventional for-profit enterprises, in order to attract the private capital that they need to develop, and to increase their efficiency. Nevertheless, in doing so, SSEOEs tend to sacrifice their competitive advantages vis-à-vis public and for-profit providers: in particular, those resulting from their connections with the community and territory wherein they operate. The available empirical evidence suggests that the emergence, consolidation and success of SSEOEs are explained by their distinctive characteristics: in particular, the pursuit of not-for-profit goals; their grounding on processes of bottom-up mobilization; and their maintenance of a collective and participatory nature (Borzaga et al. 2016). Therefore, SSEOEs should not mimic conventional for-profit enterprises. They should struggle to adopt management practices that reflect their ethics.

REFERENCES

Bakker, Linda, Jaco Dagevos and Godfried Engbersen. 2017. 'Explaining the Refugee Gap: A Longitudinal Study on Labour Market Participation of Refugees in the Netherlands.' *Journal of Ethnic and Migration Studies* 43 (11): 1775–91. https://doi.org/10.1080/1369183x.2016.1251835.

Borzaga, Carlo, Luca Fazzi and Giulia Galera. 2016. 'Social Enterprise as a Bottom-Up Dynamic.' *International Review of Sociology* 26 (1): 1–18. https://doi.org/10.1080/03906701.2016.1148332.

Borzaga, Carlo, Gianluca Salvatori and Riccardo Bodini. 2017. 'Social and Solidarity Economy and the Future of Work.' ILO. https://www.ilo.org/wcmsp5/groups/public/---ed_emp/---emp_ent/---coop/documents/publication/wcms_573160.pdf.

Del Biaggio, Cristina. 2020 'Privatisation de L'Asile: ORS, un Empire "en construction".' *Vivre Ensemble: Bulletin de liaison pour la défense du droit d'asile* VE 180/Décembre: 24–8.

European Committee of the Regions. 2020 'Integration of Migrants in Middle and Small Cities and in Rural Areas in Europe.' http://ec.europa.eu/migrant-integration/library-document/integration-migrants-middle-and-small-cities-and-rural-areas-europe_en.

Federico, Veronica and Simone Baglioni. 2021. *Migrants, Refugees and Asylum Seekers' Integration in European Labour Markets. A Comparative Approach on Legal Barriers and Enablers*. IMISCOE Research Series. Cham: Springer.

Galera, Giulia. 2010. 'Social Enterprises and the Integration of Disadvantaged Workers.' In *The Economics of Social Responsibility*. New York: Routledge.

Galera, Giulia, Leila Giannetto and Antonella Noya. 2018. 'The Role of Non-State Actors in the Integration of Refugees and Asylum Seekers.' *OECD Local Economic and Employment Development (LEED) Papers* 2018/02. https://doi.org/10.1787/434c3303-en.

Hayes, Ryan. 2019. 'Worker-Owned Apps Are Trying to Fix the Gig Economy's Exploitation. A Network of Cooperative Alternatives are Replacing Rampant Exploitation.' Vice. https://www.ilo.org/global/topics/cooperatives/publications/WCMS_573160/lang--en/index.htm.

Martini, Francesca and Maddalena Bartolini, eds. 2020. *La Liguria Duale Dell'accoglienza: Buone Pratiche, Opportunità E Problematiche Tra Aree Rurali E Area Metropolitana Genovese*. Genova: Genova University Press.

Moore, Michele-Lee, Darcy Riddell and Dana Vocisano. 2015. 'Scaling Out, Scaling Up, Scaling Deep. Strategies of Non-profits in Advancing Systemic Social Innovation.' *Journal of Corporate Citizenship* 58: 67–84. https://doi.org/10.9774/gleaf.4700.2015.ju.00009.

Patuzzi, Liam, Meghan Benthon and Alexandra Embiricos. 2019. 'Social Innovation for Refugee Inclusion. From Bright Spots to System Change.' Migration Policy Institute Europe. https://www.migrationpolicy.org/research/social-innovation-refugee-inclusion-bright-spots-system-change.

Perlink, Manfred, Giulia Galera, Ingrid Machold and Andrea Membretti. 2019. *Alpine Refugees: Immigration at the Core of Europe*. Cambridge: Cambridge Scholars Publishing.

Simsa, Ruth. 2017. 'Emergency Management by Civil Society – the Case of Austria.' *International Journal of Emergency Services* 11 (4): 78–95. https://doi.org/10.1080/19361610.2017.1228026.

Up & Go. 2022. 'Find a Better Home Cleaning Service – Up & Go Cleaners.' https://www.upandgo.coop/.

Utting, Peter. 2015. *Social and Solidarity Economy: Beyond the Fringe*. London: Zed Books.

20. Non-governmental organisations and foundations

Edith Archambault

INTRODUCTION

In many developed and developing countries, non-governmental organizations (NGOs) and foundations interact with national and local governments to provide public services or to motivate public authorities to support their causes in order to improve the capacity of governments to respond to societal challenges. Some of them deliver services or advocate inter-country or at the international level.

The term 'non-governmental organization' has several meanings. It is often used as an equivalent of an association (see entry 15, 'Associations and Associationalism'). The United Nations (UN) proposes a narrower understanding of this concept: according to its 1945 Charter, article 71, an NGO must have the following characteristics as conditions of recognition by the UN:

- Not profit-making or not distributing its eventual surplus.
- Independent from the direct control of government at any level, though often receiving public funding.
- Oriented to the public good, not member interest.

In addition, in most countries NGOs have democratic governance based on the 'one member, one vote' principle. They are not constituted as political parties and their action is nonviolent; they are not criminal groups such as mafias (Willets 2006). The narrowest understanding of the term 'NGO' is used for those operating in two or more countries, which are often called International NGOs (INGOs).

A foundation (or a charitable trust in English-speaking countries) is an organization that devotes private funds to a public purpose of its choice. It is a non-membership-based organization, therefore its governance is either the founder itself or a co-opted board rather than the democratic governance of NGOs. The other criteria are shared with NGOs: foundations are nonprofit, private, independent and public good-oriented entities. Sometimes foundations are included in the broadest understanding of NGOs (Anheier 2001).

NGOs and foundations are part of the social economy because they undertake an economic activity even when run solely by volunteers, which is the situation in most developing countries and in many developed countries' nonprofit sectors. Most of them deliver welfare services, while advocacy NGOs provide information services for their members or the public at large. Operating foundations are producers of welfare services, while grant-making foundations change income or wealth distribution (Archambault 1986).

This entry outlines a global picture of the nonprofit sector, highlighting the privileged activities in each important region through the analysis of NGOs and foundations. It also examines the different experiences of these organizations at the local and national levels. The entry critically reviews the activities of international NGOs and foundations operating at the inter-country or global levels, with a focus on challenges, limitations and opportunities. It concludes with the importance of a real partnership between authorities, NGOs and foundations to address the key societal and global problems of the 21st century.

20.1 PANORAMA OF ASSOCIATIONS AND FOUNDATIONS WORLDWIDE

As said above, NGOs have several definitions which is why empirical data, if any, deal with associations, and the legal status of most NGOs. Statistics for foundations are better in the United States (US) and European countries. The most comprehensive data on the nonprofit sectors of 41 countries, the population of which is more than half of the world's population, are the following:

- On average, the full-time paid or volunteer employment in the nonprofit sector is 5.7 per cent of the active population of these countries, the same percentage as the construction industry. The volunteer share of this workforce is 41 per cent. For example, there are 3 456 000 regular voluntary workers in charities in England and Wales; a further 944 000 trustees can be added to this estimate.
- The average share of this workforce employed in welfare services is 59 per cent (education, social services, health, development and housing, in decreasing order). The share of expressive activities, such as culture and recreation, religion, civic and advocacy, is 36 per cent.
- On average, half of the resources of nonprofit organizations come from fees, dues and sales, 35 per cent from public funding, and 14 per cent from households or corporate giving.

Of course, there is a high dispersion around these averages: the civil society workforce ranges from 16 per cent of the active population in the Netherlands to 1 per cent in Poland, Pakistan and Russia; and the volunteer share ranges from 75 per cent in Tanzania and Sweden to 19 per cent in Japan, Hungary and Brazil. Welfare services are dominant in most countries, but expressive activities are prevailing in Eastern and Nordic Europe. Commercial resources are the main part of the income of NGOs in most countries. However, in continental Europe, where the partnership with public authorities has been developed for decades, public funding affords the main part of their income (Salamon et al. 2017).

Within the nonprofit sector, the foundations of the US and Europe are the most powerful organizations, but also the most contested. In 2015, there were 86 000 foundations in the US and 147 000 in Europe. Their assets were $868 billion in the US and €511 billion in Europe. Their annual giving is nearly the same in the US and Europe ($63 billion and €60 billion) (Foundation Center n.d.; European Foundation Center n.d.). Foundations are more recent in Europe than in the US; for example, 70 per cent of German foundations were created after the 1990 reunification. They are powerful in Italy, Germany and the Netherlands, and weak in France, Poland and Ireland. Their principal activities are: religion (United Kingdom and the Netherlands), international solidarity (Belgium, Germany, Switzerland) and social services (France and Spain).

NGOs and foundations exist everywhere in the world. Their density is often seen as an indicator of democracy. However, even in dictatorial or authoritarian countries, NGOs are tolerated provided they do not engage in anti-establishment politics. In these countries, the public authorities closely control the creation and decisions of many NGOs, which therefore cease to be independent. These organizations are often called governmental NGOs (GNGOs), and they are often instruments of the social control of citizens, such as in China.

In many countries, NGOs and foundations deliver public services in addition to central or local governments. These various experiences and trajectories are discussed in the following section.

20.2 NGOS AND FOUNDATIONS PROVIDING PUBLIC SERVICES AT THE LOCAL AND NATIONAL LEVEL

Historically, NGOs have been pioneers of public services, and they continue to play this role in many developing countries today. In these countries, local, national or foreign NGOs provide education, health and social services as well as utilities. For example, in South Morocco, development NGOs have installed the electricity connection in many villages and modernized the traditional irrigation network. Service delivery NGOs provide public goods and services that governments of developing countries are unable to provide due to a lack of resources. They may be contractors or collaborate with government agencies to reduce the cost of public goods. In continental Europe, services for people with disabilities were often created by NGOs, and governments developed partnerships with these NGOs after both world wars. According to this partnership, NGOs deliver residential or day-care services or work integration to people with physical or mental disabilities, while the local or central governments pay the bulk of their expenses through grants or contracts. The relative penetration of the nonprofit sector into education and health systems follows from the historical relations between the government and the Catholic Church, which has been a pioneer in these domains since the Middle Ages. Consequently, there exists a high penetration of NGOs in Belgium and the Netherlands where these relations were peaceful, and a lower penetration in France where government–Church relations have been beset by recurring conflicts, especially in education; however, these conflicts are now resolved.

Currently, the partnership between NGOs, operating foundations and the government is not confined to continental Europe: it is beginning in many developing countries as well. Even in the United States, the country that champions liberalism, private nonprofit hospitals are publicly funded partly through the Medicaid and Medicare programmes and the Ivy League universities, most of which are foundations, and partly from public research contracts. Where the welfare partnership is long-standing and equal between both partners, a co-construction of social policies is possible where NGOs bring their knowledge of the population concerned, and of the best actions to privilege, while the government brings its ability to obtain money through taxes, and its attention to the continuity of the public service and equal access of every concerned citizen (Brandsen et al. 2018). The advantages and disadvantages of sharing welfare services between NGOs and public authorities are different locally and nationally.

Nonprofit Organizations Delivering Welfare Services at the Local Level

Locally, a good relationship between NGOs and public authorities is more likely because each partner has a good knowledge of the other, namely the results of its action, its efficiency and financial situation. That is why decentralized countries are more likely to develop local welfare partnerships. However, an example of the advantages of such a partnership in a centralized country is given in Box 20.1.

> **BOX 20.1 CHARTREUSE DE NEUVILLE, A WIN–WIN PARTNERSHIP IN FRANCE**
>
> Chartreuse de Neuville is an association devoted to heritage preservation that is currently restoring a 14th century deserted and dilapidated monastery. It partnered with the regional and local authorities to rebuild these beautiful ruins. The association created a work integration social enterprise (WISE) to train young unemployed people with no skills in heritage restoration, allowing it to receive public funding. Artists have residencies in the rebuilt parts of the monastery, and shows are regularly put on for the public. In addition, some parts of the monastery are rented for professional and family events. Chartreuse de Neuville is a real attraction for tourism in the Northern area, a disadvantaged French region.
>
> *Sources:* La Chartreuse de Neuville (n.d.); Le Labo de l'économie sociale et solidaire (n.d.); interview with the CEO for EU–Russia Report 2020 (in 2020).

Disadvantages of a local partnership also exist: proximity can induce conflicts of interest in public procurement and also between NGOs or operating foundations and their suppliers. Local governments can seek the votes of the employees, volunteers and beneficiaries of these organizations for their re-election; it could also condition their financing by control of the organizations' boards by its representatives. When the political colour of the local government changes, abrupt cessation of public funding may occur, but this is more likely for advocacy NGOs than for those which manage a public service by delegation.

Nonprofit Organizations Delivering Welfare Services at the National Level

NGOs and operating foundations provide educational, health and social services nationally as well as locally. The sharing of these welfare services provisions between central and local governments and civil society organizations obviously depends on functions that have been devolved to local governments, as well as on the level of externalization or subcontracting that authorities consider being relevant. This sharing is variable across countries, and depends on the advantages and disadvantages of central governments to outsource to civil society organizations (CSOs). The benefits are the reduction of the cost of public services (as salaries are lower in NGOs, or nonexistent for volunteers) and the reduction of public employment, considered too high in Nordic countries and France. CSOs also have a better knowledge of minority populations. Lastly, the involvement of a large part of the population is required in a crisis situation such as the COVID-19 pandemic. Another example of civil society involvement is given in Box 20.2.

BOX 20.2 THE GERMAN PARTNERSHIP FOR 2015 MIGRANTS' INCLUSION

In the years 2015–18, Germany welcomed about 1 million Syrian and Afghan refugees. *'Wir schaffen das'*, said Angela Merkel, and five years later Germany did it: half of the migrants had jobs, and most of them spoke German well or just about well. The distribution of refugees among the *Länder* was as a proportion of their population but also of their per capita income, with the richest *Länder* receiving more refugees than the poorest. Civil society's involvement was strong. In addition to the Catholic and Protestant parishes and existing NGOs providing social services, 50 000 new NGOs were created by volunteers to shelter refugees, distribute clothes, introduce the German language or help with administrative procedures. In the autumn 2021 election, the migrant issue was no longer a major one in the debates among the leaders of the diverse political parties.

Sources: L'Express (n.d.); *Le Point* (n.d.); interviews with anonymous German interviewees.

But the drawbacks of delegating public services to NGOs or foundations are also obvious: amateurism and particularism are common critiques of NGOs; operating foundations may be accused of deepening social inequalities, as is the case in education for expensive American universities or private schools in many developing and developed countries; foundations running hospitals may provide better-quality and quicker healthcare for the richest, while public hospitals welcome the rest of the population. Of course, social services for the most disadvantaged are not the subject of this criticism, but they are accused of keeping the poor in poverty. This ambiguity of NGOs and foundations seems to be reinforced when they operate internationally.

The Ambiguous Role of NGOs and Foundations at the Global Level

International NGOs (INGOs) or foundations have the source of their funding and their programmes in different countries. The most common ones link a developed country with one or several developing or underdeveloped countries; in this case, they are tools of private help to development. The best example of such an organization is the Bill & Melinda Gates Foundation (BMGF), the largest foundation in the world devoted mainly to health and agricultural development. Some INGOs are committed to reinforcing links between two or more Northern and Southern countries to advocate for specific causes or interests. An example is given in Box 20.3.

BOX 20.3 LA MAIN À LA PÂTE, A FRENCH FOUNDATION THAT IS BECOMING INTERNATIONAL

During the early 2000s in France, it was clearly apparent that science education in primary and middle schools was not up to what the 21st century demanded. Initiated by the Nobel laureate Georges Charpak, La Main à la Pâte recommends that teachers implement an enquiry-based method with pupils, and provides training to teachers in this active pedagogy. Over the last decade, it has spread internationally. Today, La Main à la Pâte is co-

> operating with more than 40 countries and three regional networks (the European Union, Southeast Asia and Latin America) and its establishment in Africa has begun. It receives grants from interested governments and large European and American foundations, such as the Siemens Foundation and the Smithsonian Institute.
>
> *Sources:* Charpak et al. (2005); Fondation La Main à la Pâte (n.d.); interview with Pierre Léna, the main founder (EU–Russia 2020 Report).

Some INGOs are confirmed by the UN for consultation, and the European Union (EU) has similarly confirmed NGOs. According to articles 70 and 71 of the UN 1945 Charter, 'specialized agencies, established by intergovernmental agreement', such as the Food and Agriculture Organization (FAO) and the World Health Organization (WHO), could 'participate without a vote in UN deliberations', while a confirmed NGO could have 'suitable arrangements for consultation' (United Nations 1945).

Therefore, there is a hierarchy between these two types of organizations, because deliberation is nearer to ultimate decisions than is consultation. Confirmed INGOs and some other organizations can be used by Northern countries or international organizations as transfer channels of public aid to development when the governments of those countries are considered corrupt or are not internationally recognized, such as the Taliban government in Afghanistan. For example, the Directorate-General for European Civil Protection and Humanitarian Aid Operations (DG ECHO) programme is mainly oriented toward INGOs. Conversely, some large foundations, mainly the BMGF, can also fund international public organizations such as the FAO, WHO and the United Nations Children's Fund (UNICEF) for specific projects. Of course, public aid to development, $152 billion, is more than 20 times private aid to development.

INGOs or foundations are either operating or campaigning. The operating ones affect small-scale change, achieved through development projects such as affording sanitary water to the population of a village or building, and running a hospital for a larger area. Service delivery INGOs provide public goods and services that governments of developing countries are unable to provide due to their lack of resources. Campaigning INGOs aim to enact broader change through influence on the political system. Once INGOs do decide to influence public policy, they organize in broad coalitions specifically for this purpose. These umbrellas, networks or caucuses are numerous, to advocate for development, humanitarian or environmental issues. An example is the World Social Forum, a rival convention of the World Economic Forum, an annual meeting focused on capitalist enterprise interests held in Davos, Switzerland. Similarly, World Social Forums, gathering hundreds of INGOs, have parallel meetings every year to influence the Conference of the Parties (COP) where representatives of the governments of most countries discuss climate change and other environmental challenges.

Foundations and INGOs have a positive impact on developing countries and the alleviation of extreme poverty in the world, but they are also the subject of significant criticism. These praises and criticisms can be illustrated by the Bill & Melinda Gates Foundation (BMGF), which alone represents half of the private philanthropy. In the field of health, the BMGF, in cooperation with the WHO and the Gavi, the Vaccine Alliance, nearly eradicated poliomyelitis, cured HIV holders and gave access to vaccines to 55 million children, and family planning, in many African and Asian countries. In the field of agriculture, this foundation was an efficient partner of the 'green revolutions' in India and some African countries. However, critics outline that the assets of the BMGF ($50 billion) are greater than the gross domestic product of many poor countries, and that its endowment is frequently invested in companies whose impact is inconsistent with its objectives because they are harmful to health and the environment. Conflicts of interest also exist with vaccine producers and Monsanto in the Indian and African green revolutions.

More generally, some critics consider INGOs and foundations as part of a neo-colonial system to maintain the domination of Northern countries over the less-developed Southern countries. They play the role that 19th century missionaries played, as Trojan horses of the predatory Northern companies. Less radical critics outline that international nonprofit organizations have a tendency to impose their system of values on countries with other traditions. In another context, the American foundations arrived in the countries of Eastern Europe as soon as the fall of the Berlin Wall; these foundations influenced Eastern countries to adopt health and education systems more similar to the American than the European ones. The Trust for Civil Society in Central and Eastern Europe also contributed to the emergence of NGOs and foundations in post-Communist countries

CONCLUSION

The European Union, where the partnership between government and the nonprofit sector is a dominant pattern, is in the best cases able to combine the strengths of both partners. On the government side, we can note a high legitimacy to decide, due to periodic elections, the weight of resources raised by the tax, the ability to create rights to benefit public services and to verify the qualifications of employees delivering these services, and finally, the concern to maintain equality between individuals and territories. On the nonprofit side, the strengths of NGOs and foundations are their roles in the detection of and response to new needs in the field of health, research, education, culture and social services, because they are nearer to the beneficiaries and more attentive to the diversity of populations. They are therefore quicker than the government to respond to emergency issues such as earthquakes, floods or other disasters. Not having to please their shareholders as corporations do, nor voters as central or local governments do, NGOs and foundations can experiment with new and unpopular fields; for example, alternatives to jail. They can also personalize public services through volunteer accompaniment and avoid the effects of silos of public social policies.

At the global level, the partnership with northern NGOs or foundations is also possible when the government of the host country is reliable and not corrupt. These organizations consider more and more that they have to cooperate with the local NGOs to avoid the above-noted criticisms of neo-colonialism, and ignorance of the history, religions and culture of the developing countries.

Finally, the fight against the great challenges of the 21st century, such as poverty of people and countries, unemployment, the marginalization of part of the youth, the ageing of society, climate change and environmental degradation, racism, xenophobia and all other forms of discrimination, presupposes collaboration between the government and the specialized SSE organizations. Reducing social and cultural inequalities for more inclusive growth, and coping with the migrations of large populations, also most often requires an effective partnership between public authorities and NGOs and foundations.

REFERENCES

Anheier, Helmut K. 2001. 'Foundations in Europe: A Comparative Perspective.' In *Foundations in Europe: Society, Management and Law*, edited by Andreas Schluter, Volker Then and Peter Walkenhorst. London: Directory of Social Change, 35–83.

Archambault, Edith. 1986. 'L'Économie Sociale Est-Elle Associée Aux Grandes Fonctions Des Pouvoirs Publics?' HAL. https://halshs.archives-ouvertes.fr/halshs-02396794/document.

Brandsen, Taco, Bram Verschuere and Trui Steen, eds. 2018. *Co-production and Co-creation: Engaging Citizens in Public Services*. Abingdon: Routledge.

Charpak, Georges, Pierre Lena and Yves Quere. 2005. *L'Enfant et La Science: L'aventure de La Main à La Pâte*. Paris: Odile Jacob.

European Foundation Center. n.d. 'EFC-Data on the Sector.' Philea. Accessed 4 October 2021. https://www.efc.be/knowledge-hub/data-on-the-sector.

Fondation La main à la pâte. n.d. 'Bienvenue Sur Le Site de La Fondation La Main à La Pâte.' Fondation La main à la pâte. Accessed 18 November 2021. https://www.fondation-lamap.org/.

Foundation Center. n.d. 'Foundation Stats: Guide to the Foundation Center's Research Database – Foundation Center.' Foundation Center. Accessed 22 September 2021. http://data.foundationcenter.org.

La Chartreuse de Neuville. n.d. 'Accueil.' La Chartreuse de Neuville. Accessed 18 November 2021. https://lachartreusedeneuville.org/.

Le Labo de l'économie sociale et solidaire. n.d. 'Accueil | Le Labo de l'Économie Sociale et Solidaire.' Accessed 28 November 2021. https://www.lelabo-ess.org/.

Le Point. n.d. 'Le Point – Actualité Politique, Monde, France, Économie, High-Tech, Culture.' Accessed 2 March 2022. https://www.lepoint.fr/.

L'Express. n.d. 'L'Express – Actualités Politique, Monde, Economie et Culture.' Accessed 18 November 2021. https://www.lexpress.fr/.

Salamon, Lester M., Megan A. Haddock and Wojciech S. Sokolowski. 2017. *Explaining Civil Society Development: A Social Origins Approach*. Baltimore, MD: Johns Hopkins University Press.

United Nations. 1945. 'United Nations Charter.' https://www.un.org/en/about-us/un-charter/full-text.

Willetts, Peter. 2006 'Article on NGOs for UNESCO Encyclopaedia.' City University London. Accessed 17 November 2021. http://www.staff.city.ac.uk/p.willetts/CS-NTWKS/NGO-ART.HTM.

21. Social enterprises
Jacques Defourny and Marthe Nyssens

INTRODUCTION

Even though not all the practices they designate are new, the recent concepts of social entrepreneurship and social enterprise (SE) are clearly fashionable, and they continue to diversify, be it in their organizational, sectoral, geographical or other expressions. This growing diversity and the rather open nature of these concepts are undoubtedly reasons for their rapid success, with both public officials and private sector actors who, each in their own way, are discovering or rediscovering new possibilities for promoting both entrepreneurial dynamics and social goals.

Most SE approaches in the literature, if not all, share the view that social enterprises combine entrepreneurial dynamics to provide services or goods with the primacy of a social mission. Beyond this minimal consensus, various tentative definitions have been put forward, but they often increased the feeling of confusion among researchers and social actors in this field. Indeed, the lack of a shared understanding is today acknowledged by most researchers, and it even seems reasonable to speak of the 'impossibility of reaching a unified definition of social enterprise'.

21.1 SOCIAL ENTERPRISES AND SCHOOLS OF THOUGHT

It is now well documented that the SE concept has emerged simultaneously in the United States (US) and in Europe throughout the 1990s, in reference to a set of new entrepreneurial initiatives seeking social goals. Defourny and Nyssens (2010) distinguish between three main schools of thought: the earned-income school, the social-innovation school, and the approach adopted by the EMES International Research Network.

For the earned-income school of thought, SE can be defined as any type of earned-income business or strategy to generate revenue in support of a social mission. Defourny and Nyssens (2010) distinguish a first stream, within this school, which they name the 'commercial non-profit' approach, with a view to underlining a key difference (namely the fact that the organisations considered to be social enterprises by scholars belonging to this first stream were all non-profits), with later development, referred to as the mission-driven business approach, which embraced all types of organization, whether non-profits or for-profits, launching business activities to address social problems. To a large extent, the concept of social business as promoted by Yunus (2010) can be related to the mission-driven business approach. This concept was mainly developed to describe a business model that focuses on the provision of goods or services to poor customers, which constitute a new market segment (often called the 'bottom of the pyramid') in developing countries. Such a social business is supposed to cover all its costs through market resources. It is owned by (often large) investors who, at least in Yunus's version, do not receive any dividend, as profits are being fully reinvested to support the social mission.

The social-innovation school of thought focuses on the very specific nature of the social entrepreneur and on their creativity, dynamism and leadership in coming up with new responses to social needs (Dees 1998). The emphasis here is on the systemic nature of innovation and the scope of its social or societal impact, rather than on the types of resources mobilized. The Ashoka organization has played a pioneering role in promoting this way of thinking; since the early 1980s, it has supported entrepreneurs of this kind.

In Europe, the EMES International Research Network developed the first theoretical and empirical milestones of SE analysis (Borzaga and Defourny 2001). The EMES approach derives from extensive dialogue among several disciplines as well as among the various national traditions present in the European Union. It preferred from the outset the identification of three subsets of indicators (Borzaga and Defourny 2001):

(1) Economic and entrepreneurial dimension of social enterprise

    (a) A continuous activity producing goods and/or selling services
    (b) A significant level of economic risk
    (c) A minimum amount of paid work

(2) Social dimension of social enterprise

    (a) An explicit aim to benefit the community
    (b) An initiative launched by a group of citizens or civil-society organizations
    (c) A limited profit distribution

(3) Governance-related dimension of social enterprise

    (a) A high degree of autonomy
    (b) A decision-making power not based on capital ownership
    (c) A participatory nature, which involves various parties affected by the activity

Such indicators were never intended to represent the set of conditions that an organization should meet in order to qualify as an SE. Rather than constituting prescriptive criteria, they describe an 'ideal-type' in Weber's terms, that is, an abstract construction that enables researchers to position themselves within the galaxy of SEs. In other words, they constitute a tool, somewhat analogous to a compass, which helps analysts to locate the position of the observed entities relative to one another, and eventually identify subsets of SEs. Those indicators allow for the identification of new SEs, but they can also lead to designate as SEs older organizations being reshaped by new internal dynamics.

These indicators are focused on the internal governance of SEs, but the EMES approach is not restricted to this aspect. Indeed, according to EMES, SEs also have a special place in society. They simultaneously pursue economic, social and political goals at large. They are economic actors, but they do not rely exclusively on the rationality of the market. Indeed, as the EMES indicators state, the financial viability of SEs depends on their members' efforts to secure the enterprise's social mission. However, these resources can have a hybrid character: they may come from trading activities, but also – to borrow concepts from Polanyi's substantive approach – from adequate resources to support redistribution and reciprocity (see entry 28, 'Finance Sector' and entry 45, 'Financing'). SEs pursue social goals connected to their social mission; their political goals refer to their 'political embeddedness', which sheds light on the fact that SEs have a role in the constitution of a democratic framework for economic activity (Laville et al. 2009).

21.2 FROM SCHOOLS OF THOUGHT TO TYPOLOGIES

In response to this conceptual diversity, various authors have attempted to identify SE categories and propose typologies. The degree of market reliance is certainly a dominant criterion in the eyes of many researchers looking for a basic SE typology. Dees (1996) paved the way for such an approach when he presented SEs along a single-dimensional continuum between two extremes corresponding, respectively, to a 'purely philanthropic' pole and a 'purely commercial' one. From the point of view of Dees's spectrum, all SEs can be seen as 'intermediate organizations' and they may all be labelled as 'hybrids' (Doherty et al. 2014).

Relying mainly on the US SE landscape, Young et al. (2016) proposed the metaphor of a 'social enterprise zoo' – in which different types of animals seek different things, behave differently, and may (or may not) interact with one another in both competitive and complementary ways – just like SEs, which combine social and market goals in substantially different ways. The authors propose 'six major species of zoo animals': for-profit business corporations developing programmes of corporate social responsibility, in which social goals play a strategic role; social businesses looking for an explicit balance between social impact and commercial success; social cooperatives maximizing their members' welfare while also including a general public-benefit dimension; commercial non-profit organizations driven by their social mission; public–private partnerships; and hybrids.

Kerlin (2017) adopted an institutional perspective and identified key features of macro-institutional frameworks to suggest how any set of socioeconomic and regulatory institutions at the country level tends to shape a specific major SE model per country.

21.3 THEORIZING THE DIVERSITY OF SE MODELS

While taking stock of these various typologies, which were inductive or/and country-specific, Defourny and Nyssens (2017) tried to go one step further by providing strong theoretical foundations to explain how various 'institutional logics' in the whole economy may generate different SE models. They developed a framework by combining principles of interest and resource mixes to identify institutional trajectories generating four major SE models. They represented this framework under the form of a triangle (see Figure 21.1).

When speaking about 'the economy', the first type of organization that is generally identified is the 'for-profit firm', which is driven by capital interest and relies mainly on market resources. For-profit enterprises, however, face market failures, which call for an intervention of the state, which is driven by the general interest, and relies mainly on non-market resources. Some associations seeking a public benefit are located close to the general interest angle, although not in the vertex itself, as their general interest (the community they serve) is usually not as wide as the one served by the state. There is also a third principle, which is often neglected when describing the socioeconomic purpose, and it is mutual interest. Mutual interest refers to services or goods provided to members under their own control. In other words, mutual benefit organizations include all the traditional types of cooperative enterprises,

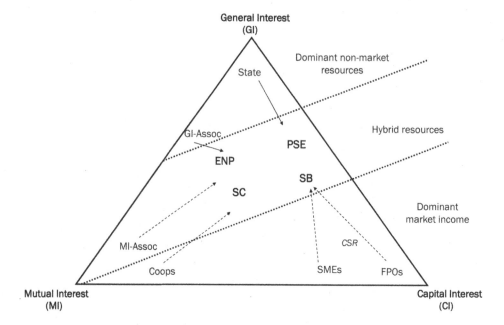

Note: ENP – entrepreneurial non-profits; PSE – public sector social enterprises; SC – social cooperatives; SB – social businesses.
Source: Defourny and Nyssens (2017).

Figure 21.1 Institutional logics and resulting SE models

which usually rely mainly on market resources, as well as voluntary associations driven by the interest of their members (such as sports clubs, professional associations, and so on), which usually rely more on non-market resources.

On the basis of this triangle, Defourny and Nyssens identified four major social enterprise models. These four models are characterized by different institutional trajectories which can be grasped through two movements.

The first movement could be observed among public and non-profit organizations, namely the movement towards marketization; it results from dramatic changes in the funding of goods and services of general interest. Both public and non-profit organizations traditionally relied mainly on non-market income; they used to be fully subsidized by public authorities, or to mix public financing and philanthropic resources. Nowadays, they are pushed towards more market-oriented activities in order to complement their existing resources, thus giving rise to two SE models:

1. Entrepreneurial non-profits (ENPs) are typically non-profit organizations developing any type of earned-income business in support of their social mission. A growing number of associations are developing income-generating strategies that can take various forms. Some associations are developing market activities as a support for their social mission. Other associations develop market activities to finance their activities linked to their social mission. Many associations are also encouraged to develop more entrepreneurial dynamics

when they find themselves competing in public markets with private for-profit enterprises and public operators.
2. Public sector social enterprises (PSEs) result from a movement toward the marketization of public services, which embraces public sector spin-offs. These SEs are usually launched by local public bodies, sometimes in partnership with third-sector organizations, to provide services that are outsourced (such as care services) or new services (such as those offered by work-integration social enterprises).

The second movement corresponds to a shift from the capital and mutual interest toward the general interest:

1. Social cooperatives (SCs) aim at implementing democratic or participatory forms of governance, that is, equal voting power in the general assembly, and a limitation of the remuneration of capital shares. However, this model goes beyond that of most traditional cooperatives, in that it combines the pursuit of the interests of its members with the pursuit of the interests of the community as a whole or of a specific target group. The legal status of the social cooperative emerged in Italy in the early 1990s. Since then, new laws, similar to the social cooperative law, have been passed in other countries. Depending on the legislation in force, other legal forms may be close to the cooperative status, even though they differ from a strictly legal point of view. Cooperative-type social enterprises may also result from the evolution of mutual-interest associations that wish to develop their economic activities in order to respond to a specific social problem and, in so doing, move towards a more explicit general-interest objective.
2. Social businesses (SBs) are rooted in a business model driven by shareholders' interest. However, they mix this logic with a social entrepreneurial drive which is aimed at the creation of a 'blended value' in an effort to balance and better integrate economic and social purposes. In this SE model, it is then a question of aiming at and balancing financial results with social – and sometimes also environmental – results (double/triple bottom line).

At first sight, when looking at Figure 21.1, the four SE models seem to arise from new dynamics at work in pre-existing organizations. Thus, it may seem that social enterprises cannot be created from scratch. Such an interpretation would clearly be misleading, as a new (social) enterprise can emerge everywhere in the triangle; its location will depend on its general-interest orientation and on the way in which it balances the social and economic objectives with the financial resources. It should also be stressed that this basic typology does not deny the existence of the many hybrid models that can be observed in the field; for example, partnerships between for-profit companies and associations, or partnerships involving local public authorities, are relatively common.

21.4 TESTING SOCIAL ENTERPRISE MODELS ACROSS THE WORLD

These theorized models were put to the test on the basis of the data collected through a large survey which was carried out by researchers from 43 countries across the world. The survey operated through an international research project named the International Comparative Social Enterprise Models (ICSEM) Project. The empirical data collected were statistically analysed with a central objective: to see whether groups of enterprises emerged that presented characteristics which made that appear as groups that were significantly homogeneous and, at the same time, significantly distinct from one another. This statistical processing of the ICSEM database confirmed the existence, at the global level, of three of the four major SE models proposed in the typology: the social-cooperative model, the entrepreneurial non-profit model, and the social-business model. The data collected shows that these three major models of social enterprise are found in almost all the countries covered, that is, 39 countries out of the 43 countries studied (Defourny et al. 2020).

Regarding the social cooperative model, two groups emerged. Although organizations in the first cooperative group produce a diversity of goods and services, practically all these activities are meant to serve social objectives. These objectives are to create jobs for the unemployed, to generate income for poor individuals, to pursue community development, to address ecological issues, and so on. In the second cooperative group, most social enterprises provide financial and insurance services. Access to financial services has always been a main concern for poor populations, and a central issue for a substantial component of the cooperative movement.

Four groups are converging towards an entrepreneurial non-profit SE model. Two of them include organizations that are mainly driven by a mission of employment generation and may therefore be considered as work integration social enterprises (WISEs) (see entry 42, 'Work Integration'), whereas the other two groups cover a wider spectrum of social missions. The largest non-profit type group includes rather large organizations providing mainly education, health and social services. The other one covers much smaller organizations, providing a very wide spectrum of services to foster local development, ecology, access to education and capacity building. These non-profit type organizations display a much wider diversity of resources than what is found in the two cooperative-type groups, with a maximum 40 per cent of income coming from the market. Such a resource mix could be seen as surprising, since a common approach to SE sees it as a market solution to a social problem. However, for the EMES school of thought, the entrepreneurial dimension of social enterprise lies, at least partly, in the fact that the initiative bears a significant level of entrepreneurial risk, but not necessarily a market risk. In this broader perspective, the resource mix which can best support the social mission is likely to have a hybrid character, as it may combine trading activities with public subsidies and voluntary resources.

A last, smaller group indicates the existence of a small and medium-sized enterprise (SME) model of social business, bringing together the newest and smallest social enterprises in the sample. It includes for-profit enterprises that combine a strong commercial orientation with a social mission. The data shows that these enterprises have business models that are very similar to those of cooperative-type organisations, and that they too rely on market resources. However, their governance models are markedly different. In this last group, many enterprises are in the hands of a single person. With regard to rules and provisions regarding profit distribution, it is striking that in the majority of organizations in this group there are no rules limiting profit distribution. Some of these companies adopt an accreditation that requires social objectives to be predominant in their mission (for example, the 'B Corp' accreditation), but generally these accreditations do not impose any limits on profit distribution. This does not mean that all or most of the profits are usually distributed to the owners, as a fairly common practice involves reinvesting the profits into the business. As this combination of economic and social objectives is implemented within less regulated frameworks than those defined by the rules and governance structures of cooperative-type social enterprises, the balance between these (potentially conflicting) objectives and its evolution over time raises the question of the sustainability of the social mission.

The existence of a public-sector SE model is not confirmed by the identification of a distinct group of enterprises. However, one should not conclude too quickly that the public sector is absent from the field of social enterprise. In fact, it is found within some clearly identified groups, often involved as a partner in the creation of social enterprises; in particular – work integration enterprises (see entry 42, 'Work Integration'). It is also possible that local researchers, considering a priori SEs as inherently private initiatives, did not consider public-sector initiatives as potential SEs.

21.5 PROMISES AND CHALLENGES

An in-depth understanding of the different SE models makes it possible to identify future challenges that are anything but trivial.

In the case of the social-business model, it can be expected that the actors of the traditional private sector will play a leading role in the development and configuration of social entrepreneurship. At play here is a belief, widely held in the business world, that market forces have the capacity to solve an increasing share of social problems. Therefore, while some stress the need to mobilize different types of resources, it is not impossible that the current wave of social entrepreneurship acts in part as a process of prioritizing and selecting social challenges according to their potential to be addressed in an entrepreneurial and market-based way. Certainly, some innovative responses may emerge from social business, but from a societal point of view, one can only doubt the relevance of such a classification of social needs. This type of questioning is increasingly relevant in countries where the logic of privatization and marketization of social services has gone the furthest.

Many SEs that are increasingly supported by proactive public policies – sometimes aimed at reintegrating marginalized workers, sometimes at providing services to vulnerable populations – face another type of challenge. The risks inherent in such public support are, on the one hand, that social innovation becomes 'frozen' at a certain stage by its institutionalization; and on the other hand, that social enterprises be instrumentalized within the framework of political agendas that take away most of their autonomy and creativity (see entry 53, 'Social Policy' and entry 51, 'Public Policy').

Despite such risks, the emergence of different entrepreneurial forms centred on social goals and the identification of three – or even four – major models open up several interesting perspectives. First, this identification constitutes an additional step in the clarification of the landscape of social enterprises, too often caricatured and described by monolithic discourses. Far from aiming at any unification, it highlights very different major models, which themselves open up to a diversity of effective practices within them. Secondly, and most importantly, it shows in a structured way that social entrepreneurship can emerge from all parts of our economies, including those – different from one part of the world to the other – that were least thought of.

So why not recognize, in these four major SE models, the emergence of new distributions of roles and tasks in the pursuit of the common good? Historically, the state has often been tempted to take sole responsibility for the general interest, even though traditions of solidarity or philanthropy have almost always coexisted with official forms of public monopoly. The recognition of the complementarities between public and associative action is, after all, very recent and, moreover, far from being achieved in many regions of the world. In this context, the emergence – or rather the strengthening – of genuine associative entrepreneurship, as well as the development of a new family of cooperatives more focused on the general interest, underlines the relevance and the potential of a new sharing of responsibilities, as well as the need to deepen partnerships of all kinds around specific issues of the common good. Within such partnerships, or along more individual lines, a growing number of entrepreneurs (concerned with integrating a general-interest dimension into the heart of economic activity) are also questioning the pursuit of profit at all cost.

Identifying this diversity is not only about recognizing that social enterprise can generate social impacts by providing goods and services to meet unmet needs through a variety of models. It also means acknowledging the institutional dimension of these different models; that is, their potential role in the development of norms and regulations, both at the level of the organization and beyond, through the 'institutional work' of all actors. It is essential not to reduce social enterprises to a space dedicated to 'alternatives'; indeed, through their innovative dynamics in many areas of activity, they carry a transformative potential for the whole economy in search of sustainable models. By going beyond mere trade-offs between economic, social and environmental performance, particularly through their articulation with the social movements that support them, they can contribute to raising society's awareness and to generating or strengthening a willingness to change on a large scale. Although the social and ecological transition cannot be fully achieved without deep systemic transformations at the macro level, social enterprises also contribute to the evolution in the patterns of production and consumption. The challenge is therefore to take the full measure of their contribution and broaden their influence. In this sense, social enterprises are indeed a driving force for the transition.

Of course, the path of the social enterprise, in the midst of isomorphic pressures, will never be an easy one (see entry 44, 'Co-optation, Isomorphism and Instrumentalisation'). This is why social enterprises undoubtedly have much to gain by maintaining and strengthening their links with the social and solidarity economy, which is their most frequent and natural melting pot, and which has acquired a great deal of experience on how to maintain its own identity while interacting with the market, public authorities and civil society.

REFERENCES

Borzaga, Carlo, and Jacques Defourny, eds. 2001. *The Emergence of Social Enterprise*. London: Routledge.

Dees, J. Gregory. 1996. *Social Enterprise Spectrum: Philanthropy to Commerce*. Boston, MA: Harvard Business School, Publishing Division.

Dees, J. Gregory. 1998. 'The Meaning of "Social Entrepreneurship".' Kansas City, MO and Palo Alto, CA: The Kauffman Center for Entrepreneurial Leadership.

Defourny, Jacques, and Marthe Nyssens. 2010. 'Conceptions of Social Enterprise and Social Entrepreneurship in Europe and the United States: Convergences and Divergences.' *Journal of Social Entrepreneurship* 1 (1): 32–53. https://doi.org/10.1080/19420670903442053.

Defourny, Jacques, and Marthe Nyssens. 2017. 'Fundamentals for an International Typology of Social Enterprise Models.' *International Journal of Voluntary and Nonprofit Organizations* 28 (6): 2469–97. https://doi.org/10.1007/s11266-017-9884-7.

Defourny, Jacques, Marthe Nyssens and Olivier Brolis. 2020. 'Testing Social Enterprise Models across the World: Evidence from the "International Comparative Social Enterprise Models (ICSEM) Project".' *Nonprofit and Voluntary Sector Quarterly* 50 (2): 420–40. https://doi.org/10.1177/0899764020959470.

Doherty, Bob, Helen Haugh and Fergus Lyon. 2014. 'Social Enterprises as Hybrid Organizations: A Review and Research Agenda.' *International Journal of Management Reviews* 16 (4): 417–36. https:doi.org/10.1111/ijmr.12028.

Kerlin, Janelle A. 2017. *Shaping Social Enterprise: Understanding Institutional Context and Influence*. Bingley: Emerald Group Publishing.

Laville, Jean-Louis, A. Lemaitre and Marthe Nyssens. 2009. 'Public Policies and Social Enterprises in Europe: The Challenge of Institutionalisation.' In *Social Enterprise: At the Crossroads of Market, Public Policies and Civil Society*, edited by Marthe Nyssens 272–95 London: Routledge.

Young, Dennis R., Elizabeth A.M. Searing and Cassady V. Brewer. 2016. *The Social Enterprise Zoo: A Guide for Perplexed Scholars, Entrepreneurs, Philanthropists, Leaders, Investors, and Policymakers*. Cheltenham, UK and Northampton, MA, USA: Edward Elgar Publishing.

Yunus, Muhammad. 2010. *Building Social Business: Capitalism That Can Serve Humanity's Most Pressing Needs*. New York: Public Affairs.

22. Women's self-help groups
Christabell P.J.

INTRODUCTION

Women's self-help groups (SHGs), one of the major types of social and solidarity economy organizations and enterprises (SSEOEs) are small informal organizations, each usually consisting of ten to 20 (mostly poor) women, formed in local areas of the Global South. They frequently meet, weekly or fortnightly, to conduct beneficial finance-related activities. The essential activities of the women's SHGs are generally mentioned as being microfinance, which includes mobilizing savings, extending credit, and initiating micro-enterprises among the members. The SHGs are self-reliant units in the sense that they mobilize their resources and conduct their activities sustainably. This mechanism indicates that these women are also 'bankable', as they could save their meagre income and extend effective credit needs, thereby promoting financial services for the poor. Experiences and research studies confirm that engaging in these various activities, mooted by the women's SHGs, ensures sustainable employment and income generation among women, thereby helping them to overcome poverty. In addition to the financial activities, many women's SHGs take up non-financial actions in social, cultural and political arenas. Hence the SHGs have become a part of the life of millions of women in the Global South.

Thus, the importance of SHGs in the lives of such women, who are generally uneducated, lack training in modern technology, and do not hold any physical assets, is highlighted. After engaging in different activities initiated by the SHGs, the women find their due space in society and are involved in various activities outside their homes through collective action. They have become loan managers, and are now interested in many other activities to which they may have been denied access previously, for cultural reasons. Many of the women have gained independence by forming micro-enterprises and also have become part of group enterprises that allow them to be visible in patriarchal societies, which give very little recognition to the role of women in the community. In short, for millions of women, the SHG movement has been proven to be a very effective mechanism through which rural credit delivery systems work. It adopts a solidarity methodology, having had a significant impact on poverty and low income in the rural arena of Asia, Africa and Latin America over the last several decades by enhancing security, autonomy, and self-confidence in local women.

22.1 DEVELOPMENT: ORIGIN AND HISTORY

Women's SHGs are formed across the world in various forms, using different solidarity methodologies (see entry 12, 'The Black Social Economy'). Despite being widespread among women in the Global South, Asia is a hotspot for women's SHG practices. The pioneer of the field, Dr Muhammad Yunus, Professor of Economics at Chittagong University, experimented with small groups of poor women near his university in Bangladesh back in 1976. Later, he built a vast empire under Grameen Bank (GB), consisting of more than 9 million women members and covering 93 per cent of all villages in Bangladesh. These members hold 40 per cent of shares in the bank, and now own GB. He encouraged the women to save tiny amounts on their own, and money was reimbursed as loans to the groups, which comprise five women. In addition, women were asked to deposit a small amount (1 taka) per week, and also encouraged to contribute to an emergency fund which could be used at times of sickness, default, or other contingencies. The contention of success was a simple lending technology which includes characteristics such as group contract, small loan size, vetting, and other standardized practices. This innovative and alternative financial mechanism was started in Bangladesh, and it even earned a Nobel Peace Prize for the great visionary and his experimentation.

The studies confirm that with a few cycles of loans with GB, if women manage the loans, there is a higher probability of the families coming out of poverty (Todd 1996). The runaway success of GB can be attributed to the notion that the institution deals with self-managed SHGs rather than individual clients. GB provides small loans with short repayment periods, which helps the women to invest in agriculture, petty trading, handicrafts, processing units, and even consumption. The administrative structure is simple, and the entire process ensures the participation of the members. These informal participatory structures, reinforced by the cultural underpinnings existing in the traditional communities, have created an atmosphere where debtors honour their obligations. The conventional system of providing collateral for credit is replaced with group liability, and group supervision is exercised on processing and repayment. Hence the repayment is relatively high, and thereby the system is sustained for decades on its own. In due course, the notion of women's SHGs had made a significant breakthrough in the rural population across the world. Given the advantages of these institutions, many non-governmental organizations (NGOs) and governments in Bangladesh itself, and neighbouring Asian countries, have utilized this strategy to reach poor women by improvising the needs of the local population. Box 22.1 describes the SHG–Bank Linkage Programme.

BOX 22.1 SHG–BANK LINKAGE PROGRAMME: A WIN–WIN MODEL

Even with a population of 1370 million, India has not reached those poor individuals who are financially excluded from the formal financial system. As part of the financial inclusion strategy, the National Bank for Agriculture and Rural Development (NABARD), the specialized institution for refinancing the rural and agricultural credit in India, initiated the Self-Help Group – Bank Linkage Programme (SHG-BLP) to facilitate financial inclusion as early as 1992. The SHGs in India, facilitated by different agencies, are tested for viability after six months of formation. Then the banks start lending to the SHGs based on their savings. Hence, the SHGs are capable of availing credit from formal financial institutions, giving their savings as collateral security. According to the NABARD annual report of 2020–21, 8.7 million SHGs mobilized Rs 195 000 million ($2602 million) in deposits and an annual loan offtake of Rs 470 000 million ($6270 million). The banks also extend credit to men and to mixed groups, as well as groups initiated under different government programmes such as Deendayal Antyodaya Yojana – National Rural Livelihoods Mission (DAY-NRLM). This is a win–win strategy, as the beneficiaries can reach the banks, and the banks get business with low transaction costs. Transaction costs relate to the cost of lenders, which can be estimated by multiplying the number of hours spent by bank personnel per loan account by salary and allowances per hour. The system of SHGs lowers the transaction costs of the formal financial institutions by reaching the maximum number of women, thereby realizing the paramount objective of financial inclusion. The formal financial institutions are relieved from arduous duties such as identification of the borrower, pre-sanction and post-sanction inspection, preparation of documents, monitoring, and following up on recoveries. The banks found that transaction costs are meagre when they lend to groups rather than to individuals. This, in turn, helps the women to gain access to formal financial institutions and thereby avail themselves of loans from the banks.

Source: NABARD Annual Report 2020–21.

For instance, the Tao Yeu May Fund (TYM), a licensed microfinance institution (MFI) in Vietnam, managed by the Vietnam Women's Union, has a client base of around 1 million women, actively engaging in various activities among poor women in the country. Indonesia's Bank Rakyat Indonesia (BRI) specializes in small-scale and microfinance-style activities including borrowing from, and lending to, approximately 30 million retail clients, who are primarily women. Khushhali Microfinance Bank Limited (KMBL), the largest MFI in Pakistan, has a client base of around 10 million people. Pro Mujer, a social enterprise offering services across Latin America (Argentina, Bolivia, Mexico, Nicaragua and Peru), reached the poor by facilitating SHGs to target prospective clients. The Aga Khan Agency for Microfinance even transcends borders: it reaches out to people in various countries across Africa and Asia, including Tajikistan, Syria, Pakistan, Mali, Madagascar, Kyrgyz Republic, Egypt, Côte d'Ivoire, Burkina Faso and Afghanistan. The Malawi Rural Development Fund (MARDEF) has given out 177 195 microloans within the landlocked country. Meanwhile, the NGO CARE has initiated the SHG programme in Niger, which has been running since 1991. Box 22.2 describes the Self Employed Women's Association (SEWA).

BOX 22.2 SEWA: A TRADE UNION OF WOMEN IN INFORMAL SECTOR

The Self Employed Women's Association (SEWA) in Ahmedabad, India, was formed in 1972 as a trade union of women working in the informal sector ranging from small-scale vendors and traders to washerwomen, cooks, and cleaners. SEWA started a bank consisting of 4000 members in 1974, and later extended its services to the women's SHGs which now consists of 6 880 000 members. SEWA is running its cooperative bank, and it initiated a group life insurance scheme; now, its members can become self-reliant. It also started several skill-training courses to enhance the income-earning potential of its members, and it provides legal services to help disadvantaged women obtain the benefits of national labour legislation previously denied to them.

Source: Bhatt (2006).

In India, many players, including private banks, NGOs, community organizations, regional governments, government departments, central government schemes, and so on, took up the methodology and effective approach to reach 93 million women. It is claimed that through 7 million SHGs, 76 million women are mobilized. The non-performing assets (NPAs) of SHG loans are at 2.83 per cent. The primary reason for this most comprehensive outreach is partly attributed to the interventions made by NABARD. As part of the laudable objective of financial inclusion of vulnerable sections of the country in the ambit of formal financial institutions, the SHGs, whether initiated by women or under different government schemes, are encouraged to link with the banks (see Box 22.1). The facilitating institutions of microfinance in the country used this excellent opportunity to reach a vast expanse of the population. Some of the other essential successful stories can be told by SEWA (see Box 22.2), Mysore Resettlement and Development Agency (MYRADA), and Kudumbashree (see Box 22.3), for example.

BOX 22.3 KUDUMBASHREE: ASIA'S LARGEST WOMEN'S COLLECTIVE

Kudumbashree (meaning 'prosperity to family') started in 1997 as a poverty alleviation programme in Kerala state, India, with a slogan 'To reach out to families through women and reach out to the community through the family'. In the initial stage, the members identified nine risk factors and formed women's SHGs of vulnerable women from the neighbourhood. These women's SHGs are known as neighbourhood groups (NHGs), *ayalkoottam* in the Malayalam language. As of 2021, they included 4 114 097 women spread across the state, with 0.29 million neighbourhood groups in urban and rural areas. Kudumbashree included members from different backgrounds – transgender people, differently abled, older women, and so on – and women belonging to marginalized sections of the society. The Kudumbashree movement is federated with NHGs as the lowest unit, with area development and community development societies at the higher level. All the NHGs have an elected president and secretary, and the activities of each SHG are governed by a written by-law. Apart from the regular activities which the women's SHGs take up (micro-savings, microcredit, micro-enterprise, and so on), training and skilling are imparted to the women in various services, information technology, logistics, and so on. Group farming initiatives are prolific in the state, which gives prominence to organic farming, value addition, imparting agricultural technology to the women, and so on. All the NHGs are linked to the nationalized banks, and subsidized bank loans are extended to them. The provisioning of a range of support and resources to the women has attracted scores of them: auditing of accounts, creation of an emergency fund, provision of poverty alleviation measures, and relief measures during crises are included. The impact is visible in the local areas, as members of Kudumbashree contested the elections of local bodies, and many of them emerged as leaders and thereby participated in the decentralized planning process. Dovetailing with the Mahatma Gandhi National Rural Employment Guarantee Act (MGNREGA) 2005 via Kudumbashree, this ensures wage employment opportunities too.

Source: Parthasarathy et al. (2018).

The success of these institutions in the Global South is attributed to various factors. One of the influential factors is the density of the population, which decreases the average administrative costs. Other factors, such as the education of the clients and the facilitating officers, the quality of the rural infrastructure, and so on, paved the way to success. In this part of the world, gender inequality is high, with biases in access to different capabilities and entitlements, including education, employment, ownership of physical assets, and access to financial services. Here the feminization of poverty is very high, and women are facing the vagaries of poverty. In addition, this part of the world ignores the importance of savings and lending among the poor, citing creditworthiness as the reason. The mechanism of women's SHGs is proved before the world that diversified and alternative financial systems can be sustainably carried forward successfully among the poor.

22.2 ORGANIZATIONAL STRUCTURE AND PATTERNS OF ACTIVITIES

The members of women's SHGs mostly hail from similar economic, social, and ethnic backgrounds. This homogenous background helps them to understand each other, and to address their problems effectively. The feelings of mutual aid, joint responsibility, peer monitoring, and overall bonding through cultural ties help the women to run their business at their own pace. They agree upon standard criteria regarding the frequency of savings, disbursement of loans, type of enterprises they engage in, and mode of activities, using a written by-law or an agreement. Many women's SHGs are federated at higher levels, which helps them to mobilize at the local level (see Box 22.3, and entry 53, 'Social Policy').

A striking feature in the case of SHGs is that the women gain an avenue to save a meagre amount in a safe place. The savings of all the group members are pooled together to produce a substantial amount, which can be rotated among these women in the form of credit. Women's SHGs work based on a solidarity methodology to bring in their resources and make the best use of them for the benefit of themselves and their families. Even though the significant women's SHGs are confined to savings and credit, some institutions have gone beyond credit to offer insurance and other financial services such as remittances, emergency funds, and so on. They even engage in various activities in the local areas, including political mobilization, and social and cultural activities, and they engage in related environmental issues, and so on. Apart from meeting the financial needs, many microfinance institutions such as Kudumbashree in Kerala and Grameen Bank try to impart various inputs in terms of legal rights, sanitation, reproductive health, nutrition, gender sensitization, and so on, to the members (Christabell 2013).

The very idea of microfinance gained ground in the poor regions of the Global South due to the inadequate inclusion of the poor in the formal financial institutions. The major constraint is that these institutions ask for collateral security to sanction loans. But the access to collateral-free credit, group actions based on cooperation, and strict terms and conditions on the part of the facilitating institution – whether governmental or non-governmental – handholding, and so on, positively influence their participation. From the point of view of financial inclusion, the SHG methodology can reach the poor people who cannot enter the premises of banks. But most microfinance institutions report that the NPAs are significantly less, so that this is a sustainable kind of mechanism which reaches the poorest of the poor also in the Global South.

Studies show that in these areas, people depend on informal sources for their credit needs. There is of evidence that because the benefits from the SHGs are greater, the reliance on informal sources of credit has reduced substantially. This is because of the cheap finance which the women can avail themselves of, with low transaction costs. As they join together, the risk of default becomes very low.

22.3   IMPACT OF WOMEN'S SELF-HELP GROUPS (SHGS)

The impacts of SHGs are multi-fold, as they are instrumental in effectively reducing poverty. For instance, a study among the participants of SHGs in Bangladesh showed an increase in gender participation in agriculture and non-agricultural activities in the local area. The economic power relations inside the households are tilted, and women have started becoming a significant force in the decision-making processes. The result can be summed up as empowerment which is fuelled by economic power.

Capacity building of the women was given special care by imparting training as part of initiating enterprises by many facilitating institutions, which helped them to engage in income-generating activities: farming, agro-processing, manufacturing, services, logistics, and so on (Christabell 2016). Gender sensitization and interventions on gender-related violence have indeed made cultural changes in the local areas.

In countries such as India, the SHGs are linked to nationalized banks and other formal financial institutions. NPAs are used to understand the level of default in the banking system. While the level of NPAs is 9 per cent for the formal financial institutions, the NPAs among the SHGs are less than 3 per cent, which is again a win–win situation for both the women and the banking system. Hence the SHGs are capable of attracting credit funds from the larger public as well as what they mobilize on their own, which in turn equips the women to avail themselves of more capital for the enterprises and also to meet their consumption needs. This again prevents them from falling prey to usurious money lenders in the local areas who charge exorbitant interest rates (Wilson 2002).

Evidence shows that microcredit support to the households has improved the nutritional status of children, and shifted them from traditional to non-traditional activities. It also enhances the people's employment opportunities, increases the per capita consumption of food in the household, and increases investments in housing, sanitation, and education, with an improved standard of living in the remote regions of the Global South.

The women are well connected at the local level and start participating in various organizations and other community-based organizations based on the experience they gain from women's SHGs which has a spillover effect in the community. The women's SHGs enhance capacity at the individual and group level, empowerment and self-efficacy, which lead to 'greater control over household decision making, wider participation in civil institutions and political processes' (Gugerty et al. 2019, 133).

22.4   CRITICISMS

In some areas, a significant question that arises is the viability of the SHGs during crises, and whether the women can manage, and also sustainability in respect of the repayment of loans.

Institutions such as Grameen Bank and other microfinance institutions can deepen their credit by giving larger loans to the members in women's SHGs. In some cases, it is reported that women cannot absorb large volumes of credit. Sometimes, large amounts of credit remain unutilized in the local areas, as the women have limits in the general cultural settings, and large amounts of credit will become a burden for them. On the other hand, women, with their practical knowledge and skill, could manifest their capability to invest credit and create profitable ventures. Illiteracy, low education, weak management skills, and so on, also hamper the efforts of some women entrepreneurs.

Even though the institutions reach scores of women at the grass-roots level, it is found that effective targeting, rendering of quality financial services, and so on, play a significant role in sustaining the activities in those regions. Many studies have hailed the positives of SHGs among women, but it is also found that most of the institutions failed to reach the poorest of the poor. The widowed, divorced, female-headed households, disabled, old, needy, and most vulnerable sections are sometimes excluded from the ambit of these local institutions. The issue of mistargeting is rampant in many parts of the world. But utmost care has been taken by various institutions to include women from divergent backgrounds.

A major criticism levelled against the women's SHGs is that the loans given to them are so small and also short term, which forces the women to spend on consumption rather than on any enterprises. Many economists question this, and are sceptical about the purpose of these loans. Thus, it is argued that this kind of arrangement does not ensure sustained longer-term changes. The reasons cited are the inadequate quantum of the loans, irregularities in distribution, and using them for consumption. A report by FUNDELAM, however, observed that even though the credit is deficient, it has enabled women to finance part of the cost of the productive assets, which helped them cushion households from worsening their socio-economic status.

The institutional innovation of microfinance which introduced the concept of women's SHGs is governed by a critical triangle comprising financial sustainability, outreach to the poor, and the impact on the poor (Christabell 2009). These institutions are more effective if the population density is high, and if the availability of homogenous women is sufficient in number in the neighbourhood.

Indiscriminate uniform replication of the success models is often made worldwide, without understanding the substance that led it to failure (Galbraith 2017). These replications give little importance to local conditions and the evaluation of earlier programmes. Yet another major issue is that several programmes are running side by side in the same locality, which prompts the members to switch from one group to another, or maintain membership in the multiple SHGs. This is a threat to the sustainability of the SHG movement, as the defaulter may move to another SHG, and the first one may feel it difficult to take disciplinary action against the member.

22.5 THE WAY FORWARD

In short, the women's self-help groups initiated by microfinance institutions across the world have become a part of the life of millions of women in the Global South. The prime objective of microfinance was to initiate micro-enterprises among the self-employed women at the grass-roots level. But some other institutional issues, such as illiteracy, low education, and deficiency of management skills, hamper the efforts of micro-entrepreneurs. Hence training and the imparting of skills, extending technical assistance in different forms, have also started becoming part of these programmes. Women's economic status, as well as household work responsibilities, severely limit the level of participation outside the house. The policies of the government, including financial and institutional barriers, hamper the women who would like to initiate micro-enterprises. This warrants a comprehensive approach to the women at the grass-roots level who try to sustain a livelihood on their own, using the solidarity methodology among them. The international community, as well as the local governments, must make an earnest effort to keep the women at centre stage, and this has to be replicated in various other scenarios across the globe to help women to pull themselves out of poverty.

Women are very resilient to crises of various types across the world. They find ways to absorb the shocks: economic, social, personal, emotional, and psychological. It is imperative to initiate these kinds of institutions across the world in all cultures to help the people in various ways to grow economically and socially.

REFERENCES

Bhatt, Ela R. 2006. *We are Poor but So Many: The Story of Self-Employed Women in India.* New Delhi: Oxford University Press.

Christabell P.J. 2009. *Women Empowerment Through Capacity Building: The Role of Microfinance.* New Delhi: Concept Publishing Company.

Christabell P.J. 2013. 'Social Innovation for Women Empowerment: Kudumbashree in Kerala.' *Innovation and Development* 3 (1): 139–40. https://doi.org/10.1080/2157930X.2013.764630.

Christabell P.J. 2016. *Inclusive Growth through Social Capital Formation: Is Microfinance an Effective Tool for Targeting Women.* New Delhi: Concept Publishing Company.

Fundacio'n de la Mujer Campesina (Fundelam). 1995. The Socio-Economic Impact of Credit Programs on Rural Women: A Study in Carchi, Ecuador. Promoting Women in Development (PROWID).

Galbraith, James K. 2017. *Seduced and Betrayed: Exposing the Contemporary Microfinance Phenomenon.* New Mexico: University of New Mexico Press.

Gugerty, Mary Kay, Pierre Biscaye and C. Leigh Anderson. 2019. 'Delivering Development? Evidence on Self-Help Groups as Development Intermediaries in South Asia and Africa.' *Development Policy Review* 37 (1): 129–51. https://doi.org/10.1111/dpr.12381.

NABARD. 2021. Annual Report 2020-21. Mumbai.

Parthasarathy, Soma Kishore, Poulomi Pal, Shubha Bhattacharya, Subhalakshmi Nandi, Nandita Bhatla and Alpaxee Kashyap. 2018. *Kudumbashree State Poverty Eradication Mission: A Model Documentation Report on Addressing Intimate Partner Violence (IPV) in India.* New Delhi: ICRW.

Todd, Helen. 1996. *Women at the Center: Grameen Bank Borrowers After One Decade.* London: Routledge.

Wilson, Kim. 2002. 'The New Microfinance: An Essay on the Self-Help Group Movement in India.' *Journal of Microfinance/ESR Review* 4 (2): 217–45.

23. Youth
Davorka Vidović

INTRODUCTION

The social and solidarity economy (SSE) is a sector that has become highly relevant for the youth as a social group, mainly because of the rising challenges that youth face in contemporary society. This entry intends to highlight the role of the SSE in addressing problems faced by youth in their transition to adult roles, economic independence, and civic and political participation.

The entry briefly describes the main challenges young people face today across the world. It offers some insights into how SSE organizations and enterprises (SSEOEs) offer various tools and models that may strengthen young people's capacities to participate in and co-create solutions in their communities in a meaningful way. Several examples of good practices of youth-led or youth-oriented SSE organizations and enterprises may serve as an illustration of how the SSE could be used to address and overcome contemporary youth challenges.

23.1 YOUTH AND CONTEMPORARY CHALLENGES

Youth is commonly understood as a large social group in the transition between childhood and adulthood. However, there is no common definition of the age frame: some define youth as individuals between the ages of 15 and 24 (for example, the United Nations) (UN 2013), others as individuals between the ages of 15 and 29 (for example, Eurostat), or even between the ages of 15 and 34 (for example, African countries) (UN 2013).

The main challenge of contemporary youth is the same as those of many youth generations, and that is integration within a broader society by taking on permanent (adult) social roles in the family, the economy and the political community: namely, starting their own family, becoming economically independent and becoming engaged in civil or political life. The focus on the transition between childhood and adulthood has been one of the dominant approaches in the research on youth over the last 70 years. It specifically focuses on different aspects and barriers that are relevant for successful transition (Ilišin and Spajić-Vrkaš 2017, 12). However, the dynamics and speed of changes in contemporary society make those challenges more numerous and complex than ever before.

In literature, youth is seen as either a resource or a social problem. The former understands young people as bearers of a desirable future and the source of innovation. The latter considers youth to be the source of social problems and deviant behaviour (Ilišin and Spajić-Vrkaš 2017, 14). In both cases, youth is recognized as one of the most vulnerable segments of society, being most intensively exposed to the changes in contemporary society. Dominant neoliberal economy and hyper-globalization increased the risks of living in today's society. Technological changes, the transformation of the labour market, migrations, climate change and overall commodification create insecurities that make it difficult for young people to take on adult roles. Let alone a smooth transition, they face a higher risk of unemployment, poverty, greater inequalities, and exclusion, increased deviant and at-risk behaviour, such as juvenile delinquency and drug abuse, than other social groups.

Among many issues, unemployment is seen as one of the key problems of youth today. However, youth is not a homogeneous social group: young people differ in their socio-economic status, ethnic background, education, values and identities. Certain youth groups, such as young persons with disabilities, rural youth, women and indigenous youth, to name just a few, are groups that are facing multiple challenges and deprivations (UN 2020), and are among the most vulnerable social groups. The share of global youth aged 15–24 not in employment, education or training (NEET), the category that is most at risk of poverty and exclusion, was 22.5 per cent in 2021. The proportion of young female NEETs (31.3 per cent) is more than double that of young male NEETs (14.2 per cent) (ILO 2000, 149).

At the same time, education systems are outdated and do not transform fast enough to meet the changing and diverse needs of today's labour market (UN 2016). In other words, training and skills that young people obtain through formal and/or informal education are highly inadequate. In addition, a high percentage of youth across the globe, mainly in less developed and more deprived areas, end up as early leavers from education and training, which weakens their job prospects.

One of the key problems of today's youth is their weak participation in political processes, mainly the institutional politics and traditional political arena (UN 2020), in comparison with both the older population and previous youth generations (Ilišin and Spajić-Vrkaš 2017). One of the main reasons is constantly low levels of trust in political institutions. As a consequence of youth remaining marginal in decision-making processes, they have less influence on the development of institutions, practices and policies that reflect the needs of youth and vulnerable youth groups. Besides political engagement, there is a perceived decline in the level of civic engagement among young people worldwide (UN 2016).

However, being marginalized from the mainstream political and social institutions, youth tend to both oppose the status quo and the traditional development path, and create the alternative arena for engagement and participation, mostly through advocacy, lobbying, volunteering, or activities in communities and/or civil society organizations (UN 2016, 2020).

23.2 THE SSE IN ADDRESSING YOUTH-SPECIFIC PROBLEMS

The SSE covers organizations and enterprises that have explicit economic and social (and often environmental) goals, but prioritize social mission over private economic interest. It is based on participative, democratic and inclusive processes, and thus provides valuable and alternative tools for young people to get engaged in social and political processes. Below are some areas where the SSE significantly contributes to strengthening young people in their complex transition to adult roles.

Innovation and Change

Being based on different values than the conventional market economy, the SSE is seen as an alternative, inclusive type of economy that prioritizes the benefits of the least privileged, marginalized, and the most vulnerable groups over a profit. Doing things opposite to the mainstream economic model requires an innovative approach, flexibility and experimentation. Research on youth shows that young people have characteristics that make them suitable for acting as agents of social justice, meaning agents 'finding solutions to social problems and accelerating social change' (UN 2020, 57).

More than any other segment of society, youth has a tendency for change, to oppose the current system and status quo. Often, young people are a home for those more progressive thoughts and visions, and a place where avant-garde ideas have been born. In other words, youth is oriented toward alternative development paths, innovation and technology usage.

Studies on youth emphasize that 'today's young people are highly motivated to generate positive social change' (UN 2020, 65) or for young women 'to have a positive impact on society' (Py & Berthélemy, 2019; Soler-i-Marti et al. 2021, 523). Practices of the SSE offer good tools and frames that will engage young people in achieving social and environmental goals, and in addressing social issues, such as unemployment, poverty, deprivation – discrimination of any kind. Engagement in SSE organizations helps them to move from their marginal position to the position of an active agent of change. In other words, they are not just active, productive members of society, but also co-creators of a better society. Through engagement in the SSE, young people are oriented to the creation of social values in a sustainable way. Young people will often create new, innovative solutions to problems and needs which they recognize in their local surroundings.

EnerGea Tecnologia Sostenible is an example of a youth-led social enterprise started in Bolivia in 2017 by two young professionals in the field of engineering, energy and sustainable technologies. This social enterprise addresses issues of energy usage and is particularly focused on achieving greater awareness around the more environmentally friendly light-emitting diode (LED) technology. Their business model relies on assembling, selling and installing LED lighting products for local businesses and industries that make their energy use more efficient and cheaper. Additionally, they have developed a system of fluorescent lighting waste management and recycling. Finally, the third stream of their activities includes science, technology, engineering, the arts and mathematics (STEAM) education programmes for children and young people in Latin America (EnerGea 2021).

Participation

Considering the lack of youth's political participation in traditional institutions, SSEOEs provide them with alternative ways to engage, participate, collaborate and regain their power. SSE organizations and enterprises are most often collective efforts that gather different individuals around a joint social objective. Democratic governance is at the core of SSE, meaning that members, users and beneficiaries participate in the decision-making process.

As such, these organizations are places where young people through their own experience can learn about democracy, collaboration and mutual support. By being a place that brings together people from different ethnic, religious or social backgrounds, but also with different values and ideological, political or other preferences, SSEOEs become platforms for learning about acceptance, tolerance, trust and humanity.

Particularly important aspects of the SSE refer to its collective and value-driven nature which produces commitment and empowerment of young people. Even though sometimes working conditions might not be much different from conventional economy, what makes young people committed to SSE organizations are shared principles, horizontal governance and co-responsibility, a 'sensation that workers are not alone and that difficulties and responsibilities are shared', and feeling that 'they are swimming together against the current' (Soler-i-Marti et al. 2021, 543) (see entry 57, 'Working Conditions and Wages').

SSEOEs are based on the democratic governance model and management principles that are more participative and inclusive. This enables young people to be heard, to create and to make a difference. More than that, the SSE is a way to 'affect social change in their own way and on their own terms' (UN 2020, 58).

Good examples of the SSE model suitable for youth and its empowerment to participate are student or school cooperatives (see entry 26, 'Education Sector'). This is an organizational model that imitates 'real' cooperatives, thus providing students with a practical experience of the functioning of such local organizations. Student or school cooperatives have a long tradition in many countries, mostly related to the expansion of the cooperative movement back in the 19th century, and with the new school movement and reformed pedagogy in the late 19th to early 20th centuries. Since the beginning of the 2000s, interest in school cooperatives has begun to grow again, especially within various (new) concepts and policy frameworks, such as entrepreneurship education, the social economy and sustainable development (Vidović 2020). School cooperatives are governed by students and teachers, but other stakeholders from the local community are often included as well.

By participating in activities of school cooperatives, student members get the experience of real production of goods, but also collective democratic governance, decision-making, participation, social entrepreneurship, local needs and resources, and social and environmental issues. Because of democratic governance, as a core principle of cooperatives, school cooperatives are seen as training grounds for democracy. For example, school cooperatives often create their activities around agriculture (related to school gardens), handicrafts, ecological and sustainable production, and revitalizing old crafts, but also around new media and information and communication technologies.

Especially in smaller local communities, student cooperatives often play an important part in the dynamics of cooperation between the school and its environment: parents, other schools, businesses, civil society organizations, other cooperatives and local authorities. In some countries, such as Germany, all student cooperatives are firmly connected from the beginning with a real cooperative from the local environment, which is their permanent partner and mentor. According to available sources, different forms of student or school cooperatives exist in Norway, Finland, Germany, Poland, Croatia (and other former Yugoslavia countries), the United States, Turkey and some Asian countries.

Different Entrepreneurial Mindset

SSE is often seen as an alternative sector over the traditional economy that has enormous potential for preparing young people to make a transition to the labour market. At the same time, the SSE offers many opportunities. Research on young people's transition into the labour market has paid very little attention to the alternative sectors such as the SSE, and the potential they have over the traditional economy.

Social entrepreneurship as an SSE model is particularly suitable for the economic empowerment of young people; either they are social entrepreneurs themselves, or they are employees or partners in youth-led social enterprises. Often, social entrepreneurship is recognized and promoted by policymakers as a model that may generate jobs for vulnerable groups, including youth. In addition, social entrepreneurship also strengthens, encourages and pushes young people in generating economic, social and environmental values. The entrepreneurial mindset which is the core of social entrepreneurship is the driving force that encourages the transition of young people to taking over adult roles, learning to accept the risks and achieving economic independence. It also enables them to be creators of change and different developmental paths, not those based on pure profit motives.

For example, Mondragon Team Academy (MTA) World, a global network of social innovation ecosystem labs, with headquarters in Irun (Basque country), uses Finnish educational methods based on the 'learning by creating' methodology. This innovative educational model was established in 2008 by the Innovation and Entrepreneurship Unit of Mondragon University Business School in cooperation with TiimiAkatemia in Finland.

Its educational model is focused on 'team-entrepreneurship', which is seen as the adoption of the new way society is organized. This model is based on teamwork and experimentation. It uses the 'learning by creating' methodology instead of teaching about entrepreneurship, giving the main tools to students to encourage them to set up their ventures. Today, MTA World has more than 2000 'team-entrepreneurs', with more than 80 team companies created and 15 MTA Labs founded in cities across Europe, Asia and South America.

Bottom-Up and Locally Embedded

SSEOEs enable young people to get involved with the development of their local communities. The SSE is all about caring about others, taking care of the benefits of the community, and above all, taking care of vulnerable individuals and groups. It is based on a bottom-up approach, which means that SSE initiatives are based on social needs identified in the local community.

Through their engagement in the SSE, youth can develop profound awareness of local social needs and environmental problems. Further, they can become knowledgeable about local resources and the ways those can be utilized to serve the common good in a sustainable way. Through the SSE, local communities may reduce environmental hazards by keeping the local economy on a smaller-scale level that benefits social justice in communities. The local embeddedness of SSE initiatives tends to perceive youth as a resource, not as a (social) problem, which in the end contributes to better integration of young people within the community and society in general.

For example, Alashanek ya balady Association for Sustainable Development (AYB) is a youth-led organization established in 2002 in Cairo (Egypt) to promote voluntarism in the local community. But it has grown into an association that provides several programmes to facilitate vulnerable populations, primarily youth and women. The programmes include training, employment programmes, microcredit, health and social services. For example, AYB trains youth in simple vocational skills such as carpentry, sewing and iron welding; and on the other side maps job opportunities in the labour market. Today, it operates through 12 franchises across Egypt, and provides services aimed at all family members of underprivileged communities, thus contributing highly to their socio-economic empowerment.

Challenges that young people face in today's world often push them to the margins of society by making them lack the vital resources to make their transition to adulthood successful and smooth. In that context, the SSE appears to be a valuable model for empowering youth, in making them more informed, engaged, sensible to needs in their communities, and more active and collaborative. The examples given above illustrate how SSE initiatives across the globe could both provide services and support for young people to enable their easier access to socially valuable resources (such as education, employment and financing), but also engage youth in active, participative and collaborative ways of addressing social and environmental issues within local communities. More comprehensive studies on the role of SSE on youth are missing, and they are much needed, as those may enlighten the area where policy support measures would contribute highly to creating more opportunities for young people in this sector.

REFERENCES

EnerGea. 2021. https://energea.com.bo

Ilišin, Vlasta and Vedrana Spajić-Vrkaš. 2017. *Generacija Osujećenih. Mladi u Hrvatskoj na Početku 21 stoljeća*. Zagreb: Institut za Društvena Istraživanja.

ILO (International Labour Office). 2020. *Global Employment Trends for Youth 2020: Technology and the Future of Jobs*. ILO. https://www.ilo.org/global/publications/books/WCMS_737648/lang--en/index.htm.

Py, Joséphine and Soazig Barthélemy. 2019. *Women-led social enterprises: A European study*. Empow'her.

Soler-i-Marti, Roger, Andreu Camprubí Trepat, Ester Oliveras and Mireia Sierra Andrés. 2021. 'The Social and Solidarity Economy: An Opportunity for Young Women's Work Transitions'. *Young* 29 (5): 529–48. https://doi.org/10.1177/1103308820986057.

UN (United Nations). 2013. 'Fact sheets on youth definition'. https://www.un.org/esa/socdev/documents/youth/fact-sheets/youth-definition.pdf.

UN (United Nations). 2016. 'World Youth Report. Youth Civic Engagement'. New York: United Nations.

UN (United Nations). 2020. 'World Youth Report. Youth Social Entrepreneurship and the 2030 Agenda'. New York: United Nations.

Vidović, Davorka. 2020. 'Učeničke zadruge kao rasadnik zadrugarstva? Refleksije zadružnih načela u djelovanju učeničkih zadruga u Hrvatskoj'. *Socijalna Ekologija* 29 (3): 389–416. https:doi.org/10.17234/socekol.29.3.3.

PART III

LINKAGES TO DEVELOPMENT

24. Care and home support services
Christian Jetté, Yves Vaillancourt and Catherine Lenzi

INTRODUCTION

The field of home support service provision has seen considerable growth over the past few decades due to ageing populations in the Global North, deinstitutionalization of people with physical or cognitive disabilities (Lenzi 2018), and demands brought by the Independent Living Movement that favour keeping individuals within their home communities. The expansion of these services was accompanied by a renewed interest from public authorities – originating in the 1990s – in certain components of the social and solidarity economy (SSE) that had historically developed expertise in responding to the needs of these populations, often as a result of the initial influence of charitable or religious organizations (Jetté and Vaillancourt 2010) (see entry 38, 'Social Services' and entry 53, 'Social Policy'). Over time, home care activities diversified in multiple territories and regions, occupying an increasingly important space in the production of these services, whether in terms of home cleaning and maintenance, meal preparation, bodily hygiene, supervision, accompaniment, paratransit, friendly visits, respite care for loved ones or advocacy. The SSE's diverse components (associations, community organizations and cooperatives) working in this field have also gained new recognition, despite the existence of certain ambiguities.

24.1 WELFARE MIX AND THE SSE IN PERSONAL SERVICES FOR PEOPLE WITH DISABILITIES

Increasing reliance on the SSE for the provision of personal services for people with disabilities has coincided with a questioning of the welfare state and a new sharing of responsibilities between the public, private, SSE and domestic (family, friends, family caregivers) sectors (Vaillancourt and Jetté 1997). Two dynamics also contributed to shaping the SSE's trajectory during the 2000s. The first, a liberatory dynamic, as previously mentioned, was brought by the Independent Living Movement, and relayed by a fringe of the feminist movement, through demands supported by an ethics of care in favour of developing and recognizing jobs held primarily by women (in particular, elder care, care for people with disabilities and childcare). The second, a dynamic with a more strategic target, was inspired by a neoclassical current in economics emphasizing government budget rationalizations, lifting the fiscal burden from the shoulders of individuals and businesses, and reducing public services in favour of the private market and the family. In some cases the force of this dynamic, associated with neoliberalism, led to a strong push for privatization and the creation of (quasi-market) competition between different service providers, both in the Americas (Browne 2003) and in Europe (Kendall 2001).

Many refer to these new social protection systems as 'welfare mix', as they leave more space not only for competitive dynamics and lucrative private sector stakeholders, but also for stakeholders from the associative, domestic and public sectors influencing aspects of financing, regulation and services (Evers and Laville 2004). These actors mobilize a mix of transactional (contributions and fees), redistributive (public financing) and reciprocal (donations, activism and volunteering) resources for the benefit of people with disabilities.

This welfare mix takes different forms based on the country of implementation, evolving according to two differentiated visions of developing services for people who are losing their autonomy (see also entry 53, 'Social Policy' and entry 38, 'Social Services'). In the first case, it may have served as a veil for commodification and privatization strategies, in which SSE organizations are prioritized primarily due to their low cost of service production, cheap labour and ability to mobilize volunteer resources. Meanwhile, in the second case, this welfare mix takes inspiration from a more participatory and democratic approach within a plural economy that falls under a perspective of social innovation, decommodification and co-construction of policies and services (Jetté et al. 2012). This second vision involves respecting organizations' autonomy (rather than their framework under a centralized body, or subordination to management principles such as new public management) to allow for the development of new practices adapted to the specific realities and needs of people, territories and communities; recognition and appreciation for expertise from different careers and professions working in the field of care; and recognition of the importance of their contribution in a more general sense. It also involves participation from the SSE, not only in terms of generating services in a simple co-production relationship (contractualization, outsourcing or subcontracting) but also in terms of co-construction: developing programmes and policies that provide guidelines for these services as part of collaborative and partner-based entities with other stakeholders (the state, users, private businesses, independent contractors, SSE organizations and enterprises, caregivers) (Vaillancourt 2012) (see entry 50, 'Partnership and Co-construction').

At a more local or organizational, and thereby micro-sociological level, this plural economy recalls the notion of multi-stakeholders heralded by the presence of a diversity of actors on the boards of directors and other avenues for participation in organizations and businesses. It follows that general interests are best served, and the balance of power is best assured within an organization, if all of the people and groups affected by the production of goods or services are represented within it. Social and solidarity economy organizations and enterprises (SSEOEs) are especially well suited for applications of this multi-stakeholder principle, as the legal frameworks related to the associative or cooperative movements already accommodate this type of participation. For example, an SSE organization or enterprise working on home support services could have seats on its board of directors for representatives from categories such as service users, family caregivers, home health aides and community members from the area where the organization operates. Decisions made pertaining to the organization's orientations or management become the subject of tripartite or even multi-party discussions that allow for each stakeholder to express their concerns and interests. Production and consumption relationships are then articulated according to a variety of configurations involving demand for, and supply of, home services as part of a process that seeks a satisfying conclusion for all parties. Certainly, these participation mechanisms do not shield SSEOEs from power struggles or a preponderance of a certain category of stakeholder to the detriment of others, especially in questions of funding, but they do allow for statutory representation of all parties involved in the services (Vaillancourt et al. 2003).

24.2 HYBRIDIZATION OF ORGANIZATIONAL AND INSTITUTIONAL FORMATS

The question of funding raises important issues for the SSE in the field of home support services (see entry 45, 'Financing'). Whether its origins are in the public, philanthropic, insurance or private sectors, this funding and its related conditions introduce dynamics that in some cases can appear unusual compared to those that define the organizational and operational models used in the SSE, such as a non-profit nature, solidarity, proximity, participation and innovation. They can therefore lead to phenomena of institutional isomorphisms within organizations (DiMaggio and Powell 1983), meaning a propensity for organizations to duplicate modes of operation, governance or management based on principles from an actor, or group of actors, that are exercising domination and structuring a field of activity. While this tendency has been observed in the home support services provided by the SSE in some territories, given the central role frequently played by the public and private sectors in the funding and regulation of these services – their influence being able to introduce regulations that are competitive or technocratic in nature and that interfere with its social and democratic ultimate goals – it remains true that the SSE rarely permits itself to be completely absorbed by an institutional environment that it is not familiar with (Jetté and Vaillancourt 2010).

The reality on the ground suggests a hybridization of governance regimes in home support services based on national territory (Quebec, the United Kingdom, Belgium, France and Italy) and further within these territories at a national, regional and local level, meaning a combination of actors, public policies, funding and interactions from competitive and partner-based regimes that call for a diversity of service providers (Lévesque and Thiry 2008). While researchers remain critical of the true ability of the SSE to extend its principles of social profitability and economic viability to the full gamut of programmes and policies in the field of personal services for people losing autonomy, they generally agree that, due to its more participatory and democratic visions, the SSE has the capacity to enable optimized socio-economic development and innovation for both service users and service providers (Laville and Nyssens 2001).

The SSE also assumes a specific intermediary role between the supply and demand for services, distinguishing it from the roles of the public and private sectors, which tend to structure their service programming based on technocratic or economic viability norms (Petrella 2012). Of course, these norms could be justified in terms of optimal informational conditions and user adaptation capabilities, but their strict application has led to exclusion of those whose social, financial, physical or cognitive conditions do not match up to the programmed service offered by the public or private sectors. As for the SSE, it tends to construct its activities from a bottom-up model, starting by jointly constructing the supply and the demand in a manner that centres on the needs of people with disabilities. This philosophy of action – inherited in part from a long pragmatic tradition that has its roots in the Americas – manifests in outreach work that is adapted to their rhythms and the specific conditions of their environments. This helps to centre interventions on the abilities of the person rather than on their functional limitations. When developing services, by including contributions from those who use these services, practices can be adjusted for the individuals' specific needs, especially for people who are living alone, isolated, marginalized or especially vulnerable (Le Goff 2013).

This approach has led to several social innovations, as the SSE is often called to meet needs that are not met by the public or private sectors. Whether in terms of information, orientation, personalized support, collective outreach or developing new partnerships on the ground between stakeholders affected by home services (whether public, private or associative), SSE actors bridge the divide between individuals and the resources that can meet their needs. These social innovations may be considered radical in the sense that they provide new approaches in an activity sector. For example, the Initiatives de travail de milieu auprès des aînés en situation de vulnérabilité (ITMAV) developed by the Quebec Association of Senior Centres took the form of outreach activities that aimed to directly contact vulnerable seniors in their familiar environments (apartments, parks, malls, and so on), creating a bond of trust to identify their needs in terms of quality of life, whether referring them to appropriate resources, providing information on government assistance, providing individual support, providing training on new technology, organizing parties, advocating, and so on (QASC 2012). Social innovations can also be of a more incremental nature when they improve on processes already in place. This is the case with the Société coopérative d'intérêt collectif (SCIC) in Versailles, France, which helps to facilitate transitions for seniors between different types of services (housing services, nursing care, day centres, home services, support from loved ones, and so on), and the Quebec-based community organization Carpe Diem that encourages developing alternative approaches for those living with Alzheimer's disease (Gil et al. 2018).

These examples of social innovations illustrate an effort of organizational and institutional hybridization that nonetheless raises questions pertaining to funding, management and working conditions (Thériault and Vaillancourt 2021). Indeed, some SSEOEs in the field of home support services have complex funding landscapes, including government subsidies, user contributions and financial resources from foundations. Frequently this is accompanied by volunteer and independent contractor management. In the latter case, these local and regional organizations act as brokers for users who have been provided with vouchers, often by a public administrative body, that can be used to partially or fully pay for expenses relating to some home care services. This formula, initially developed for people with physical disabilities, has been extended over time to include seniors who are losing autonomy. Its advantages include a great degree of flexibility in terms of service scheduling and duration (day, evening or night), the type of work performed (housekeeping, hygiene, meal preparation, supervision, and so on) and the choice of the service provider. Disabled persons' associations have long considered this formula to be an essential condition for their autonomy and continued presence in the community. However, its limitations (identified by, among others, the feminist and labour movements) include poor wages for workers (frequently women), atypical work hours and weighty administrative components of the work. SSEOEs that work with people with disabilities are therefore evolving in a complex institutional environment, faced on the one hand with contradictory tensions within its diverse components, and on the other with the powerful attraction of the private sector model and the ponderous inertia of public regulations.

24.3 ETHICS OF CARE AND HOME SERVICES

In this regard, studies conducted in France and Quebec demonstrate, among other findings, the importance of the relational aspect of these services, and workers' mastery of tasks and behaviours that suggest an emotional involvement which supports the expression of an ethics of care (Lenzi and Jetté 2020). This ethics of care is defined as: 'species activity that includes everything that we do to maintain, continue, and repair our "world" so that we can live in it as well as possible. That world includes our bodies, our selves, and our environment, all of which we seek to interweave in a complex, life-sustaining web' (Tronto 2010, 160). In home support services, it refers to a wide range of caring activities that are largely undertaken by women on a basis of diverse professional backgrounds, but also through experienced knowledge acquired from their personal trajectories and socialization that brought them to care for dependent people. Poorly recognized and often underappreciated in society at the symbolic, professional and financial levels, these jobs (whose necessity was thrown into sharp relief by the COVID-19 pandemic) play a crucial role in ensuring that people losing autonomy can remain in their homes. The SSE occupies a leading position in this activity sector, bringing together a collection of 'small jobs' with diverse qualifications to be gained on both an experiential and a professional training basis. These roles include home health aides, health and social services aides, family caregivers, and so on. It contributes to making these tasks – which are often associated with unpaid work, due to being traditionally assimilated with domestic labour enacted by women – more visible. Running counter to this essentialist vision of specific social roles for men and women, some components of the SSE will provide a framework for such careers, giving the recognition needed to create an activity sector which finds a new legitimacy within the interdependent links that connect every member of society.

It is in this same vein that the SSE plays a leading role in gathering, accompanying and supporting family caregivers. These individuals – partners, parents, friends, loved ones – themselves provide, without pay (or in return for a modest compensation), a major proportion of the services needed to ensure that people with disabilities can stay in their homes. These individuals are regularly called upon by governments, who may be struggling with the explosion of costs related to growth in demand for social and health services, and have only recently garnered the attention of social and health authorities. Their contributions to keeping people losing autonomy in their homes have been considered a given in a context of domestic reciprocity that, once again, refers back to the unpaid labour traditionally delegated to women (Petiau and Rist 2019). Several associations, community organizations, cooperatives and foundations in multiple countries have arranged to bring together these family caregivers, defend their rights, advocate for the recognition of their contribution to keeping people with disabilities in their communities, and provide them with respite measures.

CONCLUSION

The SSE plays a crucial role at the intersection of different activity sectors and in the implementation of tools for support and accompaniment that meet the needs of people losing autonomy. Its non-profit nature, its roots within the communities which it serves, its permeability to the specific situations of certain groups of people, and its capacity for the mobilization of transactional and non-transactional resources make it an especially well-adapted actor for meeting the needs of individuals who are vulnerable or have vulnerabilities on a physical or cognitive level. Such individuals may experience conditions that are far from ideal for confronting the competitive dynamics that regulate consumer choices for goods and services in other activity sectors. The primary challenges of the SSE remain, at the economic level, the mobilization of sufficient financial and material resources to carry out the mission that it shares with the public and private sectors, without compromising on working conditions. On a socio-political level, it must provide itself with the means to preserve its organizational and institutional autonomy, and participate in a broader recognition of the labour of care for people with disabilities in a context where the costs of these services are still far too often considered an unproductive expense, rather than an investment in the common good.

REFERENCES

Browne, Paul Leduc. 2003. *The Commodity of Care: Home Care Reform in Ontario*. Ottawa: Canadian Centre For Policy Alternatives.
DiMaggio, Paul J., and Walter W. Powell. 1983. 'The Iron Cage Revisited: Institutional Isomorphism and Collective Rationality in Organizational Fields.' *American Sociological Review* 48 (2): 147–60. https://doi.org/10.2307/2095101.
Evers, Adalbert, and Jean-Louis Laville. 2004. *The Third Sector in Europe*. Cheltenham, UK and Northampton, MA, USA: Edward Elgar Publishing.
Gil, Roger, Nicole Poirier and Michel Billières. 2018. *Alzheimer, de Carpe Diem À La Neuropsychologie*. Toulouse: Editions Érès, Dl.
Jetté, Christian, and Yves Vaillancourt. 2010. 'Social Economy and Home Care Services in Quebec: Co-Production or Co-Construction?' *VOLUNTAS: International Journal of Voluntary and Nonprofit Organizations* 22 (1): 48–69. https://doi.org/10.1007/s11266-010-9134-8.
Jetté, Christian, Yves Vaillancourt and Jean-Vincent Bergeron-Gaudin. 2012. 'L'économie Plurielle Dans Les Services à Domicile Au Canada: Une Comparaison Des Modes de Régulation Entre Le Québec et L'Ontario.' *Partie 2 – Le Choix Des Différents Modèles Sociaux*, 66: 155–75. https://doi.org/10.7202/1008877ar.
Kendall, J. 2001. 'Grande-Bretagne: Une Économie Plurielle de Soins Bouleversée Par Les Quasi-Marchés.' In *Les Services Sociaux Entre Associations, Marché et État: L'aide Aux Personnes Âgées*, edited by Marthe Nyssens. Paris: Éditions La Découverte / MAUSS / CRIDA.
Laville, Jean-Louis, and Marthe Nyssens, eds. 2001. *Les Services Sociaux Entre Associations, Marché et État: L'aide Aux Personnes Âgées*. Paris: Éditions La Découverte / MAUSS / CRIDA.
Le Goff, Alice. 2013. *Care et Démocratie Radicale*. Paris: Presses Universitaires De France.
Lenzi, Catherine. 2018. 'Désinstitutionnalisation.' In *Dictionnaire Pratique Du Travail Social*, edited by Laurent Ott and Stéphane Rullac. Paris: Dunod.
Lenzi, Catherine, and Christian Jetté. 2020. 'Normalisation Des Pratiques et Invisibilité Du Travail de Care Dans Les Services de Soutien à Domicile.' In *Les Territoires de l'Intervention À Domicile: Regards Croisés France-Québec*, edited by Christian Jetté and Catherine Lenzi. Paris: L'harmattan.
Lévesque, B., and B. Thiry. 2008. 'Concurrence et Partenariat, Deux Vecteurs de La Reconfiguration Des Nouveaux Régimes de Gouvernance Des Services Sociaux et de Santé.' In *Gouvernance et Intérêt Général Dans Les Services Sociaux et de Santé*, edited by Bernard Enjolras. Bruxelles: Peter Lang.
Petiau, Anne, and Barbara Rist. 2019. 'Dilemmes Moraux et Conflictualités Autour Des Frontières Du Care Entre Aidé·e·s et Aidant·e·s Rémunéré·e·s.' *Revue Française Des Affaires Sociales* 1 (1): 133. https://doi.org/10.3917/rfas.191.0133.
Petrella, Francesca. 2012. *Aide À Domicile et Services À La Personne: Les Associations Dans La Tourmente*. Rennes: Presses Universitaires De Rennes.
QASC (Quebec Association of Senior Centres). 2012. 'Cadre Pratique Des Association Québécoise Des Centres Communautaires Pour Aînés Quebec Association of Senior Centres.' In *Cadre Pratique Des Initiatives de Travail de Milieu Auprès Des Aînés Vulnérables*. https://www.aqcca.org/images/stories/pdf/cadre_pratique.pdf.
Thériault, L., and Y. Vaillancourt. 2021. 'Working Conditions in the Nonprofit Sector and Paths to Improve the Situation.' In *Intersections and Innovations: Change for Canada's Voluntary and Nonprofit Sector*, edited by Susan D. Phillips and Bob Wyatt. Edmonton, AB: Muttart Foundation.
Tronto, Joan C. 2010. 'Creating Caring Institutions: Politics, Plurality, and Purpose.' *Ethics and Social Welfare* 4 (2): 158–71. https://doi.org/10.1080/17496535.2010.484259.
Vaillancourt, Y. 2012. 'Third Sector and the Co-Construction of Canadian Public Policy.' In *New Public Governance, the Third Sector and Co-Production*, edited by Victor Alexis Pestoff, Taco Brandsen and Bram Verschuere. New York: Routledge.

Vaillancourt, Y., Aubry François and Christian Jetté, eds. 2003. *L'économie Sociale Dans Les Services À Domicile*. Québec: Presses de l'Université du Québec.

Vaillancourt, Y., and C. Jetté. 1997. 'Vers Un Nouveau Partage Des Responsabilités Dans Les Services Sociaux et de Santé.' *Cahiers du LAREPPS.* 97(5): 296.

25. Culture, sports and leisure sectors
Nadine Richez-Battesti and Francesca Petrella

INTRODUCTION

The social and solidarity economy (SSE) is a central pillar of the population's sports, recreational and cultural life. It represents the historical heart of the sports movement and popular education. It develops collective practices in which the user plays a central role in the framework of democratic organisations based on solidarity. Therefore it brings together local initiatives from the civil society and citizen involvement. It is a driver of 'living together' in harmony. In the culture, sports and leisure sectors, commitment, local anchorage and the link to the user are central. Values such as solidarity, altruism and tolerance are also highly regarded. Equal opportunities and access, the rejection of all forms of discrimination, and social ties are all principles that strengthen these sectors, which are in line with values pursued by the SSE. These values constitute the basis of ethics common to the sports and cultural communities, which differ from sports businesses and specific cultural industries marked by competition and the reign of money. These communities have in common the criticism of an elitist vision of sports and culture, and the will to anchor practices in daily life.

25.1 THE SSE CONTRIBUTING TO DEMOCRATISING CULTURE, SPORTS AND LEISURE

SSE initiatives in the field of culture, sports and leisure originated in the 19th century, promoting greater equity in the economy and alternatives to capitalism. For a long time, sport, leisure and culture were part of the elitist practices of an enlightened aristocracy and a rising bourgeoisie. This original elitism has recently been replaced by a more vigorous, business-oriented development on the one hand, and by the development of cultural and creative industries, leading to new divisions in the development of these sectors, on the other. Between these two dynamics, the democratisation of sport and leisure, and subsequently of culture, began progressively in the early 20th century, amplifying in the late 20th century with the massification of sport, leisure and culture. The SSE contributes to the development of amateur practices. Considering public school as one of the first driving forces in the development of sports practices such as gymnastics, citizens' collectives could be considered the second driving force, mobilising an essential resource: the voluntary sector. Activities were developed within the framework of amateur practices, for which the local area was the container.

25.2 THE ROLE OF THE STATE AND LOCAL AUTHORITIES

Since the 1920s, in developed countries, the development of the culture, sports and leisure sectors was accelerated by the emergence of leisure societies (Dumazedier 1962). In these societies, particularly from the 1960s, consensus that citizens should freely choose the use of free time became widespread, which was a part of a process of democratisation of sport, leisure and culture.

Although support from the public authorities is essential to the democratisation of sport, leisure and culture, it varies significantly across the countries. For instance, in many countries, laws stipulate that sports practices are mandatory in school curricula, thus gradually favouring the institutionalisation of the sports sector. Meanwhile, such countries also recognise sports practices as a matter of public goods. However, in other countries it is mainly through funding, particularly subsidies from local authorities to organisations supporting activities (sports clubs, holiday camps, cultural associations, and so on), that public authorities contribute to the development of sports, leisure and cultural activities.

The European Union is also investing more and more in the field of culture, although there is no cultural policy (Calligaro and Vlassis 2017). This commitment is often linked to support for the tourism sector in order to promote employment and creativity (see entry 41, 'Tourism Sector').

25.3 THE IMPORTANCE OF VOLUNTEERING

Voluntary work is central to the organisations – in particular, social and solidarity economy organisations and enterprises (SSEOEs) – within the culture, sports and leisure sectors. In particular, voluntary work contributes to the functioning of sports associations, where parents often take on the collective training of their children. The number of volunteers is often higher than the number of permanent staff in such cases. Box 25.1 gives the case of France.

BOX 25.1 THE CASE OF FRANCE

The sports movement encapsulating the French sports federations, has 17 million members (out of a population of 60 million individuals) and more than 300 000 associations, mobilising 3.3 per cent of the SSE workforce and 16 per cent of establishments. Three-quarters of sports establishments belong to the SSE sector, and 99 per cent of them are associations. However, there is a small share of cooperatives in leisure activities that are 100 per cent associative, unlike the case of sports activities. Ninety-five per cent of establishments employ less than ten employees, compared to 89 per cent for the rest of the economy.

In sports and leisure activities, the SSE represents 55 per cent of total employment and 74 per cent of establishments. Within the sports sector alone, the SSE accounts for 64 per cent of the workforce and 84 per cent of establishments. It is deployed in many associative clubs present throughout the country, allowing the dissemination of diversified practices to all.

Recreational and leisure activities represent at least 38 per cent of jobs and 35 per cent of establishments. They take the form of activity and leisure centres, youth and cultural centres, popular education associations offering sports and leisure activities for children during the extracurricular time, as well as recreational associations (dance clubs, card games and outdoor sports such as hiking, kayaking, and so on).

> Sports and leisure activities are not highly recruited for. They rely heavily on volunteers (Tchernonog et al. 2019), representing more than 120 000 full-time employment positions (more than the number of employees).
>
> In the culture sector, the SSE has just over 22 000 employees, representing 26 per cent of employment in the sector and three-quarters of establishments, thus signalling a large number of small establishments. As for sport and leisure, 99 per cent of SSE establishments in the culture sector are associations, and 97 per cent of them have less than ten employees. Here again, the development of cultural cooperatives can be observed. The SSE is particularly prominent in the field of performing arts, while public actors are dominant in the management of heritage or public cultural facilities. As for the for-profit sector, it mainly concerns the music industry.
>
> *Source:* Observatoire de l'ESS (2020).

25.4 COMMUNITY EDUCATION, EMANCIPATION AND EMPOWERMENT

Culture, sports and leisure activities are often historically part of community education (see also entry 16, 'Community-Based Organizations' and entry 26, 'Education Sector'). The activities are thus an opportunity for collective dynamics based on the principles of self-management, linking practices, reflection and management. Activities surrounding community education aim to give everyone the means to understand the world in order to be able to transform it. Sport, leisure and culture are thus spaces of emancipation and empowerment that allow everyone to leave the places to which they have been assigned. This is the case of the Senscot network in Scotland, which uses the arts (theatre, films, music, and so on) to help people throughout their lives, for example by helping young people to enter employment or by helping older people to combat social isolation (SENScot 2022).

Through their democratic and deliberative practices, SSEOEs have been the cradle of these initiatives. They have promoted inclusive access to sports and leisure activities, recognising a central role for the user, and promoting experimentation and access, particularly for those who have previously been excluded because of their income, disability, age or location.

Sports clubs are most often formed on a small scale. They promote sociability, the transmission of social values and a sports ethos that appreciates effort and fair play. Meanwhile, organisations in the field of culture facilitate inclusive access for the public to cultural goods and services within a territory.

25.5 THE SPECIFICITY OF CULTURE: FROM CULTURAL DEMOCRACY TO CULTURAL DEMOCRATISATION

As actors of territorial public policies, cultural groups – in particular, SSEOEs in the culture sector – can access public funding which, in some countries such as France, represents a significant part of the government's budget. However, the transformation of the financing methods of local authorities makes their development more fragile. Subsidies that used to finance the functioning of organisations are giving way to more project-oriented calls for tender. However, cultural initiatives still play a central role in local development, contributing to the animation of territories through access to culture for all. Therefore, they often exist at the heart of the co-construction of territorial public policies. At the European level, particular emphasis is placed on the role of culture in territorial attractiveness, in connection with cultural tourism and social inclusion. Here, the SSE plays a central role (Lhermitte and Hugo 2021).

Fostering collective artistic creation is a key dimension of SSEOEs' cultural projects. Beyond that, the SSE plays a driving role in the transition into the third age of cultural policies. This new dynamic is based on the conversion from cultural democracy to cultural democratisation (Benhamou 2004), leading individuals to contribute to the cultural fabric and to leave their passivity as spectators. This is clearly initiated by the 2001 United Nations Educational, Scientific and Cultural Organization (UNESCO) Universal Declaration on Cultural Diversity, alongside the ability to promote the cultural rights identified by civil society in the context of the Fribourg Declaration (Meyer-Bisch 2008). In particular, these initiatives point to the right of everyone to participate in cultural life, and contribute to making cultural rights a driver of societal transformation in favour of the emancipation of individuals. The SSE is also playing an increasingly significant role in the development of the cultural and creative industry, in order to contribute to a more inclusive and sustainable society, especially in disadvantaged cities and territories.

25.6 CHALLENGES AND OPPORTUNITIES FOR INNOVATION

The challenges of the SSEOEs in the culture, sports and leisure sectors are mainly in three areas. Firstly, professionalisation in these sectors has been supported by the emergence of specific diplomas and an increase in the number of jobs. Yet, the employment conditions in the sports, recreational and cultural activities of the SSEOEs are characterised by a fragmentation of professional activity, due to the discontinuous characteristic of some activities, their seasonality or the lack of resources of a significant proportion of the organisations. As a result, job insecurity is prevalent within the SSEOEs of these sectors. The professionalisation of the sport and leisure sector within the framework of small structures has made it necessary to share jobs between organisations. In France, this has been accompanied by the emergence of organisations such as employers' grouping, which constitute inspiring forms of social innovation. The employers' grouping, generally an association or a co-op, allows companies to join together to recruit full-time employees who could not be recruited by an individual company. By reconciling flexibility and job stability, the employers' grouping responds both to the economic realities of small and medium-sized enterprises, and to employees' legitimate need for security. In the cultural sector, the specific status of French intermittent entertainment workers makes it possible to adapt to the temporary nature of tours or shows with different employers, while guaranteeing continuity of remuneration.

The Smart project, created in Belgium in 1998, now spread across eight European countries, is a cooperative that offers support to self-employed workers in the culture sector. This enables the development of their activities by offering them a self-employed status. Smart is also a cooperative platform, based on the pooling of financial and production resources, and encouraging participation and solidarity among its members. Doc Servizi, a workers' cooperative with over 4000 members, is another innovative organisational form in Italy. This cooperative model becomes the artist's employer, managing contracts, invoicing, payment of tax and social and security contributions, and collection of payment from the customer. In other words, it deals with the needs of professional artists (Doc Servizi 2022). Thus, the SSE seems to offer relevant solutions to promote better conditions for the exercise of cultural and sports activities (Constantini 2018).

The second challenge concerns organisational transformations in these sectors. These sectors are characterised by a more entrepreneurial dimension, particularly in relation to the development of a market sector (see also entry 44, 'Co-optation, Isomorphism and Instrumentalisation'). Thus, in the sports sector, the development is observed of a more diversified and personalised commercial offer, linked to the search for well-being and relaxation, carried out by profit-making companies. The same is true for the growth of the commercial sector and the increase in cultural offers. The resulting increase in competition should lead to an evolution of these sectors characterised by the development of inter-firm cooperation and cooperatives involving a diversity of stakeholders. Indeed, a strengthened entrepreneurial dimension of cultural organisations within the SSE would give rise to new organisational forms, cooperatives and multi-stakeholders, or within territorial clusters or third places, associating a diversity of actors (public and private), but also citizens and the civil society as a whole. It would also contribute to the development of hybrid and complex organisations. For example, Gängeviertel, located in Hamburg, Germany, is a multi-purpose third sector organisation founded by social activists with a background in arts and culture. The goal is to preserve a traditional housing compound in the heart of the city which was earmarked for demolition. Gängeviertel now combines a holding for a membership-based club and a cooperative in charge of managing the housing compound, alongside organising cultural activities and events. Another example from Germany, TSG Bergerdorf Sports Club, has changed its organisational form from a traditional gymnastics club to a skills development space for young people. It also offers a diverse range of sports as part of the commercial activities provided which are linked to wellness expectations. They have been able to adapt their governance to these transformations by developing a more complex structuring in connection with the diversification of activities and the strengthening of their commercial dynamics (Zimmer et al. 2018).

These organisational transformations can also be illustrated by the strengthening of the link to the territory, with this being particularly significant in the culture sector. For example, in the city of Chuncheoon, within northern South Korea, the cultural sector has been particularly active in deploying programmes to support the development of social enterprises, with the aim of revitalising the territory according to two objectives: creating employment, and developing the attractiveness of the territory (Lee and Defalvard 2019). We can also observe the development of clusters at the local level which, by encouraging cooperation, allow the development of creativity and innovation, and contribute to local development (UNIDO 2015). In Marseille, France, la Friche la Belle de Mai is now a place of creativity and innovation, converted from the Seita tobacco factory into a cultural complex. La Friche la Belle de Mai, a multi-stakeholder cooperative, is both a workplace for 70 organisations (400 artists and creatives working here every day) and a place for cultural dissemination and events (600 public art events per year, from youth workshops to large-scale festivals). With over 450 000 visitors a year, la Friche la Belle de Mai is a multi-faceted public space comprising a sports area, restaurant, five concert and theatre venues, shared gardens, a bookshop, a crèche, 2400 square metres of exhibition space dedicated to contemporary art, an 8000 square metre roof terrace, a training centre (Friche la Belle de Mai 2022). Creative hubs (Bilbao, Barcelona, Berlin, and so on) – sometimes supported by museums, as in the case of the 'Guggenheim effect' – have been used to boost local development. The multiplier effect of culture-based investment presents an opportunity to reap local benefits in cultural, social and economic terms. It is this dynamic that can be found in the framework of the European Capital of Culture projects which, since 1985, have been a strategic tool for the development of the host city, bringing coherence to initially disparate activities.

Finally, it should be noted that the COVID-19 pandemic has weakened the whole sector. Although this sector seemed resilient throughout the 2000s in Europe, with 7.5 per cent of total employment and more than 5 per cent of European added value (Eurostat 2022), it seems to have been strongly affected by the pandemic. In Europe, the cultural and creative industries lost 31 per cent of their turnover in 2020, greater than the losses of other sectors of the economy (Lhermitte and Hugo 2021), due to the closure of establishments and their inability to be open to the public due to restrictions.

REFERENCES

Benhamou, Françoise. 2004. 'Exception Culturelle, L'Exploration d'une Impasse.' *Revue Esprit* May: 85–113.
Calligaro, Oriane and Antonio Vlassis. 2017. 'The European Policy of Culture: Between Economic Paradigm and the Rhetoric of Exception.' *Politique Européenne* 56 (2): 8–28.
Constantini, Anastasia. 2018. 'Social Economy Enterprises and Cultural and Creative Industries: Observations and Best Practices.' Brussels: Dieses. https://www.researchgate.net/project/How-social-enterprises-contribute-to-creative-industries.
Doc Servizi. 2022. 'Doc Servizi – L'arte Si Fa Valore.' Doc Servizi. https://docservizi.retedoc.net/.
Dumazedier, Joffre. 1962. *Vers Une Civilisation Du Loisir?* Paris: Editions Du Seuil.
Eurostat. 2022. 'Culture Statistics – Cultural Employment.' Eurostat. https://ec.europa.eu/eurostat/statistics-explained/index.php?title=Culture_statistics_-_cultural_employment.
Friche la Belle de Mai. 2022. 'Une Fabrique d'Art et de Culture et Un Espace de Vie.' Friche La Belle de Mai. https://www.lafriche.org/.
Lee, Ai, and Defalvard, Hervé. 2019. 'Culture et Économie Sociale En Corée Du Sud.' In *Culture & Économie Sociale et Solidaire*, edited by Defalvard Hervé. Fontaine: Presses Universitaires de Grenoble.
Lhermitte, Marc, and Alvarez, Hugo. 2021. 'Rebuilding Europe: The Cultural and Creative Economy Before and After the Covid-19 Crisis.' EY. https://www.ey.com/fr_fr/government-public-sector/panorama-europeen-des-industries-culturelles-et-creatives-edition.
Meyer-Bisch, Patrice. 2008. 'Les Droits Culturels Enfin Sur le Devant de la Scène.' *Observatoire* 1 (33): 9–13
Observatoire de l'ESS. 2020. 'Atlas Commenté de l'Économie Sociale et Solidaire.' ESS France. https://www.ess-france.org/publication-de-l-edition-2020-de-l-atlas-commente-de-l-ess.
SENScot. 2022. 'Cultural & Creative.' SENScot. https://senscot.net/thematic-sens/cultural/.
Tchernonog, Viviane, Lionel Prouteau, Hugues Sibille, Colas Amblard, Chantal Bruneau and Chantal Brutel, eds. 2019. *Le Paysage Associatif Français: Mesures et Évolutions*. Lyons and Paris: Dalloz Juris Éditions.
UNIDO. 2015. 'Creative Mediterranean Resilience through Creativity: Progress Report 2015.' Vienna: UNIDO. https://open.unido.org/api/documents/4673180/download/DEVELOPMENT%20OF%20CLUSTERS%20IN%20CULTURAL%20AND%20CREATIVE%20INDUSTRIES%20IN%20THE%20SOUTHERN%20MEDITERRANEAN.
Zimmer, Annette, Patrick Hoemke, Joachim Benedikt Pahl and Christina Rentzsch, eds. 2018. *Resilient Organizations in the Third Sector*. Münster: Westfälische Wilhelms-Universität, Institut für Politikwissenschaft. https://emes.net/publications/books/resilient-organizations-in-the-third-sector/.

26. Education sector
Christina A. Clamp and Colleen E. Tapley

INTRODUCTION

Social and solidarity economy (SSE) activities directed to enhancing the quality of education are broad in scope and encompass primary and secondary education as well as the role of higher education in support of innovation in the SSE. They also include workforce development, which may be done through higher education or other nongovernmental entities. Education at the primary and secondary levels is examined in terms of how SSE institutions have contributed resources to improve the quality of the public schools or created innovative alternatives. This can take the form of alternative models such as co-operative schools. In higher education, the challenge for the SSE is to encourage the incorporation of a curriculum about the SSE as well as resources to support research and policy work to guide the development of new SSE institutions. Literature on the SSE and education is scarce. The focus of this entry is on mapping the role of the SSE in the education sector and identifying best practices, lessons learned, and areas for future innovation. In identifying best practices, examples were selected based on their impact, sustainability, accessibility, and relevance to multiple stakeholders.

Education is key to promoting social progress. Too often, education is focused on maintaining the status quo. SSE organizations and enterprises (SSEOEs) are committed to a more civic and inclusive-minded commitment to their local communities, and this includes educational institutions (see also entry 3, "Contemporary Understandings"). Spiel et al. (2018) cite four goals in the relationship between education and social progress. Education is key to maintaining a competitive labor force in an increasingly globalized economy. Through education, people can develop skills and understanding of the importance of participation in civic life as engaged citizens. Education cultivates life skills to expand our knowledge as well as realize our full potential. Lastly, it is the most effective means for creating a level playing field and reducing the impact of social injustices and social exclusion. Primary and secondary education is considered a basic right for every child according to the United Nations. Only through the commitment of governments and SSEOEs can we hope to achieve that objective. The SSE in the form of philanthropy can influence the content of education, to focus on goals of social justice and social inclusion. SSEOEs also play a role in the promotion of educational programming to address the needs for professional capacity-building for their workforces. This can take the form of professional training such as badges or certificates as well as courses and degrees in higher education.

26.1 HIGHER EDUCATION AND THE SSE

Many universities include degrees in nonprofit management, but far fewer offer studies in co-operative management and community development. Degrees in co-operative business

Table 26.1   Universities with degrees in co-operative business studies

Region	University	Programs in co-operative studies
Africa	Ambo University, Ethiopia	BA and MA programs
	Moshi University, Tanzania	Co-operative business education
Asia	Sungkonghoe University, Korea	Co-operative business education
	University of Sydney, Australia.	Co-operative business education
Europe	University of Helsinki, Ruralia Institute, Finland	Co-operative network studies with seven affiliated universities
	Université de Bretagne Occidentale, France	Master's degree in Mutualist and Co-operatives
	European Research Institute on Cooperative and Social Enterprises (EURICSE), Italy	MA and professional trainings
	Università Di Bologna, Italy	Master's in the Economics of Co-operatives
	Mondragón University (MU), Spain	MA
	The Co-operative College, UK	Courses and programs related to co-operatives
	University of Gloucestershire, UK	MBA in Co-operative Enterprise
	University of Exeter, UK	Co-operative business education
North America	IRECUS, Université de Sherbrooke, Quebec, Canada	MA and certificate programs
	St Mary's University, Canada	Master and certificate programs in co-operative management
	Université du Québec à Montréal (UQAM), Québec, Canada	Executive MBA and professional training
	University of Saskatchewan, Canada	Co-operative business education
	University of Winnipeg, Canada	Bachelor of Business Administration concentration in co-operatives
	Cape Breton University, Canada	Co-operative business education
	Ontario Co-operative Association & York University, Canada	Cooperative Management Certificate
	Universidad Autónoma de Queretero, México	Bachelor's and technical diplomas in co-operative and social enterprise management
	University of Missouri, USA	Co-operative business education
South America & the Caribbean	Cipriani College of Labour and Co-operative Studies, Trinidad and Tobago	BA, AA and professional certificates
	Pontificia Universidade Católica do Paraná (PUCPR), Brazil	Master's and certificate programs in co-operative management
	Universidad de Habana, Cuba	Master's, diplomas and courses on co-operatives
	Universidad Federal Rural de Pernambuco, Brazil	Post-graduate programs on co-operatives
	Universidad de Santiago de Chile (CIESCOOP), Chile	Diploma and master's on SSE

Source: Miner and Guillotte (2014).

development were surveyed by Miner and Guillotte (2014) at 18 universities (see Table 26.1). Miner and Guillotte (2014) identified the following other universities with co-operative business education programs: Cape Breton University, Canada; Moshi University, Tanzania; On Co-op, York University, Canada; Sungkonghoe University, Korea; University of Exeter, UK; University of Missouri, USA; University of Saskatchewan, Canada; and University of Sydney, Australia.

Two universities that have noteworthy programs for their scale, and years in co-operative research and co-operative studies, are the University of Saskatchewan and the University of

Wisconsin, Madison. They benefit from support from co-operatives and credit unions as well as public funding. The University of British Columbia and the University of Massachusetts have established campus co-operatives. The Law Clinic at the City University of New York provides legal support to the development of co-operatives and is affiliated with 1worker1vote (http://1worker1vote.org/).

University College, Cork in Ireland has strong ties to the Irish credit unions and co-operatives and has an active research center and undergraduate and graduate teaching in support of SSE. Its online master's program reaches an international student enrollment. Strong programs with a community development focus are housed at the University of Cape Breton, Concordia University, and Carleton University in Canada, and at the University of New Hampshire in the United States.

Co-op Network Studies (CNS), a network established by a group of seven universities and coordinated by the Ruralia Institute of the University of Helsinki, offers multidisciplinary, web-based minor subject courses and modules leading to a bachelor's or master's degree (Ruralia Institute 2021). This delivery model offers students a greater variety of courses and module options while ensuring a larger enrollment pool for the courses.

An outstanding innovation in the role of universities in the promotion of SSE is Team Academy. Team Academy (Tiimiakatemia) was established in Finland in 1993 at the University of Applied Sciences in Jyväskylä, Finland (Ruuska and Krawczyk 2013). The model was then adopted at other Finnish universities and spread to universities in the United Kingdom, Hungary, Brazil, Argentina, Queretaro and Puebla Mexico, the Netherlands, and Costa Rica. There are multiple centers in Spain located in the Basque region (Irun, Bilbao, Oñate), Madrid, Barcelona, and Valencía. The network includes innovation labs in Bilbao, Berlin, and Seoul. Mondragon University (MU) in Spain has provided technical assistance for the expansion of Team Academy to other institutions. The curriculum is based on the development of skills in entrepreneurship, fostering of networks, connections with innovation labs, experience with the newest entrepreneurial methodologies, and interaction with new markets.

The Universidad Fundepos in Costa Rica, with technical assistance from MU, joined Team Academy in 2019. It has 260 participants and has served 1800 program participants. Team Academy students are organized into teams and operate as co-operatives. First-year students learn about the co-operative form of business. The learning process is to build their skills as entrepreneurs while developing their cultural competencies for engaging in international business, and to work together in a co-operative with their "teampreneurs." The students move around the globe, utilizing the various network member sites to develop their entrepreneurial skills and networks to facilitate the development of a viable business concept by the end of their studies. Post-graduation, the majority of the students secure employment as entrepreneurs or intrapreneurs. There are retention issues, as not everyone is cut out to be an entrepreneur; MU's LEINN program model allows for students to transfer to other degree programs if it is not right for them.

Costa Rica has a second program supported by SSE institutions and the government. CENECOOP (campus.co.cr) offers over 30 courses online. The cost ranges from free to $20 per course. Students rely on cell phones and loaded tablets. The curriculum includes courses on co-operative schools and student co-operatives, co-operative management, as well as more general courses in entrepreneurship, finance, and digital literacy. Since Costa Rica accepts more refugees than other countries in the region, this program is seen as accessible to all (Naves 2021).

Southern New Hampshire University's Global Education Movement (GEM) delivers associate and bachelor's degrees through a competency-based model of blended learning to low-income youth and refugees at nine sites in five countries: Rwanda, Lebanon, South Africa, Malawi, and Kenya. The goal is to improve student labor market outcomes through a combination of online coursework and in-person instruction. Over 1200 students have been enrolled, with 93 percent on track to graduate and 84 percent employed within six months of graduation.

The Korean government has been supportive of the development of SSE through the establishment of public policies related to education and training. To create skilled leaders to lead the social economy, the government-supported expansion of specialized courses in social economy leadership called the Social Economy Leadership Program (SELP). The SELP program is a non-degree program offered by colleges and universities to SSE workers which teaches skills required to lead the social economy. The program began in 2013 at three universities, and by 2018 the number had increased to four, with over 600 workers benefiting from the program (Yoon and Lee 2020). Over 20 universities are projected to host SELP by 2022. In addition to SELP, many colleges and universities are committed to offering related degree programs.

The solidarity economy in Brazil grew in the 1990s as a social movement (Cruz-Souza et al. 2011). In response to the economic dislocation created by neoliberal policies, the government appealed for the creation of incubators for co-operatives. La Red Universitaria de Incubadoras Tecnológicas de Cooperativas Populares (Rede de ITCPs) formed with 44 universities and institutions of higher education networked in five regions of Brazil in 1998. At Universidad Federal de São Carlos, the innovation resulted in the Incubadora Regional de Cooperativas Populares (INCOOP), an extension program to develop co-operatives that entailed the participation of faculty, students, workers, and professionals across a range of disciplines and professions. Twenty solidarity enterprises in areas such as food, cleaning, surveillance, laundry, recycling, sewing, production of seedlings, handicrafts, carpentry, agricultural production, and cleaning products created jobs and income for approximately 500 people. INCOOP has a practical curriculum with graduate and postgraduate programs of study. Graduates develop their own projects with the support of the INCOOP incubator. Embedded in the curriculum is a focus on solidarity finance and ethical consumption, aligned with the Solidarity Economy and Popular Cooperatives group. This group is linked to the national network, Rede de ITCPs.

26.2 PRIMARY AND SECONDARY EDUCATION AND SSE

Evidence of the implementation of initiatives and programs linked to the social and solidarity economy can be found in various forms throughout primary and secondary education. Examples of model programs can be found at both levels.

Evidence of the social and solidarity economy in Tanzania dates back to colonial times and can be observed in various forms throughout society (Bee 2013). Although data and information related to SSEs in Tanzania is limited (2013), the Tanzania Federation of Cooperatives is charged with inspecting over 200 co-operatives every three months (Daily News Reporter 2021). Tanzania continues to face many challenges in education, including teacher shortages, a lack of classroom resources, overcrowding in classrooms, lack of funding, curriculum and design, and learner retention, with fewer than 40 percent of children pursuing secondary education (Lugalla and Ngwaru 2019).

Educators in East Africa are required to implement active learning pedagogies in their teaching, yet they face numerous barriers in educating their students (Crichton and Nicholas 2018). These educators often work in overcrowded classrooms, with insufficient resources, limited funding, and are offered few professional development opportunities. In Tanzania, as well as other parts of the world, educators can be found using the Taking Making into Challenging Contexts Toolkit to model the integration design thinking, making, and science, technology, engineering, and mathematics (STEM) education in what they define as challenging contexts. Crichton and Nicholas (2018) define a challenging context as a setting "in which individuals have limited, unreliable or no access to modern-day conveniences such as electricity, running water, health care, mobile computing, and related emerging technologies due to a variety of circumstances, conditions or environmental constraints" (Crichton and Nicholas 2018, 7).

While Crichton and Nicholas (2018) note that challenging contexts can be found anywhere, a major focus of their work has been to train teachers to implement this pedagogy as a model to impact sustainable change in challenging contexts. In their model, students learn to use and apply the Design Thinking approach in innovative and creative ways to solve authentic problems that are faced by their communities. Although there are numerous benefits for any students who engage in learning through this model, children who learn making in challenging contexts have the added benefit of learning that they can become part of the change that they want to see in their own communities. Through active learning, students apply the "Four Rs" of global citizenship (rethink, reuse, reduce, and recycle) to solve authentic problems in a tangible way (Crichton and Nicholas 2018, 22). By engaging in design thinking, STEM and making, students practice and learn transferable skills that they can use in the future to solve problems in the context of their own community to create a more sustainable future. They can identify problems or issues that need solving in their communities and work together to design solutions.

Association for Sarva Seva Farms (ASSEFA) has supported the development of poor rural communities in India through the promotion of the social and solidarity economy for over 50 years. ASSEFA's core values are based upon the Gandhian principles of nonviolence, love, and truth. For over 40 years, ASSEFA has worked to establish schools in rural areas with no school facilities, and to improve access and equity in education. During this time, over 10 598 children and 474 educators have benefited from their programs (Association for Sarva Seva Farms 2020). ASSEFA promotes the holistic development of children's basic knowledge, health, and wellness, as well as providing education regarding the principles of nonviolence, love, respect, and the importance of sharing with others. ASSEFA has had a tremendous impact on education in India, expanding the number of schools that exist in rural areas. It also provided access to education during the COVID-19 pandemic when the government authorized school closures, particularly providing education for women, improving educator preparation, and educator professional development.

In India, the COVID-19 pandemic has disrupted the education of over 320 million students in primary and secondary education. This learning disruption is exacerbated by digital divides that have increased the educational inequities in gender and class that existed in India prior to the COVID-19 pandemic (Sahni 2020). Only 23 percent of households in India have access to the internet (Sahni 2020), with only a reported 8 percent of children in rural areas attending online classes (Carvalho 2021).

While many schools remained closed in India due to COVID-19 with an expected reopening date of November 2021 (Carvalho 2021), ASSEFA provided online classes in basic math,

English, and even social emotional learning for 1350 students in the coastal area of India (Association for Sarva Seva Farms 2020). Due to a lack of internet and device accessibility, over 50 percent of those students had difficulty attending classes (Association for Sarva Seva Farms 2020). In response to student needs, educators implemented creative ways to deliver content, including recording lessons and sharing them through WhatsApp.

Another example of ASSEFA's impact on education in India is the introduction of "weekend schools." The weekend schools grant proposal was submitted in September 2020 in response to the COVID-19 impact. Many parents in India must decide between working on the weekends and being home to care for their children (Association for Sarva Seva Farms 2020). For many families, there is no choice, and parents must leave their children home alone or in the care of neighbors. In response to childcare needs, ASSEFA has established two weekend school sites, in Mykudi and Kottapatti, for children aged 6 through 12 (Association for Sarva Seva Farms 2020). The goal of these weekend schools is to provide a safe environment for socioeconomically disadvantaged children to learn useful skills that will benefit them in the future, beyond simply reinforcing skills learned in the textbook. These weekend schools engage students in learning and activities aligned to the head, hand, and heart.

The weekend school project is grant-funded and over 300 children are benefiting from participation in the pilot version. After one year, the skills gained by children involved in the weekend school project will be assessed and the ASSEFA Head Office will send a progress report along with photos to the funding agency. After assessing the program, the plan is to expand the weekend school program to other areas. In addition to their work with improving rural education, ASSEFA has also played an instrumental role in preparing new teachers through the College of Education at Silarpatti and the Teacher Education Institute at Pooriyampakkam, which has also had a major impact.

ASSEFA is also responsible for implementing numerous socioeconomic welfare programs. One of ASSEFA's goals is the empowerment of rural women through various programs, including those focused on education and financial stability. ASSEFA partners with a variety of key stakeholders, including the government and private sector, to provide the resources necessary to implement these programs.

The Digital Livelihoods Program is an initiative that was created in collaboration with Hewlett Packard, FREND and the Sarvodaya Mutual Benefit Trust to offer training and education to Saathis (friends) who expressed a desire to start their own smart printer-based business (Association for Sarva Seva Farms 2020). The training was offered by FREND on how to operate the printers, and the printers were offered to the Saathis at a subsidized rate by Hewlett Packard. Over 300 Saathis have benefited from participating in this program and are now earning income (Association for Sarva Seva Farms 2020). This service, as well as providing the printing of educational materials, transportation tickets, government documents, and photos, among many other things, contributes greatly to the community.

In Germany, a secondary school co-operative program called Schulergenossenschaften allows students to develop and operate their own co-operative under the guidance of their school. As part of this program, students are required to create and implement their own business plans (Wolf and Redford 2018). Students' ideas are turned into action, as they write the statutes of their co-operatives and are responsible for the creation of the goods and services that are distributed (Wolf and Redford 2018). Students are supported throughout the process, often with the resources to implement their business plan, by the Genossenchaftsverband, the co-operative association, if needed. Participants in the student co-operatives are allotted the same time frame and are held to the same criteria and expectations as those in the adult co-operatives, including annual audits. This program, which allows students to learn while engaging in the program, lasts at least three years and offers the opportunity to renew once this time ends. One of the program's main goals is to promote sustainability. Schulergenossenschaften has been praised for the lasting impact it has had on the community, and its innovative model for educating students.

In the Basque region, the Euskal Herriko Ikastolak is an example of a European co-operative with 120 members from throughout France and Spain (Basque Country Schools 2018). Approximately 6000 teachers employed by the program educate 60 000 students, and have an impact on over 40 000 families (Basque Country Schools 2018). The Ikastola pedagogical model focuses on the promotion of the Basque curriculum, focused on social participation, responsibility, and competence development. Students are taught through engagement in active learning and innovation is highly valued. An emphasis is placed upon educating students about Basque culture and creating multilingual Basque students who are trained in information and communication technology (Basque Country Schools 2018). One of the most unique components of this program is that the co-operative is run in partnership with parents and the community. Educators partner with families and professionals to create their own learning materials, which they constantly revise and improve. While each school is part of the co-operative and adheres to the same values and model, each has its own history and unique way of operating in its own unique context. As part of the services provided by the program, published teaching materials and training are offered. The program is funded primarily (80 percent) through services it provides. Other funding comes from public subsidiaries (15 percent) and a direct cost to members (5 percent) (Basque Country Schools 2018).

The South Korean government's commitment to the social economy is also evident in its primary and secondary schools. In 2018, plans were made to revise curriculum content to focus on social economy, cooperation, and other practices related to the social economy (Yoon and Lee 2020). There was also a desire by the South Korean government to create a curriculum connected to social and solidarity economy education and to provide courses for students in primary and secondary school (Yoon and Lee 2020). In 2018, South Korea had established over 60 school co-operatives to promote student learning and curriculum related to the social economy (Yoon and Lee 2020).

26.3 CRITERIA FOR SUCCESS

One of the most critical components necessary for a successful initiative is directly tied to the ideals that are foundational to human-centered design and the work that is being done through Making in Challenging Contexts. When stakeholders fail to implement a human-centered design approach, they often apply their own context to what they think the communities, or "users" as they are often called in human-centered design, need based on their own perception. Decisions are often made because stakeholders think they know the solution, but what they really need to do is take the time to better understand the problem, the needs of the community, and the context through empathy work. By implementing human-centered design when partnering with a community, stakeholders can have a more profound impact by offering services and practices that change lives by filling an actual need.

Another critical component is the involvement of multiple stakeholders engaged in a mutual partnership. As stated previously, this partnership must work toward the best interests of the community. When multiple stakeholders collaborate and work toward the same goals with the local community and government, initiatives are much more successful. When informing practice for education it is also important for stakeholders to come from a diverse range of backgrounds, to ensure that all voices are heard and that a variety of perspectives are considered (Lugalla and Ngwaru 2019).

Funding is another critical factor that impacts the success of an initiative. Programs need to either demonstrate relatively low-cost sustainability over time, or be provided with ample funding for the program to be sustained long term. Long-term funding is necessary for any initiative to demonstrate effectiveness, or to have a true impact on a community. Many programs demonstrate strong potential for success and are ended before their impact is able to be assessed due to a lack of long-term funding (see also entry 45, "Financing").

Through a review of programs, it is clear that there are several key factors that contribute to the expansion and improvement of the quality of education. When examining various models, they were assessed for overall impact, sustainability, the program's ability to fill a need within the community, the quality of the partnerships developed with stakeholders, and the model of innovative practice. Technology and knowledge sharing is key to promoting and scaling programs at an international level, as in Team Academy, which has the potential to have a tremendous impact on the SSE.

The various ways in which the SSE provides services to education are evident in innovative programs and models across primary, secondary, and higher education. While innovative programs and models are impactful, the key to success is government and private sector support. Governments must prioritize the SSE when creating policy, and adequate funding must be provided to support SSE initiatives. If governments develop collaborative partnerships with key stakeholders and support SSE initiatives through funding and policy, these programs can flourish.

REFERENCES

Association for Sarva Seva Farms. 2020. "Social Solidarity Economy: The Gandhian Path. Annual Report, Royapettah, Chennai." Association for Sarva Seva Farms. https://www.assefawr.org/sarvodaya-mutual-benefit-trust.htm.

Basque Country Schools. 2018. *ikastolen elkartea*. https://ikastola-eus.translate.goog/ikastola/zer_da?_x_tr_sl=eu&_x_tr_tl=en&_x_tr_hl=en&_x_tr_pto=nui,sc.

Bee, Faustine K. 2013. "The Role of Social and Solidarity Economy in Tanzania." *Asian Journal of Humanities and Social Studies* 1 (5): 244–54.

Carvalho, Nirmala. 2021. "COVID-19 and Education: A Catastrophic Situation in India." *Asia News*. https://www.asianews.it/news-en/COVID-19-and-education:-a-catastrophic-situation-in-India-54081.html.

Crichton, Susan and Wachira Nicholas. 2018. *Taking Making Into Classrooms in Challenging Contexts: A Toolkit Fostering Curiosity, Imagination and Active Learning*. Innovative Learning Centre. Canada. https://www.niteoafrica.org/wp-content/uploads/2019/09/toolkit-limited-resources.pdf.

Cruz-Souza, Fatima, Ana Lucia Cortegoso, Maria E. Zanin, and Ioshiaqui Shimbo. 2011. "Las Incubadoras Universitarias de Economia Solidaria en Brasil – Un Estudio de Casos." *REVESCO Revista de Estudios Cooperativos* 106: 74–94. https://doi.org/10.5209/rev_reve.2011.v106.37373.

Daily News Reporter. 2021. "TFC Appeals for Budget Beef Up to Enhance Cooperatives." *Tanzania Daily News*. https://dailynews.co.tz/news/2021-05-3060b32f6f3389b.aspx.

Lugalla, Joe and J. Marriote Ngwaru. 2019. *Education in Tanzania in the Era of Globalisation: Challenges and Opportunities*. Dar-es-Salaam: Mkuki Na Nyota Publishers.

Miner, Karen and Claude-Andre Guillotte. 2014. "Relevance and Impact of Co-operative Business Education." Community-Wealth.org. https://community-wealth.org/content/relevance-and-impact-co-operative-business-education-boosting-co-operative-performance.

Naves, Sergio. 2021. "El modelo de la Economia Social Solidaria (ESS) en la educacion superior para el desarrollo." Cartagena, Costa Rica, September 10. Panel Presentation, 8th International Research Conference on Social Economy, CIRIEC Costa Rica.

Ruralia Institute. 2021. "Co-op Network Studies." https://www2.helsinki.fi/en/ruralia-institute/education/co-op-network-studies#section-46831.

Ruuska, Juha, and Piotr Krawczyk. 2013. "Team Academy as Learning Living Lab." *Proceedings of the University Industry Conference*. https://www.researchgate.net/publication/281775684_Team_Academy_as_Learning_Living_Lab_European_Phenomena_of_Entrepreneurship_Education_and_Development.

Sahni, Urvashi. 2020. "COVID-19 in India: Learning Disrupted and Lesson Learned." Education Plus Development. https://www.brookings.edu/blog/education-plus-development/2020/05/14/covid-19-in-india-education-disrupted-and-lessons-learned/.

Spiel, Ciristiane, Simon Schwartzman, Marius Busemeyer, Nico Cloete, Gili Drori, Lorenz Lassnigg, Barbara Schober, Michele Schweisfurth, and Suman Verma. 2018. "Chapter 19—How Can Education Promote Social Progress?" In *Rethinking Society for the 21st Century: Report of the International Panel on Social Progress*. Cambridge: Cambridge University Press. 90–93.

Wolf, Christian and Dana T. Redford. 2018. "ECOOPE Good Practice Guide." socioeco.org. https://www.socioeco.org/bdf_fiche-outil-184_en.html.

Yoon, Kil-Soon and Sang-Youn Lee. 2020. *Policy Systems and Measures for the Social Economy in Seoul*. Geneva: United Nations Research Institute for Social Development and Global Social Economy Forum.

27. Energy, water and waste management sectors
Waltteri Katajamäki

INTRODUCTION

The impact of climate change is one of the most significant challenges of our time. Our current patterns of production and consumption and the way we use natural resources are unsustainable. These hinder our path towards sustainable development and have significant implications for the environment, economies, global health, the future of work and livelihoods. Addressing and reversing the impacts of climate change and moving towards a just transition to environmentally sustainable economies and societies for all, that contributes to sustainable development in its economic, social and environmental dimensions, is a priority. Solutions such as decarbonisation of the economy and carbon neutrality are needed. However, these must align with the goals of decent work for all, social inclusion and the eradication of poverty (ILO 2015).

Moving towards a circular economy has the potential to contribute to these objectives through its focus on changing the dominant linear production and consumption patterns. In essence, a circular economy minimises the resource inputs and maximises the reuse of materials. It can be seen as an alternative approach to the current linear economy of 'take–make–use–dispose', and instead focuses on reduction of the use of raw materials and resources, reuse of materials at different stages, recycling more effectively, and increasing the lifetime of products and materials by keeping them in use for longer. Therefore, a circular economy can be a useful approach in promoting greener and more sustainable production and consumption practices, and help to achieve the Sustainable Development Goals. Currently, however, only 8.6 per cent of the global economy is circular (Circle Economy 2021).

While the environmental benefits of the circular economy are well documented and analysed, less is known about its impacts on socio-economic aspects, such as employment, inclusion and poverty reduction. To fully contribute to a just transition, the circular economy needs to place a stronger emphasis on all three dimensions of sustainable development and enhance its focus on the importance of participation, social dialogue, democracy and innovation (Circle Economy 2020). In this way, it can achieve broader sustainability objectives, including those about a human-centred recovery from the COVID-19 crisis.

A shift towards a circular economy will see millions of jobs lost or transformed. On the other hand, this transition is a significant opportunity for the world of work: the International Labour Organization (ILO) has estimated that it has a potential for a net growth of 7 million jobs globally by 2030, primarily driven by job increases in waste management and recycling and in the services sector, and through the creation of sustainable enterprises (ILO 2019a). Hence, this transition would need to include protection and investment in skills development and reskilling opportunities for those whose jobs are lost and changed, as well as ensure decent work opportunities and rights for all workers, including women and youth. With the participation of relevant ministries and employers' and workers' organisations, social dialogue should play a central role in this transition.

27.1 THE ROLE OF THE SOCIAL AND SOLIDARITY ECONOMY IN ENERGY, WATER AND WASTE MANAGEMENT SECTORS

The social and solidarity economy (SSE), with its approach based on values such as inclusiveness, innovation and democratic decision-making and community participation, while promoting entrepreneurship and, in many cases, environmental aspects, can contribute to bridging the gap between circular economy and social objectives. This includes SSE values and decent work being embedded at the core of the circular economy practices. By placing social aspects, such as community and personal well-being and quality of life, at the centre together with economic and environmental considerations, the SSE can further become a useful approach in moving towards sustainable circularity that benefits large numbers of people around the world.

The idea of combining environmental and social aspects is not new for SSE entities. From regenerative agricultural or energy cooperatives, and environmental social enterprises, to community forestry and ecological schools, they have contributed towards environmental sustainability objectives alongside care for the community and social and economic well-being. SSE values such as cooperation, solidarity and mutualism, along with its focus on complementing social innovation with technological solutions, are crucial and highly relevant as the world is moving towards human-centred recovery from the COVID-19 crisis that is inclusive, sustainable and resilient.

However, to fully leverage the potential of the SSE would require investment in and establishment of enabling policy and regulatory environments. This will allow for SSE entities to create more and better jobs and to ensure that existing jobs remain relevant, participate and provide social benefits in the circular economy, and have an established role in the environmental governance more generally to contribute to a just transition towards a circular economy.

To understand the role that the SSE can play in shaping an inclusive circular economy, it is necessary to recognise its instrumental role in the functioning of our current economies and societies. SSE entities play a key role in the provision of services such as energy, water and sanitation, and waste management. They are essential for lives and livelihoods, balancing between environmental, economic and social objectives, and responding to the need of some basic required services for allowing people to live, work and prosper.

The SSE's provision of these services demonstrates its potential to contribute to the greening of the economy in general and the circular economy. The SSE can add value in promoting innovative, locally based solutions for specific challenges. SSE entities in sectors such as energy, water and waste management are providing solidarity-based alternatives for production and consumption, where their structure allows for more inclusive and participatory decision-making, the ability to keep prices affordable, reinvestment of any profits to the community, and access to some of these vital services, including for underserved populations, and in many cases aligned with circular strategies. In addition, SSE entities provide training and skills development opportunities for their members and workers to contribute towards addressing the skills gap for a just transition.

Energy

Access to stable and affordable energy is essential for social and economic development, and the move towards cleaner energy is a key component of a just transition. Despite steady progress in the past decades, access to clean and affordable energy and energy services continues to be a major challenge in many parts of the world, and it is often the most vulnerable segments of the societies who are most impacted by these challenges. In 2019, an estimated 759 million people lacked access to energy, while 2.6 billion people remained without access to clean cooking facilities (IEA et al. 2021).

People around the world have responded to this lack of access by establishing their own enterprises providing missing or otherwise unsuitable services. SSE entities contribute to the energy transition, in terms of both providing cleaner energy services and making them available to underserved populations facing energy poverty, including in times of otherwise soaring energy prices. Energy cooperatives and social enterprises have a long history of producing, supplying and distributing energy, serving millions of people and providing significant proportions of overall energy provision in many countries, particularly in rural areas. They have also been active in promoting clean cooking energy or providing renewable energy solutions such as solar panels. SSE entities can produce solar, wind or water energy, manage biomass power plants, or organise as renewable energy villages, for example. Their main objective need not be in energy provision. Agricultural producers' associations, for instance, can move to using alternative and renewable energy sources that can provide energy for cold storage facilities, or water pumps for irrigation systems. On the other hand, housing cooperatives can aim at energy self-sufficiency through producing and using renewable energy (ILO 2013).

From a circular economy perspective, energy production through biomass holds potential for, for example, agricultural producers' or community forestry organisations that can make use of by-products. Agricultural waste and manure can be used for developing biogas or ethanol, while residues from tree harvesting or sawdust from sawmills can be turned into bioenergy. While some of the technologies for these and other innovative circular solutions can be expensive, pooling resources from members and being able to negotiate with financial service providers, for example, provide SSE entities with the possibility to access these.

Locally owned energy structures based on SSE principles and values can provide the technologies and affordable access to cleaner energy, while ensuring local ownership and the ability to decide on sustainable energy consumption and use. Their self-organised and decentralised structures that aim towards energy self-sufficiency can improve life quality and enhance sustainable resource use and management (Morandeira-Arca et al. 2021). This kind of social innovation that SSE entities contribute to in the energy sector has multiple benefits, promoting not only technologies for energy efficiency, self-sufficiency and lower carbon emissions, but also empowerment and enhanced well-being for members and communities. SSE entities also provide local populations with the opportunity to decide on aspects related to energy production and consumption, and to organise its provision themselves at an affordable cost.

SSE entities often move towards multi-purpose approaches, investing in other services as required by their members and users, such as financial services, improved infrastructure, and training and awareness-raising, including on benefits of locally produced energy. They can also create additional income in cases where surplus energy produced can be then sold to the national grid; this can be invested into further improving the facilities, or in other community projects and initiatives. Furthermore, having energy production at the local level can improve decision-making and democracy beyond the organisation, including in relation to the policy-makers and authorities (ILO 2013).

Water

The right to sufficient, safe, acceptable, physically accessible and affordable water for personal and domestic use, and the right to sanitation, are basic human rights. Globally in 2020, around 2 billion people lacked safely managed drinking water services, while 3.6 billion people lacked sanitation services (UN-Water 2021). In addition, food production is highly dependent on access to water, while at the same time it uses large amounts of global freshwater resources. Hence, access to water has direct implications on economies, human health, food security and many other aspects of human life.

Across the world, services related to water supply and sanitation are mainly organised by the public sector and managed by municipalities, but there are many types of public, private and mixed governance arrangements. Often, particularly marginal urban areas and remote rural areas can face limited water infrastructure and consequently lack of access to water and related services.

This is where SSE entities, including social enterprises, community-based water cooperatives and water user associations, have proven useful for addressing water supply challenges. These organisations are important for ensuring sufficient and good-quality water for household and productive uses at affordable prices in various countries, particularly in Europe and North and South America. While most common in rural areas, water cooperatives are sometimes the main water providers, even in major cities such as Santa Cruz de la Sierra, Bolivia. In regions such as Southeast Asia and parts of Africa, water users' associations or producers' organisations coordinate community-based irrigation management for agricultural production, for example (Arvonen et al. 2017). These organisations can improve the management of increasingly scarce water resources, provide access to technologies, finance, and skills and training, and hence improve agricultural productivity, and consequently, community and household incomes and well-being (Zhang et al. 2021).

Circular water reuse is a key strategy for water security. It can be applied through activities such as rainwater harvesting, transforming sewage sludge for biofuel production, using wastewater as organic fertiliser, and treating water for various reuse purposes, such as irrigation or industrial refrigeration, among others (UNESCO and UNESCO i-WSSM 2020). SSE entities can promote and make use of these and other circular approaches to water management, in addition to contributing to the protection and sustainable management of water resources.

Promoting local, community-based water solutions and social innovation based on SSE principles and values can also improve water treatment practices and decrease related health problems. In addition, they can have positive implications on gender equality, improving the situation of women and girls, who are often responsible for fetching water, sometimes over very long distances, meaning less time for education and earning incomes. Social enterprises and other types of SSE entities can promote sustainable entrepreneurship, particularly for women, making clean water available, and also improving the safety of those responsible for fetching it. SSE entities can also promote safer and more hygienic sanitation facilities as improved service. When the users of the service design these, they are more likely to be suitable for local conditions, improving hygiene and safety, and are often also environmentally more sustainable solutions.

When SSE entities own and manage the water structures and systems, this increases the sense of ownership and allows for deciding on their use. Water mains, wells, sanitation facilities and other structures that have been installed as part of development projects, for example, may not always have provided the expected results, when not based on the actual needs of and consultations with the communities and users of the facilities. When coordinated through SSE entities, this allows for deciding on specific technologies and solutions, including circular ones, that are suitable for the community and households, as the users themselves have been involved in the decision-making processes.

In addition to water supply, and linking to waste management, sewerage and irrigation, SSE entities can benefit the sanitation workers, who often face highly dangerous, unhygienic working conditions, with no protection and limited opportunities for organisation through trade unions. Forming or joining SSE entities can not only provide bargaining power, voice and representation, but also serve as a pathway towards formalisation and improved working conditions (World Bank et al. 2019).

Waste Management

Waste management is essential for safeguarding well-being and public health, ensuring environmental protection, and overall hygiene and attractiveness of urban and rural areas alike, all around the world. When left untreated, waste becomes a problem from both environmental and public health perspectives, with the consequences often falling on those in vulnerable situations. While most often offered as a public municipal service, in many countries the sector is underfunded and not able to keep up with increasing population and waste streams. In addition, informal waste management systems have developed in many countries alongside the formal, public systems. In this space, SSE entities such as social enterprises and cooperatives have been established to address the related issues, from recycling and reusing used textile or plastic waste, to turning food waste into fertilizer, among others. SSE entities are often the preferred and common form of organisation of informal waste workers, many of whom are women, in their attempts to move towards formalisation to improve their conditions and access to formal waste management (see also entry 42, 'Work Integration').

SSE entities in waste management can help in organising the waste systems. In countries such as Brazil, Colombia and India, there are major cities where much of the municipal waste collection system is based on cooperatives. In Brazil, for example, waste picker organisations have created networks through which they have been able to further increase their position in the waste systems, including formal arrangements with municipal authorities (Gutberlet et al. 2020).

SSE entities are increasingly active in managing electrical and electronic waste, where circularity takes place through recovery, repair, refurbishment, reuse, repurposing and recycling of used electrical and electronic equipment. Here, the role of cooperatives and other types of SSE entities has been acknowledged, including in relation to their capacity to promote the rights of informal workers through advocating for their inclusion and recognition, helping them organise to fight for their rights and improve their livelihoods, provide avenues for skills development, and create formal and decent work opportunities in the sector, while contributing to circular and environmental objectives (ILO 2019b).

Due to the lack of well-developed and effectively implemented recycling policies and systems, much of the global waste streams continue to be dumped in landfills, including plastics, electronics and other materials that would have further recycling value. Recycling is a key aspect of the circular economy, and moving from waste management to waste reuse plays a key role in this. In recycling, waste is seen as a resource that maintains some of its original value and can be further made useful. Circularity has been part of waste management cooperatives and other types of SSE entities for a long time, and their participation has not only improved local waste management systems but also generated socio-productive inclusion, in which SSE entities and their members have been able to improve their working conditions (Gutberlet et al. 2020).

Informal waste collectors join and establish SSE entities to tackle these and other challenges. SSE entities can support informal waste workers in strengthening their collective voice and representation in policy-making processes, including with both public and private actors in the waste management chains. In some cases, SSE entities have been able to enhance collaboration with trade unions for improved representation and capacity building. In other cases, waste workers have first organised into a trade union and then moved towards formal business by establishing a cooperative. Through SSE entities, waste workers can move towards formalisation, underlining their roles as recyclers, and in this way help to move towards becoming recognised as public service providers. In addition, these organisations can provide and facilitate access to social protection and services such as finance, insurance, housing, childcare and children's education, in addition to skills development and training. Sometimes, however, while cooperatives have been able to secure stable incomes for their members, decent work deficits and dangerous working conditions have remained (ILO and WIEGO 2017) (see entry 57, 'Working Conditions and Wages').

CONCLUSIONS

The social and solidarity economy and the circular economy are in many ways complementary approaches, aiming to transform global production and consumption patterns to become more sustainable. Focusing on environmental and circular aspects is not new for the SSE, which places the triple bottom line of sustainable development at the heart of its objectives and actions. Promoting a just transition in sectors such as energy, water and waste management is essential for tackling environmental and climate change, and promoting human and community well-being. Values such as community participation, solidarity, democracy and innovation help to place SSE entities in these three sectors, as well as in many others that contribute towards circularity, as key actors to function as a link between environmental sustainability, the capacity to promote decent work and social inclusion, while improving the access to vital services for their members as well as the community at large. To achieve this at a broader level, SSE entities will need to be part of the discussions on the circular economy and demonstrate the value of the SSE as playing a key role in the circular transition. This is even more relevant now, with the additional challenges brought about by the COVID-19 pandemic, and on the way towards a human-centred recovery that is inclusive, sustainable and resilient.

ACKNOWLEDGEMENTS

The author would like to thank International Labour Office colleagues Mariangels Fortuny and Shreya Goel Ashu for their valuable inputs on this entry.

REFERENCES

Arvonen, Vesa, Samuel N. Kibocha, Tapio S. Katko and Pekka Pietilä. 2017. 'Features of Water Cooperatives: A Comparative Study of Finland and Kenya.' *Public Works Management and Policy* 22 (4): 356–77. https://doi.org/10.1177/1087724x17715267.

Circle Economy. 2020. 'The Social Economy: A Means for Inclusive & Decent Work in the Circular Economy?' https://www.circle-economy.com/resources/the-social-economy-a-means-for-inclusive-decent-work-in-the-circular-economy.

Circle Economy. 2021. 'The Circularity Gap Report 2021.' https://www.circularity-gap.world/2021.

Gutberlet, Jutta, Gina Rizpah Besen and Leandro Pereira Morais. 2020. 'Participatory Solid Waste Governance and the Role of Social and Solidarity Economy: Experiences from São Paulo, Brazil.' *Detritus* 13: 167–80. https://doi.org/10.31025/2611-4135/2020.14024.

IEA, IRENA, UNSD, World Bank and WHO. 2021. *Tracking SDG 7: The Energy Progress Report*. Washington, DC: World Bank.

ILO. 2013. *Providing Clean Energy and Energy Access through Cooperatives*. Geneva: ILO.

ILO. 2015. *Guidelines for a Just Transition towards Environmentally Sustainable Economies and Societies for All*. Geneva: ILO.

ILO 2019a. *Skills for a Greener Future: A Global View*. Geneva: ILO.

ILO. 2019b. *Global Dialogue Forum on Decent Work in the Management of Electrical and Electronic Waste (e-waste). Points of consensus*. Geneva: ILO.

ILO and WIEGO. 2017. *Cooperation Among Workers in the Informal Economy: A Focus on Home-based Workers and Waste Pickers. A Joint ILO and WIEGO Initiative*. Geneva: ILO.

Morandeira-Arca, Jon, Enekoitz Etxezarreta-Etxarri, Olatz Azurza-Zubizarreta and Julen Izagirre-Olaizola. 2021. 'Social Innovation for a New Energy Model, from Theory to Action: Contributions from the Social and Solidarity Economy in the Basque Country.' *Innovation: The European Journal of Social Science Research*, 1–27. https://doi.org/10.1080/13511610.2021.1890549.

UNESCO and UNESCO i-WSSM. 2020. *Water Reuse Within a Circular Economy Context (Series II): Global Water Security Issues (GWSI) Series*. Paris: UNESCO Publishing.

UN-Water. 2021. *Summary Progress Update 2021 – SDG 6 – Water and Sanitation For All*. July. Geneva: UN-Water.

World Bank, ILO, WaterAid and WHO. 2019. *Health, Safety and Dignity of Sanitation Workers: An Initial Assessment*. Washington, DC: World Bank. https://www.who.int/water_sanitation_health/publications/health-safety-dignity-of-sanitation-workers.pdf.

Zhang, Chuan-Hong, Wandella Amos Benjamin and Miao Wang. 2021. 'The Contribution of Cooperative Irrigation Scheme to Poverty Reduction in Tanzania.' *Journal of Integrative Agriculture* 20 (4): 953–63. https://doi.org/10.1016/s2095-3119(21)63634-1.

28. Finance sector

Riccardo Bodini and Gianluca Salvatori

INTRODUCTION

A defining feature of the social and solidarity economy (SSE) is its bottom-up nature: SSE organizations and enterprises (SSEOEs) arise when groups of citizens seek to collectively provide answers to their needs or to the needs of their community. These needs can be of various kinds, including self-employment, access to consumer goods, provision of social services, organization of cultural activities, marketing of agricultural or other products, and so forth. One of the needs that has historically been at the root of many SSE initiatives is the need for financial resources. Indeed, finance plays a key role in the life of both individuals (to manage savings and investments and to access credit for a variety of purposes) and organizations (to cover start-up costs, to address cash flow issues, to fund investments, and so forth), and is thus a fundamental ingredient in the process of economic development. It is not surprising, then, that people have sought to devise collective solutions to this shared need, often pooling whatever economic means they had access to in order to supply financial resources to the members of their community.

As in many instances when it comes to SSEOEs, the specific organizational forms through which this happened have varied greatly based on different cultural and legal contexts, and range from small and informal arrangements to large, highly formal and structured organizations. At the small and informal end of the spectrum, for instance, forms of rotating savings and credit schemes based on mutual aid principles can be found in many African countries and have been around for centuries: the *abota* in Guinea-Bissau, the *tontine* in Morocco, the *iqqub* in Ethiopia are just a few examples of ways in which local communities have sought to address the issue of access to finance. At the other end of the spectrum, we find formal and structured organizations such as cooperative banks and mutual insurance companies, some of which have grown to be among the largest financial institutions in the world. In general, there is a great variety of SSEOEs that operate within the boundaries of the financial sector, providing financial products and services of various kinds to individuals, other SSEOEs, as well as public sector agencies and for-profit businesses.

These organizations have often been instrumental in the economic development of their communities, in some instances contributing to lifting entire regions out of poverty by making investments possible where other actors were unwilling or unable to operate. Their ownership and governance structure ensure that the primary focus of the organization is on serving its members and community, and their close ties with the community itself enable relationship lending practices that help to better evaluate risk and serve customers who would otherwise be excluded from the market.

This entry focuses primarily on the main actors in terms of structure and size, reviewing the different types of SSEOEs that supply financial resources through the various financial mechanisms (see entry 45, 'Financing'). Since one of the ways in which financial resources can be made available is grants and donations, this entry also includes philanthropic organizations.

These organizations are not usually considered part of the financial sector because they are not market actors, but they are an important part of the SSE and play a key role in making financial resources available to other SSEOEs. It should also be noted that this entry focuses on SSE entities providing financial products and services. There also exist public sector entities that are mandated to support the financing of the SSE, usually in partnership with SSE actors (see entry 55, 'Supporting Organizations and Intermediaries').

28.1 THE SSE IN THE FINANCE SECTOR

The main types of SSEOEs operating in the finance sector are presented below. They are classified based on the type of activity or financial products they provide: grants, banking services (including debit), risk capital (equity or quasi-equity), guarantees and insurance.

Grants

The primary actors within the SSE providing grants (that is, financial resources that do not need to be repaid) are foundations. Foundations are legal entities created to achieve specific goals related to the wellbeing of target groups of people or communities through the use of an endowment or systematic fundraising (EURICSE 2013). Foundations pursue their goals in a variety of ways, including through the direct supply of services. This entry focuses on grant-making foundations, that is, foundations which use their endowment or the funds they raise to fund projects or activities carried out primarily by other SSEOEs, or in some instances to fund the organizations themselves in order to help them grow and increase their impact. There are three basic types of grant-making foundations:

- Individual or family foundations, founded and endowed by an individual or a family, usually in support of a specific cause.
- Corporate foundations, founded and endowed by a company as a form of corporate social responsibility strategy.
- Community foundations, founded by a plurality of actors from a specific geographical area, usually with the goal of raising funds in support of the local community and economic development initiatives.

In addition to these three, which are the most common, in some countries there have also been instances of foundations arising from the privatization of state-owned enterprises, as in the case of banking foundations in Italy. Regardless of their origin, foundations typically invest their assets in equity and bond markets, and use dividends and the payment of interest to issue grants that further their social mission. While grant-making is by far the most prevalent way in which foundations make resources available to SSEOEs, it should be noted that it is not the only one. For instance, through programme-related investment (PRI), part of the endowment of the foundation consists in the investment in social enterprises expecting a repayment with some interest, albeit usually at below-market rates. Recently, forms and instruments of 'venture philanthropy' have begun to emerge, combining a customized financing strategy with non-financial services, organizational capacity-building and performance measurement by applying risk capital techniques to the grant-making activity in favour of social enterprises.

These funds typically provide grants, equity investments or debt instruments that require an economic performance as well as the expected social return (ILO 2019).

Unlike other SSEOEs, foundations do not have a democratic governance system. However, the use of their endowment is tied to the statutory purposes of the organization, and the assets cannot be appropriated by the founding or governing parties, ensuring their adherence to their mission.

Banking Services

SSEOEs have been present in the banking sector for almost 200 years, ever since the first cooperative banks were founded in Germany in the mid-19th century, first by Schulze-Delitzsch (primarily in urban centres and geared toward the needs of artisans and shop owners) and then by Friedrich Raiffeisen (mostly in rural areas and addressing the needs of small farmers for capital). From those early experiences stem the two main types of banks based on cooperative principles that are still prevalent today: (1) people's banks, deriving from the work of Schulze-Delitzsch; and (2) cooperative banks, based on the model developed by Friedrich Raiffeisen.

While there are significant differences between the two models, in both instances the banks are owned by their customers and are based on mutualistic principles. They both originated in people pooling their assets through unlimited liability schemes (that is, the legal obligation of company founders and owners to repay, in full, the debt and other financial obligations of the company) in order to leverage enough capital to start the bank. And while at the beginning the bank's business was primarily with its members and limited to the economic activities that characterized them (artisanry and trade in one instance, agriculture in the other), over time both models diversified their customer/membership base and started serving the entire population of their areas of operation. They also increasingly served non-members as well as members, shifting from a strictly mutualistic logic to a role as banks for the community at large, whose primary function became ensuring the economic development of their areas of operation.

The main difference between the two models today is that people's banks also issue stocks which are traded on public stock markets, and as such are partly owned by non-members, diluting member control on the bank's governance. They also tend to be larger institutions, with weaker ties to their local community. Cooperative banks, on the other hand, adhere to the one member, one vote cooperative principle, tend to be smaller in size (even though they can join together to form very large banking groups, as described below) and are more rooted in their geographic area of operations.

In addition to these two types, there are other SSE banks that are based on cooperative principles, such as building societies, mutual savings banks, and so on. Among these, credit unions and ethical banks are of particular significance. Credit unions are in all respects cooperative banks, but have some specificities: their members usually have something in common – for example, the same employer or profession – they are often funded only by members' deposits, avoiding outside borrowing, and in some countries they are restricted to providing only personal loans. They tend to be smaller in size, although in some instances can also grow very large (as in the case of the Navy Federal Credit Union in the United States, for instance, which has a banking income of over US$6.5 billion).

Ethical banks also adhere to cooperative principles, but have a specific focus on supporting social and solidarity initiatives and sustainable economic development. Through their lending and investment practices, ethical banks support companies and projects that have a high social or environmental value, responding to the needs of people excluded from the banking system, or of people who seek to achieve a positive social impact through their savings and investments. Ethical banks originated in Europe approximately 30 years ago and work closely with other cooperative banks in various ways, including for the sale of their social investment products.

Cooperative banks can be found all over the world, and in some instances have grown to be major financial institutions, primarily by joining together to form cooperative banking groups: from the Mouvement Desjardins in Quebec to the Crédit Agricole and Crédit Mutuel in France, to Rabobank in the Netherlands, ICCREA and Cassa Centrale Banca in Italy, CBK in Kenya, and Sicredi in Brazil, cooperative banks have become major players in the financial sector in their respective countries and are consistently among the largest cooperatives in the world (EURICSE and ICA 2021).

At the same time, there is ample evidence that their specificities in terms of governance and objectives (namely, addressing the need for credit of their members/customers rather than generating value for shareholders) result in significant differences in behaviour relative to commercial banks. They have been shown to be consistently more risk-averse than commercial banks, avoiding investment in riskier and more speculative financial products, and adopting instead a longer-term approach to financial sustainability. As a result, they tend to be more capitalized and resilient than commercial banks in times of crisis (Birchall 2013). They have also played, and continued to play, a key role in the economic development of their communities, often operating in areas that are neglected or ignored by other types of financial institutions.

Risk Capital: Equity or Quasi-Equity Investments

Equity investments are typically the domain of mainstream financial institutions, as they primarily follow a profit-maximization logic that is not in line with SSE objectives. However, over the years the SSE has given rise to its own sources of equity capital in order to address the needs of SSEOEs. Indeed, while SSEOEs can meet many of their financial needs through access to credit from the banking system, sometimes they also require equity capital to fund investments. Given their specificities, SSEOEs are ill-equipped to access the same sources of risk capital as for-profit companies: unlike shareholder companies, they are not designed to remunerate investors, and their democratic governance structures make it difficult to assign decision-making powers to those who bring capital to the firm (see entry 49, 'Participation, Governance, Collective Action and Democracy'). For these reasons, SSEOEs in need of capitalization have looked primarily to their own membership base through a variety of schemes (see entry 45, 'Financing'), and to the accumulation of surpluses over time.

In some cases, though, particularly in contexts with a very well-developed SSE ecosystem (see entry 56, 'The Institutional Ecosystem'), new SSE institutions have been created for these purposes. This is the case, for instance, of cooperative mutual funds in countries such as Italy, where cooperatives are required by law to destine at least 3 per cent of their surpluses to national or regional funds that are then used to support the development of the cooperative movement in a variety of ways, including through investments. In other contexts, the interaction between the SSE ecosystem and the public sector has given rise to a variety of financial instruments largely controlled by the SSEOEs and available to SSEOEs. In Italy, for instance, the cooperative movement and the public sector contributed to the creation of Cooperazione Finanza Impresa (CFI), a financial institution devoted to investing in worker and social cooperatives in order to help their start-up phase, including in the case of worker buyouts or business transfers to employees. Furthermore, in Quebec, for instance, the co-design of policies by SSEOEs and local government has led to the creation of initiatives such as RISQ and the Fiducie du Chantier de l'économie sociale, which provide several financial products including patient capital to support social economy enterprises at every stage of their development (see entry 55, 'Supporting Organizations and Intermediaries' and entry 50, 'Partnership and Co-construction') (McMullin 2021).

Guarantees

Risk evaluation on the part of financial institutions can sometimes be more challenging for SSEOEs relative to for-profit enterprises, for a variety of reasons including the lack of standardized data to assess creditworthiness. Moreover, SSEOEs sometimes do not have significant assets that can be used as collateral in order to access credit. As a result, one of the main hurdles facing SSEOEs in accessing financial resources (whether from cooperative banks or other types of non-SSE financial institutions) is the availability of guarantees.

As in the case of equity capital, SSEOEs have developed their own solutions to this issue, primarily through the creation of guarantee consortia. The guarantee consortium assesses the creditworthiness of the guaranteed company together with the bank. The guarantees provided by the consortium are based mainly on special money deposits established with the affiliated banks, which are meant to cover any potential loss. In the case of guarantee mutual funds (GMF), the assets that are used to make commitments to the banks are constituted by the contributions of the individual SSEOEs that might make use of them. The member companies constitute a financial asset, allowing them to make commitments towards the banking system under more advantageous conditions. In some instances, public contributions might then increase the assets available to the GMF (even sometimes with the role of ultimate guarantor or 'counter-guarantee'). In comparison, credit surety funds (CSFs) are generated by a broader range of contributors, such as well-capitalized cooperatives, local government units, government financial institutions, industrial guarantee and loan funds, and other institutions and government agencies. The beneficiaries of the CSFs are not restricted to the contributors, since the mutualistic principle is not required. Micro, small and medium-sized enterprises, as well as cooperatives and other SSEOEs, might be guaranteed to have easier access to credit from banks despite lack of collateral, regardless of whether or not they contributed to the CSFs (ILO 2019).

Insurance

The final type of SSEOEs providing financial products are mutual insurance companies. Mutual insurance companies originated in England in the 17th century to cover losses due to fires, and spread from there throughout Europe and beyond, expanding over time the range of risks they covered and the insurance products they offered.

Mutuals are insurance companies owned by the policyholders, who select the management of the company. Their primary goal is to provide their members with insurance coverage at the lowest price, making it more accessible. Profits are usually distributed to the members via a dividend payment or a reduction in premiums. Since they are not traded on stock exchanges, they do not have to reach short-term profit targets and thus can invest in safer assets and pursue long-term goals in the interest of their members. Mutual insurance companies can be found all over the world, and according to the International Cooperative and Mutual Insurance Federation (ICMIF), mutual or cooperative insurers serve more than 900 million people worldwide. As in the case of cooperative banks, mutual insurance companies can be very large organizations: in Japan, Nippon Life, the largest mutual in the world, has over 90 000 employees and a premium income of over US$50 billion.

Mutual insurance companies are included in this entry because, as most insurance companies, they also supply financial products to their members: they manage savings and investments, provide retirement plans through pension funds, and offer financial insurance policies (primarily for life insurance) for which the amounts of benefits offered are tied to the performance of an underlying investment asset.

CONCLUSION

The SSE is best understood as an alternative way to organize economic activity. SSEOEs can be found in every sector of the economy, operating according to a different logic than for-profit companies, and the financial services sector is no exception. While by no means exhaustive, the list of organization types presented above accounts for the main ways in which the SSEOEs operate in this sector, and is sufficiently complete to draw some cross-cutting observations on the specificities of SSEOEs within the broader landscape of financial service providers, and on the implications of these specificities in terms of the role and relevance of the SSE in the financial sector and beyond.

The ownership and governance structure of SSEOEs make a big difference in terms of the goals of the organizations, and ultimately in terms of their behaviour on the market. All of the SSEOEs described in this entry (with the exception of foundations) are owned by their customers, and their goal is thus not to maximize profits (although they of course need to be profitable in order to stay on the market), but to provide financial products to their members under the best conditions possible. Democratic member control on the governance of the organization helps to ensure that management responds to member needs, and that the organization's strategies are consistent with their long-term interests.

This in turn determines significant differences in the ways in which these organizations behave on the market relative to their for-profit counterparts. First, they tend to be more risk-averse, adopting long-term investment strategies and shying away from more speculative financial products. This behaviour for the most part has shielded SSE financial institutions from investment bubbles and ensuing financial crises, including most notably the 2008 financial crisis tied to subprime lending. Indeed, not only did cooperative banks avoid selling subprime loans to their customers, but they also by and large did not invest in the derivative financial products that were tied to those loans. As a result, they did not need to be bailed out by governments after the market crashed, and were the only banks that continued to lend money during the ensuing credit crunch, playing a key role in supporting the local economy. Moreover, due to their profit distribution constraints, they tend to be more capitalized than commercial banks, which also contributes to their resiliency.

Another notable difference in behaviour concerns the areas in which these organizations operate and the people they serve. From their origins forward, they have been particularly adept at serving the financial needs of people and firms that would otherwise be excluded from the financial market. By having a close and direct relationship with their members/customers, they are often better able to evaluate risk compared to standardized credit scoring systems, which enables them to be more inclusive in their lending practices. Similarly, they have traditionally also operated in areas where other banks have not been able to, sometimes as the only financial institution serving the community. As a result, they have played and continue to play an instrumental role in the economic development of rural and underserved communities.

This does not mean that they are necessarily small and marginal. As we have seen, in many cases they are major players in the market, reaching millions of customers and managing very large assets and funds. In Europe, for instance, cooperative banks have a market share of over 20 per cent for both loans and deposits (Groeneveld 2019), and mutual insurance companies are among the largest insurance companies in many countries across four continents. Moreover, SSE financial organizations have found ways to serve the needs of people, businesses (primarily small and medium-sized enterprises) as well as other SSEOEs, displaying the same dynamism and versatility that characterizes the SSE overall.

Moving forward, the ability to provide financial resources that are consistent with the specificities of SSEOEs will be increasingly important. Indeed, over the last few years, SSEOEs have started engaging in more capital-intensive activities such as urban renewal, waste management, management of facilities for cultural activities, cultural heritage management, social housing, and others, and this engagement is expected to increase in the near future. This evolution is likely to increase demand for finance, beyond what has been made available so far.

At the same time, the evolution of the financial services sector linked primarily to the advent of information and communication technologies is giving rise to new ways to make financial resources available to individuals and businesses alike, often based on the use of new information technology platforms connecting them directly to prospective donors, lenders or investors. This is the case, for instance, with new crowdfunding and crowdlending platforms, some targeted specifically to SSEOEs. Many of these platforms are set up as for-profit companies, but the SSE could play (and in some cases is already playing) a role in this space as well (see entry 33, 'Information and Communication Technology (ICT)').

In general, the scale of intervention called for by the change in our societies requires the equipment of SSEOEs with new models and new tools that are capable of coping with a greater demand for goods and services. From a financial perspective, this means the development of an adequate and accessible supply with a blended approach, mixing different tools and strategies, consistent with the specificities of SSEOEs. Based on the history of the SSE, a significant portion of these resources and tools will likely come from within the SSE itself, expanding the reach and diversity of SSEOEs operating within the financial services sector. At the same time, this should be complemented with well-crafted long-term public policies, co-constructed with SSE actors, to support the growth of SSE financial ecosystems, in terms of SSE-adapted regulatory frameworks, institutional support and resources.

REFERENCES

Birchall, Johnston. 2013. *Resilience in a Downturn: The Power of Financial Cooperatives*. Geneva: International Labour Organization.
EURICSE. 2013. *Social Europe Guide. Volume 4, Social Economy and Social Entrepreneurship*. Luxembourg: European Commission.
EURICSE and ICA. 2021. *Exploring the Cooperative Economy: World Cooperative Report, 10th Edition*. Creative Commons. https://monitor.coop/en/media/library/research-and-reviews/world-cooperative-monitor-2021.
Groeneveld, Hans. 2019. 'European Co-Operative Banks in 2019: A Concise Assessment.' http://v3.globalcube.net/clients/eacb/content/medias/publications/research/20201015_hg_research_letter_european_cooperative_banks.pdf.
ILO (International Labour Organization). 2019. 'Financial Mechanisms for Innovative Social and Solidarity Economy Ecosystems.' ILO. https://www.ilo.org/global/topics/cooperatives/publications/WCMS_728367/lang--en/index.htm
McMullin, Caitlin. 2021. 'Financial Mechanisms and the Social and Solidarity Ecosystem in Quebec.' Geneva: International Labour Organization. https://www.ilo.org/global/topics/cooperatives/sse/WCMS_829908/lang--en/index.htm.

29. Food and agriculture sector
Judith Hitchman

INTRODUCTION AND BACKGROUND INFORMATION: THE STATE OF PLAY IN FOOD AND AGRICULTURE TODAY

Traditional diets are part of our cultural heritage and therefore linked to food sovereignty (Nyéléni.org 2007). Yet over the last 50 years, food systems have become linked to the global governance of food and agriculture, with the commodification of seeds and inputs as well as commercialisation of processed foods. As a consequence, food systems have become increasingly far removed from food sovereignty. This process of removal is due to agriculture being regulated by the World Trade Organization (WTO), hence food is a commodity rather than a fundamental human right (Article 25, Universal Declaration of Human Rights) (United Nations 1948). This has led to industrial agriculture producing cash crops often for export, dispossession of small-scale local producers (despite the fact that they account for 70 per cent of all farmers and are in fact the ones who feed local markets), land and water-grabbing, and seed patenting. This situation has become considerably aggravated by the signature of an agreement by the World Economic Forum with all United Nations (UN) agencies, including the Food and Agriculture Organization (FAO). The nomination of Qu Dongyu as Director-General in August 2019 also played a role, with the situation becoming exacerbated by the signing of a partnership agreement in 2020 with CropLife International, the global trade association representing the largest agrochemical, pesticide and seed companies (La Via Campesina 2020). Dongyu is pro-private sector and has followed José Graziano Da Silva of Brazil, who strongly supported the social movements, with prior achievements including the introduction of the Fome Zero (Zero Hunger) policy in Brazil under President Lula in 2003.

Global agriculture is worth up to $2.4 trillion, accounting for an important percentage of the global economy. Food systems far removed from food sovereignty have led to considerable distortion, with countries or regions in which much of the population suffer from hunger often exporting certain crops, while local people have little access to fresh nutritious food. Some key figures include the following (ETC Group 2019):

- Twenty global corporations control the food chain.
- The three biggest corporations control over 50 per cent of the seeds.
- Four corporations control over 99 per cent of the livestock breeding.
- Ten corporations control 55 per cent of fertilisers.
- Four traders control 75 per cent of the grain and soybean market.
- Eleven corporations control 30 per cent of the food processing industry.

The results of this are quite dramatic (Nyéléni.org 2007; FAO 2020):

- One in ten people in the world are malnourished; hunger is rising.
- Thirty per cent of the global population is overweight or obese.

- One in five people in the developed world today cannot afford to consume three meals a day or to purchase fresh fruit and vegetables.
- Approximately 15 per cent of the population in developed countries such as the United States and many European countries need food support through food stamps and food banks, with this figure rising.

29.1 WHAT IS THE RESPONSE OF THE SOCIAL AND SOLIDARITY ECONOMY (SSE)?

In spite of the alarming figures shown above, 70 per cent of the world's food is produced by small-scale family farmers, using less than 25 per cent of the world's agricultural land. This food is essential to territorial and local markets all over the world, which are influenced by various forms of the SSE in significant ways. Currently, in most countries, there is an increasing awareness of the need to achieve greater food justice and improve citizens' democratic control over their food systems. Sustainable local food systems lie at the heart of this approach, with the following subsystems and typologies:

- Local farmers' markets.
- Allotments.
- Community gardens.
- Grow-it-yourself.
- Community Supported Agriculture.(CSA)
- Local food coops.
- Local collective producers' shops.
- Solidarity shops and systems.
- Farmgate sales.

At the heart of these phenomena lies the struggle for access to land, seeds and water, as well as the right to food, food justice and different ways of regaining control over food systems. Agroecology as a holistic, scientific approach to production and consumption includes, as a strong anchor, both traditional and indigenous environmentally friendly farming, and social movement-based links between production and consumption. Agroecology protects and promotes agrobiodiversity. Miguel Altieri, a Chilean-born agronomist and former lecturer at the University of California, is widely credited as the leading figure and author on this subject. Agroecology has been adopted by the broader food and agriculture social movements as a response to industrial agriculture. The '10 Elements of Agroecology' were adopted by the FAO Council in December 2019 (FAO 2018). The work was based on the participatory contributions of the Civil Society and Indigenous People's Mechanism Working Group on Agroecology. It is important to note that a circular and solidarity economy is included as one of the ten elements. This is the result of the two Forums on Agroecology held by the FAO in 2014 and 2018.

The social movements also held the Nyeleni Forum on Agroecology in Mali in March 2015. An extract from the final declaration reads (Nyeleni, 2007, 71):

IV. Build local economies
• Promote local markets for local products.

- Support the development of alternative financial infrastructure, institutions and mechanisms to support both producers and consumers.
- Reshape food markets through new relationships of solidarity between producers and consumers.
- Develop links with the experience of solidarity economy and participatory guarantee systems, when appropriate.

This clearly shows the importance of SSE-based approaches to agroecology.

29.2 THE ORIGINS OF THE FOOD SOVEREIGNTY MOVEMENT

La Via Campesina was formally constituted in April 1993 (during a conference held in Mons, Belgium) only months before the finalisation of the Uruguay Round of the General Agreement on Tariffs and Trade (GATT), which, for the first time, included agriculture and food in its negotiations. The 46 representatives (women and men) of organisations of peasants, small-scale farmers, indigenous peoples and farmworkers from the Americas, Asia, Europe and Africa who met at Mons clearly understood that the GATT Final Act, along with the creation of the WTO, represented a profound shift away from more controlled national economies to an almost exclusively market-driven global economy. They also clearly understood that the further entrenchment of neoliberalism would spur national governments to continue to dismantle the agrarian structures and programmes that peasants and farmers had won after years of struggle: these very structures and programmes that helped to ensure the viability of small-scale farming, promote production for domestic consumption and contribute to national food security. The leaders of the conference were quick to identify the threat which farming families in the North and South faced: 'their livelihoods, their way of life and, indeed, their very mode of existence were all at stake' (Aurélie Desmarais and Nicholson 2013, 3).

29.3 LEGISLATIVE FRAMEWORKS

In response, several countries have included food sovereignty and the right to food in their constitution, as well as a legal framework for solidarity economy. These include Mali, Senegal, Venezuela, Bolivia, Nepal and Costa Rica. And these same countries, as well as many more, have legislative frameworks for SSE. It is clear that in order to overcome the damaging industrial food and agricultural system outlined above, food sovereignty and agroecology must include an economic paradigm change. The policy document on 'Connecting Smallholders to Markets' (Civil Society Mechanism (CSM) Working Group 2016) is one of the most important policy documents that supports local and territorial markets for smallholder producers and consumers.

29.4 THE ISSUE OF ACCESS TO LAND

A basic requirement for food production is access to land. Over the last 50 years, much of the traditional agricultural hinterland of cities which provided the city with food has become part of the urban sprawl. The New Urban Agenda clearly mentions the need to preserve agricultural land, and recommends the use of community land trusts as a means of preservation from speculation and maintaining traditional agricultural land. Community land trusts are important forms of the SSE and are widespread around the world. They have proven especially important in many ethnic minority communities inhabiting American cities. They enable them to grow culturally appropriate food in neighbourhoods that were previously highly disadvantaged. According to Terre de Liens, the French community land trust organisation:

> They emerged in Europe in the 1970s and have rapidly developed in the past 10 years. Their focus is to facilitate and support access to land for agroecological farmers. They mobilise community support around maintaining local food production and commercialisation, ensuring environmental protection, and fostering the development of organic farming and agroecology. In some cases, they also seek to ensure that farmland is preserved in the face of urban and infrastructural sprawl. (Nyéléni Europe Food Sovereignty Movement 2020, 115)

Today in France, 100 farms are still lost every week due to land concentration and an ageing farming population. Nevertheless, there is an increasing population of young, often new farmers practising solidarity-based farming through collective farms and CSA. The most important overarching policy framework is the 'Voluntary Guidelines' for the governance of land tenure, negotiated by the Civil Society Mechanism and the UN Committee on Food Security and Nutrition in 2012, which was subsequently adopted by the FAO (FAO 2012). It clearly outlines the rights of people to land, and governance thereof, and is an instrument that can be used to protect and defend land rights around the world.

29.5   SEEDS: THE HEART OF LIFE ITSELF

Ecoagrobiodiversity has been greatly reduced by the control of large corporations. Nevertheless, the SSE and community seed-saving of traditional varieties has become an important way of preserving traditional open-pollinated varieties of plants. There is strong resistance by social movements to the Union for the Protection of New Plant Varieties (UPOV) and the International Treaty on Plant Genetic Resources for Food and Agriculture. Small-scale family farmers defend the right to freely save, exchange and replant their seeds. It should also be mentioned that this includes the struggle against genetically modified organisms and so-called 'new genomic techniques'. It has been scientifically proven that traditional, open-pollinated seeds and participatory breeding techniques allow plants to adapt to and resist climate change, and that the nutritional value of fruit and vegetables produced using agroecological approaches is higher than that produced by industrial agriculture. Open-pollinated varieties are also more resilient to climate change. Community seed-saving is an essential aspect of the SSE and genuinely sustainable food systems.

29.6   WATER, CLIMATE CHANGE AND AGROECOLOGY

Water is an essential element in agriculture (see entry 27, 'Energy, Water and Waste Management Sectors'), and the climate crisis is increasing the instances of both droughts and floods. Yet agroecology and agroforestry are powerful tools in preserving food production and overcoming many of the effects of a changing climate. Ensuring that forests and trees are part of the landscape in order to protect against soil erosion, as well as mulching to keep moisture in the soil when growing crops, are both important practices within agroecology. Agroecological practises are more labour-intensive than industrial farming; however, they do ensure much greater protection against a changing climate. This is essential within an SSE-based approach to food production, as are the social aspects of agroecology.

29.7 NOT JUST AGRICULTURE, ALSO FISHERIES

Artisanal fisheries face the same issues and threats from industrial fisheries globally as those experienced by small-scale family farms. Ocean acidification caused by excessive use of chemical fertilisers, the use of high technology to identify shoals of fish that are then targeted by factory ships that process fish at sea, and many other issues are forcing artisanal fishers away from their traditional practices and fishing grounds (Josse and Brent 2021). Practises such as community supported fisheries are now quite widespread in North America and are an effective SSE means of supporting small-scale fishers (Local Catch Network 2022). Direct sales by small-scale fishers to local communities is also a widespread practice in many countries.

29.8 HOW IS FOOD DISTRIBUTED AND CONSUMED IN SSE-BASED AGROECOLOGICAL SYSTEMS?

Distribution and consumption cannot be disassociated from production in an agroecological and SSE perspective, but instead need to be considered in a local to the global framework (Hitchman 2017).

Land use and social inclusion are two aspects that are generally the object of legislation of devolution and are considered by the local government, irrespective of whether there is a national policy framework or not. Some important examples of SSE practice include the use of municipal land to grow food for public canteens (such as schools and hospitals), thus making land and food part of the commons (see entry 13, 'The Commons')

During the COVID-19 pandemic there has been a significant increase in SSE practice relating to food in many parts of the world. For instance, Brazil's Movement of Small Farmers (MPA) has consistently delivered free food baskets of any surplus food to *favelas* to ensure that people have access to healthy fresh food in spite of the loss of salaries. This is clearly an example of community empowerment. Other examples include the way in which CSA farms in China and in the Basque country carried out weekly home deliveries of produce – to all their members in the case of China, and to the vulnerable in the Spanish Basque Country. URGENCI, the global CSA network, has written a report on the resilience of these practices during COVID-19 (URGENCI 2021).

CSA and local solidarity partnerships for agroecology have developed many different techniques of SSE to ensure social inclusion and fair income for farmers, as well as affordable food for all. These range from local government subsidies of some shares, to differentiated costs based on subscribers' income (within a trust-based system), to farm-based work in order to offset some costs for a limited number of subscribers. Solidarity also exists between consumers and the producers in the event of a shortfall due to illness of farmers or climate events. This principle of shared risks and benefits originated in Japan in the 1970s as the *teikei* system, the original version of CSA. CSA networks at the national level are federated by URGENCI. There are currently approximately 3 million families that are members of national and regional networks of URGENCI.

Producers' local cooperatives, consumer cooperatives and their shops are also part of the SSE. They include small farmers' cooperatives and processing and retail shops, which are now common across the world, particularly within Latin America. They are based on either agroecological practice or participatory guarantee system organic certification, another aspect of the SSE.

Additionally, it is important to be aware of the corporate capture of SSE initiatives by industrial agribusiness operators, including everything from food boxes to sales of local varieties of fruit and vegetables, and even of agroecology (without the social movement dimension).

CONCLUSION: THE IMPORTANCE OF SOCIAL MOVEMENTS

In the field of food and agriculture, the role played by social movements, starting with La Via Campesina, whose membership is over 250 million, has been significant. Other key social movements cover all recognised UN constituencies and include key players within the SSE such as indigenous people, herders, pastoralists, fishers, women, youth, consumers and the urban poor. They work together at the global and regional levels to defend human rights and introduce and implement the policy that supports producers and consumers through the International Planning Committee for Food Sovereignty (IPC) (IPC 2014). The IPC now includes a growing dimension of the SSE.

REFERENCES

Aurélie Desmarais, Annette, and Paul Nicholson. 2013. 'La via Campesina: An Historical and Political Analysis.' In *La via Campesina's Open Book: Celebrating 20 Years of Struggle and Hope*. La Via Campesina. https://viacampesina.org/en/la-via-campesina-s-open-book-celebrating-20-years-of-struggle-and-hope/.
Civil Society Mechanism (CSM) Working Group. 2016. 'Connecting Smallholders to Markets.' CSM. https://www.csm4cfs.org/connecting-smallholders-markets-analytical-guide/.
ETC Group. 2019. 'Plate Tech Tonics: Mapping Corporate Power in Big Food.' https://etcgroup.org/sites/www.etcgroup.org/files/files/etc_platetechtonics_a4_nov2019_web.pdf.
FAO. 2012. 'Voluntary Guidelines on the Responsible Governance of Tenure of Land, Fisheries and Forests in the Context of National Food Security or Voluntary Guidelines on Tenure.' https://www.fao.org/tenure/voluntary-guidelines/en/.
FAO. 2018. 'The 10 Elements of Agroecology: Guiding the Transition to Sustainable Food and Agricultural Systems.' https://www.fao.org/documents/card/en/c/I9037EN.
FAO. 2020. 'The State of Food Security and Nutrition in the World.' https://www.fao.org/publications/sofi/2020/en/.
Hitchman, Judith. 2017. 'Why Local Food Systems and Territorial Production and Consumption Are the New Sexy Solutions to the Food System.' In *Book of the 2014 International Colloquium*. Alava: Elikadura21. http://elikadura21.eus/en/publicaciones/.
IPC. 2014. 'Twenty-Third Meeting of the Subsidiary Body on Scientific, Technical and Technological Advice.' International Planning Committee for Food Sovereignty (IPC). https://www.foodsovereignty.org/.
Josse, Thibault, and Zoe Brent. 2021. 'How Do Communities Support Fisheries?' TNI. https://www.tni.org/en/publication/how-do-communities-support-fisheries.

La Via Campesina. 2020. 'FAO Must Withdraw from Its Agreement with CropLife International: IPC.' https://viacampesina.org/en/fao-must-withdraw-from-its-agreement-with-croplife-international-ipc/.

Local Catch Network. 2022. 'Local Catch.' https://localcatch.org/.

Nyéléni Europe Food Sovereignty Movement. 2020. *Handbook: Your Land, My Land, Our Land.* https://www.accesstoland.eu/Handbook-Your-Land-My-Land-Our-Land.

Nyéléni.org. 2007. 'Declaration of Nyéléni.' https://nyeleni.org/spip.php?article290.

United Nations. 1948. 'Universal Declaration of Human Rights.' https://www.un.org/en/about-us/universal-declaration-of-human-rights.

URGENCI. 2021. 'Enacting Resilience: The Response of LSPA to the Covid-19 Crisis.' https://urgenci.net/enacting-resilience-the-response-of-lspa-to-the-covid-19-crisis/?fbclid=IwAR1JAzCYhPPfENhqWN9lDmworLV2ohyE2DMGmWjxZvF7CFab2SywYPj-U0g.

30. Gender equality and empowerment
Bipasha Baruah

INTRODUCTION

How can we build economic systems that recognize and work within the biophysical limits of our finite planet while simultaneously reducing poverty and inequality? This has become a defining question of our time and the social and solidarity economy (SSE) is increasingly considered a vehicle via which we might address this "trilemma." Attempts to build economic alternatives to capitalism have been made all over the world for well over a century, in industrialized, emerging and developing economies. Some such efforts started from very idealistic roots (such as a desire to align the economy more closely with the workings of the natural environment), while others were more ideologically driven (such as a desire to demonstrate an alternative to capitalism that centers the safety and wellbeing of workers). Others, such as collective farms, nonprofit daycare facilities or community-based economic developments evolved out of sheer necessity to meet the survival needs of millions of people whose demands were either ignored or unfulfilled in capitalist economies.

This entry provides an overview of the SSE's engagement with gender equality and empowerment. Why did the SSE sector adopt gender equality as a core value? How successful has the sector been in addressing the root causes of gender inequality? What are the key challenges and obstacles to gender equality that the SSE sector must contend with now and in the future?

30.1 RECONCILING SHARED GOALS: THE FEMINIST MOVEMENT AND THE SSE

The feminist movement and the SSE may not have started out with a common goal of gender equality (see entry 5, "Feminist Economics"). In the early years of the feminist movement, its primary focus was on empowering women to achieve equality with men within the existing global capitalist system, via activities such as documenting the existence of male bias in economic systems and advocating for equal rights and opportunities for women. Feminist organizing and mobilizing within the capitalist system also involved documenting the value of unpaid care work and informal work to the global economy, as well as advocating for policies aimed at enabling women and girls to gain equitable access to education and employment opportunities within capitalist economic systems. Over time, different voices and experiences helped to strengthen feminism as a movement of diverse groups of people who wanted to restructure society globally along with principles of economic, political, and social justice, rather than simply as a movement of women seeking socioeconomic equality with men. The feminist movement's interest in, and active engagement with, the SSE grew in part out of the realization that succeeding within the existing global capitalist system would require women and other socioeconomically disadvantaged groups to adopt the values espoused by it. In other words, they would be narrowly self-interested, competitive, individualistic, and mercenary

(Matthaei 2009). They would also be expected to consume goods and services conspicuously and to participate in socially and environmentally irresponsible consumerism fueled by the creation of unnecessary needs, cost externalization, and planned obsolescence. Simply put, they would be compelled to adopt and reproduce a system that causes harm to the environment and exacerbates inequality. As the heavy human and environmental costs of playing the capitalist game became more evident, even feminists who had previously focused their energy on achieving gender equality within the global "zero-sum game" capitalist system began to welcome the possibility of alternative economies based on solidarity, cooperation, and collective socioeconomic empowerment rather than individualism, competition, and elimination. The opportunity to participate in a creative, "win–win" production process which seeks to benefit all stakeholders (workers, consumers, business owners and entrepreneurs, local and distant communities, environment, government, suppliers, and competitors), and which is supported by socially responsible consumers, workers, and investors, and inclusive public policy, was welcomed by millions of people around the world; people whose needs had previously been marginalized in capitalist economies.

Today, the SSE has come to represent a persistent challenge to capitalist economies around the world. New solidaristic ways of being economic and doing economic life have been developing and spreading, creating new economic practices and institutions. These new ways of economic being and doing have been propelled by late 20th century social justice movements, including feminist, anti-racist, indigenous, LGBTQ (lesbian, gay, bisexual, transgender, queer), environmental, worker, peasant, and anti-corporate globalization movements (Matthaei 2009) (see entry 1, "Activism and Social Movements," entry 18, "LGBT* Inclusion," and entry 12, "The Black Social Economy"). The growth of more solidaristic economic values, practices, and institutions has also been propelled by the severe and cross-cutting economic, environmental, and human health crises that have been experienced around the world in recent decades. The recognition that "business as usual" and "trickle-down economies" will not deliver better lives for most of humanity or lead to better environmental stewardship is the backdrop against which more just, democratic, and sustainable economic values, practices, and institutions—and revitalized forms of pre- or non-capitalist alternatives—have begun to sprout, spread, and cross-pollinate across the world (ibid.).

The major objectives of the global SSE—namely, fulfillment of human needs, dismantling of oppressive socioeconomic hierarchies, optimal development of human potential, and preservation of the environment—are entirely consistent with feminist goals of women's empowerment and solidarity, not least because women constitute more than 50 percent of the global population. Feminist scholars from various disciplinary backgrounds have demonstrated the commonalities between global aspirations of gender equality and social justice, and the aspirations of SSEs. For example, feminist scholars such as Waring (1988) and Folbre (2012) have written extensively about not just what care work and caregiving contributes to the economy, but also how vital it is for everyone to perform some form of care work to experience being fully human. Like feminism, the SSE visibilizes and values nonmarket economic activities such as (women's traditional) unpaid reproductive work and community-building work (see entry 24, "Care and Home Support Services").

In a similar vein, scholars of the informal economy have drawn attention not just to the economic contributions made by informal sector workers, but also to the ways in which formal and informal economies are mutually constitutive (Chen 2008; de Soto 2000). Furthermore, scholars working from Black, racialized, postcolonial, queer, working class, and disabled perspectives have drawn attention to the importance of subverting and dismantling intersecting oppressions and social hierarchies (hooks 2000; Garland-Thomson 2014). Ecofeminists and other scholars of the environment have emphasized the mutual inclusivity of goals of women's empowerment and environmental protection (Rocheleau et al. 1996). Cooperation, equity, economic democracy, local community control, interdependence, and sustainability are values and aspirations common to both the feminist movement and the SSE.

The compatibility between feminism and the SSE is not serendipitous. Advocates of gender equality and women's empowerment have historically played important roles in shaping the values and practices of diverse institutions such as cooperatives, mutual associations, self-help groups, community forestry groups, associations of informal sector workers, social enterprises, fair trade organizations and networks, and community banks, as well as various forms of solidarity finance–organizations that are collectively referred to as the SSE today. Globally, women also constitute the majority of people in the SSE: in Europe, women account for 66 percent of people involved in the SSE; in Canada, this figure rises to 70 percent; and it is 80 percent in Africa (Intercontinental Network for the Promotion of the Social and Solidarity Economy 2012). Given the high visibility of women in the SSE and the well-established recognition of the value of engaging with gender equality as a core organizing principle of the SSE, efforts have been made around the world to systematically take stock of the opportunities and constraints experienced by the SSE sector in advancing global goals of women's empowerment, reform of gender relations, and social change. What are the major accomplishments of the SSE sector when it comes to gender equality? What are some persistent and emerging challenges and criticisms that the sector must contend with? The following attempts to present an overview.

30.2 ACCOMPLISHMENTS AND ACCOLADES

The accomplishments of the SSE sector in advancing gender equality and social justice have been documented by scholars, practitioners, and activists in various world regional settings. The SSE in its various forms and iterations has provided access to incomes and dignified livelihoods to women and other socially and economically disadvantaged groups including, in some contexts, low-income men, racialized and ethnic minorities, people with physical and intellectual disabilities, sexual minorities, refugees, and migrants. Being part of the SSE has relieved millions of people around the world, including in some instances people who lack formal education or even basic literacy skills, from abusive working conditions or physically strenuous and unsafe work. As an example, an SSE organization called Technology Informatics Design Endeavour (TIDE) has successfully trained rural women in India, who formerly worked for daily wages as manual laborers, to build smokeless stoves from locally available materials. The training provided by organizations such as TIDE includes practical technical modules and business operation components. These organizations have been able to break down the training into components that are not intimidating, even for women who are not literate. The demonstration effect, of women with limited education and social privilege earning a living by constructing stoves for a fee, frequently motivates other women to pursue the training. Upon completion of training, some women have chosen to organize themselves in solidaristic ways to optimize their earning potential. For example, a group of women trained by TIDE to construct biogas cookstoves formed a cooperative. They travel in groups of two or more to build stoves in distant rural areas (Baruah 2015). Other SSE organizations and enterprises (SSEOEs) have also created livelihood opportunities for women by providing training in skills and services that are often weak or absent in remote or rural communities. Examples include: the "master trainers" of the Aga Khan Rural Support Programme in Pakistan who help women to transition from subsistence farming activities to commercial production; the "barefoot" doctors, vets, and lawyers of the Bangladesh Rural Advancement Committee (BRAC); the literacy workers of Proshika in Bangladesh; and the health and childcare providers of the Self Employed Women's Association (SEWA) in India (Baruah 2004). Such initiatives have enabled many people to transition from poorly paid, unskilled, or menial activities, which have few or no barriers to entry, into activities which demand improved technical skills and, in some instances, increased amounts of capital, yet provide higher returns due to greater market demand.

The successes enjoyed by organizations such as SEWA and BRAC in organizing and mobilizing millions of informal sector workers to achieve higher incomes and better working conditions are well known. Perhaps less well known are the successes such organizations have enjoyed in enabling their members to access stronger social security and protection via their housing, healthcare, childcare, education, and insurance programs. As an example, through the National Insurance Vimo SEWA Cooperative, SEWA provides financial protection to thousands of self-employed women workers and their families. When Vimo SEWA was registered in 2009 under the Multi-State Co-operative Societies Act, it was the first cooperative working in the field of microinsurance in which both insurance policyholders and shareholders are women. More than 12 000 women from five states (Bihar, Delhi, Gujarat, Madhya Pradesh, and Rajasthan) are individual shareholders, and 13 membership-based organizations of the SEWA movement are institutional shareholders. In addition to offering insurance services, Vimo SEWA prioritizes member education and awareness about various aspects of social security and financial risk management. Vimo SEWA members are also integrated into the much wider SEWA movement and have access to a wide range of services, including banking services, housing microfinance, childcare, medical care, and pharmacy services that are offered through SEWA's sister organizations. SEWA's joint strategy of unionization and formation of cooperatives in different sectors has been especially effective in addressing the needs of informal sector workers. In addition to raising public awareness about the importance of the informal economy, and demonstrating its connection to the formal economy, organizations such as SEWA and BRAC have successfully advocated for their members via the legal and labor machineries of national, state, and municipal governments; they have demonstrated the need for social services and social protection to optimize the benefits of employment; and they have influenced the formulation of responsive policies and regulations at local/municipal, national, and international levels. As examples, the International Labour Organization's (ILO) Convention on Home Workers, and the Supreme Court of India's recognition of the right to vend as a basic human right, alongside the right to a just licensing policy for street vendors, came about largely because of SEWA's advocacy. SEWA's founder, Ela Bhatt, spearheaded the establishment of Women's World Banking, based in the Netherlands and the United States, with an aim to empower low-income rural and urban women by improving their participation in sustainable livelihood activities, through access to financial services. It was also largely SEWA's work that inspired the inception of Women in Informal Employment: Globalizing and Organizing (WIEGO), a global research-policy network based at the John F. Kennedy School of Government at Harvard University. The network seeks to improve the status of the working poor, especially women, in the informal economy through better statistics, research, programs, and policies, and through increased organization and representation of informal workers (Chen 2008).

Other opportunities created and possibilities enabled by SSEOEs in various parts of the world that have helped to reduce gender inequality include: combining resources for the group ownership of assets and means of production; building forums in which people can cooperate rather than compete for economic opportunities; accessing new markets, associations, subsidies, and sources of financing; and creating new sources of affiliation and solidarity. The opportunity to associate with collectives beyond those represented by the family has been identified repeatedly as a major benefit of women's participation in SSEOEs (Schuler and Hashemi 1993). Not having to rely upon natal or marital families as the sole source of affiliation has been associated with other positive outcomes for women, including reduction in domestic and other forms of gender-based violence, alongside increases in self-confidence, awareness of rights and entitlements, and personal agency (Baruah 2021).

30.3 CHALLENGES AND CRITICISMS

Despite these remarkable accomplishments, persistent challenges remain, especially when it comes to the SSE sector's ability to support gender equality and women's empowerment. The tendency for many women in the SSE to pursue feminized, often low-paid and precarious economic activities, such as tailoring, weaving, cooking, catering, childcare, and eldercare, is frequently emphasized in the literature (see, e.g., Vadera 2013) since they normalize and entrench familial and societal gender hierarchies and divisions of labor. In recent years, some SSEOEs have attempted to break new ground by setting up cooperatives and social businesses in more skilled, non-traditional (often male-dominated) sectors such as transport services (Vadera 2013; Baruah 2021), construction, and energy services (IRENA 2019). The early evaluations of such initiatives are generally promising, but the creation of permanent and stable sources of income and livelihoods remains a challenge. For example, women who have been trained to build, install, and repair energy technology continue to face the challenge of finding permanent employment with their newly acquired skills, as they are often only able to earn incomes on an intermittent basis through contracts and orders placed by nonprofits and government agencies (Baruah 2015) (see entry 27, "Energy, Water and Waste Management Sectors"). Women trained by SSE organizations to work as commercial drivers in cities in India continue to struggle with precarious employment opportunities, deep-rooted social prejudices against women drivers, balancing long working hours with family responsibilities, and lack of a sense of community beyond their peers in the program (Baruah 2021). Such limitations highlight the need for the state to provide adequate social security to protect against market vagaries, natural disasters, illness, maternity, old age, job losses, and other risks to wellbeing. Workers can gain optimal traction from their employment or entrepreneurial efforts in the SSE only if there are wider socially progressive policies in place, including state intervention to create a robust social welfare infrastructure and accessible, high-quality public services (see entry 53, "Social Policy").

The limits that the SSE sector has experienced in terms of guaranteeing full economic empowerment for women, as well as access to quality work and social protection, highlights how crucial it is for this sector not just to replicate and "scale up" its efforts in different settings, but also to build broader productive linkages and collaborations with the public and private sectors, and to demand effective social protection policies from the state. In recent years, there have been significant advancements globally in expanding and strengthening social protection policies, as more countries transition toward developing welfare systems. Some strategies that are being tried in European, African, Asian, and Central and South American countries include basic income schemes as well as conditional and unconditional cash transfer programs that enable poor women to make priority decisions for themselves and their dependents. Programs such as Brazil's Bolsa Familia, Mexico's Prospera, Mali's Social Cash Transfer initiative, and India's basic income pilot are hopeful developments given that structural inequality constrains individual ability to exercise rights and demand entitlements.

Another persistent criticism of the SSE sector when it comes to gender equality is that the sector has been more willing to pursue apolitical means of empowering women—for example, via employment and income-generating schemes—rather than through more controversial or politically sensitive strategies such as demanding the reform of patriarchal inheritance laws and male-biased property rights, enhancing women's active participation in local and national politics, and challenging the gendered division of labor within households and in society at large. Several authors have emphasized that there may be less resistance to women taking part in income-generating activities because it is considered a "win–win" for the family (Baruah 2021). While men may not challenge such activities at all, they are likely to be far more resistant to deeper economic and political demands from women (for independent land and property rights, for example) that challenge traditional patriarchal privileges and entitlements to resources. A deeper structural engagement with reforming gender relations, as opposed to just improving women's economic status via jobs and incomes, is necessary as part of the SSE's proactive and sustainable commitment to gender equality.

The underrepresentation of women in key leadership roles within SSEOEs is another persistent criticism of the sector. Evaluations of SSEOEs have revealed that while women make up most of the sector's workers, members, and consumers, they are often still underrepresented as managers, decision-makers, and on the boards of SSEOEs. In other words, the presence of women in large numbers in the SSE sector does not necessarily translate to representation of their ideas, needs, and priorities at the institutional level. Of course, it is important to acknowledge that women's underrepresentation in executive or managerial positions and on boards of directors is not unique to the SSE sector. It is also true for most public and private sector organizations. However, women's underrepresentation in leadership roles in the SSE sector is particularly jarring and ironic given the sector's explicit commitment to gender equality and social justice.

There is significant evidence from around the world that gender diversity in leadership is good for institutions, for the economy, and for society at large. In its study of almost 22 000 organizations across the globe, the Peterson Institute for International Economics discovered that companies with women making up 30 percent of leaders can add up to 6 percentage points to their net margin, compared to other organizations in the same sector. Across the economy, the percentage of women in leadership positions is positively linked to better financial performance (Noland et al. 2016). Companies with more women board members, on average, outperform those with fewer women by 53 percent on return on investment, 42 percent on return on sales, and 66 percent on return on invested capital (ibid.). Similar findings have emerged for women in executive positions: organizations with higher percentages of women decision-makers financially outperform their peers. Women making up a minimum of 30 percent of executive officers and board members has been found to have the most positive impact on organizational performance. At lower than 15 percent female representation, it is not uncommon for women, because of their minority status, to be made to feel marginal and "invisible" in decision-making processes (Agarwal 2010). Establishing critical mass is important for creating more supportive institutional environments in which women can speak out on issues and concerns in the presence of colleagues. The SSE sector must aspire towards, and fulfill, this goal urgently.

Finally, there is emerging research which suggests that there are limits to what the SSE can accomplish for gender equality and empowerment. Interests, priorities, and needs within the SSE sector may be too variable for cohesive solidaristic activities that produce equitable gains for all women. For example, access to microcredit or other forms of solidarity finance may reduce economic stress at the household level while entrenching, rather than subverting, familial gender hierarchies. This occurs through mechanisms including exacerbating women's work burdens and putting pressure on them to borrow large sums of money, which in some instances maintains existing gender hierarchies at best, and actively defeats any gender equality agenda at worst. For example, Baruah (2010) writes about SEWA members borrowing large sums of money to fund bigger dowries for their daughters, and taking microcredit loans to perform sex-selective abortions of female fetuses. Such findings reveal how deeply problematic it may be to collapse economic empowerment goals with gender equality objectives. Most SSEOEs assume a causal link between women's higher economic performance and greater gender equality. They also tend to assume that what is good for one group of women will necessarily be good for all groups of women. Yet, the examples presented above represent just a few ways in which even innovative pro-women initiatives can sometimes be confounded in practice. That women have been implicated in female feticide and infanticide, in food and health biases against daughters, in exploitative relationships with other women, and in dowry deaths (as just a few examples) speaks rather poignantly and painfully to the unpredictability and subjectivity of women's agencies, priorities, and constraints. To engage meaningfully with these issues, SSEOEs must not only continue to be cognizant of the fact that what is good for men need not also be good for women, but they must also be open to the possibility that what may serve one group of women well may not benefit, or may actively disadvantage, other women.

Other recent studies that have evaluated SSE initiatives based on intersectional identities of gender, race, and ethnicity have arrived at the conclusion that identity politics based on race, ethnicity, class, and caste may, in some contexts, be more powerful than gender in limiting or enabling access to economic opportunities offered by the SSE (see, for example, Hossein's 2016 evaluation of microfinance programs in the Black Americas). Other authors (see, e.g., Cornwall 2011) have corroborated that men from disadvantaged, racialized, ethnic, and caste backgrounds, as well as people with disabilities and sexual minorities, irrespective of gender identity, may face greater disadvantage than able-bodied women from economically or politically dominant communities in accessing and benefiting from economic opportunities offered by the SSE. These findings confirm the need for the SSE to move beyond its present "gender equals women" framing of gender equality and empowerment, toward a broader understanding of gendered, racialized, classed, and disabled experiences that produce and maintain social hierarchies and inequality. To remain true to its commitment to inclusivity and to subverting all types of oppressive social hierarchies, the SSE must respond to a broader evidence base of emerging trends about what constitutes gender inequality.

CONCLUSION

The SSE represents the possibility of reconciling equally important global goals of securing economic security for all and preventing further environmental breakdown with reducing gender inequality and other forms of social injustice. People around the world now derive all or part of their livelihoods from this sector. The SSE sector has also enjoyed significant success in providing millions of women not just with good incomes and dignified working conditions, but also with social services and protections, and with institutional sources of affiliation and solidarity that have positive effects upon their health and wellbeing.

In the future, the SSE sector must engage with deeper persistent challenges to gender inequality, including women's underrepresentation in leadership roles within SSEOEs, their inability to access land and property rights and to participate in politics at par with men, and the fact that women all over the world continue to shoulder a disproportionate burden of household maintenance and caregiving activities. In the future, the SSE must also engage with the possibility that not all men may be beneficiaries of patriarchal privilege, just as not all women are victims of patriarchal oppression. Moving beyond the "gender equals women" conceptualization of gender inequality will enable the SSE to recognize and rectify other forms of social oppression and inequality based on race, ethnicity, class, caste, sexuality, and dis/ability.

REFERENCES

Agarwal, Bina. 2010. *Gender and Green Governance*. Oxford, UK and New York, USA: Oxford University Press.

Baruah, Bipasha. 2004. "Earning Their Keep and Keeping What They Earn: A Critique of Organizing Strategies for South Asian Women in the Informal Sector." *Gender, Work and Organization* 11 (6): 605–26. https://doi.org/10.1111/j.1468-0432.2004.00251.x.

Baruah, Bipasha. 2010. *Women and Property in Urban India*. Vancouver: University of British Columbia Press.

Baruah, Bipasha. 2015. "Creating Opportunities for Women in the Renewable Energy Sector: Findings from India." *Feminist Economics* 21(2): 53–76. https://doi.org/10.1080/13545701.2014.990912.

Baruah, Bipasha. 2021. "Women on Wheels in New Delhi, India: Can Social Innovation Promote Gender Equality?" In *Social Economy in Asia: Realities and Perspectives*, edited by Euiyoung Kim and Hiroki Miura, 173–96. New York, USA and London, UK: Lexington Books.

Chen, Marty. 2008. "A Spreading Banyan Tree: The Self-Employed Women's Association, India." In *From Clients to Citizens: Communities Changing the Course of Their Own Development*, edited by Alison Mathie and Gordon Cunningham, 181–206. Rugby: Intermediate Technology Publications.

Cornwall, Andrea. 2011. *Men and Development: Politicising Masculinities*. London, UK and New York, USA: Zed Books.

De Soto, Hernando. 2000. *The Mystery of Capital: Why Capitalism Triumphs in the West and Nowhere Else*. New York: Basic Books.

Folbre, Nancy. 2012. *For Love and Money: Care Provision in the United States*. New York: Russell Sage Foundation.

Garland-Thomson, Rosmarie. 2014. "The Future of Disability: Feminist, Queer, Crip." *Women's Review of Books* 54 (5): 11–13.

hooks, bell. 2000. *Feminism Is for Everybody*. Boston, MA: South End Press.

Hossein, Caroline Shenaz. 2016. *Politicized Micro-Banking in the Black Americas: The Fight for Social and Economic Justice*. Toronto: University of Toronto Press.

Intercontinental Network for the Promotion of the Social and Solidarity Economy. 2012. "Women in SSE." RIPESS. http://www.ripess.org/working-areas/women-sse/?lang=en.

IRENA. 2019. "Renewable Energy: A Gender Perspective." January. https://www.irena.org/publications/2019/Jan/Renewable-Energy-A-Gender-Perspective.
Matthaei, Julie. 2009. "Beyond Economic Man: Economic Crisis, Feminist Economics, and the Solidarity Economy." Paper delivered at the International Association for Feminist Economics Conference. https://base.socioeco.org/docs/matthaei_iaffe_09_paper.pdf.
Noland, Marcus, Tyler Moran, and Barbara Kotschwar. 2016. "Is Gender Diversity Profitable? Evidence from a Global Survey." PIIE; Women's Economic Empowerment Research Initiative. https://www.piie.com/publications/working-papers/gender-diversity-profitable-evidence-global-survey.
Rocheleau, Dianne, Barbara Thomas-Slayter, and Esther Wangari. 1996. *Feminist Political Ecology: Global Issues and Local Experience.* London: Routledge.
Schuler, Sidney Ruth, and Syed M. Hashemi. 1993. "Defining and Studying Empowerment of Women: A Research Note from Bangladesh." Arlington, VA: John Snow International Research and Training Institute.
Vadera, Meenu. 2013. "Women on Wheels." In *Aid, NGOs and the Realities of Women's Lives: A Perfect Storm*, edited by Tina Wallace, Fenella Porter, and Mark Ralph-Bowman, 143–54. Rugby: Practical Action Publishing.
Waring, Marilyn. 1988. *If Women Counted: A New Feminist Economics.* San Francisco, CA: Harper.

31. Health and care sector
Jean-Pierre Girard

INTRODUCTION

This entry concerns the social and solidarity economy (SSE) in the health and care sector. It encompasses a wide range of activities, including healthcare and medical treatment, childcare, early childhood education, disability and long-term care, and eldercare. The information derives from various studies and reports at the international level and focuses on the actions of cooperatives and mutual aid organizations (which seem to attract more interest than associations or non-profit organizations) to show the positive consequences that they generate for members, workers and community needs, instead of short-term financial gain (see also entry 17, 'Cooperatives and Mutuals'). Higher quality of services, improved access to services, lower delivery cost, empowerment of various stakeholders, maximized social impact, strengthened links with the community, and good wages are among these benefits (see also entry 38, 'Social Services' and entry 53, 'Social Policy'). The entry also takes into consideration matters of governance: stakeholder participation, community engagement, and accountability.

All too often, the health and care sector are seen only through two lenses: of public organizations or of for-profits. This entry, therefore, is intended to provide a clear and updated view of the role of a third actor which, while it shares the notions of the common good and general interest with public organizations, can mobilize many stakeholders, and identify innovative ways of addressing such important societal challenges as the escalating care needs of an ageing population, or better, more affordable childcare resources for young families. It also has the capacity to hybridize resources that emanate from the market, from state transfers and from volunteering. In short, SSE in this area by no means resembles a one-size-fits-all approach that is so common in public services, paying little or no heed to differences between urban and rural contexts, socio-economic status, and so on. In contrast to for-profit organizations (FPOs), SSE organizations and enterprises (SSEOEs) in the health and care sector are not driven solely by financial considerations, but instead offer ways to instrumentalize financial resources for the purpose of serving the needs of their members and the well-being of the community. In this regard, surpluses will often be reinvested to strengthen an organization's financial base, or to improve or expand services, rather than to enrich shareholders (see entry 53, 'Social Policy' and entry 38, 'Social Services')

Note that, notwithstanding the important contributions they make to the health and care sector, this entry does not address the role of individuals or families who are supporting people with health issues, nor associations whose purpose is to support individuals suffering from specific health problems (for example, cancer, Alzheimer's) or to advocate on their behalf (for example, HIV/AIDS), nor the work of diverse foundations.

31.1 HEALTH AND CARE SECTOR AND THE SOCIAL AND SOLIDARITY ECONOMY

The recognition of the SSE from an international perspective is not new. The year following its establishment (1920), the International Labour Organization (ILO), under the leadership of its first general director, Albert Thomas, set up a cooperative department and hired a French co-op specialist, Georges Fauquet, to be its first director. In 1945, the year of its founding, the United Nations (UN) reached out 'to establish a mutually beneficial partnership with the international cooperative movement' (United Nations Department for Policy Coordination and Sustainable Development 1997, iii). It granted the International Cooperative Alliance (ICA) consultative status with the Economic and Social Council of the United Nations, the highest recognition that the UN awards to non-governmental organizations. However, for the health and care sector, recognition took a long time.

A UN report (United Nations Department for Policy Coordination and Sustainable Development 1997, iii) is called upon for the following information:

> In 1987, the Interregional Consultation on Developmental Social Welfare Policies and Programmes (Vienna, 7–15 September 1987) adopted the Guiding Principles for Developmental Social Welfare Policies and Programmes in the Near Future (E/CONF.80/10, chap. III), which were subsequently endorsed by the General Assembly in its resolutions 42/125, 44/65 and 46/90. The Guiding Principles noted that:
>
>> A basic principle and objective of social welfare policy is to promote the widest possible participation of all individuals and groups, and greater emphasis needs to be placed on translating this principle into practice. This may be achieved through new partnerships in the field of social welfare policy, providing opportunities for greater involvement of beneficiaries, individually and collectively, in decisions concerning their needs and in the implementation of programmes, including community-based programmes (para. 27) …
>
> Social welfare is the concern not only of governments but also of numerous other sponsors. Non-governmental and voluntary organizations, trade unions, cooperatives and community and social action groups are major sponsors of social welfare programmes that must be recognized, supported and consulted (para. 54).
>
> There are advantages to such a diversity of sponsors and approaches including the potential for more precise identification of needs, innovation in strategies, generating broader participation and the involvement of more resources. This may result in a need for better coordination of diverse activities and programmes and for a clearer definition of areas of responsibility and function to achieve the optimal effect. (para. 55)

Included in the global agenda and general Guiding Principles was the following: 'Within the framework of national laws, there is a need to strengthen the role and contribution of non-governmental and voluntary organizations, private entities and people themselves in enhancing social services, well-being and development' (para. 64 (h)).

The Copenhagen Declaration on Social Development, adopted at the World Summit for Social Development (Copenhagen, 6–12 March 1995), called upon states and governments to make better use of resources allocated to social development, including the contribution of cooperatives for the attainment of social development goals (Commitment 9 (h)) (United Nations 1995, 16).

The United Nations itself responded to this call in a practical fashion by conducting and producing the first global survey on the role of cooperatives in the health and social care sector. Undertaken prior to widespread internet access, the report was first released in 1997 in English (which was followed by two additional versions in Spanish and French the following year). The purpose of the survey was:

> to clarify prerequisites for the further development of the health and social care component of the international cooperative movement, largely by means of its own resources, but also with the possible support of relevant agencies of national, regional and local governments and the relevant specialized agencies and bodies of the United Nations system (United Nations Department for Policy Coordination and Sustainable Development, iv).

A milestone document in the long process of gaining international recognition of SSE in the health and care sector, the survey provided updated descriptions of co-ops active in the sector and an initial typology: producer, consumer, or multi-stakeholder co-ops; their levels of activity (first level, second level, and so on); and their various health approaches (promotion, prevention, curative, rehabilitation). In addition, the survey suggested strategies by means of which co-ops in this sector could gain better recognition from other key stakeholders (unions, state, and so on).

Drawing on responses from existing health cooperatives worldwide, the survey explained in straightforward language the value-added of the co-op model in terms of a variety of dimensions key to health and social care, including participation, motivation, and partnership. Due to the special requirements of health and social care services, the organization of a cooperative enterprise places it at an advantage relative to both public sector and private for-profit sector enterprises. Of particular value is the participation of customers (users, clients and patients) in the identification of goals and in the design of operations.

This survey also served as a reminder that the very first health cooperative (with its own clinic and hospital) was launched early in the 20th century by a multi-functional agricultural cooperative in Japan to help its members avoid long journeys from the countryside to urban areas for medical consultation. This medical cooperative network, alongside a second, urban cooperative established under the leadership of the Japanese Consumers Cooperative Union, 'stress preventive health and healthy living. They have extended services from the medical to social medicine and social care, particularly for the elderly, given the demographic ageing of the Japanese population' (United Nations Department for Policy Coordination and Sustainable Development 1997, 167).

While not mentioned in the 1997 report, the 1978 Alma-Ata Declaration of the World Health Organization (WHO) focuses on the importance of individuals and community participation in primary healthcare. The Declaration states that it: 'requires and promotes maximum community and individual self-reliance and participation in the planning, organization, operation and control of primary healthcare, making fullest use of local, national and other available resources; and to this end develops through appropriate education the ability of communities to participate' (WHO 1978, VII, 5).

Unfortunately, from a global perspective, the WHO has never devoted attention specifically to the contribution of the SSE to the health and care sector. However, regarding certain concerns, such as health promotion, it does recognize the role of civil society organizations.[1]

Nearly 20 years later, under a mandate from the 2014 International Cooperative Summit, a second global survey was conducted. Its purpose was to discern how these organizations improve access to health care, and the innovations they bring to the sector. Entitled 'Better Health and Social Care: How are Co-ops and Mutuals Boosting Innovation and Access Worldwide' (Girard 2014), this survey covered cooperatives and mutuals in 59 countries from every part co-ops of the world. It illustrated innovative practices: for instance, fruitful partnerships between and public entities, and initiatives to reach isolated or marginalized populations or to address issues of gender. As the executive summary states:

- Health cooperative contractors provide high-quality, efficient services for Costa Rica's social security system.
- Continuum of care offerings by diverse types of cooperatives in Italy.
- The Espriu Foundation network in Spain runs hospitals in collaboration with the government. This has led to cost savings for the national health system and to higher satisfaction among users.
- Cooperatives provide options for innovative Personal Health Record platforms in Finland.
- Mutuals provide health care to indigenous people in Paraguay.
- Women's Health Cooperative has become a model of community empowerment due to its provision of easily accessible and affordable health care services in Tikathali village in Nepal.
- Thanks to a fruitful partnership with a Public Health Regional Centre and municipal housing office, a home care cooperative in Canada provides overall service to seven homes for the elderly and six homes for the disabled. (Girard 2014, iii)

In addition to such little-known but interesting practices as the paramedic workers' cooperative network in Quebec (Canada), the survey put on the radar the unique value-added of the co-op model: its capacity to respond to members' needs. In case after case, cooperatives active in other sectors became engaged in health and social care as a practical response to members' expectations. For the purposes of this entry, let two examples suffice. In Ethiopia, Oromia Coffee Farmers Cooperative Union uses part of its surplus to invest in improved health facilities, including health post and medical equipments, which reach thousands of beneficiaries. In Oruro, Bolivia, due to the poor treatment that members received in public health institutions, Cooperativa Multiactiva Corazón de Jesús established a health centre staffed by a doctor, an orthodontist and two nurses (Girard 2014, 17). Similarly, the survey revealed many instances in which various kinds of cooperatives (agriculture, financial, workers, and so on) and mutuals (insurance) had invested in educational material on good health practices.

The most recent global study on the role of healthcare cooperatives was initiated in 2018 by the International Health Cooperative Organisation (IHCO) and the European Research Institute on Cooperative and Social Enterprises (EURICSE). They agreed to jointly develop a multi-annual research initiative[2] on the contribution of healthcare cooperatives to improve people's health and well-being around the world. They aimed to publish an annual report containing – for a progressively larger number of countries – both quantitative and qualitative analyses of healthcare cooperatives and mutual organizations as well as the systems in which they operate.

The first year of the research study focused on 15 countries, all of which have structured healthcare systems: Argentina, Australia, Belgium, Brazil, Canada, Colombia, France, Italy, Japan, Malaysia, Singapore, Spain, Sweden, the United Kingdom and the United States. For each country, EURICSE developed a profile of the main features of healthcare cooperatives vis-à-vis the healthcare system. In-depth case studies of these cooperatives were provided for Belgium, Brazil, Canada, Italy, Spain and Japan. Healthcare cooperatives of various types were investigated (cooperatives of health practitioners, mainly doctors; user/patient cooperatives; and multi-stakeholder cooperatives), as well as cooperatives active in other sectors, such as agricultural cooperatives also providing health services.

Using both quantitative and qualitative methodologies, the researchers noted that:

> health cooperatives exist in all of the healthcare systems surveyed, although large country variations are noticeable. They deliver a wide range of services, covering risk protection, prevention and soft healthcare service delivery, pharmaceutical product distribution and healthcare clinic management. Country variations depend on several factors: the degree of coverage provided by the public healthcare system; the degree of freedom granted to private providers; cooperative traditions and cultures (social orientation); the ability of cooperative movements to self-organize to address new challenges; and the way cooperatives are recognized, regulated and supported by national laws. Such differences have helped shape the role of cooperatives within the healthcare domain in different ways across countries. (IHCO and EURICSE 2018, 6-7)

Each of these three reports shows the capacity of cooperatives and mutuals to be implemented and run under a variety of healthcare systems: those that are almost exclusively public as well as those that mix public and private healthcare provision. But such an observation should not lead us to underestimate the challenge that cooperatives face if they are to gain full recognition from the state. The reports also demonstrate the remarkable diversity of the cooperative model, ranging from small clinics to substantial networks of cooperatives that own and operate clinics, hospitals and research centres. Take, for example, the world's biggest health co-op network, UNIMED do Brasil, an organization that encompasses nearly one-third of the country's doctors. There is also room for cooperative pharmacies, including primary level user-owned and secondary-level cooperative networks of pharmacies, such as the Association of All Pharmacists Cooperatives (TEKB) in Turkey.

Finally, even if the need for health facilities is huge in many parts of the world, the first two reports highlight how underdeveloped health cooperatives are in low-income countries, especially in Africa. That raises many issues, including a lack of knowledge of the cooperative model, but also a lack of a legal framework to support such a model.

Since the UN's 1997 survey, co-ops and mutuals engaged in the health and social care sector seem to be receiving more and more attention. What, then, about the more global notion of care, for instance childcare and eldercare? To address this issue, in 2016 two agencies of the ILO, the Cooperatives Unit (COOP) and the Gender, Equality and Diversity Branch (GED) (now the Gender, Equality, Diversity and Inclusion Branch, GEDI), decided to jointly undertake a global mapping of the provision of care through cooperatives.

As the report's introduction explains:

> Across research and practice literature, various case studies have been set forth, providing a foundational understanding of the functions of care cooperatives and the barriers they face. These studies, however, tend to focus on childcare and, to a lesser extent, eldercare, mostly discussing cases from Western Europe and North America. As such, the broader understanding of care cooperatives across geographic regions and populations has been lacking. (Matthew et al. 2016)

The report uses the following definition of care: 'Looking after the physical, psychological, emotional and developmental needs of one or more other people, namely the elderly, children and people living with disabilities, physical illness and/or mental illness.'[3]

The mapping primarily uses two sources of information: an online survey (the survey sample consisted of 182 survey respondents from the care sector and cooperative movement, of which 55 per cent participated in the English version of the survey[4]), and key stakeholder interviews. The aim of the research was to:

- Determine the landscape of cooperatives that provide care, including their beneficiaries, members, objectives and scope;
- Ascertain the legislative, social and economic contexts that drive care through cooperatives;
- Identify the challenges and opportunities that cooperatives face in initiating and sustaining care provision and decent employment;
- Determine the resources that cooperatives need in order to be viable care providers, enterprises and employers;
- Assess how well cooperatives affect the livelihood of care beneficiaries, workers and the larger community, compared to private and public care provision options; and
- Determine whether and under which form care cooperatives are registered. (Matthew et al. 2016, 6)

The findings of the research in many respects lend support to the results of reports previously cited in this entry:

- Cooperatives are emerging as an innovative type of care provider, particularly in the absence of viable public or other private options;
- Cooperatives generate access to better terms and conditions of work in the care sector (for example access to benefits, more bargaining power, regularized hours) – especially for female employees;
- Compared to the public, other private and even non-profit care providers, cooperatives provide care in distinct and preferred ways;
- Cooperatives foster interdependency in care by privileging equitable inclusion and democratic decision-making across the care chain. As such, care workers, care beneficiaries and their families, and other stakeholders have a voice in the nature of the service provided and the operation of the care provision enterprise. (Matthew et al. 2016, 4)

Two other observations are in order. The authors argued that 'the cooperative approach to care is distinct from public, other private and even non-profit providers'. Why? 'When the seven cooperative principles are engaged, cooperatives foster interdependence rather than dependence in caregiving by privileging voice and inclusion.' (Matthew et al. 2016, 4) This refers to the cooperative identity, values and principles that were adopted at the congress of the ICA in Manchester in 1995.[5]

The authors also recognized that 'more evidence and data are needed in order to move forward', for example, 'more information on the social and economic impacts of care cooperatives ... if the impact of care cooperatives is to be conveyed to governments, funders and potential beneficiaries'. (Matthew et al. 2016, 33)

As mentioned in the introduction to this chapter, there appears to be no study or report that explores the impact of the three main legal forms of SSEOEs in the health and care sector from a global perspective. For example, it is only possible to find research focusing on one sector of activity concerning quality in for-profit, non-profit and public childcare provision. This is the purpose of the Child Care Briefing Notes published in 2011 by the Canadian Childcare Resource and Research Unit. Quoting research conducted over the last 30 years in various countries such as Canada, the United States, the United Kingdom and New Zealand, the Notes refer to:

> observational tools such as the Early Childhood Environmental Rating Scale (ECERS) that measure 'process quality' or with indicators of quality: staff training, wages, working conditions, professional development, staff morale, turnover, compliance with regulations, ratios and how funds are used .... the research examining multiple variables across jurisdictions shows that public and non-profit childcare is significantly more likely to be a better quality than for-profit childcare (Childcare Resource and Research Unit 2011)

In other words, non-profit organizations surpass FPOs in terms of many of the indicators directly impacting upon the quality of services, such as wages, working conditions, early childhood educator training, staff turnover, staff morale, staff–child ratios and group size.

In their conclusion, the authors supply the following reminder:

> Whether childcare is for-profit or public/not-for-profit is not the only policy issue that determines whether children and families get high quality early childhood services. Yet, it is, however, a fundamental choice that influences how well other key structural policy elements – public financing; a planned (not market) approach; well paid, early childhood-educated staff treated as professionals; a sound pedagogical approach; and ongoing quality assurance – function to ensure high quality and equitable access.

From another perspective, the impact of the recent COVID-19 pandemic on morbidity among older citizens in many countries has brought to the forefront of public debate the question of eldercare. Of particular concern are the consequences of the ownership and management of nursing homes (also known as long-term care homes) or seniors' homes (also known as retirement homes or assisted living facilities) on their residents. Given their focus on maximizing profit rather than on the well-being of their clients, relative to other ownership models (public and not-for-profit), how effectively have FPOs involved in this sector managed the consequences of the pandemic?

For sure, amongst the raft of COVID-19 post-mortems coming our way in the near future, we can expect many comparative studies on this issue. In fact, in 2016, a research team from the University of British Columbia in Canada has already released a study that reviewed the link between ownership and care quality. They used the 'Bradford Hill's Guidelines for Assessing Causation':

> These guidelines provide a useful framework for assessing evidence for a causal effect. Specifically, Bradford Hill suggested that nine relevant factors should be considered before concluding causation ... Plausibility ... Temporality ... Experiment ... Biological gradient or dose-response ... Coherence ... Analogy ... Consistency ... Strength of the association ... [and] ... Specificity. (Ronald et al. 2016, 5-12)

Using data from Canada and the United States, the authors suggest that there is a greater likelihood of inferior care when it is provided by for-profit facilities. And they ask, 'what is behind this relation between profit and inferior care? One explanation is that there is a trade-off between improving quality (for example by hiring more staff) and generating profit. In other words, where the pressure to make a profit is strong, quality may be sacrificed.' (Ronald et al. 2016, 4-12). Based on this causal link between for-profit ownership and inferior care, the authors argue that the 'precautionary principle should be applied when developing policy for this frail and vulnerable population'. (Ronald et al. 2016, 8-12)

It is evident that more research needs to be done on the value-added of the SSE in the health and care sector, particularly in the care sectors, including association legal form. However, based on what we know from the 1997 report, there is some evidence related to the quality of service, sensitivity to stakeholders' empowerment and community link. Paying more attention to a country's spending, in particular, the health and care expenses, will converge focus towards the way health and care services are delivered. We can expect that this, in turn, will contribute to a better in-depth understanding of the SSE in this field of activity.

NOTES

1. For example, the NGO Alliance For Health Promotion has been in official relation with the WHO since 2015. See Alliance for Health Promotion (2021).
2. This 2018 report appears to be the only research generated by this IHCO–EURICSE partnership as of November 2021.
3. Adapted from Maybud (2015).
4. The survey also offers options to answer in Spanish, Italian and French.
5. See International Cooperative Alliance (2018).

REFERENCES

Alliance for Health Promotion. 2021. 'Alliance for Health Promotion – A4HP.' https://allianceforhealthpromotion.org/.

Childcare Resource and Research Unit. 2011. 'What Research Says About Quality in For-Profit, Non-Profit and Public Child Care.' https://childcarecanada.org/sites/default/files/What%20research%20says%20about%20quality%20in%20fp%20np%20and%20p%20child%20care.pdf.

Girard, Jean-Pierre. 2014. 'Better Health & Social Care: How Are Co-Ops and Mutuals Boosting Innovation and Access Worldwide, Volume 1 Report.' Quebec International Summit of Cooperatives. http://productionslps.com/wp-content/uploads/2014/10/International-survey-co_op-and-mutual-Health-and-social-care-CMHSC-14.pdf.

IHCO (International Health Cooperative Organisation) and EURICSE. 2018. 'Cooperative Health Report, Assessing the Worldwide Contribution of Cooperatives to Health Care.' https://previewihco.files.wordpress.com/2018/03/cooperative-health-report-2018.pdf.

International Cooperative Alliance. 2018. 'Cooperative Identity, Values & Principles.' ICA. https://www.ica.coop/en/cooperatives/cooperative-identity.

Matthew, Lenore, Simel Esim, Susan Maybud and Satoko Horiuchi. 2016. 'Global Mapping of the Provision of Care through Cooperatives: Survey and Interview Findings.' International Labour Office. https://files.uniteddiversity.coop/Cooperatives/Global%20Mapping%20of%20the%20Provision%20of%20Care%20through%20Cooperatives.pdf.

Maybud, Susan, 2015. 'Gender. Women and the Future of Work – Taking Care of the Caregivers.' ILO's Work in Progress series, March. https://www.ilo.org/wcmsp5/groups/public/---ed_protect/---protrav/---travail/documents/publication/wcms_351297.pdf.

Ronald, Lisa A., Margaret J. McGregor, Charlene Harrington, Allyson Pollock and Joel Lexchin. 2016. 'Observational Evidence of For-Profit Delivery and Inferior Nursing Home Care: When Is There Enough Evidence for Policy Change?' *PLOS Medicine* 13 (4): e1001995. https://www.ncbi.nlm.nih.gov/pmc/articles/PMC4836753/pdf/pmed.1001995.pdf

United Nations. 1995. 'Copenhagen Declaration on Social Development Annex.' https://www.un.org/en/development/desa/population/migration/generalassembly/docs/globalcompact/A_CONF.166_9_Declaration.pdf.

United Nations Department for Policy Coordination and Sustainable Development. 1997. *Cooperative Enterprise in the Health and Social Care Sectors: A Global Survey.* New York: United Nations.

WHO. 1978. 'Declaration of Alma-Ata International Conference on Primary Health Care, Alma-Ata, U.S.S.R.' Geneva: WHO.

32. Housing sector
Alice Pittini

INTRODUCTION

The shortage of affordable housing solutions for all is a topic that has been attracting increasing attention on a global scale. There was already a housing affordability crisis prior to the COVID-19 pandemic, resulting from a combination of several long-standing elements. House prices had been increasing dramatically and housing costs were increasingly unaffordable especially for renters. Despite significant improvements over time, problems with housing quality also persist in many areas. However, the pandemic has served to reinforce the importance of adequate and affordable homes, revealing the impact that housing conditions have had on well-being and both physical and mental health. This has been supported by a growing body of literature, data and other useful evidence from international organisations and institutions.

Against this background, this entry explains the contribution of the social and solidarity economy (SSE) to affordable and decent housing for all. It particularly pays attention to a partnership with the public sector in building, renovating or putting at disposal housing for all, including those on low incomes and vulnerable groups. The entry introduces diverse forms of SSE organisations and enterprises (SSEOEs) in the housing sector and their diverse ways to contribute – sometimes together with third parties – to affordable and accessible housing provision. It also introduces good practices, lessons learned and potential areas of innovation of SSE in contributing to the accessible and affordable housing sector.

32.1 SCOPE AND DEFINITIONS

Defining the precise scope of what constitutes the SSE in the field of housing presents some significant challenges. It requires a distinction between which types of entities and activities are considered to be in and out of the scope of the SSE field, which is far from straightforward, as different interpretations and 'models' exist worldwide (see entry 54, 'Statistical Measurement').

In terms of the subjects involved, based on the working definition of the SSE, I consider this term to encompass a wide range of different legal structures, comprising mainly (but not exclusively) housing cooperatives, mutual societies, associations, foundations, trusts, charities, and not-for-profit or limited-profit companies active in the provision of housing and often additional services to residents and communities. Indeed there is a great diversity in Europe and the world in terms of – among other aspects – types of organisations providing affordable housing, their size, structure and legal form, the way they are regulated and how they finance their activities. This diversity is the result of the history of housing provision, which is very much embedded in the local realities and linked with the different paths of development of welfare states (see entry 53, 'Social Policy'). In terms of the object at stake, that is, which types and forms of housing are part of the SSE, I consider this to include different forms of social and affordable housing provision.

According to the Organisation for Economic Co-operation and Development (OECD), social (rental) housing is to be understood as 'residential rental accommodation provided at sub-market prices and allocated according to specific rules' (Salvi del Pero et al. 2016, 36). It is important to note that social housing provision is usually subject to regulation from public authorities, and it is often provided by different levels of public administration either directly or through public housing bodies/companies set up with the purpose of implementing public policy in this area. Therefore, 'some of these housing organisations can be described with traditional "state", "market" or "civil society" labels, but many correspond in fact to hybrid organisational forms, encompassing characteristics of state, market and third sector organisations' (Czischke et al. 2012, 419)

The term 'affordable housing' is also used to refer to a range of types of housing provision which is usually broader than social housing; the focus being rather on the outcomes in terms of affordability for end-users rather than on the specific framework and regulation around it. A useful definition of affordability is: 'Housing is affordable when housing of an acceptable minimum standard can be obtained and retained leaving sufficient income to meet essential non-housing expenditure' (Stephens 2017). Furthermore, in the absence of any universally agreed reference on this concept, a useful operational typology was developed in the framework of the European Union (EU) Urban Agenda Housing Partnership, which sees 'affordable housing' as part of a 'continuum' including social housing as well as other low-cost rental housing, and even access to homeownership at a reduced price (Rosenfeld 2017).

32.2 MISSION AND OBJECTIVES

Looking at the mission and objectives of SSEOEs in the housing field, they share a social and 'societal' objective that is to provide affordable and quality homes to those who need them. In this sense, although distinct from public administration, they contribute to fulfilling public policy objectives and activities in the public interest (see entry 51, 'Public Policy'). From this perspective, although public provision of housing (either by local authorities, or by other public bodies directly or through dedicated public companies) does not fall under the scope of the definition of SSE, in many cases this distinction relates purely to legal form and the public or private nature of the organisations involved, rather than to the actual output. However, while some housing providers focus on providing access to the wider public, other organisations (often those characterised by a high level of residents' co-production and self-help) may focus on a limited group of people who at the same time are users and collectively own their homes, as is typically the case in housing cooperatives or community land trusts. Also, housing organisations can develop to address the specific needs of certain vulnerable groups such as the homeless, people with disabilities, people with a migrant background, members of minorities, and so on.

While being mission-driven, SSEOEs in the housing field are typically active on the residential market. Furthermore, unlike profit-driven actors which tend to benefit shareholders, SSEOEs re-invest profits in their core mission and to the benefit of residents and the communities they work in. Furthermore, in many cases they may access public funding when contributing to a specific public policy goal.

32.3　EXAMPLES OF THE SSE IN THE HOUSING SECTOR

Interestingly, most countries with a relatively large and well-established social and affordable housing sector are characterised by a strong presence of what can be broadly be described as organisations acting within the remits of the social and solidarity economy. Four organisational qualities characterise this sector, namely:

- They are sensitive to the public interest while at the same time making their own choices.
- They are sensitive to public regulation but always bearing their values and missions in mind.
- They are sensitive to the market without letting this be conclusive to their activities.
- Their core mission is to provide affordable and decent housing.

I provide some examples below of the forms and characteristics of these SSE housing organisations across countries. The list is by no means exhaustive, but it provides an illustration of the diversity of models and organisations involved, and points at some good practices within the sector (see entry 16, 'Community-Based Organizations').

In the United Kingdom, for instance, housing associations are nowadays managing over half of the social housing stock. Housing associations are private, non-profit-making organisations that may take different legal forms including industrial and provident societies, charitable companies, not-for-profit companies, cooperatives and charitable trusts. Some associations trace their routes back to 19th century philanthropists. Newer and sometimes faster-growing associations aim principally to build more homes to rent for a widening group of households unable to afford market housing. Besides the core landlord activities, they often run community spaces and facilities, and carry out initiatives to improve the lives and well-being of residents such as employment training, advice on health and lifestyle issues, and community activities.

Austrian limited-profit housing associations are enterprises whose activities are directly geared towards the fulfilment of the common good in the field of housing and residential matters, whose assets are dedicated to the fulfilment of such tasks, and whose business operations can be regularly reviewed and monitored. They act on a limited-profit basis and represent about a fifth of the total Austrian housing stock and about 40 per cent of multi-family housing. Today in the limited-profit sector housing production is twice as high as in the private sector, at lower rents, and it provides homes that are more spacious. It is therefore not surprising that their contribution is generally highly valued by the population, to the point that a 2018 Gallup poll has shown that around nine in ten people in Austria think that housing associations play an important role in the housing market.

In Denmark, social housing is provided at cost prices by not-for-profit housing associations. A specific feature of the Danish social housing model is the principle of tenants' democracy, which is basically a way to organise the running of each housing estate based on the central role played by residents. There are about 700 housing associations, which own 8000 estates, also defined as 'sections'. They are legally regulated by the state, but owned and organised collectively by the association members themselves. These arrangements are attractive for tenants because they give influence over the management of their homes without requiring them to take responsibility for running estates themselves. Furthermore, there is evidence that the tenant democracy system has helped to strengthen the Danish social housing sector, by increasing tenants' commitment to the sector and ensuring that landlords are responsive to their needs (United Nations Economic Commission for Europe and Housing Europe 2021).

The Netherlands is the country with the largest share of social housing in the EU, accounting for about one-third of the total housing stock. Registered social housing organisations in the Netherlands (*woningcorporaties*) are private non-profit organisations (associations and foundations) with a legal task to give priority to housing households on lower incomes. They operate on the basis of registration and are supervised by the national government. They are, however, independent organisations, setting their own objectives and bearing their own financial responsibilities. Their task is not only to build, maintain, sell and rent social housing stock, but also to provide other kinds of services, directly related to the use of the dwellings, to the occupants.

In Estonia, as a result of mass privatisations of public housing stock in the early 1990s, 97 per cent of people own their own homes. Most live in multi-dwelling apartment buildings, which are managed by cooperative-style apartment associations. Members of apartment associations are responsible for managing their buildings under legally defined frameworks that support their decision-making. For example, more than 50 per cent of apartment owners in each building must agree on the scope and budget of any refurbishment work. This approach has been very successful in upgrading and improving low-quality housing, driven by collective decision-making and enabling the management of buildings by residents.

Housing cooperatives are legal entities owning real estate, consisting of one or more residential buildings. They can apply different models (from rental to ownership and limited equity schemes) but they are all membership-based, with membership granted by way of a share purchase in the cooperative. They are based on the values of self-help, self-responsibility, democracy, equality, equity and solidarity, and operate according to seven cooperative principles that are internationally recognised. The size of the sector varies significantly. It can be very large, with for instance over 1 million 'tenant ownership' units in Sweden. In Switzerland, most social landlords are small not-for-profit cooperatives; 70 per cent own fewer than 100 dwellings. Swiss housing cooperatives own the properties they manage, while members own a share but have no equity in their units. These shares are reimbursed to members upon leaving, but tenants do not have the right to buy their dwellings, so as to preserve the cooperative housing stock. To promote good practice, these cooperative organisations adopted a charter laying down the core principles such as no speculative profits, good-quality affordable and sustainable housing, integration of disadvantaged households, and tenant participation and self-determination (United Nations Economic Commission for Europe and Housing Europe 2021).

32.4 ADDED VALUE

Building or rehabilitating social and affordable housing presents a unique opportunity to meet social, economic and environmental objectives and contribute to implementing the Sustainable Development Goals.

First of all, SSEOEs which provide adequate and affordable housing solutions offer social and economic stability to residents and the society as a whole, as lower housing costs free up resources for households to access other essential goods and services.

Secondly, adequate and affordable housing can result in a number of positive spillovers in other areas. For instance, the link between housing conditions and health and well-being have been increasingly documented over the years, including by the World Health Organization, showing that better quality of housing can lead to lower healthcare costs and better social outcomes.

Similarly, good-quality housing offering sufficient space is associated with higher educational achievements for children and teenagers; conversely, overcrowding and exposure to noise has been found to negatively affect educational outcomes and children's overall development.

Investing in affordable housing has a demonstrated multiplier effect for the local economy as it creates local employment opportunities and retains investment in the local and regional economy. Furthermore, by investing for the long term and re-investing earnings into their objectives, they can contribute to countering speculative trends in the housing market (see entry 47, 'Local and Territorial Development Plans').

Also very important in the context of the fight against climate change, 'greener' housing is key to achieving a reduction of CO_2 emissions, and energy-efficient renovation can provide an efficient response to energy poverty. Integrating renewable energies and circularity in housing is a further opportunity for SSE housing organisations to rise up to this challenge (see entry 27, 'Energy, Water and Waste Management Sectors').

Last but not least, transparency, involvement of residents and stakeholders, and freedom to find innovative solutions to complex issues, are some of the key added values of SSE housing providers which can provide further immaterial benefits such as increasing social cohesion and a sense of community at the local level.

Therefore, a strong case can be made for these types of organisations, not only as a tenure of choice for those unable to afford market prices but also as a valuable partner for public authorities in achieving more and better-quality affordable housing.

32.5 LOOKING AHEAD: POTENTIAL AREAS OF INNOVATION

Housing delivery must continuously evolve to respond to changing socio-demographic contexts, new needs from different population groups, technological development and environmental challenges, to name just a few. Some of the areas where this innovation is taking place are particularly worth mentioning as they will be key to determining the sustainability of SSE housing organisations and their capacity to respond to current and future challenges: the provision of new services to residents and local communities; more democratic and collaborative practices; as well as innovation in construction and renovation techniques.

With regard to setting up new services to tenants and local communities, we find very different starting points in terms of to what extent housing providers have a culture or history of combining housing with social care. This way of working (in cooperation with other service providers) has proved to be the most effective in enhancing the quality of life for residents, and it can also lead to significant savings for the public purse in the long term. It is, however, very much driven by the changing needs at the local level, and it can target very different groups and aspects.

For instance, it is worth mentioning that social housing providers in recent years have been increasingly involved in programmes aimed specifically at helping particularly vulnerable groups, tackling homelessness and the risk of housing exclusion. In particular, models that provide housing first and then integrate health and social care support are increasingly considered to be the most effective way to tackle chronic homelessness (OECD 2015).

Another major driver for innovation in services delivery is the ageing population. New approaches are being deployed that combine physical characteristics of the dwellings (accessibility of homes) with, for instance, the use of information and communication technologies, and smart homes technologies, home-based health and care services, co-housing and intergenerational housing living models (see entry 24, 'Care and Home Support Services').

There is also a growing tendency for providers of social and affordable housing to work with local communities. Examples of this trend include, for instance, the establishment of programmes to support the creation of social enterprises or partnerships between housing organisations and employment services to help residents get into work.

Furthermore, housing providers increasingly must take an active role in guaranteeing the cohesion of the social fabric by working not only with tenants, but also with local neighbours in organising communal initiatives. Overall we can see a trend toward stronger cooperation with residents and a more active role of inhabitants in leading self-help initiatives, reflecting a societal need for a more democratic and bottom-up approach.

But perhaps the most visible and significant innovations are in the way providers of social and affordable housing mobilise to tackle environmental challenges. One of the main drivers is no doubt the need for homes to consume less and greener energy. In 2019, the buildings and construction sector accounted for 36 per cent of final energy use. CO_2 emissions from the operation of buildings have increased to their highest level yet, at around 10 $GtCO_2$ (one billion tonnes of CO_2), or 28 per cent of total global energy-related CO_2 emissions. With the inclusion of emissions from the buildings construction industry, this share increases to 38 per cent of total global energy-related CO_2 emissions (United Nations Environment Programme 2020). The decarbonisation of housing is therefore a key priority and essential to meeting the goals of the Paris Agreement and related Sustainable Development Goals (SDGs):

> Climate-neutral construction and renovation will need to become the new norm ... Furthermore, there is a growing recognition of the need to accelerate and widen policy efforts, expanding their narrow focus from just the building to a more systemic approach. This would also encompass the energy production system, neighbourhood planning and the circular and resource efficient use of building materials and services. (United Nations Economic Commission for Europe and Housing Europe 2021)

REFERENCES

Czischke, Darinka, Vincent Gruis and David Mullins. 2012. 'Conceptualising Social Enterprise in Housing Organisations.' *Housing Studies* 27 (4): 418–37. https://doi.org/10.1080/02673037.2012.677017.

OECD. 2015. *Integrating Social Services for Vulnerable Groups: Bridging Sectors for Better Service Delivery*. Paris: OECD.

Rosenfeld, Orna. 2017. 'Interpreting the Term "Affordable Housing" in the Housing Partnership 1 Goals and Objectives.' Brussels: European Commission Directorate-General for Regional and Urban Policy. https://ec.europa.eu/futurium/en/system/files/ged/briefing_note_2017_interpreting_the_term_affordable_housing_-_march_2017.pdf.

Nasarre-Aznar, Sergio (coord.), Milan Ftáčnik, Núria Lambea-Llop, Līga Rasnača. 2021. Concrete Actions for Social and Affordable Housing in the EU. Brussels, The Foundation For European

Progressive Studies (FEPS), *Brivibas Un Solidaritates Fonds, Friedrich-Ebert-Stiftung, Fundacion Pablo Iglesias, Masarykova Demokraticka Akademie*.

Salvi del Pero, Angelica, Willem Adema, Valeria Ferraro and Valérie Frey. 2016. *Policies to Promote Access to Good-Quality Affordable Housing in OECD Countries*. Paris: OECD Publishing.

Stephens, Mark. 2017. The Urban Institute, Edinburgh, Presentation on ENHR 2017, Tirana.

United Nations Economic Commission for Europe and Housing Europe. 2021. '#Housing2030: Effective Policies for Affordable Housing in the UNECE Region.' https://unece.org/sites/default/files/2021-10/Housing2030%20study_E_web.pdf.

United Nations Environment Programme. 2020. 'Global Alliance for Buildings and Construction 2020: Global Status Report for Buildings and Construction towards a Zero-Emissions, Efficient and Resilient Buildings and Construction Sector. Executive Summary.' https://globalabc.org/sites/default/files/inline-files/2020%20Buildings%20GSR_FULL%20REPORT.pdf.

33. Information and communication technology (ICT)

Raymond Saner, Lichia Saner-Yiu and Samuel Bruelisauer

33.1 BACKGROUND

Information and communications technologies (ICTs) are part of the modern infrastructure of organizing and producing services and interactions. They are generally referred to as a collection of devices, networking tools, software applications and operating systems that allow individual or corporate users to collect, access, store, transmit, analyse, compute and share data and information. Cutting-edge ICT such as high-speed internet, mobile technology, machine learning and artificial intelligence (AI), robotics, internet of things (IOT) and blockchain have transformed everyday human interactions in an unprecedented manner.

The spread of ICT has given rise to the 'digital economy', defined as 'that part of economic output derived solely or primarily from digital technologies with a business model based on digital goods or services' (Bukht and Heeks 2017). In 2016, the digital economy worldwide was worth US$11.5 trillion, or 15.5 per cent of global gross domestic product (GDP). By 2025, it is expected that the digital economy will reach 24.3 per cent of the global economy (Huawei and Oxford Economics 2017). Since 2020, the COVID-19 pandemic has accelerated the deeper adoption of the ICT technologies, and transformed core aspects of an operation or an organization when producing products or delivering services. With the prolonged pandemic restricting human interactions and curtailing mobility, it is foreseeable that these trends will continue in all sectors.

It is widely acknowledged, however, that many trends associated with the growth of the digital economy also pose major socio-economic challenges, such as rising inequality and the proliferation of non-standard work contracts in the 'gig economy' enabled by online platforms (Gurumurthy et al. 2021). The production and use of ICT also has a large and growing environmental footprint. In 2018, the sector used an estimated 3.6 per cent of global electricity and caused 1.4 per cent of global carbon emissions, while extracting large amounts of minerals and natural resources (Malmodin and Lundén 2018).

The social and solidarity economy (SSE) overlaps with the ICT sector through its production and service delivery. SSE organizations and enterprises (SSEOEs) are also affected by emerging business models that are anchored in ICT and the corresponding so-called Fourth Industrial Revolution, where the role of technologies and autonomous intelligence is expected to further impact upon human cognition and emotions. ICT enables SSEOEs to scale up and to re-image new modalities of organizing collaboration, and may also affect the manifestation of the SSE principles of solidarity, fair benefit sharing and democratic decision-making.

33.2 THE ROLE OF SSEOES IN DEVELOPING AND PRODUCING ICT

SSE principles and values have been applied to the development and production of ICT since the 1980s; a decade that was characterized by important breakthroughs which set the path for the widespread adoption of digital information and communication technology. Whereas SSEOEs play a relatively significant role in the development of software and provision of ICT services, hardware production is mostly dominated by for-profit private sector businesses. It may be due to the high entry barrier of capital requirement which SSEOEs have more difficulty in meeting. The following three subsections describe these trends.

From Free Software to the Digital Commons

A large part of software was developed in universities and corporate research centres in the 1960s and early 1970s. In these places, an academic culture of knowledge sharing was prevalent, and developers with research funding did not face the immediate pressure for cost recovery or return on investment. As commercial distribution of proprietary software increasingly came to dominate the software industry, ideals of sharing and collaboration also became less prevalent and intellectual property rights became more vigorously defended.

In 1983, Richard Stallman founded the free software movement which later became institutionalized as the Free Software Foundation (FSF). The declared mission of this non-profit organization is to 'promote user freedom' and to 'defend the rights of all software users' by advocating for and developing 'free software' (Free Software Foundation 2019). FSF formulated a set of 'four essential freedoms' which software developers must grant to users before being qualified as 'free' (not necessarily being free of charge):

1. The freedom to run a program as a user wishes, for any purpose;
2. The freedom to study how the program works and change it so it does the computing as the user wishes …
3. The freedom to redistribute copies so the user can help others;
4. The freedom to distribute copies of the modified versions to others [and to] give the whole community a chance to benefit from one's changes. (Free Software Foundation 2021)

Putting users and their interests first, together with a broader social objective beyond its own operational reach, reveals a resemblance with the principles and values of SSE. Stallman writes that '[these freedoms] are essential, not just for the individual user's sake, but because they promote social solidarity – that is, sharing and cooperation' (Stallman 2009, 31). FSF is also the main sponsor of the GNU project, which maintains a free operating system (GNU/Linux) and an extensive collection of free software packages. Another important aspect of free software is that 'free' does not prohibit commercial use or paid professional support, which the Foundation considers fundamental to achieve its aims (Free Software Foundation 2019). The free software movement can therefore be counted as an innovative interpretation of SSE principles in ICT development.

GNU/Linux (General Public License) marked the beginning of a widening community of developers who were convinced of the benefits of sharing source codes to enable collaborative improvement. But not all of them may have been just as convinced of the 'ethical imperative' to maintain and defend users' freedom against the growing dominance of proprietary software, as promulgated by free software advocates (Stallman 2009).

In 1998, some of them became engaged in creating the Open Source Initiative (OSI) and open source label. Its founders were mainly convinced by the practical benefits of sharing source codes and improving them by engaging the developer community. Instead of insisting on a commitment to the idea that all developers should uphold users' freedoms, like the FSF, the OSI founders also cherished the 'pragmatic, business-case' approach for writing open source software, and decided to create a label and position it in clear distinction to the 'philosophically- and politically-focused' free software label and movement (Open Source Initiative 2021).

Besides these ideological and strategic differences, however, the OSI's definition of open source does not contradict the four freedoms per se. Stallman (2009, 31) himself acknowledges that 'nearly all open source software is free software', although they 'stand for views based on fundamentally different values'. Similarly, FSF's free software licence GNU is listed as one of the most popular open source licences on the OSI's website, together with others that comply with the open source definition (Open Source Initiative 2021). Both open source and free software are also often associated with the 'copy left' concept and movement, which further encompasses licences that apply the conditions to other works, including writing, photography, art and scientific discoveries. Notable examples include the Mozilla Public Licence, and the Creative Commons licence.

Similar to FSF's and OSI's approach, the Creative Commons licence is based on the idea of collaboration as a source of creativity and innovation, and therefore waives a limited set of rights to any recipient or creator who wants to use the protected content for private or other creative purposes, provided that authors be attributed, and the resulting work will also enter the 'creative commons'. Creative Commons has become the most widely applied licence in the realm of ICT-based content and services. The most notable platforms using the licence are Wikipedia and the online photo sharing service Flickr.

The use of the notion of 'commons' emphasizes the nature of information and other content covered by the licence as a type of common-pool resource accessible to all members of society (see entry 13, 'The Commons'). A similar extension of the information and knowledge was later formulated by Hess and Ostrom (2006), observing the similarities between natural commons and 'social commons' which are established and maintained through the voluntary contributions of individuals and groups. Yochai Benkler of Harvard University employs the term prominently to 'commons-based peer production' as a 'socio-economic system of production that is emerging in the digitally networked environment' (Benkler and Nissenbaum 2006, 394). In 2010, Mayo Fuster Morell further applied the concept to online creation communities as a form of collective action to create and govern the 'digital commons' (Fuster Morell 2010). By extending the option of collective action from the natural commons, these authors suggest that governance arrangements can be found that may outperform market or hierarchies in managing software and other (ICT-based) content. While a general discussion on the overlap of the commons and SSE is provided elsewhere in this *Encyclopedia* (see entry 13, 'The Commons'), some writings explicitly suggest to make the connection between open source, digital commons and other related movements on the one hand, and SSE principles and values on the other. For instance, it is suggested that maintaining democratic principles in such communities is both possible and desirable. Development and application of a framework to assess the democratic quality of online platforms in general is also taking place, highlighting the role of platform cooperatives and other forms of SSE units creating and using digital content (Fuster Morell and Espelt 2018). Platform 'commoning' has also been described as a new way to build and support SSE using commons-based pool production (Ridley-Duff and Bull 2021).

SSEOEs Providing ICT Services

SSEOEs and their practices can also be found in the ICT service sector which encompasses activities such as creation and maintenance of information technology (IT) infrastructure (websites, databanks, and so on) and similar services. Examples of SSE providers of ICT services operate while observing SSE principles such as democratic self-management of workers or users, and often demonstrate a commitment to values associated with cooperation and openness which may also be expressed through the use and active promotion of open source or free software in their work. Two organisations that provide ICT-related services and are organised along SSE principles, Koumbit and Enspiral, will be briefly profiled here to illustrate the spectrum of actors.

Koumbit is a member-based not-for-profit organization based in Montreal whose primary activity is providing web services, including designing, developing and hosting websites. The individuals and organizations who become members of Koumbit must subscribe to a set of values which centre on non-hierarchical self-management by the workers, a commitment to open formats and free software, and solidarity (Koumbit 2022). Around 20 worker-members belong to the Conseil de Travail (Council of Workers), where important decisions are made. In addition, issues that affect only some workers are dealt with in committees or teams, as is the case in many cooperatives (Koumbit 2022).

Enspiral, in contrast, is a more community-oriented cooperative organised around the principles of cooperatives and SSE networks. Enspiral is attempting systemic changes at a meta-level by facilitating an 'ecosystem of purpose'. The organisation consists of full- and part-time members who work on joint projects but can also work on projects separate from Enspiral. The Enspiral Network was founded in 2010 in Wellington, New Zealand, as a collective of individuals doing contract work together, excited by the possibility of creating something more. The Enspiral Network now includes over 28 members and 124 contributors working on IT consulting projects for government, business or community organizations. Among the different modes by which people interact at Enspiral are 'stewards', or support pairs, and 'pods', which are any small group of people meeting in person or virtually generally around a common goal or discussion theme. Most of the internal work takes place through formal and informal working groups. Enspiral members share work (projects) and cherish ongoing learning opportunities (retreats) (Bevensee and Buck 2020).

Challenging Market Entry for SSEOEs Producing ICT Hardware

As for the industry sector overall, the SSEOEs occupy only a marginal presence in the production of ICT hardware, mainly comprising components for telecommunications infrastructure, as well as computers, (smart)phones, servers and other devices. In 2019, for instance, out of the 300 largest cooperatives by turnover in US dollars, only three were active in the industry sector (four if turnover is divided by GDP per capita) (EURICSE and ICA 2021). Several characteristics of the production for industrial goods, including ICT hardware, make it relatively difficult for SSEOEs to enter these markets. Particularly, the high capital intensity of machinery required for serial production of high-technology components poses an issue for entities which depend greatly on member contributions and revenue. As 'employment-oriented' organizations they further put particular emphasis on the value and rights of workers, and often face difficulties in attracting financial capital due to their democratic governance structure and limited profit distribution (Fonteneau and Pollet 2019).

However, there are a few examples of SSEOEs that participate in the industrial production of ICT hardware. One of these exceptions is the Basque worker cooperative federation Mondragon Corporation. With more than 81 000 employees and a global turnover of US$13.7 billion in 2019, it is by far the largest SSE organization in the industry and utilities sector, and the 37th largest cooperative in the world. Established in 1956 as a manufacturer of paraffin heaters, it has evolved into a multinational SSE organization active in banking, insurance, a wide variety of industry goods and services, retail (including supermarkets, petrol stations, travel agencies, and more), as well as knowledge-related activities combining education, training and innovation. From the universe of worker cooperatives that are part of Mondragon, two organizations stand out as producers of ITC-based goods and services. Mondragon Sistemas (MSI Grupo) is a group of SSE organizations specialized in the digitalization of production processes. Another SSE organization, Mondragon Telecommunications, provided telecommunication engineering services, but was dissolved in 2016.

Another company that embraces SSE principles and values in the production of ICT hardware industry is Fairphone, founded in the Netherlands. Launched in 2010 as an awareness-raising campaign about conflict materials such as cobalt, which are essential ingredients for smartphone components, the founders registered as a company in 2013 with a commitment to contribute to a 'fairer electronics industry' enshrined in the by-laws. Fairphone produces smartphones with extended longevity by making all components replaceable and easy to repair for standard users, continued software updates and long-term support. These product design features and related business practices are in stark contrast to other phone manufacturers or brands that prioritize profit over users' interests and the environment, by stimulating unsustainable consumption, short product life span and waste. These brands require users to buy a whole new phone when only parts (such as the battery or display) need to be replaced, or make it so difficult to repair that it becomes an expensive expert's job. Fairphone also demonstrates the 'SSE difference' through its organizational culture and participation of its workforce and stakeholders in decision-making, which are institutionalized in an elected governing body, a Workers Council, and ongoing communication on pay and satisfaction with in-house as well as supplier employees (Quiroz-Niño 2019).

33.3 SSEOES AS USERS AND OPERATORS OF ICT

Besides the production of ICT-related goods and services, SSEOEs are also users and operators of these technologies, as will be described in this section. As users, SSEOEs employ ICT software and hardware and consume services just like other organizations, to manage operational processes of delivering goods and services for efficiency and productivity gains. Examples include the use of ICT for farm management and advisory services (Rijswijk et al. 2019), and the use of web platforms to improve community-based healthcare provided by cooperatives (Biehl et al. 2021). They may also benefit from ICT solutions to organize internal governance, such as by using online voting in assemblies. Other SSEOEs, particularly social enterprises and foundations that are not member-based but statutorily bound to pursue social and/or environmental goals, may use ICT to contribute to their mission. They are also considered part of this ecosystem and need to think through their ICT strategy in order to scale up their socio-economic impact.

They can be qualified as operators when deploying ICT as a core element of their business activities to provide services to their customers, members or beneficiaries. SSEOEs worldwide, to varying degrees, have adopted ICT to manage their core operations in line with SSE principles and values. Others have created whole new SSEOEs as alternatives to existing online services in sectors dominated by shareholder-owned businesses. ICT operators in the SSE sector that are owned and controlled by users tend to leverage this role to strengthen users' rights and autonomy as they interact with other actors in an online platform or marketplace to earn their income, order goods and services, and engage with other governments and society at large (Brülisauer et al. 2020).

Platform Cooperatives and Other User-Centred Applications

Many sectors face major disruptions and severe challenges to their business models due to the emergence of online platforms as direct, highly automated intermediaries between providers and consumers of goods and services. Key sectors where such business models are taking hold are transport, including the delivery of food and other goods; tourism, particularly short-term rentals; and other forms of service provision, including domestic and care services, but also programming, translation, learning activities and creative work where the provision of services takes place online and contracts tend to be transactional and time-constrained. The wide variety of messenger apps, social media platforms and other communication and content sharing applications at their core complete the picture of the expansion of the 'platform economy'.

In many sectors affected by platform-caused disruptions, the SSE sector has developed alternatives within the platform economy by deploying ICT to control and operate the platform based on democratic governance and co-ownership of assets by the users themselves. As in the non-digital world, SSE platforms enable different user groups, including workers, producers, consumers, internet users and communities (for example, of residents), to gain control over the data and economic transactions in which they are engaged.

'Platform cooperatives', a term coined and promoted by Trebor Scholz, Nathan Schneider and colleagues at the Platform Cooperative Consortium, are a core component of this movement (Scholz and Schneider 2017). It comprises organizations that leverage the cooperative principles to provide services over online platforms in a wide range of sectors and activities. The underlying premise is to use the platform as an enabling tool to pivot away from a super-extractive labour practice exhibited by the likes of Uber, and to exert more influence in the gig economy so that workers could also enjoy a decent wage and a fair share of the benefits.

Examples and proposals are increasing in this ecosystem, especially in the sectors that have been most affected by the COVID-19 pandemic, such as in the ride-hailing sector. Cooperatives such as the Drivers Cooperative, Taxiapp, Green Taxi Cooperative, and so on, have started up and are growing. New funding schemes are also emerging to help finance the development of such drivers' cooperatives (Wefunder 2022).

Other economic sectors are also showing signs of emerging platform-based SSE and cooperatives. Smartcoop, for example, is an intermediary service provider that connects across Europe to support workers, entrepreneurs and organisations to invoice, to work together with other professionals, and to manage a budget on an occasional or a long-term basis. Through a hub and spoke design it is presented in nine European countries and connects 35 000 members (Smart 2022).

33.4 THREATS AND OPPORTUNITIES OF THE ICT ECONOMY FOR SSEOES

Promoting SSEOEs in the ICT industry is not without its challenges. For instance, due to the small size of SSEOE producers of ICT products (mostly intermediary goods or small market-size software consulting), these SSEOEs are in a weak position when competing with the dominant for-profit ICT enterprises over access to market opportunities. Sometimes they cannot survive in the market.

Making partnerships or alliances among ICT-producing SSEOEs, to join forces and to produce ICT goods and services through collaborative efforts while maintaining autonomy, is a strategy to address various problems associated with the small scale of SSEOEs, such as purchase, sales, and research and development. Such a strategy would help SSEOEs to have more bargaining power, obtain lower sales prices from the ICT transnational corporations, and possibly make agreements to produce intermediary ICT goods and services resulting in technology transfers, without falling into the trap of monopsony-related unfair business conditions.

Lack of financial resources undermines the potential of SSEOEs to increase productive capacity and diversify these products. Small SSEOEs have difficulties in achieving economies of scale (which would have a cost advantage that arises when there is a higher level of production for one good) and economies of scope (which has lower average costs because costs are spread over a variety of products). Without both, business entities in general will not gain sufficient market size as producers of ICT products and services.

The case of Loconomics, a former SSE platform, is illustrative. Loconomics was a sharing economy platform start-up that offered shared services to freelancers. Having started as a traditional platform company, Loconomics transformed its Articles of Incorporation and became a worker-owned cooperative. For its socially oriented business model, it became a well-publicised case study and received broad academic and media attention interested in platform cooperativism since its founding in 2014. Yet, such reputational gains were never translated into sufficient funding or users to scale. In 2020, after six years of bootstrapping and product campaigning, Loconomics was closed. The case of Loconomics shows that without a sound capitalization strategy, SSEOEs cannot gain and maintain adequate size of production and large client networks, and the chances of small ICT SSEOEs surviving the start-up stage of their business ventures may be slim.

CONCLUSION

The ICT field is characterized by rapid changes of products and services. Innovation is a key ingredient for successful entry and survival in the ICT business. SSEOEs need to find a balance between cherishing and preserving SSE values while at the same time exploring ways to foster innovation within their organisations. The example of Enspiral described above offers a way to strike this balance, which allows experimenting, sharing and collaboration without losing SSE values and principles.

SSEOEs interested or already operating in the ICT industry should consider partnerships or alliances to share financial resources, or rely on alternative funding mechanisms that could be used to fund SSEOE start-ups and pay a premium for its people-centred and socially oriented economic principles. This means more financial SSE intermediaries, jointly owned, which could offer alternative financing other than being dependent on private sector banking or venture capital are needed (see entry 28, 'Finance Sector' and entry 45, 'Financing'). SSEOEs could also create joint ventures with private sector companies in the ICT sector, as long as the agreements with private sector companies guarantee the autonomy of SSEOEs, and prevent them from being drawn into a rat race of continuously increased pressures for efficiency gains which would make it difficult to keep the spirit of SSE alive.

The fundamental question for SSEOEs in ICT, therefore, is how to strengthen the ability of SSEOEs to avoid losing the SSE spirit of joint ownership and democratic forms of governance while at the same time engaging in more risk-taking entrepreneurial initiatives needed to enter the ICT world of producing goods and services.

REFERENCES

Benkler, Yochai, and Helen Nissenbaum. 2006. 'Commons-Based Peer Production and Virtue.' *Journal of Political Philosophy* 14 (4): 394–419. https://doi.org/10.1111/j.1467-9760.2006.00235.x.

Bevensee, Emma, and Emma Buck. 2020. 'A Supportive Backdrop and a Warm Embrace: An Impact Report of the Enspiral Network.' Wellington: Enspiral & Rebellious Data. https://emmibevensee.com/wp-content/uploads/2020/01/Enspiral-external-report-FINAL.pdf.

Biehl, Verena, Heidrun Becker, Alenka Ogrin, Alenka Reissner, Johannes Burger and Andrea Glaessel. 2021. 'User-Centered Development of a Web Platform Supporting Community-Based Health Care Organizations for Older Persons in Need of Support: Qualitative Focus Group Study.' *Journal of Medical Internet Research* 23 (3): e24006. https://doi.org/10.2196/24006.

Brülisauer, Samuel, Anastasia Costantini and Gianluca Pastorelli. 2020. 'The Digital Social Economy: Managing and Leveraging Platforms and Blockchain for a People-Centred Digital Transformation.' CIRIEC Working Paper 2020–11. Liège: CIRIEC. https://www.ciriec.uliege.be/wp-content/uploads/2020/10/WP2020-11.pdf.

Bukht, R., and Heeks, R. (2017). Defining, Conceptualising and Measuring the Digital Economy. (GDI Development Informatics Working Papers; No. 68). University of Manchester, Global Development Institute 1–24. http://hummedia.manchester.ac.uk/institutes/gdi/publications/workingpapers/di/di_wp68.pdf

EURICSE and ICA. 2021. 'World Cooperative Monitor 2021.' EURICSE and ICA. Brussels: International Cooperative Alliance. https://monitor.coop/sites/default/files/2021-11/WCM_2021%20spread%20FINAL.pdf.

Fonteneau, Bénédicte, and Ignace Pollet, eds. 2019. *The Contribution of the Social and Solidarity Economy and Social Finance to the Future of Work.* Geneva: International Labour Organization. 2019. https://www.ilo.org/wcmsp5/groups/public/---ed_emp/documents/publication/wcms_739377.pdf.

Free Software Foundation. 2019. 'About.' https://www.fsf.org/about/.

Free Software Foundation. 2021. 'What Is Free Software?' GNU Project. https://www.gnu.org/philosophy/free-sw.html#four-freedoms.

Fuster Morell, Mayo. 2010. 'Governance of Online Creation Communities: Provision of Infrastructure for the Building of Digital Commons.' CADMUS. https://cadmus.eui.eu//handle/1814/14709.

Fuster Morell, Mayo, and Ricard Espelt. 2018. 'A Framework for Assessing Democratic Qualities in Collaborative Economy Platforms: Analysis of 10 Cases in Barcelona.' *Urban Science* 2 (3): 61. https://doi.org/10.3390/urbansci2030061.

Gurumurthy, Anita, Nandini Chami and Deepti Bhartur. 2021. 'Platform Labour in Search of Value: A Study of Workers' Organizing Practices and Business Models in the Digital Economy.' Geneva: International Labour Organization. https://www.ilo.org/wcmsp5/groups/public/---ed_emp/---emp_ent/---coop/documents/publication/wcms_809250.pdf.

Hess, Charlotte, and Elinor Ostrom, eds. 2006. *Understanding Knowledge as a Commons: From Theory to Practice*. Cambridge, MA: MIT Press.

Huawei and Oxford Economics. 2017. 'Digital Spillover.' Huawei Technologies. https://www.huawei.com/minisite/gci/en/digital-spillover/files/gci_digital_spillover.pdf.

Koumbit. 2022. 'Self-Management.' https://www.koumbit.org/en/content/self-management.

Malmodin, Jens, and Dag Lundén. 2018. 'The Energy and Carbon Footprint of the Global ICT and E&M Sectors 2010–2015.' *Sustainability* 10 (9). https://doi.org/10.3390/su10093027.

Open Source Initiative. 2021. 'History of the OSI.' https://opensource.org/history.

Quiroz-Niño, Catalina. 2019. 'Participatory Decision-Making Processes within a Mobile Communication Social Enterprise and SDG 16.' Geneva: UN Inter-Agency Task Force on Social and Solidarity Economy (UNTFSSE). https://knowledgehub.unsse.org/knowledge-hub/participatory-decision-making-processes-within-a-mobile-communication-social-enterprise-and-sdg-16/.

Ridley-Duff, Rory, and Mike Bull. 2021. 'Common Pool Resource Institutions: The Rise of Internet Platforms in the Social Solidarity Economy.' *Business Strategy and the Environment* 30 (3): 1436–53. https://doi.org/10.1002/bse.2707.

Rijswijk, Kelly, Laurens Klerkx and James A. Turner. 2019. 'Digitalisation in the New Zealand Agricultural Knowledge and Innovation System: Initial Understandings and Emerging Organisational Responses to Digital Agriculture.' *NJAS – Wageningen Journal of Life Sciences* 90–91 (December): 1–14. https://doi.org/10.1016/j.njas.2019.100313.

Scholz, Trebor, and Nathan Schneider, eds. 2017. *Ours to Hack and to Own: The Rise of Platform Cooperativism, A New Vision for the Future of Work and a Fairer Internet*. New York, USA and London, UK: OR Books.

Smart (n.d.). 'Smart Coop'. http://smart.coop

Stallman, Richard. 2009. 'Viewpoint: Why "Open Source" Misses the Point of Free Software.' *Communications of the ACM* 52 (6): 31–3. https://doi.org/10.1145/1516046.1516058.

Wefunder. 2022. 'Invest in Startups You Love | Wefunder, Home of the Community Round.' Wefunder.com. 28 November 2022. https://wefunder.com/home.

34. Local community development
Luis Razeto Migliaro

34.1 THE IDEA OF LOCAL COMMUNITY DEVELOPMENT (LCD)

The idea of local community development (LCD) which is integral to human development was first formulated by the French economist and priest Louis-Joseph Lebret (Lebret 1966). In his book *Dinámica Concreta del Desarrollo* (*Concrete Development Dynamics*), Lebret defined LCD as a set of coordinated and harmonic activities that allow a population or community in a given area to transition from a less humane to a more humane life phase. LCD is evaluated or measured by the intensity and rhythm of the change; the percentage of the population that participates in and benefits from the process; the degree of solidarity and cooperation experienced among the participants; and the authenticity of the human and social values that are achieved.

According to Lebret, the economic effort of this development is oriented towards the following objectives, ordered according to importance: (1) the production and distribution of the 'necessary goods' for a dignified life for all members of the community; (2) the facilitation of people's access to 'improvement goods', which will allow them to attain higher intellectual, cultural and spiritual value; (3) production of the 'comfort goods' or 'facility'.

It is notable that making efforts to produce or obtain the 'comfort goods' or 'facility' whose utility is not disdained, but whose excessive use may dehumanize personal and community life is only in third place in the order of objectives.

LCD requires, and at the same time foments, the formation of economic, social and cultural links that generate or reinforce local identity. This local identity provides people, families and organizations with a sense of belonging to an active, organized and integrated collectivity. With this collectivity, people, families and organizations act with solidarity and assist each other. In this sense, LCD coincides and converges with the objectives of the social and solidarity economy (SSE). If development is understood as expansion, perfection and transformation of the economy in a given social, ecological and environmental system, we can say that LCD and the SSE share objectives contributing to development in the social, ecological and environmental subsystem of a given locality or territory.

34.2 AGENTS FOR LOCAL ECONOMIC DEVELOPMENT AND THE SSE

The concept and theory of the SSE arise from the experience and knowledge of a number of very diverse small and medium-sized economic organizations formed from different kinds of links: of family, of the neighbourhood, of community, of cooperation, of reciprocity, of mutual aid. The study of such experiences identifies the existence of a distinctive economic rationality, which is distinguished from that of other economic forms. Central to this economic rationality is the active presence of solidarity in the organization and processes of production, distribution, consumption and accumulation. This is why it was given the name 'solidarity economy'.

This special rationality of the SSE determines a way of growing, perfecting and transforming the economy which is manifested in the LCD processes. Thus it is important to understand the properties of this solidarity rationality, which integrates the economic, social-political and cognitive-cultural dimensions of life. Simplifying the expression, it is termed 'social, economic and cultural solidarity'.

A 'rationality' is not an abstract form that acquires reality when 'applied' to organizations and processes. On the contrary, it is the set of objectives and motivations of those who are protagonists of certain experiences and ways to do economy, and the methods and modes of action and interaction with which they try to fulfil them, that generate a social-economic and cultural rationality. This explains the importance of making explicit the set of motivations that promote the actors or protagonists, that is, the people who make the SSE. There are diverse agents with various motives, but their motives converge. They are:

1. Poor people with experiences of popular economy who display activities and construct economic organizations to subsist and meet their necessities.
2. People and associations that look for alternatives to the capitalist and statist economic methods because they have understood the magnitude of the injustices, inequalities and problems of contemporary economics, politics and culture.
3. People and organizations seeking to renovate the ways of cooperation and self-management, trying to reach higher levels of efficiency in a more demanding economic, political and technological context that require more knowledge, creativity, autonomy and solidarity.
4. People and groups that become aware of the gravity of the environmental, ecological and human problems that have produced the unsustainability of the current mode of development, and consequently consider the need for 'another development' with emphasis on the local, in exploiting non-conventional resources and energy, and in self-support.
5. People and groups with cultural and social tendencies to create and disseminate new ways of working, distribution and consumption in community and service ambits, in which they express the aspiration of many Christians, Muslims, Jews, Buddhists, Hindus and humanists to live in greater coherence with the ethics and spirituality that encourage them.

These different agents, including people, groups, associations and organizations, meet with each other where they live. They meet and recognize each other, share their concerns and projects, discover the unity of their objectives and the possibility of collaborating with the resources and capacities that they all have to some degree. Thus they reinforce the organizational and community links of those who live in the same area and the initiatives that are produced to generate LCD with this social-economic and cultural rationality that they share.

34.3 RATIONALITY OF THE SSE AND LCD

The special rationality of the SSE, and of LCD, is manifested in the objectives and interests of the organizations, in the ways their members relate, in the circuits of distribution and assignment of the resources they generate, in the ownership properties they adopt, and in the relations they establish with the market, the state and local institutions. The manifestation of this rationality can be identified synthetically and schematically as follows:

- Confronting in an integrated manner a set of human, individual and societal needs; and needs of physiological subsistence, coexistence and relation with others, capacitation and cultural development, personal growth and social identity, autonomy and critical integration with society. Participation is central to this process. Participation in this process implies not only working, producing, selling and buying, but also a way of life, a complex social and group practice that tends to be integral, and 'life strategies' beyond 'subsistence strategies'.
- Establishing a close link between production, distribution and consumption. There is some division of labour, and there are commercial relations with others and monetary distribution processes in an SSE, but in their relations in their own organization and with other similar organizations they share and cooperate so that monetary mediations between production and consumption are less important. Not every job has a price or remuneration. Besides, what each receives does not always correspond to a contribution of equivalent value. The proximity of production, distribution and consumption requires establishing personal connections, which implies an emphasis on family, neighbour and territorial relations.
- Using preferably local or nearby resources and production factors, or those from their own solidarity sector, if possible favouring the poorest and small economic units instead of supplies from larger, rich and distant economies. Also, produce preferably for one's own locality, orienting production to satisfy the needs, aspirations and desires of the local community. This does not preclude using resources from other sectors or from outside the local territory, or from producing for the general local and export market, the latter especially when there is not sufficient local demand. Essential is a preference for the small and local, which is amplified in concentric circles of circuits of production and distribution.
- Operating with a qualitative and subjective concept of efficiency. The relation between objectives and methods, between costs and benefits, transcends a strictly quantitative calculation. Objectives and methods are highly intertwined, thus fulfilling an objective itself is a method to achieve another objective. For example, satisfying certain basic needs is a method to satisfy relational and coexistence needs and vice versa. Work and the community use of time may be both a cost and the achievement of certain objectives. Thus it is not always possible to measure efficiency quantitatively, because costs and benefits may not have a monetary expression or be completely separable.

SSE organizations and enterprises (SSEOEs) offer their members a set of extra-economic benefits and satisfactions that are added to the account or total value increase that each member makes. To measure the product generated by SSEOEs, it should be considered that both the physical production and a set of services, if they had not been generated in the organization, would have had to be acquired in the market.

The operation also implies a set of important savings: collective management based on traditional knowledge and customs, reduction of the costs of information and communication, self-control of the work, a number of free benefits, using partial, discontinuous and secondary labour not used in other kinds of businesses, the contribution of social creativity, using low-cost means of work, and so on, which are a set of aspects that allow SSEOEs to operate with low costs.

- Preferring family and community consumption over individual and mass consumption. It can be found in sharing goods and services within family and community, in particular when these goods and services are available and better satisfy the personal and community needs.

An important aspect of the rationality of these organizations linked to consumption is their method of accumulation. To the extent that these economic units establish market relations with others, they have the possibility of accumulating unconsumed surplus, forming a reserve capital and making productive investments in their own organization. However, the main type of accumulation is in the development of values, capacities and creative energy by those who participate in them. We may say that these organizations seek to assure the future not only by possessing material activities, but especially by cultivating the richness of social relations, and by potentiating the capacities and human resources that once acquired will always be available to confront growing, recurrent and new necessities.

In these elements constituting solidarity rationality is a special economic factor operating in the SSE and LCD. It can be called factor C (community), which is added to the conventional factors K (capital) and L (work). This factor is the presence of special community elements and solidarity values which are expressed in different ways: cooperation in work, shared use of knowledge and information, participative decision-making, social integration of different functional groups, activities of coexistence and participation, fair and solidarity-based distribution of the benefits, and so on.

By being present within the economic and social units, factor C achieves tangible positive effects, a reduction in costs or additional benefits that are added to the results of the economic operation. In other words, factor C means that the formation of a group, association or community, or the presence of integrative links and solidarity values in the companies, provides a set of benefits to each member, and better yield and efficiency to the whole economic unit, due to a combination of economies of scale, economic benefits of association and positive externalities.

34.4 POTENTIALS OF THE SSE AND LCD

What has been indicated so far about the SSE and LCD must be understood as a theoretical expression of behavioural tendencies, and not necessarily as an exact description of what really happens. Intermediating between 'what is' and 'what should be', the theoretical formulation of rationality identifies the potentials not fully realized but already present to some degree.

Study of the different forms of popular economic, cooperative and solidarity organizations has shown that:

1. The economic experiences that arise from the people and their communities carry this solidarity rationality in a way that we may consider germinal or embryonic, in the sense that they have not always been displayed in all their dimensions and aspects.

2. These inherent forms of doing economy are viable both at the subsistence level and in a perspective of growth and development, and contain potentials that can greatly transcend those which have so far been their practical manifestations.
3. The viability and possibility of development increase as the solidarity economic units and their members organize and act with more coherence in relation to this social-economic and cultural rationality of which they are budding carriers. A decisive aspect of the potential growth of the SSE is given by the degree of identification of its members with the ideals and values that characterize them, and with the kind of social utopia to which they are oriented. This identification may occur both at the level of discourse expressed as the experiences lived – that is, as a self-conscious reflection – and as concrete social practices.
4. The SSE and LCD are neither the only nor the most decisive factor for the social-economic and cultural development of a society. Socio-economic and cultural development is a process that involves the entire society, and in which there is the active participation of the market with its variety of companies, intermediaries and consumers, and the state with its institutions, rules and organizing activity. Three sectors may be distinguished in the economy: the market capitalist economy, the state economy and the SSE. Each is observed to have special advantages according to the ambits or territorial spaces in which there is human interaction.

The main agent of international development, which articulates production, commerce, finances, transport and world economic flow, is the capitalist market. The main agent that regulates and coordinates the development and economic interactions in each country is the state. The main agent of local development, which expresses social-economic coexistence in a town, neighbourhood or small locality, is the SSE. It is important to comprehend that these three modes of production, distribution, consumption and accumulation give rise to different ways of 'city-building'. This theme deserves special consideration due to its close connection with LCD.

34.5 THE SSE AND THE COMMUNITY RELATIONS IN LARGE CITIES

The morphology of modern large cities does not favour community relations. Cohabiting reduced spaces, multitudes of anonymous individuals remain in their reciprocal exteriority, showing themselves to others as competition and even potential threats, due to which precautions must be taken to guarantee their personal and property security. Contemporary metropolises have many problems (congestion, overcrowding, atmospheric contamination, personal insecurity, poverty, margination, insalubrity, and so on), which demonstrate how inadequate the current economy is for the needs and quality of life of people.

Cities do not have to be like this. A city is a social product: the historical result of the actions of persons and groups that define their way of inhabiting and living. Land occupation by different groups and social sectors, the location of infrastructure and urban equipment in the different city levels, the functional organization of the urban space are all the historical results of the organization and functioning of the economy, and reflect the rationalities that reign in the successive phases of the historical evolution. A city is constructed in different ways by the different economic sectors that develop in it, each influencing with its specific rationality according to the size and relative importance that each sector has reached.

The economic sector presided over by the state tends to occupy and structure the urban space hierarchically and according to the organization of the political power. The central government is established in the city centre, making evident the hierarchy of the executive, legislative and judicial powers. The different dependencies of public administration are built immediately around the political centre, also following a line of administrative hierarchy which is seen in the architectural forms of the buildings which house their services. The other administrative organs, with their communal structure and decentralized services, show a similar hierarchy of political power in the city. When the construction of residential neighbourhoods for the population is planned and organized by the state, they are usually monotonic populations of houses homogeneous in design, size and form, with a square arrangement of streets and plazas, transport, infrastructure and services.

The capitalist economic sector builds cities with the rationality of the market. The economic subjects compete with each other to occupy the spaces that offer better perspectives of profitability and capital gains due to their proximity to the centres of power, the capital market, the supply of commerce and consumption. Thus they constitute different industrial, commercial, residential, educational, recreational, and so on, zones corresponding to the financial capacity of the different social groups, from the most affluent in the highest and central positions, to the lowest in the periphery, producing a very evident differentiation in the quantity and quality of the infrastructure, buildings and equipment in the different sectors of a city, which is thus highly segmented.

The SSE sector constructs a city in accordance with its own special rationality. One of its features is the tendency to integrate economic, social, cultural, political and religious activities in complex organizations that aim to meet human needs in an integrated manner. The SSE sector does not favour the separation of spaces destined to different economic and social functions, but tends to re-integrate the activities of production, distribution and consumption in the urban spaces inhabited by the local communities. The productive activities of families and communities will intertwine with daily life and with the activities of work, commerce and consumption.

This is important from the perspective of development for several reasons. It means more intense and extended productive use of urban land. It largely influences the use of time, because it allows reducing the commute between work and home. From the perspective of social identity and work motivation, it avoids the feeling of marginalization and disengagement from companies which is generated when people live far away from the centres of productive activity. It may even produce a reduction in social conflict, if closeness generates sentiments of identity and internal cohesion of the human group, while distance produces feelings of alienation, separation and opposition.

Personal and community participation – which is strengthened by the SSEOEs – is manifested in the participation of the citizens in the planning, design and construction of the city in their neighbourhoods and in the design of their functional and symbolic elements (see entry 50, 'Partnership and Co-construction'). There are very interesting experiences of citizen participation in the elaboration of budgets in communities.

34.6 FINAL REMARKS

Finally, I illustrate some of the main contributions that SSE and LCD processes have made in the development, transformation and general improvement of society. One essential improvement is overcoming poverty. This is not conjunctional and transitory as are state subsidies, but structural and permanent, since it is accomplished by the deployment of the capabilities and resources of the same groups that confront problems of subsistence and marginalization.

It is worth noting that just the fact that thousands of families achieve subsistence from their previous marginal situation, and that they do so without having to use state assistance or submit to the conditions demanded by capital, is a formidable achievement in terms of creating the conditions or premises of self-sustainable and sustained development.

Another contribution of the SSE is in the use of the labour force. Less-skilled or less-productive workers may find work in solidarity organizations, the so-called secondary workforce, and partial or discontinuous jobs may be available that are unlikely to occur in other sectors of the economy.

The SSE and LCD activate creative, organizing and management capacities that are disseminated socially and have never been economically exploited. When they arise and display what could be called 'popular entrepreneurship' their contribution to development is notable, since the business factor is one of the most scarce and decisive sources.

They also favour integral human development. They satisfy physiological, self-preservation, spiritual and coexistence needs with organizations that tend to be integral, in the sense of combining strictly economic aspects with the social, cultural and political dimensions of individual and collective lives. When the economic units of the solidarity sector are more integral, they provide the participants with a superior degree of self-control with respect to their own living conditions.

Thus the SSE and LCD give rise to the constitution of new social subjects – associations, organizations, communities – as well as decreasing conflicts and providing better social integration. The expansion of the 'intermediate groups' produces new economic actors who may activate a large number of economic projects and activities; these intermediate actors are added to those usually recognized as the basic generators of economic initiatives: the individual and the state. Better social integration and decreasing conflict make it possible to create and liberate resources and capacities often inhibited by fear and distrust.

These socio-economic experiences manifest special preoccupation for the conservation and cultivation of nature, because of their specific rationality that orients them to use preferably local resources and provide the satisfaction of the needs of their community and immediate surroundings, instead of responding to more distant claimants of the goods and services they produce. Persons and human groups are especially interested in their immediate environment, in the surroundings with which they link and on which their life and progress are strictly dependent. Each human group or community tends to take responsibility for that portion of the earth, air and water which serves them vitally. Thus both the oldest and most traditional forms, as well as the new ones that compose this economic sector, tend to adapt to the microclimate and conserve the resources of the place.

If the discovery and empowerment of resources is a function of the existence of projects, the SSE and LCD are mobilizers of new resources, because they are inexhaustible sources of projects. They constitute a large, novel and creative project of transformation and human and social development, which due to the motivational force of their objectives is capable of identifying the means and resources necessary for their execution.

One important advantage of the SSE compared to other ways of doing economy is that those cultural and relational values which are not 'owned' in the way material goods are may nevertheless be possessed. The happiness of one is reinforced with that of the others; knowledge is developed as it communicates; the friendship of two or more persons grows only if it is reciprocal; the creativity of an individual is empowered in a culturally rich and creative social context; the degree of security of a person due to participation in an organized group is higher when the security of the other members of the group is higher; acting for the benefit of the others produces qualitatively superior personal satisfaction.

Another significant contribution of the SSE and LCD is that of knowledge and technology. While modern technology finds them in the knowledge possessed by scientists, engineers and specialist technologists, the popular and solidarity economy opens the immense and multifaceted field of knowledge disseminated socially and the popular creative spirit. This implies an almost infinite multiplication of the approaches and spaces of reality subject to useful knowledge. Everywhere there are realities whose knowledge allows hidden productive potentialities to surface; we can understand that nobody knows their immediate and particular reality better than those who live and experience it directly. From this, technologies arise adapted to the specific conditions in which they are to be used, understandable and acquirable (in the sense that they may be made 'their own') by many; different and alternative technologies than those which are usually used in capitalist companies.

The transmission and communication of knowledge may be done fluidly in an SSE, as a process of reciprocal learning, without interfering with the private forms of appropriation which give rise to 'technological secrets' which characterize the capitalist economic sector, and are an impediment to the necessary integration of knowledge into production.

REFERENCE

Lebret, Louis-Joseph. 1966. *Dinámica Concreta del Desarrollo*. Barcelona: Ediciones Herder.

35. Peace and non-violence
Smita Ramnarain

INTRODUCTION: THE SSE AS AN ALTERNATIVE PEACE PARADIGM

Since the 1990s, peace and peacebuilding as an active intervention in conflict-affected societies have been closely integrated with a liberal approach to state-building. The liberal (or neoliberal) peace model emphasizes good governance, law, democracy, development and constitution-building, based on the assumption that democracies tend to be more peaceful. As such, it advocates democratization and market integration as exemplary avenues for conflict resolution and peace (Duffield 2010; Murtagh 2016).

This model has come under scrutiny in recent times, as experiences in post-conflict settings have revealed its failures and omissions (see, e.g., Duffield 2010; Pugh 2006). Liberal peacebuilding is subordinated to top-down systems driven by the state or international donors, and largely devoid of local ownership. Peace projects conceived and implemented by external donors/organizations without local input or ownership have created undesirable outcomes, including disenfranchising local populations, sidelining traditional or indigenous practices, and exacerbating inequalities and resentment. Further, peace is defined narrowly as the absence of physical violence and subsumed under a securitized form of state-building. Finally, the liberal model of peacebuilding and reconstruction also comes under scrutiny for its continued espousal of neoliberal and macroeconomic adjustment policies – promoting austerity and the withdrawal of the state from the provision of basic services and social protection – and an emphasis on 'development as usual', provoking questions surrounding who benefits from the development and what is being 'reconstructed' (Pugh 2006; Ramnarain 2013).

Countering these failures of top-down, liberal approaches, diverse alternative approaches, ranging from critiques of peace conditionalities to hybrid forms of peacebuilding, community-based development (CBD) and social and solidarity economy (SSE) perspectives have emerged (Ramnarain 2013) (see also entry 16, 'Community-Based Organizations'). Notably, however, the hybrid peace and community-based peacebuilding and development models do not jettison the liberal rubric entirely, but rather make a case for the coexistence of its core norms – security and stabilization, reinforcing states, democratic governance, and marketization – alongside local agency and participatory methods. Therefore, in terms of articulating a transformative or radical alternative to existing peacebuilding paradigms, these frameworks are arguably insufficient. Using case studies from conflict-affected Burundi, Vervisch et al. (2013) argue that the CBD framework – with its overestimation of community homogeneity, translation of local participation into technocratic box-checking and tendency to elite-capture – can be entirely unsuitable for repairing trust and promoting social cohesion. Further, the nature of networks, type and effects of participation, and the kind of resources/goods distributed, play a critical role in determining the success of community-based peace interventions.

In contrast to hybrid peace or CBD frameworks, SSE offers what Murtagh (2016, 111) calls a 'critical political space' for resistance to the liberal peace model, and a more radical, transformative and emancipatory vision of peace and non-violence (see also entry 49, 'Participation, Governance, Collective Action and Democracy' and entry 1, 'Activism and Social Movements'). In addition to an emphasis on broad political engagement and participatory processes within the communities they are placed in, a key aspect of the SSE is that it offers the possibility of building alternative economics of peace from the ground up, providing a counterpoint to the neoliberal restructuring and austerity practices that generally characterize post-conflict macroeconomic policy and the liberal peace model.

The SSE is underpinned by the foundational principle that surplus arising from economic activity such as production, trade or distribution of goods and services is used for overall social benefit (as opposed to private profit) and that the tenets of redistribution, inclusion and equity govern its use (see entry 3, 'Contemporary Understandings'). The pursuit of community benefit may also include ancillary and non-economic objectives focused on the building of trust and solidarity, resilience, mutual assistance and reciprocal exchange, and community self-reliance. As such, SSE organizations and enterprises (SSEOEs) can play a critical economic role in addressing the economic exclusion, poverty and deprivation that characterize conflict-affected societies by challenging the economies that drive the perpetuation of violence, and by providing the political and the economic foundations for peace and justice.

35.1 THE SSE, PEACE AND NON-VIOLENCE

This entry examines three pragmatic contributions of SSEOEs, with respect to the pursuit of peace, justice and non-violence. These contributions include their roles within:

1. informal and 'everyday' peace and non-violence practices;
2. framing an alternative economic framework underpinning peace(building) and non-violence; and
3. fostering equitable participation in political processes, peace campaigns and solidarity movements.

In documenting these contributions, this entry draws on accounts from a variety of contexts, based on documented successes of the SSE in post-conflict contexts. While there are examples of SSEOEs developing useful interventions in many conflict-affected or fragile contexts, no systematic study of these exists. Neither is there a universal template for the evaluation of their potentially transformative or damaging effects. Equally, these examples pose questions and dilemmas for the contribution of the SSE to peace and non-violence, which are considered in the subsequent section.

35.2 THE SSE AND EVERYDAY/INFORMAL PEACE

The SSE serves as a critical locale for the performance of 'everyday' peace. Everyday peace consists of the methods and practices that individuals and groups may implement to navigate their lives in deeply divided societies, prone to direct violence as well as chronic or structural inequities (MacGinty 2014). In contrast to top-down, institutionalized and technocratic approaches to peace and peacebuilding – which may consist of programmes, projects and interventions designed by 'experts' to build peace, and which may render local actors passive – everyday peace focuses on how individuals and groups enact and perform peace as part of living. Some of these practices might simply include employing coping strategies and building resilience. Some forms of everyday peace may involve avoidance, 'ritualized politeness' or 'blame deferring', that is, practices that only permit a 'façade of normality' (MacGinty 2014, 555). But everyday peace can also be the starting point from which people and communities create dialogue surrounding the proximate sources of conflict and division, and collaborate towards finding solutions to common problems with indirect links to conflict. In their most ambitious form, everyday peace practices can be exercises in the 'pooling of micro-solidarities' (ibid.), subverting top-down liberal diplomacy discourses that are the exclusive preserve of the political elite or international donors, and become a conduit for new forms of contact between previously divided groups.

The SSE creates an arena where practices of everyday peace are intrinsic to the tackling of immediate issues around goods or service delivery. This is especially manifest in contexts where conflict has destroyed the mechanisms for their provision, or where neoliberal post-conflict restructuring has diminished capacities. Murtagh (2016) details an example from Northern Ireland where previously divided Catholic and Protestant communities established dialogue with respect to traffic and road safety measures on a major arterial road intersecting both communities, forming a social enterprise for the purpose (the Stewartstown Road Regeneration Project). This social enterprise went on to collaborate on an urban regeneration project that not only had a sizeable economic impact, but also led to a steep decline in violence and the transformation of attitudes toward the 'Other'. Murtagh (2016, 119) concludes that the generation of resources for the local economy by social enterprises enables a legitimate counter to 'sectarian, market, or neoliberal hegemonies'.

As such, in general, SSEOEs can play a critical role in creating informal channels of peacemaking and peacebuilding. In societies impacted upon by structural violence, discrimination and exploitation, the activities of cooperatives, trade unions and credit unions have served to bridge divides, unite groups in a common cause, and promote non-violence and peace. One example is that of the Self Employed Women's Association (SEWA) in Gujarat, India, which was founded in 1972 as a trade union based on the Gandhian principles of truth, non-violence and service. The trade union was initially formed in order to take up issues faced by self-employed women working in the informal sector, including home-based workers, traders, street vendors, service providers and construction workers. SEWA currently comprises a large number of cooperatives that organize women by profession, and are concerned with the provision of financial, health care and social security services for these women and their families. As such, SEWA brings together women from a variety of caste and religious backgrounds under the umbrella of its cooperatives, in a context where gender-based inequality and religious and/or caste divides are significant. Ramnarain (2011) discusses the ways in which cooperative membership has provided material resources and greater economic security to women, broadened their social and political awareness (against practices such as dowry, sexual harassment in the workplace and domestic violence), and built their capacities to translate that awareness into action, both in their daily lives and in their communities. Women interviewed in the study recognized the close relationship between peace and social justice, and the important role of the cooperative in pressing for greater equity, especially in cases of gender-based violence and harassment, and caste or religious discrimination. Similar examples emerge from a study of Ghana's 'market women', who were able to use their associations, networks and trading relations to bridge political, social and ethnic divides, promoting peace in their communities during and after ethnic clashes in 2012 (Bukari et al. 2021).

35.3 THE SSE AND AN ALTERNATIVE POLITICAL ECONOMY OF PEACE AND NON-VIOLENCE

The SSE provides an alternative economic paradigm for peace and peacebuilding. Material resources play a central role in conflicts and are integral to sustainable peace. The neoliberal macroeconomic restructuring that accompanies the liberal peace package is based on the assumption that policies which liberalize markets and globally orient an economy have the best chance of ensuring economic success, thus eliminating the rationale for conflict. Multiple commentators, however, have remarked on the counterintuitive nature of the neoliberal policy package in countries divided by conflict, structural violence and social exclusion, and its distinctly illiberal outcomes. New inequalities may be produced and old ethnic/class divisions may be inflamed, as social spending is curbed precisely when it is critical to the restoration of peace (Pugh 2006; Duffield 2010). Austerity policies, currency devaluation and the removal of food subsidies have, in several contexts, led to a rise in unemployment, social polarization and heightened tensions (see Ramnarain 2013 for examples).

SSEOEs can emerge as spaces for an alternative and radical political economy that challenges the liberal peace model, and its market- and profit-centric tenets. SSEOEs are typically characterized by the collective ownership of the means of production, cooperative forms of labour and the provision of employment as a social necessity, and/or the sharing of profits or the combined resources generated from group activities (see also entry 13, 'The Commons'). The ethos of the SSE – that of social benefit, equity and redistribution rather than the pursuit of profit – provides both a means of resistance to neoliberal ideals and a measure of protection in the face of rapid commodification of labour and resources resulting from neoliberal policies (see also Utting et al. 2014).

This is exemplified in the case of Nepal, which holds a long history of savings and credit cooperatives (SACCOs). The SACCOs provided a buffer for Nepal's member populations both during its decade-long Maoist conflict (1996–2006), as well as in the period after the conflict, through resource pooling and financial inclusion in an economy that depends significantly on remittances from migrant workers. Ramnarain (2013) details the ways in which SACCOs – especially women's SACCOs – were an integral component of members' livelihood strategies, assisting women and conflict-affected communities with the provision of credit services, livelihood programmes and training, and protection against abuse, persecution and violence during conflict. The SACCOs and other agricultural and workers' cooperatives were also platforms for local integration across caste and ethnic lines. It is worth noting that as a result of the reputation of cooperatives as institutions invested in the self-reliance, education and well-being of local communities, they were left unharmed during the violent anti-state conflict that saw several attacks on other kinds of state property.

Sentama (2009) provides examples of Rwanda's coffee cooperatives, which promoted reconciliation in the post-genocide period through a focus on poverty alleviation. Although they were started with economic motivations in mind, contact, communication, commonality of purpose and cooperation initiated progress towards the restoration of damaged interpersonal relationships. Sanchez Bajo (2019) expands on socio-economic development as a central aspect of the revitalization of Rwanda's cooperatives in the post-genocide period, ensuring greater food security domestically, and price stability for primary exports such as coffee and tea. The cooperatives ensured members' economic security by offering discounts on necessities and food to their members, the provision of credit, pooling logistics facilities such as transport fuel stations, paying members' health fees, and subsidizing equipment such as solar panels. Unlike the liberal model where peace is rendered subsidiary to economic restructuring, the SSE emphasizes the provision of these critical forms of material security as an integral component of peace and non-violence.

Neoliberal economic prescriptions for peace also tend to focus investments on programmes and infrastructure that purportedly enhance competitiveness and business innovation which, in turn, are assumed to create jobs and employment (Ramnarain 2013). Evidence indicates, however, that the SSE can play an equally significant role in generating gainful livelihood and employment opportunities at higher wages. Jaffe (2015) provides examples of worker cooperatives in New York City that have enabled its members to earn much more than the minimum wage. Similarly, worker-recuperated enterprises – defined as previously capitalist enterprises that were closed down by their owners, reclaimed by workers, and resumed under collective and democratic self-management – in many cases have prevented overall job loss, created labour sovereignty, and transformed the private property into 'collective property with a social purpose' (Azzellini 2018, 764). These accounts hold promise for the role played by the SSE in conflict- and crisis-affected societies in employment generation or revitalization, as also demonstrated in the cases of Ireland (economic regeneration through a collaborative enterprise by previously warring factions), Nepal (women's small enterprise enabled by SACCO loans) and Rwanda (coffee cooperatives bringing gainful employment to, and also reconciliation between, victims and former perpetrators of genocide).

An often neglected aspect of building sustainable peace, especially in the aftermath of conflict or crisis, is the gendered work of care provision. In conflict-affected societies and in crisis situations, the task of meeting essential material and care needs of households and communities tends to be disproportionately placed on women. The importance of unpaid work and social provisioning for the sustenance of communities is ignored in top-down approaches, which emphasize the value of paid work that occurs in markets through formal policies and schemes of job creation and employment generation. The SSE recognizes the diverse economic practices that make up the economy, including the interconnected activities of social provisioning that are essential for sustainable lives and livelihoods (Gibson-Graham 2006). For instance, besides providing financial services, other beneficial services within SACCOs in Nepal included: health camps for women and children to provide vaccination and health services in a time when the state was unable or unwilling to provide these services due to conflict; pooling of resources so that children could be sent to school; and informal pooling of childcare so that women could engage in livelihood-related activities (Ramnarain and Bergeron 2019). The SSE thus provides an alternative economic template that centralizes life-making in processes of economic recovery and sustainable peacebuilding.

35.4 THE SSE, EQUITY AND PARTICIPATION IN FORMAL POLITICAL PROCESSES AND CAMPAIGNS

Despite being a less popular strategy, SSEOEs can nevertheless play a crucial role in promoting peace through encouraging participation in formal political processes, in formal reconciliation or peacebuilding activities, and in campaigns for conflict resolution (see also entry 49, 'Participation, Governance, Collective Action and Democracy'). In particular, SSEOEs may act to represent groups that may not otherwise be represented in these exercises. If conflict and violence are exercises in perverse collective action, SSEOEs have played a countering role by restoring the inter-relationships that conflict may have eroded, and by providing local platforms for conflict resolution and peacebuilding. Indeed, the very functioning of SSEOEs in local communities depends upon consensus-building and conciliation practices.

As Nepal's violent conflict came to an end in 2006, and its transition to a democratic republic commenced, SACCOs played a key role in educating their members about the new Constitution, ensured women's full participation in the Constituent Assembly elections, and collected and delivered women's ideas and opinions on how the new Constitution might be more gender-equitable and inclusive. SACCOs thus contributed to creating the social infrastructure for participatory democracy in Nepal (Ramnarain 2013).

A *raison d'être* of SSE is movement-building and developing solidarity among workers and groups on the basis of common social and economic issues (see also entry 1, 'Activism and Social Movements'). SEWA, on multiple occasions, has mobilized street vendors against police persecution, and organized campaigns to influence municipal and national policies to better protect informal sector workers from everyday forms of violence. In the aftermath of the 2002 communal riots, SEWA ran rehabilitation and peacebuilding programmes, and SEWA members facilitated reconciliation dialogues in their communities (Ramnarain 2011).

Alvord et al. (2004) discuss the Highlander Research and Education Center in the United States, which focuses on educational interventions designed to empower local actors struggling against powerful adversaries such as mining corporations or white power structures by providing technical assistance and capacity-building for labour unions or civil rights movements. In Ghana, Bukari and Guuroh (2013) highlight the manner in which youth and women's community groups undertook a range of interventions to alleviate ethnic conflict and tensions, including peace education, arms control and mediation between groups in the aftermath of ethnic clashes.

The role of the SSE and collective action on the part of rural workers, demobilized combatants, small farmers and cooperatives to resist forces of decollectivization, marketization, privatization and economic liberalization in Nicaragua following the collapse of the Sandinista regime in 1990 is well documented by Utting et al. (2014). The issue of land redistribution was central to these struggles, and agricultural producers' organizations mobilized farmers into waves of protest and resistance in defence of their assets and livelihoods. It was the constant advocacy of the cooperative movement that led to further legislation supporting the cooperative sector in Nicaragua, thus enabling the successful participation of Nicaraguan coffee growers in the global fair-trade movement.

35.5 THE SSE, PEACE AND NON-VIOLENCE: KEY CHALLENGES

Experiences from diverse contexts demonstrate that the SSE and SSEOEs can play key roles in everyday strategies for peace and non-violence. They encapsulate an alternative political economy approach that emerges from local needs, emphasizing social provisioning, redistribution and equitable economic security, empowering political strategizing and building solidarity at the grassroots levels. Despite their contributions, the SSE is interlinked with broader political, social and economic landscapes, and is not impervious to their influences. The dilemmas created by these influences are as follows:

- elite-capture;
- the exclusionary practices embedded in fractured ethno-nationalist/classist milieus;
- the potency of the liberal peace models to mould the SSE to their own objectives through donor agendas, short project horizons, financial sustainability and marketization pressures; and
- the manipulation of the SSE to 'responsibilize' the local through self-help dicta and to socially engineer the local into governable terrain, especially on the backs of women's work in these organizations.

These dilemmas are discussed extensively elsewhere (see, e.g., Cooke and Kothari 2001; Ramnarain 2013; Murtagh 2016).

With regard to the connection of the SSE and SSEOEs to peace and non-violence, a significant question arises in how SSEOEs and their practices can transition from simply reactive approaches of peace and non-violence to more proactive and transformative modes. Everyday peace and sustainable peace are not mutually exclusive. Borowiak et al. (2018) argue that SSE may provide contact zones where people of different backgrounds are brought together, but equity, inclusion and participation do not occur without conscious efforts at trust-building. Further, peace, as Galtung (2011) suggests, could simply be the absence of violence (negative peace). Even as members of SSEOEs acknowledge that negative peace is inadequate, and that social justice and equity are prerequisites for lasting peace (Ramnarain 2011), the degree to which SSEOEs and their practices are able to realize 'positive peace' – the absence of structural violence and an egalitarian distribution of power and resources – is, ambiguous and variegated at best.

Finally, the principles of compromise and negotiation are fundamental to the operation of the SSE. Internal compromises underpin the functioning of SSEOEs which may truncate the emancipatory potential of the SSE for peace and social justice. For instance, in order for SEWA to remain functional for its women members, and to preserve its moral and practical legitimacy in the communally charged milieu of post-riot Gujarat, religious divides remain more under the radar than gender discrimination. The second type of compromise emerges due to a paucity of resources, which is an especially pertinent constraint in conflict-affected contexts, where decreasing state support – driven in turn by neoliberal macroeconomic policies – can drive SSEOEs to look to donors for assistance. SSEOEs may then be forced to defer their longer-term transformative agendas in order to conform to the pressures of meeting funding conditionalities and timelines set by external donors, some of which reflect the very neoliberal ideologies and impulses that SSE seeks to resist (Ramnarain 2013).

The emergence, scaling-up and expansion of the scope of SSEOEs is also a critical concern (Ramnarain and Bergeron 2019; Murtagh 2016). When SSEOEs are well established prior to the conflict, they emerge as a credible and legitimate alternative political or economic space. There are very few examples, however, of the SSE and SSEOEs that have emerged and remained functional in deeply divided communities (Murtagh's example from Northern Ireland, discussed above, is an exception). Continued research is required to understand the conditions under which a vibrant and inclusive SSE may emerge in socially fraught environments, and how SSE spaces and enterprises might be interlinked horizontally, vertically and in terms of depth in order to achieve sustainable peace.

REFERENCES

Alvord, Sarah H., L. David Brown and Christine W. Letts. 2004. 'Social Entrepreneurship and Societal Transformation: An Exploratory Study.' *Journal of Applied Behavioral Science* 40 (3): 260–82. https://doi.org/10.1177/0021886304266847.

Azzellini, Dario. 2018. 'Labour as a Commons: The Example of Worker-Recuperated Companies.' *Critical Sociology* 44 (4–5): 763–76. https://doi.org/10.1177/0896920516661856.

Bukari, Shaibu, Kaderi Noagah Bukari and Richard Ametefe. 2021. 'Market women's informal peacebuilding efforts in Ekumfi-Narkwa, Ghana.' *Canadian Journal of African Studies*, 1–21. https://doi.org/10.1080/00083968.2021.1939078.

Bukari, Kaderi N., and Reginald G. Guuroh. 2013. 'Civil Society Organizations (CSOs) and Peacebuilding in the Bawku Traditional Area of Ghana: Failure or Success.' *Research on Humanities and Social Sciences* 3 (6): 31–41.

Cooke, Bill, and Uma Kothari, eds. 2001. *Participation: The New Tyranny?* New York: Zed Books.

Duffield, Mark. 2010. 'The Liberal Way of Development and the Development–Security Impasse: Exploring the Global Life-Chance Divide.' *Security Dialogue* 41 (1): 53–76. https://doi.org/10.1177/0967010609357042.

Galtung, Johan. 2011.'Peace, Positive and Negative.' In *The Encyclopedia of Peace Psychology*, edited by Daniel J. Christie. Hoboken NJ: John Wiley & Sons.

Gibson-Graham, Julie Katherine. 2006. 'Imagining and Enacting a Postcapitalist Feminist Economic Politics.' *Women's Studies Quarterly* 34 (1–2): 72–8.

Jaffe, Sarah. 2015. 'Can Worker Cooperatives Alleviate Income Equality?' Al Jazeera America. Accessed 16 January 2015. https://www.occupy.com/article/can-worker-cooperatives-alleviate-income-inequality#sthash.I3MGaZPq.dpbs.

Murtagh, Brendan. 2016. 'Economics: Neoliberal Peace and the Politics of Social Economics.' In *The Palgrave Handbook of Disciplinary and Regional Approaches to Peace*, 110–22. London: Palgrave Macmillan.

Pugh, Michael. 2006.'Post-War Economies and the New York Dissensus.' *Conflict, Security and Development* 6 (3): 269–89. https://doi.org/10.1080/14678800600933464.

Ramnarain, Smita. 2011. *Women's Cooperatives and Peace in India and Nepal*. Toronto: Canadian Cooperatives' Association.

Ramnarain, Smita. 2013. 'The Political Economy of Peacebuilding: The Case of Women's Cooperatives in Nepal.' *Economics of Peace and Security Journal* 8 (2): 25–34. https://doi.org/10.15355/epsj.8.2.26.

Ramnarain, Smita, and Suzanne Bergeron. 2019. 'SSE, Gender, and Sustainable Post-Conflict Reconstruction.' In *Proceedings of the UNTFSSE International Conference, Geneva*. https://genderandsecurity.org/sites/default/files/Ramnarain_Bergeron_-_SSE_G_Sustainable_Post-Con_Reconstructn.pdf.

Sanchez Bajo, Claudia. 2019. 'Cooperatives Contribution to Positive Peacebuilding and Sustainable Development in Rwanda.' In *Proceedings of the 7th CIRIEC International Research Conference on Social Economy, Bucharest*.

Sentama, Ezechiel. 2009. 'Peacebuilding in Post-Genocide Rwanda: The Role of Cooperatives in the Restoration of Interpersonal Relationships.' Coventry University. https://pureportal.coventry.ac.uk/en/publications/peacebuilding-in-post-genocide-rwanda-the-role-of-cooperatives-in#:~:text=The%20study%20found%20that%2C%20despite,negative%2Ddehumanizing%20relationships%20(division%2C.

Utting, Peter, Amalia Chamorro and Christopher Bacon. 2014. 'Post-Conflict Reconciliation and Development in Nicaragua: The Role of Cooperatives and Collective Action.' UNRISD Working Paper No. 2014-22. https://www.unrisd.org/80256B3C005BCCF9/(httpAuxPages)/64D5CC31A7852D55C1257DB1004B81DA/$file/Utting%20et%20al.pdf.

Vervisch, Thomas, Kristof Titeca, Koen Vlassenroot and Johan Braeckman. 2013. 'Social Capital and Post-Conflict Reconstruction in Burundi: The Limits of Community-Based Reconstruction.' *Development and Change* 44 (1): 147–74. https://doi.org/10.1111/dech.12008.

36. Reduction of hunger and poverty
Judith Hitchman

INTRODUCTION

The first and second Sustainable Development Goals (SDGs) address ending poverty and hunger, respectively. These are two key aspects of the overarching goals underlying the aspirations of the SDGs. Nevertheless, the economic system that underpins the SDGs remains that of capitalism, which by its very nature implies a growth paradigm that leads to social exclusion: an increase in wealth for the richest 1 per cent comes at the expense of both people and the planet. The measures most widely proposed to end poverty and hunger are grounded in charity-based solutions and corporate social responsibility (greening the existing system), rather than in those that empower populations and communities to determine how best to achieve these aims.

The social and solidarity economy (SSE) provides many real opportunities for overturning the above paradigm. It is important to note that the real underlying cause of hunger is poverty. The fact that the hungry are also generally in precarious employment (including migrant workers), employed in the informal sector, living in geographical areas of conflict and/or victims of the climate crisis is significantly important. Malnutrition is affecting increasing numbers of the world's population, including both under-nutrition and over-nutrition in the accounting. It is estimated that up to 25 per cent of deaths in the world are due to some form of malnutrition (over- or under-nutrition combined). The most important reference document is the Food and Agriculture Organization's (FAO's) annual State of Food Security and Nutrition in the World (SOFI) report (FAO 2021b). This report shows that hunger and poverty are on the rise, largely resulting from the COVID-19 pandemic and the economic impacts and job losses it has caused. The current rise in food prices caused by a conjunction of increased fossil fuel costs, affecting chemical inputs for industrial agriculture, and long value chain breakdown, is also affecting people's ability to buy healthy nutritious food (FAO 2021a). In many cases around the world, the pandemic has produced the vicious circle shown in Figure 36.1.

36.1 SSE SOLUTIONS TO POVERTY AND HUNGER

The solutions of the SSE, on the contrary, have provided significant responses to reverse this vicious circle and build resilience through a positive, virtuous circle of policy possibilities. The examples of the resilience of SSE responses to the pandemic are manifold. Some are illustrated in Figure 36.2.

The first element of policy that is of relevance is the formalisation of employment through cooperatives. One of the most relevant ways of overcoming poverty – and consequently hunger – is through the creation of small cooperatives at the local and community level. Formalising employment opens many doors in terms of gaining access to various safety nets including decent work and salaries.

282   *Encyclopedia of the social and solidarity economy*

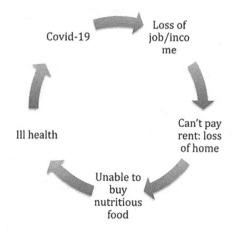

Figure 36.1   The vicious circle of food access

Figure 36.2   The virtuous circle of resilience

The second element is the provision of land and housing. One of the areas most prone to speculation globally is that of land and housing. Community land trusts and cooperative housing are vital parts of the SSE that protect agricultural land from speculation and construction. This is something mentioned in the New Urban Agenda (Habitat III 2017). Community land trusts are legally recognised in many different countries and on different continents:

> A community land trust (CLT) is a nonprofit corporation that holds land on behalf of a place-based community, while serving as the long-term steward for affordable housing, community gardens, civic buildings, commercial spaces and other community assets on behalf of a community. CLTs balance the needs of individuals who want security of tenure in occupying and using land and housing, with the needs of the surrounding community, striving to secure a variety of social purposes such as maintaining the affordability of local housing, preventing the displacement of vulnerable residents, and promoting economic and racial inclusion. Across the world, there is enormous diversity among CLTs

in the ways that real property is owned, used, and operated and the ways that the CLT itself is guided and governed by people living on and around a CLT's land. (Wikipedia 2021)

The connection between ending food poverty and land ownership is one of the key aspects of the SSE. Community gardens are one of the many ways in which urban communities can ensure access to food (see entry 29, 'Food and Agriculture Sector').

36.2   THE KEY LEVER IN THE SSE TO ENSURE THE HUMAN RIGHT TO FOOD AND NUTRITION IS FOOD SOVEREIGNTY

The definition of food sovereignty used here is that generally accepted by everyone, from institutions, to academics, and social movements, and used in the Nyéléni Declaration on Food Sovereignty 2007 (Nyéléni 2007).

It is important to distinguish food sovereignty, which entails empowerment of communities and peoples, from food security, which is simply access to sufficient food. If the food in question is based on industrial, over-processed products that have a high fat and sugar content and calories rather than nutrients, the outcome for communities is likely to be linked to the vicious rather than the virtuous circle. Access to healthy, local, nutritious foods through various SSE initiatives is generally based on short and, normally, direct supply chains. This is in stark opposition to the current general practice of the charity-based food banks, whose use had increased by up to 40 per cent in many countries at the time of writing in 2021 (Cohen et al. 2021).

A further example of communities creating their own food safety net through SSE practice during the pandemic is that of small-scale family farmers and landless people's farms in Brazil gifting surplus production to those living in the *favelas*, thus framing food as part of the commons and as a human right.

Community supported agriculture (CSA) began in Japan in the late 1960s and early 1970s. It was the result of collaboration between housewives who were concerned by the spread of Minamata disease caused by industrial pollution, and the Japan Organic Agriculture Association (JOAA). Together, they created a direct purchasing scheme known as *teikei* (meaning partnership or alliance). *Teikei* is based on ten principles, developed by JOAA in 1978, jointly between producers and consumers. It is the oldest form of SSE associated with food (Japan Organic Agriculture Association 1978). The ten principles are as follows:

1. Principle of mutual assistance. The essence of this partnership lies not in trading itself, but in the friendly relationship between people. Therefore, both producers and consumers should help each other on the basis of mutual understanding. This relationship should be established through reflection on past experiences.
2. Principle of intended production. Producers should, through consultation with consumers, intend to produce the maximum amount and maximum variety of products within the capacity of the farm.
3. Principle of accepting the produce. Consumers should accept all the produce that has been grown according to the previous consultation between both groups, and their diet should depend as much as possible on this product.
4. Principle of mutual concession in the price decision. In deciding the price of the produce, producers should take full account of savings in labour and cost, due to grading and

packaging processes being curtailed, as well as of all of their products being accepted. Additionally, consumers should take into full account the benefit of getting fresh, safe and tasty foods.
5. Principle of deepening friendly relationships. The continuous development of this partnership requires the deepening of friendly relationships between producers and consumers. This will be achieved only through maximising contact between the partners.
6. Principle of self-distribution. On this principle, the transportation of produce should be carried out by either the producers' or consumers' groups without dependence on professional transporters.
7. Principle of democratic management. Both groups should avoid over-reliance upon a limited number of leaders in their activities, and try to practice democratic management with responsibility shared by all. The particular conditions of the members' families should be taken into consideration on the principle of mutual assistance.
8. Principle of learning among each group. Both groups, of producers and consumers, should attach high importance to learning from each other and should try to prevent their activities from ending only in the distribution of safe foods.
9. Principle of maintaining the appropriate group scale. The full practice of the matters written in the above articles will be difficult if the membership or the territory of these groups becomes too large. Therefore, they should both be kept to an appropriate size. The development of this movement in terms of membership should instead be promoted through increasing the number of groups and the collaboration among them.
10. Principle of steady development. In most cases, neither producers nor consumers will be able to enjoy such good conditions as mentioned above from the very beginning. Therefore, it is necessary for both parties to choose promising partners, even if their present situation is unsatisfactory, and to go ahead with the effort to advance in mutual cooperation.

Teikei was perhaps one of the first manifestations of a counter-power to the industrial food system and the global network. It became a key actor in bridging the food sovereignty and SSE movements. It spread to both the United States and Europe at the beginning of the 21st century, and based on these principles, URGENCI, the International Network of CSA, was founded in Aubagne, in France in 2004. According to the association's article 2 in the Articles of Association, URGENCI's mission is: 'to further at the international level, local solidarity-based partnerships between producers and consumers. We define the solidarity-based partnership as an equitable commitment between farmers and consumers, where farmers receive fair remuneration, and consumers share the risks and rewards of sustainable agriculture' (URGENCI 2018). Today there are CSAs and networks in most countries, and on all continents, with Asia, Europe and North America as the strongest. The network represents approximately 3 million members of producers and consumers combined.

36.3 SSE ORGANISATIONS AND ENTERPRISES (SSEOES) BASED ON *TEIKEI* PRINCIPLES

CSA, on the basis of the *teikei* principles outlined above, is thus innately part of the SSE. The fundamental solidarity between producers and consumers ensures agreement to enable producers to access a decent living wage, irrespective of other events such as climate or illness.

However, in many cases the solidarity is carried much further, as in the case of many CSAs in the German Solidarischelandwirtshaft (SOLAWI) network, which is based on the system of a 'bidding round'. In this system, the producers state the amount they need to earn for the next year (including investments, and so on) in the annual general meeting with the consumers. The members of the CSA then discreetly write the amount that they can individually afford to pay for their annual share on a sheet of paper. If the total amounts to or exceeds the producers' needs, all is well. If it is less, there is a second round of 'bids'. The beauty of this system is that it incarnates the phrase first made by Louis Blanc in 1839 but later popularised by Marx: 'From each according to his ability, to each according to his needs' (Marx 1875).

It places food justice for eaters at the core, equally balanced with a fair and decent income for the producers. Other forms of SSE within CSA include an agreed number of solidarity shares for low-income families, farm contributions of food to soup kitchens, and 'working' shares, in which the beneficiary does an agreed number of working hours per month on the farm. These various practises all form part of the SSE, and indeed contribute to the notion of food as part of the Commons (see entry 13, 'The Commons').

Cooperative food shops, genuine farmers' markets, farmers' collective shops and the Open Food Network platform are all part of SSE in various ways. The role of local governments is also key in many areas, including solidarity public procurement from groups of local agroecological producers, and social inclusion through support to access healthy local agroecological food through either CSAs or local farmers' markets (see entry 51, 'Public Policy' and entry 45, 'Financing').

36.4 FOOD, HEALTH AND THE SSE

The links between the food we eat and our health are manifold and deep. The issue is often one of access to affordable healthy nutritious food, as opposed to industrially made, over-processed foods. It is important to distinguish calories from nutrition. A growing number of hospitals in both the United States and the United Kingdom are now linking healthcare benefits to the provision of fruit and vegetables. This can be further strengthened by the role of local governments supporting access to healthy, nutritious, locally sourced foods.

The link between soil health and human health is also paramount. Industrial agriculture uses large amounts of chemical inputs that affect both soil and human health in a detrimental manner (Terre Solidaire et al. 2021). On the other hand, recent studies on nutrition have also shown the vital importance of soil health in human health. Soil health is dependent on natural amendments from compost, manure and crop rotation. The human microbiome, largely responsible for our health, has also been proven to mirror the soil microbiome of the food we eat (Ochoa-Hueso 2017). Other studies have shown that the nutritional value of agroecologically grown local food is higher than that of foods that have been transported long distances, conserved for long periods of time or processed (many greens lose about 30 per cent of their vitamins in the first three days) (Eng 2013). Taken together, it is clear that our nutritional well-being is closely linked to how the food has been grown, and also to its geographical proximity.

Seasonality is also an important factor for sustainable local food systems and our health (SDG 2.4). All these elements are key to ending malnutrition (SDG 2.2) when linked to food justice and the right to food (Hitchman 2019). The SSE is one of the '10 Elements of

Agroecology' as recognised by the FAO (2018). As such, this is an important recognition of the role of the SSE in the production of healthy, sustainable food.

CONCLUSION

The interconnection between ending poverty and ending hunger can be seen as deeply intertwined. The role of the SSE in changing the vicious circle into a virtuous circle is a clear challenge for society, and one that can only be met by deep systemic change, the introduction of an economic vision based on the SSE and the sharing (rather than accumulation) of wealth. These questions need to be considered in a holistic manner that encompasses the overall economic system and includes a human rights-based approach to the right to food and nutrition.

REFERENCES

Cohen, Alison, Kayleigh Garthwaite, Sabine Goodwin, Wendy Heipt, Kristen Wyman, Suzanne Babb, Lorrie Clevenger and Betty Fermin. 2021. 'Food Banks and Charity as a Response to Hunger in the Wealthy but Unequal Countries.' Global Network for the Right to Food and Nutrition. https://www.righttofoodandnutrition.org/files/rtfn_watch_arti.03-2021_eng_web.pdf.

Eng, Monica. 2013. 'Most Produce Loses 30 Percent of Nutrients Three Days after Harvest.' *Chicago Tribune* 10 July. https://www.chicagotribune.com/dining/ct-xpm-2013-07-10-chi-most-produce-loses-30-percent-of-nutrients-three-days-after-harvest-20130710-story.html.

FAO. 2018. 'The 10 Elements of Agroecology: Guiding the Transition to Sustainable Food and Agricultural Systems.' Rome: FAO. https://www.fao.org/documents/card/en/c/I9037EN/.

FAO. 2021a. 'FAO Food Price Index.' Rome: FAO. https://www.fao.org/worldfoodsituation/foodpricesindex/en/.

FAO. 2021b. 'The State of Food Security and Nutrition in the World.' Rome: FAO. https://www.fao.org/publications/sofi/2021/en/.

Habitat III. 2017. 'The New Urban Agenda.' https://habitat3.org/the-new-urban-agenda/.

Hitchman, Judith. 2019. 'How Community Supported Agriculture Contributes to the Realisation of the SDGs.' In *UNTFSSE Knowledge Hub*. Geneva: UN Inter-Agency Task Force on Social and Solidarity Economy. https://knowledgehub.unsse.org/knowledge-hub/how-community-supported-agriculture-contributes-to-the-realisation-of-the-sdgs/.

Japan Organic Agriculture Association. 1978. 'Principles of Teikei.' URGENCI. November. https://urgenci.net/principles-of-teikei/.

Marx, Karl. 1875. 'Critique of the Gotha Programme.' Marxists.org. https://www.marxists.org/archive/marx/works/1875/gotha/.

Nyéléni. 2007. 'Declaration of Nyéléni.' Nyéléni.org. https://nyeleni.org/spip.php?article290.

Ochoa-Hueso, Raúl. 2017. 'Global Change and the Soil Microbiome: A Human-Health Perspective.' *Frontiers in Ecology and Evolution* 5 (71). https://doi.org/10.3389/fevo.2017.00071.

Terre Solidaire, POLLINIS and BASIC. 2021. 'Pesticides: A Model That's Costing Us Dearly.' BASIC. https://lebasic.com/en/pesticides-a-model-thats-costing-us-dearly/.

URGENCI. 2018. 'URGENCI International Network: Articles of Association.' https://cloud.urgenci.net/index.php/s/NZ5GnCg43geDHxs.

Wikipedia. 2021. 'Community Land Trust.' 29 December. https://en.wikipedia.org/wiki/Community_land_trust#:~:text=A%20community%20land%20trust%20(CLT).

37. Reduction of multidimensional inequalities
Andrea Salustri

INTRODUCTION

Reducing multidimensional inequalities is one of today's greatest social challenges. In the absence of consideration for collective and common interests, poverty, discrimination, reduced social protection, unequal growth, global crises, and the capture of political power by elites can reinforce the trend towards increasing and persistent multidimensional inequalities. To counter this process, the public sector should be empowered to fully exercise its redistributive function, but binding constraints on public finances, authoritarianism, corruption, and the existence of unobservable needs may reduce the effectiveness of public action, or even trigger non-linear dynamics (that is, situations in which public policies may increase, rather than mitigate, inequalities). Similarly, the market should be able to reabsorb the long-term unemployed, those undergoing precarious forms of employment, and informal workers; however, the existence of a "secondary labor market" seems necessary for the "primary labor market" to function properly (Frere 2013). Consequently, despite the commitment of many countries across the international community to reduce multidimensional inequalities, these are increasing worldwide at all levels, especially in the economic and social sphere.

With its origins much closer to those in need, the social and solidarity economy (SSE) often has a comparative advantage over governmental and market organizations in reducing poverty and, hence, multidimensional inequalities. Specifically, SSE organizations and enterprises can contribute to reducing multidimensional inequalities at all scales by developing alternative economies based on solidarity, cooperation, and self-management, creating the basis for inclusive and democratic development. Thus, through observation of the potential gap in the institutional matrix, which consists of the relative underdevelopment of the SSE compared to state and market entities, a process of mutual institutional recognition can facilitate a paradigm shift from inequality to solidarity (Matthaei 2018). However, participating in co-development processes can expose SSE to forms of instrumentalization and isomorphism that may reduce its commitment to achieve a transformative change towards an incremental one (Utting 2018). These risks should not be ignored, and distortions should be assessed and corrected through appropriate actions.

37.1 SSE AND IDENTITY-BASED INEQUALITIES

Within a Marxist conception of the economy, market relations are based on "multiple and interdependent forms of inequality and oppression" (Matthaei 2018). However, while deeply rooted in the paradigm of inequality, capitalism asserts an equal opportunity to compete for wealth in markets, and consequently implicitly contrasts the attribution of individuals to a social class by birthright. In addition, capitalism motivated the development of other movements for equality, such as anti-racist and feminist movements. Although these movements initially acted independently and took the capitalist class system as given, they later developed an attitude of cooperation against a "particular inequality and those privileged by it" (Matthaei 2018). Today, identity-based social movements have achieved intersectionality, so that, since the beginning of the new millennium, these movements represent the majority of oppressed individuals. Through opposition to a range of inequalities, the spread of transformative ideas underpinning these movements has led progressive social movements to adopt a politics of solidarity. This, in turn, provides the basis for solidarity economics, which are shaping alternative economies that integrate socialism with solidarity (Matthaei 2018).

SSE enterprises and organizations (SSEOEs) are key actors of alternative economies, as they reject narrow self-interest and purely (or primarily) profit-oriented behavior. The SSE calls on all individuals, regardless of whether they are privileged or oppressed by existing multidimensional inequalities, to change society towards solidarity and cooperation. Although most activities are initiated by and for the poor and excluded, the spread of the SSE could also be important for many people within the middle class, not only as mere volunteers or consumers of the goods and services it produces and distributes (Frere 2013). Moreover, many people who are not in need participate in solidarity and cooperative activities. Such participation represents their dissension to obtaining benefits from unequal relationships based on an unlevel playing field, implicitly recognizing the intrinsic value of equality and social justice. This bottom-up radicalism contributes towards reducing multidimensional inequalities at all scales, which in turn improves democracy, creating the basis for transformative social development. Finally, innovators and those who have successfully resisted the deterioration of socio-economic relations during crises may find instrumental reasons to support the development of the SSE, as the absence of concern for collective and common instances may eventually undermine their private interests as well.

Concrete examples of how the SSE may reduce identity-based inequalities are discussed as follows. In the United States (US), Cooperative Home Care Associates (CHCA) is a worker-owned cooperative of 1700 low-income women of African American and Latin American backgrounds, employing 2200 home care workers in the South Bronx area of New York City (COPAC 2018a). In India, self-help groups provide women-centered platforms for women's empowerment and collective action. Specifically, the Self-Help Group–Bank Linkage Programme (SHG-BLP) catalyzes meaningful savings and high loan repayment rates among rural women (Pal and Singh 2020). In Morocco, the Coopérative Taitmatine brings together women who process argan oil into a variety of products, which are commercialized by the cooperative for the national and international markets (Fontaneau and Pollet 2019). In South Korea, Songdo, a social enterprise established in 2010 to provide cleaning and indoor parking services, employed 35 North Korean refugees out of a total workforce of 110, with women accounting for 75 percent of the refugees employed (Fontaneau and Pollet 2019). In Mexico, the Union of Indigenous Communities of the Isthmus Region (UCIRI) is a farmers' cooperative, influenced by indigenous governance systems, gathering coffee producers from 53 different communities, including Zapotec, Mixe and Chontal ethnic groups, across five different municipalities (COPAC 2018b).

37.2 THE SSE AND SOCIO-ECONOMIC INEQUALITIES

Analyzing the tacit or explicit social norms governing the functioning of markets provides a better understanding of how the SSE contributes towards reducing economic inequalities. In particular, it highlights the issue of equity in individuals' access to, and participation in, market exchanges. This is an area in which the SSE can play a major role. Also, the financial analysis of inequality overlooks the notion that different individuals generally have heterogeneous abilities to convert economic wealth into welfare. Furthermore, within a given social group, some individuals may have less wealth due to forms of cultural, social, economic, and political discrimination (Alkire and Santos 2009). Consequently, the SSE takes on a further role in reducing economic inequalities, through identification of latent socio-economic inequalities which concern both the ability of individuals to convert economic and non-economic wealth into well-being, and the unequal redistribution of resources within formal and informal groups.

On this basis, it appears that, since the beginning of the 21st century, the concentration of wealth has increased steadily, and that the growing gap between the richest and the rest of the population has been fueled by high and persistent levels of income inequality. Returns in the private sector have privileged those who own or allocate capital to the detriment of workers in essential roles, who face increasing precariousness in working conditions (Berkhout et al. 2021). Moreover, economic incentives at all levels are now often focused on extracting wealth instead of promoting the development of resilient and equitable economic systems. This has led to a process of accumulation of wealth and income at the top of the distribution, coupled with a deterioration in the living conditions of those at the bottom, causing the rise of old and new forms of poverty (Berkhout et al. 2021).

Within this scenario, the SSE has proven to be an element of socio-economic resilience, a deterrent to exploitative dynamics, and a factor for inclusive and sustainable growth. Operating differently from business-as-usual, the SSE offers the opportunity to create stable institutional structures by or for vulnerable workers or small businesses. It responds constructively to changes in the labor market, and meets the respective needs of employees and entrepreneurs who wish to network and receive support in running their businesses (Fontaneau and Pollet 2019). Moreover, this alternative way of doing business discourages exploitative practices which are damaging to employees and the environment (UNRISD 2021).

The extractivism that often characterizes economic activity leads not only to an increase in economic inequalities of income and wealth, but also to the impoverishment of global environments (forests, seas, biodiversity, poles, and so on). To preserve these collective interests, however, it is necessary to ensure and develop open and shared access to essential goods and resources (Bance and Schoenmaeckers 2021). Consequently, another role of the SSE in reducing economic inequalities is that of being actively involved in the co-production of common goods and the regulation of their access, fostering inclusive and sustainable practices.

Worldwide, there are many alternative economies in which SSE enterprises and organizations play an important role. For example, many community services in Brazil and other Latin American countries are provided by organizations characterized by common ownership of the means of production, such as collective kitchens and gardens, self-construction pre-cooperatives, and so on (Frere 2013). Also, in India, joint liability groups (JLGs), self-help groups (SHGs) and cooperatives have made financial services accessible to the poor (such as SHG-BLP, see section 37.1). In the US, worker-owned home care cooperatives (such as CHCA, see section 37.1) provide personal and supportive services to people with long-term physical, mental, or developmental disabilities, or with short-term needs for medical or personal assistance (Borzaga et al. 2019). Finally, in response to the rapid advent of the sharing economy, numerous platform cooperatives have developed worldwide, mostly in North America and Europe, offering the same services on technologically equivalent digital platforms, while remaining jointly owned and democratically controlled enterprises (Saner et al. 2019).

Concrete examples of how the SSE contributes to reducing socio-economic inequalities include the following. In Côte d'Ivoire, the Coopérative Agricole Kavokiva du Haut Sassandra (CAKHS) has been involved in the fight against child labor in the informal and rural economy (COPAC 2018a). In Argentina, the El Amanecer de los Cartoneros is a recycling cooperative of social and ecological work that benefits *cartonero* (waste gatherer) workers – otherwise confined within the informal economy – through the promotion of rights at work and social recognition (Borzaga et al. 2019). In the Philippines, the San Francisco Association of Differently Abled Persons (SAFRA ADAP) produces quality furniture for the government education department, with a staff composed entirely of people with disabilities (COPAC 2018a). In Australia, the Earthworker Cooperative brought together the environmental/climate movement with the labor movement in 2014, to build cooperative factories enabling communities to find ways out of the climate emergency. Today, it successfully runs factories and other cooperatives in energy, water, transport, and landscaping (https://transformativecities.org/atlas/atlas-36/). Loconomics is a workers' platform cooperative in California that offers an on-demand web and mobile app for local service professionals, who use the platform as a marketplace to offer a variety of services (Saner et al. 2019). Platform cooperatives are also active in the creative industries, such as Stocksy United, a British Columbia-based enterprise that trades royalty-free photo and video content created by its professional and amateur owners (Brülisauer et al. 2020).

37.3 THE SSE AND DYNAMIC INEQUALITIES

Across the world, the poorest people have seen their incomes fall because of the coronavirus pandemic. Most of those forced into poverty are informal workers, excluded from social protection, social support programs, and access to credit. This poverty trap, which is often unrecognized by those not affected by it, means that even in the case of a rapid return to economic growth, the poorest groups will recover more slowly due to the absence of tailored policies (Berkhout et al. 2021).

Also, due to a general increase in poverty, within advanced economies, inequalities have been growing rapidly, manifesting in a hierarchy that places a class of unemployed and precarious or informal workers in a subordinate position in relation to a middle class that is disappearing from below (Frere 2013). On the other hand, the amount of wealth held by the wealthiest population has increased considerably, and after the economic crisis triggered by the outbreak of the pandemic, stock markets are now growing rapidly.

In this context, given the risk that public action may prove ineffective in reducing social and economic inequalities, the SSE must play a crucial role as an actor of last resort. Meanwhile, at the political and economic level, it must advocate for transformative social development, understood as social development that includes the eradication of all those inequalities that keep current and future generations at a disadvantage, or limit their capacity to act (UNRISD 2021).

However, over the last 50 years, the downsizing of the public sector, the expansion of the private sector, the reduction of state regulation, and the adoption of selective approaches to social policies have had a negative impact on reducing poverty and inequality. In particular, the discriminatory effects of selective transfers have created divisions even among the poor, neglecting some whilst privileging others (Yi 2010). On the contrary, society needs "transformative social policies," defined as a set of social policies focused on institutional relations between the political, economic, and social spheres, which bring about a change in relations between people and institutions towards greater cooperation and solidarity (Yi 2010) (see entry 53, "Social Policy").

Consequently, today, the SSE has an essential role to play in reducing multidimensional inequalities. By participating in public-social and solidarity economy partnerships (PSSEPs), people can cooperate in the pursuit of socio-economic demands even when the constraints imposed on public finances are binding (Bance 2018). In addition, PSSEPs can help to reduce existing boundaries among the public sector, the private sector, and the SSE, creating new opportunities for joint action to reduce multidimensional inequalities (Bance 2018).

37.4 LIMITS AND OPPORTUNITIES

Given that the SSE often operates in an unfavorable political and legal environment, and under unfair conditions compared with private businesses, there are many obstacles preventing it from achieving its full potential. Therefore, the actions promoted by the SSE must be accompanied by solidarity and redistribution expressed by the state and by its full legal recognition (Utting 2018).

A political and legal framework which recognizes the added value of the SSE in creating jobs and contributing to social welfare creates favorable conditions for the SSE to consolidate and achieve its goals. Public policies are particularly effective when they are designed to allow the SSE to contribute towards protecting general interests, recognizing and supporting its many forms and values. However, when the SSE is reduced to the role of service provider, it runs the risk of losing its transformative character, as it faces a trade-off between its economic survival and the social objectives it pursues (Utting 2018).

In summary, mainstreaming practices may help the SSE to go beyond the fringe insofar as SSEOEs are based on supportive policies and equal access to markets. However, they also run the risk of diluting or distorting the social and solidarity practices underpinning the SSE. Specifically, the SSE's commitment to achieving a transformative change can easily be reduced to a focus on incremental change; that is, a process that overlooks changes in those processes of socio-economic distribution that may reproduce or intensify inequalities. With incremental change, the poverty reduction may be modest and may coexist with increasing income and wealth inequalities (Utting 2018).

37.5 THE NEXUS AMONG INEQUALITY, HUNGER, AND POVERTY

According to the United Nations Development Programme (UNDP), besides costing millions of lives, there are several other reasons why the coronavirus pandemic and its socio-economic implications will affect global society for years to come. The severity of the crisis for the poorest countries (especially in sub-Saharan Africa) has been underestimated because of low direct mortality. The poorest countries did not adopt emergency social protection schemes during the pandemic, so they are likely to pay a higher price in terms of increased poverty. High multidimensional poverty is amplifying the negative impact of the pandemic on education and employment, while limiting the space for emergency protection programs. In addition, inequalities between racial and ethnic groups are increasing, as well as gender inequalities (OPHI-UNDP 2021).

As is well known, multidimensional poverty and hunger are closely interlinked phenomena. According to the Food and Agriculture Organization (FAO), hunger is increasing in most of Africa and, to a lesser extent, in Latin America and Western Asia. Globally, many people experience moderate to severe food insecurity, and the lack of regular access to sufficient nutritious food increases risks of malnutrition and poor health. Although mainly concentrated in low- and middle-income countries, moderate to severe food insecurity also affects parts of the population in North America and Europe. For the process of social development to be truly transformative, therefore, the reduction of socio-economic inequalities must be linked to an integrated strategy to eradicate poverty, hunger, food insecurity, and malnutrition (FAO 2019). Community supported agriculture (CSA) adopts this approach, as it is built on both food sovereignty and the SSE. Another way of tackling poverty and hunger in a cooperative and self-determining way is through the development of community-run farmers' markets. These support local farmers by charging a fair price for food produced according to the principles of agroecology.

Around the world, a variety of organizations adhere to the principles of CSA. In Japan, the *teikei* system emphasizes co-partnership between consumers and producers: consumers (usually 30–100 local families) participate in production through labor and capital, and in return receive seasonal, local, and organic food directly from the farm (Takitane et al. 2005). Similarly, the Seikatsu Club is the largest network of consumer cooperatives in Japan. The basic organizational unit of the Seikatsu Club is the Han, which is a small local group of 7–10 neighbors that is responsible for collecting and sending orders to the local center, receiving the products twice a week and distributing them to the members (Takitane et al. 2005). The Seikatsu Club operates according to two basic principles: democratic self-administration, stimulating the participation of all members; and development of a close relationship between the members of the cooperative and the producers (Takitane et al. 2005). In France, the Associations pour le Maintien d'une Agriculture Paysanne (AMAP) are groups of consumers that contract with farmers to buy their products in advance, at a mutually agreed price, for an established period. Consumers meet regularly with farmers to stock up on food, and a committee of volunteers ensures the functioning of the association (Laville 2010). In Italy, solidarity purchasing groups (SPGs) are groups of individuals who decide to self-organize to collectively buy food or other rural productions, selecting suppliers according to solidarity and critical consumption. The main objective of the participants is to align consumption with the ethical principles of political consumerism: fair prices for small producers; preference for local products; sustainability in production; and transport of goods (Maestripieri et al. 2018).

Concrete examples of how the SSE contributes towards eradicating poverty and hunger are presented as follows. In Malawi, the case of the Smallholder Coffee Farmers Trust is an example of how a sector in mountain communities, with severe physical and economic limitations, can be successfully developed, bringing income to peripheral areas of developing countries (Arnalte 2006). In the Philippines, 3408 farmers are members of the Payoga-Kapatagan multipurpose cooperative, which helps them to switch from monoculture production to integrated agriculture (that is, combining crop production with livestock farming) and to increase their livestock activity (COPAC 2018a). In China, many smallholder cooperatives have been established to sell local products. Approximately 13 percent of smallholder farmers in China are members of these cooperatives, and the income of these households is higher than that of individual farmers (Poirier 2011).

REFERENCES

Alkire, Sabina, and Maria Emma Santos. 2009. "Poverty and Inequality Measurement." In *An Introduction to the Human Development and Capability Approach*, edited by Lila Shahani and Severine Deneulin, 121–61. London, UK and Sterling, VA, USA: Earthscan.

Arnalte, Laura. 2006. "Malawi's High Grown Coffee." socioeco.org. https://www.socioeco.org/bdf_fiche-document-1790_en.html.

Bance, Philippe. 2018. "Conclusion. Public-Social and Solidarity Economy Partnerships (PSSEPs) and Collective Action Paradigm." In *Providing Public Goods and Commons. Towards Coproduction and New Forms of Governance for a Revival of Public Action (Vol. 1)*, edited by Philippe Bance, 301–12. Liege: CIRIEC aisbl. https://www.ciriec.uliege.be/wp-content/uploads/2018/03/CSS1CCL.pdf.

Bance, Philippe, and Jérôme Schoenmaeckers. 2021. "The Increasing Role and the Diversity Forms of Commons for Production and Preservation of Essential Goods and Services." *Annals of Public and Cooperative Economics* 92 (1): 5–12. https://doi.org/10.1111/apce.12318.

Berkhout, Esmé, Nick Galasso, Max Lawson, Pablo Andrés Rivero Morales, Anjela Taneja, and Diego Alejo Vázquez Pimentel. 2021. "The Inequality Virus: Bringing Together a World Torn Apart by Coronavirus through a Fair, Just and Sustainable Economy." Oxford: Oxfam International. https://Oxfamilibrary.openrepository.com/Bitstream/Handle/10546/621149/Bp-The-Inequality-Virus-250121-En.pdf;Jsessionid=2465FC344276B7D94785820F3AA3086D?Sequence=1.

Borzaga, Carlo, Gianluca Salvatori, and Riccardo Bodini. 2019. "Social and Solidarity Economy and the Future of Work." *Journal of Entrepreneurship and Innovation in Emerging Economies* 5 (1): 37–57. https://doi.org/10.1177/2393957518815300.

Brülisauer, Samuel, Anastasia Costantini, and Gianluca Pastorelli. 2020. "The Digital Social Economy-Managing and Leveraging Platforms and Blockchain for a People-Centred Digital Transformation." CIRIEC Working Paper N.11. Liege: CIRIEC International. https://www.ciriec.uliege.be/wp-content/uploads/2020/10/WP2020-11.pdf.

COPAC. 2018a. "Transforming Our World: A Cooperative 2030. Cooperative Contributions to SDG 8." http://www.copac.coop/wp-content/uploads/2018/04/COPAC_TransformBrief_SDG8.pdf.

COPAC. 2018b. "Transforming Our World: A Cooperative 2030. Cooperative Contributions to SDG 10." https://www.ilo.org/wcmsp5/groups/public/---ed_emp/---emp_ent/---coop/documents/publication/wcms_637335.pdf.

FAO. 2019. "The State of Food Security and Nutrition in the World. Safeguarding against Economic Slowdowns and Downturns." Rome: FAO. https://www.fao.org/3/ca5162en/ca5162en.pdf.

Fontaneau, Benedicte, and Ignace Pollet, eds. 2019. "The Contribution of the Social and Solidarity Economy and Social Finance to the Future of Work." ILO. https://www.ilo.org/wcmsp5/groups/public/---ed_emp/documents/publication/wcms_739377.pdf.

Frere, Bruno. 2013. "The Solidarity Economy: Emancipatory Action to Challenge Politics." In *Reducing Inequalities*, edited by R. Genevey, R.K. Pachauri, and L. Tubiana. Dehli: TERI Press 233–49. https://agritrop.cirad.fr/569731/1/01-PFL%202013%20Inequalities.pdf.

Laville, Jean-Louis. 2010. "The Solidarity Economy: An International Movement." *RCCS Annual Review*, 2: 3–41. https://doi.org/10.4000/rccsar.202.

Maestripieri, Lara, Toa Giroletti, and Antonello Podda. 2018. "Solidarity Purchasing Groups in Italy: A Critical Assessment of Their Effects on the Marginalisation of Their Suppliers." *International Journal of Sociology of Agriculture and Food* 24 (3): 393–412. https://doi.org/10.48416/ijsaf.v24i3.7

Matthaei, Julie. 2018. "URPE, Radical Political Economics, Social Movements, and Revolution—from Identity Politics to Solidarity Economics: Looking Backward, Looking Forward on the Occasion of URPE's Fiftieth Anniversary." *Review of Radical Political Economics* 50 (3): 504–21. https://doi.org/10.1177/0486613418791841.

OPHI-UNDP. 2021. "Global Multidimensional Poverty Index 2021. Unmasking Disparities by Ethnicity, Caste and Gender." UNDP-OPHI. https://ophi.org.uk/wp-content/uploads/UNDP_OPHI_GMPI_2021_Report_Unmasking.pdf.

Pal, Anirban, and Piyush Kumar Singh. 2020. "Do Socially Motivated Self-Help Groups Perform Better? Exploring Determinants of Micro-Credit Groups' Performance in Eastern India." *Annals of Public and Cooperative Economics* 92 (1): 119–46. https://doi.org/10.1111/apce.12304.

Poirier, Yvon. 2011. "Social Solidarity Economy in Rural China." http://www.socioeco.org/bdf_fiche-document-1717_en.html.

Saner, Raymond, Lichia Yiu, and Melanie Nguyen. 2019. "Platform Cooperatives: The Social and Solidarity Economy and the Future of Work." In *Proceedings of the UNTFSSE International Conference, Geneva*, 1–23. https://knowledgehub.unsse.org/wp-content/uploads/2019/06/Saner_Platform-Cooperatives_En.pdf.

Takitane, Izabel Cristina, Tania Nunes da Silva, and Eugenio Avila Pedrozo. 2005. "Food Safety and Sustainability: The Case of the New Organizational Arrangements between Rural Producers and Consumers of Organic Products in Japan." In *Proceedings 15th International Farm Management Conference*. https://ifmaonline.org/wp-content/uploads/2014/07/05Takitane-da-Silva-Pedrozo.pdf.

UNRISD. 2021. "Overcoming Inequalities: Towards a New Eco-Social Contract. UNRISD Strategy 2021–2025." Geneva: UNRISD. https://www.unrisd.org/80256B3C005BCCF9/(httpAuxPages)/DD3B34E514A44997802586D80055AC4F/$file/UNRISD-Strategy-2021-2025.pdf.

Utting, Peter. 2018. "Achieving the Sustainable Development Goals through Social and Solidarity Economy: Incremental versus Transformative Change." Geneva: UNRISD. https://www.unrisd.org/80256B3C005BCCF9/httpNetITFramePDF?ReadForm&parentunid=DCE7DAC6D248B0C1C1258279004DE587&parentdoctype=paper&netitpath=80256B3C005BCCF9/(httpAuxPages)/DCE7DAC6D248B0C1C1258279004DE587/$file/UNTFSSE---WP-KH-SSE-SDGs-Utting-April2018.pdf.

Yi, Ilcheong. 2010. "Social Protection, Social Security and Social Service in a Development Context: Transformative Social Policy Approach." *Journal of International Development Cooperation* 5(4): 57–84. https://doi.org/10.34225/jidc.2010.4.57.

38. Social services
Susanne Elsen

INTRODUCTION

This chapter concerns the growing significance of the social and solidarity economy (SSE) within social service from the perspective of social work and local social policy which fights poverty and inequality and promotes social rights. This encapsulates aspects such as social inclusion and decent employment of disadvantaged groups, as well as the social development of deprived urban and rural communities. Especially, within the context of concerns surrounding social work, the power of the SSE in achieving the core social objectives of the 2030 Sustainable Development Goals is elucidated (see also entry 40, "The Sustainable Development Goals"). The SSE has the capacity to facilitate empowerment, promote the participation of social service users, and create opportunities for improving self-determination and personal prosperity (see also entry 24, "Care and Home Support Services" and entry 49, "Participation, Governance, Collective Action and Democracy"). If people in need are not just defined as social service users and receivers of social support, yet instead have the opportunity to participate actively, in a meaningful way as co-producers of solutions, it can make a crucial difference.

Taking a cross-sector approach, the SSE, under proper conditions, can stimulate social innovation (Moulaert 2010, 6) and new local welfare models which integrate different objectives and actors into synergetic solutions and cause multiple societal effects. For social services and local social policy, SSE provides the opportunity to create new institutional arrangements in which material and non-material resources can be combined in an integrative and productive way. This will be illustrated by some best-practice examples.

38.1 THE POTENTIAL OF THE SSE IN THE FIELD OF SOCIAL SERVICES

A basic difference between public services, market providers, and SSE approaches lies in the specific bottom-linked, integrative, and participative context of the formation and management of solutions following the citizens' concrete needs, such as education and care for people with special needs, or social housing for homeless people, as well as employment or qualifications for young migrants. The hallmark of the SSE is an answer "organized by collectives directly to satisfy human needs not subject to the discipline of profit maximization or state-technocratic rationality" (Wright 2010, 141). SSE solutions predominantly manifest as voluntary associations, self-help groups, and social cooperatives, based on democratic governance and self-organization of citizens who are affected by a common concern, predominantly embedded in a local context (Elsen 2019). The SSE is a pathway to social empowerment by which civil society actors directly organize various activities, rather than simply shape the deployment of economic power (Wright 2010, 140). Thus, both the objectives of SSE approaches and their functioning and organizational culture are beneficial. The significance of SSE activities lies not only in their economic potential or capacity to cope with actual societal problems, but also in their emancipative power.

The United Nations Research Institute for Social Development (UNRISD) provides a helpful explanation of the innovative role of SSE organizations as non-state actors in the field of social work, claiming that they are increasingly associated with social transformation. The explanation is as follows: organizations and networks adopt new ideas, strategies, and practices that aim to better meet social needs and build relationships conducive to social and environmental improvements. Social innovation frequently occurs at the local level, where community organizations and social enterprises, mostly enabled by civil society networks and decentralization, organize to greater effect in order to mobilize resources and to defend their rights (UNRISD 2016, 8).

These solutions are embedded within local contexts, allowing direct communication between the people affected by these contexts, as well as other relevant actors in the public and private spheres (Habermas 1985). The spatial dimension is indeed relevant for the development of innovative and bespoke solutions to specific problems, allowing for the integration of different actors, building of networks, and implementation of bottom-linked activities. During the COVID-19 pandemic, for instance, restaurants and small shops promptly developed delivery services in collaboration with volunteers and non-profit organizations. This timely solution, serving customers and providers equally beneficially, now encapsulates one element of innovative community-based care approaches, which answer the needs of both the elderly or care-dependent citizens, and local suppliers.

SSE involves forms of "governance which are more horizontal and democratic; and often linked to collective action and active citizenship" (UNRISD 2016, 15). Members and users can control important decisions and transactions. This kind of management allows SSE organizations in the field of social objectives to function in a way in which they can attain their specific social aims while simultaneously generating social capital and gaining assets for further development. These contexts are also settings of civic learning. A productive mix of paid work, voluntary engagement, public support, and individual earnings is characteristic of these organizations. Often, they reinvest their surplus in order to further their objectives.

To understand the psychological potential of the SSE in social work, I refer to the concept of human-scale economies, put forward by the development economist Manfred Max-Neef (1992), which is based on his theory of human needs and aspirations. The analysis integrates four aspects of human needs: being, having, doing, and interacting. Max-Neef's classification demonstrates, on the one hand, the interconnection of these needs; and on the other hand, the existence of satisfiers, including subsistence, protection, affection, understanding, participation, creation, leisure, identity, and freedom (Max-Neef 1992, 199). Following this concept, how needs are satisfied makes a fundamental difference. Buying vegetables as economic goods, or producing and harvesting them in a social cooperative, have completely different qualities, related to the satisfaction of needs and to the possible contribution to individual wellbeing, social inclusion, community and capacity-building. Satisfiers relate to forms of organization, values, rules, and social practices. Actors in a social cooperative, for instance, work in a specific setting, built by norms of cooperation and common aims, ownership, rights, and obligations. The balance between needs, satisfiers, and economic goods is an important equation for the creation of the SSE in the field of social work. Operating in self-contained productive niches, such as in social agriculture, can trigger internal and synergetic satisfiers.

Synergetic satisfiers are those which stimulate and contribute to the simultaneous satisfaction of other needs, while satisfying the need in question. They can generate concrete material effects, but also improve knowledge, understanding, and social inclusion, allow freedom from market dependencies, and promote resilient communities, while yielding a sense of affection and identity (Elsen and Fazzi 2021). In this context, fundamental needs are not only goals, but can also become drivers of local development. The special potential of the SSE lies in its power to create new institutional arrangements by combining public and private institutions with civil society actors in a productive way. Notable recent developments include the use of integrative approaches in disadvantaged rural areas, which combine agricultural multifunctionality with the innovation of social and healthcare services. Social agriculture provides innovative opportunities for the synergetic development of social and healthcare structures, alongside multifunctional infrastructure within small farms, which suffer under world-market competition and are threatened by poverty. Similarly, it can benefit social cooperatives which use the multifunctional options of agriculture to offer an empowering context to their users. These approaches are also able to initiate innovation processes affecting their broader environment (Elsen 2019).

Regarding the potential of the SSE, the following are innovative aspects for the welfare sector:

- Bottom-linked governance which reduces role differences and hierarchical positions, flattens vertical structures, and enables democratic decision-making.
- Empowerment, participation, and self-determination of users in the welfare system, and the ability to co-create innovative approaches.
- Integrative and cooperative knowledge production versus concentration of knowledge and dependencies from professionals.
- Cross-sector solutions, combining resources and adapting to specific needs.
- Mix of non-material and material resources from different sources.
- Integration of collaborating social networks, volunteers, and stakeholders.

The following examples highlight the innovative aspects of the SSE for social service provision.

Italian Social Cooperatives and New Local Welfare

The social function of cooperatives is anchored in Article 45 of the Italian Constitution of 1947, with cooperatives emerging as synergetic and creative solutions for societal problems. They are connected to public administration and fostered by regional and national consortia, as well as being supported by mutual funds. Italian cooperatives indeed compensate for the shortage of public solutions for social needs. With the social changes experienced at the end of the 1970s, collective solutions for social needs gained topicality. Such needs included care for vulnerable populations, and labor integration of disadvantaged individuals or people living with disabilities, as well as new social needs, including the re-integration of drug-users. Citizens affected by these issues, along with their relatives and volunteers, built associations and cooperatives to advance specific social services. Two decades after these developments in the field, a legal framework for cooperatives with social objectives was legislated in 1991 (381/1991). Italian social cooperatives are SSE enterprises providing educational, healthcare, and social services, as well as socio-economic activities within many productive fields. They act in the market, following democratic, integrative, and participative rules based on the mandate of social inclusion of marginalized groups. Italian legislation distinguishes type A, consisting of cooperatives offering social and healthcare services, from type B, which focus on training and employment of disadvantaged groups, such as individuals living with disabilities, ex-prisoners, older unemployed individuals, and migrants.

In elucidating the specific potential of Italian cooperatives to promote human rights, social inclusion, and self-fulfillment of vulnerable individuals, the example of the reform of Italian psychiatric clinics is particularly convincing. The reform was driven by the director of the Hospital of Trieste, Franco Basaglia, and his team in 1972. The patient cooperative Cooperativa Lavoratori Uniti (CLU) was founded in response to resistance of the social, sanitary, and cooperative sectors and the labor unions. It intended to stop the exploitive and degrading so-called "ergotherapy" and to develop a decent productive context as the most important precondition for the social integration and rehabilitation of the patients. This social cooperative created an example for the positive effects of self-help and democratic self-organization in a very sensitive socio-sanitary field, and is still in existence today. The professionals involved in the medical and psycho-social care at the clinic also organized their work in social cooperatives, thereby leaving their public contracts in order to gain more freedom to act according to their visions. This had far-reaching effects to institutional innovations and encouraged the further consolidation of the psychiatric reform in the context of the so-called Basaglia law in 1978, which found followers in other regions both inside and outside of Italy (Kiesswetter 2018).

Since the turn of the millennium, in response to austerity policies and the privatization of public services and infrastructure, a new type of social cooperatives in Italy have been responding to contemporary social needs. Community cooperatives have emerged to safeguard citizen services or public infrastructure, and organize complex community needs in the form of multi-stakeholder cooperatives, involving natural and corporate members. Although filling a gap left by the state, by combining forces these new cooperatives can offer a way to prevent a closing down or purely commercial privatization of services, and instead favor organizational models controlled by citizens which offer access to all, independent of their financial power (Elsen 2019). Especially in rural areas, community cooperatives in the social field can serve to initiate and foster local development, interrupting the cycle of economic, social, and cultural decline that follows depopulation, and enabling revitalization, for instance by implementing cooperatives in the social-agricultural field.

The following example demonstrates the opportunities that can arise from the interplay of social services collaborating with public, private, and civil society actors within the SSE. In 2001, the type A social cooperative Nazareth (Società Cooperativa Sociale Nazareth) was founded in Cremona, Italy as a private supplier of educational and social services for young people and families. Acting in a broad network of public and private organizations, and supported by many volunteers, over the following years Nazareth amplified its work significantly, following the social needs and opportunities of the community. The social cooperative developed a whole chain of specific and innovative social approaches, ranging from elderly care to a child neuropsychiatric institution. A sports lab and a music lab also emerged, fostering social cohesion and community culture. In collaboration with public actors from basic medical care settings and specialists of physical therapy, the Cremona Welfare center was created. These processes of development and networking demonstrate the strength of this cooperative society, building synergetic links between the single entities and creating a new interconnected local welfare structure. Nazareth moved ever closer to core social problems such as housing and labor integration of vulnerable persons. A daycare center for people in psychological distress and a housing cooperative for young migrants were founded, followed by a project to put unaccompanied minor migrants in contact with migrant families who could host them. In 2013, Nazareth founded the social cooperative Rigenera,, a social farm for the qualification and labor integration, working in biological agriculture on 3.5 acres and processing the agricultural products for an own brand. Rigenera, is now present in local markets, not only selling their products, but also representing the producers, who normally are reduced to users of social services. Not least, Rigenera remains regularly up-to-date with recent problems and opportunities within the community (Ferrari 2020).

Social Agriculture

Over the past three decades, the role of farms and social cooperatives in maintaining and improving the health and wellbeing of vulnerable individuals who may be suffering from physical and mental difficulties, or social marginalization, has gained attention across Europe. The core idea involves using material and immaterial agricultural means to deliver social, or other, services for the benefit of the local community, thus encouraging awareness and capacity-building, fostering social integration, and creating leisure activities. Social agriculture encompasses all those approaches that combine agriculture with social, healthcare, or educational objectives. It integrates people into everyday farm work with the objective of improving or promoting physical or mental health and wellbeing, by offering meaningful activities or therapeutic tasks (Wiesinger et al. 2013). For example, organizations may implement projects focused on environmental education, food education, preservation of biodiversity, protection of the landscape, or by creating an environment in which children of preschool age or people with physical, psychological, or social problems can attend learning activities or even lodge. In addition, agricultural enterprises offer child or elderly daycare structures. Not least, labor integration of migrants and unemployed people in rural areas is often effective in the work-intensive fields of agriculture and forestry, also generating benefits for landscape ecology.

On the other hand, social agriculture acts to prevent rural poverty by providing an additional income for small farms, and it has an important impact on the economic, social, and cultural development of the territory (see entry 29, "Food and Agriculture Sector"). Combining agriculture with social, health, child, and elderly care, eco-social education and learning, the development of gainful employment or ecological restoration, and entitlement to a pension (for women in particular) can become a base for sustainable rural development, especially in remote mountain areas. Social agriculture has demonstrated its potential to prevent rural depopulation, to stimulate re-population of abandoned mountain areas, and to encourage social cohesion in rural communities (Haubenhofer 2010). In August 2015, Italy was the first European country to pass a law encapsulating the promotion of social agriculture (Law Number 141/2015). The combination of agricultural activities with social care and healthcare objectives, organized in social cooperatives, is a strategy which enables the preservation of jobs and creates income opportunities, while providing services to the community and contributing to sustainable rural development. The introduction of a legal framework for agricultural activities which have social aims also implies an advancement for the anti-mafia movement (Elsen and Fazzi 2021).

The horizontal structure makes social cooperatives especially suited to this field, and allows for interesting experiments by merging agricultural production with social, ecological, and political objectives. Actors in social agriculture are pioneers of new local welfare, but also of agricultural innovation and ecological transformation. Organic and biodynamic cultivation methods are dominant practices in social agriculture, as they are best suited to social activities involving individuals living with disability or disadvantage. According to a report published by the Italian Rete Rurale Nazionale (Giarè et al. 2017) on social agriculture in Italy, almost 70 percent of the examined initiatives (N = 367) adopt organic or biodynamic farming methods. The Italian Association for Organic Agriculture (AIAB) underlines the complementarity of the social and ecological motivations experienced by actors in social agriculture, who predominantly demonstrate a committed attitude towards the common good (AIAB 2007). Besides the creation of employment, social integration of disadvantaged people, productive use of local assets, and other socio-economic, cultural, and ecological effects, the return of young, qualified, and proactive people who commit to their territory and develop new local economies with a high moral claim is above all the most promising sign for the remote rural regions.

38.2 REQUIREMENTS FOR THE DEVELOPMENT OF SSE IN THE SOCIAL SERVICE SECTOR

The potential of the SSE depends on the integration into social, cultural, and political dynamics, and on the awareness of the interrelated processes of the creation and institutionalization of the alternatives (Laville 2016, 214). In welfare states, SSE organizations and networks evolved at the end of the 20th century in answer to growing private and public poverty (caused by deindustrialization of urban regions), changes in the labor market, unemployment, and cutbacks to welfare money (see entry 53, "Social Policy"). Thus, most of them have been initiated as bottom-up reactions to poverty, social exclusion, and the degradation of urban communities in old industrial areas. Some of them were part of active labor market initiatives or integrative social policy strategies in disadvantaged communities. The opportunity to develop their own democratic and alternative structure was limited as a consequence of their financial dependency on public money. SSE organizations and enterprises (SSEOEs) that succeeded in reaching a stable and autonomous state in the broad field of social work and social service are based on multi-stakeholder structures composed of private and public actors, and on their embeddedness within local communities, and in horizontal networks such as consumer groups. They often merge gainful employment and volunteering with mixed financing, of their own earnings, and public and private support. Mutual structures and the connection between single initiatives, cooperatives, and associations play a crucial role in the implementation and stabilization of the SSE in the field of social work and social development. As shown in the example, the Italian social cooperative movement acts on the basis of a legal framework, enrolled in a fostering structure of consortia and mutual funds.

The SSE in relation to meeting significant social needs and problems, such as qualification and meaningful employment of migrants, decent housing solutions for homeless people, and community care for elderly people, confronts core social policy duties. The SSE indeed has the capacity to develop new, synergetic, and participative welfare solutions, mostly on a local level, at the intersection of civil society actors, public entities, concerned individuals, and private supporters. This stresses the necessity of an institutional environment, allowing for and enabling social experiments through fostering practices. These experiments need a resilient space, in particular due to their hybrid and multifunctional objectives and their merged structures in new institutional arrangements, which disrupt established routines within the diverse sectors involved. "To achieve human needs satisfaction, bottom-linked institutions for participation and decision-making, embedded in wider movements and governance structures are essential. The empowerment of the local population is a precondition for democratic government and the building of connections between sections" (Moulaert 2010, 13). In addition, these processes of community development need time, and especially in disadvantaged areas, professional agents to apply the methods and instruments of community work. This plays a central role in the recent developments of new local welfare. The example of Cremona, Italy, illustrates this aspect.

Thus, the SSE is not an alternative to social policy, but a socially productive culture of active and formative local social policy, which requires social acceptance and support. The first precondition for developing a strong and creative field of the SSE in the social work or social service sector, and beyond, is the recognition of the specific culture and structure of this integrative realm and its societal effects. Awareness must be raised of the diversity it can provide to pure profit-oriented enterprises, as well as to conventional social service activities. As SSEOEs in the field have shown, this is not an easy task, disrupting well-established procedures. The SSE, for instance, should not be measured with the reductive criteria of for-profit enterprises, as it prioritizes social and also ecological objectives over profit motives. This is important to mention because many SSEOEs in labor integration have been criticized for the "distortion of competition," since they acted in productive fields with disadvantaged people and received the government's welfare budget for their activities.

REFERENCES

AIAB (Associazione Italiana Agricoltura Biologica). 2007. *Bio Agricoltura Sociale. Buona Due Volte. Risultati Dell'Indagine di AIAB Sulle Bio-Fattorie Sociali*. Roma: AIAB.

Elsen, Susanne. 2019. *Eco-Social Transformation and Community-Based Economy*. New York, USA and London, UK: Routledge.

Elsen, Susanne and Luca Fazzi. 2021. "'We Want to Change Realities Here.' Motivations of Actors in Social Agriculture Fighting Organized Crime in Southern Italy." *Zeitschrift Für Gemeinwirtschaft Und Gemeinwohl* 44 (2): 165–82. https://doi.org/10.5771/2701-4193-2021-2-165.

Ferrari, Mauro. 2020. "Coltivarci. Agricoltura Sociale e Welfare Locale." In *Perspektiven der Sozialen Landwirtschaft unter besonderer Berücksichtigung der Entwicklungen in Italien*, edited by Susanne Elsen, Sergio Angeli, Armin Bernhard, and Sara Nicli, 117–47. Bozen: Bozen-Bolzano University Press.

Giarè, Francesca, Patrizia Borsotto, Carmela De Vivo, Marco Gaito, Daniela Pavoncello, and Alessandra Innamorati. 2017. "Rapporto Sull'agricoltura Sociale in Italia." Rete Rurale Nazionale. https://www.reterurale.it/flex/cm/pages/ServeBLOB.php/L/IT/IDPagina/18108.

Habermas, J. 1985. *Die neue Unübersichtlichkeit*. Frankfurt Am Main: Suhrkamp.

Haubenhofer, D.K., M. Elings, J. Hassink, et al. (2010). "The Development of Green Care in Western European Countries." *Explore* 6: 106–11

Kiesswetter, Oscar. 2018. *Genossenschaften Made in Italy – Ein Erfolgsbericht*. Norderstedt: Books on Demand.

Laville, Jean-Louis. 2016. "Kritische Theorie und Solidarische Ökonomie. Von den Frankfurter Schulen zu den Epistemologien des Südens." *Forschungsjournal Soziale Bewegungen* 29 (3): 203–17. https://doi.org/10.1515/fjsb-2016-0238.

Max-Neef, Manfred. 1992. "Development and Human Needs." In *Real-Life Economics*, edited by Paul Ekins and Manfred Max-Neef, 197–214. London, UK and New York, USA: Routledge.
Moulaert, Frank. 2010. "Social Innovation and Community Development." In *Can Neighbourhoods Save the City?* 4–17. London, UK and New York, USA: Routledge.
UNRISD (United Nations Research Institute for Social Development). 2016. *Flagship Report Policy Innovations for Transformative Change*. Geneva: United Nations Research Institute for Social Development.
Wiesinger, Georg, Erika Quendler, Christian Hoffmann, Di Alessandro Martino, Sigrid Egartner, Nina Weber, and Josef Hambrusch. 2013. *Soziale Landwirtschaft*. Wien: Bundesanstalt für Bergbauernfragen.
Wright, Erik Olin. 2010. *Envisioning Real Utopias*. London: Verso.

39. Sustainable investment, production and consumption

Cynthia Giagnocavo

INTRODUCTION

At the core of the social and solidarity economy (SSE) is the call for a fair, inclusive and equitable global economy. In order to achieve it, the SSE envisions an alternative view of the economy which puts the environment and people at the centre (see also entry 7, 'Heterodox Economics'). In the 59th United Nations Commission for Social Development on the priority theme of socially just transition towards sustainable development (E/CN.5/2021/3), it was noted that the current course of economic development has not led to shared prosperity for all, but to high and rising inequalities, the climate crisis and unsustainable consumption and production patterns disproportionately affecting the most vulnerable. The report further analysed the relationship between inequality, consumerism and environmental degradation and climate change, making the argument that a fundamental redesign of production and consumption patterns to achieve Sustainable Development Goal (SDG) 12 is an imperative for the realisation of the 2030 goals (UN DESA 2021).

This readjustment implies a significant transformation in both values and methods of valuation, economic activities and how the predominantly market-driven economy is structured. One important example of the need for better methods stems from the fact that negative externalities of production and consumption are often not taken into account in analyses of efficiencies or optimisation of activities within market economies (see also entry 4, 'Ecological Economics').

This entry focuses on three main interlinked aspects: sustainable investment and finance; sustainable production; and sustainable consumption. Although they are interlinked, for example as set out in Box 39.1, they are located in different spheres of activities and influenced by significantly different actors. Here, each concept is described, before considering their interconnectedness and the role of the SSE, particularly with regard to circular value creation. Finally, reference is made to the comparative advantages that the SSE has in creating sustainable circuits of investment, production, exchange and consumption.

BOX 39.1 SUSTAINABLE INVESTMENT IN AGRICULTURE THROUGH SSE ENTITIES

In 1955, the Andalucían province of Almería, in southeastern Spain, was one of the poorest areas of Europe. It was a drought-ridden area with little infrastructure and a gross domestic product (GDP) per capita of less than half the national average. Most residents who had not already fled in search of better opportunities were barely subsisting, and levels of hunger were high. Today, it is the top Spanish fruit and vegetable growing area with an income among the wealthiest third of Spanish provinces in GDP per capita. This turnaround from a destitute area to a thriving province is due to the local cooperative association and marketing cooperatives, and sustainable, cooperative finance. Almería's average landholding is still only 2 hectares, and most are held by the 15 500 small-scale and family farmers who utilise greenhouses.

The dictatorship regime initiated development efforts in the 1950s and 1960s by introducing an electrification plan and installing water pumps that utilised groundwater to lure farmers to increase agricultural production in the area. However, it was an exploitative arrangement, environmentally unsustainable, and designed to ensure that farmers would continue to be subsistence farmers and cheap labour for others. Outside buyers offered abusive prices and price-fixing was common. Farmers found it extremely difficult to obtain credit and access to markets, and, frustrated by lack of access to markets, several Almería locals who had been inspired by the Raffeissen model formed the credit cooperative Caja Rural Provincial de Almería in 1963.

Although Cajamar provided financing, more importantly it acted as a catalyst in building organisational and social capital strength, providing the means by which poor farmers could turn their labour into something of value. Although an agricultural production of 3.5 million tonnes and a turnover of over €2200 million is impressive, what is most striking is the direct employment provided to more than 40 000 workers (in addition to self-employed farm families), with an equitable distribution of wealth generated in the region. More than 250 complementary or auxiliary businesses, both cooperative and investor-owned, have been created, with a turnover of more than €2000 million.

Initially, the cooperative bank offered unsecured loans and thus it had a crucial interest in making sure that the agricultural cooperatives' activities were worth financing. COEXPHAL (the association of cooperatives and producer organisations) was formed in 1977 with the support of Cajamar in order to give farmers access to external markets.

The initial catalyst role of SSE entities grew into strategic, sector-level innovation. Under the cooperative structure, the goal was to give farmers decent livelihoods, but to reinvest surplus back into the system. In the 1970s, SSE-funded experimental farms were set up to test, develop and share the results of new agricultural technologies, such as improved greenhouse design and new irrigation techniques, essentially transferring the financial and experimental risk of innovation from the farmer to the SSE entities. Almería cooperatives responded to new challenges brought about by both globalisation and climate change by investing further in research, development and innocation: sustainable greenhouses, efficient water management, biological crop control, genome research, shorter supply chains, renewable energy and conversion to organic farming systems.

The synergies created by the different SSE and cooperative institutions have allowed Almería's agricultural and credit cooperatives to thrive. Cajamar is now Spain's largest cooperative bank, and the farming area is now the largest cooperative vegetable growing area in Europe, with the majority of cooperatives using biological pest control and increasingly sustainable and climate-smart techniques (see Giagnocavo et al. 2018).

39.1 SUSTAINABLE INVESTMENT AND SSE

Sustainable investing, sustainable finance and socially responsible investing are broad categories. In their simplest form, they refer to a type of investing wherein the investor predominantly considers environmental, social and governance factors before investing funds and/or resources in a particular initiative, fund or business. In the last decade, various initiatives have been launched: in 2019 the International Platform for Sustainable Finance was formed to mobilise private capital towards environmentally sustainable investments. It focused on engagement with policymakers who are in charge of developing sustainable finance regulatory measures intended to help investors identify those investment opportunities that actually improve climate or environmental objectives (see also entry 28, 'Finance Sector').

Principles for Responsible Banking was also launched in 2019 during the United Nations General Assembly by 130 banks from almost 50 countries. This undertaking concerned a commitment to reducing negative impacts on the environment resulting from such banks' activities, and banking products and services. The European Commission published its 'Strategy for Financing the Transition to a Sustainable Economy' in 2021 (European Commission 2021), initially branded as 'financing sustainable growth', after an extensive period of drafts and consultations. It is concerned with sustainable finance standards, disclosure and labels, so as to recognise legitimate transition efforts. Inclusion, support for small and medium-sized enterprises, individuals and the real economy are noted as being important to achieving sustainability. The necessity for the financial system to become more resilient to climate change, and environmental risks posed by climate change and environmental degradation, is also highlighted in this strategy. It identifies sustainable economic activities, a European Union (EU) green bond standard, methodologies for low-carbon indices and metrics for climate-related disclosure.

Social and solidarity financing (SSF), on the other hand, although it shares certain characteristics with the sustainable investment, sustainable finance and socially responsible investing initiatives and characteristics referred to above, is connected to the SSE, where both financial and social relationships are interconnected; that is, relationships are not solely economic (see also entry 28, 'Finance Sector'). SSF as part of the SSE is concerned with the needs of people seeking finance, and ultimately in redistributive and equitable socio-economic activity. SSF is involved in both taking savings and deposits, as well as lending activity. It finances businesses that rank highly in socially desirable behaviour (environmental, educational and social welfare, and economic inclusiveness). It does not involve itself in speculative or 'casino' finance – a term used to describe the mainstream banking sector and investment and finance – and is engaged only with the productive or real economy. To understand the importance of this, it is useful to bear in mind that most shareholder-owned banks have both retail and investment arms and trade on their own account, where regulation allows, using the retail savings, pension contributions and deposits of ordinary people and small businesses to trade and invest speculatively for their own benefit, and ultimately for the benefit of their shareholders. As a result, much financial activity is not based on the real economy, but on highly speculative trading.

Amongst the type of SSE financial entities are credit unions, cooperative banks, ethical banks, microcredit and microfinance, and to a certain extent socially responsible investment. Whether an investment or finance entity may be considered to be part of the SSE depends on the degree of involvement, cooperation and associative solidarity relationships amongst workers, customers, producers and consumers, and also the extent to which the entity practices democratic governance. Ownership arrangements are also key distinguishing factors. It is these latter characteristics that create a circuit of value creation, so that there is a reinvestment of economic returns into the community, members or the organisation itself. In its simplest form, the money deposited by one member of the community is utilised or invested to meet the borrowing needs of others and to create added value for the community as a whole. It is an efficient use of financial resources that creates a virtuous circle. The profits or benefits are not diverted to outside shareholders. The more successful the community is, the more surplus value will be reinvested and available to further finance other needs, whether local or beyond.

In addition, financing systems play an important role in promoting sustainable consumption and production. In their analysis of sustainable investment, Sandberg and Sjöström (2021) consider the financial versus moral motivations of financial decision-making; that is, why investments are directed towards sustainable consumption and production practices. Sustainable investment, sustainable finance and socially responsible investment are still often motivated by financial goals, where sustainability is seen to be a method to generate long-term shareholder value. On the other hand, the motivation to 'do good' and be inclusive, not to invest in harmful industries and production, or not to extend credit for unsustainable consumption, is of a different moral logic.

Financial motivation requires investors to 'adopt a reactive and hypothetical stance', while investments motivated by moral reasons require a proactive approach to sustainability issues (Sandberg and Sjöström 2021). The nature of the return on investment may also differ greatly. The former approach to sustainable investment attempts to 'make good' by 'doing good', and the latter SSE approach is more concerned with returns on investment that have more to do with moral or ethical considerations. For example, the return on investment as a result of inclusive investment to set up a senior or child daycare centre may mean more equitable conditions for women or dignity for the elderly. Investments in training farmers in better agro-ecological techniques may mean that they spend less on chemical products and inputs, create less environmental damage, have less health and safety risk and produce healthier products for consumers.

39.2 SUSTAINABLE PRODUCTION AND CONSUMPTION (SPC)

Early approaches to sustainable consumption and production were focused on limiting negative environmental impacts, and the treatment of consumption was focused on 'green' intentions, and actual consumer behaviour (Moors et al. 2005). However, the SSE goes beyond consumer behaviour to consider social-economic systems, and endeavours to put in place or revamp an economy that can support the societal and cultural changes necessary for SCP which create shared prosperity for people and environmental sustainability (UN DESA 2021). The extensive work done by Dasgupta (2021) on the economics of biodiversity has also underlined the fact that production and consumption demands have exceeded nature's ability to continue to supply people with all the goods and services they relied on, and pointed to 'widespread institutional failure', not just a market failure. The fundamental problem identified by Dasgupta was that governments reward people more to exploit nature than to protect it, prioritising unsustainable activities, including the extraction of natural resources for production and consumption. The solution, according to Dasgupta, is to understand that our economies are embedded in nature (see also entry 4, 'Ecological Economics').

A common approach to sustainable consumption and production is to locate them in the circular economy, where the emphasis is on closing material loops. A transition to the circular economy would have significant impacts on sustainability, consumption and related investments in such activities. The circular economy upends the production and consumption patterns of using resources to produce, consume and then throwing away or disposing of the products. Instead, the circular economy seeks to keep product value circulating for as long as possible through reuse, repair, remanufacturing or repurposing, and recycling (Geissdoerfer et al. 2017). The European Commission's circular economy action plan adopted by the EU in 2015, and relied on by its new circular economy plan (European Commission 2020), defines the circular economy as:

> an economy [that] aims to maintain the value of products, materials and resources for as long as possible by returning them into the product cycle at the end of their use, while minimising the generation of waste. This process starts at the very beginning of a product's lifecycle: smart product design and production processes can help save resources, avoid inefficient waste management, and create new business opportunities. (European Commission 2015)

However, the SSE can be seen to go one step further than the circular economy, which concentrates mostly on environmental issues within an industrial context. The SSE integrates not only the environment but also the economic and social dimensions of sustainability and solidarity. Both organisational and governance aspects are included in the SSE approach, to regenerate and restore consumption and production to include more than the economic aspect, and to build inclusive and equitable economies (Geissdoerfer et al. 2017).

The SSE approach can be seen to focus on various levels, from local business and community initiatives, to overall social and economic dynamics. While circular economy scholars focus on how to close material loops, the SSE requires a more profound change of consumption and production patterns. Recently, more research has been carried out tying the SSE to sustainability and consumption, pointing to the sharing economy, collaborative consumption, reuse, second-hand, product-service system, repairs, etc. (Camacho-Otero et al. 2018). (See generally, Bali and Sweet 2021a, 2021b.)

However, the complexity of implementing such profound changes and their inter-relationships should not be underestimated. Not only are social and institutional changes that transform the upstream process of production and consumption (Bocken et al. 2017) necessary, but the redesign of actual goods and services to meet people's needs is also required (Merli et al. 2018), as well as the scaling up of such alternative sustainable and SSE systems.

Initiatives such as consumer and producer networks, a wide range of social enterprises (manufacturing, work integration, tourism, and so on) and cooperatives (supply, consumer, producer, service sharing, energy, waste, and so on) provide a different approach to SCP. Cooperatives and social enterprises combine social and economic value within their business models through their organisational design; they are essentially designed for such purposes. For example, cooperatives are 'autonomous associations of persons united voluntarily to meet their common economic, social, and cultural needs and aspirations through a jointly-owned and democratically-controlled enterprise' (ICA 2015).

39.3 THE SSE'S ROLE IN FUTURE CHALLENGES IN SUSTAINABLE INVESTMENT, PRODUCTION, CONSUMPTION

There is a need for a critical rethinking in the SSE, where sustainable production and consumption may mean not consuming or investing in the production of goods at all, rather than trying to endlessly produce and consume more sustainable goods. Since the SSE does not measure its value solely by turnover, contribution to GDP, shareholder profits or other monetised valuation methods, the SSE is not trapped within the predominantly environmentally damaging production and consumption paradigm, which needs a constant supply of energy, natural resources and other inputs, such as unfairly paid labour. Sustainable consumption and production necessarily implicate a discussion about growth. There are various perspectives on growth: degrowth refers to the need to reduce production and consumption, and looks to other indicators to define economic or societal success; post-growth focuses on decoupling economic growth from a vision of 'well-being'; green growth puts its faith in scientific and technological progress and innovation to achieve sustainability and ensure that natural assets are depleted as little as necessary; and finally, the 'doughnut economy' refers to conciliation between real needs of humans and the possibility for a sustainable future.

The SSE may be seen to fit in within all of these approaches to growth, across many sectors, representing a diversity of organisational and financial models. The SSE is flexible enough to provide innovative economic, social and environmental solutions that are often rooted in their local context, as illustrated in Box 39.2, yet help to redefine sustainable investment, production and consumption by focusing first on the real economy and outcomes that are good for people and planet.

BOX 39.2 ALTERNATIVE PRODUCTION AND CONSUMPTION SSE MODELS

The Rochdale Pioneers, founded in 1844, established the basis not only for the modern consumer cooperatives but also for the modern cooperative movement worldwide. It was formed in Lancashire, England to provide an affordable alternative to poor-quality and adulterated food and provisions, using any surplus from sales to benefit the community. The cooperative movement now extends across the globe and encompasses all sectors of the economy.

Currently, there are many forms of alternative purchasing and consumption networks, such as solidarity purchasing groups, community supported agriculture, urban gardens and, in general, the sharing economy. These SSE models relate to co-access and co-ownership and/or consumption of a wide variety of goods and services. These could include car and bike sharing, clothes trading, exchanges of housing, workspace, or sharing of tools, or any good or service used on a day-to-day basis, where ownership is not crucial to enjoying their use.

REFERENCES

Bali, Swain Ranjula and Susanne Sweet, eds. 2021a. *Sustainable Consumption and Production, Volume I*. Cham: Palgrave Macmillan. https://doi.org/10.1007/978-3-030-56371-4.

Bali, Swain Ranjula and Susanne Sweet, eds. 2021b. *Sustainable Consumption and Production, Volume II*. Cham: Palgrave Macmillan. https://doi.org/10.1007/978-3-030-55285-5.

Bocken, Nancy M.P., Paovo Ritala and Pontus Huotari. 2017. 'The Circular Economy: Exploring the Introduction of the Concept Among S&P 500 Firms.' *Journal of Industrial Ecology* 21 (3): 487–90. https://doi.org/10.1111/jiec.12605.

Camacho-Otero, Juana, Casper Boks and Ida Pettersen. 2018. 'Consumption in the Circular Economy: A Literature Review.' *Sustainability* 10 (8): 2758. https://doi.org/10.3390/su10082758.

Dasgupta, Partha. 2021. 'The Economics of Biodiversity: The Dasgupta Review.' London: HM Treasury. https://assets.publishing.service.gov.uk/government/uploads/system/uploads/attachment_data/file/962785/The_Economics_of_Biodiversity_The_Dasgupta_Review_Full_Report.pdf.

European Commission. 2015. 'Communication from the Commission of the European Parliament, the Council, the European Economic and Social Committee and the Committee of the Regions: Closing the Loop – An EU Action Plan for the Circular Economy.' https://eur-lex.europa.eu/legal-content/EN/TXT/?uri=CELEX%3A52015DC0614.

European Commission. 2020. 'Communication from the Commission of the European Parliament, the Council, the European Economic and Social Committee and the Committee of the Regions: A New Circular Economy Action Plan For a Cleaner and More Competitive Europe.' https://eur-lex.europa.eu/legal-content/EN/TXT/?uri=COM:2020:98:FIN&WT.mc_id=Twitter.

European Commission. 2021. 'Communication from the Commission to the European Parliament, the Council, the European Economic and Social Committee and the Committee of the Regions: Strategy for Financing the Transition to a Sustainable Economy.' https://eur-lex.europa.eu/resource.html?uri=cellar:9f5e7e95-df06-11eb-895a-01aa75ed71a1.0001.02/DOC_1&format=PDF.

Geissdoerfer, Martin, Paulo Savaget, Nancy M.P. Bocken and Erik Jan Hultink. 2017. 'The Circular Economy – a New Sustainability Paradigm?' *Journal of Cleaner Production* 143 (1): 757–68. https://doi.org/10.1016/j.jclepro.2016.12.048.

Giagnocavo, Cynthia, Emilio Galdeano-Gómez and Juan C. Pérez-Mesa. 2018. 'Cooperative Longevity and Sustainable Development in a Family Farming System.' *Sustainability* 10 (7): 2198. https://doi.org/10.3390/su10072198

ICA (International Co-operative Alliance). 2015. 'The Guidance Notes to the Cooperative Principles.' ICA. https://www.ica.coop/en/media/library/research-and-reviews/guidance-notes-cooperative-principles.

Merli, Roberto, Michele Preziosi and Alessia Acampora. 2018. 'How Do Scholars Approach the Circular Economy? A Systematic Literature Review.' *Journal of Cleaner Production* 178 (2018): 703–22. https://doi.org/10.1016/j.jclepro.2017.12.112.

Moors, Ellen H.M., Karel F. Mulder and Philip J. Vergragt. 2005. 'Towards Cleaner Production: Barriers and Strategies in the Base Metals Producing Industry.' *Journal of Cleaner Production* 13 (7): 657–68. https://doi.org/10.1016/j.jclepro.2003.12.010.

Sandberg, Joakim and Emma Sjöström. 2021. 'Motivations for Investment in Sustainable Consumption and Production.' In *Sustainable Consumption and Production, Volume I*, edited by Ranjula Bali Swain and Susanne Sweet. Cham: Palgrave Macmillan 125–39. https://doi.org/10.1007/978-3-030-56371-4_7.

UN DESA (United Nations Department of Economic and Social Affairs). 2021. 'UN/DESA Policy Brief #109: Accelerate Action to Revamp Production and Consumption Patterns: The Circular Economy.' Cooperatives and the Social and Solidarity Economy. United Nations. https://www.un.org/development/desa/dpad/publication/un-desa-policy-brief-109-accelerate-action-to-revamp-production-and-consumption-patterns-the-circular-economy-cooperatives-and-the-social-and-solidarity-economy/.

40. The Sustainable Development Goals

Denison Jayasooria and Ilcheong Yi

INTRODUCTION

The Millennium Development Goals (MDGs) (2000–2015) and the Sustainable Development Goals (SDGs) (2015–30) illustrate that we are one global human family. We are interconnected. Issues of poverty, ill health and natural disasters have an impact directly or indirectly on all the people and nations of the world.

Today, the SDGs represent the global development agenda. Governments have the primary responsibility for implementing the SDGs, and ensuring follow-up and review over the coming 8 years, at the national, regional and global levels. However, according to SDG 17, which concerns partnerships, there is also a place for all stakeholders (government, business, academia, civil society and local community) to play a role.

This entry, after a brief summary of the global development agenda, explains the relationship between SDGs and the social and solidarity economy (SSE) principles and models to illustrate the compatibility of the two, and showcases the SSE as a community-based strategy for the effective localising of the SDGs.

40.1 FROM THE MDGS (2000–2015) TO THE SDGS (2015–30)

The global development agenda between 2000 and 2015 was entitled the Millennium Development Goals (MDGs). It was a set of eight development goals and applied only to the developing world. It had a strong emphasis on eradicating extreme poverty and hunger, alongside a focus on addressing gender equality and women's empowerment, as well as reducing child mortality and improving maternal health. It also aimed to achieve universal primary education. Two other development agendas were: combating diseases including HIV/Aids and malaria, and ensuring environmental sustainability. These were envisioned as possible with global partnership, especially regarding financing for development of poor developing nations.

The assessment of the implementation of the MDGs revealed that while there was progress made by some countries, there were major gaps in the development agenda, as well as the delivery. This matter was the subject of the conversation at the Rio Plus 20 Summit on sustainable development held in Rio de Janeiro, Brazil from 20 to 22 June 2012. At the end of the Summit, a consensus document was released entitled the 'Future We Want' which provided a global common vision (United Nations 2012). The Summit also established a High-Level Political Forum (HLPF), and a global consultation process was instituted by engaging major groups and stakeholders in formulating the post-MDG global development agenda. Rio recognised the critical need for political leadership to ensure that the next 15-year agenda had a greater impact in addressing global concerns.

Table 40.1   Five SDG dimensions of development

5 Ps	Dimensions of development
People SDG 1, 2, 3, 4, 5	Human development including personal freedoms. Addressing poverty, health, education and gender as most essential.
Prosperity SDG 7, 8, 9, 10, 11	Wealth creation, economic growth and equitable distribution. Decent work, cities, addressing inequality, production and consultation are important aspects.
Planet SDG 6, 12, 13, 14, 15	Environment: sustainable and responsible use of resources. Sustainability and the management of natural resources as an asset is key to life in the water and on the land, including managing the forests and climate change concerns.
Peace SDG 16	Community solidarity, inter-ethnic and religious harmony. Accountability and good governance is essential, including independent institutions such as the National Human Rights Commission of India.
Partnership SDG 17	Cooperation among sectors such as public, private and voluntary at the global, regional, national and local levels is essential. Technical and financial support are also essential.

There were also shifts in the thinking behind the development agenda. The earlier work of Amartya Sen (1999), entitled *Development as Freedom*, was making inroads into policy discussions. Therefore, the linkage of development and the human rights agenda gained traction. Amartya Sen's call was a shift away from focusing on the narrow development agenda, such as increasing personal incomes or focusing on the gross national product, by expanding the development process towards linking development with capabilities. He called for an inclusive agenda by the integration of economic, social and political considerations. His was a shift in focus from income deprivation to capability deprivation, as he saw the linkage between illiteracy, ill-health and undernourishment on the one hand, and better education and health provisions which have a positive impact on earning higher incomes on the other.

The global conversation was calling for a major shift towards a far more comprehensive and integrated agenda between economic, social, environmental and human rights concerns. By 2015, there had already been some global consensus on the future agenda, and on 25 September 2015, at the United Nations (UN) in New York, world leaders accepted the SDGs as the post-2015 development agenda. They agreed to a global agenda entitled 'Transforming our World: The 2030 Agenda for Sustainable Development' (United Nations 2015).

The central theme of the SDGs is 'leaving no one behind'. It was agreed that this global agenda was relevant to all member states of the UN, not just the developing countries, as it was recognised that even within developed nations there are individuals who are disadvantaged, and might be in danger of being left behind. The SDGs contain three dimensions of sustainable development, namely economic, social and environmental concerns, including human rights and good governance. There are 17 goals compared to the MDGs which comprised only eight goals. The SDGs are a more comprehensive agenda, with 169 targets and 231 unique indicators. They form a 15-year global agenda targeting action between 2015 and 2030. The SDGs provide a unique opportunity to integrate five dimensions of development, as illustrated in Table 40.1.

These 17 goals, 169 targets and 231 unique indicators make up a very comprehensive and cross-cutting development agenda encompassing economic, social and cultural aspects, as well as civil and political rights. The SDGs have a very strong collaborative aspect and while the governments are being held accountable for their implementation, the partnership of all stakeholders is of utmost importance in the success of the implementation.

Once in four years, each country is given an opportunity to share its achievements and challenges at the HLPF which meets every year in July at the UN headquarters in New York. The process is called the Voluntary National Review (VNR). While this is not like the Universal Periodical Review (UPR), which has a more rigorous process of review, within the VNR each country gets an opportunity to showcase how it is implementing the SDGs once every four years.

The HLPF has become the global space for conversations surrounding the implementation of models via the formal process of the VNR, or through side events hosted by member states and stakeholders. Here the SSE model or approach is often featured by governments, UN agencies, civil society and academics.

The SDGs' goals, targets and indicators seem like a mammoth task for member states to deliver, and therefore there is a need for workable grassroots models in addressing the 17 concerns in an integrated and impactful way. Hence, the means of implementation and financing for development are key. This is where SSE actors are advocating that the SSE may act as a vehicle for an effective intervention strategy for the realisation of the SDGs at the local grassroots level.

40.2 RELATIONSHIPS BETWEEN THE SDGS AND THE SSE

The concepts of the SSE and the SDGs have close parallels. Explaining the relationship is a helpful exercise to establish the SSE as a vehicle for the realisation of the SDGs, especially at the grassroots local level, and in ensuring no person or community is left behind.

Peter Utting (2015) provides a useful definition of the SSE as collective action in the production of goods and services by communities, cooperatives, associations and social enterprises. All these economic activities are people-centred and environmentally sensitive. He further identifies the values associated with the SSE, such as cooperation, solidarity, triple bottom line and democratic governance (see also entry 3, 'Contemporary Understandings').

In a similar way, Ben Quinones (2020) articulates a fivefold dimension of the SSE. These dimensions include, firstly, the triple bottom line of people, planet (environment) and profits (economy); then socially responsible governance; and finally, edifying ethical values. In the SSE collective accountability, democratic decision making and transparency are important. The transformative dimension of the SSE is its edifying values, which are not about just taking a person out of poverty, but empowering individuals for a collective and collaborative vision. Figure 40.1 illustrates the five dimensions of the SSE.

Identifying the commonalities between the SDGs and the SSE in terms of their foci is an important exercise, as the five SDG dimensions appear in parallel to the SSE dimensions, with notable synergy between them. It is also important to note that the SSE provides a community focus intervention strategy and a platform to realise the potential of community-led integrated approaches in localising the SDGs. In this context, Table 40.2 draws up the parallel dimensions and points to the rich potential of the SSE for the realisation of the SDGs.

These commonalities make an increasing number of governments look at the SSE as a means of implementation of the SDGs. Given its association with localised circuits of production, exchange and consumption, SSE organisations and enterprises (SSEOEs) can be conducive not only to basic needs provisioning but also to local economic development, based on sustainable production and consumption, as well as local reinvestment. The SSE's values

Figure 40.1 Five dimensions of the SSE

Table 40.2 SDGs and SSE local community potential

SDGS	SSE	SSE potential for the SDG realisation
People	People	People are at the heart of development. The SSE sees people in an integrated and inclusive way.
Planet	Planet	The SSE has a greater appreciation of the environment and of intergenerational sustainability.
Prosperity	Profits	The SSE creates a more just and equitable share of the resources, especially wealth distribution in the context of wealth creation.
Peace	Governance	The SSE empowers local communities at the grassroots to be in direct control of the organisation and directly benefiting from it. People's participation and joint cooperation are central to all SSE organisations and enterprises. SSE governance structure is to be participatory and accountable to the people.
Partnership	Values	The SSE fosters value transformation, such as appreciation of diversity, respect of human dignity, self-respect and fundamental human rights.

and principles, centred around democracy, solidarity and social cohesion, have considerable potential to reduce inequalities. Further, given the active participation of women, the SSE can have a significant impact on women's economic, social and political empowerment. The patterns of production and consumption practised by SSEOEs tend to be more sensitive to local environmental conditions than those of for-profit enterprises. In addition to these economic, social and environmental attributes, the SSE has a political dimension: it involves forms of resistance, mobilisation and active citizenship that can challenge the structures that generate social, economic and environmental injustice.

Active in almost all economic sectors, SSEOEs have been shown to contribute to all 17 SDGs. However, specific socio-economic and environmental contexts, and sometimes political contexts at the national or local level, determine the SDGs which SSEOEs seek to achieve. According to the United Nations Research Institute for Social Development's (UNRISD) study on the contribution of SSEOEs to the SDGs in Seoul (Figure 40.2), the contribution of SSEOEs was particularly prominent in the areas of SDG 10 (reduce all forms of inequality), SDG 1 (end poverty in all its forms), SDG 11 (inclusive, safe and sustainable cities for all citizens), SDG 8 (inclusive and sustainable economic growth, and decent work), SDG 4 (quality education and lifelong learning), SDG 12 (sustainable consumption and production), SDG 3 (good health and well-being) and SDG 9 (infrastructure and industrialisation) (Yi et al. 2018).

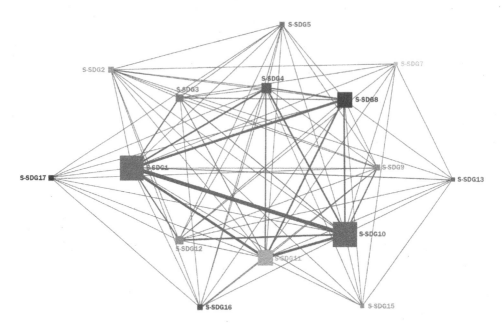

Note: The size of a square represents the number of SSEOEs directly contributing to implementation of that specific S-SDG. The thickness of a line represents the degree to which SSEOEs contributing to that S-SDG also contribute to other S-SDGs. (For example, SSEOEs contributing to S-SDG 1 are more likely to contribute to S-SDG 10 than to S-SDG17.)
Source: Yi et al. (2018).

Figure 40.2   How Seoul's SSEOEs contribute to the SDGs: tracing the pathways

Key goals such as SDG 12 on 'ensuring sustainable consumption and production patterns' are particularly relevant, as many SSEOEs have in their charters a commitment to environmental sustainability. SSEOEs also help to achieve goals such as SDG 8, and in particular target 8.4, which aims to 'improve progressively, through 2030, global resource efficiency in consumption and production and endeavour to decouple economic growth from environmental degradation'. This is because SSEOEs strive to consider the well-being of their employees a key objective, and do not solely focus on the financial return from their activities.

40.3 PROMOTING THE SSE AS A MEANS OF IMPLEMENTATION OF THE SDGS AT THE GLOBAL LEVEL

Various global or supranational processes and agreements are already under way to support the SSE as a means of implementation of the SDGs. The UN Inter-Agency Task Force on Social and Solidarity Economy (UNTFSSE) established in 2013 has been a key organisation to promote the SSE as a means of implementation of the SDGs. Composed of members (20 UN agencies) and observers (14 international and regional organisations working on SSE issues), it is taking the lead in the popularisation of the SSE through policy dialogues, research, documentation and advocacy work within and beyond the UN system. It has raised the visibility of the SSE, as well as documented the contributions of SSE actors to implementing the SDGs. In particular, in 2018, the UNTFSSE established the Knowledge Hub for the SDGs, making a great contribution to raising awareness and visibility of the SSE as a vehicle for the implementation of the SDGs. Currently the International Labour Organization (ILO) hosts UNTFSSE's secretariat, and the United Nations Research Institute for Social Development (UNRISD) plays the role of the implementing agency of the Knowledge Hub for the SDGs (see also entry 6, 'Globalization and Alter-globalization').

In June 2022, the 110th International Labour Conference (ILC) adopted a resolution and conclusion concerning decent work and the social and solidarity economy (SSE), which directly relates to the implementation of the SDGs.

International and regional organisations focusing on or based in the Global North are also active in promoting the SSE, but the connections between the SSE and the SDGs are not as explicit as the UN agencies. For instance, the Organisation for Economic Co-operation and Development (OECD) is actively promoting social economy, but its main focus is largely on entrepreneurship and local development. On 4 December 2020, the International Summit on Social Economy for an Inclusive, Sustainable and Fair Recovery was organised in Toledo, Spain, by the Spanish government. At the Summit the 'Toledo Declaration on the Social and Solidarity Economy as a Key Driver for an Inclusive and Sustainable Future' was adopted with the support of 19 EU member states. In 2021, the Commissioner for Jobs and Social Rights of the European Union adopted the European Action Plan for Social Economy after a long consultation process involving citizens and stakeholders. The Plan follows other initiatives by the European Union to support the development of social economy enterprises, such as the 2011 Social Business Initiative (SBI).

International and regional non-government organisations promoting the SSE play a significant role in increasing the potential of the SSE as a means of implementing the SDGs. The EMES International Research Network (EMES), the Global Social Economy Forum (GSEF), the Intercontinental Network for the Promotion of Social Solidarity Economy (RIPESS), the International Centre of Research and Information on the Public, Social and Cooperative Economy (CIRIEC), the International Cooperative Alliance (ICA), Social Economy Europe and the SSE International Forum are among those key organisations contributing to the achievement of the SDGs at the national and subnational levels by SSEOEs.

40.4 PROMOTING THE SSE TO ACHIEVE THE SDGS AT THE NATIONAL AND SUBNATIONAL LEVEL

As awareness of the potential of the SSE to implement the SDGs grows, an increasing number of governments, at both national and subnational levels, are adopting policies and programmes that aim to support SSEOEs. National and subnational governments (including municipal, provincial and state/regional levels of a federal government) are increasingly interested in setting up public policies to promote and support the SSE in the context of the growing importance given to local sustainable development policies (including quality local public services), but also widespread reduction of fiscal transfers from the central government (Yi et al. 2017) (see also entry 51, 'Public Policy' and entry 53, 'Social Policy'). Caught between this fiscal pressure and increased service demands, policy makers seek advice on which policies and programmes are most people-oriented, while being cost-effective in achieving objectives associated with economic, social and environmental dimensions of sustainable development in their jurisdictions. The SSE is well placed to achieve these objectives because of its defining values and principles of community-centredness, democratic self-control, solidarity, ethics and cooperation within and beyond organisations. It has considerable potential to reduce inequalities in a local context. For instance, given the active participation of women, the SSE can significantly contribute toward women's economic, social and political empowerment (Yi et al. 2018).

The links between the SSE and the SDGs at the national level are often explicitly mentioned in the VNR for the HLPF of the UN, where the performance and success of the SDGs at the national level is reported (see Box 40.1 for an example).

BOX 40.1 LINKS BETWEEN THE SDG AND THE SSE AT THE NATIONAL LEVEL: MALAYSIAN VNR

A specific reference to social and community enterprises was made in the 2021 VNR report of Malaysia. The report recognised the contribution of social economy and the role of community actors, especially cooperative and social enterprise networks, in achieving the SDGs, as follows.

The VNR acknowledged that there are alternative economic models to the dominant economic model, which is for private equity and individual business. It also highlighted the roles of community forestry, and indigenous and local communities in achieving the SDGs. There is a sense of openness, especially after the COVID-19 pandemic revealed the vulnerability of the poor and informal sector, and the role of local communities in the support for local economies.

The recognition of the links between the SSE and the SDGs are also observed in the recent public policies to promote the SSE, such as the National Entrepreneurship Policy, the Malaysian Social Enterprise Blueprint and the Malaysian Cooperative Transformation Plan.

Through these policies, the cooperative provisions and the social enterprise accreditation are recognised as creating a new avenue for businesses to undertake a greater social and environmental responsibility.

Source: Malaysia (2021).

The ambitious vision for transformation laid out in the 2030 Agenda for Sustainable Development, and its core principle of 'leaving no one behind', can be realised only if the economic, social and political structures and relations generating injustice are corrected at multiple levels of governance. With a wide range of political, economic, social and environmental problems – as well as opportunities for progress – to be found at the local level, translating this global agenda into national as well as local solutions in urban, peri-urban and rural areas is key to achieving the SDGs. While attempts were made to 'localise' the MDGs, progress towards their achievement was mainly assessed in terms of national averages, which obscured the fact that multidimensional inequalities were increasing within and between urban and rural areas in both developed and developing countries. Acknowledging the importance of implementing the SDGs in all localities and for all communities, the 2030 Agenda emphasises the role of local authorities and communities in strengthening sustainable ecosystems, promoting local culture and products, fostering community cohesion and personal security, and stimulating innovation and employment. SDG 11 (make cities and human settlements inclusive, safe, resilient and sustainable) is a manifestation of the importance of localising the SDGs (Yi et al. 2017). Box 40.2 describes links between the SDG and the SSE at the subnational level.

BOX 40.2 LINKS BETWEEN THE SDG AND THE SSE AT THE SUBNATIONAL LEVEL

One of the most interesting achievements in terms of the contribution of SSEOEs to achieving the SDGs at the subnational level is the UNTFSSE Knowledge Hub for SDGs, in particular its collection of papers submitted to the 2019 UNTFSSE International Conference 'Implementing the Sustainable Development Goals: What Role for Social and Solidarity Economy' held on 25–26 June 2019 (Yi et al. 2019). The papers submitted to the conference aimed to systematically analyse the contribution of the SSE to the SDGs at the local level, through the analysis of SSE development in different regions and territories, examination of the role of the SSE as a means of implementation for the SDGs in diverse local contexts, and identification of robust methodologies and innovative solutions for measuring the SSE and its impacts. These submitted papers – that is, 43 studies on the contribution of SSEOEs to achieving the SDGs in different parts of the world – showed that the goals on poverty reduction (SDG 1), decent work (SDG 8), gender equality (SDG 5) and sustainable production and consumption (SDG 12) are among those most strongly associated with the SSE's objectives (Alarcón et al. 2022).

40.5   THE SSE AND THE SDGS IN GRASSROOTS COMMUNITIES

The SSE can address multiple objectives of sustainable development in an inclusive, democratic and sustainable manner. Through localised circuits of production, exchange and consumption, the SSE is conducive not only to basic needs provisioning but also to local economic development more generally. It can enhance the capacity of local producers and communities to increase added value, and stimulate demand for locally produced goods and services. The SSE can also contribute to retaining a greater share of income, and generating tax revenues for the local area. Solidarity, social cohesion and collective action, which are key characteristics of the SSE, can facilitate cooperation among local actors to improve basic infrastructure and social services, as well as promote the economic, social and political empowerment of vulnerable or otherwise excluded groups, in particular women. These roles and functions of the SSE in promoting local sustainable development, specifically the SSE–SDG links, are best illustrated through the work of community-based organisations. Boxes 40.3 and 40.4 give examples.

BOX 40.3   THE ASSOCIATION FOR SARVA SEVA FARMS (ASSEFA)

ASSEFA is rooted in Gandhian philosophy of Sarvodaya (a path of non-violence) in building a society where equality and freedom for all human beings is central. It is a vision for rural development which adopts a decentralised approach of democracy, decision making and collective action.

ASSEFA is currently operating in 10 000 villages and touching the lives of more than 1 845 700 rural families in Tamil Nadu. The majority of the rural population are involved in the agricultural economy and are dependent on agriculture for their livelihood (Jayasooria 2022).

ASSEFA at the village level undertakes a holistic range of interventions that encompasses improvement of the quality of life, which incorporates health and hygiene, education, gender equality, and justice and community resources for sustainability, which are associated with multiple SDGs such as SDG 1 on poverty, SDG 2 on hunger, SDG 3 on good health, SDG 4 on education, SDG 5 on gender and SDG 16 on justice and non-discrimination.

One example of the effective economic and sustainable programmes at the village level is the dairy farms run by families, especially women, involving the care and milking of cows. These impact upon SDG 5 on gender equality, SDG 8 on creating economic opportunity, SDG 10 on addressing inequality and SDG 12 on consumption and production.

Yvon Poirier and Kumar Loganathan (2019) describe ASSEFA as a large-scale organisation which embodies all aspects of development, namely women's empowerment, business development and environmental concerns, as well as human rights, housing and food needs of the poor. It highlights how ASSEFA delivers almost all the SDGs addressing human concern.

BOX 40.4   COMMUNITY-OWNED PAWN SHOPS IN MALAYSIA

Malaysian media documented a surprising development during the COVID-19 pandemic and the lockdown in mid-2020. When the lockdown was lifted, many individuals were making a beeline for pawn shops (Hassan 2020). This incident showed the vulnerable position of low-income families, especially those from the informal sector, as well as the self-employed individuals who have neither enough savings nor a social protection plan.

One major alternative initiative was established by faith-based institutions based on Islamic principles and guidelines. It is inclusive, as this service is accessible to people of all faiths (Jayasooria 2021).

The cooperative laws (Cooperative Act 1993) were amended to enable cooperatives to establish pawn shops as collective enterprises. Among the cooperatives it is estimated that 90 of them manage Islamic pawn shops, and the cooperative bank known as Bank Rakyat manages 42 outlets (Hanifkuala 2014).

The pawn shops address both SDG 1 and SDG 10 in addressing poverty and inequality, providing access to credit in times of financial uncertainty. There is a collective dimension, as these pawn shops shown are community-owned and therefore closer to the SSE due to their compliance with SSE collective ownership and ethical values in meeting human needs.

CONCLUSION

Although development discourse and practice consistently emphasise the importance of localising international and national development strategies and goals, results thus far have been less than satisfactory. In the context of the 2030 Agenda, which is built upon the principle of 'leaving no one behind', localising the SDGs is essential for realising the vision of transformation everywhere for everyone. In this context, the SSE, rooted in the local context, plays a significant role in achieving the SDGs at the local level. SSEOEs are mostly organised by and for the most vulnerable, and are being mobilised to address their concerns at the local level. The SSE, which may be organised in different ways (such as cooperatives, self-help groups, social enterprises, village communities or informal groups), plays a role in the realisation of SDGs at the local level. As we can see in the cases of India and Malaysia, the links between the SSE and the SDGs, or the contribution of the SSE to achieving the SDGs, are particularly visible in community-based organisations, which are often intertwined with broader social struggles to promote the interests of the most vulnerable and to strengthen the collective right of communities to be engaged in designing projects and laws affecting their lands or environment. They are making a difference in the lives of ordinary and vulnerable people, and the SSE communities are contributing towards the localising of the SDGs, ensuring no one is left behind.

REFERENCES

Alarcón, Miguel Ángel, Ana Milena Silva, Leandro Pereira Morais, Juan Fernando Álvarez and Duarcides Ferreira Mariosa. 2022. 'Characterization of the UNTFSSE Knowledge Hub: 2019 Repository about the Relationship between Social and Solidarity Economy and the Sustainable Development Goals.' SSE Knowledge Hub for the SDGs. Geneva: UNTFSSE Knowledge Hub for the SDGs. 2022. https://knowledgehub.unsse.org/knowledge-hub/characterization-of-the-knowledge-hub/.

Hanifkuala, Nur Hanini Mohd. 2014. 'Ar-Rahnu Funding for Co-Ops.' *New Straits Times*. 24 December. https://www.nst.com.my/news/2015/09/ar-rahnu-funding-co-ops.

Hassan, Hazlin. 2020. 'Coronavirus: Rush on Pawnshops as Cash-Strapped Malaysians Hock Valuables.' *Straits Times*. 5 May. https://www.straitstimes.com/asia/se-asia/coronavirus-rush-on-pawn-shops-as-cash-strapped-malaysians-hock-valuables.

Jayasooria, Denison. 2021. 'Mapping the Social and Solidarity Economy Landscape in Asia: Spotlight on Malaysia.' Geneva: ILO. https://www.ilo.org/wcmsp5/groups/public/---ed_emp/---emp_ent/---coop/documents/publication/wcms_822183.pdf.

Jayasooria, Denison. 2022. 'Grassroots Solidarity in Revitalising Rural Economy in Asia, Drawing Lessons from Three Case Studies in India, Indonesia and China.' *Sociedade E Território* 34 (1): 237–60. https://doi.org/10.21680/2177-8396.2022v34n1id27979.

Malaysia. 2021. 'Malaysia Voluntary National Review (VNR) 2021.' Putrajaya: Economic Planning Unit, Prime Minister's Department. https://www.epu.gov.my/sites/default/files/2021-07/Malaysia_Voluntary_National_Review_%28VNR%29_2021.pdf.

Poirier, Yvon, and Kumar Loganathan. 2019. 'Association for Sarva Seva Farms (ASSEFA) India 50 Years of Sustainable Development Implementing the Sustainable Development Goals: What Role for Social and Solidarity Economy?' Geneva: UNTFSSE Knowledge Hub for the SDGs. https://knowledgehub.unsse.org/wp-content/uploads/2019/05/81_Poirier_new.pdf.

Quinones Jr, B. 2020. 'The Making of SSE.' YouTube. https://www.youtube.com/watch?v=Mx3T3nWJDWw.

RIPESS. 2022. 'About RIPESS.' 22 February. http://www.ripess.org/who-are-we/about-ripess/?lang=en.

Sen, Amartya. 1999. *Development as Freedom*. Oxford: Oxford University Press.

United Nations. 2012. 'The Future We Want: Outcome Document of the United Nations Conference on Sustainable Development.' https://sustainabledevelopment.un.org/futurewewant.html.

United Nations. 2015. 'Transforming Our World: The 2030 Agenda for Sustainable Development.' https://sdgs.un.org/2030agenda.

UNTFSSE. 2022. 'About the Knowledge Hub.' SSE Knowledge Hub for the SDGs. 22 February. https://knowledgehub.unsse.org/about/.

Utting, Peter. 2015. Introduction: The challenges of scaling up social and solidarity economy, Utting, Peter ed. *Social and Solidarity Economy: Beyond the Fringe*, London, Zed Books and UNRISD.

Yi, Ilcheong, Heejin Ahn, Jongick Jang, Michelle Jaramillo, Eun Sun Lee, Suyeon Lee, Peter Utting and Joon Young Yi. 2018. 'Social and Solidarity Economy for the Sustainable Development Goals: Spotlight on the Social Economy in Seoul.' Geneva: UNRISD. https://www.unrisd.org/80256B3C005BCCF9/httpNetITFramePDF?ReadForm&parentunid=C271CADE934020E0C1258315004C7DDF&parentdoctype=book&netitpath=80256B3C005BCCF9/(httpAuxPages)/C271CADE934020E0C1258315004C7DDF/.

Yi, Ilcheong, Samuel Bruelisauer, Gabriel Salathe-Beaulieu and Martina Piras. 2019. 'Implementing the Sustainable Development Goals: What Role for Social and Solidarity Economy?' Geneva: UNTFSSE Knowledge Hub for the SDGs. https://knowledgehub.unsse.org/knowledge-hub/conference-summary/

Yi, Ilcheong, Hyuna Yi, and Suyeon Lee. 2017. 'Research and Policy Brief 24: Localizing the SDGs through Social and Solidarity Economy.' Geneva: UNRISD. https://www.unrisd.org/80256B3C005BCCF9/(httpAuxPages)/3174C96290CECDFAC12581A700362DBA/$file/RPB24-Localizing%20SDGs%20through%20SSE.pdf.

41. Tourism sector
Gilles Caire

INTRODUCTION

To make a better world, the social and solidarity economy (SSE) questions tourism in terms of its socio-economic and environmental impacts, the relationship between producers of tourist services and consumer tourists, and the ways in which decisions are made in partnership with the inhabitants of the host territories.

Social and solidarity economy tourism (SSET) aims to be the bearer of a 'different kind of tourism', one that is open, respectful, supportive, responsible, qualitative and, in short, more human. The International Social Tourism Organisation (ISTO), created in 1963 and bringing together 159 member organisations from 40 countries, has two ambitions: the social ambition of 'tourism for all', aiming to 'make holidays accessible to the greatest number of people', and the solidarity ambition of 'responsible tourism, that benefits people, communities and local areas. These include responsible, solidarity, fair and community tourism' (ISTO 2020).

41.1 AN ALTERNATIVE VIEW OF TOURISM

According to the United Nations Tourism Statistical System (United Nations 2010), 'tourism is a social, cultural and economic phenomenon related to the movement of people to places outside their usual place of residence, pleasure being the usual motivation'. SSET is concerned with all dimensions of this definition and aims to contribute, at its level, to the achievement of the United Nations Sustainable Development Goals (SDGs).

Social Dimension

Regarding the social dimension, the SSE concerns the population practising tourism and workers of the tourism sector. The population practising tourism is still a minority, probably no more than one in three of the planet's inhabitants. Travel, an element of the right to leisure included in the Declaration of Human Rights (art. 24), is inaccessible to the vast majority of people in poor countries, due to a lack of financial means and paid holidays. But this is also the case for a significant proportion of disadvantaged people in rich countries. In the European Union, for example, more than one in three people do not go on holiday, half of them for financial reasons. The ambition of SSET is first and foremost to contribute to the reduction of inequalities within and between countries (SDG 10) by facilitating access to tourism.

In many countries, the working conditions and incomes of tourism workers, whether salaried or self-employed, are more unfavourable in tourism than in other economic sectors, with precarious working conditions and poorly paid work; long working hours and tight work schedules raising the issue of reconciling family and professional life; the prevalence of informal or undeclared work, and therefore lack of social security coverage; and child labour. The second ambition of SSET is to contribute to decent work (SDG 8) in the tourism sector.

Cultural and Democratic Dimension

On the cultural side, the encounter between tourists and host populations can be conflictual due to a range of issues such as inappropriate behaviour disrespecting local values, laxity and commercialisation of folklore customs or traditions of hospitality. Being rooted in the local context, SSET takes into account the opinions of local people and respects their beliefs and ways of life, and consequently contributes to democratic decision-making and mutual cultural understanding (SDG 16).

Economic Dimension

Tourist spending at a destination may destabilise food prices and local rents. Moreover, tourism revenues are very unevenly distributed among local people, in particular those involved in the tourism sector, depending on their place in the value chain (tour operator, carrier, accommodation provider, restaurant operator, activity provider, and so on), their market weight, their gender and their location. SSET seeks shared growth (SDG 8) in tourism revenues, gender equality (SDG 5) in the sector and community empowerment (SDG 11) in host territories.

Environmental Dimension

Travel, which is an integral part of tourism, also poses a major problem of environmental sustainability, both at the local level (over-frequentation of natural areas, damage to biodiversity, soil artificialisation, water and waste management, and so on) and at the global level, as with the effects of air transport on global warming. SSET aims to establish sustainable production and consumption patterns (SDG 12) through environmentally friendly tourism, by favouring soft modes of transport, waste sorting and energy saving.

Human Dimension

Finally, pleasure, a substantial element of tourism, is deeply linked to the human character of the search for connections, discoveries of other places and other people, freedom, emancipation, relaxation, and couple and family life. Emotions, imagination, play, joy, rest, social ties and contact with nature, all of which are possible thanks to tourism, are constituent elements of human development, elements of the 'good human life' as defined by Martha Nussbaum (2000). To this end, the various forms of SSET offer a wide range of sports, cultural and leisure activities, with an emphasis on group, diversity, nature, participation and discovery.

41.2   SIX HISTORICAL FORMS OF SSE TOURISM

This search for an 'other tourism' has historically been built around six major moments, leading today to a plural SSET in terms of the audience's received social objectives, and institutional forms (Caire 2012).

The Tradition of Traveller Hospitality

Most religions (Judaism, Christianity, Islam, Hinduism, and so on) and many customary practices around the world consider hospitality as a virtue. Travellers and foreigners, especially pilgrims, must be welcomed with food and shelter.

The Hospice du Grand Saint Bernard founded in 1050, the many hostels on the pilgrimage routes to Santiago de Compostela, and even certain forms of backpacker tourism based on free hospitality are one of the examples based on a non-monetary economy based on mutual aid, solidarity, selflessness and commitment.

Holiday Camps for Children

One of the first modern forms of SSET can be found in Switzerland. In 1876, Herman Walter Bion, a pastor in Zurich, created the first holiday camp (*Ferienkolonie*, in reference to the settler seeking a new and better life). With a dual intention of hygiene ('a breath of fresh air') and education, Bion took some 60 underprivileged children from working-class neighbourhoods to the mountains. Dispersed among peasant families, who were compensated to cover the costs incurred, these children were brought together several times a week to organise games, songs and hikes supervised by educators.

Very quickly, from the 1880s onwards, holiday camps expanded considerably, first in Europe (for example in Germany, Italy, France, Russia, Holland, Belgium) and then, after the First World War, in the United States, Canada, Japan, and so on. The first international holiday camp congress was held in Zurich in 1888 under the presidency of Bion. Initially, it was a philanthropic, religious or secular model, financed by subscriptions and private donations, and based on voluntary work (except for the hosts), with unpaid staff. Quite quickly, these holiday camps were to benefit from public authority subsidies and were then subject to increasing regulation and a gradual professionalisation of the staff (Downs 2002).

Today, depending on the country, these holiday camps can be based on non-monetary models (such as the scout movement), non-market models (such as camps organised by charitable organisations or municipalities), market non-profit models (associative organisations) or market profit models (particularly for language trips). But in almost all cases, the dual health and educational dimension remain central.

Youth Hostels

Also in the spirit of youth education, Richard Schirmann, a German teacher, founded the first youth hostel in Altena in 1912, on the principle that 'It is impossible to squeeze the limitless world into a crowded classroom. So the school must go out into the world' (Hostelling International 2021).

The model developed very quickly throughout Europe, then after the Second World War on other continents. As early as 1932, representatives of 11 European associations founded the International Youth Hostel Federation (IYHF) (which has operated as Hostelling International since 2006), of which Schirmann became president. The mission has remained the same since 1932:

> To promote the education of all young people of all nations, but especially young people of limited means, by encouraging in them a greater knowledge, love and care of the countryside and an appreciation of the cultural values from towns and cities in all parts of the world, and as ancillary thereby to provide hostels or other accommodation in which there shall be no distinction of origin, nationality, colour, religion, sex, class or political opinions and thereby to develop a better understanding of their fellow men, both at home and abroad. (Hostelling International 2021)

These values of accessibility, non-discrimination, social and gender diversity, peace, learning and understanding, authenticity, and contact with nature and heritage are today carried by an international movement of over 4000 youth hostels in 75 countries, with 4 million members and over 1.5 billion annual overnight stays. Although there are some youth hostels run on a for-profit basis, most organisations in the sector are not-for-profit.

Since 1947, the international federation has had a consultative seat at the United Nations Educational, Scientific and Cultural Organization (UNESCO). And during the 1980s, the Hostelling International (HI) network implemented standardised environmental commitments, resulting in an Environmental Charter in 1992 and a Sustainable Tourism Charter in line with the SDGs in 2016 (Hostelling International 2021).

Holidays for Working-Class Families

After the Second World War, paid holidays became widespread in rich countries, in particular with the adoption in 1936 of International Labour Organization Convention No. 52 on paid holidays, according to which every employee is entitled, after one year's continuous service, to at least one week of paid annual leave (increased to two weeks in 1970 by Convention No. 132). From then on, political and trade union leaders sought to democratise holidays in a context, in the aftermath of the Second World War, where the tourist offer was almost exclusively aimed at the upper classes.

The problems were quantitative, with the absence of accommodation for large numbers of people; financial, with prices higher than the purchasing power of the working classes; and qualitative, with activities not adapted to families with children. Depending on the country, popular education movements, mutual societies, political parties (particularly Christian Democrats, Social Democrats and Communists), workers' unions, joint institutions (such as works councils in France) and charitable organisations tried to respond to these problems, based on two models that were sometimes combined (Diekmann and McCabe 2020).

The first model is the construction of collective tourist accommodation aimed in particular at workers and employees, offering all-inclusive packages (accommodation, catering and activities including childcare) at accessible rates, which are sometimes adjusted according to family income. In several countries, these accommodation facilities also benefit from subsidies from the national or local authorities, as part of social policies and policies to support areas that have not been industrialised (coastline, mountains, countryside). From the 1960s to the 1980s, the numbers of these facilities, often called holiday centres, were continuously growing in France, Belgium, Switzerland, Portugal, Morocco and Brazil, for example. Many of these centres were linked to both public and private sectors where unionisation and/or company paternalism were strong (gas and electricity companies, railways, banks, aeronautics, mines, and so on). Funding is based on a combination of market resources from customer payments, and non-market, public, union and company resources. This sometimes leads to a distinction between ownership of the facilities, owned by public authorities or companies, and management delegated to an association.

The second model is that of social action, with the subsidisation of holidays of people facing obstacles that may be monetary, cultural (people not used to going away), social (isolation) or physical (disability, illness and age). These subsidised holidays were usually in for-profit tourism accommodation or in the non-profit accommodation mentioned above. This model is based on the full or almost full financial coverage of transport and accommodation costs, but also on social and cultural support. In this case, the support is provided by foundations, associations specialising in disability or charities.

North–South and North–North Fair, Solidarity and Community Tourism

At the end of the 1970s, as post-decolonisation development models were being questioned, North–South tourism was criticised for being isolated, for having little local economic impact, for being culturally distorted and for dismantling community lifestyles. Following on from these first experiences, solidarity tourism really emerged at the end of the 1990s – particularly in Africa and Latin America – in conjunction with the debates on international aid, fair trade and ecotourism. It takes the form of small group travel, far from the major tourist infrastructures, favouring encounters and exchanges with local populations. Tourist groups are hosted by local people or in accommodation run by the local population (small hotels, family-run gîtes, campsites, and so on). The aim is to promote the local economy (guides, meals, transport, handicrafts, and so on) and to travel with respect for the local people, their culture and their environment. In addition, part of the price of the trip is donated to development projects, decided upon and managed by the host communities. The organisation of these trips generally relies on the collaboration of associations in the Northern sending countries, and village associations, community groups or cooperatives in the Southern receiving countries.

In a similar vein, some Northern countries will also develop forms of internal solidarity tourism. In Quebec, more than 200 tourist cooperatives are part of a long tradition of social economy. Half of them have adopted the status of multi-party solidarity cooperatives, introduced by the 1997 Cooperatives Act. Anchored territorially, these tourism cooperatives focus on creating local jobs, pooling the means of production and financing the tourism development of their territory (Salamero et al. 2018).

Share Tourism

From the 2000s onwards, digital technologies and the collaborative economy have led to the emergence of platforms offering accommodation with local people, home exchange, carpooling, visits to non-touristy urban areas, and so on. The principles are that the service is free or very low cost, it is user-friendly and involves direct contact with the host, and the computer system used to establish contact is not-for-profit.

With the rise of these systems, some platforms will evolve towards the profit-making model of start-ups. For example, couchsurfing.com was initially established in 2004 as a non-profit association but became a joint stock company in 2011, financed by advertisement. Since 2020 it has charged a flat fee to all its users. Other platforms, on the other hand, have chosen to keep the non-profit model, such as BeWelcome or the Greeters movement, or Les Oiseaux de Passage. These matchmaking systems thus operate, in an updated form, according to the traditional principles of hospitality without charge mentioned above.

41.3 CONSIDERABLE CHALLENGES FOR THE FUTURE

Whatever form of organisation is chosen, SSET must now face the following challenges.

Social Inequalities and Tourism Inequalities

Inequalities in income and wealth are growing today, including within developed countries. At the same time, public budgets are increasingly constrained, and social policies focus on housing, food and access to employment. Leisure and holidays are not considered a priority by the public authorities. As a result, in many European countries for almost 20 years the proportion of people going on holiday has not increased, or has even decreased.

However, numerous studies (Diekmann and McCabe 2020) in France, Canada, Belgium and the United Kingdom have shown the value of holidays for children and young people (confidence-building, empowerment, social openness, acquisition of knowledge, social skills and mobility, channelling of energies, development of citizenship, re-mobilisation, and so on); for families (reduction of intra-family conflicts, strengthening of ties, less stress, perspective on daily life, feeling of social normality, and so on); and for the elderly and people with disabilities (reduction of social isolation and feelings of loneliness, improvement of physiological and psychological health, and so on).

The challenge for SSET is therefore to defend the social utility of holidays, to argue around the positive effects of travel for all categories of public, in order to regain public support.

The Environmental Unsustainability of Tourism Growth

When transport, food, accommodation and traveller purchases are taken into account, 8 per cent of global greenhouse gas (GHG) emissions are due to tourism (Lenzen et al. 2018). The growth rate of these emissions is close to 4 per cent per year, and the majority of emissions comes from countries with the highest gross domestic product per capita. Air transport is by far the most GHG-emitting mode of transport per passenger kilometre. However, as domestic tourism is largely predominant in terms of number of trips (representing 75 per cent of total emissions), it is tourist trips by car that are the most significant in terms of volume. These effects of tourism on climate change, and the problems of social and environmental pressure on the most popular destinations, are added up to be a source of a growing critical discourse on mass tourism, often described as 'tourism bashing'.

This context can generate two reactions leading to the exclusion of the 'poor' from tourism: the introduction of carbon taxes and access tolls to exceptional sites, and the prioritisation of highly profitable inbound tourism for destinations. The challenge for SSET is to make its social ambition of democratisation compatible with the growing environmental constraints. The development of 'slow' tourism (soft mobility, longer stays) and local (intra-regional) tourism, the search for a better distribution of flows in space and time to avoid the effects of overpopulation and seasonality, but also the defence of the right to travel for all, are therefore strategic elements for SSET.

Social Responsibility

The tourism industry often offers insecure, temporary and seasonal jobs with low wages and sometimes no access to social security. In addition, the threat of mass unemployment with the prolongation of the COVID-19 crisis affects the tourism sector in particular.

In rich countries, the challenge for SSET operators is to provide, in a highly competitive context, offers that remain accessible to the greatest number of people, and collective agreements that are favourable to their employees in terms of wages, working conditions and social security coverage. In developing countries, the challenge for SSET is to contribute to a step-by-step formalisation of informal jobs that are still very present in the tourism sector.

Institutional Isomorphism

Institutional isomorphism (see entry 44, 'Co-optation, Isomorphism and Instrumentalisation') is a process that leads organisations to resemble other units facing the same set of constraints. In the first place, it takes place because of the pressure exerted by regulations and the conditions for the allocation of public funding. Within the government's regulatory regime, standards of safety, supervision of minors, quality, contracts, and so on, tend to be uniform for all operators. And these standards have a greater impact on low-cost holidays and small structures, which is often the case for SSET organisations. Secondly, the influence of expertise and sectoral professionalisation leads to standardisation of practices, by copying the formulas that 'work', pushing for an upmarket approach and the same thought and management patterns.

The challenge for SSET is to avoid trivialising its offer, at the risk of having the same products, the same prices, the same audiences and, in the long term, the same values as the dominant tourism. It is also a question of knowing how to distinguish itself from the social washing and greenwashing of falsely responsible tourism. Social innovation and the need for differentiation, in a market that has become mature in many countries, are now crucial for the survival of the SSET sector.

REFERENCES

Caire, Gilles. 2012. 'Social Tourism and the Social Economy.' In *Social Tourism in Europe. Theory and Practice*, edited by Scott McCabe, Lynn Minnaert and Anya Diekmann. Bristol: Channel View Publications.

Diekmann, Anya, and Scott McCabe. 2020. *Handbook of Social Tourism*. Cheltenham, UK and Northampton, MA, USA: Edward Elgar Publishing.

Downs, Laura Lee. 2002. *Childhood in the Promised Land. Working Class Movements and the Colonies de Vacances in France, 1880–1960*. Durham, NC: Duke University Press.

Hostelling International. 2021. 'Our History: For Good, Not For Profit!' https://www.hihostels.com/pages/534.

ISTO. 2020. 'Promote a "Sensible" Tourism Tomorrow.' https://isto.international/wp-content/uploads/2020/04/Sensible-Tourism.pdf.

Lenzen, Manfred, Ya-Yen Sun, Futu Faturay, Yuan-Peng Ting, Arne Geschke and Arunima Malik. 2018. 'The Carbon Footprint of Global Tourism.' *Nature Climate Change* 8 (6): 522–8. https://doi.org/10.1038/s41558-018-0141-x.

Nussbaum, Martha. 2000. *Women and Human Development: The Capabilities Approach*. Cambridge: Cambridge University Press.

Salamero, Sylvain, Gilles Caire and Christiane Gagnon. 2018. 'Le Tourisme Coopératif au Québec: Une Forme de Tourisme Vecteur de Développement Pour les Territoires Périphériques?' *IdeAs – Idées d'Amériques* 12. https://journals.openedition.org/ideas/3390.

United Nations. 2010. 'International Recommendations for Tourism Statistics 2008.' New York: United Nations. https://unstats.un.org/unsd/publication/seriesm/seriesm_83rev1e.pdf.

42. Work integration
Kate Cooney, Marthe Nyssens and Mary O'Shaughnessy

INTRODUCTION

One field of social enterprise – WISEs, or work integration social enterprises – has become increasingly recognized as being emblematic of the dynamics of social enterprises, and it now constitutes a major sphere of their activity globally. The main objective of WISEs is to integrate those with intellectual or physical disabilities, and other disadvantaged groups, including the long-term unemployed, back into the labour market and society through a productive activity. WISEs, like the broader field of social enterprises, of which they are a part, are usually viewed as multiple-goal organizations: they mix social goals, connected to their specific mission to benefit the community (the integration of people excluded from the labour market through productive activity, but also in some cases other goals linked to community development, such as the supply of services to elderly people, children and recycling goods); economic goals, related to their entrepreneurial nature; and socio-political goals, given that many social enterprises originate in a sector traditionally involved in socio-political action (Cooney et al. 2016).

42.1 PIONEERING INITIATIVES

In many countries, WISEs have their roots in a pre-1960s era characterized by vocational rehabilitation initiatives targeted at persons deemed (at the time) unable to compete and/or participate fully in the open labour market. These first-wave WISEs combined work activities with life skills training and socialization activities for those with intellectual and/or physical disabilities. Any market activity was typically sheltered from full exposure to market competition, through government subsidies and procurement policies. As part of broader Keynesian welfare state models, government subsidies and support flowed from a commitment to provide places of decommodification, sheltered spaces where populations, deemed unable to support themselves, could participate in productive activities by selling their labour.

The second wave of WISEs emerged in the 1980s; it was characterized by a markedly different profile. These WISEs engaged with a broader set of disadvantaged populations, including long-term unemployed, immigrant and refugee populations, individuals struggling with substance misuse, former prisoners, homeless and otherwise struggling low-income individuals. Most of these WISEs were typically founded by civil society actors: social workers, community activists and trade unionists. In the context of persistent unemployment, the social actors lacked adequate public policy measures to tackle the challenges traditionally associated with these disadvantaged groups. Consequently, initiatives emerged that emphasized the limitations of public intervention on behalf of persons excluded from the labour market, such as the long-term unemployed, persons lacking qualifications or people at risk of social and economic exclusion. The aim was similar to that of the initiatives that had arisen in the 1960s: namely, to provide work activity and socializing opportunities for those at the margins. However, the context had changed. The 1970s crisis of rising structural unemployment fostered this second wave of WISEs. This second wave of WISEs emerged on the borders of the old welfare states. They created employment opportunities and services where states and markets were not providing them; they were also almost forerunners in the implementation of active labour market policies, in many instances appearing well before the emergence of such public policies (see also entry 53, 'Social Policy'). Indeed, the processes of institutionalization of WISEs is best understood in the context of the boom in national active labour market policies that emerged in the 1970s. Public bodies, faced with high rates of unemployment and a crisis in public finances, began to develop policies that aimed to integrate the unemployed into the labour market or community service provision (through professional training programmes, job subsidy programmes, and so on), instead of relying only on passive labour market policies based on a system of allocation of cash benefits to the unemployed. In this context, it seems that WISEs had come to represent a tool for implementing these active labour market policies, in essence almost becoming a 'conveyor belt' of active labour market programmes, albeit to varying degrees across country contexts.

While public policy support available to WISEs varies across countries, European WISEs have availed themselves of public funds such as the European Social Fund (ESF) and the European Structural and Investment Funds (ESIFs) and other additional public national or regional support to WISEs in the form of: (1) subsidies and/or reduction in taxes or social security contributions; and (2) non-competitive direct assignment of public works and contracts (Borzaga et al. 2020, 84). Thus, while there is some growth in other forms of resources from income-generating activities for WISEs, such as the sale of goods and services to private users, the majority of (European) WISEs continue to rely on a mix of financial resources, with a notable reliance on public funds/subsidies and a combination of paid and unpaid human resources (Borzaga et al. 2020). Public subsidies to WISEs are not as important in other parts of the world. In contrast to their European counterparts, in the United States (US) the policy supports, such as set-aside procurements, have not been extended to the newer WISEs that have emerged with a broadened focus beyond the sheltered workshop model, resulting in more exposure to market forces for these WISE businesses. The resource mix of Latin American WISEs includes much fewer public resources than the resource mix of their counterparts in other parts of the world; this feature reflects the weakness of state support to the social enterprise field in this region.

42.2 DIFFERENT MODES OF WORK INTEGRATION

The historic evolution of the WISE sector highlights the ways in which the organizational model has been adapted in response to shifting social constructions about appropriate levels of integration and norms about employment for disadvantaged groups, as well as the changing nature of jobs in the entry-level labour market. Based on the different forms of public recognition, several types of WISEs emerged which can be classified into four main groups, based on how workers are integrated into the workplace and/or mainstream labour markets.

The first type of integration mode seeks to make up for the gap between the productivity required by the conventional labour market and the actual capacities of the workers through open-ended employment contracts. Historically, this integration mode has been most prevalently offered to WISEs creating sheltered employment for persons with disabilities and subsidized by public authorities. Some newer forms of WISEs, rooted in the second wave, also offer such type of work integration, but increasingly combined with the goal of community service. This is the case for the example of the Community Services Programme (CSP) in Ireland, which is a community-based support programme for social and community enterprises with specific characteristics, including: community ownership, a local development focus and the provision of work integration opportunities for the long-term unemployed and other groups at risk of social and economic exclusion. The participating social enterprises are not required or expected to become financially sustainable, and consequently often remain reliant on statutory funding (O'Hara and O'Shaughnessy 2021).

A related open-ended employment integration mode aims to (re)socialize people by means of productive activities. These WISEs aim to serve particularly vulnerable workers. The work they provide is 'semi-informal'; that is, it is not regulated by a legal arrangement or employment contract. Voluntary work is relatively important, and market resources are limited. This is similar to the first category of WISEs previously described, except that there is no labour contract. Pertinent examples include some of the Japanese WISEs that provide opportunities for those with disabilities to enjoy a social life (Laratta and Nakagawa 2016).

Another major type of integration mode features work experience ('transit' employment) or training through work. Although social enterprises operating this mode of integration all share a common objective – to help their beneficiaries find a job in the conventional labour market – they differ in the ways in which they pursue this goal. A WISE operating in this way can provide temporary jobs with on-the-job training and social support (for example, in the US) or offer training leading to a qualification in the form of an internship (for example, in Belgium and Japan). Such initiatives typically offer term-limited job opportunities before transitioning workers to employers in the unsubsidized labour market, and increasingly work with mainstream employers to co-create training curricula and develop work skills to meet labour market demand. This integration mode is the most frequent across countries, and the diversity of approaches is matched by the diversity in the ways in which resources are mobilized. Some countries have direct subsidization schemes for the job or employment function of the WISE (for example, France, Japan and Austria). In some countries, the beneficiaries of WISEs receive subsidies directly through unemployment or social allowances, supplemented by a lump-sum reimbursement for public transport costs and meals (for example, Switzerland), while in others the job creation or employment function is practically independent of any kind of direct public subsidy, although there may be public resources for ancillary training (for example, the US). For many of these models, the ability to generate third-party resources through volunteer labour and philanthropy can be important.

A final category of integration mode describes WISEs that offer self-financed permanent employment – that is, jobs which are economically viable in the medium term – to vulnerable individuals. Worker cooperatives specifically designed to employ disadvantaged workers could be included in this category. The mode of integration is direct employment by firms that are designed with social hiring in mind. In the case of worker cooperatives operating in this mode, the firms are owned and controlled by their workers, and they typically focus on wealth building through employment as a form of community economic development. These WISEs aim to create new and democratic workplaces, and to provide services for local communities (see also entry 49, 'Participation, Governance, Collective Action and Democracy'). US worker cooperatives specifically designed to employ disadvantaged workers can be included in this category. This is also the case of many collective initiatives embedded in the informal sector in Southern countries, such as in Latin America (Gaiger and Wanderley 2019).

Finally, it must be pointed out that some types of WISEs do not fit easily into one of these main groups, because they simultaneously implement different modes of work integration, such as B-type social cooperatives in Italy, or neighbourhood organizations in France. These WISEs pursue different work integration objectives for widely differing target groups. It should also be noted that several types of WISEs, with different integration modes, can coexist in the same country.

42.3 WISES CAN ADOPT DIFFERENT MODELS OF SOCIAL ENTERPRISE

While it is one thing to identify the integration mode of workers implemented by the WISE, another is to qualify the specific type of social enterprise in which these workers are integrated. Even though not all practices tadopted are new, the concept of social enterprise has grown in popularity, and the forms they take continue to diversify. As explained in entry 21, 'Social Enterprises', in this *Encyclopedia*, four social enterprise models have been theorized within the framework of a broad international research project, the International Comparative Social Enterprise Models (ICSEM) Project, namely: entrepreneurial nonprofits, public sector social enterprises, social cooperatives and social businesses (see entry 21, 'Social Enterprises'). These models were tested based on the data collected through a large survey which was carried out by researchers from 43 countries across the world (Defourny et al. 2021). The empirical data collected were statistically analysed with a central objective: to see whether groups of social enterprises emerged that were sufficiently similar in terms of their characteristics, but at the same time demonstrating some distinctiveness from each other. Work integration is certainly one of the most emblematic missions of social enterprise which can potentially be found across the four models.

The first set of WISEs includes enterprises that can be referred to as 'entrepreneurial nonprofits'. This is the case of WISEs that are founded and managed by civil society actors, including social workers, community activists and trade unionists. Two groups emerging from the ICSEM empirical evidence are broadly classified as 'WISE entrepreneurial nonprofit'.

In the first of these two groups, most WISEs adopt the nonprofit organizational (NPO) legal form and have been launched by citizens. These WISEs rely on a diversity of resources, with half of the income coming from the market and the other half from public subsidies and donations. In the second group, legal forms are much more diverse (NPOs, foundations, limited companies, or even informal organizations). Enterprises in this group rely more heavily on market resources than those in the previous group. Most organizations in this second group have also been launched by a parent third-sector organization or by citizens. If the social enterprise terminates its activity, the net assets are transferred to another social enterprise or NPO with a similar social mission, or to the parent organization. The distribution of profit is fully prohibited, or profit is distributed to the nonprofit parent organization. These latter organizations can be defined as 'nonprofit parent-launched WISEs'.

These two types of WISEs sell a wide variety of goods or services. Their productive activities can often be considered as 'mission-related': the economic activity is a means to create jobs, whatever the types of products, and these are commercialized for a population that is much wider than the group of vulnerable workers targeted by the social mission.

In Eastern Asia, the social enterprise landscape is dominated by these two WISE NPO groups. WISEs can choose to operate under a nonprofit legal form and to be registered by public authorities in one way or another, thus gaining access to subsidies. Alternatively, and most often, a WISE can be created by a nonprofit parent organisation, such as a foundation or an association, which is likely to support it in one way or another. In this case, the WISE itself can take any legal form, adopting the form that is best adapted to the market that generates its income. Such a legal arrangement often corresponds to partnerships between for-profit companies (through their foundations) and NPOs, operating as 'social joint ventures' (Defourny et al. 2019).

In some environments, with a strong cooperative tradition, WISEs may be launched by persons excluded from the labour market and motivated by a dynamic of mutual aid. Indeed, large sections of the population living on the margins of the formal economy are involved in various types of economic practices based on self-help principles, to generate income and to improve their living conditions. These initiatives are sometimes labelled as 'solidarity economy', especially in Latin America (Gaiger and Wanderley 2019) (see also entry 10, 'Origins and Histories'). In many of these labour-managed initiatives, the quest for empowerment of the poor and for economic democracy among workers are also explicit social goals. Therefore, such WISEs are often single-stakeholder social enterprises, and may be seen as informal or semi-formal worker cooperatives. In many cases, the mutual interest pursued by member-workers lies in the creation of jobs for these workers under their own control, but it is combined with a clear and broader social orientation because these workers are generally living on the margins of society and working for the survival of poor families or local communities.

According to ICSEM results, this cooperative type – especially worker cooperatives – constitutes the dominant social enterprise form in Latin America. Workers are the core of these rather small organizations; their goal is to create their own jobs and to improve their living conditions. Some Latin American cooperatives have experienced strong isomorphic pressures which have led them, in some cases, to become more similar to capital interest-driven organisations (see also entry 44, 'Co-optation, Isomorphism and Instrumentalisation'). As a result, the cooperative legacy sometimes conveys an ambiguous image. However, the importance of this cooperative-type social enterprise group leads us to acknowledge the strong worker cooperative DNA that characterizes the social enterprise field in Latin America. In some way, these worker cooperatives reconnect with the initial roots and values of the cooperative movement.

By contrast to these single-stakeholder cooperative-type social enterprises, some social cooperatives which also integrate disadvantaged workers into the labour market, bring together different types of stakeholders in their governing bodies. This is the emblematic case of the Italian B-type social cooperatives, which generally involve permanent staff members, previously unemployed workers, volunteers and representatives of local public institutions (Poledrini and Borzaga 2021). These WISEs are multiple-stakeholder initiatives and include a clear focus on the general interest. Their efforts to create jobs for the unemployed most often take place within an overall objective of local development, thus combining members' interests with the interests of a larger community.

This type of work integration emerged through the ICSEM empirical evidence for Europe. In this group, some organisations are cooperatives; others are not legally registered as cooperatives, but they have adopted one of the new legal forms forged in close proximity to the conventional cooperative status. All activities serve strong social objectives: they mainly aim to create jobs for the unemployed, or to improve the health of vulnerable people. These social enterprises rely mainly on market resources, although they often sell some of their services or goods below the market price – a fact that reflects their public interest orientation. They have democratic governance structures, mainly under the control of their workers and managers.

Work integration can be pursued by WISEs that are promoted by local public bodies and can be considered as spin-offs of these entities. Some municipalities concerned about the integration of unemployed people on their territories launch WISEs themselves, or in partnership with civil society actors, reflecting the fact that the third sector and the public sector are often closely interwoven in such contexts (see also entry 51, 'Public Policy'). ICSEM empirical data analysis does not confirm the existence of such public-type SE models as a distinct group. However, some WISEs involve a governmental agency among their founding members. A possible interpretation is that, although they do actively support social enterprises, most public authorities prefer to act as partners, rather than as the main entrepreneur, in the creation and management of WISEs.

Finally, some WISEs may also correspond to the social business model, especially when they take the form of small and medium-sized enterprises combining a for-profit motive with the aim of creating jobs for vulnerable groups. These enterprises usually adopt commercial forms of ownership, but their willingness to develop economic activities goes hand in hand with an explicit social mission. For instance, economic activities are chosen to best suit the profile of the target groups. In Central and Eastern Europe, the largest social enterprise group is mainly made up of rather small commercial companies, run by an individual entrepreneur who is the main owner and dominant decision-maker, leading to the ownership and governance of these social enterprises being described as 'independent'. These enterprises combine a strong commercial orientation with a social mission. One of the most common social missions of these social enterprises is employment generation, constituting a sign of the importance attached to this type of mission in Central and Eastern Europe, which results, in some cases, in the concept of social enterprise being conflated with that of WISE.

42.4 PROMISES AND CHALLENGES

WISEs are present in all regions of the world and across many social enterprise models. They are a common form of social enterprise, and one that continues to evolve, taking different shapes under different policy regimes. Historically, they have emerged as organizations at the front line of the post-1970s neoliberal welfare state restructuring project, and increasingly operate in an environment coloured by the language of neoliberalism (see also entry 53, 'Social Policy'). Public policies have played a central role in shaping the organizational behaviour of WISEs over time. Many WISEs have roots in welfare regimes that created sheltered work experiences for workers deemed unable to fully compete in the labour market. As welfare state restructuring has occurred over the decades, in some countries WISEs have come to be connected to active labour market policies (ALMPs), while in other countries WISEs are viewed as entrepreneurial efforts to develop opportunities for the disadvantaged in the absence of robust active labour market policies. For those WISEs in countries where there is close integration with national or regional ALMPs, there may be a trade-off between securing public financial support for the organizational mission, and flexibility to innovate in service delivery.

Moreover, when public funds are allocated and legal frameworks designed to promote such initiatives, because work integration is ranked very high on the political agenda, a focus on WISEs might be most tempting for all actors. Although there is some growth in other resources from income-generating activities, such as the sale of goods and services to private users, the majority of (European) WISEs continue to rely on a mix of financial resources, with a notable reliance on public funds/subsidies, and a combination of paid and unpaid human resources.

The public policy preference for WISEs to be a part of the solution to the ongoing restructuring of the neoliberal welfare state, mobilizing solidarity-based resource networks, delivering public social goods and job creation for disadvantaged workers makes it more likely that public authorities will impose one or a few very precise types of WISE framework. This leaves very little space for autonomy in social enterprise, and runs the risk that all WISEs end up looking the same. For those WISEs operating in countries with minimal public/ALMP support for their work integration activity, the trade-off is between the ability to innovate and the financial risk that comes with unsubsidized commercial venturing with a disadvantaged target population who may need a lot of investment to be productive in a competitive commercial business.

In summary, many WISEs have moved beyond the sheltered workshop model, into a role as labour market intermediary, and a site of community-based employment generation aiming to utilize their innovative capacity, and the diversity of their resource mix, to create employment opportunities in a changing political and economic landscape. hey are a complex form of social enterprise, marked by country-specific contextual differences, and typically tasked with balancing the commercial sale of goods and services with the workforce development needs of the target populations they employ.

REFERENCES

Borzaga, Carlo, Giulia Galera, Barbara Franchini, Stefania Chiomento, Rocío Nogales and Chiara Carini. 2020. 'Social Enterprises and their Ecosystems in Europe. Comparative Synthesis Report.' European Commission. Luxembourg: Publications Office of the European Union. https://europa.eu/!Qq64ny.

Cooney, Kate, Marthe Nyssens, Mary O'Shaughnessy and Jacques Defourny. 2016. 'Public Policies and Work Integration Social Enterprises: The Challenge of Institutionalization in a Neoliberal Era.' *Nonprofit Policy Forum* 7 (4): 435–60. https://doi.org/10.1515/npf-2016-0028.

Defourny, Jacques, Marthe Nyssens and Olivier Marthe Brolis. 2019. 'Asian Social Enterprise Models in a Worldwide Perspective.' In *Social Enterprise in Asia: Theory, Models and Practice*, edited by Eric Bidet and Jacques Defourny, 335–56. Abingdon: Routledge.

Defourny, Jacques, Marthe Nyssens and Olivier Brolis. 2021. 'Testing Social Enterprise Models Across the World: Evidence from the "International Comparative Social Enterprise Models (ICSEM) Project".' *Nonprofit and Voluntary Sector Quarterly* 50 (2): 420–40. https://doi.org/10.1177/0899764020959470.

Gaiger, Luiz Inácio and Fernanda Wanderley. 2019. 'Social Enterprises in South America: Challenges and Perspectives.' In *Social Enterprise in Latin America: Theory, Models and Practice*, edited by Luiz Inácio Gaiger, Marthe Nyssens and Fernanda Wanderley, 239–85. Abingdon, UK: Routledge.

Gardin, Laurent, Jean-Louis Laville and Marthe Nyssens. 2012. *Entreprise sociale et insertion: Une perspective internationale*. Paris: Desclée de Brouwer.

Laratta, Rosario and Sachiko Nakagawa. 2016. 'Work Integration Social Enterprises for People with Disabilities in Japan.' *Nonprofit Policy Forum* 7 (4): 487–507. https://doi.org/10.1515/npf-2016-0006.

O'Hara, Patricia and Mary O'Shaughnessy. 2021. 'State Support Key to the Predominance of Work-Integration Social Enterprise (WISE).' In *Social Enterprise in Western Europe: Theory, Models and Practices*, edited by Jacques Defourny and Marthe Nyssens, 112–30. New York: Routledge.

Poledrini, Simone and Carlo Borzaga. 2021. 'Social Enterprise in Italy: A Plurality of Business and Organisational Models.' In *Social Enterprise in Western Europe: Theory, Models and Practices*, edited by Jacques Defourny and Marthe Nyssens, 131–57. New York: Routledge.

PART IV

ENABLING ENVIRONMENT AND GOVERNANCE

43. Access to markets
Darryl Reed

INTRODUCTION

Market access is a major problem for social and solidarity economy organizations and enterprises (SSEOEs). This entry examines access to different types of markets, including business to business (B2B), business to consumer (B2C), and government-regulated markets (for government purchases, social goods, and public utilities). It explains problems of market access encountered by SSEOEs and indicates how the social and solidarity economy (SSE) sector and allies, along with governments, can facilitate market access through good practices and supportive public policy.

43.1 SSEOES AND MARKETS

In analyzing market access, it is helpful to distinguish three types of market or market relationships, which may occur across a full range of product and service markets (see entry 29, "Food and Agricultural Sector," entry 28, "Finance Sector," entry 32, "Housing Sector," entry 27, "Energy, Water and Waste Management Sectors," entry 41, "Tourism Sector," entry 38, "Social Services," entry 33, "Information and Communication Technology (ICT)," entry 25, "Culture, Sports and Leisure Sectors," entry 26, "Education Sector," entry 31, "Health and Care Sector").

B2B Markets

SSEOEs' access to B2B markets occurs at two distinct locations. Firstly, there is the initial entry into formal B2B relationships. While their situations vary, SSEOEs typically enter B2B markets at the bottom of value chains, selling commodities or intermediary products upstream to much larger firms. The challenges that they regularly face include meeting quality standards, quantity demands, price points, delivery schedules, and so on. Agriculture is the major sector in which the majority of SSEOEs engage in B2B relationships.

Secondly, SSEOEs that are already participating in B2B relationships may want access to different positions in the value chain to capture more value-added. There are four basic ways in which this may occur: (1) providing new services (for example, transportation, exporting/importing); (2) providing new intermediary products for sale upstream; (3) creating new inputs in-house; and (4) adding value to existing intermediate products by increasing their quality. The challenges that SSEOEs face here include accessing the knowledge and resources to develop new products and services, as well as gaining support from buyers upstream.

B2C Markets

Three basic pathways exist for SSEOEs to enter B2C markets. Firstly, new SSEOEs can sell directly to consumers through retail outlets and/or online platforms. Such SSEOEs operate across a range of product markets, and are organized by different actors, including agricultural producers (for example, fresh produce), artisans (for example, handicrafts), workers (for example, food service, information technology (IT) and design services, construction), and consumers (for example, food retail, sports equipment, housing). Key challenges include accessing market knowledge, raising start-up capital, managing supply chains, ensuring quality control, and developing marketing strategies. The extent of these challenges varies with the nature of the markets in which SSEOEs are competing, and their size, and organizational capacities.

Secondly, SSEOEs that are already involved in B2B relationships can try to access consumers through these chains. Here SSEOEs develop and brand their own final products, and then work with distributors and/or retailers who mediate sales of their products to consumers. Such relationships enable SSEOEs to reach a wider consumer base, while still being able to market directly to consumers (for example, through online campaigns, live events, and so on). The primary challenge such SSEOEs face is convincing distributors and retailers to promote their branded products, when the latter may have their own brands (and those of large corporate competitors) to promote.

A third pathway into B2C relations entails SSEOEs already working in B2B markets setting up their own distribution and/or retail outlets. Historically, this has been a common practice among agricultural producers such as dairy farmers, typically through second tier cooperatives.

Government Procurement Policies, Social Goods, and Public Utilities

Governments operate in markets in two main ways. Firstly, they purchase goods and services for use by their agencies and programs. This typically involves a procurement policy with a bidding process to ensure competitive prices. Policies may also feature conditions on who can participate in the bidding process, and various product specifications reflecting political, social, and environmental policy concerns. Public institutions regulated by governments (such as universities and hospitals) may adopt similar procurement policies.

Secondly, governments can establish markets for social goods and public utilities through a combination of regulation and incentives. In social goods (health care, housing, education, and so on) the nature of markets vary depending upon who is allowed to provide services (government, non-profits, or for-profit providers), funding formulas (full funding, partial funding, and so on), eligibility requirements (universal or income-tested) and standards for service (wait times, staff–client ratios, and so on). In public utilities including water, electricity, and communications, governments may establish regulated monopoly providers or allow limited competition depending on the nature of the utility and government goals. SSEOEs' access to procurement programs and to markets in social goods and public utilities depend on both their own capacities and the conditions established by governments (see entry 55, "Supporting Organizations and Intermediaries" and entry 46, "Legal Frameworks and Laws").

43.2 PROBLEMS OF MARKET ACCESS

SSEOEs' ability to access markets depends upon three primary factors: whether actual markets approach ideal market conditions; whether governments uphold human rights; and whether certain behavioral assumptions about market actors hold. In cases in which governments do not ensure the first two conditions, SSEOEs may face structural impediments to market access. Regarding the third condition, SSEOEs may encounter organization impediments to market access, or enjoy competitive advantages, depending upon whether behavioral assumptions hold.

Justifying Markets

Markets can be justified by efficiency and/or ethical arguments. Efficiency claims are laid out most systematically in neo-classical economics. The basic argument is that under ideal market conditions, competition generates static efficiencies (efficient allocation of resources and distribution of goods) and dynamic efficiencies (innovation in production methods and new products and services). This results in consumers having access to a wide range of goods and services at low prices (consumer sovereignty), workers receiving a fair (market) price for their labor, and (economic) profits being generated only through innovation. Ideal market conditions include: a large number of buyers and sellers; no barriers to entry and exit; perfect information; negligible transaction costs; homogeneous markets (substitutability of goods); and no generation of negative externalities. A behavioral assumption in the model is that actors are (primarily) motivated by individual utility maximization.

In neo-classical economics, ethical arguments focus on fairness. Two primary types of claims are made. The first, a claim of distributive justice, basically assumes market outcomes (prices) under competitive conditions as the standard for fairness. The second type of claim focuses on fairness as individual liberty. Here, markets are deemed to be fair because individuals are not forced into exchanges, and because all actors have a fair or equal opportunity (liberty) to compete in markets. A key assumption of this last claim is that actors have (relatively) equal starting positions (Buchannan 1985).

Structural Impediments to Market Access

Three assumptions, or claims, in the neo-classical argument reveal sources of structural impediments to market access. The first, the assumption that actual markets tend to approach ideal markets, raises two issues. One, the fact that markets do not automatically self-correct, means that governments have to enforce market preserving rules (for example, anti-trust regulations, insider-trading rules) to limit anti-competitive practices and the emergence of oligopolies and oligopsonies. The other is that naturally occurring market imperfections—with respect to public goods (for example, defense), natural monopolies (for example, utilities), and, arguably, social goods (for example, health care)—require government action for efficient solutions. This may include government provision of services or the use of market-emulating rules (Buchanan 1985).

The second structural impediment relates to the normative claim that labor is treated fairly because workers receive fair wages and freely enter into labor contracts. Underlying these claims is a view of labor as equivalent to other factors of production, rather than as citizens with a range of human rights (civil, political, social, labor, and so on). If governments do not enforce these rights, then firms which do not respect them can gain a competitive advantage over SSEOEs which do.

A third impediment relates to the assumption of equal starting positions. It is important to note that this clearly counter-factual assumption relates not only to individuals but also to social groups and even nations, due to historic processes of colonization, enslavement, and other forms of oppression. These roots of unequal starting points create structural impediments to market access, requiring government action in a range of areas including social policy and trade agreements, for example (see entry 7, "Heterodox Economics").

Organizational Impediments to Market Access

SSEOEs may also face impediments to market access due to features inherent in their organizations. Three concerns are most commonly raised. The first relates to limited access to capital due to restrictions on outside investors. This may inhibit potential start-ups from forming, restrict them from entering capital-intensive industries, and may affect their competitiveness, as they are subject to being undercapitalized.

A second concern relates to democratic control of SSEOEs. The argument here is that democratic procedures can be time-consuming and/or ineffective, for example due to being overly risk-adverse, resulting in a failure to take advantage of opportunities to move into new product and geographic markets.

A third issue involves the collective ownership of SSEOEs and rules restricting salary ranges and the distribution of the surplus. The concern here is that entrepreneurs are unlikely to adopt this form of organization, as it significantly limits their potential earnings by eliminating the potential of taking the company public and by limiting executive salaries (Spear 2000).

SSEOEs' Competitive Advantages and Market Access

SSEOEs also have competitive advantages that may facilitate market access. First, their constitution as self-help groups enables them to mobilize large groups of people in the face of oligopolistic and oligopsonistic markets by appealing to a very tangible self-interest. Historically, this ability has demonstrated itself in the formation of consumer and producer cooperatives in many regions of the world.

Other SSEOE advantages derive from their commitment to the value of solidarity, which is expressed through a variety of principles and practices. The emphasis on participation and democratic decision making, for example, facilitates the empowerment of members. This leads to productive efficiencies, since organizations are able to make better use of their members, as members make better use of their time and available resources. The principles of cooperation among cooperatives and concern for the community enable SSEOEs to draw upon and create new social capital. This provides access to knowledge and resources from other SSEOEs and allies (for example, non-governmental organizations, foundations) and facilitates SSEOE business partnerships. Concern for the community also generates other advantages. It can make customers more likely to patronize SSEOEs, either out of shared values, or by generating trust that reduces the cost of or need for monitoring. In addition, it tends to result in practices and policies that generate positive externalities, which reinforce the growth of available social capital (Spear 2000).

43.3 GOOD PRACTICES

SSEOEs, along with other supporting actors, can facilitate market access by engaging in good practices, that is, practices that align with the values of the SSE.

Education and Start-Ups

For new SSEOEs to form, educational outreach is often not enough, especially in vulnerable communities. For this reason it is good practice to integrate educational efforts into programs that engage individuals within the actual organizing of new SSEOEs. This practice can be led by individual SSEOEs, SSE apex bodies, non-governmental organizations (NGOs), and government agencies. An impactful example comes from the Indian state of Kerala, which has facilitated the organization of millions of women below the poverty line into a state-wide network of self-help groups (Kudumbashree) dedicated to eliminating poverty through collective wealth building strategies and enterprises. The strategic partnership between the Peruvian producer cooperative Cepciafe (now Noradino) and the NGO Pidecafe (now Progreso) is another exemplary case. For more than 25 years the latter has facilitated the organization of new producer organizations (starting with Cepciafe), and has supported technical and organizational capacity building, while the former has increased market access by mentoring new start-ups, opening up and sharing new product markets, and developing new partnerships to develop value-added activities.

Capacity Building

Access to markets requires capacity building. SSEOEs can support each other by supplying three key resources. The first is knowledge and information, which are required across a full range of functional areas, such as knowledge about markets (for strategy and marketing), products (for quality control), production processes (for competitiveness), organizational dynamics (for good governance and management practices), and finance and accounting (for access to capital and to fulfill fiduciary responsibilities). Knowledge sharing can involve a full range of SSE actors (individual SSEOEs, national and sectoral apex bodies, and so on) and can occur through various media and programs including, but not limited to, B2B interactions, mentoring programs by other SSEOEs, and training programs sponsored by federations.

Secondly, SSE actors can provide other SSEOEs with financial support. Key institutions here include credit unions and cooperative banks (which can provide long-term, low-interest loans for capital projects and working capital), cooperative development foundations (which can provide funds for training programs and development projects), and SSEOE business partners (which can provide advance payments, loans for capital projects, and so on; see entry 28, "Finance Sector").

A third resource that SSEOEs can provide is access to their networks. These may include business partners, NGOs, industry organizations, government agencies, intergovernmental organizations, foundations, research centers, and universities. Connecting SSEOEs to such networks can multiply their access to knowledge and finance, and thereby connect them to a range of other resources. For example, SSE apex bodies and SSEOEs collaborate with development agencies and private foundations to fund projects to support SSEOEs in the South, such as Equal Exchange, a United States-based coffee roaster which has collaborated with the

United States Agency for International Development (USAID) on a capacity building project in Peru (see entry 35, "Peace and Non-Violence").

Supporting B2B Relations

Establishing B2B relationships with other SSEOEs is another good practice. Along value chains, several practices are important, especially for fledgling organizations. The first is the use of pilot purchases, which include detailed information about quality expectations, feedback on the purchase, and prospects for a second order. This mentoring provides smaller SSEOEs with the opportunity to develop capacities such as for production and quality control, in order to compete in conventional B2B markets. Long-term contracts are another good practice, as they make suppliers less susceptible to exogenous shocks. Such practices are common among Northern fair trade distributors and retailers, many of which are organized as worker co-ops (for example, JustUs!, Planet Bean, and La Siembra in Canada). SSEOEs can also cooperate horizontally to gain access to B2B markets, both contractually (with small suppliers joining together to bid on large contracts) and organizationally (through forming second-tier organizations).

Supporting Value-Added Strategies

Another good practice is to facilitate the capturing of more value-added along supply chains by SSEOEs. While not something most investor-owned firms will consider, among cooperatives this practice exemplifies the principle of cooperation. Again, the fair trade movement provides concrete examples. One practice is horizontal cooperation among Southern producer groups (often through second-tier cooperatives) to establish their own packaging and exporting facilities for their commodities (for example, cocoa beans). A second practice includes vertical collaboration between producers and SSEOE distributors and retailers (and financiers) to help producers establish processing and testing/tasting facilities for intermediate products (for example, cocoa butter) and final goods (for example, chocolate-based products). Another good practice is for SSEOE distributors and retailers to support efforts by producers to increase the quality of their products, so that they can sell into niche quality markets such as fine flavor cacao, and ethical markets including organic and fair trade markets. The French worker cooperative Ethiquable is an excellent example of a retailer providing such support.

Supporting B2C Relations

While all new SSEOEs need support, in B2C markets there is particular demand for marketing support. Within the SSE, there is a huge potential for marketing cooperatives and larger cooperatives with marketing departments to supply knowledge and resources, and actively mentor new start-ups.

SSE distributors and retailers also have a strategic role in supporting B2C relationships, as they are in a position to assist more vulnerable SSEOEs further down their chains, through (co-)branding their products, and distributing and selling these (co-)branded products. These relationships may have extra value for Southern producer SSEOEs as this support can provide the basis for them to establish their own distribution and retail channels in domestic and regional markets (including through South2South trade relations).

Apex bodies and other actors can also facilitate B2C relations by branding SSE enterprises themselves. In the United Kingdom (UK), for example, the clover leaf logo is used by a wide range of consumer cooperatives. In fair trade markets, civil society-led certification schemes provide a form of branding for cooperatively made products, insofar as they require production by SSEOEs (for example, the Small Producers Symbol exclusively, and Fairtrade International in a limited range of products).

SSE actors can also support B2C relationships as consumers. Procurement policies favoring SSEOEs are a good practice. Another good practice is to facilitate the search for SSE goods and services. Cooperatives & Mutuals Canada has recently launched an online map of all the registered cooperatives in the country. In Argentina, GCOOP, an open source software company, has developed a free SSE app which provides an interactive map with advanced search functions and the facility for SSEOEs to update their own profiles and information (see entry 33, "Information and Communication Technology (ICT)").

Innovation and Strategic Planning

Strategic planning and innovation are core good practices. The Mondragon Cooperative Corporation provides an example of how SSEOEs organized in a group can generate market access through strategic planning processes and systems designed to support innovation in member enterprises, to incubate new enterprises, and to establish strategic partnerships. RaboBank provides an example of how SSEOEs can use their strategic planning process to access sustainable markets and provide similar market access to other SSEOEs. RaboBank has done this by incorporating the Sustainable Development Goals into its plan and advising its clients on how they can do the same (see entry 40, "The Sustainable Development Goals").

However, given the limited resources of most SSEOEs, there may be important roles for apex bodies in these areas. Firstly, apex bodies can promote incubation and innovation centers and programs, either by themselves or in collaboration with universities and colleges. Working with institutions of higher education has the advantage of exposing a broad base of students and recent graduates to social entrepreneurship through SSEOE forms. Such collaboration can extend to SSE case study competitions, hack-a-thons, and innovation competitions. Secondly, apex bodies potentially have a role in supporting research and development centers which can facilitate the adoption of new technology and a more competitive presence for SSEOEs in emerging markets (for example, delivery services, transportation, and so on). Thirdly, apex bodies can promote new forms of SSEOE structures (with financial support, facilitating discussions, and so on), such as cooperative "franchising" (for example, Arizmendi cooperatives in San Francisco), cooperative conversion programs (for example, Co-operatives UK, the Co-op Convert Project in Canada) and the development of platform cooperatives (see entry 33, "Information and Communication Technology (ICT)").

43.4 PUBLIC POLICY

Government policy has a huge impact on whether and how SSEOEs can access markets. Five key policy areas and practices are identified here.

Public Recognition of the SSE

Public recognition of the importance of the SSE and SSEOEs provides a foundation for policies that can facilitate market access. Most fundamental is acknowledging the importance of the SSE and SSEOEs in constitutions. The post-World War II Constitution of Italy, for example, recognizes the "social role" of cooperatives and the state's responsibility to establish a framework favorable to cooperative development. An even more powerful example is the 2008 Constitution of Ecuador (Art. 283) which declares the economic system to be a "social and solidarity economy." A logical second step is the establishment of dedicated bodies to lead and coordinate initiatives with other ministries and agencies. Ecuador, for example, developed a series of new bodies (the Ministry for Social and Economic Inclusion, the Institute for the Popular and Solidarity Economy, and the National Popular Finance Corporation) to promote the SSE (UN Secretary-General 2021).

Business Law

Business law has several roles to play. Firstly, laws should ensure that SSEOEs can incorporate and operate in line with their values and identities. That is, laws should allow for organizations including multi-stakeholder cooperatives, non-profit cooperatives, social/solidarity cooperatives, and second-tier cooperatives. Legal provisions should also facilitate the easy formation of SSEOEs, especially by vulnerable groups, as well as the conversion to SSEOE forms by non-profits or family-owned businesses, for example (UN Secretary-General 2021).

Secondly, collaboration of national governments would harmonize laws and enable the formation of truly international, multinational, and transnational cooperatives that allow for (individual and corporate) members from different countries to cooperate in the same legal entities (and not just through contractual agreements).

Thirdly, it is imperative that SSEOEs are guaranteed equal treatment to other types of enterprises, especially investor-owned firms. This includes the right to engage in the same business activities in the same product markets, equal access to the same geographical markets, and equal access to programs for business support (see entry 46, "Legal Frameworks and Laws").

Public Procurement Policies

Governments can facilitate market access through procurement policies in three basic ways. Firstly, they can participate in existing, non-state-led procurement policies that promote products made by SSEOEs (for example, the Fairtrade Towns initiative). Secondly, they can include provisions that require the procurement of goods and services from SSEOEs (for example, a minimum percentage of contracts that must go to SSEOEs), favor SSEOEs getting contracts (for example, as preferred suppliers), and/or facilitate SSEOEs' ability to compete (for example, provisions for locally or sustainably produced goods). A third good practice is to require and/or encourage government contractors and public institutions (universities, hospitals, and so on) to adopt similar procurement policies.

Social and Economic Development Policy

Social and economic policies can facilitate market access in four main policy areas. Firstly, in social services delivery policy, governments can utilize several methods to enable this (see entry 51 "Public Policy"). One method includes restrictions on the provision of services (for example, day care services, special education programs, and so on) to SSEOEs and non-profits. A second option is to provide SSEOEs and non-profits with extra support in offering services (for example, grants, subsidies for some clients). A third option is to provide subsidized costs to the entire population and have non-profits, SSEOEs, and for-profits compete on the basis of service.

Secondly, governments can support and/or favor SSEOEs in providing public utilities (see entry 27, "Energy, Water and Waste Management Sectors"). In the United States, government support for electrification dating back to the New Deal has spurred the development of over 900 electricity cooperatives in rural regions. Subsequent impacts have included the provision of high-speed internet access to underserved rural areas by such cooperatives, as well as support for electrical cooperatives in more than two dozen developing countries by their apex body, the National Rural Electric Cooperative Association.

A third area of opportunity concerns efforts to integrate vulnerable and marginalized communities into labor markets. Work integration programs, targeting the otherly-abled and the long-term unemployed, have emerged as an important tool in many Northern countries since legislation introducing (Type-B) social cooperatives in Italy in 1991 (Defourny and Nyssens 2021). Commonly known as work integration social enterprises (WISEs) in some countries, such programs are frequently supported by government grants and/or contracts (see entry 42, "Work Integration").

In the Global South, where much larger segments of the population operate outside the formal economy, more extensive economic development policy is required to deal with problems of labor market exclusion. There is potential for this to be facilitated through what Coraggio has called a transition of the informal economy into a popular (solidarity) economy. While various governments in Latin America have introduced SSE policy initiatives, Ecuador's *Buen Vivir* strategy stands out as the most comprehensive (Coraggio 2015). Grounded in a new Law for the Popular and Solidarity Economy, and implemented through a series of strategic plans, the strategy included support for: the incubation and financing of new SSEOEs (especially in the popular economy); capacity building in export sectors (especially for small producers); extensive government procurement programs; the establishment of outdoor markets and fairs to support fledgling SSEOEs; and support for (fair trade) supply chain linkages.

Over the last four decades, Northern governments have changed the focus of their regional economic development policies, especially in relation to rural regions. Within a larger neo-liberal policy region, efforts to attract outside capital have given way to supporting local business development, often through some form of community economic development corporation. From an SSE perspective, good policy practices have included funding incubation and innovation programs which favor SSEOEs (especially among vulnerable and marginalized groups), establishing and linking other supportive programs (for example, employment training), introducing legal reforms to address historic injustices (for example, recognition of land claims), and supporting the formation of networks to facilitate the development of local circular economies (see entry 50, "Partnership and Co-construction" and entry 49, "Participation, Governance, Collective Action and Democracy").

Decentralized Planning and Co-construction of Public Policy

A final measure that will facilitate SSEOEs' access to markets is to increase the opportunities for participation in policy making. A variety of related initiatives over the last two decades or so provide good examples. These include: the state-wide decentralized planning program in the Indian state of Kerala; participatory budgeting practices, which first emerged in the Brazilian city of Porto Alegre; and co-construction of public policy practices such as those in Quebec (see entry 35, "Peace and Non-Violence" and entry 52, "Resilience in the Context of Multiple Crises"). Decentralized planning not only helps to eliminate information deficits and bureaucratic corruption, but it also aligns with Coraggio's insistence that systemic change needs to build upon and support the solidarity-based initiatives of vulnerable and marginalized communities.

REFERENCES

Buchanan, A. 1985. *Ethics, Efficiency, and the Market*. Oxford: Oxford University Press.
Coraggio, José-Luis. 2015. "Social and Solidarity Economy and its Institutionalization in Latin America: Five Countries, Five Trajectories." *Revue Française de Socio-Economie* 15 (1): 233–52. https://doi.org/10.3917/rfse.015.0233
Defourney, Jacques and Marthe Nyssens (eds). 2021. *Social Enterprise in Western Europe: Theory, Models and Practice*. Abingdon, UK: Routledge.
Spear, Roger. 2000. "The Co-operative Advantage." *Annals of Public and Cooperative Economics*, 71 (4): 507–23. https://doi.org/10.1111/1467-8292.00151.
UN Secretary-General. 2021. *Cooperatives in Social Development: Report of the Secretary-General*. United Nations Digital Library. https://digitallibrary.un.org/record/3936566?ln=en.

44. Co-optation, isomorphism and instrumentalisation

Nadine Richez-Battesti and Francesca Petrella

INTRODUCTION

Addressing the issues of co-optation, isomorphism and instrumentalisation of the social and solidarity economy (SSE) requires the examination of dynamics and trajectories of organisational transformation and the analysis of institutional arrangements. It involves the assessment of the capacity of SSE organisations and enterprises (SSEOEs) to maintain their specificities over time, and thus to escape the phenomenon of trivialisation while adapting to a changing context. Addressing these issues is also a way to discuss the contribution of the SSE to the modification of dominant principles and to social transformation. This entry defines co-optation, isomorphism, and instrumentalisation and discusses the risks associated with these three processes for the future of the SSE. It presents three approaches of the SSE to reducing the risks of co-optation, isomorphism and instrumentalisation and increasing the capacity to contribute to social transformation.

44.1 CO-OPTATION, ISOMORPHISM AND INSTRUMENTALISATION

The SSE is based on the principle of cooperation between individuals (and groups of individuals) to meet social needs that are otherwise poorly, or not at all, satisfied and to contribute, through organised collective action, to the production of goods or services. Based on Karl Polanyi's (1944) approach, existing at the crossroads of the state, the market and reciprocity, the SSE is defined as combining different modes of exchange and different registers of interaction such as competition and cooperation. Depending on the period and the institutional context, some of these modes are dominant, and the prevalence of the state or the market in production models can orient and constrain the behaviour of SSEOEs. Reciprocity and the voluntary commitment that SSE is likely to embody also varies across time and space.

Co-optation

Co-optation refers to a process of aligning the interests and practices of one social group with those of another group that is more powerful. Selznick (1948) characterised it as a 'state of tension between formal authority and social power' (Selznick 1948, 35). It has been used in the analysis of social movements and their institutionalisation, and nowadays it is frequently used in critical sociology and critical management studies.

The process of co-optation takes place in various fields. Firstly, mainstreamed principles of the new public management theory stipulate that any organisation, be it public or private, must be managed according to the management principles of a for-profit enterprise. International organisations and national governments adopting this principle treat SSEOEs as conventional for-profit enterprises insofar as they have an activity of production of goods and services, regardless of how this activity is financed. Subsequently, SSEOEs, like any other enterprise, are obliged to adjust the nature of the organisation and its activities to the key principles of for-profit enterprises, such as efficiency, responsibility and transparency. Competing with for-profit enterprises in markets, SSEOEs must signal their quality, just like other companies. The increasing number of labels and certifications in many sectors of activity contributes to the fact that SSEOEs are considered as traditional enterprises like any other, without taking into account their organisational specificities and their effects on the nature of the service provided. Therefore, there is a risk that SSEOEs will lose their identity and will be trivialised, as their specificities are not recognised.

Moreover, SSEOEs are nowadays invited to develop alliances and partnerships with for-profit enterprises (especially in the field of work integration), and to adopt growth, merger or acquisition strategies in order to reach critical mass and improve their performance. It is also notable that SSE enterprises are increasingly resorting to private financing methods from sales or services, but also from sponsorship or philanthropy, particularly in order to cope with the decrease in public subsidies (see entry 45, 'Financing'). These practices bring SSEOEs even closer to for-profit enterprises, with SSEOEs becoming increasingly for-profit business-like, following processes of marketisation and corporatisation (Maier et al. 2016).

However, the responsibility of any company to address social and environmental challenges such as inequality and climate change is ever-increasing. This is evidenced by the increased focus on corporate social responsibility and environmental, social and governance (ESG) factors in the business community, and the growing number of companies that seek to reconcile financial profitability with social purposes, such as BCorps in the United States and mission-based companies in France. While the increasing consideration of sustainable development issues can be seen as a crucial social advancement, the risks of greenwashing or social washing remain. Moreover, the rapprochement of conventional for-profit enterprises with SSEOEs in terms of the pursuit of a social or environmental goal can mask fundamentally different governance, management and profit-sharing practices. Further, it can mask the specificities of SSEOEs in these dimensions and lead SSEOEs to processes of isomorphism as described below.

As a result, the boundaries between the SSE and the for-profit business sector are becoming increasingly blurred, leading to a larger risk of SSEOEs being co-opted by the for-profit business sector. This process of co-optation raises the crucial question of SSE's identity, its autonomy, its resistance to institutional and competitive pressures and, finally, its capacity for social transformation.

Isomorphism as a Trend Towards Convergence of Organisations

In organisational sociology, the term 'isomorphism' is used to describe the process of homogenising the practices of organisations under the influence of other organisations. The concept of institutional isomorphism was introduced by DiMaggio and Powell in 1983. They characterised the convergence of the behaviours of organisations belonging to the same organisational field in a context where bureaucratisation and rationalisation were spreading to all organisations (DiMaggio and Powell 1983). DiMaggio and Powell thus highlighted the tendency to homogenise the practices of organisations in the same sector of activity, which mobilise the same resources and the same outlets, through their analysis at a meso level. This isomorphic behaviour results from the intention to reinforce the legitimacy of organisations in a context of uncertainty.

DiMaggio and Powell distinguish three main mechanisms that bring about isomorphic change:

1. Coercive isomorphism: refers to the formal or informal pressure exerted by the state or any other organisation to constrain organisations through the imposition of common standards.
2. Mimetic isomorphism: refers to organisations conforming to what they consider to be dominant behaviour. This may express organisations' difficulty in imagining new solutions and their preference for imitation strategies that appear less risky in a context of uncertainty.
3. Normative isomorphism: characterises organisations in their professionalisation process. For instance, formal education systems and professional networks which maintain and reproduce the norms conveyed by a given profession reinforce each other and create a process of increasing the homogenisation of structures.

These three forms of isomorphism affect SSEOEs to varying degrees. Coercive isomorphism affects SSEOEs in the sense that the state is increasingly guiding the activity of SSEOEs in the framework of its funding policy, through tendering and performance evaluation procedures. Mimetic isomorphism is particularly relevant for the sectors that have been progressively opened to competition, such as the banking and insurance sectors. It also concerns the medico-social sector. Finally, normative isomorphism can be observed particularly in sectors that have undergone a process of professionalisation, for example in the case of care activities (see entry 24, 'Care and Home Support Services'). While these three forms of isomorphism affect some SSEOEs' development trajectories, they nevertheless hide the complexity and the diversity of strategies implemented to resist, transform and innovate, which we will return to in the next section.

Instrumentalisation

The term 'instrumentalisation' is used in reference to public authority action towards the SSE. Indeed, especially in some European countries, some SSEOEs have strong links with the state and local authorities. This is particularly the case for associations and social enterprises within the SSE sector, in the field of social and medico-social services, as well as for work integration social enterprises (WISEs) (see entry 53, 'Social Policy'). These organisations provide goods and services in partnership with the state and public authorities, and obtain public funding in return. The process of instrumentalisation of SSEOEs by the state is shaped by the modes of financing and the forms of contracting utilised. Initially, public funding took the form of subsidies and thus left the decision of how to allocate its resources to the beneficiary organisation. Beneficiary organisations also retained a certain level of autonomy in the choice of activities they pursued. With the transformation of public funding through the development of calls for tenders and calls for projects, the autonomy of SSEOEs has been reduced, and the funding of their operation is made more difficult.

As a result, in addition to the competition between organisations that exists during these public calls for tender, the definition of production expectations prescribed by public actors –

objectives, means, audiences, results – also limits the creativity of SSEOEs, the recognition of their skills in revealing needs and the ways in which these needs are met. Furthermore, some scholars consider that the development of associations mitigates the negative impact of the disengagement of the state and local authorities in the production of services of general interest. This disengagement, however, aiming at lower production costs through contracting, results in lower-quality services and goods. Instrumentalisation is therefore a process that distorts the practices and objectives of SSEOEs.

Therefore, co-optation, isomorphism and instrumentalisation are three risks that can affect SSE over time, diverting it from its original principles and subjecting it to market or state rules.

44.2 DRIVERS OF CO-OPTATION, ISOMORPHISM AND INSTRUMENTALISATION

Several, sometimes contradictory, elements are likely to explain these trends. Firstly, a misguided belief in the virtues of the market and for-profit enterprises has reinforced the importance and legitimacy of the market mechanisms and the management tools of for-profit enterprises (see entry 7, 'Heterodox Economics'). The for-profit enterprise model was thus imposed as the gold standard, including those within public organisations, in line with the theory of new public management.

Secondly, the emergence of new frames of reference for action in terms of corporate social responsibility, and reflection on the reform of aspects of for-profit organisations, such as BCorps in the United States and the mission-based companies in France, illustrate the capacity of capitalism to adapt to the transformations of its environment and to the expectations of society. These new standards blur the boundaries between SSE and for-profit companies. Without calling into question the dogmas of competition and market regulation, these standards broaden the registers of a performance that is too often approached in its financial dimension. These standards illustrate a global demand: economic and financial performance should be accompanied by non-financial performance within social and environmental realms, in line with the Sustainable Development Goals. In the wake of this dynamic, the rise of measurement benchmarks (particularly impact measurement) can also be observed, often presented as the new 'grail' of access to funding for SSEOEs. These new frames of reference accelerate the processes of co-optation, isomorphism or instrumentalisation for SSEOEs, which assume that for-profit enterprises encapsulate aspects of these principles, albeit without any radical change in practices. For-profit enterprises, however, cannot reduce the risks of greenwashing or social washing unless they radically change their business strategies and behaviour. In this context, the following three intrinsic features, which make up the basis of SSEOEs, mitigate the risks of co-optation, isomorphism or instrumentalisation, and help the enterprises to radically change their business behaviours. The first is the logic of cooperation, in the sense of organising diverse stakeholders to respond to a social or environmental need that has not yet been met or is still emerging. The second is the inclusion of a democratic process based on deliberative processes between partners and, more broadly, between stakeholders on the basis of democratic governance, which does not distribute power in accordance with the share of capital. The third feature concerns the limited distribution of surpluses at the individual level and the necessary deliberation on the use of the profits or surpluses made.

44.3 FROM ORGANISATIONAL CONVERGENCE TO INSTITUTIONAL PLURALISM

Consideration of cooptation, isomorphism or instrumentalisation emphasises the role of context in the transformation of organisations and the trends for reducing the diversity of organisations. However, this type of analysis, focusing on cooptation, isomorphism or instrumentalisation, underestimates the voluntarist action of some organisations to produce change. In order to consider this voluntary action (Battilana et al. 2009), scholars in the school of institutionalism (e.g., Oliver 1991; Lawrence and Suddaby 2006) identify the variety of organisational practices rather than their standardisation, and promote an analysis in terms of institutional pluralism. Such analyses are based on a processual approach oriented towards understanding adaptations, rather than their results. In this perspective, different approaches emphasise the strategic capacity of organisations to adapt to the institutional pressures they face. These analyses highlight the persistence of organisational diversity and the emergence of complex hybridisation processes in an uncertain environment. They highlight the capacity of these organisations to innovate and reinvent themselves. While institutional pressures such as the search for efficiency and the increasing introduction of management instruments are often presented as powerful levers for homogenisation and standardisation, these scholars identify different strategies which, on the contrary, constitute vectors of differentiation. It is therefore a way of reintegrating a strategic or agency dimension in the face of institutional pressures.

In this perspective, the approaches explained below help to understand legitimate changes of SSEOEs which are distinguished from cooptation, isomorphism and instrumentalisation. In terms of institutional work, the approach helps to distinguish the actions and strategies of organisations to adapt to an uncertain environment. The hybridisation of institutional logics makes it possible to identify and understand the modes of coexistence of different institutional logics within the same organisation. Finally, in terms of social innovation, the approaches help to understand strategies for social transformation.

Institutional Work

Institutional work means 'creating, maintaining or destabilising institutions' (Lawrence and Suddaby 2006, 215). With this concept, Lawrence and Suddaby (2006) highlight the importance of patient work within organisations to make observable changes. They distinguish the activity from the outcome of institutional work, and point to the existence of contradictory tensions between institutional change and institutional stabilisation. They also highlight the importance of intentionality, defined as the way in which 'actors link their actions to the situations they encounter' (Lawrence et al. 2009, 13). Three distinctive types of institutional work are thus presented: creating institutions (setting up new practices, advocating for a new project, building new networks, developing new skills, and so on); maintaining institutions (supporting institutions, creating myths around institutions, and so on); and destabilising institutions (convincing people of the need for change, questioning beliefs, and so on). In this framework of institutional work, organisations are not constrained to conform to dominant, externally imposed norms as in the case of co-optation, isomorphism or instrumentalisation. They can build alternative strategies. This is illustrated through three mechanisms: when SSEOEs create new institutions such as fair trade or solidarity finance; when SSEOEs support and reaffirm the role of deliberative practices in the construction of their strategies; and when SSEOEs strive to privilege cooperation rather than competition as a mode of collective efficiency.

The Hybridisation of Institutional Logic

A second analytical approach identifies strategic responses to external institutional processes. This approach highlights the coexistence of different institutional logics within an organisation and characterises the modalities of their combination in response to external pressures. The term 'institutional logic' was introduced by Alford and Friedland (1985) to describe the contradictory practices and beliefs within the institutions of modern societies. These institutional logics can coexist, lead to forms of hybridisation or be incompatible, resulting in processes of domination. Scott and Mayer (1991) propose to consider the strategies of hybridisation and the creative combination of institutional logics specific to the different stakeholders within organisations, in order to respond to heterogeneous, competing or even contradictory demands. Oliver (1991) distinguishes five types of strategic manoeuvres used by organisations faced with these contradictory tensions: acceptance, compromise, avoidance, contestation and manipulation.

Here again, there is no single strategy of acceptance, as observed in the presence of cooptation, isomorphism or instrumentalisation, but an institutional logics approach offers a range of possible choices. From this point of view, acceptance (Oliver 1991) is the strategic scenario that corresponds to co-optation, isomorphism and instrumentalisation. Moreover, if cooptation, isomorphism and instrumentalisation refer to the pressure of one specific category of actors (a dominant social group, the market or the state), the institutional logics approach illustrates the possible confrontation of logics carried by different actors and the resulting strategies adopted by the organisation. In the field of SSEOEs, hybridisation logics have been particularly studied, showing the capacity of these organisations to favour compromises between two institutional logics, an economic one in terms of overall performance and a social one in terms of social justice, for example. This can be illustrated through work integration or childcare. For its part, fair trade exemplifies a strategy of contestation by questioning the dominant rules of the market in favour of more social logic. The diversity of forms of hybridisation of these institutional logics reflects the ability of SSEOEs to transform the pressures of homogenisation or alignment into a source of differentiation, maintenance or renewal of their specificities.

Social Innovation

Finally, the last approach concerns social innovation, which points to the renewal of SSEOEs' dynamics and their singularisation, particularly in response to the various crises that affect our society. SSEOEs are indeed recognised today, even at the European level, for their capacity to socially innovate in order to respond to social and environmental needs that are poorly, or not at all, met by public or for-profit organisations.

However, social innovation remains a polysemous notion with multiple uses. Social innovation can be defined in terms of results: social innovation is thus a new solution to a social problem that is more effective, efficient, sustainable or fairer than existing solutions, and creates value for society as a whole rather than for individuals in particular (Phills et al. 2008). But innovation can also be social in its creation and implementation process. Thus Murray et al. (2010) point out that in most cases, the success of innovation will rely on the participation and involvement of different stakeholders who pursue a wide variety of interests: of the users and beneficiaries of the innovation as well as the producers and suppliers. Social innovation can also give rise to new organisational forms, especially within the SSE. These include, in particular, new forms of cooperatives, as shown in the French case by the development of cooperative societies of collective interest, cooperatives of activity and employment, or territorial poles of economic cooperation. Other hybrid forms are also developing, not unrelated to co-optation strategies, which carry risks of isomorphism (as described above) if certain safeguards are not put in place. These safeguards relate particularly to the attention given to governance and deliberative practices, and to the discussion of property rights. The fact remains that there are avenues of organisational innovation to be explored that are created by multi-stakeholders and that contribute to the development of the SSE and its ecosystem.

44.4 TO CONCLUDE: CHALLENGES, STAKES AND OPPORTUNITIES

Analysis in terms of cooptation, isomorphism or instrumentalisation illustrates the homogenising pressures that SSEOEs are facing and the risk of degeneration. This risk is higher when democratic governance is weakened and debate is reduced. Such analyses, however, mask the diversity of responses that organisations are likely to provide to the institutional pressures they face. Institutional work is an example of this. The coexistence of institutional logic is another, as is the capacity to produce social innovation. Thus, during their transformations over time, organisations, whatever their nature, experiment with different practices that are likely to move them away from their original model. These transformations can then oscillate between trivialisation and innovation, and are increasingly reflected in the hybridisation and complexification of organisational models. The growing challenges of social and ecological transition, the new aspirations towards more social justice and the search for meaning in work make the SSE a source of inspiration, whilst contributing to the legitimisation of institutional pluralism.

REFERENCES

Alford, Robert R., and Roger Friedland. 1985. *Powers of Theory: Capitalism, the State, and Democracy*. Cambridge: Cambridge University Press.

Battilana, Julie, Bernard Leca, and Eva Boxenbaum. 2008. 'Agency and Institutions: A Review of Institutional Entrepreneurship.' HBS Working Paper Series. Boston, MA: Harvard Business School. https://www.hbs.edu/faculty/Pages/item.aspx?num=32451.

DiMaggio, Paul J., and Walter W. Powell. 1983. 'The Iron Cage Revisited: Institutional Isomorphism and Collective Rationality in Organizational Fields.' *American Sociological Review* 48 (2): 147–60. https://doi.org/10.2307/2095101.

Lawrence, Thomas B., and Roy Suddaby. 2006. 'Institutions and Institutional Work.' In *The SAGE Handbook of Organization Studies*, edited by Stewart Clegg, Cynthia Hardy, Tom Lawrence and Walter R. Nord, 215–54. London: SAGE.

Lawrence, Thomas B., Roy Suddaby and Bernard Leca, eds. 2009. *Institutional Work: Actors and Agency in Institutional Studies of Organization*. Cambridge: Cambridge University Press.

Maier, Florentine, Michael Meyer and Martin Steinbereithner. 2016. 'Nonprofit Organizations Becoming Business-Like.' *Nonprofit and Voluntary Sector Quarterly* 45 (1): 64–86. https://doi.org/10.1177/0899764014561796.

Murray, Robin, Julie Caulier-Grice and Geoff Mulgan. 2010. *The Open Book of Social Innovation*. London: NESTA.

Oliver, Christine. 1991. 'Strategic Responses to Institutional Processes.' *Academy of Management Review* 16 (1): 145–79. https://doi.org/10.5465/amr.1991.4279002.

Phills Jr, James A., Kriss Deiglmeier and Dale T. Miller. 2008. 'Rediscovering Social Innovation.' *Stanford Social Innovation Review* 6 (4): 34–43. https://ssir.org/articles/entry/rediscovering_social_innovation#.

Polanyi, Karl. 1944. *The Great Transformation: The Political and Economic Origins of Our Time*. Boston, MA: Beacon Press.

Scott, Richard W., and John W. Mayer. 1991. 'The Organization of Societal Sector: Proposition and Early Evidence.' In *The New Institutionalism in Organizational Analysis*, edited by Walter W. Powell and Paul J. DiMaggio, 108–40. Chicago, IL: University of Chicago Press.

Selznick, Philip. 1948. 'Foundations of the Theory of Organization.' *American Sociological Review* 13 (1): 25–35. https://doi.org/10.2307/2086752.

45. Financing

Gianluca Salvatori and Riccardo Bodini

INTRODUCTION

As is the case with any business, social and solidarity economy organizations and enterprises (SSEOEs) have a need for finance dictated by growth and consolidation objectives, which in turn are functional to the type and size of demand and the needs of individuals and communities on which they intend to make a positive social impact. But precisely because finance for the social and solidarity economy (SSE) must also be instrumental with respect to the social objectives that are pursued, the theme of the relationship between the SSE and financial mechanisms can be dealt with both from the point of view of demand, by analysing the financial needs that SSEOEs express in order to feed their own development, and from the point of view of supply, by looking at the financial instruments and products that the SSE developed to satisfy its own needs. The two perspectives are mutually independent, and sometimes in conflict. The low weight accorded to the SSE as a financial actor has often undermined the ability to fulfill all its needs with consistent solutions, forcing SSEOEs to use tools and products originally designed for non-SSE entities. But, due to their specific nature and mission, SSEOEs are not well suited to access financial mechanisms designed to maximize return on capital, or to assign investors ownership rights and governance powers proportional to their capital contributions. This means that many of the financial mechanisms most used by for-profit corporations are not readily applicable to the SSE. In other words, the specificities of the SSE are not aligned with the assumptions on which the most widespread forms of finance in capitalist economies are based, and this substantial difference in approach conditions access to the financial instruments. Therefore, when talking about the difficulties of access to finance for SSEOEs, one should never lose sight of the wider frame of reference, since the problem is not so much simply that of access to finance, as that of the specific ways in which this access occurs. That is, the theme to focus on should be whether these ways are coherent or in contrast with the nature and mission of the SSE.

As a result, the SSE, over time, has had to develop autonomous forms of finance able to respond, at least in part, to its specific financial needs. For this reason, this entry should be read in close connection with entry 28, "Finance Sector," dedicated to the contribution of the SSE to the creation of its own financial sector, populated by institutions and instruments conceived to satisfy requirements that univocally qualify the SSE and its mission to meet people's needs. Throughout history, the mismatch between supply and demand for financial instruments has often led SSEOEs to generate alternative approaches, as in the case of cooperative credit, mutual institutions, guarantee consortia, or member lending, which developed in parallel to the more traditional systems of for-profit finance.

Over the past few years, the traditional finance sector has increasingly opened up to approaches that value sustainability in its various meanings, including environmental and social. The diffusion of environmental, social, and governance (ESG) criteria—which establish ways of allocating financial resources that are sensitive to environmental, social, and good governance objectives—is a clear sign of this trend. In this sense, SSEOEs today may find it less difficult than in the past to access financing instruments consistent with their own identity. However, even the growing attention by the financial industry to sustainability factors does not imply that the gap between supply and demand of financial resources in the SSE perspective has been satisfactorily closed. In many cases, the new financial instruments that are created with the intention of integrating elements of social sustainability, although no longer exclusively oriented towards maximizing the benefit for investors (as in the case of impact investing), often adopt evaluation parameters and resource allocation criteria that are not fully aligned with the objectives of SSEOEs; or they in fact privilege selection criteria that favor mainly projects and organizations where the measurability of social impact is more immediate and evident, with obvious distorting consequences. An example of this can be obtained from the literature analyzing the influence of impact investment funds, social impact bonds, and pay-for-success schemes on SSEOEs. Another example can be obtained by the recent taxonomy of sustainable finance being adopted by the European Commission, based on indicators that are clearly skewed toward a notion of sustainability that is primarily concerned with environmental and climate change issues, to the detriment of social issues.

A final aspect to consider in this premise depends on the fact that within the SSE are included organizations of a very varied nature, in terms of size, sectors of activity, stage of maturity, and financial requirements. Indeed, the SSE includes an extremely diverse set of actors, with their specific financial needs. A social start-up that is just beginning its operations on very limited resources, or a community cooperative that manages the neighborhood pub, cannot be compared with a mature and adequately capitalized large cooperative (for example, in the agricultural or consumer sector), just as a worker integration social enterprise providing low-skills services in order to employ disadvantaged workers does not have the same financial profile as a philanthropic foundation that manages a hospital, or a century-old mutual insurance company with hundreds of thousands of members.

45.1 A TAXONOMY OF FINANCIAL MECHANISMS

The great variety of organizations included within the definition of SSE determines, as mentioned above, that financial needs can be very different depending on the type of activity, the degree of maturity of the organization, its size, and other distinctive factors related to the context within which it operates. Therefore, what is most specific about the relationship between the SSE and finance is not so much the type of financial needs expressed by individual organizations, which often correspond to the needs of for-profit organizations of comparable size or at a similar stage of development, but rather the types of financial resources effectively available to them and the ways in which these resources can be accessed. It is by adopting this perspective that the constraints and opportunities that distinguish the SSE emerge, as compared to for-profit enterprises that attract capital because their main goal is to remunerate investors.

With this in mind, the following is a classification of the main financial instruments used by SSEOEs, with greater or lesser frequency. For some, the correspondence with specific characteristics of the SSE is unequivocal, in the sense that they are instruments that are created with the constraints and real operating models of the SSE in mind. In contrast, for others it is clear that they are financial instruments also shared with for-profit enterprises.

The classification is organised according to five broad categories: social base, surpluses and assets, grants, debt, and equity. Tables 45.1–45.5 define and briefly present for these categories a cluster of financial mechanisms that are, at least in principle, available to SSE organizations.

Table 45.1   Social base

Main category	Subcategory	Definition
Self-financing mechanisms (social base)		Self-financing mechanisms include the act and the practice of using one's own capital to provide funding for an enterprise. It allows the firm to maintain control apart from outside influence and to grow without debt. However, the capacity to expand the business might be constrained by the lack of capital.
	Capital by members	Members' capital is the share account that shows the owner's stake in the business. This account shows how much of the company assets are owned by the members instead of creditors. In SSEOEs each member usually contributes the same amount of shares, since the non-distribution constraints do not give an incentive for accumulation of shares.
	Social loan	The social loan is a form of financing, typically for cooperatives, based on the contribution from members of repayable capital, usually in the medium and short term with the addition of interest rates.

Source: Based on ILO (2019).

Table 45.2   Surpluses and assets (management)

Main category	Subcategory	Definition
Firm's resources (surpluses and assets derived from management)		Resource management is the efficient and effective development of an organization's resources. Such resources may include financial resources, inventory, human skills, production resources, information technology (IT), or natural resources.
	Proceeds from assets	When long-term assets are sold, the amounts received are referred to as the proceeds. If the amount of the proceeds is greater than the book value or carrying value of the long-term asset at the time of the sale, the difference is a gain on the sale or disposal, otherwise the difference is a loss.
	Balance sheet assets	Balance sheet assets are listed as accounts or items that are ordered by liquidity. Liquidity means the ease with which a firm can convert an asset into cash. The most liquid asset is cash, followed by short-term deposits and accounts receivable. The most illiquid are assets such as land and buildings, often referred to as property, plant, and equipment.
	Deferred gross profit	The deferred gross profit arises from the instalment sales approach. Under this method, only the gross profits on those sales for which cash payment has been received are recognized. All gross profits associated with uncollected receivables appear on the balance sheet as an offset to receivables, where they remain until customer payments are received. The deferred amount of gross profit is stated on the balance sheet as an offset to the accounts receivable account.
	Physical assets	The availability of buildings or unused areas assigned to SSE organizations and addressed to the achievement of social purposes can be considered as a financing tool.

Source: Based on ILO (2019).

Table 45.3   Grants

Main category	Subcategory	Definition
Financial grant		A grant is an award, usually financial, given by one entity (typically a company, foundation, or government) to another, often an individual or a company, to facilitate a goal or incentivize performance. Grants are essentially gifts that under most conditions do not have to be paid back. Some grants have waiting periods, called lock-up or vesting periods, before the grantee can take full ownership of the financial reward.
	Donation	A donation is a gift for charity, humanitarian aid, or to benefit a cause, made by an individual or an organization to a nonprofit organization, charity, or private foundation. Charitable donations are commonly in the form of cash, but they can also take the form of real estate, motor vehicles, appreciated securities, clothing, and other assets or services.
	Tax share donation	The tax share donation is a portion of income tax that the state allocates to support institutions that carry out socially relevant activities, chosen directly by the taxpayer. In Italy, for instance, each taxpayer can allocate 0.5% of their own effective taxes to the institution of his choice.
	Donor-advised fund/ mutual funds	A donor-advised fund is a charitable-giving vehicle established at a public charity aimed at managing charitable donations on behalf of organizations, families, or individuals. To participate in a donor-advised fund, the donor opens an account in the fund and deposits cash, securities, or other financial instruments. They retain advisory privileges over how their account is invested, and how it distributes money to charities, even though they renounce ownership rights.
	Donation crowd-funding	Donation-based crowd-funding is a way of sourcing money for a project by asking a large number of contributors to individually donate a small amount to it. In return, the backers may receive token rewards that increase in prestige as the size of the donation increases. For the smallest sums, however, the funder may receive nothing at all. It can also be used in an effort to raise funds for charitable causes. Funders do not obtain any ownership or rights to the project.
	Foundations	A foundation is a legal category of nonprofit organization that will either donate funds to and support other organizations, or provide the source of funding for its own charitable purposes. Foundations include public foundations to pool funds, and private foundations typically endowed by individuals, families, or corporations.
	Venture philanthropy	Venture philanthropy is the application of principles and methods of traditional venture capital financing to philanthropic endeavours.

Main category	Subcategory	Definition
	Financing from public institutions	Government finance addresses the allocation of resources to not-for-profit objectives in accordance with its budget constraint.
	Challenge grant	Challenge grants are funds disbursed by one party (the grant maker), usually a government agency, corporation, foundation, or trust, typically to a non-profit entity or educational institution (the grantee) on completion of the challenge requirement(s). The challenge refers to the actions or results that must be achieved before money is released. Challenge grants, by spotlighting the recipient organization through the endorsement from a well-known entity, might enable other donors to trust the grantee. Furthermore they provide the maker the opportunity to garner positive publicity. The challenge could require a new solution to an existing problem that had been ignored. Additional requirements could be specified, from programme certification to member participation.

Source: Based on ILO (2019).

Table 45.4   Debt

Main category	Subcategory	Definition
Lending (financial debt)		Lending or debt instruments provide borrowers with funding in exchange for repayment of this funding (known as the principal) along with interest, based on pre-determined timeframes and interest rate terms. The provision of funding might require guarantees.
	Concessional/flexible loans	Concessional and flexible loans include special features such as no or low interest rates, extended repayment schedules, and interest rate modifications during the life of the loan. The public sector typically uses this financing approach provided through financial intermediaries to increase the comfort and awareness of these suppliers in lending to particular markets, such as SSE.
	Crowd-lending or peer-to-peer lending	Crowd lending, also known as peer-to-peer lending, is the practice of lending money through online services that directly match lenders with borrowers. This form of non-intermediated lending, generally based on an online platform, can run with lower overheads and provide the service more cheaply than traditional financial institutions. As a result lenders can earn higher returns compared to savings and investment products offered by banks, while borrowers can borrow money at lower interest rates. However, there is the risk of the borrower defaulting on the loans taken out from peer-lending websites.
	Bond	An IOU: i.e., a document that acknowledges a debt owed, issued by a borrower to a lender.
	Social bond	Securities representing debts (e.g. bonds) issued by banking institutions to collect resources for social impact initiatives. They offer a market return and foresee that, with the resources coming from the placed securities, the bank provides sums of money as donations or financing at competitive conditions in support of initiatives that favor social innovation.

Source: Based on ILO (2019).

Table 45.5 Equity

Main category	Subcategory	Definition
Equity and quasi-equity investments		Equity investments provide a critical capital base for a company or project to grow its operations, access other sources of finance, and reduce investment risks faced by other project/company investors, especially debt investors who are repaid before equity investors.
	Direct equity investment	Direct capital contribution to a project without the guarantee of repayment; the return on a direct equity investment will depend on the performance of a project/company over the investment period.
	Equity funds/mutual funds	Pooled investments in debt or equity of several projects and/or companies. The objective of debt funds is to preserve capital and generate income. The objective of equity funds is investment growth through capital gains or dividends. Both debt and equity funds may invest in subfunds to further leverage their investment. A mutual fund/collective fund invests money primarily in common and/or preferred stock. Stock funds may vary, depending on the fund's investment objective.
	Quasi-equity	A set of hybrid financial instruments with the nature of debt, but that assume typical characteristics of equity, such as flexible forms of repayment of capital, payments linked to corporate results, and subordinated repayment with respect to traditional debt securities (e.g. bonds).
	Financing members	A person or a legal entity that, with a financial contribution, favors the establishment of a company and the carrying out of the social activity. The financing member is of considerable importance in the case of the subscription of the joint stock company. Particular categories of financing members are banks, special credit institutions, and financial companies which subscribe the entire share capital and, once the company is established, resell all or part of the subscribed shares.
	Equity crowd-funding	Equity crowd-funding is a mechanism that enables broad groups of investors (the "crowd") to fund start-up companies and small businesses in return for equity. Investors give money to a business and receive ownership of a small piece of that business. If the business succeeds, then its value goes up, along with the value of a share in that business; the converse is also true.

Main category	Subcategory	Definition
	Social venture capital/ impact investing	A financing instrument that invests on the basis of criteria similar to those of traditional venture capital, to which impact investing criteria are added, e.g. the target companies pursue measurable and intentional social and environmental impact objectives. Social venture capital can be either "impact first" or "finance first" depending on the amount of financial returns pursued. They can be considered as a specific category of social impact funds that invest primarily or exclusively in equity of early-stage companies.
	Patient capital	Patient capital or long-term capital allows the investor to make a financial investment in a business with no expectation of returning a quick profit. Instead, the investor is willing to forgo an immediate return in anticipation of more substantial returns down the road. Although patient capital can be considered a traditional investment instrument, it has gained new life with the rise in environmentally and socially responsible enterprises. It may take the form of equity as well as debt, loan guarantees, or other financial instruments, and is characterized by the longer time horizons for return of capital. The source of capital may be philanthropy, investment capital, or some combination of the two. Patient capital is not a grant. It is an investment intended to return its principal, plus (often below market rate) interest. It does not seek to maximize financial returns to investors, but rather social impact. On the spectrum of capital available to both not-for-profit and for-profit bodies, patient capital sits between traditional venture capital and traditional philanthropy.

Source: Based on ILO (2019).

45.2 EVIDENCE FROM THE FIELD

This whole spectrum of financial instruments is available to SSEOEs, but each specific mechanism is used in proportion to its ability to comply with the need not to contradict the priority of social purpose over financial return that characterizes the SSE approach. In principle, as a general trend and in line with the distinctive elements of the SSE, various researches highlight a more widespread use of traditional and low-complexity tools, which guarantee organizations' broad control over their own development, rather than experimenting with more risks that involve opening up governance to external investors.

In general terms, and in light of the above considerations, the most commonly used financial instruments can be grouped as follows:

1. The self-financing and surpluses and assets are the financial instruments to which SSEOEs most frequently resort for their development, especially when it comes to organizations that carry out a prevalent entrepreneurial activity (except, of course, in the start-up phase, when activities are not yet consolidated enough to guarantee a constant and programmable flow of revenues).
2. Grants and donations are instead used more frequently by SSEOEs whose associative and advocacy dimension prevails, with a markedly nonprofit character (although obviously the availability of non-repayable seed money is often a necessary condition also for entrepreneurial start-ups in the initial phase).

3. The cluster of equity instruments is aimed, first and foremost, at social enterprises set up as joint stock companies, albeit within the limits established by national legislation for the distribution of profits.
4. And finally, the cluster of debt mechanisms is composed of both very traditional and widespread instruments, such as loans and mortgages obtained thanks to the use of the credit system, and more innovative instruments, such as social bonds, crowdfunding or peer-to-peer lending. Peer-to-peer lending is a more recently introduced mechanism, used by a still limited number of organizations, and its advantages from the point of view of SSEOEs are still under scrutiny.

Unlike in the world of venture capital, in which logic prevails that rewards the ability of the company to generate—in a short or very short time—a growth in value capable of satisfying the demand for a return on investment calculated in multiples of the initial capital contribution, the use of more traditional financial mechanisms by the SSEOEs implies management of projects, even innovative ones, compatible with a slower, incremental growth perspective and less-performing financial results. This approach obviously inhibits SSEOEs' access to the more traditional capital markets, but conversely encourages the spread of other forms of financing that prioritize the community's social and economic development over individual investor interests. Over time, this has led to the design of some original 'participatory' finance mechanisms, in which the power of collaboration and belonging to an ecosystem of SSEOEs that share the same goals and vision has been widely used (see also entry 39, "Sustainable Investment, Production and Consumption").

One example of this was the creation, in Quebec in 2007, of the Chantier de l'économie sociale Trust as an intermediary between the financial market and social economy enterprises. The Trust was created with contributions from the federal government and other solidarity finance actors (including a fund created by trade unions). The Trust offers a range of financial products in order to support social economy enterprises at each stage of their development. The first and most important of these is "patient capital" to support start-up or business expansion. Among the reasons for the success of the Trust is its function of offering first-loss protection to subsequent investors, symbolically guaranteeing through the federal government's intervention that the initiative would generate stable financial returns.

Switching continents, another financial instrument that arises specifically in a social economy context is that of consumer cooperation in South Korea, where the mechanism is based on monthly membership dues schemes, member loan schemes for project financing, member dues schemes, member prepayment schemes, and other various self-financing systems that can only work within a cooperative and mutualistic relationship. About half of the members' dues are used for expenses for the operation of the union headquarters, the price stabilization fund, and the store cooperation fund, while the rest are used for expenses related to the self-governing activities of the local co-op members (Park 2021).

A third example comes from Italy and concerns a national fund fed by a percentage of taxes that citizens can voluntarily allocate to third-sector organizations. The mechanism states that taxpayers can allocate 0.5 percent of their income tax to support a registered institution or in favor of a specific purpose of social interest. The funds are subtracted from public taxation, as they are paid to the state, but their use is at the discretion of the citizen-payer, who exercises direct responsibility in allocating a portion of their taxes for social development purposes.

The amount of the donation is proportional to the tax actually paid by each taxpayer, with an overall collection ceiling set by the state.

CONCLUSION

Faced with an objective need to support the development of the SSE in a historical phase in which the demand for services and goods with social aims is constantly growing, it should not be taken for granted that SSEOEs have greater difficulties accessing financial resources than traditional enterprises of a similar size, nor should it be assumed uncritically that the most innovative financial instruments are also the most effective and best suited to the needs of SSEOEs. The relationship with finance is undoubtedly a delicate issue for the world of SSE, because there is an asymmetry of approaches and values that can create tensions. The search for financial resources must see SSEOEs in an active role in the market for financial instruments, based on their own priorities and values. And financial intermediaries must also learn to deal sensitively with a sphere of economic life that is oriented by a vision in which performance and efficiency indicators are not resolved through the rate of return on investment. It is within this framework that the issue of financing for the SSE must be correctly placed.

REFERENCES

ILO. 2019. "Financial Mechanisms for Innovative Social and Solidarity Economy Ecosystems.", Euricse Research Report for the International Labour Organization, Geneva. https://www.ilo.org/wcmsp5/groups/public/---ed_emp/---emp_ent/---coop/documents/publication/wcms_728367.pdf

Park, Jonghyun. 2021. "Financial Mechanisms and the Social and Solidarity Ecosystem: The Case of the Republic of Korea." Geneva: International Labour Organization. https://www.ilo.org/global/topics/cooperatives/sse/WCMS_829911/lang--en/index.htm.

46. Legal frameworks and laws
David Hiez

INTRODUCTION

It is common nowadays to observe the multiplication of laws for the social and solidarity economy (SSE), even if their scope and number is still debated. However, two points must be made before examining their content and purpose. Firstly, the apprehension of the SSE by law has not only resulted from scientific research. The apprehension of the SSE in the law is also a political statement since it takes place in the controversial context of the definition of the SSE and/or its pertinence (see entry 54, 'Statistical Measurement'). In this sense, the existence of laws for the SSE is rather the outcome of a balance of power. And the existence of laws for the SSE and their multiplication strengthens the argument in favour of the SSE.

The second point is about the definition of the SSE itself. The definition of the SSE is usually given by the law, but laws that do not refer explicitly to SSE, which regulate firms or activities that have SSE characteristics, are also sometimes considered SSE organizations. Two very different examples can be taken to illustrate this phenomenon: the United States and Italy. Italy is known for its successful social cooperatives and social enterprise. The power of its cooperatives is also a well-known factor. Nevertheless, Italian legislation does not acknowledge the SSE; rather, it refers to the third sector. The United States (US) is also well known for the development of social enterprises and has many cooperatives, but the legislation does not refer to the SSE. Moreover, both Italy and the United States have laws on philanthropy that often deal with SSE organizations and enterprises (SSEOEs). In these contexts, to consider US or Italian legislation as SSE law, it is required to find a definition out of the law which is very tricky. Nevertheless, this is a logical necessity in order to qualify such legislations as SSE law. In this entry, to avoid any essentialist position, only laws that refer explicitly to SSE, or at least to the social economy or solidarity economy, are considered.

While limitations of space preclude a detailed description of SSE legislations and their content, this entry focuses on a few key issues raised within the literature. To present the legal framework for SSE, the starting point must be the traditional debate about the utility of law (section 46.2), followed by aspects of positive law, that is, the diverse ways it may regulate the SSE (section 46.3) and the geographic development of SSE legislation (section 46.4). And then the entry goes further in the analysis of the content of these laws (section 46.5), and the necessity of a complementary regulatory framework (section 46.6).

46.1 THE UTILITY OF LAW FOR THE SSE

The birth of the SSE is not related to the adoption of any law. In other words, the phenomenon of the SSE came first, and the term was used and defined later. In such a context, the question arose of whether a special law was necessary for promoting the SSE. Since many SSE-related laws have been passed, the answer seems obvious nowadays, but that statement has not always been true. Indeed, as a regulatory instrument, the law may be a means for the state to control the organizations concerned. The SSEOEs are private organizations, and in many cases the state has tried to control them because it feared their activity, or to utilize them as a public policy tool (see entry 51, 'Public Policy' and entry 44, 'Co-optation, Isomorphism and Instrumentalisation'). This has been observed in some European countries when SSEOEs emerged in the 19th century, but also in countries of the Global South after independence. Therefore, many SSEOEs have often preferred general rules to regulations specific to the SSE.

Two trends contributed to reversing this position. On the one hand, from a legal perspective, the strong law and development school of thought has highlighted the issue of the importance of law for economic development. On the other hand, the SSE has become less marginal in numerous societies and economies.

After decolonization, the wish to facilitate the development of newly independent countries in the so-called third world gave rise to the question of the function of law. Throughout its history, the law and development school utilized law as a tool to reach the goal of development. At that time, the point was very controversial. From a Marxist perspective, the law is only a superstructure and can only be secondary, like a mirror of the mode of production. But within the growing body of neoliberal thought, many authors claimed that liberty, if not the invisible hand, was the foundation of law (albeit in favour of legal enforcement of voluntary contract). One of the major contributions of the law and development school of thought has been the argument that law was necessary to allow and secure the perennial development of any economic and social institution. This reasoning may be transposed to the SSE, even if law and development never considered it in itself, as an appropriate legal framework that is necessary to allow the functioning of the free market, and SSE could benefit from a suitable regulation.

The second evolution derives from the SSE itself. For diverse reasons, depending on each national or regional context, the distance between SSEOEs and public powers decreased. In many countries, SSEOEs have been more or less normalized and, therefore, their relations with political power have been stabilized and strengthened. In other countries, notably in Latin America, the development of more activist SSEOEs has been accompanied and facilitated by the left-wing governments which were supportive of the SSE. In other words, mistrust between public powers and SSEOEs has diminished, leading to the harmonization of perspectives on the utility of a special regulation for SSE rather than general rules.

Nowadays, there is more of a consensus on the benefit of law for the development of the SSE. To limit the scope of this entry, it is necessary to establish a distinction between law dealing with the SSE and law for the SSE.

46.2 LAW DEALING WITH THE SSE AND LAW FOR THE SSE

While the definition of the SSE in law varies, it is always based on a reference to specific groupings or activities. The observer must distinguish between laws that regulate these enterprises or activities (which can be named 'laws dealing with the SSE') and laws that aim at establishing and promoting the SSE *stricto sensu* ('laws for the SSE'). Indeed, the SSE is a constellation and an umbrella concept composed of many various objects, with the most common groupings involving cooperatives and mutuals. These objects, or at least some of them, have been regulated for a long time. The concept of the SSE, however, is relatively new in the legal world. As already noted in relation to Italy and the US, most jurisdictions in which the SSE is unknown within the law regulate the objects which constitute the SSE. In other words, the SSE is, above all, a concept that encompasses diverse pre-existing objects.

The distinction between laws dealing with the SSE and laws for the SSE explains the coexistence of the different types of SSE laws in terms of their purpose and methods. On the one hand, laws dealing with the SSE can regulate the objects that constitute SSE (cooperatives and fair trade, for example), generally without mentioning the SSE itself. On the other hand, laws for the SSE can provide some general principles and definitions in order to recognize and legitimize the SSE. The former legislation is detailed and technical, which provides precise conditions for the creation of the grouping or the activity, whereas the latter is general and abstract. The following sections focus on these laws for the SSE.

46.3 THE MULTIPLICATION OF LAWS FOR THE SSE

For several reasons it is very difficult to count the exact number of countries in which laws for the SSE have been adopted, because the definition of law for SSE is debatable. Caire and Tadjudje (2019), for example, consider the Italian law no. 106 of 16 June 2016 as SSE law because they find it shares some common features with laws for the SSE. Yet Italy deals only with the third sector and does not experience the same institutional environment. Geographical considerations are another issue to make the debate complex, as several countries have no national laws for SSE, but some provinces have adopted such laws. In such a case, it is difficult to decide whether the country does or does not have a law for the SSE. The same difficulty can arise where a supranational regional law for the SSE has been adopted while some countries of the region have not embraced such legislation. For these reasons, this entry does not aim to provide a precise estimation.

Nevertheless, it can be said with a degree of certainty that the number of laws for the SSE has increased in the past 15 years, and that this trend continues. The first wave of legislation started in Latin America, with the first manifestation in Honduras in 1985, and more substantially in Colombia in 1998. But the real expansion started at the end of the 2000s in Latin America and Europe, and in addition the rather isolated case of Québec in North America. In Africa this came later, with the first law in Cabo Verde in 2016; Tunisia, Cameroon and Senegal have since followed suit, and several countries are still in the process, notably South Africa. Asia and Oceania remain behind, but the absence of general programmatic laws hides the adoption of regulatory measures and institutional arrangements in several countries, notably in South Korea and the Philippines. Today, there are about 20 laws for the SSE in force, and the most complete and updated data may be found on the website of socioeco.org (2022).

46.4 THE CORE CONTENT OF LAW FOR THE SSE

The Objectives of Law for the SSE

While laws for the SSE do not always explicitly outline their objectives, they have a similar purpose. They provide the legal regime of the SSE, without prejudice to special norms applicable to a specific entity. They encompass different types of SSEOEs subject to the laws, and provide the measures to incentivize SSEOEs' activity in conformity with their principles and goals. The Cabo Verde law is a good example (Lei n.o 122/VIII/2016, de 24 de março, art. 1) (ILO 2016).

Specifically, the laws contain three aspects:

- Without prejudice to special norms applicable to each entity. The point is that laws for SSE usually do not provide norms applicable to a specific SSE entity. As the SSE is a constellation of various entities, all entities belonging to the SSE are within the same legal framework; that is, the law for the SSE. As a matter of principle, the law for the SSE does not remove any previous law, nor replace any provision. The SSE is a constellation, and its law is a framework of this constellation.
- The legal regime of social economy. Positively, the first purpose of the law for the SSE is to provide a legal regime for the SSE; but this goal sounds ambitious. Indeed, the wording itself may be misleading, even if meaningful. Considering that the SSE is a constellation, it is difficult to imagine a legal regime applicable to all entities of the SSE. A universally applicable legal framework would contradict the principle of maintaining previous laws or provisions for specific SSE entities. Therefore, the legal regime in fact has a limited scope, consisting mainly of a definition, and few institutional frameworks. For instance, the provisions on the creation of SSE entities are very rare. They are considered only when the specific SSEOEs have their own registers. In that case, the conditions required to be registered must be stated. Apart from the definition, most laws for the SSE, if not all, also provide principles for the SSE. These principles are very important since they are the substitute for the special rules that cannot be adopted because of the pre-existence of special regulations for each of the various entities of the SSE. The word 'principles' designates clearly the generality, fitting with the necessity to build common elements for all these entities.
- The measures to incentivize its activity. The second positive element involves measures to incentivize its activity. Explicitly, the law is presented as support for the SSE. It is not only a regulation to allow its existence, but also a political gesture in favour of the SSE. This does not necessarily mean that the law for the SSE is ideologically oriented; for instance, the law for the SSE was adopted in Québec by the unanimous consent of Parliament.

The Definition of the SSE

It is common for a law to define its objects. This is a particularly important aspect of laws for the SSE because they aim at incentivizing the activity of SSEOEs. Therefore, it becomes crucial for public bodies to be able to decide whether an activity is included in the SSE or not. However, the definition is not only instrumental, but also provides the official recognition of the SSE. Here, at least two orientations can be found: definition by intention or by extension.

According to the Port Royal Logic (Arnauld et al. 1996), it is possible to define a concept either by intention, which indicates the internal content of a term or concept that constitutes its formal definition; or by extension, which indicates its range of applicability by naming the particular objects that it denotes. Most legal definitions of the SSE employ these two definitions simultaneously. However, these two definitions should be distinguished. The traditional definition of the SSE is usually based on the 'by extension' method, that is, a list of entities considered as SSE entities. This list differs from jurisdiction to jurisdiction, but the core of these entities are cooperatives, mutuals, associations (usually when they run an economic activity) and foundations. Some more specific entities are often added, characterized by their collective dimension, but different depending on the cultures. The examples include but are not limited to rural groupings, workers' groupings and some religious entities. Some entities such as social enterprises may or may not be included in the SSE depending on the countries' legal and cultural traditions (see entry 21, 'Social Enterprises').

The controversies about the classification of social enterprise are partly due to the various development trajectories and the nature of social enterprises worldwide. In many countries, especially where the SSE sector has a long tradition, the traditional SSE entities consider the social enterprises and their development as a stratagem by for-profit business entities to conquer new markets. In these countries, traditional SSE entities have been strongly advocating against the inclusion of social enterprises in the SSE category. At least in Europe, however, the intensity of controversies has decreased, and the latest European Union Communication on SSE clearly declares social enterprise an entity of the SSE, which means also that social enterprise must comply with SSE features and principles, defined in the Communication as: 'the primacy of people as well as social and/or environmental purpose over profit, the reinvestment of most of the profits and surpluses to carry out activities in the interest of members/users ("collective interest") or society at large ("general interest") and democratic and/or participatory governance' (European Commission 2021, 5).

The definition by extension can be applied either to the activities included in the SSE, or to the groupings that run these activities. The case of Cabo Verde is a good example as its law defines SSE by its activity. But there is a strong connection between the grouping and activity-based definitions, as in the case of the Cabo Verdean law. The Cabo Verdean law recognizes all those activities pursued by entities of the SSE as SSE activity. Although legal definition based on entities is dominant, legal definition by activities is also frequently used.

As mentioned above, the definition by extension is usually accompanied by the definition by intention. However, several countries use the definition by intention exclusively. In those countries, laws for the SSE give a substantial definition of the SSE that includes major features of the SSE or its entities. For instance, Cameroonian law defines social economy as a set of economic activities run by organizations and enterprises, based on principles of solidarity and participation, which aims at the collective interest of their members and/or the social and economic interest of the community (Cameroonian law 2019/004, 25 April 2019, art. 2 line 4.) (Republic of Cameroon 2019). Luxembourg has probably adopted the legislation that goes the furthest in this regard, since it provides absolutely no list of SSE entities, apart from the societal impact company (Luxembourg law, 12 December 2016, art. 1) (Travail, Emploi et Économie Sociale et Solidaire 2016).

These two kinds of definitions have their pros and cons. The provision of a list of SSE entities, based on their legal forms, has the major advantage of simplicity and certainty. The list of SSE entities makes it easy to provide certainty for all the SSE stakeholders, including public authorities and clients. Moreover, since the related legal forms have their own regulation, the law for SSE does not need not to state its own institutions for regulatory control. The disadvantage of the definition by the list of entities is its rigidity: even if legal entities meet the SSE principles, when they are not in the list of SSE entities, they cannot be recognized as SSE entities. Unsurprisingly, the substantial method – that is, the definition by intention – also has advantages and disadvantages which correspond to disadvantages and advantages of the definition of extension, that is, the provision of the SSE list. To take advantage of the strengths of these two approaches, many countries have chosen to adopt a definition that provides both a list of SSE entities and a residual SSE category for the legal entities which are not included in the list of SSE entities but comply with SSE principles. This means that the laws for the SSE should provide SSE principles. SSE principles also vary across the countries depending on their cultural or political specificities. Apart from these differences, there are strong commonalities that can be summed up as five principles: people-centredness, limited profitability, democratic management, collective property, and activity beneficial for the community.

These common principles have two major functions. On the one hand, they complete the legal definition of the SSE and make its identity more precise. On the other hand, they clearly distinguish SSE entities from others, such as public or for-profit private entities. As principles, they create room to allow other laws and regulations to deal with SSE entities, and sufficient grounds to allow other laws or regulations to go into these details. This should not be considered a limitation. It must be kept in mind that capitalist enterprises themselves do not rely on a unique definition and regulation. On the contrary, many legal forms are available for capitalist enterprises, and it is an illusion to expect otherwise for the SSE. In all likelihood, the more the SSE gains in extension, the more numerous will be its legal forms. Therefore, what could be considered an element that undermines the purity of the SSE may in fact be one that strengthens the SSE.

What is important here is that regardless of the forms they take, SSE laws – both laws for the SSE and laws dealing with the SSE – should serve the adoption of specific measures to promote the SSE and incentivize SSE activities.

46.5 PUBLIC POLICY AS A COMPLEMENTARY FRAMEWORK TO LAW

SSE legislation does not usually adopt specific measures incentivizing the development of the SSE's activity. Rather, it creates an institutional environment where specific measures for the SSE can be established. Among these measures are public policies including official statistics which are central to the promotion of the SSE (see entry 51, 'Public Policy' and entry 54, 'Statistical Measurement').

To create an enabling institutional environment, laws for the SSE must create the appropriate institutions to design and implement public policies. The most common approach outside of authoritarian states is to establish institutions composed of civil servants, representatives of political bodies and representatives of SSE organizations which have real powers. The success of such arrangements relies on the pre-existence of a coordinated structure of SSE organizations. In addition, many laws designate a political organ to manage the SSE. Such a structure is also important since it avoids the dilution of responsibilities among many institutions associated with SSE.

As SSE is by nature anchored in territories, laws for the SSE usually create local institutions to set up public policies. Some laws for the SSE provide orientations for public policies, for example, fiscal incentives. Other policy measures include public procurement, targeted financing, social impact bonds and subsidies for training (see entry 45, 'Financing').

When referring to public policy, a special mention must be made of statistics. It has long been noted that traditional statistics and public accounting were structurally unable to portray the reality of the SSE, and that what is not counted cannot be taken into account (see entry

54, 'Statistical Measurement'). To address this problem, many laws for the SSE stipulate the necessity to create or improve statistical systems to establish SSE statistics. A prime example is the case of Québec, where an accurate statistical system for the SSE now exists. This question is directly connected to legal questions; not only because the system is adopted through law, but also because the main difficulty for official statistics is to adjust the traditional categories by adapting to new criteria established by law.

As described above, laws have significant impacts on the SSE, but it is also important to consider how the SSE affects law. For instance, certain SSE practices have strongly influenced some legal arrangements, as demonstrated in the works of Boaventura de Sousa Santos (2015). But SSE also has another kind of influence on the law, which concerns the legal model for future enterprises. To the extent that capitalism has diverted attention from collective forms of organization and principles of solidarity, one of the benefits of the law for the SSE is that it opens up new perspectives. To realize the transformational potential of the SSE, law for the SSE must be considered and treated as a true legal question, notably by lawyers, in both its technical and its theoretical dimensions. This is necessary for the development of the SSE to allow the law to be adapted to present and future challenges.

REFERENCES

Arnauld, Antoine, Pierre Nicole and Jill Vance Buroker. 1996. *Logic or the Art of Thinking: Containing, besides Common Rules, Several New Observations Appropriate for Forming Judgment.* Oxford, UK; New York, USA; Melbourne, Australia: Cambridge University Press.

European Commission. 2021. 'Building an Economy That Works for People: An Action Plan for the Social Economy.' Luxembourg: Publications Office of the European Union. https://ec.europa.eu/social/BlobServlet?docId=24986&langId=en.

ILO. 2016. *Cabo Verde (5) Education, Vocational Guidance and Training.* Vol. 121/VIII/2016. https://www.ilo.org/dyn/natlex/natlex4.detail?p_lang=en&p_isn=109481&p_count=5&p_classification=09.

Republic of Cameroon. 2019. *Framework Bill Governing Social Economy in Cameroon.* Vol. 2019/004. https://www.prc.cm/en/news/the-acts/laws/3558-law-n-2019-004-of-25-april-2019-framework-bill-governing-social-economy-in-cameroon.

Socioeco.org. 2022. 'Socioeco.org – the Social Solidarity Economy Resource Website.' 14 February. http://socioeco.org/index_en.html.

Travail, Emploi et Économie Sociale et Solidaire. 2016. 'Loi Du 12 Décembre 2016 Portant Création Des Sociétés d'Impact Sociétal et Modifiant: A) La Loi Modifiée Du 19 Décembre 2002 Concernant Le Registre de Commerce et Des Sociétés Ainsi Que La Comptabilité et Les Comptes Annuels Des Entreprises; B) La Loi Modifiée Du 4 Décembre 1967 Concernant l'Impôt Sur Le Revenu; C) La Loi Modifiée Du 1er Décembre 1936 Concernant l'Impôt Commercial Communal; et D) La Loi Modifiée Du 16 Octobre 1934 Relative à l'Impôt Sur La Fortune.' Legilux.public.lu. *Journal officiel du Grand-Duché de Luxembourg.* https://legilux.public.lu/eli/etat/leg/loi/2016/12/12/n1/jo.

47. Local and territorial development plans
Hamish Jenkins

INTRODUCTION

Social and solidarity economy (SSE) development plans and programmes are essential for creating a favourable enabling environment for scaling up grassroots SSE initiatives within a given territory. If well crafted, they can facilitate the holistic growth of existing SSE ecosystems through effective complementary policy interventions (in areas such as capacity-building and training, access to finance and markets, awareness-raising and data collection) to bring synergies among ecosystem constituents, with a view to increase overall territorial sustainable development outcomes over time.

Advancing the SSE into mainstream development policy (or mainstreaming SSE) implies either:

- integrating the SSE into wider development plans and programmes; or
- developing SSE-specific development plans that involve all relevant parts of government, with a view to incorporate the elements of the plan in the broader development strategy of the territory over time.

In both cases, a key challenge is transcending sectoral ministerial or departmental remits effectively. Comprehensive SSE plans and programmes address multiple development objectives at the same time and involve a wide range of organizational forms and socio-economic sectors that cut across ministerial or departmental spheres of responsibility at different governmental levels. This mainstreaming approach aims to mobilize and harness all relevant forces in government and civil society to achieve the full transformational potential of the SSE, notably as a strategic means to meet globally agreed Sustainable Development Goals, especially at the local level (Jenkins et al. 2021).

47.1 DIFFERENT ROUTES TOWARDS DEVELOPMENT PLANS FOR THE SSE

Robust and comprehensive SSE development plans can be the result of different political strategies. First and foremost, they require strong political will and policy leadership from both elected government officials and civil society movements supporting the SSE. In many cases, SSE-related policies and programmes pre-date the adoption of national development frameworks. These are often the culmination of mobilization efforts to demonstrate the value of the SSE's contribution towards meeting a host of socio-economic and environmental objectives, which neither the public nor conventional private sectors can effectively address on their own. Hitherto disparate and fragmented SSE-related policies and programme areas can gradually be strengthened, completed and harmonized into comprehensive SSE development plans, or components of wider territorial development plans.

Legal frameworks regulating and promoting the SSE, which institutionalize legal recognition and policy and programme support for the SSE, also help to shape development plans and favour SSE policy continuity over the longer term. In some cases, where SSE legislation is absent or inadequate, it is possible to design development plans in which one objective promotes the adoption of new or better SSE laws as a means to consolidate the sector (Jenkins et al. 2021) (see more details in entry 46, 'Legal Frameworks and Laws').

47.2 MAINSTREAMING THE SSE IN DEVELOPMENT PLANS AND PROGRAMMES

Converging SSE Strategic Priorities in Development Plans and Programmes

At different territorial levels of government, development plans or strategies generally outline a set of sectoral priority areas in which the SSE can play a strategic role in achieving multiple objectives. These objectives include eradication of poverty and hunger; decent work promotion, including for vulnerable groups; better investment and market opportunities for self-employed workers and entrepreneurs in the informal economy, as well as support towards their formalization; youth and women's empowerment; reducing inequalities; better social services delivery, including in education, health and social protection; sustainable agriculture; ecotourism; arts and crafts; textiles; waste recycling; preservation of forests and biodiversity; climate change prevention and adaptation, among many others. Usually applying to all socio-economic sectors prioritized in a given context, policies and programmes to realize the development plan objectives through SSE promotion should include the following components:

- a well-coordinated governance mechanism based on policy co-construction with SSE stakeholders;
- as appropriate, promotion of an adequate (or more adequate) legal framework for the SSE;
- capacity-building (including training);
- access to finance;
- access to public and private markets;
- communications, promotion and awareness-raising on the SSE; and
- mapping the SSE ecosystem, including data collection, monitoring and evaluation (Jenkins et al. 2021).

Coordination and Implementation of SSE Development Plans

The coordination process of administrative or supervisory authorities at the national and subnational levels is an indispensable dynamic in effectively mainstreaming the SSE in development plans or strategies. It implies finding pragmatic ways to overcome the tendency of government institutions to 'operate in silos' with the attendant risk 'ghettoizing' the SSE (Mendell and Alain 2013). Most importantly, there needs to be strong political will and leadership to persuade government officials across bureaucracies to genuinely understand and embrace the SSE. A shift in mindsets may require training of civil servants (such as public procurement officials) on the meaning and value of the SSE. A commitment from the highest spheres of government typically makes a decisive difference.

Coordination can be institutionalized through three main channels:

- An existing ministry with a new mandate related to the SSE. Typically, national governments (and in some cases local governments) assign the SSE portfolio to a specific ministry (or department) to drive the process of implementation, requiring this entity to coordinate with other relevant parts of government. In many countries, the ministry of labour is in charge; in others, responsibility can fall to ministries dealing with economic affairs, or ministries that may cover issues related to family, community, tourism, arts, agriculture, social development and human rights (Caire and Tadjudje 2019).
- A public agency and/or administrative unit established for the SSE. Examples of such entities include the National Institute of Social Economy within the Ministry of Economy (Mexico); the National Institute for Popular and Solidarity Economy (Ecuador); the National Administrative Department of the Solidarity Economy (Colombia); the Directorate for SSE within the Ministry of Labour and Social Security (Costa Rica); the Korea Social Enterprise Promotion Agency (KoSEA) under the Ministry of Employment and Labour (Republic of Korea); the State Secretariat responsible for the Social, Solidarity and Responsible Economy under the Ministry of the Economy, Finance and Recovery (France); the Ministry of Microfinance and Social and Solidarity Economy (Senegal); and the (former) National Secretariat for Solidarity Economy (SENAES) within the Ministry of Labour and Employment (Brazil).
- Advocacy of sectoral SSE policy in the absence of ministries or public agencies dedicated to the SSE. Local governments and other actors committed to the SSE can convey desired development plans or strategies through ministries responsible for affairs relevant to the SSE, with the goal of eventually participating in the coordination or co-construction and co-production of those plans or strategies. Examples of this include agriculture, forestry and fisheries, and small and medium-sized enterprises (SMEs), among others (Jenkins et al. 2021).

Effective integration of the SSE in the coordination and implementation of development plans or strategies largely depends on the local SSE movements, whose representatives need, to various degrees, to be involved in the co-construction of appropriate policies and programmes and their implementation (see entry 50, 'Partnership and Co-construction' and entry 55, 'Supporting Organizations and Intermediaries'). Good examples of mainstreaming the SSE in development plans in multiple contexts and levels of governance are described in Box 47.1.

BOX 47.1 MAINSTREAMING THE SSE IN DEVELOPMENT PLANS AND PROGRAMMES IN MULTIPLE CONTEXTS AND LEVELS OF GOVERNANCE

Brazil (Federal)

The National Secretariat for Solidarity Economy (SENAES) was established in 2003 under the Ministry of Labour and Employment. It was created in response to demands of the

Brazilian SSE movement, which formalized its existence through the constitution of the Brazilian Solidarity Economy Forum (FBES) the same year. In the decade and a half that followed, the SENAES worked in close cooperation with the FBES, which has an extensive national structure, comprising numerous states and municipalities and a well-developed system for conducting multi-stakeholder policy dialogues at the federal, state and municipal levels. The creation of other entities further advanced the institutionalization of the SSE, notably: the Public Centres for Solidarity Economy, promoting the marketing and consumption of SSE products; and the National Council for Solidarity Economy, fostering relations between representatives of multiple state institutions and civil society with the objective of mainstreaming the SSE within the state apparatus and promoting the policy co-construction approach.

A number of key activities undertaken by SENAES were incorporated into the four-year national development plan of the federal government. Considerable emphasis was placed on designing and implementing SSE public policies at state and municipal levels, notably through regional development programmes to address spatial inequalities. This notably included the Programme for Regional Development, Territorial Sustainability and Solidarity Economy, which was an integral part of the 2012–2015 National Pluriannual Plan. This programme fostered a process whereby numerous municipal and state governments introduced laws and established councils and funds to support the SSE (Utting 2017).

Further to a major change in government policy at the federal level, SENAES was abolished by decree No. 9764 of 2 January 2019. Despite the major setbacks caused by cuts in SENAES federal-level programmes, SSE laws at the subnational level, created as a result of the aforementioned SENAES programme at subnational levels, enabled a number of states and municipalities to maintain SSE support programmes (Jenkins et al. 2021).

Quebec (Provincial)

Quebec's National Assembly adopted the province's emblematic Social Economy Act in 2013. A collaborative effort between the Government of Quebec, representatives of several provincial ministries, SSE supporting and intermediary organizations, and academic researchers underpinned the drafting of this framework legislation. The Act enforces inter-ministerial collaboration and the obligation of all ministries to integrate the social economy in the elaboration of new public policies and programmes. It also requires the Quebec government to adopt a social economy action plan. Building on the experience of an initial five-year plan, adopted in 2008 in collaboration with social economy actors, the 2013 legislation includes adoption of five-year action plans, starting with the second action plan for the period 2015–20. The key objectives are building the capacity of social economy enterprises and promoting their growth, particularly by facilitating their access to markets and social finance. The Ministry of Economy and Innovation is responsible for coordinating implementation. Several ministries have responded in different ways to this development in the law, including by:

- adopting action plans specifically for the social economy;
- recognizing the role of the social economy in related action plans; and

- adding the social economy to the mandate of an existing unit, or creating administrative units dedicated to the social economy to support social economy enterprises financially and otherwise.

For example, the Ministry of Environment and Climate Change adopted a Sustainable Development Strategy 2015–2020, which provided support for the development of social economy enterprises contributing to the transition to a green and responsible economy. Furthermore, in its action plan on sustainable development 2016–2020, the Ministry of Labour, Employment and Social Solidarity identifies supporting the development of the social economy in Quebec as one of its goals, including the training of 3400 home-care workers by 2020 (Mendell et al. 2020).

Durban (Municipal)

Durban's municipal Inclusive Development Plan aims to provide opportunities for the advancement of the SSE within the broader context of the metropolitan development plan. The Cooperative Unit of Durban recommended that its cooperative development efforts be part of this broader plan. A key to the success in the development of cooperatives in Durban is the municipality's role as a catalyst in co-constructing policy with all stakeholders. In addition to involving all the relevant line departments within the municipality, all government departments involved with cooperatives, including Agriculture, the Social Development Economic Department, Tourism, Trade and Industry, and Finance, were consulted, together with other key stakeholders, such as small business development agencies and federated cooperative organizations. Streamlining and consultation with all stakeholders contributed to the success of Durban's policy co-construction process and the implementation of the policy (Steinman 2020).

47.3 DEVELOPMENT OF SSE-SPECIFIC DEVELOPMENT PLANS OR STRATEGIES

Through coordinated action across all relevant ministries and sectors, SSE-specific development plans cover a wide range of objectives and action lines to develop the SSE ecosystem comprehensively (Jenkins et al. 2021). They need to correspond to local priorities based on a process of co-construction. For example, in the case of Senegal's national SSE development plan, key priorities identified by stakeholders during the co-construction process include: access to social protection for the informal sector and social and solidarity economy organizations and enterprises (SSEOEs); organization of key production sectors; the establishment of dedicated SSE incubators; the promotion of local trade and exchange systems linked to the SSE (fair trade, short supply chains, local exchanges, buying groups and collective sales points); the creation of SSE hubs for the labelling of local products; the development of value chains with local content; and the development of solidarity finance (Diop and Diop Samb 2021).

These types of priority measures also shape wider national or subnational development plans to incorporate the role and impact of the SSE as a core element to achieving economic, social and environmental goals. These goals can include decent work creation, poverty reduction and rural development through social policies such as microfinance, supporting SMEs and informal economy workers, public work programmes and environmental protection programmes (Utting 2017). With goals related to mobilization of local resources and community development, both SSE-specific development plans or strategies, and national or subnational development plans can create mutually reinforcing dynamics (OECD 2020).

As mentioned above, SSE-specific plans or strategies are more effective in terms of implementation when they are designed through a co-construction process with organizations representing diverse SSEOEs in terms of type, sector and size. In particular, when co-constructed, they contribute to integrating the siloed approaches of different ministries and departments into coherent and concerted actions. The promotion of diverse SSEOEs requires government policies and programmes to reflect the following priorities:

- A broader range of policy support mechanisms.
- A shift from a sectoral approach targeting one or a few particular types of SSE actors, to a more holistic approach that recognizes the concept and role of the SSE in national development plans and programmes.
- Efforts to improve policy coordination, including intersectoral policies that require the intervention of several administrative entities.
- Diverse mechanisms to scale up the SSE at national or subnational levels.
- Diverse territorial contexts to which policies should be adopted.
- A participatory process involving a diverse range of SSEOEs in policy co-construction (Utting 2017; Jenkins et al. 2021).

The city of Barcelona's SSE development plan provides a good illustration of the unfolding of a municipal level initiative that reflects many of the above elements (see Box 47.2). It also includes strong innovative features in terms of an inclusive co-construction process, as described in entry 55, 'Supporting Organizations and Intermediaries'.

BOX 47.2 PLAN TO BOOST SSE IN BARCELONA

With strong political commitment and leadership at the highest level, the city of Barcelona allocated considerable resources to deploy a broad, inclusive and ongoing process of policy co-construction for its 2016–19 SSE development plan, Pla d'Impuls de l'Economia Social i Solidària (PIESS). The plan included SSE as one of the main domains of socio-economic and cultural development within the territory, with a view to include its content in the development policy of the city in a holistic way. The two overall objectives of the plan were impetus and reinforcement:

- Impetus contained efforts to raise awareness and general social recognition of SSE, efforts to promote and enable the creation of new SSE initiatives and the transformation of conventional businesses into SSE bodies (or an approximation of them).
- Reinforcement included measures to reinforce and improve SSE initiatives and their organizational and economic structuring.

In order to advance these two general objectives, the plan was composed of six lines of work to which relevant government bodies were assigned:

1. Mentoring and training.
2. Funding.
3. Cooperation (among stakeholders).
4. Communication and reporting.
5. Facilities and resources.
6. Territorialization and community action.

Each line of work was further defined into more specific objectives, providing goals and concrete actions to be realized in the period 2016–19. The plan also incorporated follow-up and evaluation dimensions comprising both quantitative and qualitative assessments through participatory processes (Chaves-Avila et al. 2020).

47.4 KEY CROSS-CUTTING ISSUES

Ensuring the SSE is a Long-Term Development Policy Process

The growth and sustainability of a robust territorial SSE ecosystem, including the role of supportive development plans and programmes, is a long-term process. It must be upheld and improved well beyond relatively short-term electoral cycles and changes in the political orientation of successive ruling governments. There are examples, such as in Brazil, where an abrupt change in government led to the dismantling of federal SSE support programmes, causing major setbacks for the SSE movement in the country (see Box 47.1). Legal frameworks that recognize and institutionalize state support for the SSE can help to 'lock-in' the continuity of SSE policy and programmatic support. Strong civil society mobilization for the SSE, in combination with measurable targets showcasing the major difference that SSE policies can make on the ground, can also help to safeguard the continuity of the development plan or strategy. Achieving such targets may help to convince opposition parties of the merits of the SSE and increase the chances of continued political support of SSE promotion policies. For example, regardless of the frequent rotation of parties and leaders in power, SSE plans and programmes in Italy and Quebec enjoy continuous political support (albeit to different degrees), due to their good performance and the strong mobilization power of the SSE movement in these countries (Utting 2017; Jenkins et al. 2021).

Ensuring Efficient, Transparent and Accountable Administrations

SSE development plans, even if established with the best of intentions, can run into serious difficulties in implementation, as a result of excessively complex, rigid and non-transparent administrative procedures, or mismanagement by officials in public administrations. These can range from top-down methods and dysfunctional management, to corruption and clientelism. Other risks include under-resourced staff, politically motivated mass layoffs of experienced staff, and the recruitment of new staff lacking experience and understanding of the SSE.

The design and implementation of a development plan need to go hand in hand with administrative reforms to address these issues, including training of staff, measures to employ accumulated institutional knowledge and experience, simplifying paperwork, greater transparency, strengthened decision-making capacity of partner SSE organizations, and regular evaluation of the programmes by institutions external to the implementing entity (Utting 2017; Jenkins et al. 2021). Again, embedding the co-construction process in policy design and implementation is an essential safeguard and early-warning system to prevent or detect and correct such unintended flaws.

Overcoming Lack of Policy Coherence and Resource Constraints

This entry has demonstrated that policy coordination across ministries and departments is of paramount importance. Beyond surmounting entrenchment between bureaucratic turfs is the need to overcome conflicting policy orientations favoured by rival parts of the government (usually not working directly on SSE policies). The latter may still follow a classic neoliberal economic model that disregards the special needs and conditions of the SSE. What may be viewed as 'distortions' to free-market competition (such as reserved public procurement contracts for certified SSE organizations and enterprises) should rather be understood as 'corrections' to level the playing field between conventional profit-maximizing enterprises and SSE entities that place social and/or environmental objectives above profit.

Core features of the neoliberal agenda include downsizing of the state apparatus, stricter fiscal discipline and controls over public spending, also affecting the scope for meaningful implementation of SSE development plans (Utting 2017). This phenomenon also affects richer countries such as Spain, which did not follow up on the promotional measures contained in its 2011 legislation for the social economy, due to political priority being given to implementing austerity policies (Chaves-Avila et al. 2020).

Support for the SSE can find its way even into tight budgets, however, when the right arguments are put forward through proactive communication and advocacy among the general public and the most influential parts of government. It was precisely in the aftermath of the 2008–09 global financial crisis that the number of SSE laws began rising exponentially. After the crisis, which revealed the devastating consequences of neoliberal policies, arguments for SSEOEs as socially equitable and more resilient economic entities in crisis contexts attracted the attention of policymakers. A comparative study of 20 developed and developing countries showed that, with few exceptions, most SSE legislation in the studied countries was adopted between 2008 and 2016 (Caire and Tadjudje 2019). The role of SSEOEs in delivering social services and basic necessities in local communities during the COVID-19 lockdown can also be a strong element of policy arguments for SSE when faced with scarce budgets (Barco Serrano et al. 2019).

Communicating on SSE Effectively

Despite advances made in many parts of the world, the SSE is still a relatively unknown or little-understood transformational development approach both in policy circles and among the general public. Compared to other related normative concepts such as 'sustainable development', the 'green economy' or 'decent work', the SSE is a newer and perhaps more complex concept to convey to both mainstream economic development policy specialists and lay audiences. This can act as a barrier to the adoption and implementation of SSE development plans. Hence, many such plans contain an action line on communications, promotion and awareness-raising on the SSE, which builds on a robust mapping of the SSE landscape (to, among others, demonstrate quantitatively and qualitatively the economic weight and societal impact of the SSE in the territory), and proactive communication strategies within and outside government, through digital and conventional media, as well as awareness-raising strategies such as SSE fairs and other public events designed to raise the visibility of the SSE, with a view to developing and nurturing a vibrant 'SSE culture' within society and the body politic (Jenkins et al. 2021).

A particularly challenging communication issue is the plurality of SSE definitions (or understandings of the SSE), even within the same territory (this is discussed in detail in entry 3, 'Contemporary Understandings' and entry 46, 'Legal Frameworks and Laws'. It is worth underlining here that the preparation and implementation of an SSE development plan can involve a process of bringing diverse SSE organizations to converge on a common SSE definition to communicate to the public (as in the case of the Participatory Area instituted through the plan to boost the SSE in Barcelona, described in entry 55, 'Supporting Organizations and Intermediaries').

47.5 CONCRETE STEPS FOR POLICYMAKERS AND STAKEHOLDERS

If the political will and commitment is already there, a number of concrete steps need to be taken by policymakers, in cooperation with SSE stakeholders, in the elaboration and/or consolidation of SSE development plans. These are explained in detail in the publication *Guidelines for Local Governments on Policies for Social and Solidarity Economy* (Jenkins et al. 2021). They include the following requisite elements:

- There is one or more representative SSE umbrella organization(s) with which a co-construction process can be undertaken.
- There is an up-to-date mapping of SSE organizations and enterprises in the territory.
- The government has a process of drafting development plans through extensive consultations with SSE partner organizations and other relevant stakeholders, both internal and external to the government.
- During the process of drafting the development plan, its contents have been detailed, including its general and specific objectives, its various lines of work, and specific measures to be implemented.
- Implementing entities from government and partner SSE organizations in the execution of a development plan have been identified.
- Implementing entities from government and partner SSE organizations have committed to engage in the execution of a development plan.
- A comprehensive monitoring and evaluation methodology, with agreed criteria of evaluation after one or more phases of implementation, has been developed.
- There is a detailed budget to cover the costs of an SSE-specific development plan, or SSE-related elements in a general development plan, specifying for what and to whom budget lines are allocated.

If not all of these elements are met, the guidelines provide advice on how to foster such conditions (with advice found in relevant other chapters). They also provide advice on how to improve or update existing development plans.

REFERENCES

Barco Serrano, Samuel, Riccardo Bodini, Michael Roy and Gianluca Salvatori. 2019. *Financial Mechanisms for Innovative Social and Solidarity Economy Ecosystems.* Geneva: ILO (International Labour Organization).

Caire, Gille, and Willy Tadjudje. 2019. 'Toward a Global Legal Culture of the SSE Enterprise? An International Comparison of SSE Legislation.' RECMA 2019/3 No 353:74–88. https://base.socioeco.org/docs/e_recma_353_0074_1_.pdf.

Chaves-Avila, Rafael, Jordi Via-Llop and Jordi Garcia-Jané. 2020. 'Public Policies Fostering the Social and Solidarity Economy in Barcelona (2016–2019).' UNRISD Working Paper No. 2020-5. Geneva: UNRISD.

Diop, Malick, and Aminata Diop Samb. 2021. 'Public Policies for Social and Solidarity Economy: The Experience of the City of Dakar.' UNRISD Working Paper. Geneva: UNRISD.

Jenkins, Hamish, Ilcheong Yi, Samuel Bruelisauer and Kameni Chaddha. 2021. *Guidelines for Local Governments on Policies for Social and Solidarity Economy.* Geneva: UNRISD.

Mendell, Marguerite, and Béatrice Alain. 2013. 'Evaluating the Formation of Enabling Public Policy for the Social and Solidarity Economy from a Comparative Perspective: The Effectiveness of Collaborative Processes or the Co-Construction of Public Policy.' In *Proceedings of the UNRISD Conference on Potential and Limits of Social and Solidarity Economy.*

Mendell, Marguerite, Nancy Neamtan and Hyuna Yi. 2020. 'Public Policies Enabling the Social and Solidarity Economy in the City of Montreal.' UNRISD Working Paper No. 2020-4. Geneva: UNRISD.

OECD (Organisation for Economic Co-operation and Development). 2020. 'Regional Strategies for the Social Economy: Examples from France, Spain, Sweden and Poland.' OECD LEED Papers, 2020/03. Paris: OECD Publishing.

Steinman, Susan. 2020. 'Creating an Enabling Environment for the Social and Solidarity Economy (SSE) through Public Policies in Durban, South Africa.' UNRISD Working Paper No. 2020-9. Geneva: UNRISD.

Utting, Peter. 2017. *Public Policies for Social and Solidarity Economy: Assessing Progress in Seven Countries.* Geneva: ILO (International Labour Organization).

48. Management
Sang-Youn Lee

INTRODUCTION

Over recent decades, the global societies have noticed an interesting sector emerging where member organizations are required to be good at two contradictory missions. Borzaga and Defourny (2004) define the organizations as social enterprises, in both social and economic dimensions. These firms have an inborn requirement of ambidexterity with both social and economic achievements.

For a chief executive officer (CEO) or the top management team of a new social enterprise, however, pursuing social and economic goals at the same time is challenging. There are tensions in pursuing both the social and the economic goals. The costs incurred in pursuing social and economic value at the same time puts young social enterprises in a relatively disadvantageous situation compared to conventional young start-ups seeking growth. Therefore, it is very likely that social enterprises send out different signals to resource providers than for-profit enterprises, in order to gain legitimacy when acquiring resources. This entry introduces signaling knowledge required to acquire important resources. It first introduces various mechanisms to provide consultant and management support for social and solidarity economy organizations and enterprises (SSEOEs).

48.1 UNDERSTANDING INSTITUTIONAL ENVIRONMENTS

Young start-ups are generally small and they often lack internal resources. Since they are new to the market and have limited track records, they are less likely to secure external investors, suppliers, and buyers. Delmar and Shane (2004) argue that in order for a start-up to survive, it must first of all gain legitimacy. In other words, it is necessary to secure the legitimacy in order to be seen as a reliable entity, even if there is a lack of information about the start-up, so that it can access the necessary resources and lower the transaction costs, thereby increasing the survival and success of the company. On the other hand, Aldrich and Fiol (1994) define the 'legitimacy' of a start-up as the degree to which people perceive that it adheres to generally accepted principles, rules, norms, standards, and ways of working. Examples of legitimacy-creating activities for start-ups include establishing a corporate personality and writing a business plan, and also establishing an alliance network (Baum et al. 2000). Of course, there are various ways to secure legitimacy depending on the institutional and cultural environment surrounding the new company.

A social enterprise is an organization that pursues both social and economic values, and may benefit from or be limited by various rules and regulations (see entry 21, "Social Enterprises"). The growth of social enterprises requires positive interactions between social entrepreneurs, organizations, and institutions. These interactions enable social enterprises to make value-based decisions and extend their social mission (Davies et al. 2018). In order for entrepreneurship to be expressed in a society or a country, an appropriate system is essential.

In the case of Seoul, for instance, the consultative body based on public–private partnerships became a catalyst in generating political momentum in favor of SSE. The Public–Private Policymaking Partnership for the Social Economy in Seoul (PPPPSES) was established in 2012 to discuss and develop basic plans and measures for social economy policy. The PPPPSES has continued to hold regular meetings to share updates on the initiatives of the Seoul Metropolitan Government and non-governmental actors, which jointly decide and monitor policy measures and budgets on the social economy in Seoul. With a strong record of effective social and solidarity economy (SSE) governance, the Seoul Metropolitan Government inspired the creation of the Social Economy Forum in the National Assembly. Social economy committees within the political parties prompted election candidates to announce manifestos on the social economy during their campaigns for general and local elections. They also helped to create a political environment favorable to the social economy nationwide by giving rise to the Council of Local Governments on the Social and Solidarity Economy. It contributed to creating positive political momentum for SSE in other municipalities and nationally (Yoon and Lee 2020). The Seoul case can be viewed as an excellent example of strong SSE "policy entrepreneurship" (Jenkins et al. 2021).

In addition, the importance of the active intervention of public funds can be confirmed through the results of Paunov's (2012) study of companies in eight Latin American countries from 2008 to 2009 on how the innovativeness of these organizations was affected by the long-term global economic crisis. He mentioned that many innovative projects were stopped during this period due to lack of funds and other reasons, while showing that companies receiving public funding from the government were less likely to give up on innovative projects. Such experiences have provided the evidence for expanding the scope of public support for small and medium-sized enterprises (SMEs) and start-ups in the face of new global crises such as COVID-19.

Overall, institutions play an important role when social entrepreneurs enter new businesses with new ideas. The institutions for SSEOEs increase their impacts especially in situations of high uncertainty, such as COVID-19. The direct support budget and rapid increase in programs from public institutions related to the COVID-19 pandemic are the cases in point. For example, the COVID-19 support budget in South Korea and Canada has played a significant role in sustaining SSEOEs together with other types of SMEs. In particular the SME subsidy budget, the size of which has been rapidly increasing, helped to strengthen entrepreneurs' sustainability (Deschryvere et al. 2020). More comprehensive and effective institutions such as legal frameworks are also needed to promote SSEOEs (see entry 46, "Legal Frameworks and Laws"). For instance, in South Korea where the SSE sector grows rapidly, the bill for the Framework Act on the Social Economy (FASE), a legislative draft to support the SSE, is under review before the National Assembly and aspiring to provide a comprehensive legislative basis for the entire social economy. Since 2016, the political parties in Korea have motioned various bills for the FASE with a comprehensive scope. Their aim was to introduce legal and policy grounds for integrating and streamlining policy support, now provided by disparate agencies, into a single channel to foster the ecosystem for the nationwide social economy more efficiently.

48.2 SIGNALING FOR RESOURCE ACQUISITION

Signaling theory is based on the need to resolve information asymmetry in decision making. Spence (1974) formulated his signaling theory by utilizing a job market to model the signaling function of education. The basic premise of signaling theory is that an organization cannot usually obtain all of the necessary information to predict an individual's future performance. Therefore, decision makers need to rely on other information to evaluate whether the individual has potential to be a productive employee of their organization. Applied to organizations, signaling theory has been adopted by a range of research areas of management, including strategic management, entrepreneurship and human resource management (Connelly et al. 2011). According to these studies, organizations send signals with partially formed information that is meant to be disclosed to outsiders to obtain important resources and capabilities (Zimmerman 2008).

Signaling theory has been studied heavily in the context of new firms because it captures information asymmetry and uncertainties surrounding enterprises (Connelly et al. 2011). SSEOEs, and in particular social enterprises, signal potential investors to demonstrate that they are socially and economically rational investments, and that they will perform well in the future. Social enterprises showing that they are socially and economically rational investments can gain legitimacy which provides firms with access to resources which they need to survive and grow. Many entrepreneurship studies reported that specific firm characteristics can be used as signals, including firm activities, alliance reputation, firm size, venture capital, top management teams, and CEOs (Connelly et al. 2011). According to these studies, for early-stage firms a founder-CEO's abilities and the specificity of business plans can be very important signals to reduce information asymmetry.

Both SSEOEs and the government promoting the SSE can institutionalize this signaling process. For instance, The Seoul Metropolitan Government formed a social investment fund in 2012 and delegated the lending business to a non-governmental social financial organization. The social financial organization considers both aspects of social value creation and repayment capabilities in making loans to applicants. In South Korea, the range of social enterprises includes social ventures, commercial activities of non-profit organizations, co-operatives with clear social missions, and community enterprises (Lim et al. 2020).

The environment in which signals are communicated between SSEOEs and resource holders also affects the overall process of signal creating, sending, and receiving. Regardless of whether it is intra-organization or inter-organization, a signaling environment affects the degree of reducing information asymmetry. SSEOEs, in particular social enterprises, should consider a specific signaling context where various social enterprises send out signals conveying information about their social and economic qualities in order to acquire necessary resources, such as loans with favorable terms and conditions from a single social finance institute (Lim et al. 2020). The following examples are some of the key pieces of information the receiver of the signal would like to obtain.

Ambidexterity of Social Enterprises

One of the most representative qualities that resource holders such as social finance institutes want to confirm for CEOs would be their social entrepreneurship. Social entrepreneurs engage in entrepreneurial activities with the goal of addressing neglected social problems (Pache and

Chowdhury 2012). It would be difficult to believe that social mission of a social enterprise can be achieved and maintained without a socially motivated CEO. Resource holders will look carefully at the social motivation of the CEO and verify this through collecting and interpreting various signals giving relevant information. In addition, much literature in the field of strategic management has studied top management and their abilities and firm performance. To successfully sustain their operations, social enterprises typically also rely on a web of commercial stakeholders including clients, industrial supporters, and suppliers of goods and services (Pache and Chowdhury 2012). A CEO's management capabilities and experiences are central to the process (Lim et al. 2020).

Corporate Pursuit of Social Value

While one of the ways in which social enterprises can send out signals is based on the social entrepreneurism or the social motivation of the CEO, firm-level signals related to pursuing social value can be perceived through its proclaimed social mission and its track record of executing the mission. The pursuit of social value by social enterprises should be distinguished from conventional corporate social responsibility (CSR) because CSR activities may not be directly related to corporate business, while the social mission of social enterprises tends to accompany their economic mission. In other words, while social enterprises' social value creation is internalized in their business objectives, investor-owned companies' CSR is externalized as an additional element. However, in a broader meaning of the pursuit of social value, CSR has a thread of connection with social enterprises' social missions. The proclaimed social mission and track record of a social enterprise, that is, the pursuit of social value, can be regarded as a social dimension of the ambidextrous social enterprise and can be expected to have a positive influence on acquiring loans from social finance, because they act as important signals to confer social legitimacy to social enterprises (Lim et al. 2020).

Validity of Business Plans

For resource holders it is crucial to verify the intention and purpose of social enterprises applying for resources, in order to avoid any moral hazard, such as use of public subsidies for personal gain. For example, one of the most effective ways to ascertain the intention and purpose of loan seekers is to analyze the feasibility of their business plans. Lim et al. (2020) made an empirical analysis of the relationship between the loan approval and the level of disclosure of details about the plan to utilize the social loan. The result shows that the more detailed the business plan to use the loan, the higher the chance of achieving the loan. This implies that a more detailed purpose of raising capital can reduce information asymmetry between SSEOEs and resource holders. In other words, providing more detail about a business plan can increase the validity of the proposed plan requiring financial resources, by alleviating information asymmetry. The validity of business plans can be regarded as an important signal for social enterprises to acquire relevant resources.

Partnership

Both corporate networks and an entrepreneur's social networks influence organizational performance. New firms can benefit from strategic partnership because diverse information flows, and complementary resources provided by partners, can be instrumental in the earliest stage of SSEOEs. For instance, Eisenhardt and Schoonhoven (1996) argue that alliance formation is affected by a social calculus related to skills, status, and reputation, and that new entrepreneurial firms can leverage relevant resources by having an alliance partnership. In particular, the network structure, relationship in the network, and governance are closely related to performance (Hoang and Antoncic 2003). Network diversity also affects corporate performance, and partnership with networks for marketing information has a positive impact on business performance. Network management is costly, as maintaining dominance in existing industrial networks is perceived as a signal that an organization is spending a lot of money. However, networks with well-known funders have a positive effect on the formation of future strategic alliances, as the funder's reputation also affects start-ups. In other words, it is important for start-ups or SSEOEs in their early stage to form strategic alliances or networks that are diverse, but not overlapping or complex. This gives them an opportunity to learn, and it reduces the risk of unnecessary competition with companies in alliances and networks.

48.3 TOWARDS SUSTAINABILITY

External and internal environmental conditions in the early stages of establishment are important factors that determine the survival and growth of new SSEOEs. The capabilities and networks of SSEOEs developed at an early stage have a positive effect on future performance, and institutional intervention such as legal frameworks or policy systems, and measures for support for SSEOEs at this time, can play a significant role in enhancing performance. In addition, the entrepreneur team's composition is crucial to emit important ambidextrous signals to external resource holders. Resource acquisition is influenced by the characteristics of the entrepreneurial team such as functional background, age, and gender diversity. Furthermore, various factors, such as team resources, structure, and leadership, influence the long-term performance of entrepreneurial teams (Pearce and Sims 2002; Mitchell and Boyle 2015).

REFERENCES

Aldrich, Howard E., and C. Marlene Fiol. 1994. "Fools Rush In? The Institutional Context of Industry Creation." *Academy of Management Review* 19 (4): 645–70. https://doi.org/10.2307/258740.

Baum, Joel A.C., Tony Calabrese, and Brian S. Silverman. 2000. "Don't Go It Alone: Alliance Network Composition and Startups' Performance in Canadian Biotechnology." *Strategic Management Journal* 21 (3): 267–94. https://doi.org/10.1002/(sici)1097-0266(200003)21:3<267::aid-smj89>3.0.co;2-8.

Borzaga, Carlo, and Jacques Defourny. 2004. *The Emergence of Social Enterprise*. London: Routledge.

Connelly, Brian L., S. Trevis Certo, R. Duane Ireland, and Christopher R. Reutzel. 2011. "Signaling Theory: A Review and Assessment." *Journal of Management* 37 (1): 39–67. https://doi.org/10.1177/0149206310388419.

Davies, Iain Andrew, Helen Haugh, and Liudmila Chambers. 2018. "Barriers to Social Enterprise Growth." *Journal of Small Business Management* 57 (4): 1616–36. https://doi.org/10.1111/jsbm.12429.

Delmar, Frédéric, and Scott Shane. 2004. "Legitimating First: Organizing Activities and the Survival of New Ventures." *Journal of Business Venturing* 19 (3): 385–410. https://doi.org/10.1016/s0883-9026(03)00037-5.

Deschryvere, Matthias, Markku Mikkola, and Steffen Conn. 2020. "On the Structural Barriers to Public Innovation Support for SMEs and the Opportunity COVID-19 Can Offer to Overcome These

Barriers." *Journal of Innovation Management* 8 (2): 16–25. https://doi.org/10.24840/2183-0606_008.002_0003.

Eisenhardt, Kathleen M., and Claudia Bird Schoonhoven. 1996. "Resource-Based View of Strategic Alliance Formation: Strategic and Social Effects in Entrepreneurial Firms." *Organization Science* 7 (2): 136–50. https://doi.org/10.1287/orsc.7.2.136.

Hoang, Ha, and Bostjan Antoncic. 2003. "Network-Based Research in Entrepreneurship." *Journal of Business Venturing* 18 (2): 165–87. https://doi.org/10.1016/s0883-9026(02)00081-2.

Jenkins, Hamish, Ilcheong Yi, Samuel Bruelisauer, and Kameni Chaddha. 2021. "Guidelines for Local Governments on Policies for Social and Solidarity Economy." Geneva: UNRISD. https://www.unrisd.org/unrisd/website/document.nsf/(httpPublications)/EC42DDF4C2DDA1208025866B00481C54?OpenDocument.

Lim, Chang Gue, Sang-Youn Lee, and Jinseon Seo. 2020. "The Signaling Effect of Ambidexterity of Social Enterprises on Acquiring Financial Resources in South Korea." *Annals of Public and Cooperative Economics* 91 (4): 633–47. https://doi.org/10.1111/apce.12272.

Mitchell, Rebecca, and Brendan Boyle. 2015. "Professional Diversity, Identity Salience and Team Innovation: The Moderating Role of Openmindedness Norms." *Journal of Organizational Behavior* 36 (6): 873–94. https://doi.org/10.1002/job.2009.

Pache, Anne-Claire, and Imran Chowdhury. 2012. "Social Entrepreneurs as Institutionally Embedded Entrepreneurs: Toward a New Model of Social Entrepreneurship Education." *Academy of Management Learning and Education* 11 (3): 494–510. https://doi.org/10.5465/amle.2011.0019.

Paunov, Caroline. 2012. "The Global Crisis and Firms' Investments in Innovation." *Research Policy* 41 (1): 24–35. https://doi.org/10.1016/j.respol.2011.07.007.

Pearce, Craig L., and Henry P. Sims. 2002. "Vertical versus Shared Leadership as Predictors of the Effectiveness of Change Management Teams: An Examination of Aversive, Directive, Transactional, Transformational, and Empowering Leader Behaviors." *Group Dynamics: Theory, Research, and Practice* 6 (2): 172–97. https://doi.org/10.1037/1089-2699.6.2.172.

Spence, Michael. 1974. *Market Signaling*. Cambridge, MA: Harvard University Press.

Yoon, Kil-Soon, and Sang-Youn Lee. 2020. "Policy Systems and Measures for the Social Economy in Seoul.' Working Paper No. 2020-6. Geneva: UNRISD. https://www.unrisd.org/80256B3C005BCCF9/search/969A3AAE861EBAFA802585A8004C25AF?OpenDocument.

Zimmerman, Monica A. 2008. "The Influence of Top Management Team Heterogeneity on the Capital Raised through an Initial Public Offering." *Entrepreneurship Theory and Practice* 32 (3): 391–414.

49. Participation, governance, collective action and democracy

Jeová Torres Silva Junior

INTRODUCTION

Organizations identifying themselves as pertaining to the social and solidarity economy (SSE) exhibit or pursue the following characteristics: equity, citizen political empowerment, territorial belonging, the plurality of economic principles, and democratic management. This entry addresses the aspect of democratic management, seeks to highlight the meaning of democracy in the governance and collective action of SSE organizations, and explores why participatory processes and active citizenship are essential to their survival. This entry argues that even if an SSE organization claims to achieve its mission and meet its goals, it is critical to observe the method and processes through which it got there.

In this entry, "SSE organization" is used as an umbrella concept encompassing various organizations or collective efforts that aim to achieve the collective purpose and common goals. They include, but are not limited to: cooperatives, associations, productive groups, consortiums of people supporting solidarity finance funds, community banks, resident forums and councils, exchange clubs, and temporary projects, such as people's joint effort or group mobilizations (see also entry 3, "Contemporary Understandings"). This remark is relevant because it delimits an understanding of the SSE and its organizations that goes beyond the logic of economic regulation of human life, based only on market relations.

Further, the economy should be understood as a process of interaction between humans and their natural and social environment, which is based on a plurality of regulatory principles (Polanyi 2001). In this way, the expanded approach to SSE organizations used in this entry allows the clear presentation of at least two other regulatory principles. These two other patterns are key to determining a more integrated economic reality of SSE organizations to be added to the already conventionally institutionalized regulatory principle of market exchange. They are the principles of reciprocity and redistribution. The principle of reciprocity is established in non-monetary economic relations of proximity and neighborhood. As for the principle of redistribution, it is based on resource transfers and interventions that seek societal economic balance at the state level. Reciprocity, redistribution, and market exchange combine in the SSE to enable the hybridization of economies, showing that in society, SSE organizations are diverse and have market, non-market, and non-monetary patterns of regulation. These economic regulatory patterns may manifest themselves in combination with each other, or an SSE organization may even comprise all these patterns simultaneously in their actions.

In the SSE, gains, benefits, and revenues obtained, whether individual, collective, organizational, or territorial, should result from shared conventions that express the ways in which subjects and social forces participate in this common decision-making process. Participatory forms of decision-making, even involving different stakeholders, tend to be more balanced. In these processes, democracy is central, and without it everything is half-baked. In this perspective, participatory processes and democratic management are fundamental principles of SSE organizations, showing the collective ambitions that these types of organizations seek to achieve, together with social justice, alterity, and freedom.

Sen (2000) states that development requires the elimination of freedom deprivation, which limits people's choices and opportunities to exercise their condition as agents. In the context of the SSE, this condition requires active citizenship, full participation in decision-making, and democratic governance. In addition to liberty expansion, the extension of democratic processes is critical to effective development. The extension of democratic processes must be pursued simultaneously with the expansion of freedom. Therefore, democracy, as an exercise of participation and collective action, must be a guiding principle of the SSE in at least two levels: organizational and societal. The organizational level regards internal action in the organization, namely its democratic management and participatory practices in decision-making processes. At the societal level, the operation of the SSE organization encourages the participation and mobilization of individuals or groups within its domain, aiming to act in the public sphere through deliberative citizenship.

49.1 DEMOCRATIC MANAGEMENT, GOVERNANCE, AND PARTICIPATION AT THE ORGANIZATIONAL LEVEL

By deepening democracy at the organization level, a management model is established which uses a privileged space of social relations to foster participation, where everyone has the right to express themselves without any kind of coercion. Likewise, this democratic management is a managerial process with emphasis on dialogue and horizontal relations, where decision-making authority is shared among the organization's participants. In democratically managed organizations, the legitimacy of decisions must originate from discussion processes, guided by the principles of inclusion, pluralism, participatory equity, autonomy, and the common good. For this democratic management of SSE organizations to work, it is necessary to ensure the mechanisms of participation and to reflect on the rationality that guides these practices.

In this entry, in the context of organizational management, rationality is defined as the set of principles that orient the purposes, strategies, and actions of the individuals when managing an organization. In a private company, for example, the management focus is utilitarian rationality, with a market-economic purpose which results in using all necessary means to maximize market-economic return, regardless of the negative social or ecological consequences of that action. According to Guerreiro Ramos (1984), utilitarian rationality conceives a society centered on the market, responsible for the degradation of social relations and the waste of natural resources, often without any ethical questioning. In such a case, the only measure is the maximization of market-economic return for the organization's success. In contrast, there is substantive rationality that has the attributes of self-fulfilment, ethical judgment, valuation of collective social well-being, and the autonomy of participants in the management process (Eynaud and França Filho 2019). Therefore, substantive rationality is the principle that best guides the democratic management model of SSE organizations.

In practice, this democratic management model adopts procedures that strengthen self-management, participatory governance, and the empowerment of individuals involved in the organization's actions. In addition, the model stimulates the engagement of people in the internal decision-making processes of the SSE organization, enabling the consolidation of relationships and ties of primary sociability, which comprise the social relationship between individuals based on the proximity ties that are indispensable for social existence such as family, relatives, friends, allies, and neighborhoods (Caillé 2007). In society, the primary social relationships or primary bonds are pursued for their own sake, while the secondary relationships or bonds are seen as a means to an end. In this sense, the rationality and the instruments of democratic management employed by SSE organizations go beyond the explicit achievement of the goals in their field of action. Through this substantive rationality and the instruments of democratic management, SSE organizations pursue verifiable collective learning of shared management and the consolidation of mutual trust, increasing equity, reducing the information asymmetry among participants, and strengthening relations of proximity and solidarity.

49.2 ACTIVE AND DELIBERATIVE CITIZENSHIP, AND PARTICIPATION AT THE SOCIETAL/PUBLIC SPHERE LEVEL

To address the democracy issues fostered by SSE organizations at the societal level, in particular in the public sphere, it is necessary to consider a crucial aspect of these organizations. Assuming that SSE organizations were established from a matrix of hybridization of economic regulation principles which are structured under more substantive rationality, it is imperative to recognize that this type of organization should not focus and restrict their operation only to achieving their internal organizational mission. In other words, SSE organizations should not be limited to exclusively meeting the needs of their audience or acting only towards improving their institutional environment. SSE organizations must have a wider mission to improve the collective, community/local, territorial, national, and global conditions of sustainable development.

Although SSE organizations are created for a specific purpose (to produce goods, provide services, finance projects, share or exchange products, mobilize a community, or fight for a cause), their actions should always go beyond this purpose. SSE organizations must always add the goal of encouraging individuals to act as active citizens in the public sphere, either as pressure groups or as active individuals engaged in planning, implementing, evaluating, and exerting social control over public policies. They should act not only on SSE public policies, but on all those aiming to achieve better conditions of collective life (housing, health, social assistance, environment, culture, education, work, employment, rural development, urban planning, and gender, race, ethnicity, and religious equalities).

It is about extending the arena of democratic management beyond the SSE organization and promoting pedagogical actions that encourage the participation and mobilization of the exercise of participatory democracy, deliberative citizenship, and social management (Silva Junior et al. 2015) at local, regional, or even national level. The practices of democratic management built at the organizational level, such as strengthening social ties, building cooperation networks, accumulating established social relations, and learning from internal democratic processes, should contribute to deepening democracy at the local, territorial, or national level. In this spillover of democracy beyond organizations, it is crucial that SSE organizations encourage their members to claim, occupy, enjoy, and build their places of active citizenship in the public sphere.

This encouragement may begin with public debates at the local level, in an exercise of direct deliberative democracy (see entry 10, "Origins and Histories"). In these debates, individuals, regardless of their role (for example, members, partners, participants in organizations or projects, entrepreneurs, students, residents, and so on), should plan and decide on their actions, products, or services, according to identified local/community demands. Next, or simultaneously, these active citizens must mobilize and express themselves as pressure groups so that their various demands toward sustainable human development (in resonance with the SSE) are recognized as legitimate by civil society. Finally, there is an expansion of deliberative citizenship in the public sphere when the citizens' participation reaches the formal spaces of the state structures, such as district, municipal, provincial, departmental, regional, or national assemblies, councils, and forums.

The public sphere, at the societal level of democracy practice, should be recognized as a space for presenting and debating demands and projects for legislation and public policies. In summary, this process can start from an idea discussed within SSE organizations, go through collective debate in the local arena, and even take to the streets in the form of citizens' claims. Next, this could be close to becoming an Act or public policy (not limited to only those related to the SSE), in cases in which it reaches the prime arena for the exercise of participatory democracy: the public sphere. Understanding that the public sphere encloses the citizens, the state, the market, and civil society, constantly in cooperation and conflict, is essential to understanding what this environment means for democracy.

The state officially recognizes public demands within the public sphere, as well as public policies and government actions, built and decided in that space. Thus, for citizens to become more active and decisive in the public sphere, it is necessary to raise deliberative citizenship to a level of importance as relevant as that of the state's representative democracy. In addition, citizens need to be better educated and prepared to act collectively in the public sphere when defending the substantive interests of human life. In these two aspects, SSE organizations contribute effectively to the participation of individuals or groups linked to the SSE in the public sphere, not just quantitatively but, above all, qualitatively. These contributions are nurtured in the democratic management of SSE organizations and matured by the period of training in claim-making environments, pressure groups, social movements, and local/territorial arenas, under the aegis of democratic governance.

49.3 FINAL REMARKS

As explained in this entry, democracy in SSE organizations is present in the set of participatory management processes which emphasize cooperation, conversation, dialogue, discussion, debate, and claim as the imperative values of planning and implementing collective and public decisions. These decisions should be oriented towards solving demands and achieving the purposes of SSE organizations, not limiting their performance by utilitarian rationality. The SSE organizations should also not restrict their actions to the standards of market-economic regulation, and not reduce their political role in civil society to the compliance of social and environmental responsibility. Furthermore, participation and democratic governance practices in SSE organizations are a constant process of conquests, losses, learning, and redefinitions.

This is also how, in SSE organizations, the democratic management mode strengthens active and deliberative citizenship towards the spaces of a public sphere.

In turn, risks arising from democratic participation and management in SSE organizations also exist. For example, there is the possibility of cooptation of individuals, members, and influential leaders by the managers, coordinators, and directors of SSE organizations (Hoarau and Laville 2013). There is also the possibility, in more fluid management, to overvalue a leader who coordinates an activity, or to grant too much power to the manager (see entry 44, "Co-optation, Isomorphism and Instrumentalisation"). In addition, there will always be the challenge to overcome the inherent slower speed of decision-making processes in participatory arenas. As Arnstein (1969) mentioned in her seminal paper, there are adverse conditions under which the practice of citizen participation can be manipulated or used as validation.

Therefore, it is necessary that members of SSE organizations be vigilant around such dysfunctions of democratic management processes. These risks and challenges should not be used as arguments to prevent achieving democracy and participation in the SSE. On the contrary, it is important to acknowledge them, so that individuals, groups, and collectives within SSE organizations can safeguard themselves in all processes, stages, and levels of implementation of democratic governance and deliberative citizenship.

Finally, as mentioned previously in this entry, democratic management, democratic governance, and deliberative citizenship in the SSE, with their practices and their conceptual characteristics and components, can be identified under other terminologies, but with close definitions and attributes. The closest terms are self-management (Lee and Edmondson 2017), associative governance (Hoarau and Laville 2013), management of associations (Bernet et al. 2016), social management (Cançado et al. 2019; Eynaud and França Filho 2019), and shared and participatory local governance (Amaro 2018).

REFERENCES

Amaro, Rogério. 2018. *Manual de Práticas e Métodos sobre Grupos Comunitários*, 1st edn. Lisboa: Leigos Para o Desenvolvimento.
Arnstein, Sherry R. 1969. "A Ladder of Citizen Participation." *Journal of the American Institute of Planners* 35 (4): 216–24. https://doi.org/10.1080/01944366908977225.
Bernet, Julien, Philippe Eynaud, Olivier Maurel, and Corinne Vercher-Chaptal. 2016. *La Gestion des Associations*, 1st edn. Toulouse: Éditions Érès.
Caillé, Alain. 2007. *Anthropologie du Don: Le Tiers Paradigme*, 2nd edn. Paris: La Découverte.
Cançado, Airton, Fernando Tenório, and José Pereira. 2019. *Gestión Social: Epistemología de Un Paradigma*, 1st edn. Cuenca: Universidad del Azuay/Casa Editora. http://publicaciones.uazuay.edu.ec/index.php/ceuazuay/catalog/book/67.
Eynaud, Philippe, and Genauto C. França Filho. 2019. *Solidarité et Organisation: Penser une Autre Gestion*, 1st edn. Toulouse: Éditions Érès.
Guerreiro Ramos, Alberto 1984. *New Science of Organizations: A Reconceptualization of the Wealth of Nations*, 2nd edn. Toronto: University of Toronto Press.
Hoarau, Christian, and Jean-Louis Laville, eds. 2013. *La Gouvernance des Associations: Économie, Sociologie, Gestion*, 2nd edn. Toulouse: Éditions Érès.
Lee, Michael Y., and Amy C. Edmondson. 2017. "Self-Managing Organizations: Exploring the Limits of Less-Hierarchical Organizing." *Research in Organizational Behavior* 37 (November): 35–58. https://doi.org/10.1016/j.riob.2017.10.002.
Polanyi, Karl. 2001. *The Great Transformation: The Political and Economic Origins of Our Time*. Boston, MA: Beacon Press.
Sen, Amartya. 2000. *Development as Freedom*, 1st edn. New York: Anchor Books.

Silva Junior, Jeová T., Ariádne S. Rigo, and Ósia A. Vasconcelos. 2015. "Gestão Social nas Finanças Solidárias: Reflexões sobre a Necessidade da Avaliação da Utilidade Social dos Bancos Comunitários de Desenvolvimento no Brasil." *NAU Social* 6 (10): 151–64. https://doi.org/10.9771/ns.v6i10.31328.

50. Partnership and co-construction
Marguerite Mendell

INTRODUCTION

The social and solidarity economy (SSE) invites a broader reflection on existing social, economic and political relationships bound by structures, norms and institutional culture. It invites an even broader reflection on process, on how, where and by whom decisions are taken. The SSE is committed to the intersecting goals of sustainable development, social justice and equity. Its contribution to local and regional development, job creation and the production of goods and services in the public interest in the Global North and South is well documented. Indeed, the SSE is an economic actor in a plural economy made up of private, public and SSE actors. But limiting the SSE to its economic performance reinforces the separation of social, political, economic and environmental goals embedded in the dominant market paradigm and in its failure to address today's complex societal challenges. Partnership is a relationship that exists within the SSE between actors, or between SSE actors and different levels of government, social movements and at times with the private sector. These are not necessarily bound by contract but rather rest on trust and proven benefits for all parties. Co-construction is a process; it is an ongoing dialogue between actors designing development tools for the SSE such as finance, labour market and business development, knowledge mobilization and transfer, access to markets, as well as a dialogue between government and the SSE in the design of enabling public policy measures

50.1 PARTNERSHIP AND THE SSE

A discussion on partnership and co-construction refers to two different and interrelated features of the SSE that can be distinguished as relational and process. In the first instance, partnership is most frequently a relationship that is not legally bound but rather rooted in advantageous arrangements between actors. In other words, it reflects a common awareness and appreciation of the benefit of collaboration, the term which better describes the reality of non-legal forms of partnership. This includes relationships between SSE entities within or across sectors, between the SSE and social movements (see entry 1, 'Activism and Social Movements'), and at times, between SSE entities and different levels of government. While these relationships are not static, they are often based on long-standing relationships. Depending on how partnerships or collaboration emerge and evolve, they range from informal, to institutionalized or regulated, delineating roles and responsibilities of partners.

One example of a sectoral partnership with significant impact for the development of the SSE is the collaboration between SSE and social finance institutions to generate broad access to capital for SSE organizations and enterprises (SSEOEs) (see entry 28, 'Finance Sector'). The impact of this collaboration is positive for both the social financial institutions involved, or the supply side, and the SSEOEs in which they invest, the demand side. Pooling investments reduces the risk for individual financial partners, allowing them to create a viable and growing social finance sector while simultaneously leveraging the ability of SSE entities to access additional investment and develop capacity. Partnerships between the SSE and social finance sector in the province of Quebec in Canada, for example, are at the heart of an SSE social finance ecosystem, a best practice frequently cited by other regions in many parts of the world, where access to capital for SSE entities remains a challenge (Mendell et al. 2018).

Recently, social finance actors across Canada collaborated with the federal government to design a national social finance and social innovation strategy including a considerable investment by the government. This is an important illustration of how established relationships galvanized social finance institutions across Canada to engage in a process of co-design of policy with the national government.

Other examples of collaboration include those between SSEOEs in many diverse sectors underpinning the formation of intersectoral networks with greater representational and political capacity. They also include collaboration between the SSE and divisions within government. This is certainly the case for ministries and departments responsible for the promotion of cooperatives in many regions. In recent years, mandates for cooperatives have widened to encompass the SSE more broadly in some parts of the world. In other regions, the responsibility for cooperatives and other SSE entities remains separate. Complicating this is the further fragmentation into sub-categories to distinguish social enterprise and non-profit organizations, in some cases (see entry 54, 'Statistical Measurement'). Where there are more inclusive definitions and representations of the SSE, while acknowledging its diversity, the impact of collaboration with government is far greater. How this occurs depends on the ability and willingness of government to participate in new processes of policy design. This is where collaboration and co-construction converge, or where collaboration is a pre-condition for the co-construction of public policy for the SSE.

50.2   CO-CONSTRUCTION

Co-construction is a process; it is an ongoing dialogue between actors designing development tools for the SSE such as finance, labour market and business development, knowledge mobilization and transfer, access to markets, as well as a dialogue between government and the SSE in the design of enabling public policy measures (see entry 51, 'Public Policy'). Where co-construction of public policy in the SSE exists, it demonstrates an openness on the part of government otherwise constrained by structures and mandates with little room for flexibility or innovation. The co-construction of public policy describes a multi-stakeholder process of policy design to enable the development of the SSE. It is not a linear process. Co-construction is a dynamic and circular flow of knowledge and information, involving many actors. It is distinct from co-production, which refers to collaborative forms of programme delivery between government and service providers.

Even though many regions around the world are committed to policy innovation, they confront impermeable barriers. Ironically, many governments support and promote innovation, including social innovation, but are unable to introduce institutional innovation within government itself, with some important exceptions. Co-construction challenges traditional policy formation, breaking down institutional boundaries within government as well as between government and socio-economic actors. To meet the intersecting and multi-layered objectives of the SSE, boundaries within government have to be crossed, including institutional culture, often the most difficult obstacle to overcome.

Administrative architecture in the public sector is dominated by structures and norms; it is not conducive to flows. The SSE requires institutional flexibility, fluidity and collaboration across ministerial or departmental silos within government, and a willingness to engage with stakeholders in the co-design of new or adapted policy measures. The need for more horizontal dialogue within government and the creation of multi-stakeholder spaces bringing non-governmental actors into the conversation is increasingly acknowledged. While this openness to innovation is positive and has resulted in some important changes in policy formation, research reveals that unless it is institutionalized, it is unlikely to go beyond ad hoc pragmatic responses to short-term, complex challenges.

Any discussion of co-construction must include not only illustrations of why, how, where and with whom this exists to demonstrate its effectiveness, but a broader conversation about different conceptions of democracy which support such a process (see entry 49, 'Participation, Governance, Collective Action and Democracy'). Discussions about democracy have been subordinated to the predominance of intransigent processes of governance and decision making for the most part. Discussion, persuasion, debate and consultation are vital to democratic decision making. (Dewey 1935). Co-construction is distinguished from periodic public consultations, forums, ad hoc committees including non-governmental members, commissions of inquiry, and so on. Rarely do these disrupt the status quo, as once information is gathered and analysed, it generally lands squarely inside existing structures and processes of decision making.

Democracy is experimental, a process to question and challenge the established order. It cannot be considered exclusively as a form of government; it is embedded in social relationships. The fragility of a static form of democracy and its institutional architecture has been demonstrated time and again. Co-construction responds to the need for deepening democracy, for the democratization of democracy. Dialogic cooperation between individuals, organizations, divisions within government and between government and SSE stakeholders underlie co-construction. But cooperation has to be fostered. Cultural barriers are deep; long-established norms and ways of working are not easily transformed.

Many ways to exercise democracy have not been part of a debate within the public domain wedded to existing rules and procedures for governance and policy formation. Where there are different, more open and inclusive approaches to decision making, these are either ignored or considered as marginal or tangential. In many parts of the world the SSE has imposed the need for more reflexive governance to meet complex, inseparable challenges, as is occurring in environmental and public health policy in many countries and promoted by international organizations such as the World Health Organization (WHO), for example (Feindt and Weiland 2018). Spaces are needed for social conversation or discursive democracy, collective intelligence and social learning. Where they exist, they effectively challenge democratic governance as commonly practised (Sennett 2012). Disciplinary boundaries must also come down in order to learn from innovative practices in other fields with possible replicability or adaptability to public policy. Design-driven innovation theory in which a diversity of actors participate in a process of co-creation, for example, provides a powerful conceptual framework for how to democratize processes of policy formation (Manzini 2015). The effectiveness of polycentricity or multiple sites of stakeholder decision making has also been extensively documented and is receiving much attention. It resonates with the needs for public policy enabling the SSE to be both situated, or place-based corresponding with its territorial roots, as well as coordinated with higher levels of government for policy coherence (McGinnis and Ostrom 2011). But the challenge is not only to maintain flexibility and fluidity, including recombinant linkages between all levels of government (Fung and Wright 2003), but to institutionalize these processes. Calling for the institutionalization of flexibility is not contradictory; it is essential.

New public management was widely accepted as an alternative to the post-war welfare state model of public administration, as it conformed with an ideological shift in the size and role of government (see entry 53, 'Social Policy'). That this implied less capacity to represent the needs and desires of citizens, and a threat to democracy, was not questioned. While co-construction also questions the existing framework of governance, it does not argue for less government. Co-construction offers an alternative to the pendulum swing of more government or less government, associated with market imperatives. Its steadfast commitment to the values of the welfare state is foundational. Co-construction presents a more democratic and effective means to embrace these values, reconfiguring relations between government and social actors to instill a discursive culture.

50.3 BROADENING THE PROCESS OF POLICY FORMATION

There are numerous examples of governments and institutions around the world that recognize the need to broaden the process of policy formation. In 2010, the European Commission stated that the 2020 ten-year goal to achieve smart, sustainable and inclusive growth could only be met with a coordinated European response that included social partners and civil society. The European Commission's Social Economy Action Plan released in January 2022, while salutary as it places the social economy firmly among the objectives of the European Commission, did not move beyond extensive consultations with numerous SSE networks and organizations to engage them in a process of co-construction in drafting the final Action Plan. This is an example of the resistance to open social conversation, in this case perceived as too unwieldy, involving too many actors, thereby justifying the absence of representatives of the SSE in the drafting process.

Where is co-construction more feasible? Is it at the national or regional or local level? Of course the answer depends on institutional context, as juridical divisions of power vary considerably across nations, determining the roles and responsibilities of different levels of government. Increasingly, co-creation or co-design of public policy occurs most frequently at local and regional levels. Two questions go begging. The first concerns the need for institutionalizing processes of co-construction, without which it risks being put into action in response to specific challenges, with little impact on established forms of governance or policy formation. It is also vulnerable to electoral politics if newly elected parties do not share the same commitment to institutional innovation. The second question concerns the necessity for harmonization between different levels of government to ensure policy coherence.

In response to the first question, SSE framework legislation in some regions includes clauses inscribing processes of co-construction in law. Quebec and France are two examples where horizontality within government and stakeholder participation are bound by SSE framework legislation. Recent reform of Italian law has established a new code for the 'third sector', the term used in Italy to refer to the SSE, binding government to practise 'shared administration' with non-profit organizations, to co-create enabling policy measures for the third sector. This legal reform has institutionalized dialogue or co-construction between government and a plurality of actors (Salvatore 2022).

Several cities have created stakeholder spaces of co-construction to develop the SSE. Examples include the city of Bilbao and its Ekonpolo platform, the main instrument of the Bilbao City Council to support the SSE in Bilbao and in the region. The City Council recognizes the contribution of the SSE to urban economic development, quality of life and welfare of the city, and its capacity to meet the Sustainable Development Goals (SDGs). It also acknowledges that the transformative capacity of the SSE requires collaboration between the administration, universities, companies, civil society and SSE networks in Bilbao and across Spain to co-construct enabling policy measures.

The City of Montreal established a Secretariat for the Social Economy and in 2009 signed a Social Economy Partnership for Community-Based and Sustainable Development with representatives of the social economy, local development intermediaries and researchers, creating a space for dialogue on municipal policy for the SSE in Montreal. This conversation continues within very tight juridical limitations imposed by the Canadian Constitution on the autonomy of municipal governments. Still, within these limitations, an ongoing process of dialogue and co-construction has generated innovative urban policy measures and broad support for the SSE (Mendell et al. 2020).

These examples, as well as many case studies of co-construction of public policy for the SSE over several years in the Global North and South, produced the following findings. They may be summarized as follows (Mendell and Alain 2015). Co-construction and ongoing dialogue with SSE actors and networks:

- allows the SSE to realize its potential;
- reduces information asymmetry and transactions costs for government; and
- ensures policy effectiveness by developing more innovative, adapted and effective policy measures and programmes than those designed or implemented unilaterally by government.

The case studies also confirmed that SSE networks are necessary for effective co-construction of enabling public policy. These are present in several regions around the world, including France, Spain, Quebec and Brazil, to name a few. They include local, regional and national networks that engage with all levels of government, corresponding to juridical divisions of power with possibilities to scale with higher levels of government as needed. The case studies concluded that where individual sector networks participated in this process on their own, they created tension or rivalry within the SSE. Co-construction is most effective with broad integrated SSE representation. However, while integrated SSE networks mediate between the SSE and government, they must not crowd out or conflate the diversity of constituent organizations, enterprises and sectoral associations.

CONCLUSION

Governments are faced with intersecting problems that cannot be addressed in silos. Governing in complexity requires policy innovation (Christiansen and Bunt 2012). The COVID-19 pandemic has called upon central governments to intervene in ways that have not been seen since the mid-1970s. But it has also imposed more flexibility on governments around the world to transcend the limitations of existing institutional architecture, and the difficulty of working outside relatively rigid mandates imposed on ministries and departments. Until recently, working horizontally across these boundaries has been exceptional. The pandemic has also raised the need for more comprehensive and integrated approaches to public policy formation, and for greater collaboration with social actors. Will the demonstrated benefit of collaboration during a global health crisis provide important lessons for the future? Paradoxically, actions currently taken mirror innovative processes of co-construction of public policy with SSE practitioners and networks already in place in numerous regions around the world. Engaging directly with SSE actors increases the transformational capacity of government.

The ability of the SSE to transmit useful knowledge, by identifying SSE needs and how best to respond, transforms traditional top-down policy formation. Policy measures are co-designed, drawing upon collective intelligence in a new public and dialogical space. This is key to the development of the SSE, and where it occurs it is foreshadowing a new paradigm of public governance.

REFERENCES

Christiansen, Jesper, and Laura Bunt. 2012. 'Innovation in Policy: Allowing for Creativity, Social Complexity and Uncertainty in Public Governance.' Nesta. https://www.bl.uk/collection-items/innovation-in-policy-allowing-for-creativity-social-complexity-and-uncertainty-in-public-governance.

Dewey, John. 1935. *Liberalism and Social Action: The Page-Barbour Lectures*. New York: Putnam.

Feindt, Peter H., and Sabine Weiland. 2018. 'Reflexive Governance: Exploring the Concept and Assessing Its Critical Potential for Sustainable Development. Introduction to the Special Issue.' *Journal of Environmental Policy and Planning* 20 (6): 661–74. https://doi.org/10.1080/1523908x.2018.1532562.

Fung, Archon, and Erik Olin Wright. 2003. *Deepening Democracy: Institutional Innovations in Empowered Participatory Governance*. London: Verso.

Manzini, Ezio. 2015. *Design, When Everybody Designs: An Introduction to Design for Social Innovation*. Cambridge, MA, USA and London, UK: MIT Press.

McGinnis, Michael D., and Elinor Ostrom. 2011. 'Reflections on Vincent Ostrom, Public Administration, and Polycentricity.' *Public Administration Review* 72 (1): 15–25. https://doi.org/10.1111/j.1540-6210.2011.02488.x.

Mendell, Marguerite, and Béatrice Alain. 2015. 'Enabling the Social and Solidarity Economy through the Co-Construction of Public Policy.' In *Social and Solidarity Economy: Beyond the Fringe?*, edited by Peter Utting. London: Zed Books.

Mendell, Marguerite, Nancy Néamtan, Émilien Gruet, Jongick Jang, Vanessa Sorin, Jinhwan Kim and Garam Lee. 2018. 'Strategy for Knowledge Transfer of Social Finance Best Practices of Québec and Strategy for Adaptation to Seoul.' socioeco.org. http://www.socioeco.org/bdf_fiche-document-6622_en.html.

Mendell, Marguerite, Nancy Néamtan and Hyuna Yi. 2020. 'Public Policies Enabling the Social and Solidarity Economy in the City of Montreal.' UNRISD. https://www.unrisd.org/80256B3C005BCCF9/search/0A7D20A258646194802585580047D114F?OpenDocument.

Salvatore, Gianluca. 2022. Telephone Interview on Legislative Reform for the SSE in Italy. Interview by Marguerite Mendell.

Sennett, Richard. 2012. *Together: The Rituals, Pleasures, and Politics of Cooperation*. New Haven, CT: Yale University Press.

51. Public policy
Peter Utting

INTRODUCTION

While the social and solidarity economy (SSE) is often seen as an alternative space in relation to both the public sector and the mainstream market-based economy, it is closely connected to both. With regard to state institutions, public policies are central to this relationship. The way they impact upon the SSE, however, is multifaceted, complex and often contradictory.

During much of the 20th century, the marginalization of many workers, producers, traders, consumers and citizens comprising the SSE was partly a consequence of state inaction or public policies that skewed resource allocation and regulation in favour of other actors and sectors. Furthermore, the chequered history of cooperatives and non-governmental organizations (NGOs) (see entry 17, 'Cooperatives and Mutuals' and entry 20, 'Non-governmental Organizations and Foundations') had much to do with political interference and dependency on state institutions. During the past two decades, there have been signs that these features of inaction, bias and control are ceding ground to a different political and policy agenda: one that recognizes the potential of the SSE in relation to social, economic and environmental goals (see entry 10, 'Origins and Histories' and entry 3, 'Contemporary Understandings') and is more enabling.

This entry describes and assesses what states are doing to promote the SSE. It begins by highlighting key trends and innovations that characterize the turn towards the SSE within public policy, before providing an overview of the expanding portfolio of policy measures available to governments and parliaments. It then considers the opportunities, risks and challenges that confront the transformational process associated with the SSE in contexts where public policy supports it. The entry ends by noting certain institutional and political conditions that could address the ongoing fragility and fragmentation of public policy support for the SSE.

51.1 THE CHANGING POLICY AGENDA

A combination of conditions and contexts emerged in the late 20th and early 21st centuries to alter policy related to the SSE. Various drivers of this policy change have been attributed to global phenomena such as the impacts of the global financial crisis, increased attention to the benefits of socially oriented business models, networked forms of advocacy, and the need for green transitions. Sometimes the drivers assumed regional characteristics: in Asia, heightened social pressures and demands linked to democratization in countries such as South Korea, Indonesia and the Philippines, as well as the Asian financial crisis; in Latin America, ideological shifts associated with the so-called turn to the left and social movements activism; and in Europe, welfare state reform linked to neo-liberalism and austerity policies, as well as growing interest in social enterprise.

Analysis of how public policies are evolving reveals signs of a shift from what has been referred to as 'first' to 'second' generation policies (Chaves-Avila and Gallego-Bono 2020). The former are characterized by a fragmented, piecemeal and vertical approach; one focused on specific types of SSE organizations and enterprises (SSEOEs), particular economic sectors such as agriculture and finance, and a narrow range of policy incentives such as subsidies and training. It also leans towards top-down hierarchical policy making. Second-generation policies, in contrast, tend to adopt a broader focus, are better integrated in national policy and are more participatory. Key legal and institutional innovations include the following.

The Promotion of New Types of SSEOEs

These include social enterprises and non-traditional forms of cooperatives. The former comprise organizations that blend entrepreneurial practices and social priorities and/or serve the general public interest rather than that of members. The latter include social cooperatives providing social services to members and/or the wider public, worker cooperatives comprising employees that reconstitute failed or failing companies, and multi-purpose cooperatives which engage in activities associated with various sectors (Borzaga et al. 2020; Defourny et al. 2019).

Focusing on the SSE as a Sector

Governments and policy makers are recognizing the potential of the SSE as a sector in itself; one comprising organizations and enterprises that have in common an institutional logic or set of economic, social and democratic principles and practices that differ from conventional business and public sector activities. From Brazil to the European Union (EU), governments are attempting to map and quantify the scale and impact of this sector in terms of geographical spread, employment and gross domestic product (GDP). Excluding decrees or laws targeting particular types of SSEOEs, national parliaments in 16 countries of Europe, Latin America and Africa had passed framework law or similar broad-based laws promoting SSE by mid-2021. Examples include Mexico (2012), France (2014), Uruguay (2019) and Senegal (2021). Passing such laws, however, is often a protracted process that can be stalled or blocked by party politics and changing priorities. In lieu of laws, or additionally in certain cases, some governments have drafted comprehensive national development plans for the SSE. Such plans include the National Strategy for Social and Solidarity Economy 2010–2020 in Morocco, the 2018 Master Plan for Human Resource Development for the Social Economy in the Republic of Korea, and the Public Policy for SSE 2021–2025 in Costa Rica.

Integrating the SSE in the Welfare System

While many SSEOEs have traditionally provided services relating to health, care and work integration, several governments have scaled up and formalized their participation in national welfare systems and employment generation strategies. Examples include the role of community health or mutual health organizations in West Africa; the promotion of social enterprises generating employment for those with disabilities in Japan, the Republic of Korea and Poland; and the provision of childcare services in Quebec and Uruguay.

Institutionalizing the SSE in Public Policy

Measures are being taken to ensure that public sector support for SSE is not dependent on particular political parties or transitory circumstances, but is a consistent feature of state policy (Coraggio 2015). Increasing bipartisan or multi-party support for the SSE is apparent, as governments and parties of quite different ideological persuasions are recognizing the SSE in their policy discourse and agendas. Beyond laws, national development plans or policies targeting the SSE, governments are establishing entities with direct responsibility for supporting this sector. Such institutions include ministries (Luxembourg, Nicaragua, Senegal) or vice-ministries (Costa Rica), as well as departments (France, Morocco), secretariats (Brazil), specialized and technical agencies (Republic of Korea, Ecuador) and decentralized institutes (Argentina, Mexico) within a ministry or similar entity.

Co-construction of Policy

A key component of this institutionalization process is the establishment of consultative processes comprising SSE actors and intermediary organizations that speak and advocate on their behalf (Mendell and Alain 2015). Such processes may involve formal structures, such as within the Consultative Council for SSE in Uruguay, or institutionalized informal interactions, as has occurred in Quebec and the Republic of Korea, where large SSE umbrella organizations are recognized as key interlocutors. In several countries and jurisdictions, co-construction has played an important role in overcoming the limitations of top-down policy design and implementation, and ensuring that policy making, evaluation and review are aligned with the diversity, needs and preferences of SSE actors. Important in this regard are decentralized consultative structures at the territorial level, as seen in the case of Brazil, or multi-stakeholder working groups organized on a sectoral or thematic basis, as in Costa Rica.

Towards an Ecosystemic Approach

Early efforts to promote the SSE often centred on inter-agency coordination and ad hoc initiatives related to training or access to finance and markets. Increasingly, governments are recognizing the importance of a broader 'ecosystemic' approach which has several components (Borzaga et al. 2020; Jenkins et al. 2021; Chaves-Avila and Gallego-Bono 2020). It recognizes that an effective enabling environment for the SSE involves actors, institutions, partnerships and other interactions associated with multiple sectors (public, private, NGOs and civil society). It also acknowledges the nested nature of governance at multiple scales, and the need to mobilize resources and coordinate support and regulation at municipal, provincial/state, federal/national, and supranational or international levels. Furthermore, central to an ecosystemic approach is the notion that promoting the SSE requires efforts to strengthen its asset base in relation to multiple forms of 'capital': financial, human, social, knowledge and physical, among others. This approach is being actively promoted at the supranational level by the EU and the Organisation for Economic Co-operation and Development (OECD); nationally in countries such as South Korea and Uruguay; and regionally in areas such as Quebec in Canada, and Emilia Romagna in Italy, where the SSE has a strong presence.

51.2 THE PUBLIC POLICY TOOLKIT

Public sector engagement with the SSE in recent decades has resulted in a broad portfolio of regulatory and support measures. The types of measures related directly to the SSE include the following (Borzaga et al. 2020; Jenkins et al. 2021; Serrano et al. 2019; Utting 2017):

- Recognizing and integrating the SSE in law and policy:
  - locking in state oversight and support via constitutional clauses, laws and regulations which govern and promote the SSE or specific types of SSEOEs;
  - incorporating the SSE into sectoral, territorial or national development policies and plans; and
  - promoting the SSE within regional and international policy forums and networks.
- Financing:
  - direct financial support for SSEOEs via grants, subsidies and concessionary or flexible financing, as well as co-financing arrangements with private banks and matching grants;
  - indirect support via loan guarantees, capitalization of loan intermediaries, social and green bonds; and
  - regulations that facilitate access to banking and micro-finance institutions along with the use of other mechanisms including crowd-funding, complementary currencies, social impact investing and Islamic finance.
- Fiscal incentives:
  - tax exemptions for SSEOEs;
  - reduction in social insurance costs;
  - tax relief for investors in SSEOEs; and
  - tax share donations which allow taxpayers a degree of tax relief if they donate to a cause or organization.
- Market access:
  - public procurement, including preferential procurement;
  - regulatory measures requiring private companies such as supermarkets to purchase a share of their produce from SSE producers;
  - vouchers to encourage consumers to buy SSEOE products and services, promotion of market fairs, and fair trade for SSE producers and retailers; and
  - premium (above-market) prices.
- Governance:
  - facilitation of participatory forms of governance or co-construction;
  - promotion of multi-scalar governance to ensure that public policy support for the SSE involves authorities and public sector institutions at local/municipal, provincial/state and national levels;
  - effective coordination of the responsibilities and initiatives of multiple public sector entities;
  - rationalization of bureaucratic procedures that impede the emergence and expansion of SSEOEs; and
  - certification to validate social enterprises.
- Training and education:
  - capacity building via skills development, basic education, financial literacy and

values-oriented learning, which involves SSE practitioners, managers and civil servants; and
- university incubators to assist new SSEOEs.
- Advocacy and knowledge building:
  - awareness raising and dissemination about the concept, benefits and potential of SSE;
  - mapping the SSE and measuring its scope, scale and impact via research and data collection;
  - developing SSE satellite accounts;
  - participating in 'observatories' that monitor conditions and trends; and
  - participating in advocacy networks promoting the SSE.
- Public–SSE partnerships:
  - participation in multi-stakeholder policy and planning forums;
  - preferential procurement;
  - matching grants in joint fundraising initiatives;
  - subcontracting the provision of social welfare services to SSEOEs;
  - direct investment by municipal authorities in SSEOEs;
  - participation of SSEOEs in government work integration programmes via training services;
  - SSE education and training via public universities and government agencies; and
  - waste recycling and provision of water services, rural electrification and wind power in collaboration with municipal authorities.

This type of overview of public policy focuses on measures that relate directly to SSEOEs. Also key, however, are other aspects related to rights-based, public investment and macro-economic policies. These include building physical and social infrastructure such as roads, rural electrification, water services and clinics in communities and territories where the SSE is present. Many factors fundamentally determine the life chances and possibilities for emancipation and empowerment of disadvantaged groups, as well as the ability for the SSE to expand and operate on a level playing field. These include land rights, civil, political and cultural rights, universal social protection, as well as macro-economic and fiscal policy.

51.3 CHALLENGES AND TRADE-OFFS

While recent policy innovations often support the scaling up and strengthening of SSE, they can occur in political, institutional and macro-economic contexts that constrain their effectiveness (UNRISD 2016). How the SSE is impacted upon as it interacts more closely with the state and the market has long been an issue of concern. A key question is whether the transformative potential of the SSE is realized or, in fact, undermined by public policy, and what trade-offs are involved. Such potential extends beyond specific benefits related to basic needs provisioning, decent work and environmental protection: it also involves democratic practices and the political empowerment of disadvantaged groups. And at a systemic level, the potential of the SSE extends to its role as an alternative to market-led development and in reconfiguring the hierarchy of economic, social and environmental objectives within development strategy (see also entry 3, 'Contemporary Understandings').

The analysis of both state–SSE and market–SSE relations and their impacts has identified two major issues, often referred to as 'instrumentalization' and 'isomorphism' (see entry

44, 'Co-optation, Isomorphism and Instrumentalisation'). Under instrumentalization, SSE is employed as a policy tool to achieve specific government objectives. During this process, core features and attributes of SSE can be marginalized or diluted. Concerning isomorphism, SSEOEs assume practices and norms that characterize or are promoted by the organizations they are interacting with, including for-profit orientation, managerial culture and hierarchy. While both of these dynamics present opportunities for scaling up or strengthening aspects of the SSE, they also generate risks.

Key concerns include the following (Borzaga et al. 2020; Coraggio 2015; Cotera 2019; Fonteneau and Pollet 2019; ILO 2022; Serrano et al. 2019; Utting 2017). First, targeting versus diversity. The diversity of SSE practices and organizations, and the transformational potential of the SSE, can be undermined when state incentives are tied to a narrow range of social policy objectives, activities and enterprise forms. The focus on promoting certain forms of social enterprise and social entrepreneurship, or stretching the definition of the SSE to include corporate social responsibility, runs the risk of diverting attention from community, indigenous and collective forms of organization. Similarly, core aspects of the SSE related to democratic governance, active citizenship and collective action can be sidelined as attention focuses on service provisioning, social inclusion, enterprise development and social entrepreneurship. Government policies and legislation often emphasize the role of the SSE in relation to social purpose and economic empowerment, rather than its emancipatory potential and the political empowerment of disadvantaged groups (see entry 3, 'Contemporary Understandings'). A six-country study of the SSE in East and Southeast Asia found that state sector framings of the SSE and policy tools and innovations often ignore the democratic dimension (ILO 2022).

Second, minimalist resource allocation. Despite changes in government discourse that promote SSE, resource allocation often remains highly constrained. Furthermore, incentives and regulations, including procedures for legally establishing an enterprise, continue to be skewed in favour of conventional forms of for-profit business. Both policy discourse and existing literature on the SSE often highlight positive institutional developments with limited, if any, reference to actual resource allocation. For example, under the preferential public procurement system in South Korea, only 2.5 per cent of purchases in 2019 actually involved SSEOEs. Similarly in Brazil, the highly regarded National Secretariat for Solidarity Economy (SENAES) and other SSE-related government institutions experienced major fluctuations in budgetary support, even under the two administrations that formally promoted the SSE between 2003 and 2016 (Morais and Bacic 2020).

Third, unsustainable organizations. The sudden availability of financial support and other incentives for particular types of SSEOEs and activities can encourage the emergence of unsustainable entities that lack key assets and capabilities associated with human capital (such as managerial skills and technical know-how) and social capital (such as support networks and relations of trust), let alone access to affordable sources of finance. This often results in significant failure rates of cooperatives and social enterprises after policy support declines, as demonstrated in examples such as wind energy cooperatives in Denmark and agricultural cooperatives in Indonesia during different periods. Financial incentives, when coupled with limited oversight, can also give rise to free-riders, that is, entrepreneurs or enterprises that fictitiously assume the form of an SSEOE to access benefits. Certification schemes, such as that introduced for social enterprises in South Korea, can provide a means to address this issue, but run the risk of introducing burdensome administrative requirements.

Fourth, political tensions. Political support for the SSE can be a double-edged sword. It can mobilize much-needed resources to grow and consolidate SSEOEs, but it can also undermine their autonomy via political influence, as is the case for many agricultural cooperatives, particularly under authoritarian regimes. Revision of cooperative law within several East and Southeast Asian countries in recent decades has been partly aimed at reasserting cooperative principles, including autonomy. Furthermore, state support and the scope for co-construction at different levels of governance can change significantly with the rotation of parties and leaders in power. This can affect not only budgetary support and outreach, but also progress in institutionalizing the SSE. For example, it can result in blocking or delaying the enactment of laws supporting the SSE, and downsizing or eliminating state institutions set up to support the SSE, as occurred in Brazil when SENAES was dissolved.

Fifth, policy (in)coherence. Contradictory policies and weak implementation often undermine the effectiveness of public policy in promoting the SSE (Utting 2017). Policies can simultaneously support and constrain the SSE. Some such inconsistencies have already been noted: for example, when policy discourse supporting the SSE contrasts with a highly constrained fiscal reality of tight or declining budgetary support. Furthermore, policies often foster an uneven playing field for the SSE: for example, when laws and regulations make it far easier to establish conventional for-profit private companies than SSEOEs; when public procurement is skewed towards private enterprise; or when corporate welfare dwarfs support for the SSE, as experienced in the United States and Europe. Additionally, policy incoherence occurs when the life chances and capabilities of SSE actors are undermined by a host of other policies that affect well-being, the environment and active citizenship. These include: (1) labour market regulations and social policy that exclude workers in the informal economy; (2) the failure to effectively allow indigenous peoples to realize their cultural rights, empower women through women's rights, grant land rights to landless farmers, or respect civil and political rights that facilitate self-organization, collective action and advocacy; and (3) regressive tax policy, de-regulation or privatization that favours corporate and elite interests; macro-economic policy that promotes austerity measures; and investment policy that is skewed towards corporate-led and extractivist models of development.

States can adopt very different approaches when promoting the SSE. A review of state–SSE relations in several Latin American countries identifies three different models, that can also be found in other countries (Coraggio 2015). They are: an assistentialist social policy model where the SSE constitutes an important welfare policy tool; a co-constructed approach that sees SSE actors influencing policy in ways that foster both the economic and political empowerment of SSE actors; and a systemic approach which includes not only comprehensive legal and policy reforms and innovations, but also a focus on structural change regarding the relationship between the economy and nature, as well as controls on aspects of market-led development such as privatization. Such approaches have very different implications for how the SSE can realize its potential and impact development.

The challenges facing SSEOEs and the SSE more generally tend to be quite context- and country-specific. A study of social enterprises in 35 EU and neighbouring countries revealed multiple scenarios that had different development and governance implications (Borzaga et al. 2020). In countries with traditionally weak welfare provisioning and strong civil commitment (such as Greece and Portugal, for example), social enterprises have served to fill important gaps, and subsequently diversified their activities to address community needs and demands. Countries such as Denmark and the United Kingdom, with more-developed welfare states, have turned to social enterprises as a substitute for direct public provisioning, contracting out services. Countries such as Bulgaria, Czech Republic and Hungary, with relatively weak public sector and associative traditions, have turned to social enterprises as a form of targeting disadvantaged groups. Finally, countries such as Belgium and France, with a well-developed associative sector with strong relations with the public sector, have witnessed NGOs transitioning from non-profits to social enterprises.

On balance, despite the upsurge in public policy discourse and initiatives promoting SSE over the past decade, state support remains inchoate and fragile. It is also somewhat fragmented, in the sense that economic and social dimensions of sustainable development tend to be emphasized within public policy while other core attributes of the SSE may be given short shrift. Beyond the democratic aspect, as noted above, these include the environmental dimension. Notwithstanding important developments in particular countries – for example, enshrining the rights of nature in constitutional law in Ecuador and Bolivia; promoting sustainable agriculture in Cuba and Kerala, India; community-based forest management in Nepal; waste recycling in Brazil; and renewable energy in Germany – public policy has focused more attention on aspects of the SSE related to social welfare, targeting vulnerable groups and socially oriented enterprise forms.

Research on how the SSE can contribute to the United Nations Sustainable Development Goals (SDGs) suggests that the transformative potential of the SSE will only be realized if governments also recognize the environmental potential of the SSE. This potential derives from the fact that the SSE has a relatively light environmental footprint, has few incentives to externalize environmental costs, and in certain sectors involves practices that protect the environment and manage natural resources sustainably (see also entry 4, 'Ecological Economics', entry 8, 'Indigenous Economies', entry 39, 'Sustainable Investment, Production and Consumption' and entry 27, 'Energy, Water and Waste Management Sectors'). Public policy can play a far more proactive role in positioning the SSE to meet the increasing demand for environmental goods and services, and enabling a process of green transition that is also fair and inclusive (UNTFSSE 2014).

Certain strands of scholarship and advocacy, not least within Latin America, also question other ways in which the welfare/social enterprise approach dilutes the transformative potential of the SSE (Coraggio 2021; Laville and Eynaud 2019). It not only reduces the role of SSE to fairly specific policy goals and stakeholders, but also tends to see the SSE as a niche sector that complements the dominant mode of capitalist production, rather than a fundamentally different option.

A growing body of research suggests that what are key for addressing these challenges are measures to lock in public policy support legally and fiscally, strong multi-stakeholder governance institutions, and intermediary organizations and networks that can advocate for the SSE at different levels of governance (Jenkins et al. 2021). But if the SSE is to be more than palliative, also key are broad-based alliances of social and political forces which recognize that an enabling policy environment for the SSE ultimately requires deeper changes in macro-economic and fiscal policy, a shift from fragmented to universal social protection systems, and structural changes related to investment, production, exchange and consumption patterns.

REFERENCES

Borzaga, Carlo, Giulia Galera, Barbara Franchini, Stefania Chiomento, Rocio Nogales and Chiara Carini. 2020. *Social Enterprises and their Ecosystems in Europe: Comparative Synthesis Report*. Luxembourg: European Commission.

Chaves-Avila, Rafael, and Juan Ramon Gallego-Bono. 2020. 'Transformative Policies for the Social and Solidarity Economy: The New Generation of Public Policies Fostering the Social Economy in Order to Achieve Sustainable Development Goals. The European and Spanish Cases.' *Sustainability* 12 (10): 1–29. https://doi.org/10.3390/su12104059.

Coraggio, José Luis. 2015. 'Institutionalizing the Social and Solidarity Economy in Latin America.' In *Social and Solidarity Economy: Beyond the Fringe*, edited by Peter Utting, 130–49. London: Zed Books/UNRISD.

Coraggio, José Luis (ed.). 2021. *Miradas Sobre la Economía Social y Solidaria en América Latina*. Buenos Aires: CLACSO / Los Polvorines: Universidad Nacional de General Sarmiento.

Cotera, Fretel Alfonso. 2019. 'Avances y limitaciones en la implementación de normatividad sobre economía solidaria en América Latina y el Caribe: Estudio sobre marcos regulatorios de la economía social solidaria y su relación con políticas de protección social en américa latina.' socioeco.org. https://socioeco.org/bdf_fiche-document-7192_pt.html.

Defourny, Jacques, Marthe Nyssens and Olivier Brolis. 2019. 'Mapping and Testing Social Enterprise Models Across the World: Evidence from the International Comparative Social Enterprise Models (ICSEM) Project.' ICSEM Working Papers, No. 50. International Comparative Social Enterprise Models (ICSEM) Project. https://orbi.uliege.be/bitstream/2268/233219/1/SE%20Models%20-%20Defourny%20et%20al..pdf.

Fonteneau, Bénédicte, and Ignace Pollet (eds). 2019. *The Contribution of the Social and Solidarity Economy and Social Finance to the Future of Work*. Geneva: International Labour Organization.

International Labour Office (ILO). 2022. 'Mapping the Social and Solidarity Economy Landscape in Asia: Towards an Enabling Policy Environment.' ILO Brief. https://www.ilo.org/wcmsp5/groups/public/---ed_emp/---emp_ent/---coop/documents/publication/wcms_834832.pdf.

Jenkins, Hamish, Ilcheong Yi, Samuel Bruelisauer and Kameni Chaddha. 2021. *Guidelines for Local Governments on Policies for Social and Solidarity Economy*. Geneva: UNRISD.

Laville, Jean-Louis, and Philippe Eynaud. 2019. 'Rethinking Social Enterprise through Philanthropic and Democratic Solidarities'. In *Theory of Social Enterprise and Pluralism: Social Movements, Solidarity Economy, and Global South*, edited by Philippe Eynaud, Jean-Louis Laville, Luciane Dos Santos, Swati Banerjee, Flor Avelino and Lars Hulgård, 18–44. Abingdon: Routledge.

Mendell, Marguerite, and Béatrice Alain. 2015. 'Enabling the Social and Solidarity Economy through the Co-construction of Public Policy'. In *Social and Solidarity Economy: Beyond the Fringe*, edited by Peter Utting, 236–49. London: Zed Books/UNRISD.

Morais, Leandro Pereira, and Miguel Juan Bacic. 2020. 'Social and Solidarity Economy and the Need for its Entrepreneuring Ecosystem: Current Challenges in Brazil.' *CIRIEC-España: Revista de Economía Pública, Social y Cooperativa* 98: 5–30. https://doi.org/10.7203/ciriec-e98.14138.

Serrano, Samuel Barco, Riccardo Bodini, Michael Roy and Gianluca Salvatori. 2019. *Financial Mechanisms for Innovative Social and Solidarity Economy Ecosystems*. Geneva: ILO.

United Nations Research Institute for Social Development (UNRISD). 2016. 'Promoting Social and Solidarity Economy through Public Policy.' *Policy Innovations for Transformative Change: UNRISD Flagship Report 2016*. Geneva: UNRISD.

United Nations Task Force on Social and Solidarity Economy (UNTFSSE). 2014. *Social and Solidarity Economy and the Challenge of Sustainable Development*. Geneva: UNTFSSE.

Utting, Peter. 2017. *Public Policies for Social and Solidarity Economy: Assessing Progress in Seven Countries*. Geneva: ILO.

52. Resilience in the context of multiple crises
Beverley Mullings and Tinyan Otuomagie

INTRODUCTION

The social and solidarity economy (SSE) refers to a myriad of institutions guided by principles and practices that value cooperation, reciprocity, redistribution, solidarity, ethics, and democratic self-management. Including cooperatives, mutual benefit societies, not-for-profits, foundations, and social enterprises, social and solidarity economy organizations and enterprises (SSEOEs) exist at every level within the global economic system, influencing all manner of economic exchange including finance, production, distribution, exchange, and governance. The SSE includes a wide variety of institutions and practices that range from totally voluntary organizations on the one hand, to social enterprises that use the tools and some of the methods of business, to provide social, cultural, economic, and health services to communities.

Global development organizations such as the Organisation for Economic Co-operation and Development (OECD), the European Union and the International Labour Organization are very supportive of SSEOEs, viewing their activities as key to building models of inclusive growth. While policy makers in Europe and North America have become more attuned to the important role that SSEOEs play in enabling communities to adapt to uncertainty, vulnerability, and crises. For example, during the 2008 financial crisis, and more recently the COVID-19 pandemic, not only did SSEOEs such as cooperative banks prove to be more resilient than their for-profit equivalents, the forms of civic engagement that mutual aid and not-for-profit organizations such as food banks, time banks, and soup kitchens generated helped the most vulnerable to respond to rising levels of unemployment, food and housing insecurity, and general social need. The turn towards the SSE within policy circles can be seen in the number of programs that have been launched both to support their activities and to measure and maximize their social impact. The 2013 United Nations Inter-Agency Task Force on Social and Solidarity Economy (UNTFSSE), the 2020 OECD/European Union Global Action "Promoting Social and Solidarity Economy Ecosystems," and the European Union's 2021 Action Plan for the Social Economy (European Commission 2021) represent some of the initiatives that are being undertaken to position the SSE as a possible alternative model of development, and to identify and create the conditions for them to flourish. Governments have also begun to recognize the value of SSEOEs during periods of crisis, with several in Latin America passing laws and constitutional articles, and creating secretariats dedicated to the SSE.

To fully understand what constitutes an enabling environment for SSEOEs it is necessary to examine the role that different types have played during periods of crisis. While the organizations and enterprises defined as part of the SSE generally share a commitment to collective social and environmental goals, how these goals have been executed during different periods of crisis is as varied as the different types of institutions that fall under this umbrella term, their location in time and space, and the particular crises to which they respond.

52.1 SOCIAL REPRODUCTION AND SSE

As early as the 1980s, feminist scholars documented the important role that SSEOEs played in the social reproduction of communities afflicted by the global recession in the wake of the 1970s debt crisis. Writing largely about communities in the Global South, these studies aimed not only to bring a human face to their experiences of increasing levels of inflation, soaring unemployment, and rising levels of sovereign debt, but also to examine the forms of agency, mutuality, and collective action that communities engaged in to survive the widespread austerity policies that many governments were obliged to implement as a condition for access to loans from international lending organizations. Feminists were some of the earliest scholars to document the close relationship between SSEOEs and the care economy, and the important role of women within them. Many of the self-help, mutual aid, and cooperative activities documented in the 1980s and 1990s emerged during periods of intense crisis, when neither states nor private enterprises were able to adequately provide for collective consumption. With their attentiveness to the social reproductive practices of everyday life, feminist scholars documented how communities collectively organized to address eroding levels of access to employment, health, food, and housing, by drawing attention to the importance of these practices to the health and welfare not only of households and communities, but also of the environments within which they lived.

Although studies throughout the 1980s and 1990s drew attention to the importance of SSEOEs to the survival of households and communities, their role in the market economy, or what is often referred to as the 'real' economy, was rarely acknowledged. The broader concept of the SSE was largely marginalized within government economic agendas. Notable exceptions were SSEOEs that were large with economic contributions had were significant (the Mondragon cooperative is one such case in point). The general lack of attention to the SSE in policy circles began to change at the start of the new millennium, however, as civil society organizations mobilized to reflect upon, debate, and strategize ways to build an alternative, post-capitalist economic system, and governments began to pay greater attention to the benefits that could be derived from SSEOEs playing an expanded role in the delivery of social services (see entry 53, "Social Policy").

Gibson-Graham's (2006) book entitled *A Postcapitalist Politics* is illustrative of the way in which scholars have sought to bring renewed attention to the value that marginalized and often invisible non-market and unpaid economic activities within the SSE bring to the overall functioning of market economies. They argue that by restricting our definition of 'the economy' to the market economy we obscure the vastly different ways that exchange is negotiated, the different ways that labour is performed, and importantly, the diverse ways in which we could produce a kinder, gentler, and just world. Developing the concept of community economies –economies that put "ethical negotiations of our interdependence with each other and the environment center stage" (Gibson-Graham, Cameron and Healy 2013, 13)–they highlight the sociality of all economic relations and the interdependence that exists between a broad variety of economic and non-economic activities. They are emphatic that in recognizing the value of these diverse economies, it is important to avoid the practice of "singling out certain activities as necessarily or invariably more important, more independent, more determining of economic 'health' and distinguishing them from those that are more expendable, dependent, and less determining or potentially destructive within the economy" (ibid., 95). Such a practice, they argue, would suppress the ethic of "being in common", interdependence and care that has been so integral to the responsiveness of SSEOEs to social need during periods of crisis, and vital to the challenge of re-socializing the economy in the future. While mutuality, and a commitment to the creation of ethical spaces of care, are instrumental elements in the success of community economies, Ferreira (2021) warns that they should be understood as commitments that are not exempt from ongoing practices of coloniality, racism, and gender-based exclusion. For, as she argues, these relations of power are not entirely absent in the efforts of SSEOEs to support and build resilient communities.

52.2 FINANCIAL COOPERATIVES AND THE 2008 FINANCIAL CRISIS

The 2008 global financial crisis, and more recently the COVID-19 pandemic, have brought into sharp relief the possibilities and limits that face SSEOEs as they take on an expanded role in the provision of services to meet social needs. In the case of banking, for example, Birchall and Kelitson (2009) found that during the 2008 financial crisis when many private investor-owned banks required public bailouts, cooperative banks not only remained financially sound, but some even saw increases in members, assets, deposits, and loans. In the immediate aftermath of the crisis when other banks stopped lending to small and medium-sized enterprises, cooperatives were able to draw on the surpluses that they would normally have distributed to members, in order to weather the financial crisis. Because financial cooperatives are member-owned and funded, and because they operate within democratic governance structures, they have tended to be more risk-averse than private banks. So, for example, in the United States, cooperatives were not embroiled in the sub-prime mortgage crisis because of the moral constraint that the direct relationship between member savings and loans imposed. That some financial cooperatives even thrived during the 2008 crisis speaks also to the level of trust held for these institutions by their members. For, as reports show, membership levels increased after the 2008 financial crisis as consumers looked for safer and more ethical alternatives.

Cooperatives owned by historically marginalized communities also offer financial stability, but even more important is the access to employment, and services like pensions, retail services, renewable energy, and food distribution that many have maintained during periods of crisis because of the level of trust that they cultivate among their members. In Canada, for example, Arctic Cooperatives Limited, a service federation of 32 independently owned and controlled Inuit, Metis, and First Nations cooperatives in Nunavut, Northwest Territories, and Yukon, experienced their best year of operation in 2008 when revenues increased by 12 percent over the year before because of alignment of cooperative goals with the value placed on reinvesting in local community. The success that financial cooperatives have demonstrated in the face of crisis should not, however, be seen as evidence of the effectiveness of all cooperatives in responding to medium- and long-term crises in every community. As numerous scholars have documented, there is a long and ongoing history of racial discrimination against Indigenous and Black communities within banking and finance, from which mainstream financial cooperatives have not been exempt. Without an acknowledgement of the systemic nature of racism, gender discrimination, and other forms of exclusion in finance, the success of cooperatives in meeting social need during periods of crisis will continue to be limited to only those who gain access to them (see entry 28, "Finance Sector").

Like the 2008 financial crisis, the COVID-19 pandemic represents another kind of challenge, one that is revealing the possibilities for and limits to the capacity of SSEOEs to meet social needs during periods of crisis. With the spread of the pandemic many countries have had to contend with food shortages, rising levels of unemployment, and social infrastructures stretched to their limit. In the poorest countries, where access to vaccines has been limited, the virus has ravaged their populations, disrupting markets and fueling levels of inflation to historic highs. As indicated below, various types of SSEOEs have responded proactively to enable people to cope during the pandemic.

52.3 SOCIAL MOVEMENTS: THE CASE OF THE LANDLESS RURAL WORKERS' MOVEMENT

With the second-highest death toll of any country in the world, as of January 2023, Brazil is one of the countries most affected by the COVID-19 pandemic. Limited state support, coupled with a long history of racialized injustice affecting Black and Indigenous peoples, meant that the right to food quickly became a social crisis, impacting women and especially women heads of families. It is in this context that the Landless Rural Workers' Movement (MST), a social movement that seeks to transform the lives of poor Brazilians by securing access to land and campaigning for land reform, intervened to reduce the impact of the crisis on the most vulnerable populations. A non-hierarchical collective inspired by liberation theology, and the pedagogy of Paolo Freire, the MST is part of an extensive network of SSEOEs that include 100 agricultural cooperatives, 170 community clinics, 66 food processing factories, and almost 200 farmer associations. In the context of the pandemic and the state's refusal to assist, the MST has stepped in to help poor families, donating over 6000 tons of food and 1 150 000 lunch boxes to food-insecure people and families across the country.

The success of the MST's Christmas without Hunger campaign, which mobilized and distributed food during the pandemic, can be attributed to its broad vision of agrarian reform through education, solidarity, and a commitment to living sustainably with the environment, as well as the trust that the MST has cultivated among the neediest of families and communities. Its consistent denunciation of Brazil's ongoing practices of land dispossession and racialized social inequality, combined with its programs to promote job creation, stimulate trade, guarantee income and decent living conditions, have greatly contributed to its fundraising success.

52.4 SOCIAL ENTERPRISES AND COVID-19

As Rasheda Weaver (2020) observes, there remains much to learn about the role of social enterprises in periods of crisis. Social enterprises are organizations that use commercial or business strategies for the benefit of society or the environment. They exist in a variety of corporate forms ranging from non-profit organizations that operate revenue-generating businesses, to for-profit businesses with a social goal. At their core, social enterprises are organizations that are governed by business principles, and in the context of COVID-19, like many other small and medium-sized enterprises, they were adversely affected by the social distancing restrictions that most governments imposed. In the early days of the pandemic, some scholars saw the dual mission of social enterprises as crucial to the ability of economies to bounce back quickly in the post-COVID-19 recovery, given their contribution to employment and the economic health of communities. As the pandemic has worn on, however, it has become clear that there has been much variability in the ways that social enterprises have fared in the crisis, and that for some long-term economic uncertainty has shifted the balance between their social mission and their economic goals.

A recent survey by the British Council, Social Enterprise UK and the United Nations found that at the start of the crisis, social enterprises worldwide reported that there was a high risk that they would have to close their operations if not given government support (Darko and Hashi 2020). As many as a third of social enterprises reported that they had no access to government support; and among those which did, assistance varied significantly, with levels of support being highest in South-East Asia and Europe and lowest in sub-Saharan Africa and South Asia. Crucially, the survey found that social enterprises led by women fared the worst, with a third reporting having to reduce their activities and 3 percent closing altogether. The survey also found social enterprises to be agile, however, with 90 percent of those surveyed stating that they were operating under different business models to the ones they had before the pandemic. Social enterprises in the information technology, software, and computer services sector and the childcare sector appeared to have fared better than those in tourism, hospitality, radio, or television, given the optimism they expressed about the growth of their businesses three to six months after the survey. Conversely, social enterprises that were small or that served vulnerable and marginalized groups were the least optimistic about growth. The findings of the British Council survey suggest that how social enterprises address and mitigate the short- and long-term impacts of social and economic crises depends on the sectors within which they operate, their dependence on external finance, and, in the context of COVID-19, their use of online technologies. These observations were especially true for social enterprises that offered financial services during the pandemic.

The Kenyan mobile money service provider M-Pesa, for example, was hailed as a social enterprise success story because of the way that its mobile phone-enabled money transfer system facilitated the movement of money, primarily among poor people without access to formal financial services at the beginning of the pandemic. Africa's largest FinTech firm on the African continent, with profits of US$765 million in 2021, M-Pesa has been credited with making a significant social impact, with one 2016 study estimating that it had lifted 2 percent of Kenyans out of poverty (Suri and Jack 2016). Claims of M-Pesa's contribution to poverty reduction, however, have not gone unchallenged. Questioning the assumption that financial inclusion is instrumental to social transformation, Bateman et al. (2019) argue that FinTech firms concentrate the bulk of their value in the hands of a global digital financial elite, with little redirected to the poor communities that they serve.

In the case of M-Pesa charges on transactions under KAS1000 (USD 8) were suspended at the request of Kenyan regulators between March to December. The removal of transaction charges was part of a general effort to discourage people from engaging in physical cash monetary transactions, by providing an incentive for them to use its digital platform instead. While M-Pesa's revenues fell briefly during the period when the fees were waived, they quickly rebounded, when charges were reinstated, as the number of subscribers swelled from approximately 20.5 million in March 2021 to 50 million active subscribers in September 2021. Digital payments technologies across East Africa helped informal businesses and mutual aid groups to stay in touch with their customers and supporters, and hence stay afloat. Unlike cooperatives, however, their approaches to financial inclusion have tended to rest upon their ability to provide fee-based opportunities, rather than collective redistributive measures (Natile 2020). As such, the benefits offered by social enterprises in periods of crisis are constrained by the relative emphasis placed on individual wealth creation rather than collective wealth distribution.

CONCLUSION

While institutions guided by principles and practices that value cooperation, reciprocity, redistribution, solidarity, ethics, and democratic self-management have existed since time immemorial, their value to the functioning of economies and societies has taken on new meaning since the start of the new millennium. Examining the practices of cooperatives, self-help groups, and social enterprises during periods of crisis, this entry has examined how these institutions and their activities collectively function to support and sustain local communities in times of crisis, the conditions under which they are successful in doing so, and the challenges that they face as they are called upon to play an expanded role.

Given the broad spectrum of SSEOEs, ranging from mutual aid groups to social enterprises, it is difficult to be definitive about the effectiveness of their role in mitigating the impacts of multiple crises. Mutual aid groups, for example, that prioritize caring for each other and meeting basic survival needs are very different from social enterprises that try to balance profitability with a social vision. As examples from the MST movement show, their success in responding to social need in the face of the COVID-19 crisis has been largely due to the philosophical perspective of the organization and its members. But like many mutual aid groups, it too must rely on external financial support and the unpaid labor of members; resources that are severely tested in the context of overlapping and long-term structural crises embedded in histories of coloniality, racism, gender inequality, and state violence. Cooperatives have proven to be effective in responding to the impacts of crisis because of their structures of accountability that engender trust among members, the fact that members share in both profits and losses, and the balance that many have struck between the interests of their members and those of the communities they serve. But without a framework attentive to ongoing forms of coloniality, racism, and patriarchal oppression, cooperatives can exclude certain communities, fulfilling a social mission only for a favored group.

As governments and development organizations create larger roles for SSEOEs within their crisis response agendas, some will experience pressures to expand their mandates in ways that force them to drift away from their social mission and the ethical principles behind them. External support for SSEOEs has often also meant the imposition of state control and a habitual disregard for their independence and autonomy (see entry 44, "Co-optation, Isomorphism and Instrumentalisation"). Among social enterprises the danger of mission drift–a shift away from principles and practices that value cooperation, reciprocity, redistribution, solidarity, ethics, and democratic self-management–is especially high (see entry 21, "Social Enterprises"). Unlike cooperatives, social enterprises are neither bound by structures and mechanisms to ensure democratic control, nor obliged to redistribute the profits they earn. Thus, in periods of crisis such as the COVID-19 pandemic, they may exhibit a greater propensity for mission drift as economic opportunities expand. Paramount to the effectiveness of SSEOEs in the context of multiple and overlapping crises is the trust and the validation of inclusive communities. Without trust that SSEOEs are committed to principles of sustainability and equity, and the redistribution of wealth, their contribution to an alternative vision of human development will be limited.

REFERENCES

Bateman, Milford, Maren Duvendack, and Nicholas Loubere. 2019. "Is Fin-Tech the New Panacea for Poverty Alleviation and Local Development? Contesting Suri and Jack's M-Pesa Findings Published in Science." *Review of African Political Economy* 46 (161): 1–16. https://doi.org/10.1080/03056244.2019.1614552.

Birchall, Johnston, and Lou Hammond Ketilson. 2009. "Resilience of the Cooperative Business Model in Times of Crisis." ILO. Geneva: International Labour Office, Sustainable Enterprise Programme. https://www.ilo.org/wcmsp5/groups/public/---ed_emp/---emp_ent/documents/publication/wcms_108416.pdf.

Darko, Emily, and Faisal M. Hashi. 2020. "A Global Snapshot of Social Enterprise Responses to Covid-19." British Council, UNESCAP, Social Enterprise. https://www.britishcouncil.org/sites/default/files/socialenterprise_covidresponsesurvey_web_final_0.pdf.

European Commission. 2021. "Building an Economy That Works for People: An Action Plan for the Social Economy." European Commission. December. https://www.socialeconomy.eu.org/wp-content/uploads/2021/12/Building-an-economy-that-works-for-people-an-action-plan-for-the-social-economy.pdf.

Ferreira, Priscilla. 2021. "Racial Capitalism and Epistemic Injustice: Blindspots in the Theory and Practice of Solidarity Economy in Brazil." *Geoforum*. 132: 229–237. https://doi.org/10.1016/j.geoforum.2021.04.020.

Gibson-Graham, J.K. 2006. *A Postcapitalist Politics*. Minneapolis, MN: University of Minnesota Press.

Gibson-Graham, J.K., J. Cameron; and S. Healy. 2013. *Take Back the Economy: An Ethical Guide for Transforming Our Communities*: p. 13. University of Minnesota Press.

Natile, Serena. 2020. "Digital Finance and the Mobile Money 'Social' Enterprise: A Socio-Legal Critique of M-Pesa in Kenya." *Historical Social Research* 45 (3): 74–94.

Suri, Tavneet, and William Jack. 2016. 'The long-run poverty and gender impacts of mobile money.' *Science* 354 (6317): 1288–92.

Weaver, Rasheda L. 2020. "The Impact of COVID-19 on the Social Enterprise Sector." *Journal of Social Entrepreneurship* 1–9.

53. Social policy
Ilcheong Yi

INTRODUCTION

The relationship between the social and solidarity economy (SSE) and social policy as a specific system of collective intervention against the laissez-faire or, more typically, the welfare state has attracted the attention of scholars, policymakers and practitioners for a long time. Social policy, understood as a means to correct the dysfunctions of the capitalist economy, has an elective affinity with the SSE, which subordinates the economy to the social, often expressed as 'economy embedded in social relations' (Polanyi 1957). Welfare pluralism often frames the discourse on this relationship in which voluntary and self-managed initiatives play a significant role in shaping social policy or a welfare state. However, if understood as a means to secure the long-term circumstances of the continued accumulation of capital (Pierson 1998), social policy or the welfare state may not have much common ground with the SSE as a means of transformation of economy and society.

The interaction of SSE organizations and enterprises (SSEOEs) with social policy also reflects these normative tensions. For instance, a new organization of society and relationship based on association and cooperation was promoted by social reformers such as Robert Owen (1771–1858), Charles Fourier (1772–1837) and Charles Gide (1847–1932) in the 19th century and early 20th century. It is considered an attempt to incorporate the cooperative principle into a new form of political economy or social policy to correct the laissez-faire (Celle 2016). Further, until the public sector assumed the responsibility and functioned as the primary agency to deliver services to beneficiaries, SSEOEs played a critical role in helping people in need by providing basic social services such as education, health care, training, residence, counselling, and so on, in-kind and through cash support.

As welfare states grew in many countries, many International Conventions within the United Nations system, such as R127 – Co-operatives (Developing Countries) Recommendation, 1966 (No. 127) and R193 – Promotion of Cooperatives Recommendation, 2002 (No. 193), also emphasized cooperatives, a specific type of SSE, as an effective means of social policy at the global level.

When the welfare state retrenchment began, many SSEOEs, together with other forms of not-for-profit organizations, were called upon as critical players in the provision of social services to take the leading role in addressing social problems. Often conceptualized as the third sector or non-profit organizations, the SSE also has constituted a part of a welfare mix or mixed welfare system, otherwise made up of the state, the market and the informal private household spheres. Therefore, we can understand the roles of the SSE in enabling social policy, and in social policy or welfare state regime changes, particularly in the context of welfare pluralism.

This entry explains social policy discourse and practices in both developed and developing countries concerning the evolution of the SSE, and the opportunities and challenges of the SSE strengthening the welfare state or vice versa.

53.1 SOCIAL POLICY AND THE SSE

The social policy concept does not have a universally accepted clear definition. Its understandings and conceptualizations vary across countries with diverse socio-economic and political conditions, social questions or problems, and political ideologies. The boundary of social policy as an academic discipline is not clear cut either. The central questions, methodologies and approaches of social policy are not drawn from or shaped by specific logics defining disciplines, but are dependent upon the nature of the social question which social policy aims to address. Therefore, like the SSE, social policy as an area of academic investigation is a research field rather than a discipline, in which scholars from different disciplines try to define, clarify and provide solutions to specific social questions related to social services and social welfare. Social policy as a concept, therefore, is socially constructed, and its scope, subjects and objectives are shaped by the interactions of diverse groups with different ideas, motivations, beliefs and values, resources and practices.

However, diverse definitions of social policy have two common elements: objectives or purposes, and the means of social policy. The more comprehensive the purposes or objectives, the more diverse the means. Those definitions with a comprehensive purpose, such as planning for social externalities, redistribution and equitable social benefits, especially social services, often have more means than conventional core social services such as personal social services. In contrast, those definitions with relatively limited purposes have a small set of means of social policy, mainly those of conventional core social services (Yi and Kim 2015).

Debates over the SSE's relationship with social policy are usually based on the understandings of social policy with relatively limited purposes, and focused on its contribution to conventional social services as a delivery agent. However, in the context of social policy with comprehensive purposes, particularly in a development context, we can find more linkages between social policy and the SSE than those associated with a contribution to social services, such as its contribution to shaping and changing the nature of social policy.

The broad range of contributions of the SSE to social policy development is particularly visible in development discourse and practice. Development models and strategies always have a social policy as a critical element, albeit with varying prominence. In particular, those models and strategies which could significantly reduce poverty and inequality invariably have had some forms of solidarity-based redistributive, productive, protective and reproductive social policy programme as a complement to policies and institutions for industrialization and economic growth (Mkandawire 2004).

53.2 CHANNELS LINKING THE SSE WITH SOCIAL POLICY

Perspectives that understand social policy as means of embedded liberalism, or subjugating economy to the social structure, and focus on diverse aspects of the contribution of social policy to the political economy such as democratization, social cohesion, resource mobilization, redistribution, production, protection and reproduction, allow us to identify more diverse linkages between the SSE and social policy than those associated with the delivery of social services.

For instance, when realized in economic relations and activities, the solidarity principle can be expressed as reciprocity, cooperation and redistribution, rather than competition and winner-takes-all. In this way, the SSE's solidarity values help SSEOEs to reach the poor. Democracy and participation facilitate empowering the vulnerable, which consequently counters the welfare reform favouring the better-off. Prioritizing social objectives over profit motives, SSEOEs tend to have more substantial quality commitments than for-profit service providers. SSEOEs rooted in local networks tend to be more responsive to the needs of beneficiaries. Independent from the state and the market, SSEOEs also play a vital role in advocacy and contestation. The research also showed that SSEOEs' entry into a social policy arena gave citizens more options and increased efficiency and efficacy in using resources. The values and principles of the SSE, such as solidarity, cooperation and democracy, provided a basis for a new model of cooperation between the state and the SSE in the social policy field.

As the size and impacts of SSEOEs in the social service delivery grow, the SSE with accumulated professional skills and knowledge also influenced social policy formulation processes. When acting as delivery agencies, organizations and enterprises based on the SSE values and principles became strong advocates of the public nature of social services in civil society, and acted as players to extend public services to a broader community.

Participating in social policy delivery, SSEOEs often promote values such as solidarity, autonomy and democratic self-control and incorporate them in social policy programme design and implementation. Boxes 53.1 and 53.2 give examples of incorporating SSE values in education policy reform and achieving universal coverage of health care.

BOX 53.1   INCORPORATING SSE VALUES IN EDUCATION POLICY REFORM IN THE UK

The case of the 2006 Education and Inspections Act in the United Kingdom (UK) demonstrates how the SSE interacts with social policy in education, a key area for the productive function of social policy. The Act introduced the idea of trust schools, which would remain funded by local authorities but establish a long-term partnership with outside groups, such as local businesses and charities, which would then become involved with the school's governance and leadership. Local activists and educators soon utilized this opportunity to develop and promote the cooperative-based model for trust schools run by the cooperative values and principles of equality, equity, democracy, self-help, self-responsibility and solidarity, as well as the principles of education, democratic control and community ownership, which became one of the fastest-growing sectors of the UK co-op economy. This co-op school movement is considered a bulwark against the increasing and relentless neoliberal forms of privatization of education (see also entry 26, 'Education Sector')

Source: Based on Woodin (2019).

BOX 53.2   THE SSE ACHIEVING UNIVERSAL COVERAGE OF HEALTH CARE IN RWANDA

Community-based mutual health insurance schemes, which have been rapidly increasing in low and middle-income developing countries since the 2000s, offer an interesting case of how SSE contributes to mobilization and redistribution of resources for national-level social policy. In Rwanda, the widespread community-based mutual health insurance schemes originate from the pre-independence years of faith-based non-governmental organization (NGO)-run community mutual schemes. From 1999, the government promoted voluntarism and encouraged non-governmental actors to organize community-based health insurance (CBHI) schemes. Participation in CBHI schemes is voluntary. With organizational structures including general assemblies, the board of directors, surveillance committees and executive bureaus to regulate contract relations between members and service providers, CBHI schemes establish contractual relations with health care providers such as health centres and hospitals to purchase health care services. Laws provided measures to minimize risks associated with health insurance such as adverse selection, moral hazard, cost escalation and insurance fraud. Technical and financial assistance from foreign donors and the international financial instruments for health, such as the Global Fund, was channelled into CBHI schemes. After its pilot phase of 2008, the government established a specific legal framework, making affiliation with health insurance in principle mandatory for Rwandan nationals and residents alike. CBHI members can access health care in any public and faith-based organization across the country. Population coverage increased from 7 per cent in 2003, to 85 per cent in 2008, and over 90 per cent in 2010. Access to health care also increased from 31 per cent in 2003, to almost 100 per cent in 2012. The increase of CBHI contributed to lifting Rwanda's overall health insurance coverage to 96.15 per cent as of 2012, including other health insurance schemes. Relying on community organizations at the grassroots level and partnering with local micro-finance schemes, the scheme offered comprehensive coverage to the poor. In this Rwandan case, the resources of SSEOEs rooted in the local areas such as finance, and networks and information on the poor and the vulnerable, contributed to achieving the universal coverage of health insurance in a short time.

Source: Based on Yi et al. (2018).

53.3 THE SSE'S UNIQUE ROLE IN THE CONTEXT OF NEOLIBERAL WELFARE REFORM

Since the late 1970s, in developed countries with relatively advanced systems of welfare service provisions or welfare states, challenges including fiscal constraints, and inefficiency of centralized bureaucracy to address increasingly diverse needs and expectations of the citizens, accelerated welfare reform agendas to the top of the national policy agenda. They facilitated the adoption of privatization or marketization as a reform policy. In developing countries, international financial organizations such as the World Bank and the International Monetary Fund played a significant role in changing social policies. Questioning the quality of governance in developing countries, they promoted neoliberal reform of still very much immature social policies.

Neoliberal ideas gradually became the dominant norms and principles shaping the social policies of many developed and developing countries. Under the neoliberal principles, the redistributive function of social policy was treated as a source of market distortion. Government spending on social policy, with goals of redistribution in health, education and pensions, was reduced to market principles so as not to impose constraints on the instruments and the scale of macroeconomic policies. Under the fiscal constraints, central governments also delegated responsibilities and functions of welfare service provisions to local authorities.

The reduced role of the central government and increased role of local authorities in delivering social services was accompanied by changes in the views on the public and private sectors, notably, non-profit or voluntary sectors to which SSEOEs belonged (see entry 38, 'Social Services'). The public sector increasingly became seen as a source of economic instability and inflation, rather than a solution to welfare services. Instead, the voluntary sector has been spotlighted as an excellent substitute to fill the gaps that governments otherwise should have addressed (Kendall 2003; Deakin 2001). Not only prevailing views of the state as a source of the problem rather than a solution, but also growing pressure from NGOs for popular participation, helped to create an interface between social policy and the non-government sector, which was not integrated into macro-level government policies and mostly remained at project levels (Mkandawire 2004).

The consequence is the increased role of the non-government sector in delivering social services, particularly in developing countries. For instance, in many countries in Africa, Asia and Latin America, public agencies to provide social services were either dismantled or changed into private agencies. Diverse forms of organizations entering this newly created public–private interface – that is, implementation of social policy by the non-government sector – started to grow in size and influence in social policy discourse, design and implementation in this context of neoliberal reform. For instance, in these countries, up to one-third of health care services were provided by voluntary organizations in the 1990s (Hecht and Tanzi 1994).

SSEOEs working in social policy sector also grew in size and influence in this context (Rossel 2015). Many governments, in particular those in the developed world, have introduced or strengthened support mechanisms for the voluntary or non-profit sector. They include the introduction of payroll donation, the extension of tax advantages for registered charities, an increase of service contracts, expanding public sector subsidies to voluntary organizations, and empowerment of mediating institutions. SSEOEs, which the government schemes treated as one type of voluntary or non-profit sector, started to grow in size and influence in social policy arena, particularly in social service delivery.

The SSE's role in shaping social policy in this context of neoliberal welfare reform is particularly notable since the values and principles of the SSE are qualitatively different from the market exchange principle pursued as a solution in the neoliberal welfare reform process.

The growth of SSEOEs organized by people to defend or improve their livelihoods, and the growing pressure from non-profit organizations, including SSEOEs, for popular participation, also shape social policy at the national level. In the 1990s, when the market-oriented development strategies began to be challenged, often termed the 'Post-Washington Consensus' or 'social turn', social policy and the state's role not as a problem but as a solution became re-emphasized in the discourse of development strategies of developing countries. Sometimes even in rhetoric, donors' policies emphasized the need to work together with recipient governments to implement development projects. Donor institutions established new aid instruments such as budget support and sector-wide approaches to channel aid directly to recipient governments. In particular, between the 1990s and 2008, when the global economic crisis happened, social protection programmes such as conditional cash transfers rapidly increased in developing countries, albeit with significant variations in terms of coverage, quality and sectors. In this process, donors and governments needed partners to deliver services with lower costs but high performance. Civil society actors who had accumulated knowledge and experience in local contexts became key partners for expanding various social policy programmes. In particular, SSEOEs, with their organizational characteristics such as participation, solidarity and democratic self-control, played a unique role in shaping a unique nature of the partnership for expanding social protection programmes, compared to a non-profit voluntary or for-profit organization. The Kudumbashree initiative (Box 53.3), the poverty eradication and women's empowerment programme implemented by the State Poverty Eradication Mission of the Government of Kerala, India, is an excellent example of how a government's social policy programme and SSEOEs create synergies in improving livelihoods and empowering women politically and economically (see also entry 22, 'Women's Self-Help Groups').

BOX 53.3 KUDUMBASHREE INITIATIVE: CREATING SYNERGIES BETWEEN SSE AND SOCIAL POLICY

The origin of the Kudumbashree initiative is traced back to a small pilot programme that sought to address poverty and women's empowerment through the organization of neighbourhood groups represented by resident community volunteers, primarily women, in Alappuzha municipality and Malappuram district, Kerala in the 1990s. As these groups increased, the Kerala local government organized them into a three-tiered women's community network and registered them as an official organization. The Kerala government launched it in 1998 as a state-wide programme. As of September 2021, the Kudumbashree initiative has 294 436 neighbourhood groups with a total membership of 4 585 677. Kudumbashree membership is open to all adult women and limited to one membership per family.

The three-tiered network of women of the Kudumbashree functions in conjunction with the local self-government institutions to implement government initiatives for: (1) 'economic empowerment' such as micro-finance, micro-enterprises, collective farming, livestock farming, market development, and so on; (2) 'social empowerment' such as 'destitute identification and rehabilitation', 'rehabilitation of mentally challenged persons', and 'children's programmes'; and (3) 'women empowerment' consisting of a 'gender self-learning programme' and 'programmes for the elimination of violence against women' (https://participedia.net/method/6314).

For women to join the Kudumbashree programme, they have to organize themselves as a Neighbourhood Group. This group is a basic unit of Kudumbashree, providing a forum for members to plan and act with principles of democracy and solidarity and, in many cases, act as cooperatives or social enterprises (Mukherjee-Reed 2015). The Neighbourhood Groups send elected representatives to the ward-level Area Development Societies, and Area Development Societies send their representatives to the village or community-level Community Development Societies. The three-tiered system facilitating Kudumbashree members' participation in development planning and implementation is contiguous with the local self-governance system (the Panchayat Raj system) composed of three tiers.

One of the enabling factors to create synergies of SSEOEs included in the women's community network and Kudumbashree initiative is the institutions and policies of participatory planning processes, which had already been established in Kerala, such as the People's

Planning Campaign and the Community Development Society. The government's social policies at both national and state levels, which are discussed, planned and implemented by the Kudumbashree's and local governments' networks, have achieved successful outcomes in poverty eradication and inequality reduction, and empowerment of vulnerable and marginalized individuals and groups, particularly women. The case of the Mahatma Gandhi National Rural Employment Guarantee Scheme (MGNREGS), a rights-based employment guarantee programme in rural areas established in 2005, demonstrates how these community-level women's organizations, one of the most significant SSE sectors in India, contribute to realizing the goals and objectives of MGNREGS. In Kerala, the government addressed two challenges in the process of implementations of MGNREGS: male workers' low interests in the works of MGNREGS whose wages were only a half of the workers' average wage; and the traditional exclusion of women – the potential workers of the MGNREGS programme – from the public space. To address these problems, the government appointed the members of Kudumbashree affiliated with Area Development Societies as the programme supervisors of MGNREGS. The appointments resulted in creating interesting dynamics to strengthen MGNREGS and the ecosystem of the SSE. Most of all, Kudumbashree women who are appointed as supervisors actively participate in planning the work of MGNREGS, and they mobilize their Kudumbashree members to participate in the MGNREGS work.

Regarding women's participation in MGNREGS, Kerala was ranked first according to surveys in 2011 and 2012. The government trained these women programme supervisors to enhance their capacities to manage the projects. These elements of training are associated with their various responsibilities. The maxim of responsibilities includes: 'identifying work opportunities, mobilizing groups for work, preparing estimates in consultation with the overseer or engineer, supervising work, providing amenities at the worksite, preparing and submitting muster rolls, and handling emergencies' (Mukherjee-Reed 2015, 307). With this active participation in the programme as supervisors or workers, Kudumbashree women found the opportunity to utilize infrastructure development work in MGNREGS for various projects of the Kudumbashree programmes. In particular, they could relate those rural infrastructure programmes to farming, such as Sangha Krishi (group farming), a part of the Kudumbashree programme. Under Sangha Krishi, the government provides 10 million acres of land for agriculture to more than 44 000 collectives with more than 250 000 women farmers. Kudumbashree women linked the MGNREGS works such as the reclamation of fallow land and the improvement of infrastructure to enhance productivity, and consequently developed the group farming under Sangha Krishi into a new agricultural business (Varier 2016)

Source: Based on Yi et al. (2018).

53.4 CHALLENGES OF THE SSE IN THE SOCIAL POLICY SECTOR

Despite its contribution to making social policy better, gradually increasing the involvement of the SSE into social policy design and implementation poses various challenges to both social policy and the SSE. In the longer term, when the government relies on social service delivery by the SSE sector without strengthening its capacity to design and implement social policies, it may run the risk of hollowing out of the welfare state, particularly weakening redistributive functions at the government level (Roberts and Devine 2003). As government funding for SSEOEs grows, the government tends to establish mechanisms to make SSE management and operation more bureaucratic and marketized, which may create the so-called institutional isomorphism. It raises the question of the very identity of the SSEOEs: that is, whether SSEOEs would have a capacity to preserve the very values that make them SSEOEs. Although the centralist idea and culture have been somewhat weakened, they have not disappeared entirely in the social policy sector. There is an increasing trend to define the rules of the partnership between SSEOEs and the public sector. It threatens the diversity and flexibility of SSEOEs in responding to specific local needs. Finally, the overall framework in which SSEOEs play a significant role in shaping social policy differently from marketization is based on the public–private partnership and a neoliberal idea, rather than public–SSE partnership. As dependence on the funding of the public sector which pursues values of competition and cost–benefit efficiency grows', SSEOEs can risk being instrumentalized and co-opted by the public sector. A new paradigm of public–SSE partnership and its rules and standards need to be established and strengthened for meaningful participation of the SSE in social policy design and implementation (Bance 2018).

REFERENCES

Bance, Philippe. 2018. 'Providing Public Goods and Commons. Towards Coproduction and New Forms of Governance for a Revival of Public Action.' socioeco.org. CIRIEC. 1 January. http://www.socioeco.org/bdf_fiche-document-7301_en.html.

Celle, Sylvain. 2016. 'The Metamorphosis of the Cooperative Ideologies in French Capitalism during the Interwar Period (1919–1939).' Working Paper Presented at 28th Annual EAEPE Conference 2016. Manchester, UK. https://hal.archives-ouvertes.fr/hal-02280726/document.

Deakin, Nicholas. 2001. *In Search of Civil Society*. London: Routledge.

Hecht, R.M., and V.L. Tanzi. 1994. *The Role of Non-Governmental Organizations in the Delivery of Health Services in Developing Countries*. Washington, DC: World Bank.

Kendall, Jeremy. 2003. *The Voluntary Sector: Comparative Perspectives in the UK*. London: Routledge.

Mkandawire, T. 2004. 'Social Policy in a Development Context: Introduction.' In *Social Policy in a Development Context*, edited by Thandika Mkandawire, 1–33. New York: UNRISD and Palgrave Macmillan.

Mukherjee-Reed, Ananya. 2015. 'Taking Solidarity Seriously: Analysing Kerala's Judumbashree as a Women's SSE Experiment.' In *Social and Solidarity Economy: Beyond the Fringe*, edited by Peter Utting, 300–12. London: Zed Books.

Pierson, Christopher. 1998. *Beyond the Welfare State?* Cambridge: Polity Press.

Polanyi, Karl. 1957. *Great Transformation: the Political and Economic Origins of Our Time*. Boston, MA: Beacon Press.

Roberts, John Michael, and Fiona Devine. 2003. 'The Hollowing Out of the Welfare State and Social Capital.' *Social Policy and Society* 2 (4): 309–18. https://doi.org/10.1017/s1474746403001386.

Rossel, Cecilia. 2015. 'State and SSE Partnerships in Social Policy and Welfare Regimes: The Case of Uruguay.' In *Social and Solidarity Economy: Beyond the Fringe*, edited by Peter Utting, 236–49. London: Zed Books.

Varier, Megha. 2016. 'The Kudumbashree Story: How Kerala Women's Grassroots Scheme Grew Into a Multi-Crore Project.' The News Minute. 15 October. http://www.thenewsminute.com/article/kudumbashree-story-how-kerala-womens-grassroots-scheme-grew-multi-crore-project-51420.

Woodin, Tom. 2019. 'Co-Operative Schools: Democratic Values, Networks and Leadership.' *International Journal of Inclusive Education* 3 (11): 1164–79. https://doi.org/10.1080/13603116.2019.1617359.

Yi, Ilcheong, and Taekyoon Kim. 2015. 'Post-2015 Developmental Goals (SDGs) and Transformative Social Policy.' *Oughtopia* 30 (1): 307–35.

Yi, Ilcheong, Hyuk-Sang Sohn, and Taekyoon Kim. 2018. 'Synergistic Interactions between Social Policy and SSEs in Developing Countries: Interfaces in Discourse and Practice.' *Development and Society* 47 (2): 313–40. https://doi.org/10.21588/dns/2018.47.2.008.

54. Statistical measurement
Marie J. Bouchard

INTRODUCTION

There is a growing interest in the statistical measurement of the social and solidarity economy (SSE). Policymakers pay increasing attention to the SSE, in particular its potential to address social, economic and environmental issues in alternative ways. Yet, assessing the role played by the SSE is not an easy task, as it very often remains under the radar of national statistics. As the SSE is gaining recognition, the question of how best to measure it comes to the fore.

The purpose of measuring the SSE is to counteract the lack of visibility and improve overall knowledge and recognition of the field; namely, to support public policy development (Chaves 2021; see entry 51, "Public Policy"). Over the last three decades, significant work has been devoted to developing approaches and methodologies to gather data about the SSE at national and international levels. Many countries and regions have produced statistical portraits and mappings of the SSE (Compère et al. 2021). Despite these achievements, many of them lack statistical information about the SSE. Moreover, the statistics available do not cover a homogenous field of the SSE (Bouchard and Salathé-Beaulieu 2021), making aggregation and comparison difficult.

At the national level, the absence of a clear concept of the SSE, the lack of resources of national statistics offices, and the absence of political will are often to blame. Moreover, a globally agreed statistical definition, which ensures systematic data collection and coordination between various statistical offices, has yet to be established. Part of this is due to the perimeter defined by the notion of the SSE, which varies from one country or region to another. Another issue manifests in the different conceptualizations of what distinguishes the SSE from the rest of the economy (see entry 3, "Contemporary Understandings").

Due to space limitations, this entry focuses on the issue of delineating and enumerating the SSE population for statistical measurement purposes. It first examines how the statistical definition of the SSE is constructed, based on statistical standards and on the common structural characteristics that allow identifying and classifying SSE entities in national statistics accounts (Bouchard and Rousselière 2015). Next, this entry exposes the tools that have been developed to support the production and harmonization of statistics concerning the SSE across countries. These tools carry visions of what differentiates the SSE from other statistical entities, based mainly on either limited profitability or democratic governance. The entry then briefly examines issues surrounding the measurement of the SSE's contributions. As national accounts are not yet well equipped to measure non-economic dimensions, other methodologies are required to assess the full contributions of the SSE. We conclude by sharing some concerns about the potential effects of measurement on the definition of the SSE.

This entry has a clear focus on the features that should apply to SSE statistics. Firstly, they must enable the comparability of the measure of the SSE with the rest of the economy, while at the same time recognizing its specific modes of action. Secondly, statistics must ensure the compatibility of the measurement with the perimeter covered by each country's definition of the SSE, while still enabling comparison across countries. Finally, statistics need to ensure the relevancy of the categories and variables used to document the SSE, in order to reflect the nature of its contribution to the economy and to society.

54.1 IDENTIFYING AND CLASSIFYING SSE IN NATIONAL STATISTICS ACCOUNTS

The production of statistics requires defining the "objects" to be measured, classifying them, and enumerating the units forming the population or "universe of reference" they constitute. A statistical definition is derived from the legal or pre-agreed institutional definition of the phenomenon to be measured (see entry 46, "Legal Frameworks and Laws"). It is based on operational (empirically observable) characteristics of the phenomenon, helping to identify and screen in-scope entities, and to classify them in relevant categories.

Identifying the entities that make up the SSE in national statistics generally includes three main steps:

1. Identification of economic sectors most likely to contain SSE organizations. National economic accounts compile measures of economic activity and classify them by institutional sector and by industry, as defined in the 2008 System of National Accounts (hereafter, 2008 SNA) (EC et al. 2009). SSE organizations belong mainly to the institutional sectors of non-financial corporations (S11), financial corporations (S12), and non-profit institutions serving households (NPISH) (S15). The SSE is active in all types of industries (or activity sectors). Some are generally excluded from the definition of the SSE, depending on the culture and tradition of countries: professional associations, employer groups, political parties, religious organizations and unions. These exclusions can usually be easily identified by referring to the industry classification system (as discussed below).
2. Selection of entities by the legal statuses of organizations most likely to belong to the SSE. The SSE constitutes organizations that share common structural characteristics, namely a social purpose, democratic governance, limited or prohibited distribution of profits, and management autonomy. The "core" of the SSE that shares this bundle of characteristics is generally composed of cooperatives, mutual societies and non-profit institutions (also called non-profit organizations or associations) engaged in economic activities. Other similar forms of organizations that share SSE structural characteristics are also identified in different national contexts. In several countries, these are supplemented by philanthropic foundations and, more recently, social enterprises (see entry 21, "Social Enterprises"), which may or, controversially, may not, be incorporated as classic for-profit businesses. In some cases, the SSE includes informal businesses participating in the solidarity economy.
3. Filtering of entities that match a set of SSE operational characteristics. The operational characteristics of the SSE help to identify and discriminate entities. Tests about the presence of such characteristics can be administered through examining organizations' documents or asking filter questions. The criteria need to be empirical and observable, with features that are easy to agree upon. Examples include:

- Social purpose: serving individual and community needs; aiming at the amelioration of their well-being; giving primacy to persons over capital; limiting profit distribution.

- Democratic governance: legislation; organizational bylaws; composition, roles and rights of the governing body.
- Limited or prohibited profit distribution: legislation; organizational constitutive Acts and bylaws; obligation to distribute retained earnings and assets to a similar organization in the event of dissolution.
- Management autonomy: organizational constitutive Acts and bylaws; authority and responsibilities of the governing body.

The above are examples of filters. The number and types of operational characteristics these filters help test may vary according to the definition of the SSE used in different national contexts. The screening of SSE entities within national accounts is illustrated in Figure 54.1.

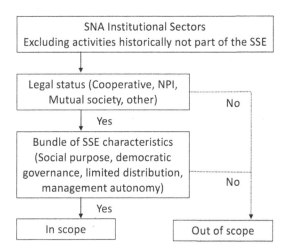

Note: NPI – non-profit institutions.
Source: Based on Bouchard et al. (2011).

Figure 54.1   Filters to identify SSE entities in national statistics accounts

Similar to other enterprises, SSE organizations produce or sell goods and services, which can be classified within a standard industry nomenclature. This enables measurement of the contribution of SSE enterprises in comparison to other economic entities (see, for example, the International Standard Industrial Classification of All Economic Activities, the Central Product Classification, and their national and multinational equivalents). Where the SSE is active in non-market production, an additional classification helps to capture some specific fields of activities of the non-profit institutions in more detail. Examples include affordable housing and some of its specific functions, such as community development; see the International Classification of Non-profit and Third Sector Organizations (UN 2018) and the Classification of the Purposes of Non-Profit Institutions Serving Households (EC et al. 2009). For cooperatives, a classification relating to the main stakeholder helps to classify cooperatives based on the members' interest, which differs according to whether members are workers, producers, or consumers, or a combination of these within multi-stakeholder cooperatives (ILO 2018; Eum et al. 2020).

54.2 INTERNATIONAL FRAMEWORKS FOR SSE STATISTICS

The statistical standards used to produce economic statistics help to ensure the comparability of SSE statistics with the rest of the economy at the national level. However, since the definition of the SSE varies across countries, so will its statistical perimeter. This makes it difficult to aggregate and compare statistics concerning the SSE across countries.

Several studies have been carried out to provide common reference frameworks for SSE statistics at the international level. All of them refer to the 2008 SNA, the underlying framework used to compile national economic accounts, as mentioned above.

Three manuals and one set of guidelines have been produced over the years to facilitate the measurement of the SSE in the national accounts. These do not all cover the same components of the SSE. The first reference framework, the *Handbook on Non-profit Institutions in the System of National Accounts* (UN 2003), hereafter referred to as UN 2003, was developed in 2003, and focuses on non-profit institutions and foundations. A second conceptual framework, the *Manual for Drawing up the Satellite Accounts on Cooperatives and Mutual Societies* (CIRIEC 2006), hereafter called CIRIEC 2006, was developed in 2006 by CIRIEC at the request of the European Commission to also cover the other main components of the social economy, that is, cooperatives and mutual societies. In 2018, *Guidelines Concerning the Statistics of Cooperatives* were adopted by the International Labour Organization (ILO 2018), hereafter referred to as ILO 2018. Also in 2018, a revised version of the UN 2003 handbook was published: the *Satellite Account on Non-profit and Related Institutions and Volunteer Work* (UN 2018), hereafter referred to as UN 2018. This new framework expands the scope of the non-profit sector to include some – but not all – cooperative and mutual entities, as well as social enterprises and direct (non-organizational) volunteering. It also includes some of the activity sectors that, while being organized as non-profit institutions, traditionally do not belong within the institutional definition of the SSE (see above). Figure 54.2 exposes the various organizational components within the SSE field and their coverage by different international frameworks for SSE statistics.

These frameworks provide considerable knowledge about the SSE and how to measure it, each offering a particular focus on the field. While the perimeter covered by each varies, these manuals can be used as references to enhance the comparison of the SSE statistics at the international level. To cover a given national definition (and statistical perimeter) of the SSE, it is sometimes necessary to combine them in a modular approach, requiring alignment of understandings and methods to ensure compatibility, as shown in the case of Portugal (INE and CASES 2019; Ramos 2019).

54.3 MEASURING THE SSE AND ITS IMPACTS

The inventory and exhaustive enumeration of the units that constitute the SSE population require compilation and screening of various databases (for example, statistical registers, business registers, SSE sectors' lists of members) and the use of filter questions to verify whether

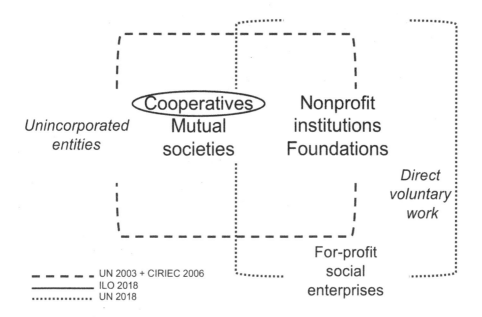

Figure 54.2   The SSE field and its coverage by international SSE statistics frameworks

all potential units meet the operational criteria. Once the delineation and enumeration of the universe of reference is completed, measurement can be made in a satellite account, based on data extracted from the national accounts. This methodology helps to compile the economic variables related to a specific aspect or domain of the economy that is poorly legible in the central national accounts. Measurement may also be based on a census, followed by a sample survey of the listed units. A combination of these methods helps to ensure the exhaustivity of the coverage, and the measurement of variables that are most relevant to the SSE.

National accounts contain the statistics which describe a country's economy. They integrate, reconcile and balance different official data sources (administrative sources and national surveys), which have already gone through rigorous processes of validation and quality analysis. National accounting makes it possible to expose what the SSE produces in terms of economic activity, namely the contribution to job creation, and to the gross domestic product (GDP) and gross value added (GVA). However, for many SSE organizations, such measurements may be either over- or under-estimated, since part of this contribution may be attributed to subsidies or to volunteering, or statistically captured by users through patronage refunds. Other accounting approaches are being developed to integrate not only the values resulting from market flows, but also the values effectively created by the resources mobilized but not visible in the accounts (Rousselière et al. 2020).

Although standard economic indicators can accurately inform about some aspects of the SSE, such as sales figures or employment, they fail to shed light on aspects such as non-monetary production, the combination of market and non-market resources, the internalization of social costs, and the reduction of environmental externalities. Recommendations can be found in international SSE statistics frameworks regarding, for example, the measurement of non-market and non-monetary inputs and outputs, membership and types of members, and work created directly or in the scope of the SSE activity.

Moreover, national accounts do not provide much information about other functions of economic units. As the main purpose of SSE enterprises is to improve the social, economic, cultural, or environmental conditions of the members of the organization, of a particular group or community, or of the whole of society, documenting it by referring only to economic variables may not be entirely sufficient, although nonetheless very important.

Numerous jurisdiction and international organizations have, over the years, worked to develop alternative statistical measurement to go beyond GDP, focusing on social progress, the well-being of population, quality of life, inclusive growth, sustainable development and human development: the Organisation for Economic Co-operation and Development (OECD) Better Life Index (OECD n.d.), United Nations (UN) Sustainable Development Goals (UN n.d.-a), UN Human Development Index (UN n.d.-b) (Stiglitz et al. 2009). As such improvements are made to national accounts, the identification of the SSE organizations housed within them will enable measurement of the contribution of the SSE and comparison to that of other economic agents. Until then, additional information may be captured through specific surveys that will measure outcomes relevant to the SSE (see, for example, the proposal for measuring SSE contribution to sustainable development goals in UN 2018).

Other impact measurement methodologies exist, namely experimental and quasi-experimental designs to evaluate policies or programs (Government of Canada 2019). These can be applied to the SSE, provided that they are adapted, and that the issues they raise are well understood by the stakeholders concerned (TIESS 2017).

CONCLUSION

The primary function of SSE statistics is to measure the contribution of the SSE within the overall economy. In seeming contradiction to this, another aim is to convey the aspects of this type of economy that are not economic in the strict sense of the term, as well as the role that the SSE plays in the different contexts where it takes root. This triple requirement of SSE statistics entails adopting methodologies that make SSE statistics: comparable to other economic agents and to the SSE across countries; compatible with the pre-agreed or legal definition of the SSE in national, regional, and international contexts; and relevant with regard to what else the SSE produces for society beyond jobs and economic added value. This entry has focused on the issue of delineating and enumerating the SSE population for statistical purposes. In this conclusion, we share some concerns about the effect of measurement on the definition of the SSE.

The SSE is usually defined by a bundle of characteristics that operationalize its fundamental values and principles. Two streams of research have nourished the work on SSE statistics: one focusing on the non-profit aspect of the SSE, a vision mostly present in Anglo-American countries; and the other focusing on its democratic governance, a vision mostly present in continental European and Latin American countries (as well as some sub-national jurisdictions such as Québec). The tools that these streams of research produce are robust, and consistent with international statistical standards. They do not cover the same statistical perimeter of the SSE, however.

Three manuals and one set of guidelines have been produced over the years to facilitate the measurement of the SSE in national accounts. Two manuals, produced between 2003

(UN 2003) and 2006 (CIRIEC 2006), aim to identify the core of the SSE, including entities related in terms of values and principles. The ILO Guidelines Concerning the Statistics of Cooperatives (ILO 2018) shows continuity with these manuals. Together, they draw a statistical perimeter that is consistent with the generally agreed-upon definition of the SSE, including legal statuses and entities that share the SSE values, principles, and operational characteristics (see Figure 54.2).

By introducing the notion of a "third or social economy" sector (UN 2018, 9–14), the UN 2018 manual (a revision of UN 2003) made a first significant attempt to reconcile these two streams. While seeking to cover the whole of the SSE, this manual in fact shows a deviation from the past, covering only the components that distribute little or no surplus, notwithstanding the difference that should be made between the distribution to members on account of their activity (patronage refund) (see entry 17, "Cooperatives and Mutuals"), versus to shareholders on account of their financial investment (dividends). This new UN 2018 framework is very much influenced by the non-profit approach on the one hand, and by the social enterprise approach on the other. It focuses on the social purpose of the SSE and not on the economic and political democracy it brings about, hence the exclusion of the perimeter of many cooperatives and mutual societies. This has generated discomfort both in the SSE sector and in the scientific community. Indeed, this posture is at odds with the generally accepted definitions of the SSE.

Not all of these tools have been developed with the same degree of operational precision, nor have they been used with the same intensity. It is most likely that the newest and most developed tool, the UN 2018, promoted by the United Nations and presently being tested in six European countries (four of which have received conditional funding from Eurostat on agreement to use it), will be most influential. It will be instructive to see how national statistical agencies in Europe adjust the scope of their study to respect (or not) the legal definition of the SSE, especially when this includes all cooperatives and mutual societies. Until a unified statistical definition and measurement tool of the SSE are produced, a modular approach, referring to more than one framework, will probably be the solution adopted, as in the case of Portugal mentioned above.

But not all countries have a long SSE tradition, nor do they all have an institutional, legal, or agreed-upon, clear definition of it. It is therefore important to consider the risk that the statistical tool leads to an overly limited definition of the SSE, at least from the point of view of national and supra-national governments and institutions. Indeed, once produced, statistics contribute to the rigidity of concepts, often at the cost of simplification and even at the risk of compromising their validity with respect to the reality they are supposed to represent. Once produced, statistical data on the SSE will serve as proof of the reality they represent. Statistical tools should help to capture data on national realities and make them comparable with each other through international standards. The SSE definition provided in a statistical framework should not, however, substitute for a legal or consensual definition within a given country or region. A strictly non-profit view of the SSE would leave unexposed and unmeasured the democratizing effects that the SSE aims to achieve. Of course, statistical tools and standards can evolve to reflect the changes in the economy and how these are conceptualized. A better coordination between international agencies involved in promoting statistical frameworks for the SSE seems advisable in view of their next revisions.

The SSE is of a multi-faceted nature, crossing economic, social, cultural, and political aspects of economic development. Therefore, the categories by which standard statistical instruments capture the reality may, in some cases, be ill-fitting. But what if, on the contrary, it was the SSE that influenced statistical standards? This could reverse the burden of proof vis-à-vis the differentiated contribution of economic agents to more sustainable, equitable, and just economic development. Future work is therefore needed to raise awareness about SSE statistics, and to further explore the tools that would seem most relevant for measuring its contribution.

REFERENCES

Bouchard, Marie J., Paulo Cruz Filho, and Martin St-Denis. 2011. *Cadre conceptuel pour définir la population statistique de l'économie sociale au Québec*. Cahier de la Chaire de recherche du Canada en économie sociale. Collection Recherche, No. R-2011-02. Montréal: Université du Québec à Montréal. https://www.economie.gouv.qc.ca/fileadmin/contenu/publications/administratives/economie_sociale/cadre_conceptuel_economie_sociale.pdf.

Bouchard, Marie J., and Damien Rousselière (Eds). 2015. *The Weight of the Social Economy. An International Perspective*. Brussels: CIRIEC and PIE Peter Lang.

Bouchard, Marie J., and Gabriel Salathé-Beaulieu. 2021. *Producing Statistics on the Social and Solidarity Economy: The State of the Art*. UNTFSSE "Opportunities and Challenges of Statistics on SSE" Project. Geneva: United Nations Research Institute on Social Development (UNRISD). https://knowledgehub.unsse.org/wp-content/uploads/2021/08/WP-2021-SSE-Stats-Bouchard-Salathe-Beaulieu.pdf.

Chaves, Rafael. 2021. *Producing Statistics on Social and Solidarity Economy: Policy Recommendations and Directions for Future Research*. UNTFSSE "Opportunities and Challenges of Statistics on SSE" Project." Geneva: United Nations Research Institute on Social Development (UNRISD). https://knowledgehub.unsse.org/wp-content/uploads/2021/08/WP-2021-SSE-Stats-Chaves-Avila.pdf.

CIRIEC. 2006. *Manual for Drawing Up the Satellite Accounts on Cooperatives and Mutual Societies*. Authored by Barea, José, and José Luis Monzón. Brussels: CIRIEC and European Commission, Enterprise and Industry Directorate-General. https://www.ciriec.uliege.be/en/publications/etudesrapports/manual-for-drawing-up-satellite-accounts-of-companies-in-the-social-economy-co-operatives-and-mutual-societies-2006/.

Compère, Coline, Barbara Sak, and Jérôme Schoenmaeckers. 2021. *Mapping International SSE Mappings*. 'UNTFSSE Opportunities and Challenges of Statistics' on SSE Project. Geneva: United Nations Research Institute on Social Development (UNRISD). https://knowledgehub.unsse.org/wp-content/uploads/2021/08/WP-2021-SSE-Stats-Compere-et-at.pdf.

Eum, Hyungsik, Chiara Carini, and Marie J. Bouchard. 2020. "Classification of Cooperatives. A Proposed Typology." In ILO, CIRIEC, and COPAC, *Statistics on Cooperatives. Concepts, Classification, Work and Economic Contribution*, edited by Marie J. Bouchard, 13–22. Geneva: International Labour Organization. https://www.ilo.org/global/topics/cooperatives/publications/WCMS_760710/lang--en/index.htm

European Commission (EC), International Monetary Fund, Organisation for Economic Co-operation and Development, United Nations, and World Bank. 2009. *System of National Accounts 2008*. New York: United Nations.

Government of Canada. 2019. "Measuring Impact By Design: A Guide to Methods for Impact Measurement." https://www.canada.ca/en/innovation-hub/services/reports-resources/measuring-impact-design.html#toc44.

ILO. 2018. *Guidelines Concerning the Statistics of Cooperatives*. Geneva: International Labour Organization. https://www.ilo.org/global/topics/cooperatives/news/WCMS_732326/lang--en/index.htm.

Instituto Nacional de Estatisticas (INE) and CASES. 2019. *Conta Satélite Da Economia Social – Social Economy Satellite Account 2016*. Lisbon: Instituto Nacional de Estatística.

OECD. n.d. *Better Life Index*. Accessed March 4, 2022. https://www.oecdbetterlifeindex.org/#/55555555555.

Ramos, Ana Cristina. 2019. "Conta Satélite da Economia Social (CSES) – Como Se Constrói a Conta Satélite." *Revista Economia Social* 6. http://www.revista-es.info/ramos_6.html.

Rousselière, Damien, Marie J. Bouchard, and Madeg Le Guernic. 2020. "On the Economic Contribution of Cooperatives". In ILO, CIRIEC, and COPAC, *Statistics on Cooperatives. Concepts, Classification, Work and Economic Contribution*, edited by Marie J. Bouchard, 39–56. Geneva: International Labour Organization. https://www.ilo.org/global/topics/cooperatives/publications/WCMS_760710/lang--en/index.htm.

Stiglitz, Joseph E., Amartya Sen, and Jean-Pierre Fitoussi. 2009. "Report by the Commission on the Measurement of Economic Performance and Social Progress." https://ec.europa.eu/eurostat/documents/8131721/8131772/Stiglitz-Sen-Fitoussi-Commission-report.pdf.

TIESS. 2017. "Evaluation and Impact Measurement for the Social Economy." Territoires Innovants En Économie Sociale et Solidaire Liason et Transfert. https://tiess.ca/en/evaluation-and-impact-measurement-for-the-social-economy/.

United Nations (UN). n.d.-a. *Human Development Index*. http://hdr.undp.org/en/content/human-development-index-hdi.

United Nations (UN). n.d.-b. *Sustainable Development Goals*. https://www.un.org/sustainabledevelopment/.

United Nations (UN). 2003. *Handbook on Non-Profit Institutions in the System of National Accounts*, edited by Johns Hopkins and University Center for Civil Society Studies. New York: United Nations Department of Economic and Social Affairs, Statistics Division.

United Nations (UN). 2018. *Satellite Account on Nonprofit and Related Institutions and Volunteer Work*. Studies in Methods: Handbook of National Accounting. New York: United Nations Department of Economic and Social Affairs, Statistics Division.

55. Supporting organizations and intermediaries
Hamish Jenkins

INTRODUCTION

Supporting organizations and intermediaries are essential components to the growth and sustainability of well-functioning social and solidarity economy (SSE) ecosystems at different territorial levels. They range from public sector agencies to private or non-governmental organizations (including SSE associations and networks, universities, and research and training centres), with a variety of hybrid institutional set-ups in between, such as formal and informal consultative bodies, subcontractual agreements and public–private partnerships. These organizations undertake multiple supporting activities for SSE organizations and enterprises (SSEOEs), which can include design and implementation of SSE legislation, SSE development plans, policies and programmes; and a range of support services, varying from advocacy and promotion of SSE interests in public policy arenas to capacity building and access to finance and markets.

A defining feature of supporting organizations and intermediaries is a strong relationship with the SSE community within the territory. Whether primarily governmental or non-governmental, these entities should enjoy a sufficient degree of trust within the SSE community and be able to ensure that diverse interests and needs, especially for under-represented sectors, are fully factored into policy and programme design and implementation. In addition, a broad coalition of SSEOEs and social movements is essential for the success of the SSE in establishing better collaborative relations with the government, developing innovative SSE initiatives, and creating and occupying policy spaces for SSE promotion (Mendell and Alain 2013; Jenkins et al. 2021).

55.1 CATEGORIES OF SUPPORTING ORGANIZATIONS AND INTERMEDIARIES

Supporting organizations and intermediaries play multiple roles in SSE ecosystem development, strengthened by appropriate co-constructed policy action, described in the next section. From an institutional perspective, they can be classified in terms of the types of relationship between supporting organizations and government (see Table 55.1).

There are two main categories of supporting organizations:

1. government ministries, departments and other bodies supporting the SSE; and
2. intermediaries between government and the SSE community.

Table 55.1 Types of relationship between supporting organizations and government

High level of public sector involvement					Low level of public sector involvement
Public sector agencies: government ministries and departments	Agencies designed and built by the government	Joint agencies with public and private co-ownership and co-responsibility	Private agencies with equity or grants provided by the government	Private agencies with service contracts with the government	Private or non-government sector without government funding

Source: Jenkins et al. (2021).

Government Ministries, Departments and Other Bodies

Government ministries, departments and other bodies with a mandate to work on SSE promotion alongside SSE organizations exist at various territorial levels of government. Examples at national and local levels include:

- The (former) National Secretariat for Solidarity Economy (SENAES) which was established under the Ministry of Labour and Employment in Brazil in 2003 (see below, and Box 47.1 in entry 47, 'Local and Territorial Development Plans').
- The Korea Social Enterprise Promotion Agency (KoSEA), established under the Ministry of Employment and Labour in the Republic of Korea in 2011.
- The State Secretariat responsible for the Social, Solidarity and Responsible Economy under the Ministry of the Economy, Finance and Recovery of France.
- The Ministry of Microfinance and Social and Solidarity Economy of Senegal.
- The Ministry of Economy and Innovation of Quebec, responsible for the social economy.
- The General Directorate of Employment, Training and Cooperative Promotion of Mexico City's Ministry of Labour and Employment Promotion.
- The Commission for the Cooperative, Social and Solidarity Economy of the Barcelona City Council, which was set up as a driver and catalyst for Pla d'Impuls de l'Economia Social i Solidària (PIESS), the impetus plan for SSE (2016–19), notably through one of its main agencies, Barcelona Activa (see Box 55.1).

BOX 55.1 GOVERNMENTAL SUPPORTING ORGANIZATION IN BARCELONA

One of the main governmental supporting organizations for implementation of Barcelona's SSE development plan (Pla d'Impuls de l'Economia Social i Solidària, 2016–19) is Barcelona Activa, a municipal-level body focused on employment promotion and local development. Barcelona Activa's strategic lines of action include the 'facilitation of the plural economy, promoting the SSE, collective entrepreneurship and social innovation'. Barcelona Activa carried out this line of action through economic development plans in larger districts of the city, with a particular emphasis on SSE advice and training, which doubled between 2016 and 2018. Half of the participants taking part in its SSE-related actions and services did so for the first time, showcasing an increasing interest in the SSE, which can be attributed to successful outreach, an integral part of the plan. Barcelona Activa also runs a new municipal institution called InnoBa, which was launched at the end of 2018 as the reception and orientation point for SSE projects. This facility offers activities, specialist services, research, training, and spaces for experimentation and incubation for SSE and socioeconomic innovation (Chaves-Avila et al. 2020).

Intermediaries Between Government and SSE

Intermediaries are generally autonomous bodies (even when created through government initiative), which mediate between government and the SSE community. They undertake a range of supporting functions for SSE development in both policy co-construction and implementation, and other functions not directly linked to government action. In most cases, intermediary organizations are established through non-governmental initiatives or public–private partnerships, to mediate between SSE actors and the government on the interface between the SSE movement and public policy actors. Examples include:

- The Chambres Régionales de l'Économie Sociale et Solidaire (CRESS) in France, whose Observatory is coordinated by the Conseil National des CRESS (CNCRESS) in partnership with institutions of the French national government.
- The Observatorio Español de la Economía Social and the Confederación Empresarial Española de la Economía Social (CEPES) in Spain.
- The Social Policy Observatory of Malopolskie and the Social Economy Development Academy in Krakow, Poland.
- The Fórum Brasileiro de Economia Solidária (FBES) in Brazil (see below, and Box 47.1 in entry 47, 'Local and Territorial Development Plans').
- The Comité Sectoriel de Main-d'œuvre – Économie Sociale Action Communautaire (CSMO-ESAC), in Quebec.
- The Chantier de l'économie sociale and the Quebec Council of Cooperatives and Mutual Associations in Canada (see below).
- The Seoul Social Economy Centre (SSEC) in the Republic of Korea (see below).

55.2 CORE ACTIVITIES OF SUPPORTING ORGANIZATIONS AND INTERMEDIARIES

Supporting organizations can carry out SSE-empowering activities independent of government action. However, to a large extent, the growth and sustainability of SSE ecosystems depend on enabling public policy tailored to the distinctive characteristics of the SSE. Therefore, the range of activities often covers both policy advocacy, co-design and monitoring (policy 'co-construction'), and implementation ('co-production') (Mendell and Alain 2013). These activities include the following:

- Mobilizing and representing SSEOEs and multiple SSE sectors' interests.
- Reinforcing the common identity and values of the SSE.
- Educating policy makers on the specificities and diversity of the SSE sector.
- Helping SSE enterprises to navigate the policy environment.

- Analysing the impact of existing government measures on SSEOEs.
- Contributing to capacity building at various stages of organizational/enterprise development.
- Identifying and disseminating best practices and the conditions under which these can be replicated.
- Facilitating SSEOEs' access to finance and markets (including financial mechanisms adapted to SSE specificities and ways to tap into public and private markets) through financial and technical support (Mendell and Alain 2013; Jenkins et al. 2021).

These activities can be regrouped into two broad categories:

1. Policy co-construction and representation.
2. Capacity building and other support services (often in the form of co-production with government entities).

Policy Co-construction and Representation

The meaningful involvement of representative SSE intermediary organizations and networks in SSE policy formulation and implementation is essential to ensure that measures taken correspond to local conditions and needs. Top-down policy design and implementation (meaning without genuine inclusion of SSE intermediaries) are often prone to fail, and tend to instrumentalize the SSE to serve state, political or market interests (Jenkins et al. 2021). The institutional method of embedding the relationship between non-governmental supporting organizations/intermediaries and governments in policy co-construction can be through formal or semi-formal/informal arrangements. These are also manifest in international SSE relations.

Formal relations
In formal settings, the role of intermediary organizations can be instituted in co-constructed laws or signed agreements between the government and SSE intermediaries. For example, in the case of Quebec, the 2013 Social Economy Act (co-constructed at the provincial level) includes a clause which creates a permanent committee of stakeholders overseeing the application of the legislation and/or future amendments, and mobilizing knowledge on the SSE as it evolves. Creation of a multistakeholder space for ongoing dialogue ('table of partners') which advises the government on the elaboration of action plans for the social economy is required by the Act. The Chantier de l'économie sociale and the Quebec Council of Cooperatives and Mutual Associations are explicitly mentioned in the law, which they largely contributed to shape (Mendell and Alain 2013; Mendell et al. 2020).

Intermediaries operating within institutionalized formal settings enjoy greater official status, enhancing the visibility of the SSE on the policy agenda, and contributing to creating a favourable policy and political environment for the SSE (Jenkins et al. 2021). For instance, in 2012, the Mayor of Seoul agreed with the Seoul Social Economy Network (SSEN) to create the Public–Private Policy Making Partnership for the Social Economy in Seoul. Its purpose is to discuss and establish basic plans and measures for SSE policy in the metropolitan area, including joint decisions on monitoring of policy measures and budgets. This process notably contributed to the founding of the Council of Local Governments on the Social Solidarity Economy (CLGSSE), whose mission is to create jobs and revitalize local communities through promotion of the social economy. The members of the CLGSSE currently consist of

47 local governments across South Korea, including 18 of the 25 self-governing boroughs of Seoul (Yoon and Lee 2020).

Semi-formal/informal relations

Informal arrangements and processes can be an alternative or a complement to official institutions, especially when existing institutions are dated and may lack inclusivity. They have the advantage of greater flexibility in bringing a broader range of SSE actors to the table, such as representatives of social movements that do not necessarily belong to a registered organization, and informal SSEOEs that would otherwise not be represented, as in the case of the Fórum Brasileiro de Economia Solidária (FBES) in Brazil (Utting 2017; Jenkins et al. 2021). Likewise, in Barcelona, the city's Plan to Boost the Social and Solidarity Economy, PIESS (2016–19) contains one landmark innovation: the creation of the Participatory Area of the SSE policy. This played an essential role in bringing diverse SSE organizations to converge on a common SSE definition and policy priorities that work for the highly diverse spectrum of SSEOEs operating in the territory. In the absence of an adequate formal body, the Participatory Area plays the role of an informal consultative and joint policy decision-making body between SSE stakeholders and those in charge of public administration. An added strength in Barcelona's City Council approach was to choose an SSE activist, external to the public administration apparatus and political parties, to lead its 2016–19 SSE development policy. This element facilitated participation of the SSE community in the drafting of the SSE policy, and internalization of the sector within the government fabric (Chaves-Avila et al. 2020).

International SSE relations

SSE networks and coalitions also act in policy co-construction at the supra-national regional and global levels. At the regional level, co-construction is particularly advanced within the European Union (EU), through the research and advocacy undertaken by the independent European Economic and Social Committee (the EU's main consultative body with an explicit mandate on promotion of the social economy) and a range of SSE networks, such as Social Economy Europe and the European wing of the Intercontinental Network for the Promotion of Social Solidarity Economy (RIPESS – Europe). At the global level, international SSE networks, such as RIPESS, the SSE International Forum (formerly known as the Mont-Blanc Meetings) and Global Social Economy Forum (GSEF), among many others, provide indispensable expertise and activism as observers in the United Nations Inter-Agency Task Force on Social and Solidarity Economy (UNTFSSE), which advocates for the SSE in international policy fora, including promotion of this socioeconomic model as a strategic means of implementation of the globally agreed Sustainable Development Goals (www.unsse.org). (The public policy co-construction dimension of supporting and intermediary organizations' activities is discussed in more detail in entry 50, 'Partnership and Co-construction'.)

Capacity Building and Other Support Services

Supporting organizations and intermediaries, whether primarily public or non-governmental entities, provide capacity building and other services aimed to empower SSEOEs through a range of activities that gravitate around the five following clusters:

1. Training and education.

2. Advisory functions (such as tailor-made mentoring and coaching).
3. Incubating services such as SSE hubs, incubators and parks.
4. Financial support.
5. Networking and marketing.

In practice, supporting organizations provide one or more of these inter-related clusters of services, in particular, financial support, the effectiveness of which depends on the skills and additional support acquired in the other clusters. These support functions are collectively designed to cater to distinct needs at different stages of SSEOEs' development with the most appropriate interventions to strengthen SSEOEs in their given context. Co-constructed public policy for SSE capacity building can help identify and fill gaps, and facilitate missing institutional connections in the existing territorial SSE support landscape (Jenkins et al. 2021).

Training and education

Training and education can cover business administration-type dimensions pertaining to SSEOE creation and development. These include management, governance, product and service quality, market and finance access, and impact or performance measurement, described in detail in entry 48, 'Management'. SSE-specific modules can also be integrated into training programmes for small and medium-sized enterprises, as in the case of the Durban city branch of South Africa's Small Enterprise Agency (Steinman 2020; Jenkins et al. 2021). Training and education by supporting organizations can also cover knowledge of SSE law and policy, as well as advocacy capacity building. They offer training for SSEOs, but also for government officials, providing them with the tools to best fulfil their responsibilities in relation to the creation and implementation of SSE laws and policies, budgeting for the SSE, promoting the engagement of SSE actors, and ensuring transparency and accountability in the whole administrative process (Jenkins et al. 2021).

Supporting organizations provide diverse forms of training courses tailor-made for different target groups, which can be provided online and offline. The Social Economy Academy established by the Seoul Metropolitan Government, and the Social Enterprise Academy, a public–private partnership in Scotland, are examples of supporting organizations specialized in SSE training (see Box 55.2). Partnerships between international organizations, governments and other stakeholders also exist for training and education programmes, such as the SSE Academy of the International Labour Organization, and GSEF's Training and Workshop Series.

BOX 55.2 SUPPORTING ORGANIZATIONS SPECIALIZED IN SSE TRAINING

Social Economy Academy, Seoul

In 2013, the Seoul Metropolitan Government established the Social Economy Academy as a result of a series of consultations with diverse, relevant stakeholders to develop a road map for enhancing human resource capabilities in the SSE. The core mission of the academy is to provide the basic capability development and practical training required to start and manage social economy enterprises. The road map also included plans to expand the network of experts and trainees. According to a survey on past trainees conducted in August 2016, 88 per cent of them continued to work in the SSE; and 31 per cent of the trainees who had not initially worked in the field, entered it by either finding jobs or starting their own social enterprises. An online learning platform was also set up to provide information on education and training courses, instructors, learning materials, and jobs available in Seoul's social economy sector (Yoon and Lee 2020).

Social Enterprise Academy, Scotland

In Scotland, the Social Enterprise Academy was established through a partnership between the Scottish Government, a social enterprise and a conventional private enterprise as both a social enterprise and a charity. The academy provides a wide range of learning and development programmes for individuals and organizations to enable social change. The tutor network is spread across Scotland, enabling a wide delivery of programmes to communities throughout the country. Most of the programmes are developed in partnership with networks, community organizations and other support bodies, so that they are tailored and adapted to meet specific local needs. By 2018, over 10 000 individuals were beneficiaries of the academy's programmes. The academy's model is currently being replicated globally through a network of Social Enterprise Academy Hubs managed by partners from local communities and support ecosystems (OECD 2018).

Advisory services (mentoring and coaching)
Supporting organizations also provide expert advice to SSEOEs, through consultancies, coaching and mentoring services for SSE actors, in particular on niche areas of expertise. They can provide more flexible and individualized support through tailor-made services, notably to address specific needs and challenges faced by SSEOEs at various stages of development. For example, the Territorial Development Fund (Fonds de développement des territoires; FDT) established by Quebec's National Assembly, funds PME MTL, the largest network of experts in Montreal, providing coaching, training and financing for private sector and social economy entrepreneurs in all industries, to support them in launching and growing their enterprises. It offers subsidies to social economy enterprises to support their development from pre-start-up to consolidation and growth (Mendell et al. 2020).

Incubating services
The activities of supporting organizations can also include incubating services. These consist of a combination of capacity building services aimed at helping to establish or scale up SSEOEs, and include examples such as co-working spaces, training, coaching, consulting services, networking and funding. These services are often combined with other supportive programmes offered to social enterprises such as direct financial support and preferential procurement. Supporting organizations offering incubating services target organizations that aim to establish themselves as SSEOEs, improve their product range and quality, and increase their organizational, managerial, financial, as well as social/environmental impact. For example, in Brazil, the National Programme of Incubators for Popular Cooperatives (which was implemented by SENAES in coordination with the Ministry of Science and Technology

and the National Council for Scientific and Technological Development) had, by the end of 2015, provided training and technical support to approximately 1000 SSE organizations and support organizations via partnerships with universities throughout the country (Utting 2017). Incubating organizations and programmes see their primary goal as accompanying SSEOEs until they become independent, financially viable organizations upon completion of the programme (OECD n.d.; Steinman 2020).

Financial support
The primacy of social and environmental objectives makes it more difficult for SSEOEs to attract funding, especially in the early stages, compared to conventional enterprises aiming for profit maximization, as discussed in detail in entry 45, 'Financing'. Supporting organizations and intermediaries (whether public, private or a combination of the two) play an essential role in providing appropriate forms of financing for SSEOEs, corresponding to different stages of their life cycle. These range from direct government subsidies and public or private grants, start-up capital, low- (or zero-) interest rate loans, loan guarantees, to more innovative financial mechanisms such as crowd-funding and complementary social currencies. Social banking and other variants of 'solidarity finance', such as cooperative mutual funds, are common features in SSE ecosystems (Jenkins et al. 2021).

Intermediaries can channel and/or match public and private funds to support SSE development through well-adapted and innovative means. For example, the Seoul Social Investment Fund was established by the Metropolitan Government in 2012 through partnerships with intermediary organizations and partners in private social finance. These organizations would receive investments and loans without interest on the condition that they would match the amount they received from the Social Investment Fund one-to-one, or one-to-three at the very least, reinvesting or loaning the funds to SSEOEs at interest rates no higher than 3 per cent per annum (Yoon and Lee 2020). Likewise, the Chantier de l'économie sociale and the Conseil québécois de la coopération et de la mutualité receive funds from the Ministry of Economy and Innovation of Quebec to undertake projects in collaboration with other social economy organizations and actors to support SSEOEs. Their intermediary nature allows greater civil society engagement with the social economy, while pursuing projects which reflect their mandate (Mendell et al. 2020). Ten years after its creation, in 2007 the Chantier also established its own trust (the Fiducie du Chantier de l'économie sociale). The trust acts as an intermediary between the financial market and social economy businesses, thereby mutualizing the risk associated with investing in the SSE, while simultaneously creating financial products that are better adapted to social enterprises (Barco Serrano et al. 2019).

Networking and marketing
Networking and marketing are also essential dimensions of services provided by supporting organizations and intermediaries, especially in the more advanced stages of SSEOE development. These tools facilitate the exchange of knowledge and experiences across SSEOEs. Networking also offers opportunities to develop synergies and complementarities among SSE actors and with private and public actors. Similarly, networks are useful to create business partnerships and value chains among SSEOEs that enable access to markets or facilitate access to finance. For instance, networks can help SSEOEs to identify partners to share and co-own infrastructure and facilities such as storage space or e-commerce platforms, which can be especially useful when they are small, lack resources or are located in remote areas (albeit

depending upon adequate access to information and communication technology infrastructure) (Jenkins et al. 2021).

Linked to policy co-construction, networking also enables 'political capacity building', in terms of collectively mobilizing resources to advocate for SSE-friendly policies with governments. Many SSE networks, some primarily funded by governments, carry out on-the-ground SSEOE development support, as well as advocacy functions to improve the legal and policy-enabling environment for SSE in their territory (OECD and EU 2017; Jenkins et al. 2021). As mentioned above, supporting organizations and intermediaries can carry out simultaneously many of the activity clusters described in this section. For example, the Seoul Social Economy Centre (SSEC), a leading intermediary SSE support organization also set up as a public–private partnership, includes among its tasks: recruiting and providing development support for the actors of the social economy; identifying and supporting the commercialization of business models of SSEOEs; providing management consulting and marketing support for SSEOEs; fostering online and offline hubs of networking among SSEOEs; facilitating public procurement of products from SSEOEs; as well as researching and developing SSE policy measures (Yoon and Lee 2020) (see entry 56, 'The Institutional Ecosystem' for additional insights on functions, characteristics, diversity and complementarity of supporting organizations and intermediaries in SSE ecosystems).

REFERENCES

Barco Serrano, Samuel, Riccardo Bodini, Michael Roy and Gianluca Salvatori. 2019. *Financial Mechanisms for Innovative Social and Solidarity Economy Ecosystems*. Geneva: ILO (International Labour Organization).

Chaves-Avila, Rafael, Jordi Via-Llop and Jordi Garcia-Jané. 2020. 'Public Policies Fostering the Social and Solidarity Economy in Barcelona (2016–2019).' Working Paper No. 2020-5. Geneva: UNRISD.

Jenkins, Hamish, Ilcheong Yi, Samuel Bruelisauer and Kameni Chaddha. 2021. *Guidelines for Local Governments on Policies for Social and Solidarity Economy*. Geneva: UNRISD.

Mendell, Marguerite, and Béatrice Alain. 2013. 'Evaluating the Formation of Enabling Public Policy for the Social and Solidarity Economy from a Comparative Perspective: The Effectiveness of Collaborative Processes or the Co-Construction of Public Policy.' In *Proceedings of the UNRISD Conference on Potential and Limits of Social and Solidarity Economy 2013*. Geneva: UNRISD.

Mendell, Marguerite, Nancy Neamtan and Hyuna Yi. 2020. 'Public Policies Enabling the Social and Solidarity Economy in the City of Montreal.' Working Paper No. 2020-4. Geneva: UNRISD.

OECD (Organisation for Economic Co-operation and Development). 2018. *Inclusive Entrepreneurship Policies: Country Assessment Notes: United Kingdom 2018*. Paris: OECD/ EU.

OECD (Organisation for Economic Co-operation and Development). n.d. 'Guidance note: Skills and Business Development Support: Better Entrepreneurship Policy Tool.' Accessed 22 September 2020. https://betterentrepreneurship.eu/ en/node/46.

OECD and EU (Organisation for Economic Co-operation and Development/European Union). 2017. *Boosting Social Enterprise Development: Good Practice Compendium*. Paris: OECD Publishing.

Steinman, Susan. 2020. 'Creating an Enabling Environment for the Social and Solidarity Economy (SSE) through Public Policies in Durban, South Africa.' Working Paper No. 2020-9. Geneva: UNRISD.

Utting, Peter. 2017. *Public Policies for Social and Solidarity Economy: Assessing Progress in Seven Countries*. Geneva: ILO (International Labour Organization).

Yoon, Kil-Soon and Sang-Youn Lee. 2020. 'Policy Systems and Measures for the Social Economy in Seoul.' Working Paper No. 2020-6. Geneva: UNRISD.

56. The institutional ecosystem
Jean-Marc Fontan and Benoît Lévesque

56.1 THE ECOSYSTEM CONCEPT

The term 'ecosystem', a neologism created in 1935 by the British botanist George Tansley, comes etymologically from the words 'ecology' and 'system'. Thus, the ecological ecosystem designates a set of components forming an observable entity, which is of various sizes, such as a wetland, a savannah, a continent or the Earth. These components are self-organizing and do not require an architect. The term 'entrepreneurial ecosystem' was used as an analogy to the notion of an ecological ecosystem as proposed by James F. Moore in 1993. In management, the term 'ecosystem' was generalized from a very specific use to refer to the environment surrounding private companies. At the end of the first decade of the 2000s, the ecosystem approach was generalized to the study of all businesses: private, public or in the social and solidarity economy (SSE).

Despite similar dimensions, such as high complexity, interdependence and feedback between its entities, entrepreneurial ecosystems have significant qualitative differences from ecological ecosystems. Ecological ecosystems are self-organizing and operate based on objective factors without reflexive capacity. Entrepreneurial ecosystems, on the other hand, include entities based on subjective factors, such as the reflexivity and preferences of entrepreneurs or consumers. These components are subject to institutional regulation based on political choices that vary according to specific ideological orientations. Consequently, the functioning of ecosystem approaches, and support in the development of private enterprises, cannot be mechanically induced from the functioning modalities of natural ecosystems.

56.2 WHY IS THE INSTITUTIONAL ECOSYSTEM NEEDED FOR SSE?

The factors explaining why the SSE needs a specific institutional ecosystem fall into two broad categories. In addition to these categories, there are two relatively recent conjunctural aspects, which have strongly contributed to a rise in the relevance of ecosystems.

The first category of factors involves the fact that the dominant ecosystem, that of private businesses, has developed without taking into account the needs and aspirations of SSE components. To grow and develop, SSE enterprises and organizations were unable to take advantage of their immediate and even global environment, which offered advantages to all other forms of business, whether private or public. For example, financial institutions often withhold support from SSE enterprises because they consider them a greater risk. Similar difficulties have affected a variety of other elements, such as the services offered to private companies, which are often inadequate to the needs of SSE enterprises and organizations. These considerations partly explain the need for public support from national governments toward SSE enterprises and organizations.

The second major category of factors relates to the global economic framework, which has been relatively closed to social transformation carried out, in large part, by the SSE. Until recently, the dominant institutional environment at both the global and national levels was relatively hostile to, or at least unconcerned with, the originality and relevance of SSE enterprises and organizations. Fortunately, there are national exceptions. The countries and regions where the SSE has been most vigorously deployed (for example, the Basque Country and Scotland in Europe, and Quebec in North America) had a more favourable institutional environment and relied on the presence of a developmental model that was more sensitive to the values of equity, solidarity and democracy.

Finally, the recent appearance of the term 'ecosystem' in the SSE coincides with a new two-aspect situation. Firstly, there has been a neoliberal repositioning of economic and social policies which focus on supply factors that value entrepreneurship and innovation. From this perspective, social enterprises, led by collective or individual entrepreneurs, are emerging without necessarily being linked to user groups and SSE historical networks.

Secondly, there has been an emergence of new social issues pertaining to all SSE components. These components, in the context of neoliberal policies, are now strongly solicited by public authorities with a focus on social cohesion and the energy transition. For a complementary, non-instrumental contribution, let alone an alternative to the existing system, the SSE needed a unified, renewed and strengthened ecosystem.

56.3 WHAT CONSTITUTES THE SSE ECOSYSTEM?

The institutional ecosystem of the SSE includes not only all of the enterprises and organizations that combine economic and social objectives, but also all the institutional and organizational entities that shape their immediate and distant environment (see entry 10, 'Origins and Histories').

Thus, the SSE ecosystem can be viewed from two perspectives. On the one hand, institutional conditions have been put in place by formal institutions (for example, public policies, market mechanisms) or informal identities (for example, culture, values, tradition). On the other hand, organizational conditions are planned in terms of skills, leadership, networks, finance, support services (communication, research, and so on), and the development of intermediary training, liaison and transfer organizations. All of this constitutes an organized ecosystem populated by specific subsystems.

Thus, an ecosystem can be composed of other ecosystems, which are more or less well integrated with each other. Although the term was not used at its inception in the 19th century, historically the SSE has long had an international ecosystem to support its development. This has brought together, under a diversity of geography and identity, a variety of national and regional sub-ecosystems that are more or less autonomous from each other but remain dependent on the same set of values and guiding principles. By geographical diversity, we mean SSE ecosystems that have been established on a spatial scale. They are transnational, national, regional or local in nature. By identity diversity, we refer to specializations that are sectoral or thematic, which might include the activities carried out (for example, the social finance ecosystem), the mission of the organizations (for example, ecosystem of social integration companies) or the legal status used (for example, cooperative or social enterprise ecosystems).

56.4 HOW ARE SSE ECOSYSTEMS ESTABLISHED?

The modalities for the emergence and development of SSE ecosystems are highly contrasted. They can result from self-organization: a process of institutionalization from below, where the actors have particular justifications to implement values and rules to achieve a collective interest (that of its members) or general interest (that of the citizens). They can also emerge from a directed or imposed approach: either by public authorities, in the name of the general interest (that of citizens), or by top-down initiatives from philanthropic or private organizations. These two processes are occasionally combined through formal or informal collaborations or well-established partnerships.

The historical SSE components have acquired specific ecosystemic identities by grouping together based on their status (cooperative, mutual and associative) or according to their activities (for example, agriculture, credit and savings, food). They have also done so at the request of political authorities to co-produce sectoral policies in terms of economic, social or territorial development. Gradually, and in very different ways, governments – especially national governments – have supported these various ecosystem identities through sectoral policies (for example, agriculture), and more recently through cross-cutting policies aimed at all SSE sectors (for example, specific policies to support SSE enterprises and organizations).

From the 1980s onwards, in a context of market liberalization and a neoliberal state wanting to facilitate and decentralize rather than intervene, the historical SSE components began to unite under the 'social economy', and then the 'social and solidarity economy'. Under this new identity, the historical components established relationships and demanded recognition of their new identity by the public authorities. At the same time, and in a more organized way from the 1990s onwards, the social enterprises that emerged within the perimeter of non-profit organizations, and under the impetus of philanthropic and private organizations, also sought recognition of a new status representing a hybrid innovation between the private and social economies.

This twofold process of gaining recognition will not be without tensions between the historical SSE ecosystem and the emerging ecosystem of social enterprises. It will result in a proposal for unification in which the key SSE actors will coexist without necessarily sharing the same conception of their ecosystem, nor promoting a homogeneous vision of the transformations to be achieved in terms of social and ecological transition (see entry 4, 'Ecological Economics'). Some researchers do not hesitate to speak of an institutionalization conflict within this new ecosystem. This conflict concerns, among other things, the legal form or forms that would be the most appropriate for the organizational components of the social economy, or the institutional framework to be favoured: that of the social economy, or that of the social enterprise (see entry 46, 'Legal Frameworks and Laws').

56.5 KEY CHARACTERISTICS AND POLICY AREAS OF SSE ECOSYSTEMS

The processes and dynamics involved with the various functions and activities of an ecosystem mean that some components are more strategic and influential than others. In sum, the key components or actors can be grouped into four broad categories whose respective importance is a result of the state of social relations and the respective place occupied by the state, the market and civil society in the overall regulation of a given society.

The first category consists of the actors that make up the sector. These are organizations and enterprises that identify themselves as part of the historical or new social and solidarity economy, including social enterprises (fairly widespread worldwide) and foundations (mainly in Europe). These actors have a particular relationship with the field of civil society. The latter plays a key role in the emergence processes of SSE organizations and enterprises. Civil society is characterized by a greater or lesser capacity of citizens to organize, associate and respond to needs and aspirations through new projects. This large institutional field represents very fertile ground for the social economy and social business. The territorial anchoring of SSE initiatives favours self-institutionalization based on justifications and values that reinforce experimentation while challenging public authorities. In a bottom-up approach, self-institutionalization represents a prerequisite for their recognition by public authorities.

The second category involves the presence of public authorities at various scales to ensure regulation (laws and policies), redistribution, support and access conditions to public markets. The public sector includes a range of institutions that can influence the supply factors for SSE enterprises (for example, universities, research centres, business services). Public policies, which affect the SSE, can be of two types. Firstly, sectoral policies (employment, integration, regional development), which call for the implementation of the SSE. Secondly, transversal policies, which explicitly aim to strengthen the SSE through measures relating to its financing, access to public procurement, specific legal framework, social clauses, and so on (see entry 46, 'Legal Frameworks and Laws'). The first type of policy can strengthen thematic or sectoral ecosystems, but with a risk of instrumentalization. The second type is more favourable to the constitution of a so-called integrated ecosystem (Chaves-Avila and Gallego-Bono 2020)

The third category is that of actors who provide many resources to the various SSE components, including goods and services, funding, training and expertise (see entry 55, 'Supporting Organizations and Intermediaries'). These suppliers include SSE companies and organizations, and also private companies that are essential for services and expertise not offered by SSE. Some private foundations facilitate liaisons between SSE organizations and private enterprises because of their expertise and success (see entry 20, 'Non-governmental Organizations and Foundations').

Finally, the fourth category of key actors in the ecosystem (but only weakly identified as strategic) is that of the users, beneficiaries and clients of SSE enterprises. These actors may be grouped in voluntary associations. In addition, they are often present as volunteers in SSE bodies.

56.6 KEY CHARACTERISTICS OF INTERNATIONAL SSE ECOSYSTEMS

The support of institutional authorities in the development of SSE ecosystems can be observed at the international level. This can be illustrated by the actions developed by SSE actors, by the state or by foundations. Support is provided through a bottom-up or top-down approach. These two approaches can also be deployed in concert.

At the international level, in 1895 in Manchester, members of cooperative networks created an International Cooperative Alliance. The Alliance's objective was to affirm the values, principles and operating rules that support the development of this type of association. Through this, they laid the foundations of the first international SSE ecosystem (Lévesque 2016). This system benefited from the advances that were being made at the national level. Sectoral clusters (for example, agriculture, finance and credit) took shape in their national markets, and cross-sectoral clusters promoted a common identity within the SSE in terms of governance and purpose. Some of these clusters have proposed strong democratization of the economy and a profound societal transformation of institutional arrangements. At the heart of this international ecosystem, inter-cooperation aimed at both self-institutionalization and the strengthening of modalities for its sustainability.

Fairly quickly, SSE European actors sought the support of the European Union (EU) through its various bodies, including the European Commission. In 2011, the Social Enterprise Initiative (SEI), launched by the European Commission, proposed a dozen priorities to strengthen the SSE ecosystem, grouped under three main themes. The main objective was to support the development of social enterprise through more accessible financing, greater visibility, a more appropriate legal environment, the development of new technologies, support for innovation and for the development of its international dimension. Finally, while the SEI was initially focused on social enterprise, the evaluation of the SEI now invites the EU to adopt an inclusive vision of the social economy, including social enterprise and social or solidarity-based enterprises and organizations.

Two collective research studies, commissioned by the EU, have assessed the impact of two main measures put in place following the SEI introduction (Haarich et al. 2021; Borzaga et al. 2020). These studies have identified the actions taken by public authorities, intermediary actors and private firms on a range of issues:

- Policymaking and regulation.
- The public procurement framework (for example, access to public markets).
- Funding: from European funds – the European Regional Development Fund (ERDF) for regional development and the European Social Fund (ESF) for social development accessible for SSE from 2014 – with other financial intermediaries (loans and grants, social impact bonds, and so on).
- Accompanying and supporting social enterprises by promoting them through, among other things, mapping, impact measurement and monitoring.
- Skills training: including management and apprenticeships.
- Research and transfer: from universities, third sector organizations and consulting firms.

Through its policies, funds and projects, the EU is clearly one of the main key drivers in the development of a specific ecosystem to improve social enterprise and the social and solidarity economy. Mostly, the EU's contributions are made indirectly through its member states, the action of the regions and the major cities. This institutional ecosystem defines an environment where social enterprises, and the social and solidarity economy, are entities that must be supported and strengthened by public authorities. Finally, with few exceptions, these enterprises are not perceived as key players at the national level, especially since they can only ensure, with difficulty, the governance of the international ecosystem that concerns them; hence the importance of a pan-state action.

The support for the development of the social entrepreneurship ecosystem is also illustrated in the work done by philanthropic organizations active at the international level. One example is the support provided and promoted by Ashoka. Ashoka is a non-profit organization registered in the United States, and has a philanthropic foundation status in Switzerland. With its resources and networks, it has developed a mindset where anyone can become a change-maker and a giver. This working posture argues that entrepreneurship and competition will close the productivity gap between civil society organizations and private companies (Drayton and Budinich 2010).

Ashoka's social enterprise ecosystem approach is the result of experimentation that dates back to the early 1980s in Asian countries (for example, India, Bangladesh, Indonesia), then in Latin American and Eastern European countries. Since 2000, the approach has been deployed in North America (the United States and Canada) and in Europe (France and the United Kingdom). With a few exceptions, it is centred on the social entrepreneur and evolves in parallel with the social economy ecosystem in countries where the latter is well established.

56.7 FROM NATIONAL TO LOCAL SSE ECOSYSTEMS

Most of the institutional SSE ecosystem components are localized or even anchored at the national level. Moreover, these national ecosystems are contrasted, in terms of both their components, and the types of regulation and control to which they are subject. Structural factors, often of an informal nature (culture, values and traditions) and mechanical factors (policies, programmes, legislation) have influenced the forms and modalities of the SSE ecosystems' development. Thus, the French, Italian, Brazilian and American SSE ecosystems have historically had distinctly different characteristics.

Richard Hazenberg et al. (2016) showed that European countries differed according to the role played by the state in supporting social enterprise development. They produced a typology consisting of four types of national public ecosystems.

- The first type is called 'statist-macro' (for example, France and Poland). The initiatives and interventions, in terms of financing, support and legislation for social enterprise, are initiated by the national government and transnational bodies (including the European Union).
- The second type is called 'statist-micro' (for example, Scotland and Sweden). National and international interventions to fund and support social enterprise are embedded in local government and community initiatives.
- The third type is called 'private-macro' (for example, England and Germany). State funding for social enterprises is reduced while market mechanisms are encouraged with the idea that the actions of the third sector, and of social enterprise, are likely to take over public services with the help of philanthropy.
- The fourth type is called 'private-micro' (for example, Holland and Italy). State funding for social enterprises is low. Market mechanisms are privileged. They are based on the local level, via associations and regional cooperation, while benefiting from municipal funding.

While typology is interesting, it overlooks the fact that within the same country, we are often faced with different SSE ecosystems. For example, in the United Kingdom, Scotland's SSE ecosystem is more focused on the social economy, whereas England is more oriented toward social enterprise. Similarly, in Canada, Quebec's SSE ecosystem, which is dominated by historical SSE enterprises and organizations, is different from those of other provinces and territories, where social enterprise is more present. Another interesting territorial case is that of Spain, where the Basque Country is recognized for the importance and success of its cooperatives.

Finally, at the regional or local level, there are more geographically circumscribed ecosystems that are supported by public authorities. This is the case of Brazilian incubators: Technological Incubators for Popular Cooperatives (Incubadora Tecnológica de Cooperativas Populares; ITCP) or incubators of a solidarity economy and participatory democracy. This is also the case in France with the Territorial Business Clusters for Economic Cooperation (Pôles territoriaux de coopération économique; PTCE) (see entry 47, 'Local and Territorial Development Plans').

In the United States, at the city or even neighbourhood level, many incubators are also helping to lay the foundations of social enterprise ecosystems. They foster the networking of partners, organizations and enterprises to support the emergence (start-up) and development (scale-up) of social enterprises. These social enterprises seek to generate revenue from market activities for a social mission, either by offering services to a disadvantaged population or by contributing to sustainable development and the ecological transition from several sectors of activity (Sours et al. 2020).

Finally, it should be noted that these emerging ecosystems do not develop without tensions and conflicts, as can be observed in several Latin American countries (Veltmeyer 2018). For example, in Brazil, two visions are opposed: that of a social economy, which complements the economic system in place; and that of a solidarity economy, which aims to be an alternative to the capitalist system.

56.8 HOW TO IMPROVE THE INSTITUTIONAL SSE ECOSYSTEM?

The concept of an institutional SSE ecosystem is an interesting one for policy and for government interventions. It opens up more interesting options for public authorities than those associated with notions of national innovation systems. Indeed, the institutional ecosystem takes into account not only the immediate environment (for example, factors and conditions of production) but also the global environment (regulations, culture, and so on). Moreover, this approach considers not only the interactions between actors, partners and other affected entities, but also their interdependence. This makes it possible to generate transformation perspectives going beyond the isolated company and that can more easily be generalized.

For several reasons, the potential of this institutional ecosystem approach for public policy has not yet been fully realized. The regulation and even coordination of an institutional ecosystem are problematic. In addition to their number and diversity, actors and partners may make rational decisions about themselves, but these decisions may be detrimental to their own ecosystem. This is for two reasons: on the one hand, they often have a different view of the interests of the SSE and its purpose; on the other hand, very few strategic actors, including public authorities, understand the dynamics and complexity of the institutional ecosystem of the social economy.

The fact that SSE ecosystems can be circumscribed at various scales raises the question of the relevance and coherence of policies and interventions affecting higher levels. While ecosystems are often contrasted at the local and even national levels, interventions at higher levels can have highly contrasting effects, sometimes even unintended and negative effects.

To the extent that the institutional SSE ecosystem is understood as a system of innovation, the challenges mentioned above can be addressed with greater ease. Moreover, if states are to take full advantage of this ecosystem proposal, it is imperative that they understand what is new about the interdependence and broadening of relationships among ecosystem components. It is also important for them to be able to characterize the strengths of ecosystems according to their various scales of action. For states, this means using the national scale, which is the most appropriate for defining the legal framework required to ensure the self-institutionalization of an ecosystem, and thus give it a broader institutional capacity. This favours the development of institutionalization anchored at the local and regional levels, which remains an option that is very promising for supporting the emergence of social and solidarity economy enterprises.

Finally, the relevance of international bodies and organizations has also proven to be important, playing a complementary role to interventions aimed at supporting the development of national institutional SSE ecosystems. Certainly, with the creation of the International Cooperative Alliance at the end of the 19th century, the need to be part of the globalization process was quickly established as a necessity (see entry 6, 'Globalization and Alter-globalization').

In the 21st century, in the unavoidable context of social and ecological transition, the need to strengthen SSE ecosystems at all scales and in all areas is more important than ever, in order to empower an inclusive, supportive and sustainable response to the challenges of social and ecological justice (see entry 13, 'The Commons').

REFERENCES

Borzaga, Carlo, Giulia Galera, Barbara Franchini, Stefania Chiomento, Rocío Nogales and Chiara Carini. 2020. *Social Enterprises and Their Ecosystems in Europe: Comparative Synthesis Report*. Luxembourg: Publications Office of the European Union.

Chaves-Avila, Rafael, and Juan Ramon Gallego-Bono. 2020. 'Transformative Policies for the Social and Solidarity Economy: The New Generation of Public Policies Fostering the Social Economy in Order to Achieve Sustainable Development Goals. The European and Spanish Cases.' *Sustainability* 12 (10). https://doi.org/10.3390/su12104059.

Drayton, Bill, and Valeria Budinich. 2010. 'A New Alliance for Global Change.' *Harvard Business Review* 88 (9): 56–64. hbr.org/2010/09/a-new-alliance-for-global-change.

Haarich, Silke N., Frank Holstein, Sandra Spule, Giulia Galera, Barbara Franchini, Carlo Borzaga, Stefana Chiomento, Wolgang Spiess-Knafl, Barbara Scheck and Giacomo Salvatori. 2021. 'Impact of the European Commission's Social Business Initiative (SBI) and Its Follow-up Actions.' Publications Office of the European Office. https://op.europa.eu/en/publication-detail/-/publication/8731e1ac-6697-11eb-aeb5-01aa75ed71a1/language-en.

Hazenberg, Richard, Meanu Bajwa-Patel, Micaela Mazzei, Michael James Roy and Simone Baglioni. 2016. 'The Role of Institutional and Stakeholder Networks in Shaping Social Enterprise Ecosystems in Europe.' *Social Enterprise Journal* 12 (3): 302–21. https://doi.org/10.1108/sej-10-2016-0044.

Lévesque, Benoît. 2016. 'Économie Sociale et Solidaire et Entrepreneur Social: Vers Quels Nouveaux Écosystèmes?' *Interventions Économiques* 54. https://doi.org/10.4000/interventionseconomiques.2802.

Sours, Patrick, Mariela Machado and Grace Burleson. 2020. 'Social Innovation in the USA: A Landscape Analysis of Social Enterprise Incubators.' Engineering For Change. https://www.engineeringforchange.org/wp-content/uploads/2020/12/E4C-Villgro-Landscape-Analysis-USA.pdf.

Tansley, A.G. 1935. 'The Use and Abuse of Vegetational Concepts and Terms.' *Ecology* 16 (3): 284–307. https://doi.org/10.2307/1930070.

Veltmeyer, Henry. 2018. 'The Social Economy in Latin America as Alternative Development.' *Canadian Journal of Development Studies / Revue Canadienne d'Études Du Développement* 39 (1): 38–54. https://doi.org/10.1080/02255189.2017.1294052.

57. Working conditions and wages
Kunle Akingbola and Carol Brunt

INTRODUCTION

Social and solidarity economy organizations and enterprises (SSEOEs) are vibrant entities characterized by their focus on social and economic objectives. From the traditional non-profits and cooperatives to unincorporated mutual associations, community groups, social enterprises and broadly defined social movement groups, the social and solidarity economy (SSE) is a broad umbrella coalesced around social and economic objectives (see entry 3, 'Contemporary Understandings'). Irrespective of their specific mission, the SSE includes some of the top grassroots employers within their respective countries. Thus, the objectives of the SSE, the diversity of organizations and the players in the sector portend a unique context for the working conditions of employees and stakeholders of these organizations.

This entry explores working conditions and wage levels of SSEOEs in different regions, countries, sectors and of different sizes. As part of this objective, the entry highlights the challenges that small SSEOEs encounter in ensuring decent wages for their employees or members. A starting point may be the Organisation for Economic Co-operation and Development's (OECD) report on job creation in the sector in 2013: it suggests that workers within the SSE may receive lower pay and, in fact, work in perilous working conditions (OECD 2013, 13).

57.1 CHARACTERISTICS OF THE SSE WORKPLACE

To explain the working conditions of organizations in the SSE, it is important to highlight four fundamental characteristics of the SSE workplace that recognize its complexity, the primacy of its human resources, the importance of interpersonal interactions, and mission commitment.

First, SSEOEs are complex organizations. The social and economic objectives of SSEOEs implies that they hold multidimensional roles that are critical to the wellbeing of people and the effectiveness of core institutions in society. The roles of the SSEOEs, which have been categorized broadly as both expressive and instrumental (Frumkin 2002), benefit diverse demographic and interest groups in the community. Expressive roles include the services and activities of SSEOEs aimed at supporting internal stakeholders or participants, such as mutual associations and self-help groups. Instrumental roles, on the other hand, are services and activities of SSEOEs that benefit stakeholders external to the organization. Many forms of cooperatives and social enterprises are examples of SSEOEs that perform instrumental roles. However, it is common for many SSEOEs to perform both instrumental and expressive roles. The implications of the multidimensional roles require SSEOEs to: continuously interact with multiple stakeholders who sometimes have conflicting interests; navigate a more institutionalized environment that emphasizes social and cultural factors; and perennially manage resource dependency to support the mission and service delivery of the organization. The interactions and processes embedded in these roles are the major relationships that define the complexity of SSEOEs (Akingbola 2013). Since complexity underlies the environment of the SSE, it is relevant to the explanation of the working conditions of the organizations.

Second, the employees and volunteers – that is, the human resources of SSEOEs – are the most important asset of the organization. Irrespective of the type of SSE, the operations, effectiveness and growth of the SSE depend significantly on the human capital provided by employees and volunteers. In many countries, the phenomenal growth of SSEOEs over the past four decades – spurred largely by emergent community needs – revitalized social movement, downloading of services previously provided by the government, and new funding environments, accentuated the critical importance of employees and volunteers. While some of these factors may be more relevant to subsections of the SSE than others, the fact remains that employee and volunteer labour are not replaceable. Employees and volunteers are fundamental to the existence of many SSEOEs for their role in delivery of mission and essential services. Examples include supported social enterprises that are founded by people with disabilities, and associations of informal sector workers.

Third, the SSE provides goods and services, engaging in activities that typically require significant interpersonal interactions with inherent emotional components. In other words, managing interpersonal interaction and emotions are a core part of work processes in the SSE, including service delivery, stakeholder engagement, advocacy and funding relationships. The interpersonal transactions and emotional commitment to the operations and activities of the SSE have implications for the performance and outcomes that stakeholders expect from the SSE. On the one hand, employees and volunteers within the SSE must have the skills and abilities required to meet this essential job requirement and be able to work in an environment in which emotions and interpersonal transactions are important beyond what is written in a job description or role profile. On the other hand, the SSE must create and sustain a work environment that incorporates consideration and flexibility for interpersonal transactions to achieve the goals of the organization.

Fourth, employees and volunteers of the SSE tend to have an inherent commitment to the mission and values of the organization. This means that SSE employees and volunteers are attracted to the social objectives of the organization which, in turn, highlight the importance of intrinsic motivation factors to them. This alignment between objectives and values among employees, volunteers and stakeholders influence how the behaviour patterns play out in the working conditions of the SSE. For example, SSE employees typically volunteer their time to participate in activities of the organization beyond the specific tasks in their job description.

Together, the four fundamental characteristics of the SSE workplace highlight the broad underlying contextual factors of the working conditions of the SSE, irrespective of country, subsector and organizational size. The characteristics are important to understanding not only the operating realities of the SSE, but also how employee and volunteer working conditions are an integral part of internal and external system and process issues that define work and employment in the SSE. As a result, working conditions and related challenges have implications for the ability of SSEOEs to respond to opportunities to achieve their mission and address threats to organizational survival.

57.2 COMPONENTS OF WORKING CONDITIONS AND WAGES

Working conditions are the core elements of work relationships determined by the social, psychological and physical factors that influence the workplace and the interaction that employees experience at work. Regardless of the type of work, working conditions typically include the nature of employment, working hours, job characteristics, compensation, work interactions, physical work environment, and written and unwritten work expectations. The working conditions of SSEOEs are related to the characteristics that define the unique context of the organizations and social enterprises. Given that the knowledge, skills and engagement of employees and volunteers are critical to organizational performance, the SSE must understand the importance of working conditions in driving employment relationships, which are essential to meeting organizational goals. It is therefore necessary to review the dimensions and trends in SSE working conditions.

SSE Work is Labour-Intensive

The labour-intensive nature of working conditions stems from the fact that service delivery is a direct interpersonal exchange between the employee and the consumer. Since the services of the SSE, including economic and financial services, are often personal and social in nature, the activities and operations are entirely dependent on employee and volunteer labour. Employees and volunteers routinely work and support clients beyond scheduled working hours. The intensive labour environment translates into heightened working conditions that leave little flexibility for employees and volunteers. Accountability is emphasized and enforced to the detriment of both the employee and organization wellbeing. Ultimately, achieving organizational objectives will not happen without competent and committed employees and volunteers.

Compensation is Low

Employees within SSEOEs generally receive lower compensation compared to business and public sector organizations. Although the differential may be minimal or non-existent, the average compensation for managerial and professional categories of SSE employees are generally lower than those of their comparative categories in the other sectors. Low pay in SSEOEs is a major factor in employee recruitment and retention challenges. British Council-sponsored surveys conducted over a period of five years find that staff and volunteer recruitment pose operational challenges for SSEOEs. The following examples illustrate the variance across surveyed countries: 17 per cent of SSEOEs in Thailand report recruitment challenges, 40 per cent in Vietnam, 29 per cent in Indonesia, 33 per cent in Malaysia, and 11 per cent in Sudan (British Council 2021).

Employees Participate in Decision Making

Whether explicitly or implicitly, the working conditions of SSEOEs tend to present opportunities for employees and volunteers to participate in decision making in their organization (see also entry 50, 'Partnership and Co-construction'). Since most SSEOEs are small and operate a close-knit workplace, there is an inherent opportunity for employees to participate in decision making. Moreover, the practice is related to the values of the SSE that emphasize democratic and egalitarian principles. Based on this value orientation, SSE employees tend to provide inputs on varied organizational systems and processes, including services, project and strategic planning, and governance. The opportunity to participate in decision making is a source of intrinsic benefit that reinforces the congruence of values between the employees and the SSE, thus enhancing the commitment of employees. The Association of Finnish Work encourages social enterprises to provide employees with an opportunity to participate in decision making, including in relation to working conditions (European Commission 2015, 83–4).

Contingency (Precarious) Contract

SSEOEs generally offer jobs based on temporary and other forms of contingency employment contracts. The adoption of contingency staffing practices, including part-time, casual and temporary employment arrangements, means that working conditions are tenuous at best. Employees often work on unstable contracts and are barely integrated within organizations before the employment contract ends. Employees do not get the opportunity to understand the mission and values of the organization. The revolving door of temporary and casual employees is a major factor in the significant employee turnover in the SSE. Similarly, this working condition affects the quality of work life, health and wellbeing of SSE employees. Contingency employment creates job insecurity and increases employee vulnerability, thereby creating greater commonality between SSE employees and the clients using SSE services.

Informal Working Conditions

In many SSE organizations, especially unincorporated mutual associations, community organizations and social enterprises, working conditions are primarily informal. Employees in these organizations may not have written employment contracts, job descriptions and performance expectations. Often a lack of clear delineation between work and interpersonal activities makes it difficult to differentiate between employees, volunteers and stakeholders who are directly involved in organizational activities. There are no policies and procedures to guide the practices and processes of the SSE. The informal working conditions are generally related to the small size of many SSEOEs. While informality is challenging from an employee perspective, job creation itself translates into positive community impact and economic benefits in many countries (British Council 2021).

Employment Benefits are Favourable

SSEOEs typically offer competitive benefits that demonstrate a commitment to employee wellbeing (Chen et al. 2014). In some segments of the SSE, the range of employee benefits is comparable to those in the business and public sectors in countries such as Canada, the United States and the United Kingdom (UK). Despite generous vacation and paid leave in some instances, only large SSEOEs are likely to offer such compensation packages.

Voluntary Labour

SSE depends on volunteer labour to complement staff in areas of service provision, organizational management and governance. For SSEOEs, volunteers are an important source of human resources for the organization (see also entry 25, 'Culture, Sports and Leisure Sectors'). Research shows that the contribution of volunteer labour to SSEOEs is growing faster than that of employees (Baines et al. 2014). In addition, SSEOEs rely significantly on the voluntary effort of employees to meet their operational and management needs. The role of volunteers in the co-production of outputs alongside employees, and the interchangeability of these roles, are key factors in SSE working conditions. Although co-production is a useful tool for the human capital pool available to the SSE, the working conditions that it facilitates could be considered a challenge to the organization.

Labour Cost

A major factor in SSE working conditions is labour cost. The SSEOEs must continuously grapple with funding and revenue pressures that require them to manage and balance their need for qualified staff with the financial sustainability of the organization. Short- and long-term staffing plans are not possible, and training to equip the employees and volunteers with the knowledge and skills to perform on the job are generally beyond the available financial resources of the SSE. The constant and significant challenge of labour costs inhibit the ability of SSEOEs to plan and implement policies and practices that have direct implications for working conditions of employees and volunteers. This challenge became apparent during surveys in 2016, in SSEOEs in both Bangladesh and Pakistan which included team investment and capacity-building in their growth plans (British Council 2021). Since labour cost is a constant challenge, related workplace costs, including costs of technology and resources that support work processes, are out of reach. Labour cost is a factor in the increasing use of voluntary labour in some SSEOEs.

Accountability

In response to environmental factors, especially funding and competition in social enterprises, SSE working conditions emphasize accountability. Accountability means developing, implementing and evaluating organizational outputs and outcomes. These are typically tied to measures of organizational effectiveness and, therefore, the working conditions of employees and volunteers. Accountability requirements play out in multiple ways. From narrowing the focus of recruitment and performance management, to displacing the skills highlighted in training objectives, accountability means that organizations in the SSE must stick only to measures of outcomes dictated by the funder and dominant stakeholder. Since accountability is an important source of social legitimacy for the SSE, working conditions of employees and volunteers include the burden of responsibility to implement and evaluate imposed measures of service and programme outcomes.

Mission and Values

The mission and values of the organization underlie the working conditions of SSE. Job descriptions, work processes, interactions and outcomes are predicated on the conflicting importance of concepts relating to the mission and values of the SSE. On the one hand, mission and values provide the reference point or base line for the type of working conditions that the SSE would implement and support in the organization. From this angle, the mission and values

Table 57.1   Working conditions and wages in the SSE

Characteristics	Working conditions	Challenges	Recommendations
Complexity (domain or operating environment)	Mission and values Multiple stakeholders Multidimensional roles	Government Funding Resource dependence	Revise regulatory frameworks to promote new funding relationships Create new SSEOEs separate from NPO structures
Staff and volunteers as critical asset (operational level)	Supports this characteristic: • Employee benefits • Volunteer labour • Mission and values Undermines recognition of value of staff and volunteers: • Labour-intensive • Low compensation • Informality • Mission and values	Small workplaces Business professionalization Funding and financial resources Low compensation and lack of human resource development (HRD)	Changes to employment regulations encourage investment in improved working conditions
Primacy of interpersonal relations and emotional commitment (operational level)	Supports this characteristic: • Participation in decision making Undermines development of interpersonal relations and emotional commitment: • Contingency contracting • Accountability	Business professionalization	Engage employees and volunteers Optimize co-production
Commitment to mission (organizational level)	Undermines this characteristic: • Contingency contracting • Labour costs • Accountability (measure only what told to)	Mission drift	Leverage mission and values

are a key part of the employment brand that is used to attract, recruit and retain employees and volunteers. On the other hand, the mission and values can become an albatross for the organization if the mission is derailed or de-emphasized by the realities of the complex operating environment. Similarly, employees and volunteers are likely to experience job dissatisfaction if the values of the organization are not reflected in the working conditions of the SSE. Thus, the mission and values of SSEOEs are an inherently challenging component of the working conditions.

Summary

The pictures of working conditions and wages highlight the critical dimensions of employment relations in the SSE. While the points explained above are the core overview of working conditions that are consistent across continents and countries, there are regional and national variations that are relative to the social, economic and political context of the region. Components of working conditions and wages in the SSE are summarized in Table 57.1.

57.3 CHALLENGES IN IMPROVING WORKING CONDITIONS

The components of the working conditions and wages in the SSE have inherent and dynamic challenges that the organization must address to improve employment relations and volunteer management. Each of the factors highlighted in the working conditions has challenges that are unique to the sector. However, it is important to highlight the following as major challenges to consider in the effort to improve working conditions.

Small Workplace

SSEOEs are typically small organizations. Irrespective of the country, most SSEOEs are very small and therefore likely to have informal structures and organizational practices based on interpersonal factors. The small size of the SSEOE workplace also means there are limited human resource capacities and financial resources to support improvement of working conditions and risk management related to working conditions. For example, most SSEOEs in the UK and Canada are unincorporated, and those that are incorporated have less than 20 employees.

Business Professionalization

The need to address the funding, accountability and competition challenges has resulted in a wholesale shift to business-oriented professionalization in the SSE (see also entry 44, 'Co-optation, Isomorphism and Instrumentalisation' and entry 48, 'Management'). This is creating tension and contradiction in the policies and practices of the SSE. The advantages of the organizational mission and values that attract employees and volunteers are negated by business-like approaches that permeate working conditions. While efficiency goals and evidence-based management practices are important, business professionalization erodes the core psychological contract that is based on the mission and values. This transforms the orientation of SSE working conditions away from long-term sustainability to short-term survival-based intrapreneurial discretion (Canet-Giner et al. 2010).

Funding and Financial Resources

Social enterprises face particular challenges in improving working conditions and wage levels. A lack of access to funding, whether in the form of capital, grant funding or cash flow, poses significant challenges for organizations in achieving their social and economic goals (see also entry 45, 'Financing'). These financial barriers also limit the ability of social enterprises to increase wage levels and improve working conditions, due to limited investment and operational resources.

An example of such funding challenges is in Romania, where banking regulation classifies nonprofit social enterprises as high risk, thus limiting access to institutional finance (European Commission 2015, 98). Further compounding the financial challenges is the definition of nonprofit organizations that prevents the distribution of profits and renders organizations unattractive to the majority of external investors, who might otherwise provide loans to SSE organizations (European Commission 2015, 94).

Low Compensation and Lack of Investment in Human Resource (HR) Development

The difference in salary between public, for-profit and SSE employees is compounded relative to its comparable position. However, regardless of the scope of salary differences, the inability to offer competitive compensation is a major challenge to attracting and retaining employees. Low pay raises questions about the viability of SSEOEs as supportive places of work.

Moreover, despite acknowledging existing challenges in staff and volunteer recruitment, few SSEOEs invest in team development and capacity-building. In Slovakia, employment regulations stipulate that: 'At least 30 percent of financial resources gained from own activities that remain after paying all costs associated with own activities must be re-invested into creation of new job positions or into improving working conditions' (European Commission 2015, 117). However, this provision for organizational investment in staff and volunteers is not the norm.

Government

Social enterprises and their mutual counterparts have varying degrees of interaction with the government; a relationship that is critical to the organizational effectiveness of SSEOEs. Government policies and programmes are an important underlying factor in the working conditions of SSEOEs. For SSEOEs that depend on government funding, the relationship directly influences the structural challenges of the organization. Low pay and precarious employment are two relevant examples. The inability of SSEOEs to plan and implement employment policies that reflect the unique characteristics of their organization is due, in part, to the lack of government legislation that correctly classifies many types of SSE. In many countries, a significant number of SSEOEs are not incorporated or registered due to this gap in government classification. This in turn impacts upon the working conditions and employment relations of SSEOEs.

Summary

The challenges of working conditions are particularly emblematic of the unique environment that characterizes the context of the SSE. Together with the components of working conditions and wages, the challenges highlight the need to prioritize issues required for the attainment of organizational goals. Whatever SSE organizations undertake to address the challenges of working conditions and wages, these initiatives must integrate both external and internal environmental factors with the mission and values of the organization.

CONCLUDING REMARKS: RECOMMENDATIONS

The challenges of working conditions and wages in the SSE are multifaceted, and unique in many ways. However, there are numerous opportunities for organizations in the SSE to improve working conditions and mitigate the existing challenges and their impacts. The opportunities are presented here as recommendations for the sector.

Reinforce the Organizational Mission

The mission of the SSE is the most unique value proposition of the organization. It communicates the problem(s) the SSE intends to address and the people it wants to serve. It is the most important factor underlying the working conditions of SSEOEs. By adhering to the mission, the working conditions are shaped by organizational policies and practices and guided by mission principles.

Define Strategy

SSEOEs need to define a clear workplace or human resources strategy to guide the coordinated steps towards the achievement of their organizational objectives in relation to working conditions. The strategy should articulate the external opportunities and challenges, outline the internal resources to be allocated, and address the process of challenging any threats to the organization. By outlining a clear human resources strategy, the SSE is driving employee and volunteer motivation and commitment to the organization. Through the strategy, employees and volunteers understand the behaviours required to support organizational objectives, and their role in the process of strategic implementation. Strategy links the performance of employees and volunteers to the outcomes and mission of the organization.

Engage Employees and Volunteers

Employees and volunteers are at the core of SSE working conditions. Moreover, as stakeholders who are attracted to the mission and values of the SSE, and essential to effective operations, it is imperative that employees and volunteers be engaged. In fact, the SSE must encourage employees and volunteers to lead the process of developing workplace policies and practices, and helping to effectively position the organization to address its challenges in the environment. Engaging employees and volunteers means enabling employees and volunteers to bring their input and learning from the front line into planning and implementation of practices on working conditions.

Enhance the Skill Set of Managers

The unique characteristics and context of SSEOEs require employees and managers to possess distinct skills specific to the SSE environment. The challenges of working conditions are an integral part of the context. Thus, the management talent pool must have the required knowledge and skills to effectively prioritize, adapt and manage SSE working conditions. Enhancing the skill set of employees and managers will equip SSEOEs with the necessary competencies to address the dynamic challenges of the working conditions.

Optimize Co-production

SSEOEs should deploy the talent pool and promote seamless collaboration between employees and volunteers for service delivery and organization management. This should be done through co-production, by orienting employees and volunteers to develop interchangeability of mutual support roles. Co-production between volunteers and employees has the benefit of enhancing the human resources pool. It is an advantage that SSEOEs could leverage to mitigate the challenges posed by working conditions, and replace the subtle but existing tension that arises with employees' concerns that their roles could be substituted with volunteers.

Enhance Access to Funding Mechanisms

SSEOEs would like to invest in their staff through capacity-building programmes and other initiatives as well as improved working conditions and wages. By enhancing access to funding mechanisms through a combination of recommendations, SSEOEs can focus on overcoming hurdles posed by challenges of limited access to financial resources.

Summary

A revision of employment regulations into regulatory frameworks would ease the process of financial investment, facilitating the ability of investors to provide much-needed capital to SSEOEs. Encouraging nonprofit organizations to create separate social enterprises, operating at arm's length, is an option to enhance access to external investor loans. Revising employment regulations will require SSEOEs to invest a percentage of profits towards improving working conditions

Due to their basic characteristics, working conditions and wages are critical to the mission and effectiveness of the SSE. Working conditions underpin how and what SSEOEs do to attract, motivate and retain employees and volunteers. At its heart, these are fundamental to the community problem-solving and social transformation roles of the SSE.

REFERENCES

Akingbola, K. 2013. 'A Model of Strategic Nonprofit Human Resource Management.' *Voluntas* 24 (1): 214–40. https://doi.org/10.1007/s11266-012-9286-9.

Baines, Donna, Ian Cunningham, John Campey and John Shields. 2014. 'Not Profiting from Precarity: The Work of Nonprofit Service Delivery and the Creation of Precariousness.' *Just Labour: A Canadian Journal of Work and Society* 22: 74–93. https://doi.org/10.25071/1705-1436.6.

British Council. 2021. *The State of Social Enterprise*. https://www.britishcouncil.org/society/social-enterprise/reports/state-social-enterprise.

Canet-Giner, Maria Teresa, Rafael Fernández-Guerrero and Marta Peris-Ortiz. 2010. 'Changing the Strategy Formation Process in a Service Cooperative.' *Journal of Organizational Change Management* 23 (4): 435–52. https://doi.org/10.1108/09534811011055412.

Chen, Xinxiang, Ting Ren and David Knoke. 2014. 'Do Nonprofits Treat Their Employees Differently? Incentive Pay and Health Benefits.' *Nonprofit Management and Leadership* 24 (3): 285–306. https://doi.org/10.1002/nml.21093.

European Commission. 2015. 'A Map of Social Enterprises and Their Eco-systems in Europe.' https://ec.europa.eu/social/BlobServlet?docId=12987&langId=en.

Frumkin, Peter. 2002. *On Being Nonprofit: A Conceptual and Policy Primer*. Cambridge, MA: Harvard University Press.

OECD. 2013. 'Job Creation through the Social Economy and Social Entrepreneurship.' https://www.oecd.org/cfe/leed/130228_Job%20Creation%20throught%20the%20Social%20Economy%20and%20Social%20Entrepreneurship_RC_FINALBIS.pdf.

Index

advocacy 404
absolutism 119
access to finance 356
access to land 225, 226
accountability 454, 456, 458
accumulation of wealth 289
Action Emploi Réfugiés (AER) xxi, 152
Action Plan 397
action research 13
active citizenship 21, 25, 388, 389, 390, 391
active labor-market-initiatives 300
active labour market policies (ALMPs) 334
active learning 204, 206
activism 2
actors 19, 23
ad hoc pragmatic responses 396
administrative architecture 396
administrative unit 374
advisory services 440
advocacy 379
aesthetic rationality 64
affordable housing 248, 249, 252, 254
African American cooperative ownership 110
African Americans 76, 92, 107, 108
African diaspora 40, 95
Agenda for Sustainable Development 317
agentivity 65
agriculture 224, 225, 226, 227, 228, 229, 338
agroecological consumer-producer movements 4
agroecology 225, 227, 228, 229, 285, 286
Aldrich, H.E. 382
Alexander 143
Alford, Robert R. 353
alliance network 382
alliance partnership 386
Almería 303, 304
alter-globalization 2, 6, 7, 8, 44, 69
   and SSE 46
alter-globalization movement 6, 46
alternative purchasing 308
altruism-based international scaling strategies 49, 50
Alvord 277
América Latina 16
Amigos Siempre Amigos (ASA) 144
Amul Dairy cooperative 135
anarchism 117
Andalucían 303

Andean insurgency 101
animacy 65
antagonisms 97
Anthropocene 17
anti-black white supremacist violence 16
anti-colonialist social movements 74
anti-globalization 8
Antigonish movement 4
apex bodies 344
A Post-Capitalist Politics 410
Arctic Cooperative Limited 411
Aristotle 59
Arnstein, S.R. 392
artisanal fisheries 228
Ashoka organisation 164, 447, 448
Asia Solidarity Economy Council (ASEC) 8
ASSEFA 205
assessment guidelines 89, 90
assets 358
assistentialist social policy model 406
associationalism 56, 58, 73, 75, 76, 113, 115, 116, 118
   as mutualism 113
associationalist socialism 113
Association for Sarva Seva farms (ASSEFA) 204, 318
Association of Finnish Work 455
associations 113
Associations pour le Maintien d'une Agriculture Paysanne (AMAP) 292
associative governance 392
associativism 103
asylum seekers 147, 148, 149, 150, 151, 152, 153
awareness-raising strategies 380

B2B markets 338
B2C markets 339, 343
Badgett 139
banking services 218
Bank Rakyat Indonesia (BRI) 174
Barcelona 377, 435
Barcelona Activa 435, 436
Basaglia-law 298
Bateman, Milford 413
Being Black in the EU 87
Belgium 197
beneficiary organisations 350
Benkler, Yochai 257

Bhabha, Homi 84
Bilbao 398
Bill and Melinda Gates Foundation (BMGF) 159, 160, 161
bioeconomics 55, 58
biological markers 62
Bion, Herman Walter 323
Birchall, Johnston 411
Black cooperatives 108
Black Lives Matter 16
Black organizations 74
Black-owned businesses 108
Black Political Economy
    defining 92
Black Social Economy 92, 95
blame deferring 274
Blanc, Louis 118, 285
blended value 167
Borowiak 278
Borzaga, J. A. C. 107, 382
bottom-linked governance 297
bottom-up radicalism 288
Boulding, Kenneth E. 27
Brazil 5, 289, 374, 378
British Council 413, 454
Brundtland Report 29
budget 380
Buen Vivir 21, 63
Bukari 277
Burundi 272
business law 345
business plan 385
business professionalization 458

Cabo Verdean law 369
Caire, Gilles 367
Cajamar 304
Cameroonian law 369
Canada 383, 395
Canadian Constitution 398
Canuts 114
capacity-building 342, 437, 438
capitalism 23, 42, 44, 54, 56, 58, 73, 99, 113, 115, 119, 287, 371
capitalist accumulation 99
capitalist economic sector 269
capitalist market 268
Capitalocentrism 13
care 41
caste 238
CBOs 123, 124, 125, 126, 127, 129
    general trends in 128
    organizational structure of 125
    partnership of 126
    suggestions for improvements in 128

various areas of activities of 124
Chambres Régionales de l'Économie Sociale et Solidaire (CRESS) 436
Chantier de l'économie sociale Trust 363
charity-based food banks 283
charity-based solutions 281
Charpak, Georges 160
Chartreuse de Neuville 158
Charusheela 85, 88
CHETNA 127
China 293
Chinmaya Organization for Rural Development (CORD) 125
Chomsky, Noam 118
Christenson, James A. 122
CICOPA 51
circular economy 209, 210, 211, 213, 214, 307
circularity 214
circular water reuse 212
city building 268
City of Montreal 398
civic activism 149
civic learning 296
civil society 156, 159, 329, 421, 446
Civil Society Mechanism 227
civil society mobilization 378
civil society organizations (CSOs) 113, 158
civil war 76
class 232, 237, 238
classical economic science 68
clientelism 378
climate change 209, 214, 227
climate change prevention 373
CO/CBO
    origins of and developments in 122
co-construction 376, 377, 379, 394, 395, 396, 397, 403, 406
    feasibility 397
    law 397
    networks 398
    public policy 347, 398, 402
    SSE actors 398
co-design of policy 395
co-development processes 287
coercive isomorphism 350
coexistence 12
COEXPHAL 304
coffee cooperatives 275
collaboration 394, 395
collaborative enterprise 276
collective artistic creation 197
Collective Courage: A History of African American Cooperative Economic Thought and Practice 93
collective decision making 17, 46

collective dignity 75
collective identity 3, 6, 7
collective intelligence 396, 399
collective ownership 106
collective socio-economic empowerment 232
collective tourist accommodation 324
Colombia 5
colonialism 84
colonization 73
commercialisation 65
commercial non-profit approach 163
commodification 71
commodities 55
common 100
commonalities 22
common goods 100
common-pool resources (CPR) 98
commons 97, 101, 228
    and social and solidarity economy 102
    from antagonistic point of view 99
communalism 110
communication 44, 369
community 121, 250, 252
community-based health insurance (CBHI) schemes 418, 419
community-based irrigation management 212
community-based organizations (CBOs) 121, 319
community-based peacebuilding 272
community benefit 273
community-care 300
community consumption 267
community cooperatives 298
community development (CD) 121
community economy (CE) 12, 17, 65, 316, 318, 319, 410
community education 196
Community Gardens 283
community labour 74
community land trust (CLT) 226, 249, 282, 283
community networks 101
community organisation (CO) 121, 296
community-owned pawn shops 318, 319
community relations 268
Community Services Programme (CSP) 331
community-supported agriculture (CSA) 225, 227, 228, 283, 284, 292
community tourism 325
comparability 425
competitive labour force 200
complementarity 62, 69, 71
complementary policy 372
Concrete development dynamics (Lebret) 264
consumption 64
contemporary associationalism 117
contract 455
control-based international scaling strategies 49
conveyor belt 330
Coopérative Agricole Kavokiva du Haut Sassandra (CAKHS) 290
cooperative banks 216, 218, 219, 221
cooperative business education 201
cooperative businesses 105
cooperative business ownership 108
Cooperative Business Studies 201
cooperative economic efforts 93
cooperative economics 105
Cooperative Home Care Associates (CHCA) 288
Cooperative laws 319
cooperative movement 131
    origins of 133
co-operatives 205
cooperatives 77, 78, 106, 131, 132, 134, 135, 136, 219, 244, 245, 250, 251, 274, 275, 307
    benefits and impacts 105
    impact of 134
Cooperatives Act (1997) 325
Cooperatives and Mutuals Canada 344
Cooperatives and Mutual Societies (CIRIEC 2006) 428
cooperative structure 304
Coopérative Taitmatine 288
Cooperative Unit of Durban 376
cooperativism 133, 134, 261
cooperatization 79
Co-op Network Studies (CNS) 202
co-optation 348, 351
coordination process 373
    national governments 374
    public agency 374
co-partnership 292
Copenhagen Declaration 241
Coraggio 346
corporate performance 386
corporate social responsibilities (CSR) 281, 351, 385
corporations
    internationalization of 45
cosmovisions 101
Council of Local Governments on the Social Solidarity Economy (CLGSSE) 437
Covid-19 lockdown 379
Covid-19 pandemic 199, 255, 260, 281, 296, 316, 318, 383, 398, 399, 411, 412, 414
CPRs 98
CREA (Creating Resources for Empowerment and Action) 143
creative commons 257
credit scoring systems 222

Crichton 204
critical entrepreneurship studies (CES) 85
criticism 177, 178
crowdfunding 222
cultural democracy 196
cultural determinants 84
cultural dimension 322
cultural groups 196
culture 85, 194, 196, 197
Curl, John 133
Cusicanqui, Rivera 101

Dalits 129
Daly, Herman 27, 33
Dardot 100
Dasgupta 306
Daston, Lorraine 68
debt 360
de Castro, Viveiros 63
decentralized planning program 347
decision making 14, 388, 396, 454
Declaration of Human Rights 321
decolonisation 366
Deendayal Antyodaya Yojana-National Rural Livelihoods Mission (DAY-NRLM) 173
Dees, J. Gregory 165
Defourny, J. 163, 165, 382
degrowth 308
deinstitutionalization 187
deliberative citizenship 389, 390, 391, 392
Delmar, F. 382
democracy 73, 388, 389, 396
    spillover 390
democratic decision making 396
democratic dimension 322
democratic governance 183, 389, 391, 429
democratic government 301
democratic management 284, 388
    organizational 389, 390
    societal 390, 391
democratic management model 389
democratic possibilities 59
democratic self-administration 292
democratic social change 59
democratic solidarity 71, 75, 80
democratic sovereignty
    weakening of 45
democratisation 59, 81, 194, 195, 196, 197
dependent people 191
Design Thinking approach 204
Desjardins 134
de Sousa Santos, Boaventura 371
dialogic cooperation 396
dialogue 394, 395, 396, 398
digital commons 256, 257

digital economy 255
Digital Livelihoods Program 205
digital technologies 255
DiMaggio, Paul J. 349, 350
direct communication 296
dis/ability 238
disadvantaged groups 330
disciplinary boundaries 396
distributive justice 105
Diverse Economies Iceberg 13
diversity 170
Doan 141
Doc Servizi 197
domestic domain 66, 67
domestic economies 46
domestic workers' cooperatives 41
Doughnut economy 308
Drew, Benjamin 134
Du Bois, W.E.B. 74, 108, 134
Durban 376
Dussel 84
dynamic inequalities 290
dysfunctional management 378

Early Childhood Environmental Rating Scale (ECERS) 246
Earthworker Cooperative 290
ecclesiastical movement 5
ecoagrobiodiversity 227
ecological economics 27, 28, 29, 30, 31, 32, 33, 34, 35
    and sustainability 29
    as transdiscipline 28
ecological ecosystems 443
ecology and system 443
economic activity 273
economic autonomy 114
economic backwardness 76
economic crisis 290
economic democracy 110
economic determinism 59
economic development 139, 141
economic dimension 164, 322
economic empowerment 421
economic federalism 116
economic globalization 45, 46
economic incentives 289
economic inequalities 289
economic instability 45
economic integration 63, 66
economic integration principles 67
economic liberalization 45
economic power 116, 177
economic reality 388
economic reductionism 57

economic sociology 53, 54
economic strands 85
economic success 38
economic system 281, 286
economic volatility 15
economic wealth 289
economism 81
economy 165, 265, 268, 388, 410
ecosystem 443
ecosystemic approach 402
ecosystem services 32
education 88, 231, 403, 439
Education and Inspections Act (2006) 420
education policy 418
education sector 200
education systems 181
educators 204
Eendragt Maakt 133
efficiency 266
egalitarian reciprocity 56
Eisenhardt, K. 386
Ekonpolo platform 398
El Amanecer de los Cartoneros 290
elitism 194
emancipation 196
emancipatory project 21
EMES International Research Network (EMES) 163, 164, 315
employees 453, 455, 460
employment 209, 281
employment benefits 455
"employment-oriented" organizations 259
employment regulations 459
empowerment 196, 231, 235, 237, 295, 297, 301
empresas recuperadas 132
EnerGea Tecnologia Sostenible 182
energy 209, 210, 211, 215
England 74, 77
Enspiral 258, 262
entrepreneurial dimension 164
entrepreneurial ecosystems 443
entrepreneurial mindset 183, 184
entrepreneurial nonprofits (ENP) 166, 168, 332
entrepreneurship 74
environmental consequences 46
environmental dimension 322
environmental movement 69
environmental protection programmes 377
environmental, social and governance (ESG) 356
epistemological surveillance 67
equality 138
equity 362
equity investments 219
equity-sharing 136
ergotherapy 298

Estilo Diversa 142
Estonia 251
ethical bank 218, 219
ethics of care 187, 190
Ethiquable 343
ethnicity 237, 238
Euricse 243
Eurocentric bias 83
Europe 74, 290
European Action Plan for Social Economy 315
European Commission 305, 397, 447
European Community Humanitarian Office program (ECHO) 160
European Economic and Social Committee 438
European Social Fund (ESF) 330
European Structural and Investment Funds (ESIF) 330
European Union 161, 195, 447
Euskal Herriko ikastolak 206
EU Urban Agenda Housing Partnership 249
evaluation 380
everyday peace 273
external environmental conditions 386
extractivism 289

factor C 267
Fairbairn, John 133
fairness 27
Fairphone 259
fair trade 80
'Familia Galan' 143
family foundations 217
Farmers' Alliance 76
Fassin, Didier 68
FE 38
   and social provisioning approach 38
federal economic governments 114
Federici, Silvia 99, 100
feminism 94
feminist economics (FE) 37
feminist movement 231
feminists 410
Ferreira 411
FE scholarship 38, 42
finance entity 305
finance mechanisms 363
finance sector 216, 217, 356
financial capital 45
financial co-operatives 411
financial crisis 15
financial goals 306
financial instruments 357, 362, 363
financialisation 70
financial mechanisms 356, 357
financial motivation 306

financial resources 356, 357, 364
financial support 441
financing 356
financing sustainable growth 305
Fiol, M.C. 382
first-generation neoliberalism 70
"first" to "second" generation policies 401
fiscal incentives 403
fisheries 228
flexibility 397
food access 282
food sovereignty 224, 226, 283
forced labour 73
formal relations 437
for-profit organizations (FPOs) 240, 246
Fórum Brasileiro de Economia Solidária (FBES) 436, 438
Forum for the Empowerment of Women (FEW) 144
foundation 155
Foundation for Public Interest (FPI) 127, 156
four essential freedoms 256
Fourier, Charles 416
Framework Act on Social Economy (FASE) 383
France 4, 75, 79, 195, 197
Franco Basaglia 298
Freedom Farm Collective (FFC) 95
free-market competition 379
Free Software Foundation (FSF) 256, 257
Freire, Paolo 123
Fribourg Declaration 197
Friedland, Roger 353
full economic empowerment 235
FUNDELAM 178
funding and financial resources 458
funding mechanisms 461
fund manager 94

Galera 107
Gallup 250
Gängeviertel 198
GATE 142
GCOOP 344
gender diversity 236
gender equality 231, 232, 233, 235, 236, 237
gender-equitable SSE 42
gender inequalities 39, 69, 123, 238
   conceptualizing and addressing 40
gender justice 123
gender relations 236
General Agreement on Tariffs and Trade (GATT) 226
Genossenchaftsverband 205
'Genuine Progress Indicator' (GPI) 33
Georgescu-Roegen, Nicolas 27

German partnership 159
German SOLAWI 285
Ghana 277
Gibson-Graham, J.K. 12, 13, 41
Gide, Charles 416
gig economyss 255
global development organizations 409
global economic crisis 383
global economic framework 444
global equilibrium 29
global financial crisis 16, 34
global financial crisis (2008-9) 379, 413
globalization 44, 45, 46, 48
   consequences of 45
global movement 6
Global North 83, 84, 138, 141, 143, 187
global or supranational processes 315
Global Social Economy Forum (GSEF) 438
global social movement 7
Global South 58, 83, 84, 86, 122, 123, 125, 143, 172, 346
GMF 220
GNU/Linux 256
good human life 322
governance 240, 396, 397, 403
governance-related dimension 164
Government 179, 459
government agencies 126
Governmental NGOs (GNGOs) 157
government funding 423
government partnership 157
governments 191, 339, 345
Graham, Gibson 410
Grameen Bank (GB) 173
grant-making 217
grant-making foundations 217
grants 217, 359, 362
grassroots communities 317
Great Depression 109
Green growth 308
green revolutions' 161
GRIN 142
group liability 173
group scale 284
guarantee mutual funds (GMF) 220
guarantees 220
Guatemalan indigenous governance 101
Guggenheim effect 199
Guidelines for Local Governments on Policies for Social and Solidarity Economy 380
Guillotte, Claude-Andre 201
Gujarat 278
Gung-Ho (Gōngyè Hézuòshè: Industrial Cooperatives) 132
Gutiérrez 101

Guuroh 277

Hamer, Fannie Lou 95
Handbook on Non-profit Institutions in the System of National Accounts (UN 2003) 428
Hansalim 4
Hardin, Garret 97
Hardt, Michael 100
harmonization 397
Hayek, Friedrich 70
Haynes, Curtis 93
Hazenberg, Richard 448
health and care expenses 247
health and care sector 240, 241, 242, 245, 246
health cooperatives 242, 243, 244
health facilities 244
Helem 144
heterodox economics 53
heterogeneous indigenous economies 61
heterosexist culture 140
heterosexuality 140
higher education 200
High-Level Political Forum (HLPF) 310, 312
high-technology components 259
holiday camps 323
holiday centres 324
holistic approach 150, 151
home services 190
home support services 187, 188, 189, 191
homo economicus 38
homonationalism 143
homosexuality 138
horizontal structure 300
Hospice du Grand Saint Bernard 323
hospitality 323
Hossein, Caroline Shenaz 40, 92, 95
Hotokusha 133
householding 55
housing 248, 249, 250, 251, 252, 253
housing cooperatives 248, 249, 251
Hudson, Lauren 16
human-centered design 206
human development 322
'Human Development Index (HDI)' 34
human dimension 322
human economy 27, 68, 69, 70, 71
    SSE as 70
human motivations 38
human resource (HR) 459, 460
hunger 281, 286, 292
hybrid international scaling strategies 49, 50
hybridisation logics 353
hybridization 189, 190
hybrid strategies 50

ICSEM 333, 334
identity-based inequalities 287, 288
IGLYO 142
ILGA World 142
ILGLaw 142
ILO Guidelines Concerning the Statistics of Cooperatives 209, 431
impact measurement 430
impetus 377
inclusion 253
income-generating activities 177
income inequality 289
INCOOP 203
Incubadora Tecnológica de Cooperativas Populares (ITCP) 5
incubating services 440
Independent Living Movement 187
indigenous aesthetics 64
indigenous communities 61, 65, 67
indigenous economies 61, 62, 63, 64, 65, 66
    key aspects in 61
indigenous organizations 78
individual sector networks 398
industrial agriculture 224, 225, 227
industrial networks 386
Industrial Revolution 133
inequalities 45, 88, 326
inferior care 246
informal economy 23
informal peace 273
informal relations 438
informal working conditions 455
Information and communications technologies (ICT) 255
    platform cooperatives 260
    SSEOEs 256
    threats and opportunities 261
    user-centred applications 260
    users and operators 259
information asymmetry 384, 385
Initiatives de travail de milieu auprès des aînés en situation de vulnérabilité (ITMAV) 190
InnoBa 436
innovation 181, 197, 241, 252, 297, 344, 396, 397
innovation theory 396
innovative community-based care approaches 296
innovative educational model 184
innovativeness 383
innovative projects 383
institutional architecture 398
institutional ecosystem 443, 444, 449
    SSE 444
institutional environments 382

institutionalism 352
institutional isomorphism 80, 189, 327, 423
institutionalist analysis 58
institutionalization process 397, 402
institutionalized dialogue 398
institutional logic 165, 166, 353, 354
institutional matrix 287
institutional pluralism 352
institutional SSE ecosystem 448, 450
   concept of 449
institutional work 170, 352, 354
instrumentalisation 287, 348, 350, 351, 404
insurgent community-based aesthetics 64
integrated ecosystem 446
integration 147, 148, 149, 150, 151, 152, 374
integration mode 330, 331
integrative approaches 297
intended production 283
Intercontinental Network for the Promotion of
   Social Solidarity Economy (RIPESS) 315
intermediaries 434, 436
intermediate groups 270
internal environmental conditions 386
international community 287
International Comparative Social Enterprise
   Models (ICSEM) 167, 168, 332
International Cooperative Alliance (ICA) 51,
   131, 241, 315
International Cooperative Summit 242
International Labour Conference (ILC) 315
International Labor Organization (ILO) 21, 142,
   241, 324, 428
International Monetary Fund 39
International Network of Community Supported
   Agriculture 284
International NGOs (INGOs) 155, 159, 160, 161
international organisations 142
International Planning Committee on Food
   Sovereignty 229
international public–private partnerships 51
International Social Tourism Organisation
   (ISTO) 321
International Society for Ecological Economics
   (ISEE) 28
International Summit on Social Economy 315
intersectionality 288
inter-sectoral networks 395
intersectoral policies 377
isomorphism 170, 287, 348, 349, 351, 404
   normative isomorphism 350
Italian Association for Biological Agriculture
   (AIAB) 300

Jaffe 276
James, Paul 2, 3, 7, 10

Japan 292
Japanese Organic Agriculture Association
   (JOAA) 283
Jeeta Vimukti Karnataka xxiv, 129
Jim Crow segregation 109
Jobel 151
joint responsibility groups (JLGs) 289
justifying markets 340
just transition 209, 210, 214

Kabeer, Naila 39
Kaleidoscope Trust 143
Kawano, Emily 7
Kerlin, Janelle A. 165
Ketilson, Lou Hammond 131, 411
Keynesian methods 57
Khushhali Microfinance Bank Limited
   (KMBL) 174
Kilimanjaro Native Cooperative Union Ltd 133
kilombos 74
knowledge building 404
knowledge sharing 207
Korea Social Enterprise Promotion Agency
   (KoSEA), 435
Koumbit 258
Kudumbashree 175, 421, 422

labour cost 456
labour force 270
labour intensive 454
labour market 330, 331, 333
La Friche la Belle de Mai 198
La Main à la Pâte 159, 160
Lambda Istanbul 143
land and housing 282
landless workers movement 412
large cities 268
Latin America 16, 101
Laval 100
Laville 86
laws 365
learning 284
Lebret, L.J. 264
legal definition 368, 369
legal forms of SSE 369
legal frameworks 365, 373
legal regime 368
legislation 367
legislative frameworks 226
legitimacy 382
leisure 194, 195, 196, 197
Levett's model 30
Lévi-Strauss 62
Levitt 44
LGBT* 138, 139
   work and social inclusion of 139

cooperatives 142
inclusion 138, 139, 144
national organisations 141
people 141, 144
Place of Refuge 142
national-local organisations supporting 143
SSE organisations supporting 141
liberal feminism 40
liberal model 276
libertarian socialism 113, 117
life strategies 266
Lim, C.G. 385
local authorities 194
local communities 299, 379
local community development (LCD) 264
SSE 265, 267, 271
local community potential 313
local development 151
local economic development 264
Local Exchange Trading Systems (LETS) 79
local governance 374, 392
local identity 264
local population 301
Local Solidarity-based Partnerships for
Agroecology (LSPAs) 4
local welfare 297
loconomics 261, 290
Logathan, Kumar 318
long-term care homes 246
long-term unemployed 287
Luc-Nancy, Jean 13
Luxembourg Commission 118

macro-syntheses 54
Mahatma Gandhi National Rural Employment
Guarantee Act 2005 (MGNREGA) 175
Mahatma Gandhi National Rural Employment
Guarantee Scheme (MGNREGS) 422
Mahila Housing SEWA Trust (MHT) 127
"mainstreaming" SSE approach 372, 373, 374
Malawi Rural Development Fund
(MARDEF) 174
Malaysian Cooperative Transformation Plan 316
Malaysian Social Enterprise Blueprint 316
Malaysian VNR 316
male bias 231
malnutrition 281, 285
management autonomy 429
management of associations 392
management team
institutional environments 382
signaling theory 384
managers 460
market access 338, 403
B2B relations 343

B2C relations 343
capacity building 342
education 342
innovation and strategic planning 344
justified 340
organizational impediments to 341
problems of 340
SSEOEs' advantages and 341
structural impediments to 340
value-added strategies 343
market-driven economy 303
market economies 303
market economy 58, 73, 77
market emulating rules 340
market exchange 388
marketing 441
market preserving rules 340
market principle 54
market women 275
Marxist 366
material culture 65
materiality 61
material resources 295, 297
Mauss, Marcel 56, 58, 61, 62
Max-Neef, Manfred 296
Mayer, John W. 353
McIntosh 107
mediated communication 10
Mexico 288
microbiome 285
microcredit 40
microenterprise 172
microfinance 40, 172, 176, 178
Microfinance Institution (MFI) 174
microinsurance 234
micro-sociological level 188
migrants 147, 149
integration 150
self-organization 149
worker cooperatives 149
Millenium Ecosystem Assessment 32
Millennium Development Goals (MDGs) 310
implementation 310
Mills, Charles W. 93
mimetic isomorphism 350
Miner, Karen 201
minimalist resource allocation 405
Ministry of Economy and Innovation 375
Ministry of Environment and Climate
Change 376
Ministry of Labour and Employment 374
Ministry of Labour, Employment and Social
Solidarity 376
mission-driven business approach 163
modern economy 33

Mondragon Cooperative Corporation 131, 259, 344
Mondragon Team Academy (MTA World) 184
monitoring 380
Moolanivasis 129
Moore, James F. 443
moral economy 68, 69, 70, 71
   concept of 68
   from oblivion to renaissance 69
movement activism 12
movements 2, 3, 4, 5, 6, 7, 8, 9, 10
M-Pesa 413
MST (Movimento dos Trabalhadores Sem Terra: Landless Workers' Movement) 132, 414
'Mujeres Creando' 143
multidimensional inequalities 287
   alternative economies 287
   change in society 288
multifaceted indigenous aesthetic rationale 64
multi-stakeholder process 395, 396
Multi-State Co-operative Societies Act 234
Murra 62
Murray, Robin 353
Murtagh 273, 274
mutual 133
mutual aid 76
mutual aid societies 75
mutual assistance 283
mutual concession 283
mutual funds 219, 220
mutual insurance 216, 220, 221, 222
mutual interest 165
mutualism 114
mutually reinforcing dynamics 377
mutuals 131, 132, 135, 136, 220
   impact of 134
mutual structures 300

Namibia 144
National Bank for Agriculture and Rural Development (NABARD) 173, 175
National Entrepreneurship Policy 316
National Federation of Colored Farmers (NFCF) 109
national fund 363
national governments 316, 374
National Pluriannual Plan 375
national scale 450
National Secretariat for Solidarity Economy (SENAES) 374, 375, 435
national statistics accounts 425, 426, 427
National Strategy for Social and Solidarity Economy 2010-2020 401
nation-state 117
Nazareth 298, 299

Negri, Antonio 100
Nelson, Nici 135
Nembhard, Jessica Gordon 93, 108, 110
neo-classical approach 71
neo-classical argument 340
neo-classical economics 38, 40, 340
neoliberal economic model 379
neo-liberal economics 105
neoliberal globalization 2, 8, 9, 45, 46
neoliberal ideas 419
neoliberalism 23, 45, 103, 117, 123
neoliberal model 35
neoliberal policies 118
neoliberal welfare reform 419
Nepal 275, 276
Netherlands, the 259
network diversity 386
networking 441
New Community Organising 122
New Genomic techniques 227
New Public Management 348, 351
New Urban Agenda 226, 282
New York City 276
NHGs 175
Nicaragua 277
Nicholas 204
non-economic wealth 289
non-governmental actors 396
non-governmental organisations 155
non-governmental organization (NGOs) 155, 156, 315
   and foundations 155, 157
   public services 157
   role of 159
   service-delivery 157
non-governmental social financial organization 384
non-material resources 295, 297
Non-performing assets (NPA) 175, 176, 177
non-profit 191
Non-Profit Organisational (NPO) 332
non-profit organizations 158, 166, 447, 458, 461
nonprofit sector 155, 156, 157, 161
nonprofit-type 168
non-violence 275
North America 75, 290
North Carolina 109
not for profit 248, 250
Nussbaum, Martha 322
Nyssens, Marthe 163, 165

Obeidat, Adnan 133
objects 426
"Occupy Wall Street" movement 10
ocean acidification 228

Oliver, Christine 353
Olson, Mancur 97
online survey 244
Open Source Initiative (OSI) 257
organisational convergence 352
organisational sociology 349
organisational transformations 198
organizational management 389, 390
organizational mission 460
organizations, definition 382
Ostrom, Elinor 59, 97, 98, 99
Othering 88
Otherness 66, 83, 89
outreach 175, 178
Owen, Robert 416
ownership 149
ownership arrangements 306

participation 182, 240, 241, 242, 266, 295, 296, 297, 301, 438
Participatory Area 438
participatory processes 377, 388, 389, 390, 391, 392
Partido dos Trabalhadores (PT) 6
partnership 158, 161, 241, 242, 243, 247, 385, 394, 395
   German 159
paternalism 76
Paunov, C. 383
Payoga-Kapatagan 293
peace 272, 273, 278
peacebuilding 272
peace conditionalities 272
peasant conceptions 68
people economy 312, 316
Philadelphia Declaration 77
philanthropic solidarity 69, 70, 76
philanthropy 69
Philippines, the 290, 293
pioneering initiatives 329
Pla d'Impuls de l'Economia Social i Solidària (PIESS) 377, 378, 438
planetary boundaries 30
planetary health 21
plasticity 84
Platform Cooperative Consortium 260
platform cooperatives 260, 290
platform economy 260
plural democracy 71
pluralisation 58
pluralism 12
pluralist approach 55
plurality 13
Polanyi, Karl 55, 56, 348
Polanyi's substantive approach 164

police violence 108
policy agenda 400
policy co-construction 436, 437, 438, 442
policy coherence 379
policy formation 397
policy (in)coherence 406
policy innovation 395, 398, 404
policymakers 380, 409, 425
political capacity building 442
political consumerism 293
political economy 69, 275
political engagement 181
political federalism 115
political goals 164
political power 115
political tensions 406
Politicized Microfinance: Money, Power, and Violence in the Black Americas 94, 95
polycentricity 396
pooling of micro-solidarities 274
Popular and Solidarity Economy 63
popular discontent 8
popular economy 74, 346
popular entrepreneurship 270
Porirer, Yvon 318
Port Royal Logic 368
postcolonial criticism 84
postcolonial perspective 89
postcolonial theories 83, 84, 85, 89
post-decolonisation development models 325
Post-Washington Consensus 420
poverty 87, 122, 270, 281, 286, 290, 291, 295, 299, 300, 373
Powell, Walter W. 349, 350
power dynamics 38
power relations 21
price decision 283
primary education 203
primary labor market 287
primary social relationships 390
Priola, Vincenza 140
priority measures 376
private capital 305
private-macro 448
private-micro 448
private sector 289, 291
proactive communication 379, 380
productivism 56
professionalisation 197
profit distribution 427
program-related investment (PRI) 217
Proshika 234
Proudhon, Pierre-Joseph 113, 115, 116, 118
Puar, Jasbir, K. 143
public action 290

public authorities 195, 449
public governance 399
public management 397
public policy 169, 330, 334, 335, 344, 370, 397, 400, 401, 404, 407, 438, 446
  challenges 404
  financing 403
  fiscal incentives 403
  governance 403
  market access 403
  measuers 395
  toolkit 403
  training and education 403
public-private partnerships 51, 423
Public-Private Policy-making Partnership for the Social Economy in Seoul (PPPPSES) 383
public procurement policies 345
public recognition 345
public sector 287
public-sector social enterprises (PSE) 167
public-sector spin-offs 167
public services 155, 157, 158, 159, 161, 295
public-social and solidarity economy partnerships (PSSEPs) 291
public sphere level management. *See* societal management
public-SSE partnerships 404

quality of services 240, 246
quasi-equity investments 219
Québec 371, 375, 395, 397
Quilombola system 133
Quinones, Ben 312

race 237, 238
racial capitalism 105, 107, 110
racial discrimination 110
radical democracy 100
Raffeissen model 304
Raiffeisen, Friedrich 218
Ramnarain 274
Rastafari community 95
rational economic agent 38
rationality 53, 265, 267, 269, 270
reciprocity 54, 62, 63, 64, 68, 114, 264, 388
redistribution 54, 63, 64, 388
redistributive function 287
redistributive solidarity 57
re-embeddedness process 66
reflexive confrontation 16
reflexive governance 396
refugees 147, 148, 150, 151, 152, 153
regional economic development 346
regional economic integration 45
regulatory patterns 388
regulatory principles 388

reinforcement 377
representative democracy 57, 71
Republic of Korea 4
research initiative 243
residual paternalism 69
resilience 282, 409
resource acquisition 384, 386
Rete Rurale Nazionale 300
retirement homes 246
Rigenera 299
right to food. *See* food sovereignty
Rochdale Equitable Pioneers Society 131
Rochdale Pioneers 308
Rotating Savings and Credit Associations (ROSCAs) 92, 93, 94, 95
Rwanda 276

SAATH 127
Saathis 205
Sabourin, Éric 62
Said, Edward 84
Sanchez Bajo 276
Sandberg, Joakim 306
San Francisco Association of Differently Abled Persons (Safra-Adap) 290
Santos, Luciane Lucas dos 84
Savings Credit and Cooperatives (SACCOs) 135, 276, 277
scale-based solutions 89
scaling deep 151
Schirmann, Richard 323
school cooperatives 183, 206
school of thought 163, 164, 165, 168
Schoonhoven, C.B. 386
Schulergenossenschaften 205
Schulze-Delitzsch 218
Schuyler, George 108
Scott, James C. 68
Scott, Richard W. 353
SDGs 253
seasonality 285
secondary education 203
secondary labor market 287
secondary workforce 270
Second World War 77
sectoral approach 377
seeds 227
Seikatsu Club 292
self-centred individualism 23, 25
self-determination 297
self-distribution 284
Self-Employed Women's Association (SEWA) 126, 174, 234, 274, 277
self-employed workers 373
self-financing 362

self-governance 100
self-help groups (SHG)
  Bank Linkage Programme 173, 288
  criticisms 177
  development 172
  impact of 177
  movement 172
  organisational structure 176
  system of 174
  women 172
self-help groups (SHGs) 172, 289
self-interest 68
self-management 48, 265, 392
self-organization 102
self-regulating market 55, 102
Selznick, Philip 348
semi-formal relations 438
Sen, Amartya 39, 311, 389
Sentama 275
Seoul 383
Seoul Metropolitan Government 383, 439
Seoul Social Economy Centre (SSEC) 436, 442
Seoul Social Economy Network (SSEN) 437
Seoul Social Investment Fund 441
Sepas 5
service economy 59
sexuality 238
sexual orientation 139, 140
Shane, S. 382
shared goals 231
share tourism 325
short-term electoral cycles 378
short-term rentals 260
signaling environment 384
signaling theory 384
Sjöström, Emma 306
skills assessment tools 152
Smallholder Coffee Farmers Trust 293
small jobs 191
small/medium enterprises (SMEs) 374
Smartcoop 261
SME 383
Smith, Adam 68
social action 325
social agriculture 298, 299, 300
social and solidarity economy (SSE). *See* SSE.
Social and Solidarity Financing (SSF) 305
social base 358
social bonds 69
social businesses (SB) 71, 163, 165, 167, 168, 169
Social Business Initiative (SBI) 70, 315
social-business model 169
social capital 47
social change 59, 75

social cohesion 46
social conversation 396
social cooperatives (SC) 140, 141, 165, 167, 168, 296, 297, 298
social currencies 114
social democracy 57, 71
social dimension 164
social economy 7, 8, 15, 16, 19, 21, 22, 24, 25, 56, 57, 73, 76, 78, 80, 92, 206, 368, 431, 445
  recognition of 77
Social Economy 398
Social Economy Academy 439
  Seoul 439
Social Economy Act (2013) 375, 437
Social Economy Action Plan 397
social economy actors 7
Social Economy Forum 383
Social Economy Leadership Programme (SELP) 203
social economy organisations 85
Social Economy Partnership for Community-Based and Sustainable Development 398
social elites 77
social emancipation 63
social empowerment 421
Social Enterprise Academy
  Scotland 440
social enterprise ecosystem approach 448
Social Enterprise Initiative (SEI) 447
social enterprises (SE) 15, 139, 163, 174, 182, 274, 307, 329, 332, 334, 369, 375, 384, 412, 413, 414, 448, 458, 459
  alternatives 170
  and schools 163
  approaches 163
  concept 163
  cooperative-type 168
  diversity of 165
  economic dimension of 164
  entrepreneurial dimension 164
  entrepreneurial nonprofits (ENP) 166
  galaxy of 164
  governance-related dimension of 164
  institutional logics 165, 166
  isomorphic 170
  models 166, 169
  public-sector social enterprises (PSE) 167
  social dimension of 164
  theorised models 167
  trade-offs 170
  zoo 165
social entrepreneurship 86, 115, 116, 167, 183, 184, 344, 383

social finance 385
social finance institutions 394
social finance sector 395
social financial organization 384
social groups 75, 289
social housing 252
social identity 269
social inclusion 295
social inequalities 326
social injustice 238
social innovation 184, 188, 189, 190, 295, 296, 327, 353, 354
social integration 298
socialism' 23
social joint ventures 333
social justice 278
social loan 385
social management 392
social medicine 242
social movements 2, 3, 4, 7, 8, 69, 81, 155, 224, 225, 227, 229, 288, 412
social networks 297, 385
social norms 68
social order 68
social policy 295, 300, 301, 416, 417
   and SSE 417
   boundary of 417
   channels linking SSE with 417
   concept 417
   context of 417
   diverse definitions of 417
   sector 422
social practices 81
social protection policies 187, 236, 376
social provisioning 276
social provisioning approach (SPA) 38
social purposes 25, 70, 71
social relationship 122
social reproduction (SR) 41, 42, 410
social responsibilities 118, 327
social role 345
social service provision 297
social services 159, 300
social services delivery policy 346
Social Solidarity Economy (SSE) 16, 24, 281
   education 206
   food 285
   food sovereignty 283
   health 285
   solutions to poverty and hunger 281
social stability 77
social state 117
social transformation 15, 97, 103
social turn 420
social value 385

social value creation 384
social versus solidarity economy 19
social work 123
societal management 389, 390, 391
Société coopérative d'intérêt collectif (SCIC) 190
society extracts 33
socio-economic activities 297
socio-economic development 136
socio-economic inequalities 289, 290
socio-economic sectors 373
socio-labour instability 45
soil health 285
solidarity 76, 172, 176
solidarity-based associationalism 69, 73, 75
solidarity-based associations
   diverse profiles of 73
solidarity economy 5, 6, 7, 8, 14, 15, 16, 17, 19, 20, 21, 22, 58, 63, 73, 80, 89, 92, 105, 131, 203, 333, 445
Solidarity Economy Forum (FBES) 375
solidarity economy initiatives 85
solidarity enterprises 203
solidarity finance 441
solidarity initiatives
   emergence of 78
solidarity purchasing groups (SPG) 292, 308
solidarity tourism 325
South Africa 133, 144
South America 74, 78
South Korea 288, 383, 384. *See also* Republic of Korea.
SPA 38
spaceship economics 27
Spain 379
Spence 384
Spivak, Gayatri 84
sports 194, 195, 196, 197
SR 42
SSE 2, 3, 6, 19, 20, 21, 23, 24, 25, 34, 35, 37, 44, 54, 61, 70, 80, 83, 102, 134, 147, 180, 182, 183, 187, 189, 194, 210, 255, 295, 303, 321, 345, 383, 388, 394, 400, 409, 416, 430, 453
   actors 398, 399
   approach 307
   challenges of 58, 422
   classifying 426
   co-construction 395, 396, 397
   community relations 268
   contract 455
   co-optation 348
   core of 426
   culture 194
   definition of 365, 368, 431
   democratic strengthening 47

dimensions 312, 313
dynamic inequalities 290
economic stability 47
ecosystems 373, 376, 378, 434, 436, 441, 442, 449
employees of 453
enterprises 430
entrepreneurial mindset 183
environmental contribution 48
exchange economy 64
filters to 427
function of 430
future challenges 308
global or supranational processes 315
governance 383
grassroots communities 317
hubs 376
identity-based inequalities 287, 288
identifying 426
in education policy 418
in law and policy 403
in national statistics 426
innovation 181
in public policy 402
international frameworks for 428
international relations 438
in welfare system 401
isomorphism 349
instrumentalisation 350
landscape 380
law dealing with 265, 366
legal definition of 370
legal framework 365
leisure 194
limitations 291
local community development 265, 267, 271
local economic development 264
migrants 147
mission of 460
movement 8, 10
multi-layered objectives 395
multiplication of laws for 367
national and subnational levels 316
networks 398
non-violence 273, 278
objectives of law for 367
operational characteristics of 426
organizations 182, 287, 380, 388, 389, 391, 392, 426, 427, 429
partnership 394, 395
patterns of evolution 148
peace 272, 273, 278
phenomenon of 365
political economy 275
political processes 277

postcolonial agenda of 87
public policies 375, 390
public recognition of 345
public services 295
refugees 147
response of 225
role of 147, 416, 420
SDGs 312
social finance institutions 394
social policy and 417
social reproduction and 410
social services 295, 300
socio-economic inequalities 289
statistics 425, 428
tourism 321, 326
training 439
unique role 419
utility of law 365
volunteers of 453
wages 457
workplace 452, 453
youth-specific problems 181
SSE-based agroecological systems 228
SSE development plans 372, 376
   accountable administrations 378
   Brazil 374
   communicating effectively 379
   coordination process 373
   different routes 372
   Durban 376
   ecosystem 376
   policy coherence 379
   policymakers 380
   policy process 378
   Quebec 375
   stakeholders 380
   strategic priorities 373
SSE enterprises and organizations (SSEOEs) 7, 21, 23, 32, 47, 48, 49, 51, 141, 144, 148, 200, 212, 216, 217, 219, 220, 221, 222, 234, 235, 236, 238, 240, 249, 255, 260, 261, 262, 266, 274, 275, 277, 278, 279, 284, 300, 312, 313, 314, 317, 319, 377, 379, 383, 384, 385, 386, 394, 401, 410, 414, 416, 418, 420, 421, 434
   ICT 256
   global scaling of 48
   growth of 420
   synergies of 421
SSEOs 438, 439
SSET 322, 323, 327
stakeholder decision making 396
stakeholders 380
Stallman, Richard 256, 257
start-ups 382, 386

state 445, 446
state-building 272
State Secretariat 435
state violence 16
statistical measurement 425
statist-macro 448
statist-micro 448
steady development 284
steady-state economy 27
STEM education 204
stereotypes 88
Stockholm Resilience Centre 34
Stocksy United 290
strategic priorities 373
strategies 353
structural violence 274, 278
subaltern aesthetics 64
subaltern studies 83
subnational governments 316
subprime lending 221
subsidy budget 383
subsistence strategies 266
substantive economics 54, 56
    theoretical analysis 54
supporting organizations and intermediaries 434, 446
    activities of 436
    categories of 434
    definition 434
    types of 435
surplus production 283
survival skills 150
sustainability 32, 386
    nested model of 30
sustainable consumption and production 306, 307
sustainable development 29, 30, 88, 209, 214
Sustainable Development Goals (SDGs) 99, 295, 281, 303, 310, 311, 319, 321, 351, 372, 407
    dimensions 311
    global or supranational processes 315
    grassroots communities 317
    national and subnational levels 316
    SSE 312
Sustainable Development Strategy (2015–2020) 376
sustainable finance 306, 357
sustainable investment 303, 305
sustainable local food systems 225
sustainable production 303, 308
sustainable rural development 299
sustainable societies 88
Sustainable Tourism Charter 324
synergetic satisfiers 297
systemic approach 406

System of National Accounts (SNA) (2008) xxvi, 428
system thinking 28

Tadjudje, Willy 367
Tansley, George 443
Tanzania Federation of Cooperatives 203
targeting vs. diversity. diversity 405
tax 363, 364
Team Academy 202, 207, 208
team-entrepreneurship 184
teampreneurs 202
technological changes 180
technological inventions 121
technological secrets 271
technology 207
Technology Informatics Design Endeavour (TIDE) 233
Teikei system 283, 284, 292
Temple, Dominique 62
Terre de Liens 227
territorial contexts 377
Territorial Development Fund xxiii, 440
The Cooperative Movement: Globalization from Below 131
The Economics of the Coming Spaceship Earth 27
The Entropy Law and the Economic Process 27
The Globalization of Markets 44
The Rainbow Project (TRP) 144
The Tragedy of the Commons 97
Third Sector frameworks 88
Thompson, Edward Palmer 68
TIDE 233
top-down methods 378
top-down policy formation 399
top management team 382, 384, 385
tourism 321
    bashing 326
    cultural dimension 322
    economic dimension 322
    environmental dimension 322
    growth 326
    historical forms of 322
    human dimension 322
    industry 327
    inequalities 326
    social dimension 321
    social inequalities 326
    social responsibility 327
    tourism inequalities 326
trade-offs 404
trade unionism 117
traditional knowledge 266
traditional statutory actors 24

Training 439
transformation 350, 354, 444, 445, 447, 449
transformative social policies 291
transgressing solutions 297
transition 180
Transition Initiatives movement 15
transnational corporations 45
transversal policies 446
Trans Welfare Cooperative Society 142
travel 321, 322
traveller hospitality 323
Trust 363
Trust for Civil Society 161
TSG Bergerdorf Sports Club 198
"tutelised" associations 115
TYM (Tao Yeu May Fund) 174
Tyrrell County School 109
Tzul Tzul, Gladys 101

Uganda Cooperative Alliance 135
Uganda shoe-shiners 135
umbrella legislation 366
unemployment 181
UNESCO Universal Declaration on Cultural Diversity (2001) 197
UN Inter-Agency Task Force on Social and Solidarity Economy (UNTFSSE) 93, 315, 438
   International Conference 317
   Knowledge Hub 317
Union of Indigenous Communities of the Isthmus Region (UCIRI) 288
United Kingdom 79
United Nations Commission for Social Development 303
United Nations Research Institute for Social Development (UNRISD) 296, 313, 315
United Nations Tourism Statistical System 321
United Nations (UN) 155
United States 122, 157, 365
universal coverage 418, 419
Universal Periodical Review (UPR) 312
universe of reference 426
unsustainable organizations 405
Up & Go 149
URGENCI 284
user-centred applications 260
users and operators 259
Utting, Peter 277, 312

value chain breakdown 281, 376
values-based enterprises 105
van Seters, Paul 2, 3, 7, 10
venture capital 363
Verschurr, Christine 41, 42

Vervisch, Thomas 272
Vimo SEWA 234
voluntary labour 455
Voluntary National Review (VNR) 312
voluntary work 195
volunteers 453, 460
voter suppression 93

wage equity 114
wages 452
Waldeck-Rousseau law 114
Wallerstein, Immanuel 84
Walras, Léon 68
war on poverty 123
waste 209, 213
waste management sectors 209, 210
water 209, 210, 212, 215, 227
Weaver, Rasheda 412
Weber, Max 164
web of life 32
welfare mix 187, 188
welfare partnership 157
welfare pluralism 416
welfare states 76, 77, 416
welfare-statism 71
welfare system 401
well-being 21, 27, 33, 38, 43
Williams, Richard 131
win–win strategy 173
WISE Entrepreneurial Nonprofit 332
women 74, 76, 95, 172, 179, 231, 232, 233, 234, 235, 236, 237, 238
women empowerment 421
Women in Informal Employment Globalizing and Organizing (WIEGO) 234
women-owned catering 106
Woningcorporaties 251
worker cooperatives 105, 106, 107, 110
worker-owned businesses 107
worker-owned home care cooperatives 289
worker-recuperated enterprises 276
workers' associative practices 74
working-class families 324
working conditions 452, 454, 457
   accountability 456
   business professionalization 458
   compensation 454
   components of 458
   employment benefits 455
   funding and financial resources 458
   government 459
   human resource (HR) development 459
   informal 455
   labour cost 456
   labour intensive 454

mission and values 456
  small workplace 458
  voluntary labour 455
work integration 329, 330, 333
Work Integration Social Enterprises
    (WISEs) 158, 168, 329, 346
  aim 331
  entrepreneurial nonprofits 332
  historic evolution of 330
  institutionalisation of 330
  public policy 335
  second wave of 329
  social enterprises 332
  spin-offs 334
work motivation 269
workplace 452, 458
workplace democracy 106
World Bank 39, 124

World Cooperative Monitor 132
World Social Forum 9, 46, 160
World Trade Organization (WTO) 224
Wuttunee, Wanda 133

Yanesha theory 65
Yoruban 94
Young, Dennis R. 165
youth 180, 181, 182, 184
    political participation 182
youth hostels 323
Yunus, Muhammad 163, 172

Zapatista uprising 8
Zein-Elabdin 85, 88
"zero-sum game" capitalist system 232
Zinn, Howard 76